PAUL
and the
MIRACULOUS

PAUL
and the
MIRACULOUS

A Historical Reconstruction

GRAHAM H. TWELFTREE

B
Baker Academic
a division of Baker Publishing Group
Grand Rapids, Michigan

© 2013 by Graham H. Twelftree

Published by Baker Academic
a division of Baker Publishing Group
P.O. Box 6287, Grand Rapids, MI 49516-6287
www.bakeracademic.com

Printed in the United States of America

Library of Congress Cataloging-in-Publication Data
Twelftree, Graham H.
    Paul and the miraculous : a historical reconstruction / Graham H. Twelftree.
        pages cm
    Includes bibliographical references and index.
    ISBN 978-0-8010-2772-7 (pbk.)
    1. Paul, the Apostle, Saint. 2. Miracles. I. Title.
BS2506.3.T84 2013
225.9'2—dc23   2013012180

13   14   15   16   17   18   19   7   6   5   4   3   2   1

To
Stephen H. Travis

Contents

Preface

I am now convinced that performing miracles, particularly exorcisms, took up a great deal of Jesus' public ministry. Moreover, Jesus appears to have considered these miracles of central significance in how he understood himself and his mission.[1] Turning to Paul, however, we are faced with a puzzle. In his letters, in what are almost universally agreed to be our earliest interpretations of Jesus, miracles and the miraculous appear of much less interest, some would say of no interest. Therefore, my motivation for undertaking this project on Paul is that expressed by Albert Schweitzer (1875–1965): "Anyone who deals with the teaching and the life and work of Jesus and offers any kind of new reading of it, ought not to stop there, but must be held under obligation to trace, from the standpoint at which he has arrived, the pathway leading to the history of dogma. Only in this way can it be clearly shown what this discovery is worth."[2]

Therefore, in this study I want to explore what was touched on in my *In the Name of Jesus: Exorcism among Early Christians* (Grand Rapids: Baker Academic, 2007), chapter 3. I am attempting to solve the riddle of the profound difference between, on the one hand, the miraculous ethos of Jesus' ministry, the Gospels and Acts, and the Christianity reflected there and, on the other hand, the letters of Paul, in which miracles and the miraculous appear of much less or perhaps of no interest. In this I am also attempting to shed light on the nature of earliest Christianity.[3] Although what follows will, in

1. Graham H. Twelftree, "The Miracles of Jesus: Marginal or Mainstream?" *JSHJ* 1 (2003): 104–24.
2. Albert Schweitzer, *Paul and His Interpreters: A Critical History*, trans. W. Montgomery (London: Black, 1912), v.
3. As Heikki Räisänen points out, "The term *Christian* smacks of anachronism but is difficult to avoid; it would be cumbersome to dispense with it altogether" (*The Rise of Christian Beliefs:*

places, build on earlier work, I cannot promise exact consistency with what
I have already written. I discover new evidence and new ways of looking at
old evidence, so that I continue to change my mind. Indeed, the results of this
project are much different from what I anticipated when I began. I cannot say
that I found what I was looking for!

Initial impulse for this study came from the invitation to provide the "Healing, Illness" and "Signs, Wonders, Miracles" articles for the *Dictionary of
Paul and His Letters*.[4] I was surprised, despite the overwhelming number and
continuing stream of studies on Paul, how little work had been carried out on
the subject, and since then I have maintained an interest in the topic. Although
this project subsequently took unexpected twists and turns over the years, I
am grateful to those who offered guidance in the initial stages: Colin Brown,
Richard Hays, Martin Hengel, Andrew Lincoln, and John Meier. Since then,
a whole cadre of folk has kindly come to my aid: Jeremy Barrier, Stephen
Barton, Richard Bell, James Bowley, John Clabeaux, Andrew Clark, Tony
Cummins, Peter Davids, Joey Dodson, Karl Donfried, David Downs, Eric
Eve, Mark Finney, Keith Hacking, Paul Hartog, Philip Kern, Michael Lattke,
Timothy Lim (Edinburgh), Steve Mason, Michael Matlock, Lidija Novakovic,
Randall Pannell, Jeremy Perigo, Lloyd Pietersen, Timothy Savage, Patrick
Schembri, Jeroen Speybroeck, Bradley Storin, Geoffrey Treloar, Brenton Wait,
John Walton, Jason Wermuth, and Magnus Zetterholm read and commented
on chapters or parts of the evolving text. I am also glad to be able to express
my gratitude to Roland Deines for an invitation to read a paper at a research
seminar of the Nottingham University Department of Theology and Religious
Studies, and to Steve Walton for an invitation to present a paper as a guest at
a research conference of the London School of Theology (Middlesex University), as well as to the faculty members (notably William Atkinson of LST)
and students of these institutions for the stimulating discussions that helped
refine a number of points for this project. Thanks are due to a Baker Academic anonymous reader who was able to offer suggestions that caused me to
clarify a number of points and to trim material, especially from the footnotes.
I hope the zealous cutting has not left too many debts unacknowledged. In
particular, I am deeply grateful to Doc Hughes, Gene Mills, and especially to

---

The Thought World of Early Christians [Minneapolis: Fortress, 2010], 1). In this project the use
of the term does not imply a movement or religion over against Judaism. To follow Räisänen,
in this study "It should be understood here in a weak sense: the noun *Christian* denotes all
persons in whose symbolic worlds Jesus of Nazareth held a central place, one way or another;
the adjective refers to their qualities and views" (pp. 1–2).

4. Gerald F. Hawthorne, Ralph P. Martin, and Daniel G. Reid, eds., *Dictionary of Paul and
His Letters* (Downers Grove, IL: InterVarsity, 1993), 378–81, 875–77.

Stephen Travis, a longstanding friend whose work I greatly admire, for giving a close reading and providing detailed comments on the nearly completed text. However, mentioning and thanking these generous people is not intended to burden them with any responsibility for what follows. Other help has come from Bob Sivigny, the long-suffering Regent University divinity librarian (now emeritus), who answered many questions and tracked down hard-to-find items, from Patty Hughson and her highly efficient interlibrary loan team, and from most diligent graduate assistants, especially in recent years, Josh Albrecht, Chevette Alston, Nick Daniels, Jackie Duckett, Alicia Eichmann, Jonathan Etheridge, Peter Guinther, Vince Lee, Alicia Panganiban, N. J. Robinson, and Kara Schmidt. Finally, the text that follows has benefited considerably from the careful attention of Brian Bolger and his editorial team at Baker Academic. Thank you. The support of Barbara, my wife, has extended beyond the home to include library work to locate materials and search databases to build bibliographies, for which I am very grateful.

Graham H. Twelftree

Regent University

Abbreviations

General

//	parallel text(s)	Gk.	Greek
c.	circa	Heb.	Hebrew
cf.	compare	ibid.	in the same source
chap(s).	chapter(s)	i.e.	that is
col(s).	columns	MS(S)	manuscript(s)
e.g.	for example	n(n).	note(s)
esp.	especially	p(p).	page(s)
ET	English translation	repr.	reprint
fasc(s).	fascicles	rev.	revised
frg(s).	fragment(s)	v(v).	verse(s)

Ancient Texts, Text Types, and Versions

LXX	Septuagint	Θ	Theodotion
MT	Masoretic Text		

Modern Editions

NA²⁷	*Novum Testamentum Graece*, Nestle-Aland, 27th ed.	NA²⁸	*Novum Testamentum Graece*, Nestle-Aland, 28th ed.

Modern Versions

ASV	American Standard Version	NIV	New International Version
ESV	English Standard Version	NJB	New Jerusalem Bible
JB	Jerusalem Bible	NKJV	New King James Version
KJV	King James Version	NLT	New Living Translation
NAB	New American Bible	NRSV	New Revised Standard Version
NASB	New American Standard Bible	RSV	Revised Standard Version
NASU	New American Standard Updated	TEV	Today's English Version (= Good News Bible)
NEB	New English Bible		
NET	New English Translation		

Apocrypha and Septuagint

Bar.	Baruch	Pr. Azar.	Prayer of Azariah
Jdt.	Judith	Pr. Man.	Prayer of Manasseh
1–4 Kgdms.	1–4 Kingdoms	Sir.	Sirach
1–4 Macc.	1–4 Maccabees	Tob.	Tobit
Odes	Odes of Solomon	Wis.	Wisdom of Solomon

Old Testament Pseudepigrapha

Acts Paul	Acts of Paul	T. Sol.	Testament of Solomon
As. Mos.	Assumption of Moses	T. 3 Patr.	Testaments of the Three Patriarchs
2 Bar.	2 Baruch (Syriac Apocalypse)		
1 En.	1 Enoch (Ethiopic Apocalypse)	T. Ab.	Testament of Abraham
2 En.	2 Enoch (Slavonic Apocalypse)	T. 12 Patr.	Testaments of the Twelve Patriarchs
Ezek. Trag.	Ezekiel the Tragedian	T. Ash.	Testament of Asher
4 Ezra	4 Ezra	T. Benj.	Testament of Benjamin
Jos. Asen.	Joseph and Aseneth	T. Gad	Testament of Gad
Jub.	Jubilees	T. Iss.	Testament of Issachar
L.A.B.	Liber antiquitatum biblicarum (Pseudo-Philo)	T. Jos.	Testament of Joseph
		T. Jud.	Testament of Judah
Let. Arist.	Letter of Aristeas	T. Levi	Testament of Levi
Liv. Pro.	Lives of the Prophets	T. Naph.	Testament of Naphtali
Pss. Sol.	Psalms of Solomon	T. Sim.	Testament of Simeon
Sib. Or.	Sybilline Oracles	T. Zeb.	Testament of Zebulon

Dead Sea Scrolls and Related Texts

1QH^a	1QHodayot^a
1QM	1QWar Scroll
1QpHab	1QPesher to Habakkuk
1QS	1QRule of the Community
1Q20 (1QapGen ar)	1QGenesis Apocryphon
1Q22 (1QDM)	1QWords of Moses
1Q28a (1QSa)	1QRule of the Congregation
1Q28b (1QSb)	1QRule of Benedictions
1Q29	1QLiturgy of the Three Tongues of Fire
4Q163 (4Qpap pIsa^c)	4QIsaiah Pesher^c
4Q166 (4QpHos^a)	4QHosea Pesher^a
4Q169 (4QpNah)	4QNahum Pesher
4Q171 (4QpPs^a)	4QPsalms Pesher^a
4Q174 (4QFlor)	4QFlorilegium
4Q177 (4QCatena A)	4QCatena A
4Q185	4QSapiential Work
4Q196 (4QpapTob^a ar)	4QpapTobit^a ar
4Q197 (4QpapTob^b ar)	4QpapTobit^b ar
4Q210 (4QEnast^c ar)	4QAstronomical Enoch^c ar

4Q226 (4QpsJub^b)	4QPseudo-Jubilees^b
4Q242 (4QPrNab ar)	4QPrayer of Nabonidus ar
4Q252 (4QCommGen A)	4QCommentary on Genesis A
4Q339	4QList of False Prophets ar
4Q365 (4QRP^c)	4QReworked Pentateuch^c
4Q374	4QDiscourse on the Exodus/Conquest Tradition
4Q375 (4QapocrMoses^a)	4QApocryphon of Moses^a
4Q376 (4QapocrMoses^{b?})	4QApocryphon of Moses^{b?}
4Q377 (4QapocrPent B)	4QApocryphon Pentateuch B
4Q381	4QNon-Canonical Psalms B
4Q387a (4QpsMoses^b)	4QPseudo-Moses^b
4Q397 (4QMMT^d)	4QHalakhic Letter^d
4Q398 (4QMMT^e)	4QHalakhic Letter^e
4Q400 (4QShirShabb^a)	4QSongs of the Sabbath Sacrifice^a
4Q478	4QpapFragment Mentioning Festivals
4Q504 (4QDibHam^a)	4QWords of the Luminaries^a
4Q509+4Q505	
(4QpapPrFêtes^c)	4QFestival Prayers^c
4Q510 (4QShir^a)	4QSongs of the Sage^a
4Q511 (4QShir^b)	4QSongs of the Sage^b
4Q521	4QMessianic Apocalypse
4Q558	4QVision^b ar
4Q560	4QExorcism ar
6Q18 (6QpapHymn)	6QHymn
11Q5 (11QPs^a)	11QPsalms^a
11Q11 (11QapocPs)	11QApocryphal Psalms
11Q19 (11QT^a)	11QTemple^a
CD-A	Damascus Document^a
CD-B	Damascus Document^b

Philo

Abr.	De Abrahamo (On the Life of Abraham)	*Ebr.*	De ebrietate (On Drunkenness)
		Flacc.	In Flaccum (Against Flaccus)
Aet.	De aeternitate mundi (On the Eternity of the World)	*Fug.*	De fuga et inventione (On Flight and Finding)
Conf.	De confusione linguarum (On the Confusion of Tongues)	*Gig.*	De gigantibus (On Giants)
		Her.	Quis rerum divinarum heres sit (Who Is the Heir?)
Congr.	De congressu eruditionis gratia (On the Preliminary Studies)		
Contempl.	De vita complativa (On the Contemplative Life)	*Hypoth.*	Hypothetica (Hypothetica)
		Leg.	Legum allegoriae (Allegorical Interpretation)
Decal.	De decalogo (On the Decalogue)		
Det.	Quod deterius potiori insidari soleat (That the Worse Attacks the Better)	*Legat.*	Legatio ad Gaium (On the Embassy to Gaius)
		Migr.	De migratione Abrahami (On the Migration of Abraham)
Deus	Quod Deus sit immutabilis (That God Is Unchangeable)	*Mos.*	De vita Mosis (On the Life of Moses)

Mut.	*De mutatione nominum (On the Change of Names)*	QE	*Quaestiones et solutiones in Exodum (Questions and Answers on Exodus)*
Opif.	*De opificio mundi (On the Creation of the World)*	QG	*Quaestiones et solutiones in Genesin (Questions and Answers on Genesis)*
Plant.	*De plantatione (On Planting)*		
Post.	*De posteritate Caini (On the Posterity of Cain)*	*Sacr.*	*De sacrificiis Abelis et Caini (On the Sacrifices of Cain and Abel)*
Praem.	*De praemiis et poenis (On Rewards and Punishments)*	*Somn.*	*De somniis (On Dreams)*
Prob.	*Quod omnis probus liber sit (That Every Good Person Is Free)*	*Spec.*	*De specialibus legibus (On the Special Laws)*
		Virt.	*De virtutibus (On the Virtues)*

Josephus

Ag. Ap.	*Against Apion*	*J.W.*	*Jewish War*
Ant.	*Jewish Antiquities*	*Life*	*The Life*

Mishnah, Talmud, and Related Literature

b.	Babylonian Talmud
m.	Mishnah
t.	Tosefta
y.	Jerusalem Talmud

'Abot	*'Abot*	*Sanh.*	*Sanhedrin*
B. Bat.	*Baba Batra*	*Šebu.*	*Šebuʿot*
Ber.	*Berakot*	*Soṭah*	*Soṭah*
'Erub.	*'Erubin*	*Taʿan.*	*Taʿanit*
Mak.	*Makkot*	*Ter.*	*Terumot*
Meg.	*Megillah*	*Yebam.*	*Yebamot*
Šabb.	*Šabbat*	*Yoma*	*Yoma (= Kippurim)*

Other Rabbinic Works

'Abot R. Nat.	*'Abot de Rabbi Nathan*	*S. ʿOlam Rab.*	*Seder ʿOlam Rabbah*
Rab.	*Rabbah (+ biblical book)*		

Apostolic Fathers

Barn.	*Barnabas*	Ign. *Pol.*	Ignatius, *To Polycarp*
1–2 Clem.	*1–2 Clement*	Ign. *Rom.*	Ignatius, *To the Romans*
Did.	*Didache*	Ign. *Smyrn.*	Ignatius, *To the Smyrnaeans*
Diogn.	*Diognetus*	Ign. *Trall.*	Ignatius, *To the Trallians*
Herm.	*Shepherd of Hermas*	*Mart. Pol.*	*Martyrdom of Polycarp*
Ign. *Eph.*	Ignatius, *To the Ephesians*	Pol. *Phil.*	Polycarp, *To the Philippians*
Ign. *Magn.*	Ignatius, *To the Magnesians*	*Vit. Poly.*	*Vita Polycarpi (Life of Polycarp)*
Ign. *Phld.*	Ignatius, *To the Philadelphians*		

New Testament Apocrypha and Pseudepigrapha

Acts Pet. Paul	*Acts of Peter and Paul*
Acts Pil.	*Acts of Pilate*

Ep. Apost.   *Epistle of the Apostles (Epistula Apostolorum)*
Ps.-Clem. Hom. *Pseudo-Clementine Homilies*
Ps.-Clem. Rec. *Pseudo-Clementine Recognitions*

Greek and Latin Works

Aelian

Nat. an.   *De natura animalium (Nature of Animals)*

Aelius Aristides

Or.   *Orationes (Orations)*

Aeschylus

Eum.   *Eumenides*

Apollodorus

Bib.   *Bibliotheca*

Apollonius Paradoxographus

Hist. mir.   *Historiae mirabiles*

Appian

Punica   *History of Rome: The Punic Wars*

Apuleius

Metam.   *Metamorphoses (The Golden Ass)*

Aristophanes

Av.   *Aves (Birds)*
Vesp. *Vespae (Wasps)*

Aristotle

An. post.   *Analytica posteriora (Posterior Analytics)*
Eth. nic.   *Ethica nichomachea (Nichomachean Ethics)*
Metaph.   *Metaphysica (Metaphysics)*
Rhet.   *Rhetorica (Rhetoric)*
Top.   *Topica (Topics)*

Arrian

Anab.   *Anabasis*

Athenaeus

Deipn.   *Deipnosophistae*

Athenagoras

Leg.   *Legatio pro Christianis (Embassy for the Christians)*

Augustine

Conf.   *Confessionum libri XIII (Confessions)*
Pelag.   *Contra duas epistulas Pelagianorum (Against the Two Letters of the Pelagians)*

Cebes

Tab.   *Tabula*

Cicero

Att.   *Epistulae ad Atticum*
Clu.   *Pro Cluentio*
Fam.   *Epistulae ad familiares*
Flac.   *Pro Flacco*
Inv.   *De inventione rhetorica*
Mur.   *Pro Murena*
De or.   *De oratore*
Rosc. com.   *Pro Roscio comoedo*
Tusc.   *Tusculanae disputationes*

Clement of Alexandria

Exc.   *Excerpta ex Theodoto (Excerpts from Theodotus)*
Paed.   *Paedagogus (Christ the Educator)*
Prot.   *Protrepticus (Exhortation to the Greeks)*
Strom.   *Stromata (Miscellanies)*

Cyril of Jerusalem

Catech.   *Catecheses*

Demosthenes

Chers.   *De Chersoneso (On the Chersonese)*
Cor.   *De corona (On the Crown)*
Lept.   *Adversus Leptinem (Against Leptines)*

Meg.   *Pro Megalopolitanis (For the*
            Megalopolitans)
Mid.   *In Midiam (Against Meidias)*

Dio Cassius
Hist.   Roman History

Dio Chrysostom
2 Glor.   *De gloria ii (Or. 67) (Popular*
            Opinion)
Ness.   *Nessus (Or. 60) (Nessus, or*
            Deianeira)

Diodorus Siculus
Bib. hist. *Bibliotheca historica (Library of*
              History)

Diogenes Laertius
Vit.   *Vitae philosophorum (Lives of*
            Eminent Philosophers)

Dionysius of Halicarnassus
1–2 Amm. *Epistula ad Ammaeum i–ii*
Ant. rom. *Antiquitates romanae*

Epictetus
Diatr.   *Diatribai (Dissertationes)*
Ench.   *Enchiridion*

Epiphanius
Pan.   *Panarion (Refutation of All*
            Heresies)

Euripides
Bacch.   *Bacchae (Bacchanals)*
Hipp.   *Hippolytus*
Ion   *Ion*

Eusebius
Hist. eccl. *Historia ecclesiastica (Ecclesi-*
               astical History)
Praep. ev.   *Praeparatio evangelica (Prepa-*
               ration for the Gospel)

Gellius
Noc. att. *Noctes atticae (Attic Nights)*

Herodian
Fig.   *De figuris (On Figures)*

Herodotus
Hist.   *Historiae (Histories)*

Heron
Def.   *Definitiones (Definitions)*

Hippolytus
Comm. Dan. *Commentarium in*
              Danielem
Haer.   *Refutatio omnium haere-*
              sium (Refutation of All
              Heresies)

Homer
Od.   *Odyssea (Odyssey)*

Horace
Carm.   *Carmina (Odes)*
Ep.   *Epistulae (Epistles)*
Sat.   *Satirae (Satires)*

Iamblichus
Vit. pyth. *De vita pythagorica (On the*
              Pythagorean Way of Life)

Irenaeus
Epid.   *Epideixis tou apostolikou*
            kērygmatos (Demonstration of the
            Apostolic Preaching)
Haer.   *Adversus haereses (Against*
            Heresies)

Isocrates
Bus.   *Busiris (Or. 11)*
Demon.   *Ad Demonicum (Or. 1)*

Jerome
Vir. ill. *De viris illustribus*

John Chrysostom
Adv. Jud.   *Adversus Judaeos (Dis-*
              courses against Judaizing
              Christians)
Hom. 1 Cor. *Homiliae in epistulam i ad*
              Corinthios
Hom. 2 Cor. *Homiliae in epistulam ii ad*
              Corinthios
Hom. Gal.   *Homiliae in epistulam ad*
              Galatas commentarius

Hom. Heb.	Homiliae in epistulam ad Hebraeos
Hom. Rom.	Homiliae in epistulam ad Romanos

Justin

1 Apol.	Apologia i (First Apology)
Dial.	Dialogus cum Tryphone (Dialogue with Trypho)

Juvenal

Sat.	Satirae (Satires)

Lactantius

Epit.	Epitome divinarum institutionum (Epitome of the Divine Institutes)

Livy

Hist.	History of Rome

Lucian

Alex.	Alexander (Pseudomantis) (Alexander the False Prophet)
Dial. mort.	Dialogi mortuorum (Dialogues of the Dead)
Icar.	Icaromenippus
Men.	Menippus (Necyomantia) (Menippus, or Descent into Hades)
Peregr.	De morte Peregrini (The Passing of Peregrinus)
Philops.	Philopseudes (The Lover of Lies)
Tox.	Toxaris
Trag.	Tragopodagra (Tragic Gout)
Ver. hist.	Vera historia (A True Story)

Origen

Cels.	Contra Celsum (Against Celsus)
Comm. Rom.	Commentarii in Romanos
Hom. Gen.	Homiliae in Genesim

Orosius

Hist.	Historiae adversus Paganos

Ovid

Metam.	Metamorphoses

Philostratus

Her.	Heroicus
Vit. Apoll.	Vita Apollonii
Vit. soph.	Vitae sophistarum

Pindar

Ol.	Olympionikai (Olympian Odes)
Pyth.	Pythionika (Pythian Odes)

Plato

Apol.	Apologia (Apology of Socrates)
Charm.	Charmides
Ep.	Epistulae (Letters)
Leg.	Leges (Laws)
Menex.	Menexenus
Phaed.	Phaedo
Phaedr.	Phaedrus
Phileb.	Philebus
Resp.	Respublica (Republic)
Symp.	Symposium
Tim.	Timaeus

Pliny the Elder

Nat.	Naturalis historia

Plutarch

Aem.	Aemilius Paullus
Ages.	Agesilaus
Alex.	Alexander
Apoph. Iac.	Apophthegmata Iaconica
Cleom.	Cleomenes
Def. orac.	De defectu oraculorum
De laude	De laude ipsius
Mor.	Moralia

Polybius

Hist.	Historiae (Histories)

Porphyry

Abst.	De abstinentia
Antr. nymph.	De antro nympharum
Vit. Pyth.	Vita Pythagorae

Pseudo-Aristotle

Mir. ausc.	De mirabilibus auscultationibus (On Marvelous Things Heard)

Quintilian

Inst.	Institutio oratoria

Seneca

Ben.   De beneficiis

Sextus Empiricus

Math.   Adversus mathematicos (Against
         the Mathematicians)

Simplicius

In Phys.   In Physica Aristotelis (On Aristo-
            tle's Physics)

Strabo

Geogr.   Geographica (Geography)

Suetonius

Claud.   Divus Claudius
Dom.   Domitianus
Nero   Nero
Otho   Otho
Tib.   Tiberius
Vesp.   Vespasianus

Tacitus

Dial.   Dialogus de oratoribus

Terence

Eun.   Eunuchus

Tertullian

Adv. Jud.   Adversus Judaeos (Against the
             Jews)
Apol.   Apologeticus (Apology)
Bapt.   De baptismo (Baptism)
Marc.   Adversus Marcionem (Against
         Marcion)
Or.   De oratione (Prayer)
Pud.   De pudicitia (Modesty)
Res.   De resurrectione carnis (The
        Resurrection of the Flesh)

Theocritus

Id.   Idylls

Thucydides

Hist.   History of the Peloponnesian War

Virgil

Ecl.   Eclogae

Xenophon

Anab.   Anabasis
Oec.   Oeconomicus

Secondary Sources

AASF   Annales Academiae scientiarum
        fennicae
AB   Anchor Bible
ABD   Anchor Bible Dictionary. Edited
        by D. N. Freedman. 6 vols. New
        York, 1992
ABR   Australian Biblical Review
ABRL   Anchor Bible Reference Library
ACCS   Ancient Christian Commentary
        on Scripture
ACNT   Augsburg Commentary on the
        New Testament
AGJU   Arbeiten zur Geschichte des antiken
        Judentums und des Urchristentums
AJSR   Association of Jewish Studies
        Review
ALBO   Analecta lovaniensia biblica et
        orientalia

AnBib   Analecta biblica
ANRW   Aufstieg und Niedergang der
         römischen Welt: Geschichte
         und Kultur Roms im Spiegel der
         neueren Forschung. Edited by
         H. Temporini and W. Haase.
         Berlin, 1972–
ANTC   Abingdon New Testament
         Commentaries
Anth. pal.   Anthologia palatina. 2 vols.
             Leiden, 1911
ApOTC   Apollos Old Testament
         Commentary
APOT   The Apocrypha and Pseudepig-
         rapha of the Old Testament.
         Edited by R. H. Charles. 2 vols.
         Oxford, 1913
AThR   Anglican Theological Review
ATJ   Ashland Theological Journal

AUS	American University Studies	CBC	Cambridge Bible Commentary
BAFCS	The Books of Acts in Its First-Century Setting	CBET	Contributions to Biblical Theology and Exegesis
BAR	*Biblical Archaeology Review*	CBQ	*Catholic Biblical Quarterly*
BBR	*Bulletin for Biblical Research*	CC	Continental Commentaries
BDAG	Bauer, W., F. W. Danker, W. F. Arndt, and F. W. Gingrich. *Greek-English Lexicon of the New Testament and Other Early Christian Literature.* 3rd ed. Chicago, 1999	CCWJCW	Cambridge Commentaries on Writings of the Jewish and Christian World, 200 B.C. to A.D. 200
		CGTC	Cambridge Greek Testament Commentary
BDF	Blass, F., A. Debrunner, and R. W. Funk. *A Greek Grammar of the New Testament and Other Early Christian Literature.* Chicago, 1961	CGTSC	Cambridge Greek Testament for Schools and Colleges
		CIJ	*Corpus inscriptionum judaicarum*
		CIL	*Corpus inscriptionum latinarum*
BECNT	Baker Exegetical Commentary on the New Testament	CJT	*Canadian Journal of Theology*
BEFAR	Bibliothèque des ècoles françaises d'Athènes et de Rome	CNT	Commentaire du Nouveau Testament
BETL	Bibliotheca ephemeridum theologicarum lovaniensium	COL	Christian Origins Library
		ConBNT	Coniectanea neotestamentica or Coniectanea biblica: New Testament Series
BFCT	Beiträge zur Förderung christlicher Theologie		
BHT	Beiträge zur historischen Theologie	ConcJ	*Concordia Journal*
		CPJ	*Corpus papyrorum judaicarum*
Bib	*Biblica*	CRINT	Compendia rerum iudaicarum ad Novum Testamentum
BibInt	*Biblical Interpretation*		
BibJudSt	Biblical and Judaic Studies	CSJH	Chicago Studies in the History of Judaism
BibTS	Biblical Tools and Studies		
BJRL	*Bulletin of the John Rylands University Library of Manchester*	CTQ	*Concordia Theological Quarterly*
		CurBR	*Currents in Biblical Research*
BJS	Brown Judaic Studies	DJD	Discoveries in the Judaean Desert
BLS	Bible and Liberation Series		
BNTC	Black's New Testament Commentaries	*DPL*	*Dictionary of Paul and His Letters.* Edited by G. F. Hawthorne and R. P. Martin. Downers Grove, 1993
BSac	*Bibliotheca sacra*		
BSP	Bochumer Studien zur Philosophie	*DSD*	*Dead Sea Discoveries*
		EAC	Entretiens sur l'antiquité classique
BTB	*Biblical Theology Bulletin*		
BTS	Biblical Tools and Studies	EB	Echter Bibel
BTZ	*Berliner theologische Zeitschrift*	EBib	Etudes bibliques
BZ	*Biblische Zeitschrift*	EC	Epworth Commentaries
BZAW	Beihefte zur Zeitschrift für die alttestamentliche Wissenschaft	*EDNT*	*Exegetical Dictionary of the New Testament.* Edited by H. Balz and G. Schneider. 3 vols. Grand Rapids, 1990–1993
BZNW	Beihefte zur Zeitschrift für die neutestamentliche Wissenschaft		

EGGNT	Exegetical Guide to the Greek New Testament		*HistT*	*History and Theory*
EgT	*Église et théologie*		*HJ*	*Historisches Jahrbuch*
EKKNT	Evangelisch-katholischer Kommentar zum Neuen Testament		HNT	Handbuch zum Neuen Testament
EncJud²	*Encyclopedia Judaica.* 2nd ed. 22 vols. Detroit, 2007		HTKNT	Herders theologischer Kommentar zum Neuen Testament
EpRev	*Epworth Review*		*HTR*	*Harvard Theological Review*
ERT	*Evangelical Review of Theology*		*HUCA*	*Hebrew Union College Annual*
ETL	*Ephemerides theologicae lovanienses*		IBC	Interpretation: A Bible Commentary for Teaching and Preaching
EUS	European University Studies		IBRBib	IBR Bibliographies
ExAud	*Ex auditu*		ICC	International Critical Commentary
ExpTim	*Expository Times*		*IG*	*Inscriptiones gracae.* Editio minor. Berlin, 1924–
FCBS	Fortress Classics in Biblical Studies		*IGRR*	*Inscriptiones graecae ad res romanas pertinentes.* Edited by R. Cagnat et al. 3 vols. Paris, 1901–27
FEUNTK	Forschungen zur Entstehung des Urchristentums des Neuen Testaments und der Kirche		*Int*	*Interpretation*
FilNeot	*Filología Neotestamentaria*		Jastrow	Jastrow, M. *A Dictionary of the Targumim, the Talmud Babli and Yerushalmi, and the Midrashic Literature.* 2 vols. in 1. Peabody, MA, 2005
FM	*Faith & Mission*			
FRLANT	Forschungen zur Religion und Literatur des Alten und Neuen Testaments			
FTMT	Fortress Texts in Modern Theology		*JBL*	*Journal of Biblical Literature*
GAP	Guides to Apocrypha and Pseudepigrapha		*JCE*	*Journal of Christian Education*
GD	Gorgias Dissertations		*JCSBR*	*Journal of the Chicago Society of Biblical Research*
GOTR	*Greek Orthodox Theological Review*		*JE*	*The Jewish Encyclopedia.* Edited by I. Singer. 12 vols. New York, 1925
GP	Gospel Perspectives			
GR	*Greece and Rome*		*JECS*	*Journal of Early Christian Studies*
GRBS	*Greek, Roman, and Byzantine Studies*		*JEH*	*Journal of Ecclesiastical History*
HALOT	Koehler, L., W. Baumgartner, and J. J. Stamm, *The Hebrew and Aramaic Lexicon of the Old Testament.* Translated and edited under the supervision of M. E. J. Richardson. 4 vols. Leiden, 1994–1999		*JETS*	*Journal of the Evangelical Theological Society*
			JFSR	*Journal of Feminist Studies in Religion*
			JHC	*Journal of Higher Criticism*
			JJS	*Journal of Jewish Studies*
HBT	*Horizons in Biblical Theology*		*JR*	*Journal of Religion*
HCS	Hellenistic Culture and Society		*JRS*	*Journal of Roman Studies*
HE	Hermes Einzelschriften		*JSHJ*	*Journal for the Study of the Historical Jesus*
Hen	*Henoch*			

JSHRZ	Jüdische Schriften aus hellenistisch-römischer Zeit	NCBC	New Century Bible Commentary
JSJ	*Journal for the Study of Judaism in the Persian, Hellenistic and Roman Periods*	NClarB	New Clarendon Bible
		NDST	Notre Dame Studies in Theology
		NedTT	*Nederlands theologisch tijdschrift*
JSJSup	Journal for the Study of Judaism: Supplement Series	*Neot*	*Neotestamentica*
JSNT	*Journal for the Study of the New Testament*	NGS	New Gospel Studies
		NIB	*The New Interpreter's Bible.* Edited by Leander E. Keck et al. 12 vols. Nashville, 1994–2002
JSNTSup	Journal for the Study of the New Testament: Supplement Series		
		NICNT	New International Commentary on the New Testament
JSOT	*Journal for the Study of the Old Testament*	NIGTC	New International Greek Testament Commentary
JSOTSup	Journal for the Study of the Old Testament: Supplement Series	*NovT*	*Novum Testamentum*
		NovTSup	Novum Testamentum Supplements
JSP	*Journal for the Study of the Pseudepigrapha*	NTAF	The New Testament and the Apostolic Fathers
JSPSup	Journal for the Study of the Pseudepigrapha: Supplement Series	NTD	Das Neue Testament Deutsch
		NTL	New Testament Library
JSS	*Journal of Semitic Studies*	NTM	New Testament Monographs
JTC	*Journal for Theology and the Church*	NTOA	Novum Testamentum et Orbis Antiquus
JTS	*Journal of Theological Studies*	NTR	New Testament Readings
KEK	Kritisch-exegetischer Kommentar über das Neue Testament (Meyer-Kommentar)	*NTS*	*New Testament Studies*
		NTT	New Testament Theology
		NTTS	New Testament Tools and Studies
LCL	Loeb Classical Library	OBT	Overtures to Biblical Theology
LD	Lectio divina	OECS	Oxford Early Christian Studies
LNTS	Library of New Testament Studies	OTL	Old Testament Library
		OTM	Oxford Theological Monographs
LPS	Library of Pauline Studies	*OTP*	*The Old Testament Pseudepigrapha.* Edited by J. H. Charlesworth. 2 vols. New York, 1985
LQ	*Lutheran Quarterly*		
LSJ	Liddell, H. G., R. Scott, and H. S. Jones. *A Greek-English Lexicon.* 9th ed., with revised supplement. Oxford, 1996		
		PBM	Paternoster Biblical Monographs
LTJ	*Lutheran Theological Journal*	PBS	Pamphlet Bible Series
LumVie	*Lumière et vie*	PBTM	Paternoster Biblical and Theological Monographs
MBCBSup	Mnemosyne, bibliotheca classica Batava: Supplementum		
		PCNT	Paideia Commentaries on the New Testament
MNTC	Moffatt New Testament Commentary	PFES	Publications of the Finnish Exegetical Society
NCB	New Century Bible		

PG	Patrologia graeca [= Patrolo-giae cursus completus: Series graeca]. Edited by J.-P. Migne. 162 vols. Paris, 1857–1886	SBLMS	Society of Biblical Literature Monograph Series
PGM	*Papyri graecae magicae: Die griechischen Zauberpapyri.* Edited by K. Preisendanz. Berlin, 1928	SBLSCSS	Society of Biblical Literature Septuagint and Cognate Studies Series
		SBLSP	*Society of Biblical Literature Seminar Papers*
PIBA	*Proceedings of the Irish Biblical Association*	SBLSymS	Society of Biblical Literature Symposium Series
PL	Patrologia latina [= Patrologiae cursus completus: Series latina]. Edited by J.-P. Migne. 217 vols. Paris, 1844–1864	SBT	Studies in Biblical Theology
		SC	Sources chrétiennes. Paris: Cerf, 1943–
		SCHT	Studies in Christian History and Thought
PMS	Patristic Monograph Series	*ScrB*	*Scripture Bulletin*
PNTC	Pelican New Testament Commentaries	SCS	Septuagint and Cognate Studies
		SEÅ	*Svensk exegetisk årsbok*
PRSA	Problemi e richerche di storia antica	SFSHJ	South Florida Studies in the History of Judaism
PRSt	*Perspectives in Religious Studies*	SHR	Studies in the History of Religions
PSB	*Princeton Seminary Bulletin*		
PSt	Pauline Studies	SIG	*Sylloge inscriptionum grae-carum.* Edited by W. Ditten-berger. 4 vols. 3rd ed. Leipzig, 1915–24
PTSDSSP	Princeton Theological Seminary Dead Sea Scrolls Project		
QD	Quaestiones disputatae		
RB	*Revue biblique*	SJC	Studies in Judaism and Christianity
RBL	*Review of Biblical Literature*		
RelSRev	*Religious Studies Review*	SJCA	Studies in Judaism and Chris-tianity in Antiquity
ResQ	*Restoration Quarterly*		
RevExp	*Review and Expositor*	SJCiv	Studies in Jewish Civilization
RevQ	*Revue de Qumran*	SJSHRZ	Studien zu den jüdischen Schriften aus hellenistisch-römischer Zeit
Rhet. Gr.	*Rhetores graeci.* Edited by C. Walz. 10 vols. Stuttgart and Tübingen, 1832–36		
		SJT	*Scottish Journal of Theology*
RivB	*Rivista biblica italiana*	SNT	Studien zum Neuen Testament
SAAA	Studies on the Apocryphal Acts of the Apostles	SNTSMS	Society for New Testament Studies Monograph Series
SAOC	Studies in Ancient Oriental Civilization	*SNTSU*	*Studien zum Neuen Testament und seiner Umwelt*
SB	*Sammelbuch griechischer Urkun-den aus Aegypten.* Edited by E. Preisigke et al. Vols. 1– , 1915	SNTW	Studies in the New Testament and Its World
		SP	Sacra Pagina
SBL	Studies in Biblical Literature	*SocRel*	*Sociology of Religion*
SBLAB	Studies in Biblical Literature Academia Biblica	SP	Sacra Pagina
		SR	*Studies in Religion/Sciences religieuses*
SBLDS	Society of Biblical Literature Dissertation Series	*ST*	*Studia theologica*

STDJ	Studies on the Texts of the Desert of Judah	TPM	Tyndale Press Monographs
StM	*Studia missionalia*	*TRu*	*Theologische Rundschau*
StPB	Studia post-biblica	TS	Texts and Studies
STRev	*Sewanee Theological Review*	*TS*	*Theological Studies*
SUNT	Studien zur Umwelt des Neuen Testaments	TSAJ	Texte und Studien zum antiken Judentum
SVTP	Studia in Veteris Testamenti pseudepigraphica	*TSK*	*Theologische Studien und Kritiken*
SwJT	*Southwestern Journal of Theology*	TTECLS	Texts and Translations: Early Christian Literature Series
TADAE	*Textbook of Aramaic Documents from Ancient Eygpt*. Edited by B. Porten and A. Yardeni. 4 vols. Winona Lake, Ind., 1986–99	TTPS	Texts and Translations: Pseudepigrapha Series
		TTS	*Trierer theologische Studien*
		TUGAL	Texte und Untersuchungen zur Geschichte der altchristlichen Literatur
TCH	Transformation of Classical Heritage	*TynBul*	*Tyndale Bulletin*
TDNT	*Theological Dictionary of the New Testament*. Edited by G. Kittel and G. Friedrich. Translated by G. W. Bromiley. 10 vols. Grand Rapids, 1964–1976	*TZ*	*Theologische Zeitschrift*
		VC	*Vigiliae christianae*
		VCSup	Vigiliae christianae Supplements
		VT	*Vetus Testamentum*
		VTSup	Vetus Testamentum Supplements
TDOT	*Theological Dictionary of the Old Testament*. Edited by G. J. Botterweck and H. Ringgren. Translated by J. T. Willis, G. W. Bromiley, and D. E. Green. 8 vols. Grand Rapids, 1974–	WBC	Word Biblical Commentary
		WC	Westminster Commentaries
		WestBC	Westminster Bible Companion
		WMANT	Wissenschaftliche Monographien zum Alten und Neuen Testament
TeolSt	Teologiske Studier	WUNT	Wissenschaftliche Untersuchungen zum Neuen Testament
TF	Theologische Forschung		
THKNT	Theologischer Handkommentar zum Neuen Testament	*WW*	*Word and World*
		ZAC	*Zeitschrift für Antikes Christentum/Journal of Ancient Christianity*
TLNT	*Theological Lexicon of the New Testament*. C. Spicq. Translated and edited by J. D. Ernest. 3 vols. Peabody, MA, 1994	ZECNT	Zondervan Exegetical Commentary on the New Testament
		ZNW	*Zeitschrift für die neutestamentliche Wissenschaft und die Kunde der älteren Kirche*
TNTC	Tyndale New Testament Commentaries		
TPINTC	TPI New Testament Commentaries	*ZTK*	*Zeitschrift für Theologie und Kirche*

Part 1

PAUL

1

Who Was Paul?

Who was Paul—the historical Paul? Tension between the Paul of history and the apostle of faith is already apparent in the New Testament. Most notably, although Luke portrays him as a great miracle worker,[1] critics have concluded that his opponents at Corinth were able to deny his ability to perform miracles.[2] Then, for example, the letter to the Colossians, probably not from Paul's hand, if not betraying and subverting him,[3] at least shows a figure remembered and redrawn for the needs of a later period without even the hint of miracle working on Paul's part.

Which, if any, of these portraits best represents the historical Paul?[4] Was Paul, as Luke would have us believe, a great miracle worker? Or, if we understand them, were his critics at Corinth correct, so that Colossians is more

1. Ernst Haenchen, *The Acts of the Apostles: A Commentary*, trans. Bernard Noble et al. (Oxford: Blackwell, 1971), 113. The contrast in the apparent importance of miracle working between the Paul of the Epistles and the Paul of Acts has long been noted; see the brief discussion by Frans Neirynck, "The Miracle Stories in the Acts of the Apostles: An Introduction," in *Les Actes des Apôtres: Traditions, rédaction, théologie*, ed. Jacob Kremer (BETL 48; Gembloux: Duculot; Louvain: Leuven University Press, 1979), 173n10. Further, see chap. 9 below.

2. E.g., Ernst Käsemann, "Die Legitimität des Apostels: Eine Untersuchung zu II Korinther 10–13," ZNW 41 (1942): 35. Further, see §§1.1, 8.6 below.

3. On the Deutero-Paulines and Ephesians 2:15, cf. Neil Elliott, *Liberating Paul: The Justice of God and the Politics of the Apostle* (BLS; Maryknoll, NY: Orbis, 1994), 26.

4. See Martinus C. de Boer, "Comment: Which Paul?" in *Paul and the Legacies of Paul*, ed. William S. Babcock (Dallas: Southern Methodist University Press, 1990), 45–54; Dennis R. MacDonald, "Apocryphal and Canonical Narratives about Paul," in Babcock, *Paul*, 55–70.

accurate in carrying no memory of Paul as a miracle worker or even as interested in the miraculous? Or, again, do Paul's letters need to be read more carefully to recover some other relation that the historical Paul had to miracle working and the miraculous?

The critical study of Paul has been dominated by an interest in him as an intellectual and a theologian, not as a person involved in the miraculous or performing miracles. For Origen (c. 185–c. 254 CE), Paul "values reason above miraculous workings" (*Cels.* 3.46).[5] Rudolf Bultmann (1884–1976) assessed Paul's historical position in terms of being "the founder of Christian theology."[6] C. F. D. Moule (1908–2007), perhaps the most influential British New Testament scholar of the twentieth century, designated Paul "the prince of thinkers."[7] The result is that Paul is generally discussed in terms of being a thinker and considered "the first and greatest Christian theologian."[8] In particular, the last generation and more of Pauline studies, dominated by the so-called, but increasingly contested,[9] New Perspective on Paul, gives the impression that Paul's thinking was preoccupied with the law, and that he is to be understood primarily through the lens of this discussion.[10] Even more recent studies do not contest this general perception.[11]

These various scholarly conversations about Paul, dominated by the assumption that he was primarily a thinker and a theologian, and the contrasting portraits of Paul in the New Testament raise the question of how he would have understood himself and how he would have been seen by those who knew him. Would they, along with Paul himself, have taken his work to be primarily that of a thinker and a theologian or of a practical missionary?

At least initially, Paul's literary legacy certainly gives the impression of coming from the pen of a person who solves theological problems through careful thought and interaction with his literary traditions. But we have probably fallen into a trap by assuming that Paul's literary achievements accurately

---

5. See the comments by Andrew Daunton-Fear, *Healing in the Early Church: The Church's Ministry of Healing and Exorcism from the First to the Fifth Century* (SCHT; Milton Keynes: Paternoster, 2009), 105–6.

6. Rudolf Bultmann, *Theology of the New Testament*, 2 vols. (London: SCM, 1952–55), 1:187. In the long line of discussions to the present, see, e.g., Udo Schnelle, *Apostle Paul: His Life and Theology*, trans. M. Eugene Boring (Grand Rapids: Baker Academic, 2005).

7. C. F. D. Moule, "Interpreting Paul by Paul: An Essay in the Comparative Study of Pauline Thought," in *New Testament Christianity for Africa and the World: Essays in Honour of Harry Sawyer*, ed. Mark E. Glasswell and Edward W. Fashole-Luke (London: SPCK, 1974), 89.

8. James D. G. Dunn, *The Theology of Paul the Apostle* (Grand Rapids: Eerdmans, 1998), 2.

9. See Gregory K. Beale, "The Overstated 'New' Perspective?" *BBR* 19 (2009): 85–94.

10. Cf. A. Andrew Das, "Paul and the Law: Pressure Points in the Debate," in *Paul Unbound: Other Perspectives on the Apostle*, ed. Mark D. Given (Peabody, MA: Hendrickson, 2010), 99–117.

11. Cf. N. T. Wright, "Paul in Current Anglophone Scholarship," *ExpTim* 123 (2012): 367–81.

characterize his accomplishments. For, as we will see, a closer reading of Paul's letters, taking into account more than his literary activities—his life, his experiences, and his missionary accomplishments—reveals a different Paul. While not denying his genius and creative power as a theologian, to see him only or primarily as such is to caricature rather than describe him. Nearer the mark is the assertion by Adolf Deissmann (1866–1937) that "He is far more a man of prayer, a witness, a confessor and a prophet, than a learned exegete and close thinking scholastic."[12] Also, in an attempt to capture the essence of his ministry or his contribution to the history of Christianity, Heikki Räisänen suggests that Paul was "first and foremost a missionary, a man of practical religion who develops a line of thought to make a practical point, to influence the conduct of his readers."[13] Yet, even these turn out to be inadequate representations of Paul.

The question of how to describe Paul and his ministry and theology also confronts us when we take into account the apparent disconnect between the portraits of Paul and Jesus in the New Testament. On the one hand, Jesus is reported to have been a powerful and prolific miracle worker, giving this aspect of his ministry a high profile in his self-understanding and how he interpreted his mission. Yet, on the other hand, when we turn to the letters of Paul, not only does he show little interest in the pre-Easter ministry of Jesus but he also appears to say little or nothing of performing miracles in his own ministry. Paul offers no narrative of a miracle relating to his ministry; at best he only appears to hint at miraculous activity.[14] Indeed, from a perspective broader than just the miraculous, Bultmann said, "I do not believe it is possible to state sufficiently sharply the contrast in the NT canon between the Synoptic Gospels on the one hand and the Pauline letters and later literature on the other."[15]

How the ministry of Jesus became the religion of Paul is a central problem for students of Paul and the New Testament, as well as for all Christian theology.[16] Although it is beyond the scope of this study to attempt solving the problem of the relationship between Paul and Jesus, by the end of our

12. Adolf Deissmann, *Paul: A Study in Social and Religious History*, trans. William E. Wilson (New York: Harper, 1957), 6.

13. Heikki Räisänen, *Paul and the Law*, 2nd ed. (WUNT 29; Tübingen: Mohr Siebeck, 1987), 267.

14. Cf. Jacob Jervell, "The Signs of an Apostle: Paul's Miracles," in *The Unknown Paul: Essays on Luke-Acts and Early Christian History* (Minneapolis: Augsburg, 1984), 91.

15. Rudolf Bultmann, *History of the Synoptic Tradition*, trans. John Marsh (New York: Harper & Row, 1963), 303.

16. Cf. Albert Schweitzer, *Paul and His Interpreters: A Critical History*, trans. W. Montgomery (London: Black, 1912), v; Alexander J. M. Wedderburn, introduction to *Paul and Jesus: Collected Essays*, ed. Alexander J. M. Wedderburn (JSNTSup 37; Sheffield: JSOT Press, 1989), 11.

discussion it will be apparent that while Bultmann's statement about the pro-claimer becoming the proclaimed remains basically correct,[17] Jesus and Paul had both less and more in common than is generally supposed. On the one hand, as I have attempted to demonstrate for Jesus,[18] in relation to Paul, this study will show that the more we distance Paul from the miraculous, the less we understand him, his theology, and his mission. On the other hand, we will see that for Paul the miraculous was both broader and functionally different than for Jesus. We will also have evidence that earliest Christianity was much more deeply characterized by the miraculous than it is presently assumed to have been. Thus, through a discussion of the miraculous in relation to Paul, this study is an attempt to make a contribution to the understanding of the historical Paul. (It is to be noted that this is not an attempt to offer a complete sketch of the historical Paul, but only to argue for an essential part of that picture.) In turn, this study also attempts to contribute to the understanding of the relationship between the religion of Jesus and the religion of Paul. More broadly, this study is to be taken as a contribution to understanding the nature of earliest Christianity and the place and function of miracles in it.

1.1 Specific Issues

In relation to Paul and the miraculous—the focus of this study—what follows seeks to answer a series of six interrelated questions. (1) What was Paul's ex-perience of and his view of his involvement in miracles and the miraculous? Did he, for example, consider himself a miracle worker? Walter Schmithals says, "The Pauline epistles contain no sort of suggestion that Paul was such a miracle-worker, or that he practiced healing and exorcisms."[19] Paul then, as Bruno Bauer had put it, was fighting by means of word alone.[20] For Paul, the true signs of an apostle were the hardships and the persecutions he endured.[21]

Nevertheless, as we will see, since the beginning of the scientific study of Paul there have been occasional statements made, and studies concluding, that Paul performed, or thought he performed, miracles. My aim is to examine the data in an attempt to contribute to and give a place to this small, though

17. Bultmann, *Theology*, 1:33.
18. Graham H. Twelftree, "The Miracles of Jesus: Marginal or Mainstream?" *JSHJ* 1 (2003): 104–24.
19. Walter Schmithals, *The Office of Apostle in the Early Church*, trans. John E. Steely (Nashville: Abingdon, 1969), 36–37, citing 1 Cor. 2:4; 1 Thess. 1:5.
20. Bruno Bauer, *Die Apostelgeschichte: Eine Ausgleichung des Paulinismus und des Juden-thums innerhalb der christlichen Kirche* (Berlin: Hempel, 1850), 7–25.
21. Günther Bornkamm, *Paul*, trans. D. M. G. Stalker (London: Hodder & Stoughton, 1971), 76.

increasingly clear, voice that Paul considered himself involved in the miraculous. However, we will also find that Paul's view of himself as a miracle worker and his perceived relationship to the miraculous is to be viewed quite differently from how Jesus saw himself.

Equally significant is the question: (2) How important did Paul consider miracle working, and what profile did he think it took in his ministry? Over against Ernst Haenchen, who concluded that miracles were not very significant to Paul, we have, for example, Jacob Jervell's assertion that "miracles assume a quite central role in Paul's preaching, almost to a greater degree than in Acts."[22] The related question is (3) what meaning or significance did Paul give to his miracles? This question arises from what Paul has written, but we are also prompted to read Paul carefully in light of Jesus seeing his miracles as having eschatological and salvific significance.

A further question relating to Paul himself is (4) if he understood his ministry involved conducting miracles, how does he relate such a power-based ministry to his theology of weakness, suffering, and the cross?[23] Or, how can Paul write that he is a man of weakness, yet at the same time claim or be credited with works of power? Hence, we will go on to ask: (5) How does Paul relate the miraculous to other aspects of his theology and ministry? In doing so, we will test F. Gerald Downing's assertion that Paul achieved "very little integration" of the miraculous with his message and lifestyle.[24] Finally, if Paul thought he conducted miracles then (6) what kinds of miracles did he perform?

1.2 The Discussion So Far

If the major studies of Paul over the last century and more are a gauge, with some important exceptions (which I will discuss in a moment), there has been little interest in him in relation to the miraculous. Moreover, where the topic has been addressed, rarely and inadequately has it been shown what impact the miraculous should have on the interpretation of Paul's life, theology, and mission. Taking into account Pauline studies of enduring significance,[25] we

22. Jervell, "Signs," 91, citing Haenchen, *Acts*, 114.
23. E.g., Jacob Jervell, "Der schwache Charismatiker," in *Rechtfertigung: Festschrift für Ernst Käsemann zum 70. Geburtstag*, ed. Johannes Friedrich, Wolfgang Pöhlmann, and Peter Stuhlmacher (Tübingen: Mohr Siebeck, 1976), 185.
24. F. Gerald Downing, *Cynics, Paul, and the Pauline Churches* (London: Routledge, 1998), 223.
25. For recent surveys of Pauline studies see, e.g., Bruce N. Fisk, "Paul: Life and Letters," in *The Face of New Testament Studies: A Survey of Recent Research*, ed. Scot McKnight and Grant R. Osborne (Grand Rapids: Baker Academic; Leicester: Apollos, 2004), 283–325; James D. G. Dunn, "Paul's Theology," in McKnight and Osborne, *New Testament Studies*, 326–48.

begin with those in which the miraculous has a low profile or has been inadequately related to an overall assessment of Paul. In the next brief section I
will piece together the results and implications of this survey.

(a) Little or no interest in miracles. Of the olympian figures in the scientific study of the New Testament who are celebrated in Albert Schweitzer's
masterly and readable *Paul and His Interpreters: A Critical History* (1912),
we need only draw attention to two individuals who remain significant for
Pauline studies, Ferdinand Christian Baur (1792–1860) of Tübingen and William Wrede (1859–1906) of Breslau.

Baur, who placed the critical study of early Christianity on sound methodological footings in allowing the New Testament texts to speak for themselves,[26]
concluded that Acts (with its miracle stories associated with Paul) was not
historically reliable and could not be brought into harmony with Paul's letters.
Notably, however, Baur's historical method ruled out a miraculous interpretation of the texts.[27] What might appear in the narrative as a miracle was, in
reality, no miracle at all.[28] Baur says that the "consciousness of miraculous
power, the δύναμις τοῦ κυρίου ["power of the Lord"], was of course felt by
the Apostles, and in this consciousness they may have looked upon the special
results of their ministry as operations of a powerful energy, as σημεῖα, τέρατα,
and δυνάμεις ["signs, wonders, and miracles"]."[29] In other words, miracles and
the miraculous (having no reality) need not be taken into consideration in our
reconstruction of the historical Paul. Wrede, whose shadow also still falls across
Pauline studies,[30] showed little interest in Paul in relation to the miraculous,
leaving a portrait of Paul that does not include performing miracles.[31]

Though not covered in Schweitzer's history, J. B. Lightfoot (1828–89) should
be mentioned here not only because of his engagement with Baur,[32] but also
because he may be the finest Pauline commentator Britain has produced.[33]
He makes his view clear in concluding that, "There are but few allusions

26. Schweitzer, *Paul and His Interpreters*, 13.
27. Ferdinand Christian Baur, *Paul the Apostle of Jesus Christ: His Life and Works, His Epistles and Teachings*, 2 vols. in 1 (1845; repr., Peabody, MA: Hendrickson, 2003), 1:78; also 1:9, 13, 94–95, 153, 201–3.
28. Ibid., 1:203.
29. Ibid., 1:312–13n, citing 1 Cor. 10:21, 10–28; 2 Cor. 12:12.
30. See, e.g., E. P. Sanders, *Paul and Palestinian Judaism: A Comparison of Patterns of Religion* (London: SCM, 1977), 433n10; J. Christiaan Beker, *Paul the Apostle: The Triumph of God in Life and Thought* (Edinburgh: T&T Clark, 1980), index; Dunn, *Theology of Paul*, 3n3, 3n7, 9n30, 340n22.
31. William Wrede, *Paul*, trans. Edward Lummis (Eugene, OR: Wipf & Stock, 2001).
32. Bruce N. Kaye, "Lightfoot and Baur on Early Christianity," *NovT* 26 (1984): 193–224.
33. Cf. James D. G. Dunn, "Lightfoot, J(oseph) B(arber) (*1828–1889*)," in *Dictionary of Major Biblical Interpreters*, ed. Donald K. McKim, 2nd ed. (Downers Grove, IL: IVP Academic, 2007), 662.

in St Paul to his power of working miracles."[34] The paucity of references to miracles, Lightfoot supposes, is "partly because he [Paul] assumes the fact as known to his hearers, and partly because doubtless he considered this a very poor and mean gift in comparison with the high spiritual powers with which he was endowed."[35]

Schweitzer himself makes only passing reference to what he calls "the sensible manifestations of the spiritual" in Paul.[36] Schweitzer takes it to be of tremendous importance that Paul, "in spite of sharing with his contemporaries the high estimation of the sensible manifestations of the spiritual, maintains . . . the higher right of the rational manifestations of the spiritual."[37] Not surprisingly, Schweitzer leaves aside the miraculous in his assessment of Paul.

Going further into the twentieth century, Bultmann also sees Paul simply sharing, without reflection, popular notions of the time that the Spirit causes such strange phenomena as glossolalia, prophecy, and miracles of healing.[38] Yet, while Schweitzer saw Paul rising above the miraculous in giving preference to the rational, Bultmann sees Paul similarly rising, but in contesting the meaning of the miraculous. In Paul seeing the ministrations of love in the congregation as the "really characteristic feature of his conception of the Spirit," he only "recognizes them to be caused by the Spirit of God as they produce unity in the congregation."[39] Adolf Schlatter (1852–1938), a contemporary of Bultmann, argued that the Gospel record never consisted merely of Jesus' words. It is surprising, therefore, that Schlatter makes only a brief passing reference to the "proofs of divine power" in discussing Paul.[40]

Martin Dibelius (1883–1947) also makes only passing reference to the miraculous in his brief publication *Paul* (1949). He says, "There is no doubt that the young Christian churches experienced extraordinary things in their midst: cures and other 'mighty works'; ecstatic rapture, especially a beatific stammering of sounds that were unintelligible to other people (they called it

34. J. B. Lightfoot, *Notes on Epistles of St Paul from Unpublished Commentaries* (London: Macmillan, 1895), 13.

35. Ibid.

36. Albert Schweitzer, *The Mysticism of Paul the Apostle*, trans. William Montgomery (Baltimore: Johns Hopkins University Press, 1998), 169–72.

37. Ibid., 171.

38. Bultmann, *Theology*, 1:337; cf. 1:333, citing Rom. 15:19; 1 Cor. 2:4.

39. Ibid., 1:337. Further on Bultmann's view of miracle, see Rudolf Bultmann, "The Question of Wonder," in *Faith and Understanding*, ed. Robert W. Funk, trans. Louise Pettibone Smith (Philadelphia: Fortress, 1987), 247–61; Eldon R. Hay, "Bultmann's View of Miracle," *LQ* 24 (1972): 286–300.

40. Adolf Schlatter, *The Theology of the Apostles: The Development of New Testament Theology*, trans. Andreas J. Köstenberger (Grand Rapids: Baker Academic, 1998), 192–93, referring to Rom. 15:19; 2 Cor. 6:6–7; 12:1–6, 12; cf. 279.

'speaking in tongues'); clairvoyance, which could tell what was in other people's minds."[41] Yet, these observations play no appreciable role in understanding Paul, who is described primarily in terms of being a preacher.[42]

In more recent Pauline studies the vast majority of scholars either give little attention to the miraculous or say nothing about how it relates to Paul's life, ministry, and theology.[43] For example, in his *Jesus and the Spirit*, a study of the religious and charismatic experience of Jesus and the first Christians, James D. G. Dunn says there can be no doubt that miracles took place in Paul's ministry and in his communities. Yet, turning to Dunn's *Theology of Paul the Apostle*, we find the miraculous appears to be of little interest. Most of what Dunn says about Paul and the miraculous is in his discussion of Paul's apostolic authority.[44] Otherwise, Dunn does not spend any time directly on Paul and his involvement in the miraculous,[45] and in an otherwise masterly concluding chapter on Paul's theology—his "Postlegomena to a Theology of Paul"—Dunn gives no place to Paul and the miraculous.[46]

---

41. Martin Dibelius, *Paul*, ed. Werner Georg Kümmel, trans. Frank Clarke (London: Longmans, 1953), 92, citing 1 Cor. 14:25.

42. Ibid., e.g., 68–69, 87.

43. Among many examples, see Johannes Munck, *Paul and the Salvation of Mankind*, trans. Frank Clarke (London: SCM, 1959), 159; Bornkamm, *Paul*, e.g., 187; Hans Dieter Betz, *Der Apostel Paulus und die sokratische Tradition: Eine exegetische Untersuchung zu seiner "Apologie" 2 Korinther 10–13* (BHT 45; Tübingen: Mohr Siebeck, 1972), 71; D. E. H. Whiteley, *The Theology of St. Paul*, 2nd ed. (Oxford: Blackwell, 1974), 36, 126; Herman N. Ridderbos, *Paul: An Outline of His Theology*, trans. John Richard de Witt (London: SPCK, 1977), 463; Beker, *Paul*, 114, 151, 295; cf. 286, 296; Thomas F. Best, "St Paul and the Decline of the Miraculous," *Encounter* 44 (1983): 213–41; Gary W. Derickson, "The Cessation of Healing Miracles in Paul's Ministry," *BSac* 155 (1998): 299–315; Ben Witherington III, *The Paul Quest: The Renewed Search for the Jew of Tarsus* (Downers Grove, IL: InterVarsity, 1998), 212; Peter Bolt and Mark Thompson, eds., *The Gospel to the Nations: Perspectives on Paul's Mission; In Honour of Peter T. O'Brien* (Downers Grove, IL: InterVarsity; Leicester, Apollos, 2000); Erich Grässer, *Forschungen zur Apostelgeschichte* (WUNT 137; Tübingen: Mohr Siebeck, 2001), 234–35; Thomas R. Schreiner, *Paul, Apostle of God's Glory in Christ: A Pauline Theology* (Downers Grove, IL: InterVarsity; Leicester: Apollos, 2001), 93, 351, 355–56, 358, 464–65; L. J. (Bert Jan) Lietaert Peerbolte, *Paul the Missionary* (CBET 34; Louvain: Peeters, 2003); Eckhard J. Schnabel, *Early Christian Mission*, 2 vols. (Downers Grove, IL: InterVarsity; Leicester, Apollos, 2004), 2:1357; Schnelle, *Paul*, 153, 174, 201, 259, 261–64; Eckhard J. Schnabel, *Paul the Missionary: Realities, Strategies and Methods* (Downers Grove, IL: IVP Academic; Nottingham, Apollos, 2008), e.g., 354, 368, 453–55; Marcus J. Borg and John Dominic Crossan, *The First Paul: Reclaiming the Radical Visionary behind the Church's Conservative Icon* (New York: HarperOne, 2009), 196, 201; Trevor J. Burke, "The Holy Spirit as the Controlling Dynamic in Paul's Role as Missionary to the Thessalonians," in *Paul as Missionary: Identity, Activity, Theology, and Practice*, ed. Trevor J. Burke and Brian S. Rosner (LNTS 420; London: T&T Clark, 2011), 142, 145–46.

44. Dunn, *Theology of Paul*, 580; cf. 557n138.

45. Cf. ibid., e.g., 48, 456, 483.

46. Ibid., 713–37. Similarly, Beker (*Paul*, 151, 286) mentions but does not discuss Paul and the miraculous or Paul as a miracle worker.

Though we await what N. T. Wright calls his "fuller treatment" of Paul, he says his *Paul: In Fresh Perspective* is a pointer to what he has in mind.[47] Nevertheless, the miraculous is not discussed.[48] Also, in his commentary on Romans Wright had noted that Paul mentions "the various ways in which his work has been accomplished: word and deed, the power of signs and wonders, and (though hardly a separable phenomenon) the power of God's Spirit." From this, and citing a number of passages, Wright concludes that Paul "clearly assumed that powerful deeds, particularly healings, were part of his gospel ministry. This is his regular modus operandi."[49] Yet, so far, this modus operandi plays no role in informing how Wright understands Paul's thinking or ministry.

The first book-length treatment on our topic, which compares the portraits of Paul in Acts and in the authentic Pauline letters, is Stefan Schreiber's *Paulus als Wundertäter (Paul as Miracle Worker)*.[50] Schreiber finds that Luke takes the miracles as important in legitimizing, and making concrete, Paul's proclamation of the gospel. In Acts Paul's miracles establish him as part of the history of salvation. Moreover, Paul's suffering and powerlessness are not underlined, as they are by Paul himself, for whom miracles are not essential in his theology, for in his letters this theme can only be faintly traced. Important in being able to come to these results is Schreiber concluding that three key statements by Paul—1 Corinthians 2:4; Galatians 3:5; 1 Thessalonians 1:5 (see chap. 7 below)—do not refer to miracles but to the wondrous power of the proclamation. Schreiber also concludes that only two of the miracles associated with Paul in Acts can be taken as historical: the healing of the lame man (Acts 14:8–10) and the exorcism of the slave girl (16:16–18).[51] In the course of this study I will be challenging some of Schreiber's conclusions and supporting others, as well as coming to a different understanding of Paul in relation to the miraculous.

(b) Paul as miracle worker. There have been a number of studies taking more seriously, or giving a higher profile to, the issue of Paul and the

---

47. N. T. Wright, *Paul: In Fresh Perspective* (Minneapolis: Fortress, 2005), xi.

48. A discussion of the miraculous is also absent from, e.g., Gerd Lüdemann, *Paul, the Founder of Christianity* (Amherst, NY: Prometheus, 2002); Paul W. Barnett, *Paul: Missionary of Jesus* (Grand Rapids: Eerdmans, 2008). Reports by Otto Merk ("Paulus-Forschung 1936–1985," *TRu* 53 [1988]: 1–81) and Hans Hübner ("Paulusforschung seit 1945: Ein kritischer Literaturbericht," *ANRW* II.25.4 [1987]: 2649–840) also do not mention the miraculous.

49. N. T. Wright, "Romans," *NIB* 10:754, citing 1 Cor. 2:4; 2 Cor. 12:12; Gal. 3:5; 1 Thess. 1:5; "and the various scenes in Acts, e.g., 14:8–18."

50. Stefan Schreiber, *Paulus als Wundertäter: Redaktionsgeschichtliche Untersuchungen zur Apostelgeschichte und den authentischen Paulusbriefen* (BZNW 79; Berlin: de Gruyter, 1996).

51. Ibid., 287.

miraculous. We can note them in order of their appearance. Back in 1888, in publishing what became "the father of a myriad of books,"[52] when he was only twenty-six, Hermann Gunkel (1862–1932) assailed the Hegelian idea that the Spirit was the equivalent of human consciousness or the principle of the religious-moral life.

Gunkel does not offer a long or developed study of Paul and the miraculous. However, he takes Paul to be "a pneumatic to an exceptionally high degree," not only because of his experience of becoming a Christian (2 Cor. 4:6; Phil. 3:12), or because he united "almost all the gifts of the Spirit in one person," but also because of his "signs, wonders, and mighty works" that were taken to legitimize an apostle (2 Cor. 12:12) and to be an essential part of his apostolic activity.[53] Such conclusions, though only intimations, will become significant as well as confirmed, even if modified, in this study.

In his discussions of Paul and the Spirit W. D. Davies (1911–2001), a key figure in Pauline studies in the latter half of the twentieth century, says that Paul's speaking in tongues, his hearing God's voice, his preaching and words being "in the Spirit," his experience of being "caught up in the third heaven" (2 Cor. 12:2) are not isolated phenomena in Paul's experience.[54] However, Davies says that miracles were, like ecstatic experiences, accorded a secondary place by Paul.[55] Notwithstanding, even if he did not explore or develop the point, Davies has maintained miracles and the miraculous as having an important, if subordinate, place in Paul's life, theology, and ministry.

Ernst Käsemann (1906–98) briefly touches on Paul's miracle working in his commentary on Romans.[56] Also, in a discussion on Paul's concept of ministry or office ("Amt") Käsemann draws the notion of miracle into the matrix of Paul's theology. Käsemann notes that Paul's concept of *charisma* (χάρισμα) "describes in a theologically exact and comprehensive way the essence and scope of every ecclesiastical ministry and function."[57] For, the *charismata* (χαρίσματα), which include miraculous healing and exorcism,[58] exist only as

52. Edgar M. Krentz, review of *The Influence of the Holy Spirit: The Popular View of the Apostolic Age and the Teaching of the Apostle Paul*, by Hermann Gunkel, WW 2 (1982): 96.

53. Hermann Gunkel, *The Influence of the Holy Spirit: The Popular View of the Apostolic Age and the Teaching of the Apostle Paul*, trans. Roy A. Harrisville and Philip A. Quanbeck II (Philadelphia: Fortress, 1979), 77; cf. 112. Further, see §6.7 below.

54. W. D. Davies, *Paul and Rabbinic Judaism: Some Rabbinic Elements in Pauline Theology*, 4th ed. (Philadelphia: Fortress, 1980), 197.

55. Ibid., 198, 213.

56. Ernst Käsemann, *Commentary on Romans*, trans. and ed. Geoffrey W. Bromiley (London: SCM, 1980), 394.

57. Ernst Käsemann, "Ministry and Community in the New Testament," in *Essays on New Testament Themes*, trans. W. J. Montague (SBT 41; London: SCM, 1964), 64.

58. Ibid., 69.

manifestations and concretions of eternal life (Rom. 6:23).[59] Though Käsemann has given little space to the discussion of Paul and the miraculous, like Davies, he has successfully brought the theme into a direct relationship with Paul's theology, soteriology, and ecclesiology in a way that will require our attention later (see §10.3 [a] and [e] below).

For Hans Joachim Schoeps (1909–80) miracles and the miraculous are important to Paul. Schoeps argues that Paul, in his engagement with his opponents, invokes the Spirit-inspired "signs of the (or, a true) apostle" (σημεῖα τοῦ ἀποστόλου) as attesting the genuineness of his apostolic ministry. Schoeps takes these signs to be "the charismata connected with the outpouring of the Holy Spirit (Rom. 15:19; Gal. 3:5)."[60] Schoeps goes on to suggest that a detached survey of Paul's polemic shows that his visionary gift stands out, that he has seen Christ "in a trance" (ἐν ἐκστάσει, Acts 22:17), and that his preaching seems to depend on these very visions and revelations. Although he does not develop his argument,[61] Schoeps, along with John Ashton, as we will see, is among the few who take Paul's ministry to have had an important ecstatic base and aspect (see 158n36 below).

A particularly important figure in the present discussion of Paul and the miraculous is Jacob Jervell, who in 1976 called attention to the scholarly avoidance of dealing with Paul and the miraculous. Jervell discusses Paul's response to his opponents, bringing into relationship Paul's admitted weakness and his supposed miraculous activity.[62] In 1980 Jervell continued to explore this theme.[63] He begins by noting Bruno Bauer's comment back in 1850—still the generally accepted opinion for many exegetes[64]—that through sufferings and temptations Paul waged war with the word alone.[65] It was in Acts, by contrast, that Paul emerged as a miracle worker, a magician.[66] In Jervell's view the perceived difficulty in finding links between Luke and Paul has to

59. Ibid., 64.
60. Hans Joachim Schoeps, *Paul: The Theology of the Apostle in Light of the Jewish Religious History*, trans. Harold Knight (London: Lutterworth, 1961), 81.
61. Ibid., 87, citing, e.g., *Ps.-Clem. Rec.* 4.35; *Ps.-Clem. Hom.* 17.14–19.
62. Jervell, "Der schwache Charismatiker," 185–98.
63. Jacob Jervell, "Die Zeichen des Apostels: Die Wunder beim lukanischen und paulinischen Paulus" *SNTSU* 5 (1980): 54–75; Jervell, "Signs," 77–95, 169–72.
64. E.g., Bernd Kollmann, "Paulus als Wundertäter," in *Paulinische Christologie: Exegetische Beiträge; Hans Hübner zum 70. Geburtstag*, ed. Udo Schnelle, Thomas Söding, and Michael Labahn (Göttingen: Vandenhoeck & Ruprecht, 2000), 76–77.
65. Bauer, *Die Apostelgeschichte*, 7–25, cited by Jervell, "Signs," 77; Kollmann, "Paulus als Wundertäter," 76–77n4; cf. T. Michael McNulty, "Pauline Preaching: A Speech-Acts Analysis," *Worship* 53 (1979): 207–14. See also below, and those cited by Jervell, "Der schwache Charismatiker," 187.
66. Jervell, "Signs," 77.

do with our working with an imperfect portrait of Paul from occasional letters, in which, *per definition*, not all is said. Notwithstanding, Jervell seeks to
show that Luke and Paul are not as disconnected as is often assumed. Jervell
grants that Luke says more about Paul being a miracle worker than any other
of the apostles and missionaries. However, on the one hand, Jervell argues
not only that Luke's portrait of Paul is based on Paul's call and the speeches
rather than the miracles, but also, on the other hand, that the miracles in
relation to other material are given a remarkably modest place in Acts. At
this point Jervell also seeks to establish that the Paul of Acts remains consistent with the suffering Paul of the letters.[67] Indeed, Jervell goes so far as to
say, "I wish to assert here that miracles assume a quite central role in Paul's
preaching, almost to greater degree than in Acts."[68] Jervell's confidence is
based largely on taking Paul's phrase "signs of the apostle" (2 Cor. 12:12)
to refer to miraculous deeds only and, therefore, for them to be everywhere
occurring in, and also fundamental to, Paul's understanding of his mission.
Although often executed through broad brushstrokes, and therefore lacking
detail and thorough argument, Jervell's pieces are suggestive and important
for my enterprise. I will take the opportunity to test and, where necessary,
correct Jervell's work.

E. P. Sanders says it is "not to be doubted" that Paul "did things which were
counted in the ancient world as miracles,"[69] but also that these were part of
his gospel and, for his readers, established his authority as a "true apostle, or
at least a good one."[70] Sanders notes that Paul says that he speaks in tongues
"more than all of you" (1 Cor. 14:18) and saw visions (2 Cor. 12:2–4, 7), and
that Acts includes healings and exorcisms in its portrait of the apostle (Acts
16:16–18; 19:11–12). But "Paul himself says nothing of his own miracles."
Instead, "when pressed for signs of his apostolic authority Paul appealed
more to 'weakness' than to miracles, and more to the results of his missionary work than his prowess."[71] Although not extensive, in these comments
Sanders adds his voice to those who consider that Paul not only was involved
in the miraculous but also functioned as a miracle worker, and that this was
important in his ministry.

The exhaustive nine-hundred-page treatment of Pauline pneumatology by
the Pentecostal scholar Gordon D. Fee deals with statements of Paul that are

67. Ibid., 78 and n. 6; cf. 246.
68. Ibid., 91.
69. E. P. Sanders, *Paul* (Oxford: Oxford University Press, 1991), 25; cf. Sanders, *Paul and Palestinian Judaism*, 450, citing, e.g., 1 Cor. 2:4; 2 Cor. 12:12; 1 Thess. 1:15.
70. Sanders, *Paul*, 24.
71. Ibid., 25.

likely to have to do with the miraculous.[72] He concludes that Paul's proclamation was regularly accompanied by signs and wonders or miracles.[73] He says, "It would never occur to him [Paul] that the miraculous would *not* accompany the proclamation of the gospel, or that in another time some would think of these two empowerings [word and deed] as 'either-or.'"[74] Further, Fee takes Galatians 3:5 to show that miracles "were also the regular expectation of the Pauline churches. . . . He would simply not have understood the presence of the Spirit that did not also include such manifestations of the Spirit that he termed 'powers,' which we translate 'miracles.'"[75] In my attempt to explore the miraculous more broadly in relation to Paul's life, theology and ministry, I will have cause to return to Fee's work.

In arguing that Paul resembled a shaman—a person of spiritual experience, power, and influence in a community—John Ashton may have done for Paul in recent times what Morton Smith once did for Jesus.[76] That is, Ashton argues for the need to assess Paul in first-century terms, and in categories that may not be comfortable for Western Christianity.[77] He argues that the performance of miracles was characteristic of Paul's ministry and gave rise to a literary evolution of the picture of Paul that can be traced through the canonical book of Acts and the *Acts of Paul and Thecla*. In suggesting that Paul be placed among the shamans, Ashton has alerted us to the potential importance of religious experience and the miraculous in attempting to recover both Paul as a miracle worker and his attitudes toward the miraculous.

In an article, "Paulus als Wundertäter" ("Paul as Miracle Worker"), Bernd Kollmann argues that miracles or powerful works—part of the experience of the eschatological presence of God—were an aspect of Paul's ministry.[78] However, the low profile of the miraculous shows that they did not have a central place to Paul's ministry, and in the sequence "by word and deed" (Rom. 15:18) the miracles are shown to be subordinate to the proclamation. In fact, overall, Paul expected miracles to be the obvious side effects of his ministry.[79]

72. Rom. 15:19; 1 Cor. 2:3–4; 12:4–11; 2 Cor. 12:12; Gal. 3:5; 1 Thess. 1:5.
73. Gordon D. Fee, *God's Empowering Presence: The Holy Spirit in the Letters of Paul* (Peabody, MA: Hendrickson, 1994), 849.
74. Ibid., 849–50, emphasis original.
75. Ibid., 887.
76. Morton Smith, *Jesus the Magician* (London: Gollancz, 1978).
77. John Ashton, *The Religion of Paul the Apostle* (New Haven: Yale University Press, 2000); e.g., chap. 2, "Paul the Enigma."
78. Kollmann, "Paulus als Wundertäter," 76–96.
79. Ibid., 82–83. Audrey Dawson (*Healing, Weakness and Power: Perspectives on Healing in the Writings of Mark, Luke and Paul* [PBM; Milton Keynes: Paternoster, 2008], 207–8) is another who has concluded that healing was not a significant feature of Paul's ministry.

The work of Stefan Alkier on miracle and reality in the letters of Paul has a different focus from this present study.[80] Alkier deals with the issue and debate about "fact and fiction" in Paul, concluding that for Pauline Christianity miracles are events brought about by God and beyond human capabilities.

The burden of Bert Jan Lietaert Peerbolte's contribution is that, on the basis of the evidence from later interpreters—especially canonical Acts, but also the *Acts of Paul* and the *Martyrdom of Paul*—as well as from his own writings, Paul performed miraculous deeds.[81] Moreover, Lietaert Peerbolte concludes that these miracles presented Paul as a "legitimate envoy of Christ."[82] He notes that in both Paul and his later interpreters "the emphasis is consistently on the fact that Paul did not perform his miraculous deeds through his own power, but rather through the power of Jesus Christ."[83] Notwithstanding, Lietaert Peerbolte says that we are, unfortunately, in total darkness as to the character of Paul's miraculous deeds.[84] In this study I will attempt to probe the darkness to make some firm and, hopefully, reasonable suggestions about the nature, extent, and significance of Paul's miraculous activity.

Finally, and more recently, rather than giving specific examples of miracles, Craig A. Evans takes Paul to allude to performing works of power.[85] Then, having discussed the portrait of Paul as a healer and exorcist in Acts, Evans concludes, "The stories of Paul in Acts not only cohere with comments in his letters, they explicate these comments and thus help us understand better what Paul means when, for example, he reminds his readers that he performed 'the signs of the apostle' while with them."[86] While not disagreeing with Evans that Paul's letters allude to the miraculous, on the one hand, I am not setting out to support any particular relationship between Acts and Paul, and on the other hand, we will see that Luke's understanding of Paul as a miracle worker is very different from that of Paul himself.

80. Stefan Alkier, *Wunder und Wirklichkeit in den Briefen des Apostels Paulus: Ein Beitrag zu einem Wunderverständnis jenseits von Entmythologisierung und Rehistorisierung* (WUNT 134; Tübingen: Mohr Siebeck, 2001).

81. Bert Jan Lietaert Peerbolte, "Paul the Miracle Worker: Development and Background of Pauline Miracle Stories," in *Wonders Never Cease: The Purpose of Narrating Miracle Stories in the New Testament and Its Religious Environment*, ed. Michael Labahn and Bert Jan Lietaert Peerbolte (LNTS 288; London: T&T Clark, 2006), 180–99.

82. Ibid., 199.

83. Ibid.

84. Ibid., 197.

85. Craig A. Evans, "Paul the Exorcist and Healer," in *Paul and His Theology*, ed. Stanley E. Porter (PSt 3; Leiden: Brill, 2006), 363–64.

86. Ibid., 379.

1.3 Results

This survey of significant Pauline studies since the rise of a critical approach to religion has shown clearly that the topic of the miraculous has not been prominent. In some cases, even in the major studies of Paul, the miraculous has not even featured. When the subject has been broached, it has not often been given a significant profile. Some studies, perhaps most, while supposing that miracles took place in Paul's churches and that Paul conducted miracles, made little attempt to show how this conclusion should shape our view of Paul's life, mission, and theology.

An early exception to this pattern was Hermann Gunkel arguing for the importance of the pneumatic in understanding the apostolic age, and in concluding that Paul's involvement in the miraculous was an essential aspect of his life, theology, and ministry. Of recent studies, it is Jacob Jervell who has been the most alert to the lack of attention to the subject, and the most adamant that miracles and the miraculous were a central activity of Paul and fundamental to understanding the apostle. How his results would play out in our understanding of Paul and his theology and mission we are not told.

My task is to test these results through reexamining Paul's letters and his early interpreters, and to extend and deepen the discussion, in order to recover the historical Paul in relation to the miraculous. I will pay particular attention to how any miraculous aspects and any miracle working that may legitimately be associated with the historical Paul and his ministry should cause us to rethink his life, theology, and mission.

1.4 My Approach

I readily acknowledge that this project is beset with difficulties. Notably, there is a paucity of immediately obvious data from which we can answer our questions. Not only is our Pauline corpus incomplete (1 Cor. 5:9; cf. Col. 4:16), but what we have that most likely comes from Paul's hand, on a first reading, has little to say about him in relation to the miraculous, and perhaps nothing to say about him performing miracles. To begin with, therefore, although ignorance may be, as Lytton Strachey drolly supposed, the first requisite of the historian, in that it simplifies and clarifies the endeavor,[87] we have to take seriously Aristotle's advice that we must not expect more precision from our

---

87. Lytton Strachey, *Eminent Victorians* (1918; repr., New York: Modern Library, 1999), xiii. More fully on the problems of interpreting Paul, including in relation to the use of Acts, see Thomas E. Phillips, *Paul, His Letters, and Acts* (LPS; Peabody, MA: Hendrickson, 2009), 42–47.

sources than they permit (*Eth. Nic.* 1.3.24–25). Notwithstanding, to be in a position to read profitably with as much sensitivity and insight as possible the small amount of material available, my approach will involve three inter-related enquiries.

The first step will be to enquire what views Paul is likely to have inherited in relation to the miraculous (part 2). It was his Jewish heritage that he claimed determined his life (Phil. 3:4b–6; cf. 2 Cor. 11:22; Gal. 1:13–14), a point W. D. Davies reestablished for understanding Paul.[88] Therefore, I will examine Paul's Jewish traditions to see what he and those who knew him may have expected of him in relation to the miraculous. However, since Paul lived in a Greco-Roman world, through attention to the writings of Philo of Alexandria and Josephus, we will be able to see how Hellenized Jews like Paul are likely to have viewed miracles and the miraculous (chap. 2). Then, there is so much evidence that Paul saw himself as a prophet that I will enquire what impact this self-perception is likely to have had on his involvement in the miraculous (chap. 3). In that Paul became involved in missionary activity, in chapter 4 I will ask what implications and expectations this is likely to have had for him and those who knew him in terms of involvement in the miraculous. Further, since Paul makes claims in relation to Jesus and earlier Christians and their traditions, in chapter 5 I will examine what influence the Christianity he in-herited—including knowledge of Jesus or traditions about him—is likely to have had on his understanding of, and practical interest in, the miraculous in his theology, life, and ministry. Taken together, these chapters on Paul's background and heritage can be expected to allow us to see what influences are likely to have been on him, and what attitudes and practices in relation to the miraculous he is likely to have brought with him into Christianity.

In light of the results of understanding Paul's inheritance, we will be in a stronger position to take a second step in reading his letters, or what are sometimes called his "orthonymous" writings.[89] In the first of two chapters in part 3 I will examine how Paul describes aspects of his own experience that relate most directly to the miraculous (chap. 6). This can be expected to help not only in drawing conclusions about his basic disposition toward the miraculous but also in seeing the possible place and significance of the miraculous in his thinking and ministry. Then, in chapter 7 I will examine carefully what Paul has to say about his ministry, as well as the experience of

88. Davies, *Paul.*
89. Cf. Hans-Joseph Klauck and Daniel P. Bailey (*Ancient Letters and the New Testament: A Guide to Context and Exegesis* [Waco: Baylor University Press, 2006], 200): "an artificial word coined on the analogy of 'pseudonymity' . . . and composed of the two components ὀρθός, 'correct,' and ὄνομα, 'name.' . . . the true name."

his readers, for their experiences are likely to shed light on Paul's understanding and experience of the miraculous.

The third step of these enquiries involves looking back on Paul through the lenses of his interpreters: first the canonical Acts of the Apostles, then the way he was remembered in pseudepigraphical literature associated with him, and finally the literature beyond the canon (part 4). It is recognizing Acts as a later and secondary source for possible knowledge of Paul (see §8.1 below) that I turn to Luke's text only after I have the results of the discussions of the primary literature from Paul in hand (chap. 8). Following the methodological principle of giving primacy to the letters of Paul,[90] I am attempting to avoid allowing Luke's portrait of Paul to exercise any decisive control over my reading of his letters.[91] (Although Acts is a secondary source, and in Paul's letters we are dealing with firsthand information about him, we still need to read Paul critically because, like Luke, he had particular agendas that influenced his selection of material, his objectivity, and his expressions.)[92] As a result of my discussion of Acts, I can expect also to make a small contribution to the question of the nature of the book of Acts, at least in terms of its usefulness in telling us about the historical Paul. Further, I will be able to contribute to the conversation about the problem of the difference between the Paul of his letters and the Paul of Luke's second volume.[93] Finally, in the pseudepigraphical

90. Cf., e.g., Jerome Murphy-O'Connor, *Paul: A Critical Life* (Oxford: Oxford University Press, 1996), vi; Lüdemann, *Paul*, 26.

91. The criticism by Murphy-O'Connor (*Paul: A Critical Life*, vi) of, e.g., Joseph A. Fitzmyer, "A Life of Paul," in *The New Jerome Biblical Commentary*, ed. Raymond E. Brown, Joseph A. Fitzmyer, and Roland E. Murphy (Englewood Cliffs, NJ: Prentice-Hall, 1990), 1329–37; M.-F. Baslez, *Saint Paul* (Paris: Fayard, 1991); Simon Légasse, *Paul apôtre: Essai de biographie critique* (Paris: Cerf, 1991); the criticism by Lüdemann (*Paul*, 63) of Rainer Riesner, *Paul's Early Period: Chronology, Mission, Strategy, Theology*, trans. Doug Stott (Grand Rapids: Eerdmans, 1998).

92. Cf. Anthony J. Saldarini, *Pharisees, Scribes and Sadducees in Palestinian Society: A Sociological Approach* (Grand Rapids: Eerdmans; Livonia, MI: Dove, 2001), 134. In relation to the study of Paul, Colin J. Hemer (*The Book of Acts in the Setting of Hellenistic History* [WUNT 49; Tübingen: Mohr Siebeck, 1989], 244) seeks to dispense with the distinction between primary and secondary evidence on the grounds that it imports the tacit presupposition that the sources are in conflict. However, the distinction is important in allowing the voice of each witness to be heard, and the voice of Paul, in whom we are particularly interested, be given preference over his later interpreters.

93. Once an assured result of scholarship (see the survey by Michael F. Bird, "The Unity of Luke-Acts in Recent Discussion," *JSNT* 29 [2007]: 425–48), the assumption that the same author is responsible for the Gospel of Luke and the canonical Acts of the Apostles has been reopened and called into question by Patricia Walters, *The Assumed Authorial Unity of Luke and Acts: A Reassessment of the Evidence* (SNTSMS 145; Cambridge: Cambridge University Press, 2009). For critical assessments of Walters, see the reviews by, e.g., Joel B. Green, *RBL* 12/2009 (http://www .bookreviews.org/pdf/7084_7695.pdf); Paul Foster, *ExpTim* 121 (2010): 264–65. Against Gilbert Bouwman (*Das dritte Evangelium: Einübing in die formgeschichtliche Methode* [Düsseldorf:

and postcanonical literature (chap. 9)[94] I may find some support for, or at least clarification of, some of the conclusions already emerging from the discussion of Paul's letters and Acts. In these three interrelated enquiries—bracketing the interpretation of Paul's letters between an attention to the impact of inherited traditions on his thought and practice, and looking back on what he says through the lens of his early interpreters—I anticipate likely being able to reach conclusions about Paul and the miraculous in which I can have considerable confidence. These conclusions will be set out in the final chapter, particularly in the section carrying the title of this book (see §10.3). Before beginning this study, however, I need to consider how miracles and the miraculous should be defined in relation to this project.

1.5 Defining the Miraculous

In beginning his discussion, the English philosopher John Locke (1632–1704) warned, "To discourse of miracle without defining what one means by the word miracle, is to make a shew, but in effect to talk of nothing."[95] In turn, Harold Remus has shown that people of the Greco-Roman world "had various and differentiated canons by which to demarcate extraordinary from ordinary phenomena," and that these canons varied "from one period to another, from one people and group to another, and often within a group and with social status, education and profession."[96]

    In discussing what Paul may have thought about miracles and the miraculous, and what part this motif may have played in his life, theology, and ministry, there are two initial problems to consider in relation to a definition. First, whereas the miraculous was generally accepted in an ancient society,[97] this

---

Patmos-Verlag, 1968], 62–67), who, on the grounds of its more primitive theology and lack of reference to the Gospel, argues that Acts was written before the Gospel of Luke, see I. Howard Marshall, "Acts and the 'Former Treatise,'" in *The Book of Acts in Its Ancient Literary Setting*, ed. Bruce W. Winter and Andrew D. Clarke (Grand Rapids: Eerdmans; Carlisle: Paternoster, 1993), 163–82. Marshall, on the basis of the prologues, material in the Gospel anticipating Acts, and the ending of the Gospel, argues for the traditional order: Luke-Acts.

    94. For this study, Romans, 1 and 2 Corinthians, Galatians, Philippians, 1 Thessalonians, and Philemon are taken to be by Paul. As reflected in the discussions in chap. 9, Ephesians, Colossians, 2 Thessalonians, and the Pastoral Epistles are taken not to have been published by Paul.

    95. John Locke, "A Discourse of Miracles" (1706), in *The Reasonableness of Christianity*, ed. I. T. Ramsey (Stanford, CA: Stanford University Press, 1958), 79.

    96. Harold Remus, *Pagan-Christian Conflict over Miracle in the Second Century* (PMS 10; Cambridge, MA: Philadelphia Patristic Foundation, 1983), 182.

    97. Cf. Robert Garland, "Miracle in the Greek and Roman World," in *The Cambridge Companion to Miracles*, ed. Graham H. Twelftree (Cambridge: Cambridge University Press, 2011), 73–94.

is no longer the case. For many readers, miracles do not—cannot—happen, and therefore did not happen then.[98] While both careful enquiry and personal experience have caused me to conclude that miracles are possible and probably can be experienced, this is a historical study. The subject of interest is not my views, but rather those of Paul and his contemporaries. And, "if the past is to be understood," as Geoffrey Elton put it, the past "must be given full respect in its own right."[99] Therefore, as far as it is possible, it is important to bracket out my views—either for or against the possibility of the miraculous—in order to read the data with either as little credulity or, alternatively, as much sympathy as possible in order to recover more nearly the Paul of history rather than only the Paul of our presuppositions.[100]

A second and more complex problem in relation to defining the miraculous is that we need to be working with ideas Paul would recognize. Moreover, since part of my larger project is an attempt to explain the apparent discontinuity between the ministries of Jesus and Paul in relation to the miraculous, I must work with a definition of miracle that is also appropriate to understanding the ministry of Jesus.

Since the debates in the Enlightenment of the eighteenth century, a "miracle" has come to refer to an occurrence, generally taken to be caused by a god, that violates a law of nature.[101] However, for the biblical writers, what we call a miracle involved no infringement of any laws; rather, a miracle was simply a striking or surprising phenomenon that was humanly impossible and was thought to be brought about by and reveal a god.[102] What were called "strange," "wonderful," or "remarkable" things (παράδοξοι)[103] included a range of the

98. See Michael P. Levine, "Philosophers on Miracles," in Twelftree, *Companion to Miracles*, 291–329.

99. Geoffrey R. Elton, *The Practice of History* (Oxford: Blackwell, 2002), 42.

100. Ashton puts the point sharply: "It is surely impossible to get any real understanding of the religious Paul whilst wearing blinkers that shut out the sight of the spiritual and demonic world in which he lived" (*Religion of Paul*, 177).

101. Cf., e.g., Locke, "Discourse of Miracles," 79; David Hume, *Enquiries Concerning the Human Understanding and Concerning the Principles of Morals*, ed. L. A. Selby-Bigge, 2nd ed. (Oxford: Clarendon, 1902), 114–15; Colin Brown, *Miracles and the Critical Mind* (Grand Rapids: Eerdmans; Exeter: Paternoster, 1984), 23–100.

102. John Dominic Crossan, *The Birth of Christianity: Discovering What Happened in the Years Immediately after the Execution of Jesus* (San Francisco: HarperSanFrancisco, 1998), 303; Eric Eve, *The Jewish Context of Jesus' Miracles* (JSNTSup 231; Sheffield: Sheffield Academic Press, 2002), 1–2.

103. In the NT: Luke 5:26. In the LXX: Jdt. 13:13; 2 Macc. 9:24; 3 Macc. 6:33; 4 Macc. 2:14; Sir. 43:25; Wis. 5:2; 16:17; 19:5. In Josephus: *Ant.* 2.91, 223, 267, 285, 295, 345, 347; 3.1, 14, 30; 5.28, 125; 6.171; 8.130; 9.60; 10.28; 12.87; 13.140, 282; 14.455; 16.343; *J.W.* 1.518; 4.354; 6.102; *Ag. Ap.* 1.53; 2.114. In Philo: *Opif.* 1.124; *Sacr.* 1.100; *Det.* 1.44, 48, 94, 153; *Post.* 1.19, 50; *Deus.* 1.127; *Plant.* 1.62, 69; *Ebr.* 1.66, 178; *Conf.*1.31, 59, 132; *Her.* 1.81, 95; *Congr.* 1.3;

inexplicable: genetic anomalies, strange natural phenomena, and reports of events bringing human health and safety.[104]

In his public ministry Jesus associates bringing human health in his healings, exorcisms (Matt. 12:28 // Luke 11:20), and raisings of the dead (Matt. 11:2–6 // Luke 7:18–23) with the activity and disclosure of God (cf. Matt. 11:20–24 // Luke 10:12–15).[105] That, in our terms, Jesus would have taken these as miracles, not only in that they are caused by and reveal God, but also in that they are extraordinary or would not otherwise have taken place, is suggested by the crowd's enthusiastic response to them, which is embedded in the earliest traditions about Jesus.[106]

Turning to Paul, it is in his lists of gifts, or *charismata* (χαρίσματα), phenomena he took to be activated by and to express God,[107] that we probably gain access to a similar view of miracle. In one of his lists of gifts "helps" (ἀντιλήμψεις) and "administration" (κυβέρνησεις), as well as "healings" (ἰάματα) and "powers" or "miracles" (δυνάμεις), are expected in his churches as the result of the activity of God (1 Cor. 12:28–29). This eclectic, but hardly entirely supernatural, list is consistent with the ancient view, well represented in the Old Testament, that the miraculous involved any activity of a god.[108]

However, earlier in his discussion of *charismata* there is a catalogue of more obviously humanly impossible or supranatural activities of God that he chooses, such as tongues, as equally extraordinary,[109] and that are directed to the health and welfare of the community (1 Cor. 12:7). Paul lists wisdom, knowledge, faith, healings, miracles, prophecy, discernment, tongues, and the interpretation of tongues (12:8–10). Various suggestions have been made regarding what the order of the items in this list might imply about Paul's thinking.[110] At least

---

Fug. 1.180; *Somn.* 2.23, 136, 185; *Abr.* 1.196; *Mos.* 1.143, 202, 203; 2.125, 213; *Prob.* 1.58, 105; *Aet.* 1.48, 109; *Legat.* 80; *QG* 3.18. See also Gerhard Kittel, "παράδοξος," *TDNT* 2:254; BDAG, "παράδοξος," 763.

104. For a concise discussion, see Wendy Cotter, *Miracles in Greco-Roman Antiquity* (London: Routledge, 1999), 1–2; more broadly, see Remus, *Pagan-Christian Conflict*, 27–72.

105. On the possibility of these passages reflecting Jesus' view, see Graham H. Twelftree, *Jesus the Miracle Worker: A Historical and Theological Study* (Downers Grove, IL: InterVarsity, 1999), 266–77.

106. Cf. Mark, e.g., 1:45; 2:4; 3:9; 5:21, 24; 7:33; and Q: Matt. 11:7 // Luke 7:24; Matt. 12:23 // Luke 11:14. Further, see Twelftree, "Miracles of Jesus," 108–9.

107. 1 Cor. 12:4–7, 18, 24, 28.

108. Cf. Walther Eichrodt, *Theology of the Old Testament*, 2 vols. (London: SCM, 1961–67), 2:162n4, citing Exod. 34:10; Num. 16:30; Isa. 48:7; Jer. 31:22.

109. Fee says, "What distinguishes this listing is the concretely visible nature of these items . . . chosen because they are, like tongues itself, extraordinary phenomena" (*God's Empowering Presence*, 165). See also ibid., 168.

110. For various suggestions how Paul may have intended his list to be categorized, see Archibald Robertson and Alfred Plummer, *A Critical and Exegetical Commentary on the First*

part of what Paul has in mind is probably reflected in his change of word for "other" from ἄλλος to ἕτερος when he mentions faith early in the list (12:9) and tongues later in the list (12:10). In classical Greek ἕτερος signaled a definite division.[111] Even though, by Paul's time, the distinction between ἄλλος and ἕτερος had largely been lost (cf. Gal. 1:6–7),[112] he can appear to use ἕτερος to indicate specific, qualitative differences,[113] as he does here, probably reflecting a deliberate arrangement of his list. His use of ἕτερος separates the initial two items (wisdom and knowledge), which not only were of great interest to the Corinthians[114] but also were related to the opening discussion on speaking by the Spirit of God (1 Cor. 12:1–3). The last two gifts (tongues and their interpretation), which he considered overrated gifts (e.g., 14:19), are separated off at the end of the list by the use of ἕτερος.[115] This, therefore, probably intentionally leaves together a set of five gifts—faith, healings, miracles, prophecy, and discernment of spirits.[116]

It is in this cluster of supranatural activities that we see the meaning and compass of Paul's idea of miracle. For, along with the obviously miraculous gifts—healings and powers or miracles (also kept together in another list, 1 Cor. 12:28–29, suggesting their similarity)—he includes faith, prophecy, and discernment of spirits. Understanding the nature of each of these gifts, considered as a class, will help us see what Paul understood by the miraculous. First, "faith"

Epistle of St. Paul to the Corinthians (ICC; Edinburgh, T&T Clark, 1914), 265; Arnold Bittlinger, Gifts and Graces: A Commentary on I Corinthians 12–14, trans. Herbert Klassen (Grand Rapids: Eerdmans, 1968), 20–22; F. F. Bruce, 1 and 2 Corinthians (NCB; London: Marshall, Morgan & Scott, 1971), 119; George G. Findlay, "St. Paul's First Epistle to the Corinthians," in The Expositor's Greek Testament, ed. W. Robertson Nicoll, vol. 2 (Grand Rapids: Eerdmans, 1980), 888; Jack W. MacGorman, The Gifts of the Spirit (Nashville: Broadman, 1974), 34–35; W. R. Jones, "The Nine Gifts of the Holy Spirit," in Pentecostal Doctrine, ed. P. S. Brewster (Cheltenham: Grenehurst, 1976), 47–61; Ralph P. Martin, The Spirit and the Congregation: Studies in 1 Corinthians 12–15 (Grand Rapids: Eerdmans, 1984), 11–14; Gordon D. Fee, The First Epistle to the Corinthians (NICNT; Grand Rapids: Eerdmans, 1987), 662–63.

111. James Hope Moulton, et al., A Grammar of New Testament Greek, 4 vols. (Edinburgh: T&T Clark, 1908–76), 3:197; LSJ, "ἕτερος," 702; cf. Matt. 10:23; 12:45; Luke 4:43; 10:1; 23:32.

112. Moulton, et al., Grammar, 3:197; A. T. Robertson, A Grammar of the Greek New Testament (Nashville: Broadman, 1934), 749; BDF §306.

113. 1 Cor. 15:39–41; 2 Cor. 11:4, cited by Findlay, "St. Paul's First Epistle to the Corinthians," 888.

114. Cf. 1 Cor. 1:17–2:16; 8:1–3, 7; James D. G. Dunn, Jesus and the Spirit: A Study of the Religious and Charismatic Experience of Jesus and the First Christians as Reflected in the New Testament (London: SCM, 1975), 217–21.

115. Robertson and Plummer, First Epistle of St. Paul to the Corinthians, 265; Fee, First Epistle to the Corinthians, 590–91.

116. For similar divisions of the list of gifts in 1 Cor. 12:8–10, see, e.g., Robertson and Plummer, First Epistle of St. Paul to the Corinthians, 265; Findlay, "St. Paul's First Epistle to the Corinthians," 887–88; Fee, First Epistle to the Corinthians, 662–63.

(πίστις) in this context (cf. 12:9) is not related to salvation.[117] Nor is faith a
sovereign or overarching *charisma*,[118] nor is it particularly associated with the
operation of the gifts of healings or miracles.[119] The structure of the sentence—
"to another faith, to another healings, to another powers" (12:9)—accords
faith its own identity and function. Occurring in a list of activities or tangible
expressions of the Spirit, faith probably involves more than an "invincible
confidence . . . assured by a supernatural instinct."[120] Rather, as it emerges from
the hyperbole of his argument for the necessity of love (13:1–3), containing his
only other use of the word in this section, faith is the gift to remove mountains
(13:2).[121] Since the removal of mountains was a proverbial expression for the
impossible or improbable,[122] taking into account Paul's hyperbole (he uses "all"
[πᾶς] three times in 12:2–3), faith in a list of *charismata* probably referred to
the ability to be instrumental in accomplishing the ordinarily difficult or impossible. Given that Paul's interest here is the corporate value of the gifts (12:7),
the outcome of the faith is likely expected to relate at least to the health and
well-being of the group and its members. We can only guess what they might
be; perhaps it was perceived protection during travel or in a time of danger or
persecution, or the provision of food or money, for example.

Second, since the singular "healing" (ἴαμα) would already carry the idea of
repeated use, the plural gift of "healings" (ἰάματα) suggests Paul has in mind
different kinds of healing (1 Cor. 12:9).[123] It is worth noting that the gift or

117. Raymond F. Collins speaks for most commentators: "The charismatic faith of which Paul
writes is something different from the faith that characterizes all believers" (*First Corinthians* [SP
7; Collegeville, MN: Liturgical Press, 1999], 454). See also Dunn, *Jesus and the Spirit*, 211–12;
Fee, *God's Empowering Presence*, 168.

118. Thomas W. Gillespie, *The First Theologians: A Study in Early Christian Prophecy* (Grand
Rapids: Eerdmans, 1994), 112–13.

119. Anthony C. Thiselton (*The First Epistle to the Corinthians: A Commentary on the Greek
Text* [NIGTC; Grand Rapids: Eerdmans, 2000], 947) cites Lang, Kistemaker, Allo, and Senft as
associating faith with the healing referred to in 1 Cor. 12:9. Similarly, Hans Conzelmann, *1 Corinthians: A Commentary on the First Epistle to the Corinthians*, trans. James W. Leitch, ed.
George W. MacRae (Hermeneia; Philadelphia: Fortress, 1975), 209; Dunn, *Jesus and the Spirit*, 211.

120. Dunn, *Jesus and the Spirit*, 211 (depending in part on Ferdinand Prat, *The Theology of
Saint Paul*, trans. John L. Stoddard, 2 vols. [London: Barns, Oates & Washbourne, 1945], 1:426).

121. The noun, πίστις, occurs in 1 Cor. 2:5; 12:9; 13:13; 15:14, 17. The verb, πιστεύω, occurs
in 1 Cor. 1:21; 3:5; 9:17; 11:18; 13:7; 14:22 (2x); 15:2, 11.

122. See W. D. Davies and Dale C. Allison, *The Gospel According to Saint Matthew*, 3 vols.
(ICC; Edinburgh: T&T Clark, 1988–97), 2:727, citing Isa. 54:10; Josephus, *Ant.* 2.333; *T. Sol.*
23:1; *b. Sanh.* 24a; *b. Ber.* 64a; *b. B. Bat.* 3b; Homer, *Od.* 5.480–485; also Morna D. Hooker, *A
Commentary on the Gospel According to St. Mark* (BNTC; London: Black, 1991), 269; and the
detailed discussion by Maureen W. Yeung, *Faith in Jesus and Paul: A Comparison with Special
Reference to "Faith That Can Remove Mountains" and "Your Faith Has Healed/Saved You"*
(WUNT 2/147; Tübingen: Mohr Siebeck, 2002), 21–30.

123. Thiselton, *First Epistle to the Corinthians*, 946.

expression of grace is, therefore, not the possession of healing power but its tangible realization in the healings.[124]

Third, in Paul's world the plural "powers" (δυνάμεις) could refer to heavenly beings or bodies,[125] or, as the context requires here, to deeds that exhibited or expressed power—that is, miracles.[126]

Fourth, "prophecy" (προφητεία, 1 Cor. 12:10) is a revelatory gift,[127] for Paul uses the word "revelation" (ἀποκάλυψις) referring to prophecy and knowledge when he is dealing with disclosing divine mysteries (cf. 14:6, 26). He also uses the term "revelation" for visionary experiences (2 Cor. 12:1, 7) and the gospel (Gal. 1:12) or God's will being revealed to him (2:2).[128] In this we see that Paul takes revelation to be in the same orbit of the miraculous with healing and miracles.[129]

Fifth, the meaning of the "discernment of spirits" (διακρίσεις πνευμάτων) is not immediately obvious (1 Cor. 12:10).[130] It could refer to judging which spirit—holy or otherwise—is the source of some phenomena (cf. 1 John 4:1). More likely, here it is to be taken to relate to prophecy. For, further on in his discussion of the gifts, Paul pairs prophecy with the need to "judge" or "weigh" (διακρίνω) what is said. Also, in the only other place Paul discusses the use of prophecy among believers (1 Thess. 5:20–21) he also mentions the need to "examine" or "test" (δοκιμάζω) everything. Further, the two pairs of tongues/interpretation and prophecy/testing also found later in this section (1 Cor. 14:27–29) support the view that in the "discernment of spirits" following prophecy Paul has the testing of prophecy in mind.[131] Thus, for Paul, discernment of spirits belongs with prophecy as a revelatory gift.

From this list of gifts—solidified expressions of grace[132]—or humanly impossible activities of God, expressed in individuals, two things in particular

124. Cf. Dunn, *Jesus and the Spirit*, 211.
125. In the NT, see Matt. 24:29; Mark 13:25; Luke 21:26; Rom. 8:38; Heb. 6:5.
126. In the NT, see Matt. 7:22; 11:20, 21, 23; 13:54, 58; 14:2; Mark 6:2, 14; Luke 10:13; Acts 8:13; 19:11; 1 Cor. 12:28, 29; Gal. 3:5. On the singular δύναμις ("power"), see §7.1 below.
127. Cf. Dunn, *Jesus and the Spirit*, 212–25.
128. Fee, *First Epistle to the Corinthians*, 662–63.
129. Wayne A. Grudem (*The Gift of Prophecy in 1 Corinthians* [Washington, DC: University Press of America, 1982], 136–38, esp. 137) resists the conclusion that prophecy is miraculous for Paul in that it would mean that all the gifts would have to be deemed miraculous, and that the term "miracle" would be void of value in distinguishing various activities. Not only does this conception of miracle appear to arise from a post-Enlightenment perspective but it is exactly the opposite to what Paul wishes to convey.
130. See the summary of the debates by Thiselton, *First Epistle to the Corinthians*, 965–70.
131. Note Fee, *God's Empowering Presence*, 171.
132. Cf. Käsemann ("Ministry and Community," 73), who defines *charisma* "as the concretion and individuation of grace or of the Spirit."

emerge about Paul's idea of the miraculous. First, the context leads the reader to assume that all these activities contribute to the health and welfare of both the community and its members. The miraculous could, therefore, be expected to include healings, exorcisms, as well as, perhaps, provision and protection.[133] Also, second, the close association of extraordinary faith, healings, and powers or miracles with revelatory gifts shows that Paul saw them as of the same order (1 Cor. 12:9–10): healings and miracles, the accomplishment of the impossible, and the experience and assessment of revelation were of a piece for Paul. This is an important conclusion for, as I examine literature of the period with a notion of miracle consistent with Paul's, I must take into account not only healings and works of power but also feats or experiences of the impossible, and prophecy and other revelatory experiences. (The implications for this study of the close connection that Paul sees between miracle and revelatory experience will be taken up in chap. 7.) For my use of terms, the understanding of the miraculous as covering a range of phenomena—from what we would term the apparently commonplace to the extraordinary—is also an important conclusion. Therefore, in line with the thinking that Paul shared with his readers, I will use the word "miraculous" to encompass the whole range of phenomena understood to be from God, and "miracles" and "miracle working" to refer to the occurrence of or direct involvement in, for example, healings or exorcisms or revelatory experiences. Since the terms overlap, I sometimes will use them interchangeably.

1.6 Conclusion

Not least in terms of the importance of the miraculous, our earliest witnesses to Paul—his own letters and his early interpreters—appear to offer conflicting portraits. Further, over against the high profile of miracle working in the reliable traditions about the historical Jesus, we have seen that it is generally agreed that performing miracles was not important to Paul, some scholars suggesting that Paul had little or no interest in miracles. When it is suggested that miracle working was important to Paul, it is not shown what impact this should have in our reconstruction of the historical Paul.

The proposal of this project is that, despite scholarly interest being almost entirely in him as a thinker and theologian, the historical Paul is to be understood not only in terms of his theological enterprise but also through taking into account his life and work, which includes his understanding and experience of the miraculous and the place of miracle working in his mission.

133. Cf. Bultmann, *Theology*, 1:325.

In what follows I will be examining Paul's testimony, as well as enquiring what his interpreters—Luke and the Pauline pseudepigraphical writings—can contribute to a reconstruction of the historical Paul in relation to the miraculous. I begin, in the next chapter, by setting out what views on miracles and the miraculous Paul is likely to have brought with him when he became one of the Christians.

Part 2

Paul's Inheritance

2

Jews and the Miraculous

With so little direct evidence from Paul on which to base conclusions about him in relation to the miraculous—and taking into account that he is writing occasional letters—we run the risk of misreading and misunderstanding what he has to say. Therefore, in this and the next three chapters I will examine those aspects of Paul's religion and religious traditions, as well as his environment, that likely shed light on his and others' expectations in relation to him and the miraculous. I am not attempting to sketch a complete picture of Paul's religion or his religious world; rather, given his tradition and the way he portrays himself, I want to draw attention to those aspects of his religious tradition and environment that most likely have a bearing on his perspective on the miraculous, as well as how others are likely to have viewed him in relation to miracles and the miraculous.

Miracles and the miraculous loom large in some periods of the histories of the Jewish people. In particular, the times of Moses and of Elijah and Elisha stand out in the Hebrew Bible, as well as in writings from Paul's period, as periods of concentrated miraculous activity.[1] However, our interests here are not the statements and assumptions Jews made in relation to miracles and the miraculous in their past, but what was considered important about miracles

---

1. See, e.g., Erkki Koskenniemi, *The Old Testament Miracle-Workers in Early Judaism* (WUNT 2/206; Tübingen: Mohr Siebeck, 2005).

and the miraculous in the period in which Paul lived and might reasonably reflect, or help us understand, his views.

Paul, a Jew, lived in and moved through a complex Hellenistic world that was ruled by the Romans. Though he was highly assimilated into Greco-Roman society,[2] not attempting to reconcile his particular Jewish (Christian) faith with Greek thought shows that he is to be understood primarily as a Jew[3] in a culture that was thoroughly Hellenized.[4] Since, through often complex letters, Paul shows himself to be highly educated,[5] in this chapter I will take into account three large bodies of literature—the Dead Sea Scrolls, Philo, and Josephus—as representatives of the thinking of learned Jews on the miraculous at the time (§2.1). Then, Paul's zeal for the traditions of his ancestors causes us to look at a number of pieces of Jewish literature of the period that reflect the passions of those zealous for the law and Jewish traditions (§2.2). Also, Paul's claim to be a Pharisee prompts an investigation into how these particular people understood miracles and the miraculous (§2.3).[6] In that the synagogue was important in Jewish life and learning, I will also consider what may have taken place in them in relation to the miraculous and, therefore, have informed Paul and his peers on the subject (§2.4). Further, Paul says that he was a person with a message that God had fulfilled eschatological expectations in sending his Son (Gal. 4:4) for salvation to everyone who has faith, Jew and Gentile alike (Rom. 1:16–17).[7] Therefore, I will complete this chapter by setting out the place of the miraculous in the Jewish eschatological expectations that would have been familiar to Paul and those who knew his ministry (§2.5). Paul also, arguably, portrays himself as part of the prophetic tradition. So significant is this topic for this enquiry into Paul and his religion in relation to the miraculous that I will set it aside for discussion in the next chapter.

2. A number of passages show the comfort with which Paul lived in the Greco-Roman world as a Jew. See Rom. 13:1–7; 14–15; 1 Cor. 7:12–16; 2 Cor. 6:14–7:1; 8; Gal. 2:11–14.

3. See John M. G. Barclay, "Paul among Diaspora Jews," *JSNT* 60 (1995): 89–120; Thomas E. Phillips, *Paul, His Letters, and Acts* (LPS; Peabody, MA: Hendrickson, 2009), 86–87; E. P. Sanders, "Paul's Jewishness," in *Paul's Jewish Matrix*, ed. Thomas G. Casey and Justin Taylor (SJC; Mahwah, NJ: Paulist Press; Rome: Gregorian and Biblical Press, 2011), 51–73.

4. E.g., Daniel Boyarin, *A Radical Jew: Paul and the Politics of Identity* (Berkeley: University of California Press, 1994), 268n30.

5. Cf. Martin Hengel, *The Pre-Christian Paul* (London: SCM, 1991), esp. chap. 2.

6. Phillips (*Paul*, 90) warns that scholarship may have overemphasized Paul's Pharisaic commitments.

7. In more detail, see, e.g., Hans Joachim Schoeps, *Paul: The Theology of the Apostle in Light of the Jewish Religious History*, trans. Harold Knight (London: Lutterworth, 1961), 126–27.

2.1 The Scrolls, Philo, and Josephus

Paul, considered highly educated,[8] claimed he was "circumcised on the eighth day," an "Israelite" (a term denoting an "insider"),[9] and "of the tribe of Benjamin," all of which he summed up by saying he was "a Hebrew born of Hebrews" (Phil. 3:5). In order to see what views on the miraculous such a person is likely to have had on becoming a follower of Jesus, I will begin by examining the Dead Sea Scrolls. Yet, Paul's world was wider than that reflected in the scrolls. He has such control of the Greek language and such command of the Greek Bible that he must have grown up with it and its language and been part of the culture it reflected.[10] Moreover, Paul's writing his first letter, 1 Thessalonians, in Greek only about twenty years after Easter[11] attests both to his Hellenization and the astonishing speed at which Christianity was Hellenized.[12] Paul was, therefore, also immersed in the same world as Hellenized Jews such as Philo of Alexandria and Josephus.[13] These large bodies of Jewish literature can be expected to enable a contextualized examination of ideas of the period that are likely to reflect the views of Paul as he describes and discloses himself, and of those who knew him.[14]

8. E.g., Paul's letters were said to be "weighty and strong" (2 Cor. 10:10); on which, see Margaret E. Thrall, *A Critical and Exegetical Commentary on the Second Epistle to the Corinthians*, 2 vols. (ICC; London: T&T Clark, 1994–2000), 2:630. On Paul's education, see Hengel, *Pre-Christian Paul*, 18–62; Jerome Murphy-O'Connor, *Paul: A Critical Life* (Oxford: Oxford University Press, 1996), 46–51.

9. Phil. 3:5: ἐκ γένους Ἰσραήλ ("of the race of Israel"); cf. Rom. 11:1; 2 Cor. 11:22; also see Rom. 9:4. See Karl G. Kuhn, "Ἰσραήλ, κτλ.," *TDNT* 3:359–68; James D. G. Dunn, *The Theology of Paul the Apostle* (Grand Rapids: Eerdmans, 1998), 505–6.

10. Hengel, *Pre-Christian Paul*, 35, 54–62; Murphy-O'Connor, *Paul: A Critical Life*, 46–51. On the possibility that Paul spoke Latin, see Stanley E. Porter, "Did Paul Speak Latin?" in *Paul: Jew, Greek, and Roman*, ed. Stanley E. Porter (PSt 5; Leiden: Brill, 2008), 289–308.

11. Robert Jewett, *The Thessalonian Correspondence: Pauline Rhetoric and Millenarian Piety* (Philadelphia: Fortress, 1986), 60; Jorge Sanchez Bosch, "La chronologie de la premiere aux Thessaloniciens et les relations de Paul avec d'autres eglises," *NTS* 37 (1991): 336–47.

12. Samuel Sandmel, "Philo Judaeus: An Introduction to the Man, His Writings, and His Significance," *ANRW* II.21.1 (1984): 37–38.

13. Cf. Charles H. Dodd, "Hellenism and Christianity," in *Independence, Convergence, and Borrowing in Institutions, Thought, and Art* (Harvard Tercentenary Publications; Cambridge, MA: Harvard University Press, 1937), 109–31, esp. 110.

14. The early rabbinic literature has not been taken into account, since the Mishnah, the earliest codification of the traditions, was not compiled until the end of the Tannaitic period (c. 200 CE). Also, this literature, concerned with halakic and exegetical issues, shows little interest in miracles and the miraculous until the next generation, when a debate on miracles emerges (cf. *t. Yebam.* 14:6). See Michael Becker, "Miracle Traditions in Early Rabbinic Literature: Some Questions on Their Pragmatics," in *Wonders Never Cease: The Purpose of Narrating Miracle Stories in the New Testament and Its Religious Environment*, ed. Michael Labahn and Bert Jan Lietaert Peerbolte (LNTS 288; London: T&T Clark, 2006), 48–69, esp. 50–51.

(a) *The Dead Sea Scrolls*. Over 860 texts from between late third century
BCE and the middle of the first century BCE were discovered in eleven caves
near Khirbet Qumran.[15] If, as is widely agreed, these scrolls were the product
or property of the Essenes at Qumran, they were from a group well connected with society.[16] Only twenty kilometers east of Jerusalem and twelve
kilometers south of Jericho, the Qumran community was not isolated from
the rest of society, and it was also part of the wider Essene movement spread
across Palestine (Josephus, *J.W.* 2.124). Moreover, roughly one-third of the
writings, those that are not sectarian[17]—the noncanonical psalms and wisdom
material, for example[18]—enable us to glimpse not only Qumranite thinking,
but also that of others in the wider community. Alternatively, if the scrolls,
though originating in numerous libraries of a variety of Jewish groups, were
the hidden treasures deposited in the caves for safekeeping by Jerusalemite
refugees on their way to Masada, fleeing Roman suppression (66–70 CE),[19]
these documents can still be treated as a corpus, as they reflect the mix of
ideas from that city.[20] Either way, we can reasonably expect the scrolls to reflect views and values widely held in the period. Moreover, Paul's passion for
traditional Jewish practices, as well as ideas distinctive of him, are paralleled
in the scrolls: the sinfulness of all humans (Rom. 3:9–20, 23; 1QH^a XII, 30);
the inability to earn God's forgiveness (Rom. 3:28; Gal. 2:16; 1QH^a XII, 31);
the righteousness of God (Rom. 3:25–26; 1QS IX, 24–XII, 22); only God is
able to make a person righteous (Rom. 3:23–34; 1QH^a XV, 29–30; 4Q381 31;

15. Emanuel Tov and S. J. Pfann, "Lists of the Texts from the Judaean Desert," in *The Texts
from the Judaean Desert*, ed. Emanuel Tov and Martin G. Abegg (DJD 34; Oxford: Clarendon,
2002), 27–89; Greg Doudna, "Dating the Scrolls on the Basis of Radiocarbon Analysis," in *The
Dead Sea Scrolls after Fifty Years: A Comprehensive Assessment*, ed. Peter W. Flint and James C.
VanderKam, 2 vols. (Leiden: Brill, 1999), 2:430–65.

16. For a recent critical assessment of the widely agreed "Essene Theory," identifying the
occupants of the Qumran community with the Essenes, see Steve Mason, "Did the Essenes Write
the Dead Sea Scrolls? Don't Rely on Josephus," *BAR* 34, no. 6 (2008): 61–65.

17. For the classification of the scrolls into sectarian and nonsectarian texts, see, e.g., Carol A.
Newsom, "'Sectually Explicit' Literature from Qumran," in *The Hebrew Bible and Its Interpret-
ers*, ed. William Henry Propp, Baruch Halpern, and David Noel Freedman (BibJudSt 1; Winona
Lake, IN: Eisenbrauns, 1990), 167–87.

18. Devorah Dimant, "The Qumran Manuscripts: Contents and Significance," in *Time to
Prepare the Way in the Wilderness: Papers on the Qumran Scrolls*, ed. Devorah Dimant and
Lawrence H. Schiffman (STDJ 16; Leiden: Brill, 1995), 23–58.

19. See Norman Golb, *Who Wrote the Dead Sea Scrolls? The Search for the Secret of Qumran*
(New York: Scribner, 1994), critically reviewed by, e.g., Lester L. Grabbe, *DSD* 4 (1997): 124–28;
F. García Martínez and A. S. van der Woude, "A 'Groningen' Hypothesis of Qumran Origins
and Early History," *RevQ* 56 (1990): 521–42.

20. On the idea that the Qumran manuscripts are to be regarded as a homogeneous library,
see Newsom, "'Sectually Explicit,'" 167–87; Dimant, "Qumran Manuscripts," 23–58.

4Q400 1 I); and God predestines some for salvation, for example.[21] In particular, there are parallels between Paul's vocabulary, and way of theorizing, in Galatians and the Dead Sea Scrolls (4QMMT [4QHalakhic Letter]).[22] Also, in 2 Corinthians Paul's discussion that follows his statement "Do not be mismated with unbelievers" (2 Cor. 6:14; cf. 6:15–7:1)—with his use of Beliar, and seeing the world in terms of light or dark, as well as dividing people into believers and unbelievers, and identifying the church with the temple[23]—points in the same direction. Paul shares the same milieu as the scrolls.[24] In short, even if he was not familiar with the literature itself, Paul was at least reflecting the same thought world as the scrolls, so that their views on the miracles and the miraculous can be taken to reflect the world in which he lived and wrote.

These texts show considerable interest in miracles or mighty deeds and healing and exorcism.[25] There are references to unspecified mighty deeds by God,[26] as well as to those associated with the exodus (4Q185 1–2 I, 14–15; 4Q374 2 II, 6–8). There is also interest in the miraculous in the messianic age (see §2.5 below), but here our concern is how the miraculous was understood in the present.

According to the *Temple Scroll* (11Q19), produced to make God's laws more obviously applicable to the readers,[27] prophets were expected to perform miracles ("a sign and a wonder," אות או מופת [11Q19 LIV, 8–9]). These miracles were intended to gain a hearing of, or to be the basis for, a message. However,

21. Rom. 9:15–18; 1QS III, 13–IV, 14; CD-A II, 2–16; 1QM XIII, 7–11. See James H. Charlesworth, foreword in *Paul and the Dead Sea Scrolls*, ed. Jerome Murphy-O'Connor and James H. Charlesworth (COL; New York: Crossroad, 1990), ix–xvi; Joseph A. Fitzmyer, *The Impact of the Dead Sea Scrolls* (New York: Paulist Press, 2009), 98–106.

22. On the parallels between 4QMMT and Galatians, see, e.g., Martin G. Abegg, "Paul and James on the Law in Light of the Dead Sea Scrolls," in *Christian Beginnings and the Dead Sea Scrolls*, ed. John J. Collins and Craig A. Evans (Grand Rapids: Baker Academic, 2006), 63–74.

23. 1 Cor. 3:16–17; 2 Cor. 6:16; 1QS III; 1QS VIII, 4–6; IX, 6–7; 4Q174 1 I, 6. On shared vocabulary and ideas, see Joseph A. Fitzmyer, "Qumrân and the Interpolated Paragraph in 2 Cor. 6:14–7:1," *CBQ* 23 (1961): 271–80.

24. Karl P. Donfried, "Paul the Jew and the Dead Sea Scrolls," in *The Dead Sea Scrolls in Context: Integrating the Dead Sea Scrolls in the Study of Ancient Texts, Languages, and Cultures*, ed. Armin Lange, Emanuel Tov, and Matthias Weigold, 2 vols. (VTSup 140; Leiden: Brill, 2011), 2:721–33. There is a worthy minority arguing that 2 Cor. 6:14–7:1 was not written by Paul. See the discussion by Margaret E. Thrall, "The Problem of II Cor. vi.14–vii.1 in Some Recent Discussion," *NTS* 24 (1977–78): 132–48.

25. See, e.g., Eric Eve, *The Jewish Context of Jesus' Miracles* (JSNTSup 231; Sheffield: Sheffield Academic Press, 2002), 174–216.

26. E.g., 1QS I, 21; 1QM III, 5; X, 8–9; XIV, 5–6; XVIII, 10.

27. On the problem of the purpose of the *Temple Scroll*, see Steven L. Jacobs, *The Biblical Masorah and the Temple Scroll: An Orthographical Inquiry* (Lanham, MD: University Press of America, 2002), 91–102.

if the message conflicted with the Torah, not only was the message—and presumably the value of the miracle—to be ignored, the prophet was also to be executed (11Q19 LIV, 15) (further, see §3.3 [a] below).

In the *Festival Prayers* there is mention of healing. However, the reference is general;[28] "healing" (רופא) is expected for those who have stumbled in their sin (4Q509+4Q505 3 XII, 3–5).[29] Similarly, in the daily prayers or liturgies led by priests within the community there is the declaration "you heal us of madness <and blindness> and confusion" (4Q504 1–2 II, 14). It is not possible to be sure that physical or miraculous healing is in mind, either by the scribe who entered "and blindness" above the line to conform the text more closely to Deuteronomy 28:28 (cf. 4Q166 I, 8; 4Q387a 3 II, 4)[30] or in his original text. Rather, the vocabulary[31] and dependence on Deuteronomy, with its corporate focus, suggest the corporate life rather than bodily illness of individuals needing healing. However, in the hymns there is praise for what is more likely to be physical healing of "disease" or "plague" (נגע [1QHᵃ XVII, 24–25]).[32]

Beyond this reference in the hymns—prayers that suggest a slight contemporary interest in miracles of healing—other references in the scrolls are to exorcisms.[33] The fragmentary 4Q560 is probably a list of sicknesses followed by a script for exorcism, rather than a defense against an evil spirit.[34] The spirit that is thought to have entered the flesh or body (4Q560 1 I, 3) is addressed and adjured (4Q560 1 II, 5–6). In 11Q5 David is said to be responsible for composing four "songs for making music over the possessed" (11Q5 XXVII, 9–10).[35]

---

28. The scrolls also use רפא ("heal") in relation to exorcism (1Q20 XX, 28) and for the positive impact of the wind on the earth (4Q210 1 II, 2).

29. Further, see M. L. Brown, "רָפָא," *TDOT* 13:601–2.

30. See Maurice Baillet, "504. Paroles des Luminaires (Premier Exemplaire: DibHamᵃ)," in *Qumrân Grotte 4. III (4Q482–4Q520)* (DJD 7; Oxford: Clarendon, 1982), 139–40 and plate L; Dennis T. Olson, "Words of the Lights (4Q504–506)," in *The Dead Sea Scrolls: Hebrew, Aramaic, and Greek Texts with English Translations*, vol. 4A, *Pseudepigraphic amd Non-Masoretic Psalms and Prayers*, ed. James H. Charlesworth and Henry W. L. Rietz (PTSDSSP; Tübingen: Mohr Siebeck; Louisville: Westminster John Knox, 1994), 127n20.

31. שגע ("Madness") (in the OT: 2 Kings 9:11; 1 Sam. 21:15–16; cf. CD-A XV, 15) and תמהון ("confusion") (in the OT: Deut. 28:28; Zech. 12:4); U. Berges, "תָּמַהּ," *TDOT* 15:684; "שגע," *HALOT* 4:1415.

32. Cf. "נגע," *HALOT* 2:669; L. Schwienhorst, "נָגַע," *TDOT* 9:209.

33. 4Q560; 11Q5; 11Q11; 4Q510; 4Q511. On the *Prayer of Nabonidus* (4Q242) not being an exorcism see Eve, *Jewish Context*, 182–89.

34. As suggested by Philip S. Alexander, "'Wrestling against Wickedness in High Places': Magic in the World View of the Qumran Community," in *The Scrolls and the Scriptures: Qumran Fifty Years After*, ed. Stanley E. Porter and Craig A. Evans (JSPSup 26; Sheffield: Sheffield Academic Press, 1997), 330.

35. On the "stricken" or "possessed" (הפגועים [11Q5 XXVII, 9–10]) as those possessed or tormented by evil spirits, see James A. Sanders, *The Psalms Scroll of Qumrân Cave 11 (11QPsᵃ)* (DJD 4; Oxford: Clarendon, 1965), 93, citing, e.g., *y. Šabb.* 6:8b; *y. ʿErub.* 10:26c; *b. Šebu.* 15b.

Given that these poems or songs[36] would have been consistent with Qumran's apotropaic psalms,[37] the exorcisms probably were conducted by a *maskil* or scribe in public worship,[38] perhaps with the people present responding, "Amen, Amen" (cf. 4Q511 63 IV; 11Q11 V).[39] The Tobit fragments (4Q196 14 I, 12; 4Q197 4 I, 13)[40] probably can be taken as indicating endorsement of the divinely ordained (Tob. 6:4; 11:4, 7–8) method of fumigation, for popular use, to cause potentially fatal daimons to flee from attacking people.[41] Then, in rewriting stories of some of the patriarchs for his own time, the author of the *Genesis Apocryphon* says Abraham prays, lays hands on the king, and an evil spirit is expelled (1Q20 XX, 1–34, esp. 29–30).[42] This story shows that those responsible for the scrolls thought not only that miracles were able to be performed through the use of traditional incantations, but also that individuals, in their own right, though depending on God, were able to perform healings. One is left with the impression that the miracles familiar to the people responsible for the scrolls were healings, particularly exorcisms.

(b) Philo of Alexandria. In the case of Philo (c. 20 BCE–c. 50 CE), we know little about this wealthy and well-educated Jew, most important for his allegorical interpretation of the Old Testament in which he found much Greek

36. Cf. 11Q11. On the possibility the use of texts was accompanied by music, including instruments, see Bilhah Nitzan, *Qumran Prayer and Religious Poetry*, trans. Jonathan Chipman (STDJ 12; Leiden: Brill, 1994), 228n8.

37. See 11Q11; 4Q510; 4Q511; 6Q18. Cf. Bilhah Nitzan, "Hymns from Qumran—4Q510–4Q511," in *The Dead Sea Scrolls: Forty Years of Research*, ed. Devorah Dimant and Uriel Rappaport (STDJ 10; Leiden: Brill; Jerusalem: Magnes, 1992), 53–63. See also Esther Eshel, "Genres of Magical Texts in the Dead Sea Scrolls," in *Die Dämonen: Die Dämonologie der israelitisch-jüdischen und frühchristlichen Literatur im Kontext ihrer Umwelt* [= *Demons: The Demonology of Israelite-Jewish and Early Christian Literature in Context of Their Environment*], ed. Armin Lange, Hermann Lichtenberger, and K. F. Diethard Römheld (Tübingen; Mohr Siebeck, 2003), 395–415. Eshel takes 11Q11 to be exorcistic rather than apotropaic.

38. See 4Q511 63–64 IV, 1–3; on which, see Alexander, "'Wrestling against Wickedness,'" 321.

39. See the brief discussion by Geza Vermes, *The Complete Dead Sea Scrolls in English* (London: Penguin, 1997), 310.

40. 4Q478 is no longer considered a fragment of Tobit. See E. Larson and L. H. Schiffman, "Miscellaneous Texts," in *Qumran Cave 4.XVII, Parabiblical Texts, Part 3*, ed. George Brooke et al. (DJD 22; Oxford: Clarendon, 1996), 295–96.

41. 4Q196 14 I, 12; 4Q197 4 I, 13–14. On Jews taking up Greek medicine—which was considered pagan and forbidden (cf. Tob. 2:10)—when it was divinely ordained (cf. Sir. 37:27–38:15), see Armin Lange, "The Essene Position on Magic and Divination," in *Legal Texts and Legal Issues: Proceedings of the Second Meeting of the International Organization for Qumran Studies, Cambridge, 1995; Published in Honour of Joseph M. Baumgarten*, ed. Moshe Bernstein, Florentino García Martínez, and John Kampen (STDJ 23; Leiden: Brill, 1997), 384–85.

42. Cf. Graham H. Twelftree, *Jesus the Exorcist: A Contribution to the Study of the Historical Jesus* (WUNT 2/54; Tübingen: Mohr Siebeck; Peabody, MA: Hendrickson, 1993), 43–46.

philosophy.[43] Apart from Philo's own writing, toward the end of the first century CE Josephus gives the only near contemporary information about Philo, saying that he "stood at the head of the delegation of the Jews [to the emperor Gaius, or Caligula], a man held in the highest honour, brother of Alexander the alabarch and no novice in philosophy" (*Ant.* 18.259; cf. Philo, *Spec.* 3.1).[44] In any case, Philo shared with Paul a number of views: God could be known from creation;[45] faith and knowledge of God are gifts;[46] humans are composed of the material and immaterial;[47] and those who did not worship God were characterized as worshiping the creature rather than the creator,[48] for example.[49] Thus, although no demonstrable contact between these two bodies of literature is being argued or assumed, Philo's extensive writings, drawing from the same well as Paul, are invaluable for understanding Paul and his world,[50] including in relation to the miraculous.[51]

Philo associates miracles primarily with Moses and the exodus (e.g., *Mos.* 1.65–70), though it is God rather than Moses or Aaron who is often credited with, or is said to direct, the miracles (e.g., *Mos.* 1.95–97, 130–139). Most significantly for our project, Philo has no miracle stories in his writings after

43. See Ronald Williamson, *Jews in the Hellenistic World: Philo* (CCWJCW 1/2; Cambridge: Cambridge University Press, 1989), 1–27; Ellen Birnbaum, "Two Millennia Later: General Resources and Particular Perspectives on Philo the Jew," *CurBR* 4 (2006): 241–76.

44. On the value of this statement, and Josephus's possible knowledge of Philo, see Louis H. Feldman, *Josephus's Interpretation of the Bible* (Berkeley: University of California Press, 1998), 51–54. On ἀλαβάρχος ("tax official"), see Louis H. Feldman, *Josephus*, 10 vols. (LCL; Cambridge, MA: Harvard University Press; London: Heinemann, 1926–65), 9:103–5nf. For other later references to Philo, see Emil Schürer, *The History of the Jewish People in the Age of Jesus Christ (175 B.C.–A.D. 135)*, trans. T. A. Burkill et al., 3 vols. (Edinburgh: T&T Clark, 1973–86), 3.2:814n12.

45. Rom. 1–2; cf. Philo, *Leg.* 3.97–98; *Somn.* 1.203–204; *Spec.* 1.33; *Praem.* 40–42; *Mos.* 1.212; *QG* 2.34.

46. Philo, *Abr.* 80; *Fug.* 164; *Leg.* 3.136; *Migr.* 27–32; 216–222; *Praem.* 45–46; *Somn.* 1.60; *Spec.* 1.41–43.

47. Cf. Rom. 8:5 and Philo, *Her.* 57; *Mos.* 1.29.

48. Cf. Rom. 1:20–23 and Philo, *Ebr.* 109; *Decal.* 53.

49. On the echoes of Paul and Philo in each other's work, see, e.g., Wilfred L. Knox, *St. Paul and the Church of Jerusalem* (Cambridge: Cambridge University Press, 1925), 130–32; Henry Chadwick, "St. Paul and Philo of Alexandria," *BJRL* 48 (1966): 286–307; David T. Runia, *Philo in Early Christian Literature: A Survey* (CRINT 3; Assen: Van Gorcum; Minneapolis: Fortress, 1993), 68–70; George W. E. Nickelsburg, "Philo among Greeks, Jews and Christians," in *Philo und das Neue Testament: Wechselseitige Wahrnehmungen; 1. Internationales Symposium zum Corpus Judaeo-Hellenisticum, 1.–4. Mai 2003, Eisenach/Jena*, ed. Roland Deines and Karl-Wilhelm Niebuhr (WUNT 172; Tübingen: Mohr Siebeck, 2004), 70; Gregory E. Sterling, "The Place of Philo of Alexandria in the Study of Christian Origins," in Deines and Niebuhr, *Philo und das Neue Testament*, 21–52.

50. "Philo is the one from whom the historian of emergent Christianity has most to learn" (Chadwick, "St. Paul and Philo," 287).

51. Eve, *Jewish Context*, 53.

the pentateuchal period. Indeed, Philo has no miracle stories in the materials that deal with his own time.[52] Even in his discussion of the Essenes Philo gives no hint of them being interested in miraculous healing (cf. *Hypoth.* 11.13).

Moreover, although Philo is interested in health,[53] and although there is mention of God giving health (*Leg.* 3.178), and there is the expectation of healing on the payment of the firstfruits or ransom money to the temple (*Spec.* 1.77), Philo has no stories of healing miracles. This is probably because he sees physical health dependent on spiritual health (*Contempl.* 2), and God using physicians in healing (*Leg.* 3.178).[54] Also, Philo has no interest in exorcism. This is not surprising, since, in the Greek tradition,[55] he takes "souls," "demons," and "angels" to be different names for the intermediary angels or messengers between God and people, dispensing with the fear and superstition related to demons (*Gig.* 16).

Philo's leaving aside any possible contemporary reference to miracles is consistent with both his rationalism[56] and his view that the age of miracles was in the Mosaic past.[57] In relation to healing, Philo's rationalism may find expression in his statement, "What is called word-medicine [λογιατρεία] is far removed from assistance to the sick, for diseases are cured by drugs and surgery and prescriptions of diet, but not with words" (Philo, *Congr.* 53; cf. *Leg.* 3.178). In any case, it shows that Philo did not think that miracles, including healing, were or should be particularly important among his contemporaries.

(c) Josephus. Later taking the name "Flavius" from the dynasty of his patrons, Josephus ben Matthias was born into a priestly and aristocratic family in Jerusalem in 37 or 38 CE (Josephus, *Life* 5; 7). He was well educated (*Life* 8–9) and was writing only a generation after Paul,[58] and he may have lived into the second century CE.[59] Josephus was both thoroughly immersed in the

52. Ibid., 66–67, 74, 78, 80.

53. Philo, *Legat.* 106; *Leg.* 3.178; *Sacr.* 70; *Somn.* 1.112; *Aet.* 63.

54. Eve, *Jewish Context*, 79–80.

55. See Plato, *Apol.* 27c–d; *Phaedr.* 246e; *Symp.* 202d–203a; *Tim.* 40d; *Leg.* 717a–f; Xenocrates, frgs. 23; 225; cf. Plutarch, *Def. orac.* 13.2.416e.

56. See, e.g., Philo, *Mos.* 1.176, 179, 185, 200, 202, 211, 269–271. See Erwin R. Goodenough, *By Light, Light: The Mystic Gospel of Hellenistic Judaism* (New Haven: Yale University Press; London: Oxford University Press, 1935), 187–88; Harry Austryn Wolfson, *Philo: Foundations of Religious Philosophy in Judaism, Christianity, and Islam*, 2 vols. (Cambridge, MA: Harvard University Press, 1968), 1:350–54; Sandmel, "Philo Judaeus," 38.

57. Eve, *Jewish Context*, 84.

58. *Jewish War* cannot be dated exactly, but it probably came out after 75 CE; *Jewish Antiquities* appeared in 93/94 CE (*Ant.* 20.267). See Tessa Rajak, *Josephus: The Historian and His Society* (London: Duckworth, 2002), 195n23, 237–38.

59. Steve Mason, *Josephus and the New Testament* (Peabody, MA: Hendrickson, 1992), 51. Cf. Rajak, *Josephus*, 11n2.

philosophical schools of the Jews (*Life* 10) and exposed to the wider world in that, at the age of twenty-six, he went on a diplomatic mission to Rome (*Life* 13–16). Also, he later secured the favor of Rome through predicting Vespasian's becoming emperor (*J.W.* 3.400–401; *Ag. Ap.* 422; 425), and he lived in Rome for around the last half of his life, on a pension, in Vespasian's former home (*Life* 423). It is reasonable, then, to take the writings of Josephus as particularly valuable in helping us understand the world of Paul. It is not that we can expect to find Paul's views mirrored in Josephus, but that along with the scrolls and Philo he is able to show us how educated people in Paul's time and milieu, all relying on the same traditions, thought about miracles and the miraculous.

In his reworking of the biblical narrative Josephus retells miracle stories,[60] including healings (*Ant.* 8.325–327; 10.29) and a resuscitation (9.183), clustering the stories around the great figures of history.[61] There is no doubt that Josephus accepted the veracity of what he recounts. For example, in relating the longevity of the patriarchs (1.104–108), he urges the reader not to think that what he has recorded is false, even if it conflicts with contemporary experience (1.105). However, as this suggests, he holds his commitment to the integrity of the miracles stories in the face of Hellenistic rationalism (cf. §3.3 [g] below). Indeed, after affirming his belief in the miraculous nature of a story (1.105; 3.7, 24, 26; 17.354), including a recent account (17.349–355), he will offer a rational explanation (1.108; 3.8, 25, 26–27) or will pick up a well-known formula[62] to conclude with a courtesy statement for his skeptical readers along the lines: "But as to these matters, let everyone take them as he thinks fit" (3.322).[63]

The stories Josephus includes from his own time show not only that he considered miracles—stories sometimes modeled on heroes from Scripture[64]— to be part of contemporary experience, but they also show the significance

60. Recently on miracle stories and the miraculous in Josephus, see, e.g., Eve, *Jewish Context*, 25–37; Koskenniemi, *Miracle-Workers*, 229–80.

61. Cf. Eve, *Jewish Context*, 34. See also §3.3 (g) below.

62. Cf. Herodotus, *Hist.* 2.123; 3.122; Thucydides, *Hist.* 6.2.1; Dionysius of Halicarnassus, *Ant. rom.* 1.48.1, 4; 2.40.3; 2.70.5; Lucian, *Ver. hist.* 60.

63. In Josephus, see *Ant.* 1.108; 2.348; 3.81, 268, 322; 4.158; 8.262; 10.281; 17.354; cf. 19.108; see also Horst R. Moehring, "Rationalization of Miracles in the Writings of Flavius Josephus," in *Studia Evangelica VI: Papers Presented to the Fourth International Congress on New Testament Studies Held at Oxford, 1969*, ed. Elizabeth A. Livingstone (TUGAL 112; Berlin: Akademie-Verlag, 1973), 376–83; Eve, *Jewish Context*, 24–52; Koskenniemi, *Miracle-Workers*, 229–80.

64. Cf. rain falling as a result of prayers by Elijah (*Ant.* 13.322, 346) and Onias or Honi (*Ant.* 14.22); see also Otto Betz, "Miracles in the Writings of Flavius Josephus," in *Josephus, Judaism, and Christianity*, ed. Louis H. Feldman and Gohei Hata (Detroit: Wayne State University Press, 1987), 219–20.

he attached to the miracles. Josephus says the story of Eleazar the Jewish exorcist performing a healing in front of Vespasian (8.46–49)[65] demonstrates the ongoing value of the wisdom that God had given to Solomon (8.42, 45).[66] The favorable weather, with rain falling only during the night while Herod was building the temple, Josephus takes as an example of the manifestation of God's power (15.425). And the shower of rain that came after the speech of Petronius to the Jews was an indication of God being with him in his protest against Caligula setting up his statue in the Jerusalem temple (18.285). Also, rain in the night bringing much-needed water to those besieged on Masada is an example of God's providential care and encourages those within (14.390–391; cf. *J.W.* 1.286–287). Notwithstanding, the fall of Masada is aided by a change in the wind, the Romans being said to be blessed by God's aid (*J.W.* 7.318). Further, a herd of elephants trampling on Ptolemy Physcon, rather than the Jews, is said by Josephus to be God's deliverance (*Ag. Ap.* 2.53–56; cf. 3 Macc. 5:1–51). Yet, Josephus is not certain whether the death by fire of Herod's two bodyguards, when they attempted to enter David's tomb (*Ant.* 16.182), was to be credited to God's wrath or to Fortune (16.188).[67] He does, however, for example, attribute a mighty and violent wind destroying the crops of the entire country to God's punishment for killing Onias (or Honi) (14.24–28). Alcinius, the high priest, planning to pull down the wall of the Holy Place, suffers a sudden "blow" (πληγή) from God, is brought down speechless to the ground, and after days of suffering dies (12.413; cf. 1 Macc. 9:54–56). Josephus says that all suspected a deadly pestilence destroying a greater part of the people and Herod the Great's friends had been brought about by God in his anger over the execution of Mariamme, his second wife (*Ant.* 15.232–247), and that Herod's increasing illness was God's punishment for his lawless deeds (17.167).[68]

In his narrative of the burning of the temple Josephus sets out seven portents, including a comet and the birth of a lamb from a cow (*J.W.* 6.288–309).[69] He sums up by saying, "Reflecting on these things one will find that God has a care for men, and by all kinds of premonitory signs shows his people the way

65. J. B. Lightfoot (*Saint Paul's Epistles to the Colossians and to Philemon* [London: Macmillan, 1890], 89–90) noted the connection between the story of Eleazar and the description by Josephus of the Essenes' interest in the prophylactic (ἀλεξητήριος) properties of roots (*J.W.* 2.136). Further, see Steve Mason and Honora Chapman, *Flavius Josephus: Translation and Commentary*, vol. 1B, *Judean War 2* (Leiden: Brill, 2008), 110–11.

66. Betz, "Miracles," 220–21.

67. Cf. Eve, *Jewish Context*, 38.

68. Further, see the discussion in ibid., 40–43.

69. George MacRae, "Miracle in *The Antiquities* of Josephus," in *Miracles: Cambridge Studies in Their Philosophy and History*, ed. C. F. D. Moule (London: A. R. Mowbray, 1965), 127–47.

of salvation" (6.310; cf. *Ant.* 2.287). Josephus also relates dreams in which God speaks to and directs people (*Life* 208; *J.W.* 2.116 // *Ant.* 17.349–353; *J.W.* 3.351),[70] and he tells of prophecies in which the future is told.[71]

According to Josephus, miracles are also promised by false prophets (*Ant.* 18.85; 20.97, 167–172). These prophets, responsible for much of the suffering of the Jewish people (20.168), are false not because they do not deliver their promised miracles. Rather, Josephus's narrative casts them in a negative light because they are acting and speaking against the events God is overseeing.[72] Thus, in each case the impostor is apprehended before the proposed miracle is scheduled to take place.[73] In this, Josephus's view is that a miracle would not be sufficient, and could not be used, to counter what God intends, a view we will come across among Pharisees (see §2.3 [c] below).

The stories of the miraculous that Josephus relates from his own time are primarily natural phenomena, or coincidences that he takes to be miraculous; there are no healings other than one exorcism. They are important to him as evidence of God's involvement not only in history, but also in the present expressing his providential care, his power, as well as protection, direction, and even punishment of people.

(d) Conclusions. From what we can see in these three major bodies of Jewish literature reflecting the views of well-educated Jews from around Paul's time, the miraculous was solidly associated with the great biblical figures and events of the past. Nevertheless, in contrast to the rationalist approach of Philo, who expressed no interest in miracles in his own time, Josephus (though sensitive to the pressure of rationalism), and those affiliated with Qumran, understood the miraculous to be part of present experience: prophecy or foreknowledge, healings, exorcisms, unexpected natural events in nature, and portents that indicated God's care and guidance of people. Josephus shows that Jews could see miracles as God's powerful involvement in life. As we saw in the *Temple Scroll*, miracles could be used by prophets in drawing attention to their message. However, the integrity of the message or, as Josephus would see it, God's intention, was more important than the miracle.

That the rationalist approach to the miraculous, which we have noted in Philo, is not likely to have been part of Paul's thinking becomes clearer as we proceed. Indeed, despite the similarities between them, the difference between Paul and Philo in relation to the miraculous becomes obvious as we look at other and more immediate roots of Paul's religion.

---

70. Josephus, *Life* 208; *J.W.* 2.116 // *Ant.* 17.349–353; *J.W.* 3.351.
71. Josephus, *J.W.* 1.78–80 // *Ant.* 13.311–313. Further, on prophecy in Josephus, see §3.2 below.
72. Betz, "Miracles," 216, 222–23.
73. Cf. Moehring, "Rationalization of Miracles," 381–83.

2.2 Zealous Jews and the Miraculous

Not only does Paul say he had confidence in his Jewish heritage (Phil. 3:4b–5a), he also says that he expressed this confidence in his way of life: "as to the law, a Pharisee; as to zeal, a persecutor of the church; as to righteousness under the law, blameless" (3:5b–6). Testifying to his passion for the distinctive practices of the Jewish people, he also says: "I advanced in Judaism ['Ιουδαϊσμός][74] beyond many among my people of the same age, for I was far more zealous for the traditions of my ancestors" (Gal. 1:14).[75] Therefore, as well as the three large bodies of literature we have examined that have enabled us to contextualize the ideas of educated Jews concerning the miraculous, there are smaller bodies of literature that are thought to be from the hand of particularly zealous Jews from Paul's time that will help us see how he could have viewed the miraculous. An examination of the book of Judith, *Lives of the Prophets*, Pseudo-Philo's *Liber antiquitatum biblicarum*, 2 Maccabees, and *Psalms of Solomon* shows that zealous Jews had a variety of views on miracles.

At one end of a spectrum are those Jews represented by Judith,[76] a ficti-tious rescue story probably from mid-second-century BCE Jerusalem.[77] In view of other documents from such Jews of the period, it is striking that the miraculous does not feature in the book. Even though there are references to the miraculous in ancient narratives (e.g., Jdt. 5:10–13), there are no angelic

74. Until it was picked up in later Christian discourse, 'Ιουδαϊσμός was a rare word, occurring only in 2 Macc. 2:21; 8:1; 14:38; 4 Macc. 4:26 and here in the NT (Gal. 1:13–14). Steve Mason ("Jews, Judaeans, Judaizing, Judaism: Problems of Categorization in Ancient History," *JSJ* [2007], 511) notes that from this use it is apparent that it is "usable only in the special context of movement toward or away from Judean law and life, in contrast to some other cultural pull."

75. On Paul's Jewishness, both from his perspective and those of his compatriots, see Jörg Frey, "Paul's Jewish Identity," in *Jewish Identity in the Greco-Roman World* [= *Jüdische Identität in der griechisch-römischen Welt*] ed. Jörg Frey, Daniel R. Schwartz, and Stephanie Gripentrog (AGJU 71; Leiden: Brill, 2007), 285–321.

76. Hebrew being the probable original language suggests a Jewish author. See, e.g., Carey A. Moore, *Judith: A New Translation with Introduction and Commentary* (AB 40; Garden City, NY: Doubleday, 1985), 66–67. From time to time Judith is considered to come from the hand of a Pharisee, see, e.g., Moore, *Judith*, 70–71. However, the view has not been well received. See the summary discussion by Benedikt Otzen, *Tobit and Judith* (GAP; London: Sheffield Academic Press, 2002), 135. If anything, the national and religious zeal reflects pre-Pharisaic values (cf. Jdt. 9:1–14; 15:14–16:17). See George W. E. Nickelsburg, "Stories of Biblical and Early Post-Biblical Times," in *Jewish Writings of the Second Temple Period: Apocrypha, Pseudepigrapha, Qumran, Sectarian Writings, Philo, Josephus*, ed. Michael E. Stone (CRINT 2/2; Assen: Van Gorcum; Philadelphia: Fortress, 1984), 50–51.

77. Judith is controlled by the Maccabean crisis (Jdt. 2:28; 3:10). See Moore, *Judith*, 67. On the precise date, see the summary discussion by Otzen, *Tobit and Judith*, 132. The book's provenance is suggested by the central role of Jerusalem (also represented by Bethulia, Jdt. 4:6). Cf. Otzen, *Tobit and Judith*, 94–97.

interventions, nor are there any frightening displays of supernatural power in Judith.[78] Similarly, *Lives of the Prophets* (*Vitae prophetarum*), also from the hand of a zealous Jew,[79] associates miracles with the past, in this case the scriptural prophets.[80] From these two pieces of literature we have evidence that some zealous Jews, though proposing miracles may have taken place in the past, like Philo, expressed no interest in miracles in the present.

In Pseudo-Philo's *Liber antiquitatum biblicarum*,[81] by another Jew (perhaps from Palestine) from between 50 CE and 150 CE[82] zealous for his[83] traditions,[84] the miraculous is often associated with the past, and with Moses and the exodus in particular.[85] However, while this period may be paradigmatic for the author, there is an emphasis on miracles continuing to occur; they are portrayed as taking place across the narrative (*L.A.B.* 25:6; 61:5–7; 64:7). Hannah, for example, rejoices in the birth of Samuel (51:6), and David is portrayed as an exorcist and as giving Saul ongoing protection from the evil spirit (60:1–3). Changes in the biblical text[86] of this story of Saul's trouble with an evil spirit suggest a contemporary interest in exorcism; no longer is the Lord responsible for the evil spirit (60:1 // 1 Sam. 16:14), and a text that could be used in exorcism is provided (60:2–3).[87]

78. George T. Montague, *The Books of Esther and Judith* (PBS 21; New York: Paulist Press, 1973), 11.

79. Anna Maria Schwemer, *Vitae prophetarum* (JSHRZ 1/7; Gütersloh: Gütersloher Verlagshaus, 1997), 547–48.

80. See *Liv. Pro.* 1:2–8; 2:2–3, 11; 3:8–17; 4:12–13, 17; 21:2–3; 22:1–3 and the discussion in §3.3 (e) below; cf. Schwemer, *Vitae prophetarum*, 550.

81. Certainly since the sixteenth century this rewriting of the biblical story from Adam to Saul has been recognized not to have been by Philo. See Howard Jacobson, *A Commentary on Pseudo-Philo's Liber Antiquitatum Biblicarum: With Latin Text and Translation*, 2 vols. (AGJU 31; Leiden: Brill, 1996), 1:195–96.

82. C. Perrot and P.-M. Bogaert, *Pseudo-Philo*, 2 vols. (SC 229; Paris: Cerf, 1976), 2:38–39, 74; George W. E. Nickelsburg, "The Bible Rewritten and Explained," in Stone, *Jewish Writings*, 109; Jacobson, *Liber Antiquitatum Biblicarum*, 1:199–210.

83. For a case that the author was a woman, see Mary Therese Descamp, "Why Are These Women Here? An Examination of the Sociological Setting of Pseudo-Philo through Comparative Reading," *JSP* 16 (1997): 53–80; more cautiously, see Pieter W. van der Horst, "Portraits of Biblical Women in Pseudo-Philo's Liber Antiquitatum Biblicarum," *JSP* 5 (1989): 29–46.

84. E.g., the author is opposed to sexual relations with and marriage to Gentiles (*L.A.B.* 9:1, 5; 18:13–14; 21:1; 30:1; 43:5; 44:7; 45:3) and at one point says the Lord "does not need a great number but only holiness" (*L.A.B.* 27:14). There has been little success in linking the author with a particular group in Palestine. Daniel J. Harrington, "Pseudo-Philo," *OTP* 2:300.

85. E.g., *L.A.B.* 9:7; 12:2; 19:11; 25:6; 53:8. Cf. Eve, *Jewish Context*, 123.

86. On the difficulty of identifying *Liber antiquitatum biblicarum*'s biblical text, see Daniel J. Harrington, "Biblical Text of Pseudo-Philo's Liber Antiquitatum Biblicarum," *CBQ* 33 (1971): 1–17; Jacobson, *Liber Antiquitatum Biblicarum*, 1:254–57.

87. Graham H. Twelftree, *Christ Triumphant: Exorcism Then and Now* (London: Hodder & Stoughton, 1985), 38–39.

As most of the miracles in *Liber antiquitatum biblicarum* relate God's interventions on behalf of his people (e.g., 30:5; 35:2; 53:8), the miraculous is seen as God revealing himself for the sake of his people.[88] In using the verb *ostendere* (ראה, "show, display, manifest") in connection with the "miracles" (*mirabilia*, פלאות),[89] the author of *Liber antiquitatum biblicarum* also draws attention to their evidential value.[90] Probably to be included in the idea of the miraculous for this writer is Deborah being understood to speak for God (chaps. 30–33).[91] For the author of *Liber antiquitatum biblicarum*, the miraculous could also include events that were "signs" (*signa*) indicating God's will, as in water becoming half blood and half fire as a guiding sign for Gideon.[92] Therefore, for zealous Jews reflected in *Liber antiquitatum biblicarum*, the miraculous was not only part of the history of God's people, but also a present expectation, and likely to include exorcism and God's obvious intervention in life, including speaking through his representatives.

For 2 Maccabees, somewhere between the late second and early first centuries BCE,[93] miracles were also a present reality. The miraculous element in this history of the Maccabean revolt by a zealous Jew[94] is dominated by apparitions[95] reflecting and fulfilling classic prophecies (e.g., Isa. 30:31; Zech. 9:30). For example, in response to Jewish prayer, a magnificently caparisoned horse appears and attacks the Seleucid court official Heliodorus and his men as they attempt to rob the treasury. Two remarkably strong, gloriously beautiful young men also appear and flog Heliodorus, causing him to lay prostrate and speechless in light of the divine intervention (2 Macc. 3:22–30; see also 10:29–31; 11:1–12). In turn, he recovers when Onias III, the high priest, "offered sacrifice for the man's recovery" (3:32; cf. 3:31–35). Also, when Antiochus made his second invasion of Egypt, for almost forty days "there appeared over all the city [of Jerusalem] golden-clad cavalry charging through the air" (5:2), which everyone prayed would be a good omen (5:4). Not only is it said that victory in battle comes about with God's

88. Cf. Frederick J. Murphy, *Pseudo-Philo: Rewriting the Bible* (Oxford: Oxford University Press, 1993), 244–46.

89. E.g., *L.A.B.* 26:5; 27:7; 30.5; 28:1; cf. 9:7–8.

90. So Eve, *Jewish Context*, 120.

91. See van der Horst, "Portraits of Biblical Women," 34–38; Murphy, *Pseudo-Philo*, 136; Eve, *Jewish Context*, 122.

92. *L.A.B.* 35:7; cf. 27:7; 31:5; 53:4; 56:7; 59:5.

93. See Jonathan A. Goldstein, *II Maccabees: A New Translation with Introduction and Commentary* (AB 41A; Garden City, NY: Doubleday, 1983), 71–84.

94. Since devotion to the law and the temple is important to the authors (e.g., 1 Macc. 2:8, 27, 42, 50; 4:36–61; 2 Macc. 5:27; 6:18–19; 7:1), the text at least reflects the thought of zealous Jews.

95. 2 Macc. 3:24–25, 29–30; 5:2–3; 10:29–30; 11:8–10; cf. 12:22; 15:27.

help[96] to those who pray,[97] or that a town is taken by the will of God (12:16), but also, God appears to the enemy causing terror, fear, and flight in every direction (12:22).

Aside from these positive aspects of the miraculous in 2 Maccabees, there is a punishment miracle in the story of God striking Antiochus with an incurable and invisible blow (9:5). And Jews fall in battle because they were, as God revealed (12:41), wearing "sacred tokens of the idols of Jamnia" under their tunics (12:40; cf. Deut. 7:25–26). There is also the story of the miracle of spontaneous combustion of the wood for sacrifice (2 Macc. 1:19–24; cf. 1 Kings 18:33–38). Therefore, insofar as 2 Maccabees reflects the thinking of zealous Jews, our understanding of their view of the miraculous is to include the ideas that God intervenes in human affairs through apparitions to thwart an enemy and to bring military victory, and that healing could take place through offering sacrifice.

The last text to take into account, the eighteen pseudepigraphical *Psalms of Solomon*, also by pious or zealous[98] first-century CE[99] Jerusalemites,[100] similarly affirms at least God's ability to intervene in the present to bring about changes that could be called miraculous. For example, echoing and in the style of the prophets of Scripture (11:1; cf., e.g., Joel 2:1, 15), God is expected to gather his children to Jerusalem (cf. Bar. 4:37) and to level mountains for them (*Pss. Sol.* 11:4; cf. Isa. 40:4; Bar. 5:7). The psalmist pleads with God to remember his people and to care for them rather than allow them to be destroyed.[101] For the hypocrite, God is asked and expected to perform miracles of punishment: taking sleep, bringing poverty, and causing childless loneliness, for example (4:16–18).

All the texts that we have reviewed very briefly in this section show that, much like the educated Jews, a zealous Jew such as Paul could hold one of a number

---

96. 2 Macc. 12:11; cf. 12:28, 36; 15:27.

97. 2 Macc. 15:22; cf. 8:19; 2 Kings 19:35.

98. On the zeal reflected in *Psalms of Solomon* see, e.g., an "us" ("holy ones") and "them" ("the unrighteous") perspective, and a concern for the sanctity of the sanctuary, as well as an implied criticism of aspects of the priesthood (e.g., 1:7–8; 2:34–35; 3:3–8; 4:1–22; 8:9–12; 9:3; 15:4–13; 17); the work of sinners and the righteous are set over against each other (3:6–12; 4:8; 12–16); a concern for prayer and fasting (3:3, 8; 5:1; 6:1–2; 7:6–7; 15:1). See Roland Deines, "The Pharisees between 'Judaisms' and 'Common Judaism,'" in *Justification and Variegated Nomism*, vol. 1, *The Complexities of Second Temple Judaism*, ed. D. A. Carson, Peter T. O'Brien, and Mark A. Seifrid (WUNT 2/140; Tübingen: Mohr Siebeck; Grand Rapids: Baker Academic, 2001), 480. *Psalms of Solomon* has been attributed to each of the known Jewish sectarian groups of the period. See Kenneth Atkinson, *I Cried to the Lord: A Study of the Psalms of Solomon's Historical Background and Social Setting* (JSJSup 84; Leiden: Brill, 2004), 8.

99. Perhaps written in the time of Pompei; see *Pss. Sol.* 2:1–5, 26–27; 8:18–22; 17:7–9.

100. *Pss. Sol.* 1; 2; 4:1; 8; 11; 17.

101. E.g., *Pss. Sol.* 2:25; 5:5; 7:3–7; 8:28–30; 10:4; 11:8.

of views on the miraculous. Some of Paul's peers appear to express no interest in the miraculous beyond assuming it was important in the past. Others with a similar outlook to Paul appear to consider that exorcism, healing, and God intervening to speak and reveal himself through people and in events and apparitions, and to use miracles to punish, were part of their present experience. At the other end of the spectrum from the zealous Jews who associated miracle with the past were those who anticipated the miraculous in the eschaton. For example, as well as assuming that miracles took place in their own time, *Psalms of Solomon* and *Liber antiquitatum biblicarum* also expected the miraculous in the last days. We will pick up this theme later in this chapter (§2.5).

2.3 Pharisees and the Miraculous

Not only did Paul claim to be zealous for the traditions of his ancestors (Gal. 1:14; cf. Phil. 3:6), but in relation to the law he also said he was a Pharisee,[102] a claim supported by that zeal, a distinguishing feature of Pharisaism (e.g., Josephus, *Ant.* 13.279).[103] However, since the Pharisees formed a Palestinian lay holiness movement centered in Jerusalem,[104] leaving little trace of its activities in the Diaspora,[105] Paul would need to have spent considerable time in Jerusalem for his training as a Pharisee,[106] even if not with Gamaliel (cf. Acts 22:3).[107] Doubt about Paul's claim arises from him saying that he was not known by sight to the churches in Judea (Gal. 1:22).[108] However, this is

---

102. Phil. 3:4b–6; cf. 3:8–9; Gal. 1:14; also Acts 23:6; 26:5.

103. See the discussion by Udo Schnelle, *Apostle Paul: His Life and Theology*, trans. M. Eugene Boring (Grand Rapids: Baker Academic, 2005), 66–67. Note Paul's ongoing use of ζηλόω ("zealous"[1 Cor. 12:31; 13:4; 14:1, 39; 2 Cor. 11:2; Gal. 4:17 [2x], 18) and ζῆλος ("zeal" ([Rom. 10:2; 13:13; 1 Cor. 3:3; 2 Cor. 7:7, 11; 9:2; 11:2; 12:20; Gal. 5:20; Phil. 3:6]), which may be a legacy from Pharisaism.

104. Cf. 4Q163 23 II, 10–12; 4Q169; 4Q177 II, 4–5. See the discussion by James C. Vanderkam, "The Pharisees and the Dead Sea Scrolls," in *In Quest of the Historical Pharisees*, ed. Jacob Neusner and Bruce D. Chilton (Waco: Baylor University Press, 2007), 227–28.

105. See Hengel (*Pre-Christian Paul*, 29–34) and Murphy-O'Connor (*Paul: A Critical Life*, 56–59) for discussion of the primary data and Seán Freyne (*Galilee from Alexander the Great to Hadrian* [Wilmington, DE: Michael Glazier; Notre Dame, IN: University of Notre Dame Press, 1980], 319–23) on the gospel data. Freyne concludes that before 70 CE Pharisaism had made only limited inroads into Galilee.

106. Cf. Bruce Chilton and Jacob Neusner, "Paul and Gamaliel," in Neusner and Chilton, *Historical Pharisees*, 175–223.

107. E. P. Sanders (*Paul* [Oxford: Oxford University Press, 1991], 8) notes that Paul would not have learned his harshness and interest in persecution from Gamaliel (cf. Acts 5:34–39).

108. On the debate about Paul's claim to be a Pharisee, see, e.g., Anthony J. Saldarini, *Pharisees, Scribes and Sadducees in Palestinian Society: A Sociological Approach* (Grand Rapids: Eerdmans; Livonia, MI: Dove, 2001), 134–43.

but a recognition that Jerusalem was a large city, of forty thousand people or more,[109] where he had not been for some years.[110]

Paul mentions being a Pharisee to explain his attitude toward the law (Phil. 3:5). However, he goes on to say that whatever gains he had, he has "come to regard them as loss because of Christ" (3:7), giving the impression that having been a Pharisee could no longer help us understand who he was as a follower of Christ. Yet, Paul is not repudiating being an Israelite or a Pharisee, but their grounds for boasting.[111] And it was not being a Pharisee that he saw as loss, but rather his Pharisaic attitude toward the law (3:9). Indeed, Paul continued to call himself an Israelite, valuing being a Benjaminite (Rom. 11:1), and he referred to the Israelites as "my own people, my kindred according to the flesh" (9:3). He also continued to maintain the Pharisaic belief in the resurrection (1 Cor. 15), even though he no longer saw himself as a Pharisee.[112] Therefore, despite the impression of an initial reading, knowing the perspective of the Pharisees on miracles and the miraculous will contribute to our understanding of Paul not only as a Pharisee, but also in the beliefs he is likely to have continued to hold after being found in Christ.

However, in contrast to a century ago,[113] there is now less confidence in being able to identify, with certainty, any texts—save those by Paul—having been written by a Pharisee.[114] In the face of the disarray in the study of the

109. Magen Broshi, "Estimating the Population of Ancient Jerusalem," *BAR* 4, no. 2 (June 1978): 12, 14.

110. E.g., Murphy-O'Connor, *Paul: A Critical Life*, 52–59.

111. Gordon D. Fee, *Paul's Letter to the Philippians* (NICNT; Grand Rapids: Eerdmans, 1995), 316.

112. Although Paul continued to value highly his Jewish heritage (e.g., Rom. 3:1–2; 9:1–5; 11:1; 2 Cor. 11:22; Gal. 2:15), in that he came to regard these particular gains as loss (Phil. 3:7), and in that he never otherwise refers to being a Pharisee, even when he wishes to press the point of his present pride in his Jewishness (2 Cor. 11:21b–22), and in that he is part of the church rather than its persecutor, it is unlikely that he continued to see himself as a Pharisee. In contrast, Markus Bockmuehl says, "Paul in no way suggests that he has ceased to be a Pharisee" (*Philippians* [BNTC; Peabody, MA: Hendrickson, 1998], 198). However, the present tense of Paul's grammatical construction to which Bockmuehl points is to be taken as historic (cf. διώκων, "persecuting," present participle); on which, see the general discussion by A. T. Robertson, *A Grammar of the Greek New Testament* (Nashville: Broadman, 1934), 866–69.

113. Cf., e.g., APOT 1:1, 6, 8 (*Jubilees*), 282, 289, 290 (*Testament of the 12 Patriarchs*), 411 (*Assumption of Moses*); Steve Mason, *Flavius Josephus on the Pharisees: A Composition-Critical Study* (Leiden: Brill Academic, 2001), 1–17.

114. R. B. Wright, "The Psalms of Solomon, the Pharisees, and the Essenes," in *The International Organization for Septuagint and Cognate Studies and the Society of Biblical Literature Pseudepigrapha Seminar, 1972 Proceedings*, ed. Robert A. Kraft (SCS 2; Missoula, MT: Society of Biblical Literature, 1972), 136–47; Mason, *Josephus on the Pharisees*, 7–10. Cf. Antonio Pitta ("Paul, the Pharisees, and the Law," in Casey and Taylor, *Paul's Jewish Matrix*, 107) who says, "The only Pharisee whose writings we still have . . . remains Paul."

Pharisees,[115] the most secure way forward to reconstruct Pharisaic thought before the fall of Jerusalem in 70 CE is to use (at least initially) only the material of the period that mentions the Pharisees by name. This limits our sources to Josephus, the New Testament, and early rabbinic literature.[116]

(a) *Josephus.* The writings of Josephus have been considered an obvious and fruitful place to turn for insight into how Paul, a Pharisee, may have thought about the miraculous.[117] Yet, the once almost unanimous view that Josephus was a Pharisee,[118] or at least wanted to be understood as one,[119] has been all but dismantled by Steve Mason.[120] From the critical section of Josephus's *Life*, on which the view that he was a Pharisee for the most part depends, it is clear that he was not raised as a Pharisee or he would not have had to include them in his experiment. Also, his experience with the Pharisees did not satisfy him, for he says he went on to follow Bannus, an ascetic (*Life* 10–12), and nothing Josephus otherwise says about the Pharisees points to any attachment to them.[121]

This means we cannot take what Josephus says about the miraculous as reflecting the views of a Pharisee. Notwithstanding, there are two hints in what Josephus says about the Pharisees that suggest the miraculous was part of their worldview and experience. First, Josephus says the Pharisees were able to help Herod the Great because of their "foresight" (προμηθής, *Ant.* 17.41). Josephus goes on to explain "foresight" as "foreknowledge" (πρόγνωσις, 17.43), gained through God appearing to them.[122] Second, Pollion the Pharisee foretold Herod's persecuting Hyrcanus II and the judges (15.4; cf. 15.174–178, 266). In other words, the slight evidence we have from Josephus suggests that he took the Pharisees to be involved in the miraculous, if only in terms of foresight and prophecy in relation to hearing the voice of God.

115. Mason, *Josephus on the Pharisees*, 1–17, esp. 7–10.

116. Ellis Rivkin, *A Hidden Revolution* (Nashville: Abingdon, 1978), 31; Jacob Neusner, *From Politics to Piety: The Emergence of Pharisaic Judaism* (Eugene, OR: Wipf & Stock, 2003), 1–2.

117. Cf. Steve Mason, "Josephus's Pharisees: The Narratives," in Neusner and Chilton, *Historical Pharisees*, 3–40; Steve Mason, "Josephus's Pharisees: The Philosophy," in Neusner and Chilton, *Historical Pharisees*, 42–66.

118. Mason, "Was Josephus a Pharisee? A Re-examination of *Life* 10–12," *JJS* 40 (1989) 31–45; Mason, *Josephus on the Pharisees*, 325–56.

119. E.g., Jacob Neusner, "Josephus's Pharisees," in *Ex Orbe Religionum: Studia Geo Widengren*, 2 vols. (SHR 21, 22; Leiden: Brill, 1973), 1:231.

120. Mason, "Was Josephus a Pharisee?"; Mason, *Josephus on the Pharisees*, 325–56.

121. Mason (*Josephus on the Pharisees*, citing *J.W.* 1.110–114; 2.162–166; *Ant.* 13.288–298, 400–432; 17.41–45; 18.15, 17; *Life* 191–307) concludes that Josephus "consistently denigrates the Pharisees" (p. 373).

122. On prophecy coming from proximity to, or the appearance of, God, see Josephus, *Ant.* 13.300; *J.W.* 1.69.

(b) The New Testament. Save for Paul's self-reference (Phil. 3:5), all of our information about the Pharisees in the New Testament postdates Paul and is, obviously, also influenced by Christian concerns. Nevertheless, there are places where we may be able to see that the Pharisees were involved in, or had an interest in, miracles. Luke credibly says that they believed in the resurrection, angels, and spirits (Acts 23:8). For, other zealous Jews believed in the resurrection (*Pss. Sol.* e.g., 3:12, cf. 2:31; cf. below), and the belief in angels and spirits is consistent with what we will see of their interest in exorcism.

Matthew has the Pharisees charge Jesus with performing his exorcisms by Beelzebul (Matt. 12:24; cf. Mark 3:22 // Luke 11:15). Jesus' response is to ask who their followers (οἱ υἱοὶ ὑμῶν)[123] rely on to perform exorcisms (Matt. 12:27). Although we can no longer be sure who leveled the charge,[124] it is likely to have been the Pharisees. We know that they had disciples,[125] and we have no information from Josephus or the New Testament about there being disciples of the Essenes or Sadducees.[126] In any case, having Jesus reply in this way, Matthew assumes, and his readers are likely to find credible, the idea that the Pharisees had disciples and performed exorcisms.

In Acts Luke says that in the dissension that broke out after Paul made his defense before the Sanhedrin "certain scribes of the Pharisees' group stood up and contended, 'We find nothing wrong with this man. What if a spirit or an angel has spoken to him?'" (23:9). This is in line with our earlier finding in Josephus that Pharisees expected God to speak to and through humans. From the New Testament, then, we have evidence that the Pharisees believed in the resurrection, angels, and spirits and were predisposed to belief in miracles. The New Testament also gives us strong hints that Pharisees were involved in the conducting of exorcisms, and that they assumed that God spoke to people.

(c) Early rabbinic literature. In view of these texts intending to promulgate laws for the community,[127] it is not surprising that in the material that mentions the Pharisees, or can be confidently deduced to be about them,[128] no direct light is shed on their views of miracles and the miraculous (cf. 33n14 above).

---

123. For υἱός ("son") as a term for a disciple or follower, see BDAG, "υἱός," 2a.
124. Twelftree, *Jesus the Exorcist*, 104.
125. E.g., Josephus describes Pollion as having a μαθητής ("disciple"), Samais (*Ant.* 15.3). See also Mark 2:18 // Luke 5:33; and Matt. 22:15–16. Cf. Josephus, *Life* 11.
126. Deines, "The Pharisees," 484n147.
127. Neusner, *From Politics to Piety*, 2; cf. 81–96.
128. Ellis Rivkin, "Defining the Pharisees: The Tannaitic Sources," *HUCA* 40 (1970): 205–49; Jacob Neusner, *The Traditions about the Pharisees before 70*, 3 vols. (SFSHJ 202, 203, 204; Atlanta: Scholars Press, 1999), 3:301–19.

Nevertheless, some information can be gleaned from this body of material that merits our attention.

The story told by Josephus concerning John Hyrcanus hearing from the Deity (*Ant.* 13.254, 289) is also told in the rabbinic literature in relation to Yohanan ben Zakkai. Whatever the relationship between the stories,[129] all that can be said is that the rabbinic tradition in the Tosefta of around 300 CE[130] reinforces the view we are seeing that Pharisees expected God to speak to, and through, people.

The famous miracle workers Ḥanina ben Dosa and Honi the Circle Drawer, from the century before Paul was writing, probably were not Pharisees.[131] Instead, Honi and, possibly, Hanina were retrospectively "Pharisaized."[132] Ḥanina has a considerable number of miracle stories associated with him,[133] all based on the mishnaic story of his healing ability being related to the fluency of his prayers (*m. Ber.* 5:5).[134] However, although he probably was a disciple of Yohanan ben Zakkai, if these stories had appeared in nonrabbinic sources, he would not have been thought a Pharisee, for none of the stories related to Ḥanina is quintessentially Pharisaic.[135]

Though Honi was not a Pharisee himself, there is a response to him by Simeon ben Shetaḥ, a leading Pharisee and president of the Sanhedrin in the early first century BCE.[136] After Honi had prayed for rain, its increase and then its moderation, Simon reluctantly says, "If you were not Honi, I should decree a ban of excommunication against you. But what am I going to do to you? For you importune before the Omnipresent so he does what you want, like a son who importunes his father, so he does what he wants" (*m. Ta'an.* 3:8).[137] This

---

129. See *t. Soṭah* 13:5; *y. Soṭah* 9:13; *b. Soṭah* 33a. See also Neusner, *Traditions*, 1:172–76, favoring Josephus and the rabbinic tradition referring to independent sources.

130. Jacob Neusner, *The Tosefta: Translated from the Hebrew with a New Introduction*, 2 vols. (Peabody, MA: Hendrickson, 2002), 1:xiv.

131. As argued by Adolf Büchler, *Types of Jewish-Palestinian Piety from 70 B.C.E. to 70 C.E.: The Ancient Pious Men* (London: Jews' College, 1922), 264.

132. Neusner, *Traditions*, 3:314.

133. See the discussion by Geza Vermes, "Hanina ben Dosa: A Controversial Galilean Saint from the First Century of the Christian Era," *JJS* 23 (1972): 28–50; *JJS* 24 (1973): 51–64; Geza Vermes, *Jesus the Jew: A Historian's Reading of the Gospels* (London: Collins, 1976), 72–78; Baruch M. Bokser, "Wonder-Working and the Rabbinic Tradition: The Case of Hanina ben Dosa," *JSJ* 16 (1985): 42–92; Joseph Blenkinsopp, "Miracles: Elisha and Hanina ben Dosa," in *Miracles in Jewish and Christian Antiquity: Imagining Truth*, ed. John C. Cavadini (NDST 3; Notre Dame, IN: University of Notre Dame Press, 1999), 57–81.

134. Neusner, *Traditions*, 1:394.

135. Ibid., 1:395–96.

136. Yitzhak Dov Gilat and Stephen G. Wald, "Simeon Ben Sheta," *EncJud*[2] 18:600–601.

137. See the discussion by Neusner, *Traditions*, 1:177; cf. 1:120–21, a synopsis of Simeon's rebuke of Honi.

response betrays an ambivalence on the part of the Pharisees regarding the miraculous, or at least a tension between miracle working and institutional Judaism (cf. Matt. 7:21–23).[138] The miracle was in response to God answering a person who did not conform to accepted behavior and religious observance.[139] However, this Pharisaic response to the miraculous is not integral to the story and is generally agreed to have been added later.[140]

(d) Conclusions. Results from asking what having been a Pharisee may have contributed to Paul's understanding of the miraculous, though slight, are significant for this study. Not least, we have seen they shared with Judaism at large the belief that God is able to bring great changes to the lives of people and his creation, and that miracles and the miraculous were part of the history of God's people, especially in the time of Moses and of Elijah and Elisha. Importantly for our understanding of Paul, in their contemporary world, we have seen that God speaking to or through humans, foresight and prophecy, exorcism, and belief in the resurrection and angels and spirits were part of the mental furniture of the Pharisees. Rabbinic traditions can assure us of no more than that they claimed to hear and speak for God.

2.4 The Synagogues

As well as the views we have seen in the Dead Sea Scrolls, Philo, and Josephus, and among the texts that reflect those of the Pharisees and other zealous Jews, what probably took place in the synagogues will also help us understand more about Paul's religion in relation to the miraculous. Paul never mentions the synagogue, but it is inconceivable that he did not spend a great deal of his time in them before his conversion. His high level of zeal for the traditions of his ancestors (Gal. 1:13–14; Phil. 3:6) would have caused him to frequent the synagogue, a community focus for meeting, prayer, reading the Torah, study, and instruction.[141] Then, as a follower of Jesus, his five times receiving "forty lashes minus one" from the Jews (2 Cor.

138. See David Flusser, *Jesus* (Jerusalem: Hebrew University Magnes Press, 1997), 114, 117–18; Vermes, *Jesus the Jew*, 80–82. Cf. Becker, "Miracle Traditions," 69.

139. Vermes, *Jesus the Jew*, 80. Cf. Shmuel Safrai, "Teaching of Pietists in Mishnaic Literature," *JJS* 16 (1965): 19–20.

140. See Neusner, *Traditions*, 1:92, 177; William S. Green, "Palestinian Holy Men: Charismatic Leadership and Rabbinic Tradition," *ANRW* II.19.2 (1979): 636–38; Michael Becker, *Wunder und Wundertäter im frührabbinischen Judentum: Studien zum Phänomen und seiner Überlieferung im Horizont von Magie und Dämonismus* (WUNT 2/144; Tübingen: Mohr Siebeck, 2002), 301.

141. See Lee I. Levine, *The Ancient Synagogue: The First Thousand Years* (New Haven: Yale University Press, 2005), 135–74, 381–411.

11:24), which would have been administered by the synagogue,[142] suggests significant (unappreciated!) involvement in the synagogue;[143] and, as corroborated by Acts, both before and after becoming a follower of Jesus,[144] as a Jewish traveler he can be expected to have gravitated to the synagogue as a meeting place[145] and likely as a hostel.[146]

Notably, it is in the synagogue that Paul is most likely to have come across not just charitable work,[147] but also the practice of healing. Our earliest direct evidence of healing taking place in a synagogue comes from Mark's Gospel, perhaps written around 70 CE or a little before.[148] Mark portrays Jesus meeting sick people in the synagogue and healing them (Mark 1:21–28; 3:1; 6:1–2).[149] The other Synoptic writers also expect the synagogue to be a place of healing.[150] Later, the Tosefta mentions praying for the sick in the house of the assembly (*t. Šabb.* 16:22), and in the fourth-century Diaspora John Chrysostom lamented that Christians sought healing in the synagogues (*Adv. Jud.* 1.6.2; 8.6.6–11),[151] practices that are not likely to have been of interest if they were not thought at least occasionally successful. Although the evidence is not strong or extensive, it is enough to suppose that Paul's involvement in the synagogues would have exposed him to, and perhaps involved him in, praying for the sick, including the demon-possessed, reinforcing his understanding of this aspect of his Jewish heritage. Finally, since Paul considered he was living in a period of eschatological fulfillment, we will examine what he may have expected in relation to the miraculous.

142. Susanna; Josephus, *Ant.* 14.235, 260; Levine, *Synagogue*, 41, 143, 390, 395–96. See also Epiphanius, *Pan.* 30.11; *m. Mak.* 3:12; A. E. Harvey, "Forty Strokes Save One," in *Alternative Approaches to New Testament Study*, ed. A. E. Harvey (London: SPCK, 1985), 79–96.

143. Rom. 1:16, "to the Jew first and also to the Greek" (cf. 2:10), may also express Paul's inclination to gravitate toward the synagogue.

144. Acts 9:20; 13:5, 14, 43; 14:1; 17:1, 10, 17; 18:4, 7, 19, 26; 19:8; 22:19; 24:12. On Paul's pre-Christian involvement in the synagogue, see Acts 9:2; 26:11.

145. On Josephus, *Life* 66–67, 69, 133, 271, 277, 294, 300, see Graham H. Twelftree, "Jesus and the Synagogue," in *Handbook for the Study of the Historical Jesus*, vol. 4, *Individual Studies*, ed. Tom Holmén and Stanley E. Porter (Leiden: Brill, 2011), 3105–134, esp. 3117–118, 3123.

146. E.g., *CIJ* ii 1404; cf. 979; also see *y. Meg.* 3:3; Catherine Hezser, *Jewish Travel in Antiquity* (TSAJ 144; Tübingen: Mohr Siebeck, 2011), 96–100.

147. On the synagogue as the focus of charitable work, see *t. Ter.* 1:10; *t. B. Bat.* 8;14; *b. Šabb.* 150a, and the discussion by Levine, *Synagogue*, 396–98, 406–410.

148. For those suggesting earlier dates, see those cited by John S. Kloppenborg, "*Evocatio Deorum* and the Date of Mark," *JBL* 124 (2005): 419–50, esp. 419n1.

149. The controversial point in Mark's narrative is not that the sick are in the synagogue, but that Jesus heals on the Sabbath (Mark 3:2).

150. See Matt. 4:23; 9:35; 12:9–14; 13:54–58; Luke 4:31–37; 6:6–11; 13:10–17.

151. See the discussion by Robert L. Wilken, *John Chrysostom and the Jews: Rhetoric and Reality in the Late Fourth Century* (TCH 4; Berkeley: University of California Press, 1983), 83–88.

2.5 Miracles in the Messianic Age

In response to tragic times, filled with suffering and uncertainty, the scriptural prophets had spoken and written of both judgment[152] as well as better days ahead, which would be brought about by God doing something new.[153] The expectation that the present would give way to a new age in which all would be put right is both distinctive of the Hebrew people and an idea that developed in a variety of ways.[154] In a few places the eschatological hope included the coming of a messiah[155] and involved him conquering ungodly powers, including spiritual or heavenly ones,[156] which would mark the transition from the old age to the new.[157]

For at least some of the people represented in the Dead Sea Scrolls, the establishment of their community was at least a part realization of the future.[158] The Christian conviction,[159] which Paul shared, was that the coming of the Messiah, the midpoint or hinge of history, was no longer anticipated in the future; it had already taken place in the coming and, especially, the resurrection of Jesus (1 Cor. 15).[160] Paul says that God sent his son "when the fullness of time had come" (Gal. 4:4; cf. 3:23–26).[161] He also describes himself and his readers as those "on whom the ends of the ages have come" (1 Cor. 10:11), and for those whom "everything has become new" (2 Cor. 5:17).[162]

152. E.g., Isa. 24:17–23; 51:9–11; 66:15–16.

153. E.g., Isa. 25:8; 26:19; 34–35; 40:4; 45:2; 49:3–7; 51:3; 52:13–53:12; 65:17–25; 66:22; Jer. 23:1–8; 29:10–14; 31:31–34, 38–40; Ezek. 34–37; Zech. 3:8; 6:12–13.

154. See, e.g., Paul D. Hanson, *The Dawn of Apocalyptic: The Historical and Sociological Roots of Jewish Apocalyptic Eschatology* (Philadelphia: Fortress, 1975).

155. E. P. Sanders (*Paul and Palestinian Judaism: A Comparison of Patterns of Religion* [London: SCM, 1977], 296 [cf. 295–98]) notes how few passages attest to the expectation of a messiah: Isa. 9:7; Jer. 23:5–6; *Pss. Sol.* 17; 1QS IX, 11; CD-A VI, 11; XIV, 19; CD-B XX, 1; 4Q174 1 I, 11–13; 4Q252 V, 1–7; 1Q28b III, 22–IV, 28; 1QM XI, 1; XVII, 7; XVIII, 1.

156. E.g., *As. Mos.* 10:1–10; *1 En.* 45:3; 46:4–6; 55:4; 61:8–10. See Schürer, *History*, 2:526–29.

157. See, e.g., *Sib. Or.* 3:652–56; *Pss. Sol.* 17:24, 26, 27, 31, 38, 39, 41; 4Q171; 4Q174; 4Q252 V, 1–7; CD-A XII, 23–XIII, 1; XIV, 19; CD-B XX, 1; 1QS IX, 11; 1Q28a II, 11–12; 1Q28b V, 27; Philo, *Praem.* 16; 91–97.

158. George W. E. Nickelsburg, "Eschatology (Early Jewish)," *ABD* 2:588, citing the *Damascus Document*.

159. E.g., Mark 1:15; 12:6; Matt. 11:2–19 // Luke 7:18–25; Matt. 12:28 // Luke 11:20.

160. See J. Christiaan Beker, *Paul the Apostle: The Triumph of God in Life and Thought* (Edinburgh: T&T Clark, 1980), 135–81. In some Jewish literature, after Paul's time (see 55n172 below), the new age is preceded by a messianic reign; see *4 Ezra* 7:26–33; *2 Bar.* 29–30; 72–74; cf. *1 En.* 91:12–13; and also the discussion of Paul's relation to this scheme by Schoeps, *Paul*, 97–110.

161. Cf. Herman N. Ridderbos, *When the Time Had Fully Come: Studies in New Testament Theology* (Grand Rapids: Eerdmans, 1957), 48, 68–69.

162. For a discussion of Paul's use of Isa. 43:18, see, e.g., T. Ryan Jackson, *New Creation in Paul's Letters: A Study of the Historical and Social Setting of a Pauline Concept* (WUNT 2/272; Tübingen: Mohr Siebeck, 2010), 119–23.

Yet, though, Christ had been raised,[163] and those "in Christ" already participated in new life,[164] on the other hand, the resurrection of the dead[165] and the judgment[166]—"the day"[167]—had not taken place. Also, still "creation waits with eager longing for the revealing of the children of God" (Rom. 8:19), still the Son from heaven was awaited (1 Thess. 1:10),[168] and participation in a resurrection like Christ's remained in the future (Rom. 6:4–5).[169] For Paul and the early Christians, then, the anticipated middle *point* of history had become its middle *period*, extended from an eschatological event to an eschatological age. In this period, continuous with the past, yet connected with the future,[170] Paul conducted his ministry.

Our particular interest is in seeing what bearing these realized eschatological expectations may have had on Paul's view of the miraculous, his performing miracles, or on those who knew him and his work expecting him to be involved in the miraculous. Given the impact of the fall of Jerusalem on eschatological expectation, which reflects the war, famine, and confusion of the time, for example,[171] we need to give attention to material that likely reflects the period before 70 CE.[172]

---

163. Rom. 1:4; 4:24–25; 6:4, 9; 7:4; 8:11, 34; 10:9; 1 Cor. 6:14; 15:4, 14; Gal. 1:1; cf. Eph. 1:20; 5:14; Col. 2:12.

164. See 2 Cor. 5:17; Gal. 6:15; cf. Rom. 7:6; Murray J. Harris, *The Second Epistle to the Corinthians: A Commentary on the Greek Text* (NIGTC; Grand Rapids: Eerdmans; Milton Keynes: Paternoster, 2005), 432–33.

165. 1 Cor. 15:12–58; 2 Cor. 4:14; 1 Thess. 4:13–18.

166. Rom. 2:5–11, 16; 14:10; 1 Cor. 4:5; 2 Cor. 4:3–5; 5:10; 1 Thess. 5:3; cf. 2 Thess. 1:6–10.

167. Rom. 2:16; 1 Cor. 1:8; 5:5; 15:31; 2 Cor. 1:14; Phil. 1:6.

168. Although this is the only occurrence of the term ἀναμένειν ("to wait") in Paul, it is a theme in 1 Thess. (cf. 1:3; 2:19; 3:13; 4:13–18; 5:1–11), and the idea is not uncommon in his other letters: 1 Cor. 1:7; Phil. 3:20; also Rom. 8:23; Gal. 5:5.

169. Robert C. Tannehill, *Dying and Rising with Christ: A Study in Pauline Theology* (BZNW 32; Berlin: Töpelmann, 1967), 12. On the much discussed Rom. 6:5, see Ernst Käsemann, "On the Subject of Primitive Christian Apocalyptic," in *New Testament Questions of Today* (London: SCM, 1969), 132–33; Robert Jewett, *Romans: A Commentary* (Hermeneia; Minneapolis: Fortress, 2007), 401–2. Cf. Rom. 6:8.

170. See the summary discussion by Anthony C. Thiselton, *The First Epistle to the Corinthians: A Commentary on the Greek Text* (NIGTC; Grand Rapids: Eerdmans, 2000), 743–45.

171. See the discussion by Schürer, *History*, 2:510–12.

172. Thus, I leave aside *4 Ezra* (c. 100 CE). Critical in dating *4 Ezra* is the first vision, beginning, "In the thirteenth year after the destruction of our city" (*4 Ezra* 3:1)—see Bruce M. Metzger, "The Fourth Book of Ezra," *OTP* 1:520—and chaps. 11–12, in which the third head is Domitian (81–96 CE), the time of composition. I also leave aside from consideration *2 Baruch*, which is generally agreed to have been written between the end of the first century and the end of the first third of the second century CE. See J. Edward Wright, "The Social Setting of the Syriac Apocalypse of Baruch," *JSP* 16 (1997): 81–96; Mark F. Whitters, *The Epistle of Second Baruch: A Study in Form and Message* (JSPSup 42; Sheffield: Sheffield Academic Press, 2003), 155, and those cited.

Insofar as the eschaton—in all its variously expected expressions and changes over time—was to be brought about on God's initiation (e.g., Sir. 36:1–22) and by his direct intervention (e.g., Dan. 2:44; 7:9), it was understood as miraculous. Even what we might categorize as the political aspects of the eschaton are portrayed as God's direct work and also, therefore, miraculous: gathering the tribes of Jacob,[173] the salvation of the Gentiles,[174] rebuilding Jerusalem,[175] and defeating the Gentile enemies (e.g., Isa. 60:12; 1 En. 90:18–19), for example.[176] In the case of the *Assumption of Moses*, God arises to punish the Gentiles and destroy their idols, and Israel is then said to trample on their necks (10:7–8); *Jubilees* expects the servant of the Lord to drive out their enemies (23:30).

Other aspects of what was expected in the future might be more obviously deemed miraculous: a bright light shining to all the ends of the earth (Tob. 13:11), the moon changing its behavior and stars going astray (1 En. 80:4–7), and the transformation or renewal of the earth.[177] In the third book of the *Sibylline Oracles*, in the oracles against the nations (3:350–488), serene peace and freedom from storms and hail are expected (3:367–69). However, these miraculous features of the eschaton, even if they were not symbols or metaphors,[178] are cosmic (cf. *As. Mos.* 10:1–10), not related to human behavior or anything in which Paul might reasonably be expected to be involved.

Closer to human experience, Philo anticipates that wild animals will live together peacefully and also not attack humans, and that snakes and scorpions will not be harmful (*Praem.* 15.89–90; cf. Acts 28:3–6). In describing the constant threat of some animals to humans (*Praem.* 15.85–87), and looking forward to the day "when savage creatures become tame and gentle" (15.88), Philo seems to be expecting his hope to be fulfilled literally. *Jubilees*, saying that "there shall be no Satan nor any evil destroyer," is expecting that "in those days" there will be healing (23:26, 29).[179] In a number of Qumran texts

---

173. E.g., Sir. 36:13; 2 Macc. 2:18; 14:15; *Pss. Sol.* 11; cf. Isa. 4:6; 11:12; 27:13; 35:10; 40:3–5; 49:6; 52:12; Jer. 23:7–8; Zech. 9:14.

174. E.g., Tob. 13:11; Sir. 36:11–17; 1 En. 48:4; cf. Isa. 2:2–4; 11:10; 40:5; 42:4–13; 49:6–7; 45:3–6, 14–25; 51:4–5; 52:10; 54:12; 60:3, 6; 62:10; Mic. 4:1–5; Zeph. 3:9; Zech. 8:20–23.

175. Tob. 13:12–18; 14:7; cf. Isa. 54:11–13; 60; Ezek. 40–48; Hag. 2:7–9; Zech. 2:6–17, and the discussion in Schürer, *History*, 3:529–30.

176. George Foot Moore, *Judaism in the First Centuries of the Christian Era: The Age of the Tannaim*, 3 vols. (Cambridge, MA: Harvard University Press, 1958), 2:324–32; Schürer, *History*, 2:514–37; Sanders, *Paul and Palestinian Judaism*, 289–98.

177. E.g., 1 En. 45:4–5; 91:16; cf. Isa. 65:17; 66:2; Joel 2:30.

178. See the discussion by N. T. Wright, *The New Testament and the People of God* (Minneapolis: Fortress, 1992), 280–86; John J. Collins, *The Apocalyptic Imagination: An Introduction to Jewish Apocalyptic Literature* (Grand Rapids: Eerdmans, 1998), e.g., 14–21.

179. *Fourth Ezra* alludes to "healthful habitations" (7:121) and says that illness will be banished and death hidden (8:53).

healing is also anticipated in the eschaton: sight for the blind, straightening
out for the twisted (4Q521 2 II, 8), healing for the badly wounded and the
dead made alive (4Q521 2 II, 12).[180] In the idealized future, a Qumran text
interpreting the last days (4Q177 III, 2), as well as the *Damascus Document*,
also anticipate healing (CD-A VIII, 4).[181] Indeed, one text lists healing as the
chief eschatological reward (1QS IV, 6),[182] if not the image of the eschaton:[183]
"the reward . . . will be healing."

Isaiah had looked forward to the eyes of the blind being opened, the ears
of the deaf being unstopped, the lame leaping as a deer, and the tongue of
the stammerer speaking plainly (35:5–6; cf. 42:18). He also seems to expect
the dead in their tombs to be raised to life (26:19),[184] a hope that eventually
finds clear expression in Daniel 12:2 and comes to be taken as part of the days
of the Messiah.[185]

Not many years after Paul, Q and then Matthew and Luke were interpreting these hopes as fulfilled in the miracles Jesus was said to have conducted
(Matt. 11:5 // Luke 7:22).[186] Later still, early church writers, such as Clement
and Irenaeus, were also taking these Old Testament passages to have been
fulfilled in the coming of Jesus and his miracles and those of his followers.[187]

Some of the references to healing—painted on a large canvas with color-
ful, grand and general metaphors to match—are general and probably were
initially only intended as metaphors for the future.[188] Yet, in the case of Philo

---

180. For the intertextuality involved in this line, see Émile Puech, "Une apocalypse messianique (4Q521)," *RevQ* 15 (1992): 493.

181. Ben Zion Wacholder, *The New Damascus Document: The Midrash on the Eschatological Torah of the Dead Sea Scrolls; Reconstruction, Translation and Commentary* (STDJ 56;
Leiden: Brill, 2007), 313.

182. Geza Vermes, *The Complete Dead Sea Scrolls in English* (London: Penguin, 1997), 23.

183. P. Wernberg-Møller, *The Manual of Discipline: Translated and Annotated* (STDJ 1;
Leiden: Brill; Grand Rapids: Eerdmans, 1957), 79, citing Jer. 8:15; 14:19; Mal. 3:20.

184. On the problems associated with interpreting Isa. 26:19, see Otto Kaiser, *Isaiah 13–39: A
Commentary*, trans. R. A. Wilson (OTL; Philadelphia: Westminster, 1974), 215–20; Hans Wild-
berger, *Isaiah 13–27*, trans. Thomas H. Trapp (CC; Minneapolis: Fortress, 1990), 456–57, 567–70.

185. See also, e.g., 2 Macc. 7:9; 12:44; 14:46; cf. 1QHᵃ XI 10–14.

186. Cf. James D. Tabor and Michael O. Wise, "4Q521 'On Resurrection' and the Synoptic
Gospel Tradition: A Preliminary Study," *JSP* 10 (1992): 158–62; Stephen Hultgren, "4Q521, The
Second Benediction of the *Tefilla*, the *ḥăsîdîm*, and the Development of Royal Messianism,"
RevQ 23 (2008): 313–40, esp. 340.

187. On Isa. 26:19, see Clement, *Protr.* 114.3; Irenaeus, *Epid.* 67; *Haer.* 4.33.11; 5.15.1;
5.34.1; Tertullian, *Res.* 31.6. On Isa. 35:5–6, see Clement, *Protr.* 6.1; Irenaeus, *Haer.* 4.33.11;
Justin, *1 Apol.* 22.6; 48.2; 54.10; *Dial.* 69.3; Tertullian, *Adv. Jud.* 9.30; *Marc.* 4.24.12; 4.26.10;
Res. 20.6. On Isa. 42:18, see Justin, *Dial.* 27.4; Tertullian, *Apol.* 21.17.

188. Hans Kvalbein argues that the miracles listed in 4Q521 (see above) are "metaphorical
expressions for the saving acts of God concerning the whole people of Israel in the age of salvation" ("The Wonders of the End-Time: Metaphoric Language in 4Q521 and the Interpretation

(*Praem.* 15.85–90) and the *Community Rule* from Qumran (1QS IV, 6), for example, for the images to be taken other than in some sense literal would be to deny the hopes expressed and render them hollow for those in need.[189]

Paul's use of the exodus theme[190] corroborates this idea that, because they were living in the eschatological age, miracles and the miraculous could be expected. In alluding to imagery and ideas of the exodus in 1 Corinthians 10:1–13, Paul says "these things occurred as examples [or types, τύποι] for us" (10:6). A type was, among other things, a mold or model used to form or produce copies.[191] Thus, Paul sees the exodus as a formative model,[192] that is as prefiguring the present; or the present was seen as replicating the exodus,[193] a correspondence that he emphasizes (καθώς, "just as" [10:6, 7, 8, 9]) as a way of describing the "ends of the ages" (10:11). Given that the exodus was strongly associated with miracles and the miraculous,[194] in Paul seeing the present in terms of a new exodus it is highly likely he would have assumed the miraculous would be involved. Notably, with both the widespread early Christian tradition about Jesus and his first followers making the connection between these eschatological hopes and the miraculous, and Paul being convinced that the time of the end had impinged on the present, it would be quite reasonable for him, as well as those who knew him, to expect his ministry to involve the miraculous. Indeed, in chapter 7 we will see that Paul understood that expectations were fulfilled. He uses the same "signs and wonders" (σημεῖα καὶ τέρατα) formula to describe an aspect of his ministry (Rom. 15:19) that his Scriptures used to describe miracles associated with the exodus (see §7.8 below).[195]

---

of Matthew 11.5 Par.," *JSP* 18 [1998]: 104). So, also Årstein Justnes, *The Time of Salvation: An Analysis of 4QApocryphon of Daniel ar (4Q246), 4QMessianic Apocalypse (4Q521 2), and 4QTime of Righteousness (4Q215a)* (EUS 23/893; Frankfurt: Peter Lang, 2009), 269–73.

189. Justnes (*Time of Salvation*, 270), lists Otto Betz, John J. Collins, Hermann Lichtenberger, Florentino García Martínez, Émile Puech, Rainer Riesner, James D. Tabor, and Michael O. Wise as taking the future wonders literally.

190. See, e.g., 1 Cor. 5:7; 10:1–13; 11:25; 2 Cor. 3:6–11; Gal. 4:24–27. Further, see Sylvia C. Keesmaat, "Paul and His Story: Exodus Tradition in Galatians," *HBT* 18 (1996): 133–68; Sylvia C. Keesmaat, *Paul and His Story: (Re)interpreting the Exodus Tradition* (JSNTSup 181; Sheffield: Sheffield Academic Press, 1999).

191. Dio Chrysostom, *Ness.* 60.9; Lucian, *Alex.* 2. Further, see Gerd Schunack, "τύπος," *EDNT* 3:373; cf. Leonhard Goppelt, "τύπος, κτλ," *TDNT* 8:246; Thiselton, *First Epistle to the Corinthians*, 731–32; Jewett, *Romans*, 378. In Christian behavior Paul saw himself (Phil. 3:17), as well as his readers (1 Thess. 1:7), as molds or types to be replicated.

192. Cf. Thiselton, *First Epistle to the Corinthians*, 731.

193. Cf. Leonhard Goppelt, *Typos: The Typological Interpretation of the Old Testament in the New*, trans. Donald H. Madvig (Grand Rapids: Eerdmans, 1982), 220.

194. See §§2.1 (a), (b) and 2.2 above; cf. Jer. 32:20–21.

195. Exod. 7:3; 11:9, 10; Deut. 7:19; 29:3; 34:11; Neh. 9:10; Ps. 135:9; Isa. 20:3; Jer. 32:20.

2.6 Conclusions: The Miraculous among Paul's Contemporary Jews

If I was attempting to describe Paul's entire religious world, the results would have been different, not least through including what can be learned from non-Jewish Greek literature, the magical papyri, and other material from the Second Temple period. However, I have been examining only literature that likely sheds the most direct light on how a highly educated Jew, describing himself as having been a Pharisee and zealous for his traditions, would have viewed the miraculous.

It seems that most, if not all, of Paul's peers associated miracles with the great figures of the past, particularly Moses. Otherwise, as an educated, zealous Jew, Paul could have held one of a number of views on the miraculous. Like some of his peers, he could have taken little or no interest in the present experience of the miraculous. Or, like others, he could have taken miracles not only as part of his history, but also as something to be expected in the present. This would have been through prophecy or knowing the future, in healings, exorcisms, and unexpected events in nature, or portents, that were taken as evidence that God cared for and led as well as punished people. He could also have seen miracles as drawing attention to a prophet's message.

However, having been a Pharisee, and continuing to value some Pharisaic beliefs, we may be confident that Paul would have been among those who understood God continued to intervene in the lives of people and the natural world to bring about changes. Given that the ideas of claiming to hear from and speak for God, and being able to foretell the future, are found in a number of documents, they are likely to have been practices common among the Pharisees and part of Paul's mental furniture. Also, there seems to be good reason to think that Pharisees in general believed in the resurrection, angels, and spirits and carried out healings and exorcisms, activities with which Paul may have been familiar, at least because of the important place of the synagogue in his life.

Notwithstanding, although Jews are said to have had a reputation as successful healers, exorcists, and magicians,[196] we have found surprisingly few stories or specific references to the present experience of miracles among Paul's peers. This suggests that, despite his theological disposition and sensitivity to the miraculous, Paul may have had little experience of them.

---

196. Lucian, *Philops.* 16; *Trag.* 171–73. Cf., e.g., P. S. Alexander, "Incantations and Books of Magic," in Schürer, *History*, 3:342–79. Louis H. Feldman and Meyer Reinhold suggest that the reputation of the Jews "may have arisen because so many of the 613 commandments are concerned, in one way or another, with hygiene and health" (*Jewish Life and Thought among Greeks and Romans: Primary Readings* [Minneapolis: Fortress, 1996], 380).

In any case, widespread among Paul's contemporaries was the expectation that miracles or signs were to be part of the end of the age. Therefore, if he considered that the eschaton had been realized, at least in some way, his general outlook would probably have been one that expected the miraculous to take place. We have yet to see how far these views are reflected in his life and ministry, but my discussion predisposes us to consider that what I have laid out is also likely to describe the beliefs of Paul, as an educated Jew and not least as a Pharisee, before he joined the followers of Jesus.

The most significant aspects of this conclusion for the present study are that, as a person zealous for his traditions and as a Pharisee and frequenter of the synagogue, Paul would have come to Christianity, and would likely have been viewed as presupposing that God communicated with people and intervened in daily life to bring about miracles that showed his power. Also, Paul likely witnessed and, at least to a limited extent, may have been involved in healings and exorcisms. Further, he would have assumed that, with an eschatological shift having taken place in God's economy, there was a heightening of expectation of the miraculous taking place. My next task in examining the religious traditions and environment that most likely bear on Paul's approach to the miraculous is to extend the enquiry to bring into view what he and those of his period would have concluded about the relationship between contemporary prophecy, prophets, and the miraculous.

3

Prophets, Prophecy, and the Miraculous

I nterest in Paul as a prophet is generally in him as a speaker and writer with a message of salvation.[1] Our interest, on the other hand, is in enquiring how Paul seeing himself as a prophet can provide insight into his perspective on miracles, the possibility of him performing them, and, if so, what they might have meant to him and his readers.[2]

3.1 Paul as Prophet

At the very least, first, Paul not only shows an interest in prophecy (cf. 1 Cor. 13:2; 1 Thess. 5:20), he also implies that he prophesies. In 1 Corinthians 14:1–33 he implies that he prophesies when he advocates the value of prophecy. He says, "If I come to you . . . how will I benefit you unless I speak to you in some revelation or knowledge or prophecy" (1 Cor. 14:6; cf. 14:18–19, 39).[3] Also, in

1. Note, e.g., David Hill, *New Testament Prophecy* (Basingstoke, UK: Marshall, Morgan & Scott, 1979), 110–40; Karl Olav Sandnes, *Paul—One of the Prophets? A Contribution to the Apostle's Self-Understanding* (WUNT 2/43; Tübingen: Mohr Siebeck, 1991), 243–44; Anthony C. Thiselton, *The First Epistle to the Corinthians: A Commentary on the Greek Text* (NIGTC; Grand Rapids: Eerdmans, 2000), 1087–94.

2. See also Hans Windisch, *Paulus und das Judentum* (Stuttgart, Germany: Kohlhammer, 1935), 77–85.

3. E.g., David E. Aune, *Prophecy in Early Christianity and the Ancient Mediterranean World* (Grand Rapids: Eerdmans, 1991), 248–49.

his earliest letter, 1 Thessalonians, through what is probably a prophecy, Paul offers some encouragement to his readers about those in the church who had died. He prefaces his remarks about the parousia by saying, "we say to you in a word of the Lord" (1 Thess. 4:15, my translation). In saying that he was speaking "in a word of the Lord," Paul takes up a phrase used in the Old Testament prophetic tradition to represent a claim to speak for God.[4] Moreover, taking Paul's statement about "the word of the Lord" as prophecy is consistent with Paul claiming to have revelations and visions.[5] Already, therefore, we have clear signals that Paul saw himself as a prophet in the tradition of the Old Testament prophets. All our other evidence of Paul's relationship with prophecy points in the same direction.

That is, second, Paul describes his call and conversion (see §6.6 below) in terms that echo stories of scriptural prophets.[6] Given that he shares ideas and vocabulary with both Isaiah and Jeremiah (Gal. 1:15–16; Isa. 49:1–6; Jer. 1:5, 10), it is hard to deny that Paul is portraying his call not so much in terms reminiscent of a particular prophetic figure—the Servant of the Lord in Isaiah or Jeremiah—but of Old Testament prophets in general.[7] Paul's readers were unlikely to miss this clue, for the idea of being called from the womb remained in currency as the mark of a prophet (see Sir. 49:7).

Third, that Paul sees himself as a prophet in the Old Testament tradition is further suggested in him seeing his mission as having its roots in the work of the Old Testament prophets. In the beginning of Romans he says that he was "called to be an apostle, set apart for the gospel of God, which he promised beforehand through his prophets in the holy scriptures" (Rom. 1:1–2; cf. 16:25–26), and that they had borne witness to what he is proclaiming (cf. 3:21). Moreover, in the sequence "Jesus and the prophets and us" ('Ιησοῦν

---

4. See LXX 3 Kgdms. (ET 1 Kings) 20:17 (ET 21:17); cf. 13:1, 2, 5, 32; Hos. 1:1; Ezek. 34:1; 35:1. See also Sir. 48:3. The whole of 1 Thess. 4:15–17 may be "the word in the Lord," which Paul adapted and used in later correspondence. See Abraham J. Malherbe, *The Letters to the Thessalonians: A New Translation with Introduction and Commentary* (AB 32B; New York: Doubleday, 2000), 267–68.

5. 1 Cor. 15:8; 2 Cor. 12:1–10; Gal. 1:12; 2:2; cf. 1 Cor. 2:13; 2 Cor. 13:3; Aune, *Prophecy*, 249–50, cf. 94–95.

6. E.g., Krister Stendahl, "The Apostle Paul and the Introspective Conscience of the West," *HTR* 55 (1962): 204; Johannes Munck, *Paul and the Salvation of Mankind*, trans. Frank Clarke (London: SCM, 1959), 11–35; Aune, *Prophecy*, 202 (cf. 405n74); and those cited by Bruce N. Fisk, "Paul: Life and Letters," in *The Face of New Testament Studies: A Survey of Recent Research*, ed. Scot McKnight and Grant R. Osborne (Grand Rapids: Baker Academic; Leicester: Apollos, 2004), 303n79.

7. See Johannes Munck, "La vocation de l'Apôtre Paul," *ST* 1 (1947): 131–45; Munck, *Paul*, 24–33; J. Louis Martyn, *Galatians: A New Translation with Introduction and Commentary* (AB 33A; New York: Doubleday, 1997), 156–57.

καὶ τοὺς προφήτας καὶ ἡμᾶς, 1 Thess. 2:15)[8] he aligns his ministry with the Old Testament prophets, notably drawing attention to the failure he shared with them.[9] Not surprisingly, then, Paul frequently quotes from the prophets.[10] Fourth, more particularly, in various ways Paul relies on Old Testament prophetic traditions to define and describe his mission. In Romans, for example, he refers to the prophets in making the general point that God's present activity includes his own ministry (11:1–6, 13).[11] Also, his self-consciousness in having a role like an Old Testament prophet is obvious when he describes the good news being proclaimed using a slightly amended quotation from Isaiah: "How beautiful are the feet of those who bring good news!" (10:15; cf. Isa. 52:7).[12] Moreover, Paul expresses his compulsion to proclaim the gospel in terms reminiscent of Jeremiah, saying, "Woe to me if I do not proclaim the gospel" (1 Cor. 9:16; cf. Jer. 20:9).[13]

Fifth, in establishing that Paul saw himself as a prophet, are what Ernst Käsemann called "sentences of holy law." For example, Paul has sayings such as "If anyone destroys God's temple, God will destroy that person" (1 Cor. 3:17),[14] which Käsemann argued had their origin in prophetic proclamation modeled on Old Testament utterances.[15] Also, parts of Paul's letters not only appear to be oracles of his,[16] or reveal divine mysteries (1 Cor. 2:6–16; cf.

8. See Ernest Best, *The First and Second Epistles to the Thessalonians* (BNTC; Peabody, MA: Hendrickson; London: Continuum, 1986), 115–16.

9. Noting the shared use of ἀκοή ("hearing" as a faculty, 1 Thess. 2:13), Tony Cummins drew my attention to the possible echo of Isa. 6:9–10, also later used by the Fourth Gospel to explain the lack of belief in Jesus (John 12:38).

10. Rom. 1:17 // Hab. 2:3–4; Rom. 2:24 // Isa. 52:5; Rom. 9:13 // Mal.1:2–3; Rom. 9:32 // Isa. 8:14; Rom. 9:25 // Hos. 2:23; Rom. 9:26 // Hos. 1:10; Rom. 9:27 // Isa. 10:22–23; Rom. 9:29 //Isa. 1:9; Rom. 9:33; 10:11 // Isa. 28:16; Rom. 10:13 // Joel 2:32; Rom. 10:15 // Isa. 52:7; Rom. 10:16 // Isa. 53:1; Rom. 10:20–21 // Isa. 65:1–2; Rom. 11:26 // Isa. 59:20; Rom. 11:27 // Jer. 31:33; Rom. 11:33–35 // Isa. 40:13–14; Rom. 14:11 // Isa. 45:23; Rom. 15:12 // Isa. 11:10; Rom. 15:21 // Isa. 52:15; 1 Cor. 1:19 // Isa. 29:14; 1 Cor. 1:31 // Jer. 9:24; 1 Cor. 2:9 // Isa. 64:4; 1 Cor. 2:16 // Isa. 40:13–14; 1 Cor. 14:21 // Isa. 28:11–12; 1 Cor. 15:32 // Isa. 22:13; 1 Cor. 15:54 // Isa. 25:8; 1 Cor. 15:55–56 // Hos. 13:14; 2 Cor. 6:2 // Isa. 49:8; 2 Cor. 6:17 // Isa. 52:11; Gal. 3:11 // Hab. 2:3–4; Gal. 4:27 // Isa. 54:1.

11. Cf. James D. G. Dunn, *Romans 9–16* (WBC 38B; Dallas: Word, 1988), 645; John Ziesler, *Paul's Letter to the Romans* (TPINTC; London: SCM; Philadelphia, Trinity Press International, 1989), 268–69.

12. Cf. Rom. 10:16 // Isa. 53:1. See also Rom. 15:21 // Isa. 52:15; 2 Cor. 3:7–11 // Exod. 34:29–35; 2 Cor. 10:8; cf. 2 Cor. 13:10 // Jer. 1:10.

13. See also Ezek. 3:17–19; 33:7–9; Sandnes, *Paul*, 122–24.

14. Cf., e.g., Rom. 2:12; 1 Cor. 14:28, 30, 35, 37, 38; 16:22; 2 Cor. 9:6; Gal. 1:9.

15. See Rom. 10:11 // Isa. 28:16; Rom. 10:13 // Joel 2:32; Gal. 3:12 // Lev. 18:5; and Ernst Käsemann, "Sentences of Holy Law in the New Testament," in *New Testament Questions of Today*, trans. W. J. Montague (NTL; London: SCM, 1969), 66–81, esp. 76.

16. Cf. Rom. 8:12–22; 11:25–26, 31–32; 13:11–14; 16:17–20; 1 Cor. 3:17; 7:10, 29–31; 11:23–25; 13:13; 14:38; 15:20–29, 51–52; 16:22; 2 Cor. 5:20–21; 11:13–15; Gal. 1:9–10; 5:21b; Phil. 2:6–11; 3:17–4:1; 1 Thess. 2:15–16; 4:15–17; 5:1–11; on which, see M. Eugene Boring, *Sayings of the*

Rom. 11:25–36),[17] but also resemble forms of prophetic utterances in the Old Testament. Claus Westermann noted that preexilic judgment pronouncements involved a summons to hear, an accusation, and an announcement of judgment.[18] In turn, Calvin Roetzel observed that Paul can employ this prophetic form in a straightforward way.[19] In Galatians 1:6–11, for example, there is the introductory summons ("I am astonished," 1:6), then the offense is identified ("some who are confusing you," 1:7), and then he sets out the punishment ("let that one be accursed," 1:9). To this Paul adds a hortatory conclusion ("for I want you to know," 1:11) that expresses his pastoral concern for his readers.[20]

Similarly, Paul's announcement of the nearness of salvation reflects Old Testament prophetic categories (Rom. 13:11–14; cf. Isa. 43:19; 55:6). Further, in announcing salvation as a consolation, Paul may understand himself to be functioning as a prophet.[21] Despite Roetzel's hesitation,[22] in light of the other indications of Paul functioning as a prophet that we have noted, it is reasonable to assume that, in this form, he understands that he is playing a role that can be traced to Old Testament prophets.

To these points others can be added that suggest Paul understood himself not simply as a prophet, but as one in the tradition of those found in his Scriptures. Paul said he experienced a wilderness period (Gal. 1:17), perhaps reminiscent of the prophets Moses and Elijah.[23] Also, Paul claimed to have received visions (see 62n5 above), as did the prophets of old,[24] and, like the prophets who stood in the council of the Lord to receive their message,[25]

Risen Jesus: Christian Prophecy in the Synoptic Tradition (SNTSMS 46; Cambridge: Cambridge University Press, 1982), 34.

17. Sandnes, *Paul*, 77–116, esp. 115–16; cf. 172–81.

18. Claus Westermann, *Basic Forms of Prophetic Speech*, trans. Hugh Clayton White (London: Lutterworth, 1967), esp. 142–63.

19. See Rom. 1:18–32; Gal. 1:6–9; 5:18–26; 6:7–10; 1 Cor. 3:16–17; 5:1–13; 10:1–14; 11:17–34; 1 Thess. 4:3–8; cf. 2 Thess. 1:5–12; 2:1–8; 9:15; and the discussion by Calvin J. Roetzel, "The Judgment Form in Paul's Letters," *JBL* 88 (1969): 305–12. See also Rom. 16:17–20; Phil. 3:17–4:1; on which, see Ulrich B. Müller, *Prophetie und Predigt im Neuen Testament: Formgeschichtliche Untersuchungen zur urchristlichen Prophetie* (SNT 10; Gütersloh: Mohn, 1975), 185–96.

20. See Roetzel, "Judgment Form," 305–12; Boring, *Sayings*, 33.

21. Rom. 11:25–26; 1 Cor. 15:51–52; 1 Thess. 4:13–16. For a critique of the view of Müller, *Prophetie und Predigt*, 118–40, that the introductory formula λέγω δὲ ὑμῖν or its variations (e.g., Gal. 1:9; 5:2) or τοῦτο δέ φημι (1 Cor. 7:29; 15:50) and παρακαλῶ (Rom. 15:30; 1 Cor. 1:10) are prophetic legitimation formulae, see G. Dautzenberg, "Zur urchristlichen Prophetie," *BZ* 22 (1978): 130; Sandnes, *Paul*, 9–10, 160.

22. Roetzel, "Judgment Form," 312.

23. Cf. Jacob M. Myers and Edwin D. Freed, "Is Paul Also among the Prophets?" *Int* 20 (1966): 40–53.

24. See 2 Chron. 32:32; Isa. 1:1; Jer. 38:21; Ezek. 11:25; Amos 7:1, 4, 7; 8:1; 9:1; Zech. 1:18; 2:1; 5:1; 6:1.

25. Jer. 23:16–22; cf. 1 Kings 22:19–23; 2 Chron. 18:18–22.

Paul says he has seen the Lord (1 Cor. 9:1) and received his message through a revelation of Jesus Christ (Gal. 1:12; cf. 2:1–2; 1 Cor. 11:23). Then, as the Old Testament prophets are described as "servants" (δοῦλοι) of the Lord,[26] so also Paul calls himself a "servant" or "slave" (δοῦλος) of Christ.[27] Further, as signs and wonders were associated with the scriptural prophets (e.g., Deut. 13:2–3; Isa. 8:18; 20:3), so Paul used the phrase in relation to his ministry (Rom. 15:19; 2 Cor. 12:12).[28] Moreover, sometimes, like the prophets of earlier times, Paul found himself at odds with, and critical of, official representatives of religion.[29]

In light of all these points of contact between Paul and the Old Testament prophets—the description of his call, the roots and definition of his ministry, the form and content of some of his writing, and his experiences and descriptions of himself—it is hard to escape concluding that Paul understood himself to be functioning as a prophet in that tradition.[30] It is not that he takes himself to be a scriptural prophet or that he is acting as one, but that his ministry has its roots in, is shaped by, and continues in that tradition.[31] Moreover, in that he makes these connections between himself and the scriptural prophets for Gentile readers (e.g., Gal. 4:8; 1 Thess. 1:9)[32] shows that he assumes and expects even his Gentile readers to interpret his ministry in terms, not of the Greek traditions, but of the scriptural prophetic traditions.

It is not surprising, then, that Luke numbers Paul among these prophets. Broadly, Luke portrays Paul as a prophet in linking him to Jesus,[33] the prophet like Moses,[34] and interpreting the failure of Paul's mission to the Jews in terms

26. 2 Kings 9:7; 17:13, 23; 21:10; 24:2; Ezra 9:11; Jer. 7:25; 25:4; Ezek. 38:17; Dan. 9: 10 (LXX Θ); Amos 3:7; Zech. 1:6.

27. Rom. 1:1; Gal. 1:10; Phil. 1:1; cf. Rom. 15:16.

28. Bert Jan Lietaert Peerbolte, "Paul the Miracle Worker: Development and Background of Pauline Miracle Stories," in *Wonders Never Cease: The Purpose of Narrating Miracle Stories in the New Testament and Its Religious Environment*, ed. Michael Labahn and Bert Jan Lietaert Peerbolte (LNTS 288; London: T&T Clark, 2006), 196. Further, see §§7.7–8 below.

29. Isa. 1:10–31; Jer. 7:1–15; Hos. 4:1–6; 6:4–11; 8:11–14; Amos 4:4–5; 5:4–5; Mic. 3:1–12; 6:6–8. Cf. Gal. 2:11–14; 1 Thess. 2:14–15.

30. See, e.g., Myers and Freed, "Is Paul Also among the Prophets?"; Aune, *Prophecy*, 248–62; Sandnes, *Paul*, 2–4. To the contrary, see, e.g., Walter Schmithals, *The Office of Apostle in the Early Church*, trans. John E. Steely (Nashville: Abingdon, 1969), 55–56.

31. Cf. Albert-Marie Denis, "L'Apôtre Paul, prophète 'messianique' des Gentils," *ETL* 2 (1957): 316.

32. See the respective comments by Best, *Thessalonians*, 82; James D. G. Dunn, *Galatians* (BNTC; Peabody, MA: Hendrickson; London: Continuum, 1993), 6, 223.

33. See, e.g., Luke 9:7 // Acts 19:21; Luke 9:52 // Acts 19:22; see the discussion by David P. Moessner, "Paul and the Pattern of the Prophet Like Moses in Acts," *SBLSP* 22 (1983): 203–12, esp. 209–11. On the parallels between Luke's miracle stories related to Jesus and Paul, see §8.2 below.

34. See, e.g., esp. Luke 9:31–35, 41 // Deut. 18:15–18; Acts 3:22–23; 7:37; and Moessner, "Paul and the Pattern of the Prophet."

of prophetic failure (e.g., Acts 28:23–28; cf. Isa. 6:9–10).[35] At another level, though they are in the form of throne visions[36] rather than divine dialogues,[37] Luke's three stories of Paul's call or conversion (Acts 9:1–19; 22:1–21; 26:2–23) are cast to conform to Old Testament prophetic calls.[38] In this Luke is consistent with the way we have just seen Paul understood his call. Then, notably, Luke lists Paul among the "prophets and teachers" (Acts 13:1)[39] at Antioch.[40] Later, Hippolytus (c. 170–c. 236) also regarded Paul as a prophet (*Haer.* 8.20.1). Just why Paul never claimed the title prophet for himself,[41] at first a puzzle, will become clear in light of discussions in this chapter (see §3.4 below). Notwithstanding, how Paul's self-understanding as a prophet is to be interpreted generally, and specifically in relation to miracles and the miraculous, depends on how prophecy was interpreted at the time.

3.2 Prophecy in Paul's Time?

The ancient men of Greece were assumed to have both the power to prophesy and to heal.[42] More recently, in the context of the specialization of functions in the Greco-Roman world, individuals were known for either prophecy or miracle (or signs), though each, to varying degrees could take up the other.[43]

---

35. See, e.g., Moessner, "Paul and the Pattern of the Prophet"; Greg Perry, "Paul in Acts and the Law in the Prophets," *HBT* 31 (2009): 160–77, esp. 165–66.

36. Cf. 1 Kings 22:19–22; Isa. 6; Ezek. 1:4–28. See Walter Zimmerli, *Ezekiel: A Commentary on the Book of the Prophet Ezekiel*, trans. Ronald E. Clements, ed. Frank Moore Cross and Klaus Baltzer, 2 vols. (Hermeneia; Philadelphia: Fortress, 1979–83), 1:97–100, esp. 100.

37. Cf. Exod. 2:23–4:17; 6:2–7:7; Judg. 6:15–16; 1 Sam. 9:21; Jer. 1:4–10.

38. See, e.g., Paul S. Minear, *To Heal and to Reveal: The Prophetic Vocation According to Luke* (New York: Seabury, 1976), 142–47; Aune, *Prophecy*, 202.

39. That all of those listed, including Paul, are understood to be προφῆται καὶ διδάσκαλοι ("prophets and teachers," Acts 13:1) is the natural meaning of Luke's statement, made clear by the Western Text replacing ὅ τε ("and the") with εν οις ("in whom" [D²]) or εν οις ην και ("and in whom was" [D vg]). See, e.g., Gerhard Schneider, *Die Apostelgeschichte*, 2 vols. (HTKNT 5; Freiburg: Herder, 1980–82), 2:112–14; C. K. Barrett, *A Critical and Exegetical Commentary on the Acts of the Apostles*, 2 vols. (ICC; Edinburgh: T&T Clark, 1994–2002), 1:602.

40. For a possible indirect reference to Paul as a prophet, see Acts 15:22, 32; on which, see F. F. Bruce, *The Acts of the Apostles: The Greek Text with Introduction and Commentary*, 3rd ed. (Grand Rapids: Eerdmans; Leicester: Apollos, 1990), 344, 348; Sandnes, *Paul*, 3; Barrett, *Commentary on the Acts*, 2:749.

41. Cf., e.g., John Ashton, *The Religion of Paul the Apostle* (New Haven: Yale University Press, 2000), 179, 184.

42. Empedocles, *Katharmoi* 112; Diodorus Siculus, *Bib. hist.* 1.25; 34.2.5; Lucian, *Icar.* 24.

43. Anitra Bingham Kolenkow, "Relationships between Miracle and Prophecy in the Greco-Roman World and Early Christianity," *ANRW* II.23.2 (1980): 1472. On the seer, including in Paul's Hellenistic world, transmitting the signs and messages of the gods, see Michael Attyah Flower, *The Seer in Ancient Greece* (Berkeley: University of California Press, 2008).

Thus, as a prophet in a Hellenistic context, Paul would have been understood to have options in relation to the importance of the miraculous in his work.[44] However, since we have just seen that Paul, a Jew, interpreted his prophecy in terms of classic Jewish prophecy—and expected his readers to do the same—we need to give our attention to how prophecy and the miraculous were related in that tradition. Initially, however, we have to take into account the long-held dogma that prophecy in his tradition had ceased and was "defunct" by Paul's time.[45] For, if prophecy was considered only a historical phenomenon or an eschatological hope at the time, then Paul's supposed prophetic mind-set and activity will have different connotations than if prophecy was part of the cultural landscape he shared with his readers.

A number of pieces of evidence suggest that Paul had been raised within a Judaism without prophecy.[46] For example, the writer of 1 Maccabees (late second or early first century BCE)[47] says that "there was great distress in Israel such as had not been since the time that prophets ceased to appear among them" (1 Macc. 9:27).[48] Similarly, the Prayer of Azariah (mid-second century BCE)[49] laments, "In our day we have no ruler, or prophet, or leader" (Pr. Azar. 15).[50] However, in these statements the lamented prophets are key figures associated with national leadership.[51] Whether or not prophecy or prophets of other kinds existed in the period is not in view.[52]

Josephus, whom we have already taken to reflect the thinking of Jews such as Paul and his contemporaries (see §2.1 above), also makes a statement that

44. See the discussion by Kolenkow, "Miracle and Prophecy," 1472–82.
45. John R. Levison, "Philo's Personal Experience and the Persistence of Prophecy," in *Prophets, Prophecy, and Prophetic Texts in Second Temple Judaism*, ed. Michael H. Floyd and Robert D. Haak (London: T&T Clark, 2006), 194–96. Levison cites C. K. Barrett, W. D. Davies, James D. G. Dunn, Gordon D. Fee, F. W. Horn, Joachim Jeremias, George Foot Moore, and Erik Sjöberg as holding varying aspects of the dogma. However, at least Dunn's position is more nuanced; see James D. G. Dunn, *The Theology of Paul the Apostle* (Grand Rapids: Eerdmans, 1998), 417–18.
46. L. Stephen Cook's work, *On the Question of the "Cessation of Prophecy" in Ancient Judaism* (TSAJ 145; Tübingen: Mohr Siebeck, 2011), arrived too late to be taken into account.
47. See John R. Bartlett, *1 Maccabees* (GAP; Sheffield: Sheffield Academic Press, 1998), 33–34.
48. See also 1 Macc. 4:46; 14:41; and see the discussions by Rudolf Meyer, "προφήτης, κτλ.," *TDNT* 6:813–16.
49. See Carey A. Moore, *Daniel, Esther, and Jeremiah: The Additions* (AB 44; Garden City, NY: Doubleday, 1977), 46.
50. Erik Sjöberg ("πνεῦμα, κτλ.," *TDNT* 6:385), cites 1 Macc. 4:46; 9:27; 14:41; *2 Bar.* 85:1. Alex P. Jassen ("Prophets and Prophecy in the Qumran Community," *AJSR* 32 [2008]: 302n12) draws attention to Ps. 74:9; Josephus, *Ag. Ap.* 1.14; *Bar.* 1:21; Pr. Azar. 15; *m. Soṭah* 9:12; *t. Soṭah* 13:2–3; *b. Sanh.* 11a; *b. Yoma* 9b; *b. Soṭah* 48b; *Rab. Song* 8.9.3; *S. ʿOlam Rab.* 30.
51. Meyer, "προφήτης, κτλ.," *TDNT* 6:815–16.
52. For a helpful discussion taking into account the misreading of John 7:39 ("as yet there was no Spirit"), see John Goldingay, "Was the Holy Spirit Active in Old Testament Times? What Was New About the Christian Experience of God?" *ExAud* 12 (1996): 14–28.

could be read as prophecy being defunct.[53] In a discussion of the literary remains of his people Josephus admits that reliable histories no longer exist because, since Artaxerxes, there had been a "failure of the exact succession of the prophets" (Josephus, *Ag. Ap.* 1.41).[54] However, the context of Josephus's statement shows that he has in mind not the general demise of prophecy, but only of the prophets who composed historical narrative.[55] For, also, while Josephus may have thought there were no longer any writing prophets, he still happily reports the title "prophet" being claimed—by Felix, for example (*Ant.* 20.169)—and that the Hasmonean ruler John Hyrcanus conversed with the deity and knew the future in the manner consistent with a prophet (*J.W.* 1.69; cf. *Ant.* 13.282–283). Indeed, Josephus himself claimed to predict "the fate of the Jews and the destiny of the Roman sovereigns" (*J.W.* 3.351; cf. 3.399–408; see below).[56]

Moreover, in line with the ability of prophecy to take on new forms in Israel,[57] it can readily be shown that prophecy and prophets of a number of different kinds[58] were not only part of Paul's historical tradition—and eschatological expectations—but also were a lively and important part of his world.[59] Since our concern is with prophecy as persons and how Paul perceived himself functioning socially, depending on and developing categories suggested by Robert L. Webb,[60] I will use the categories of (a) charismatic prophets, (b) seers, and (c) oracular or traditional prophets, though recognizing that the categories overlap. In setting out these types and how the miraculous was related to them, we will see more clearly what it meant for Paul in relationship to the miraculous to see himself, and to be seen, in the tradition of the scriptural prophets.

(a) Charismatic prophets. There is evidence from Paul's time—from the time of the procurator Crispus Fadus (44–46 CE)—of individuals who led popular movements of large numbers of people. For example, Josephus says

53. On Josephus and prophecy, see Rebecca Gray, *Prophetic Figures in Late Second Temple Jewish Palestine: The Evidence from Josephus* (Oxford: Oxford University Press, 1993); Robert Karl Gnuse, *Dreams and Dream Reports in the Writings of Josephus: A Traditio-Historical Analysis* (AGJU; Leiden: Brill, 1996), 21–33.
54. For those who cite this passage as evidence that Josephus considered prophecy to have ceased, see Gray, *Prophetic Figures*, 9n5.
55. For important discussion, see ibid., 8–16; on Josephus's chronology, see ibid., 13.
56. See the discussion by Robert G. Hall, *Revealed Histories: Techniques for Ancient Jewish and Christian Historiography* (JSPSup 6; Sheffield: JSOT Press, 1991), 24–30; cf. 57–60.
57. Meyer, "προφήτης, κτλ.," *TDNT* 6:828.
58. For various typologies of prophetism, see Robert L. Webb, *John the Baptizer and Prophet: A Socio-Historical Study* (JSNTSup 62; Sheffield: Sheffield Academic Press, 1991), 312–48.
59. See Levison, "Philo's Personal Experience," 194–96.
60. Webb, *John*, 312–17.

that Theudas, who claimed to be a prophet, persuaded a large mass of people to follow him to the Jordan River, stating that he would part the river so that, in a reverse conquest, people could be freed from the Romans (Josephus, *Ant.* 20.97–98).[61] Also, an Egyptian who considered himself a prophet is said to have come to Jerusalem and caused thirty thousand people to follow him to the Mount of Olives, proposing to cause the walls of the city to fall in a re-enactment of the battle of Jericho in order to provide a way in to overpower the Romans (*J.W.* 2.261–262 // *Ant.* 20.169–170). Though with less detail, Luke also includes stories of these two figures (Acts 5:36; 21:38).

Since the leadership of these individuals involved actions of miraculous deliverance that, corresponding to the acts of the prophets Moses and Joshua, were supposed to be eschatological,[62] they have been called "sign prophets."[63] More accurately, they are charismatic prophets, for they are described primarily as leading large numbers of common people from one place to another.[64] In any case, apart from one of these prophets (an unnamed figure who did not claim to conduct any miracle [Josephus, *Ant.* 20.188]), these charismatic leaders or (false) prophets included, or intended to include, conducting dramatic signs or miracles as part of their leadership.[65] Therefore, they are of interest as potential models for understanding Paul as a prophet in relation to the miraculous. However, it is immediately obvious that Paul would not have found this category important in his self-understanding, nor would he have been seen by others in terms of one of these charismatic prophets. Paul took leadership responsibility for a large number of people in clusters across the northeast of the Mediterranean, but he neither considered himself leading any of them anywhere as a group, nor did he think that he led them in relation to any eschatological act he oversaw.

61. Richard A. Horsley, *Bandits, Prophets, and Messiahs: Popular Movements in the Time of Jesus* (San Francisco: Harper & Row, 1985), 160–72; Richard A. Horsley, "'Like One of the Prophets of Old': Two Types of Popular Prophets at the Time of Jesus," *CBQ* 47 (1985): 457.

62. Horsley, "'Like One of the Prophets,'" 454.

63. Paul W. Barnett, "The Jewish Sign Prophets—AD 40–70: Their Intentions and Origin," *NTS* 27 (1981): 679–97. Aside from a general description of theme by Josephus (*J.W.* 2.258–260; *Ant.* 20.167–168), the usual list of these prophets is Theudas (*Ant.* 20.97–99; Acts 5:36); an unnamed group in the time of Felix (*J.W.* 2.258–260; *Ant.* 20.167–168); an Egyptian (*J.W.* 2.261–263; *Ant.* 20.169–172; Acts 21:38); an unnamed person in the time of Festus (*Ant.* 20.188); an unnamed person who led his followers to the temple (*J.W.* 6.283–287); Jonathan (*J.W.* 7.437–450; *Life* 424–425); and another unnamed person, presumably a Samaritan (*Ant.* 18.85–87).

64. See Gray, *Prophetic Figures*, 113.

65. Horsley ("'Like One of the Prophets,'" 456n46) suggests that signs are secondary to these figures. But in not taking into account either the prophet who led his followers to the temple (Josephus, *J.W.* 6.283–287) and Jonathan (*J.W.* 7.437–450; *Life* 424–425), Gray (*Prophetic Figures*, 199n2) is right to say, "Horsley has played down the significance of the miracles and signs promised by these prophets to an unacceptable degree."

(b) Seers. As well as charismatic prophets, there existed a category of seers
or prophets among the Essenes and Pharisees that probably was familiar to Paul
and his readers. Josephus, who tells us nothing else about these individuals,
mentions the Essenes, Judas (*J.W.* 1.78–80; *Ant.* 13.311–313) and Menahem
(*Ant.* 15.373–379) predicting the future, and Simon interpreting a dream of
Archelaus (*J.W.* 2.112–113; *Ant.* 17.345–348). Josephus also says that Pollion,
a Pharisee, predicted persecution by Herod (*Ant.* 14.174; 15.4); and he says
that in the court of Herod there were Pharisees who aided the ruler with their
"foresight" (προμηθής, 17.41).[66] Also, having foretold the future of Vespasian
(*J.W.* 3.399–408; cf. 3.352–354), Josephus is likely to have seen himself among
these kinds of prophets.[67] While foresight or prediction was an aspect of Paul's
ministry (1 Thess. 4:15), as we have seen (§3.1 above), his portrait of himself
as a prophet was broader than that of a seer, so that this category probably
was unimportant both to his self-understanding and for how his readers would
have understood him in relation to the miraculous.

(c) Oracular or traditional prophets. As Richard Horsley put it, these individuals, echoing the ministry of the classical prophets, "interpreted the deeper
significance of their contemporary situation . . . in the form of oracles of
judgment or deliverance."[68] Josephus mentions "numerous" (πολλοί) prophets
falsely encouraging people to wait for God's deliverance (*J.W.* 6.286), and he
tells of one particular individual, whom he calls a "false prophet" (ψευδο-
προφήτης), commanding people to go to the temple "to receive their tokens
of deliverance," as the Romans were sacking the city (6.285–286). Josephus
also tells of Jesus, son of Ananias, under "supernatural impulse" (δαιμο-
νιώτερον, 6.303), going to the temple and speaking out judgment in a time of
peace (6.300–309). Thus, these oracular prophets claimed revelatory experiences, as well as to speak for, or represent, divinity. Philo, as we will see, also
understood prophets—both scriptural and contemporary—to be, essentially,
persons overtaken by divine power (see §3.3 [d] below).

From Josephus saying that crowds went and heard John the Baptist talk
about righteous living, and that Herod feared his power to raise a rebellion
(*Ant.* 18.117–118), we can conclude that he is describing John as an oracular
prophet. New Testament writers also describe John as such a prophet, in that
he is said to interpret the contemporary situation in terms of judgment or
deliverance.[69] Jesus is also described by New Testament writers as an oracu-

66. On foresight or prediction in Josephus, see Jassen, "Prophets," 304n20, and those cited there.
67. See Markus N. A. Bockmuehl, *Revelation and Mystery in Ancient Judaism and Pauline
Christianity* (WUNT 2/36; Tübingen: Mohr Siebeck, 1990), 87–89.
68. Horsley, "'Like One of the Prophets,'" 450.
69. See, e.g., Mark 1:1–8; 6:14–29; Matt. 11:1–19 // Luke 7:18–35.

lar prophet in, for example, his reported assertions about the contemporary nature of the kingdom of God (e.g., Mark 1:15). Notably, in relation to the present project, not only is Jesus described as involved in the miraculous and in performing miracles[70] but there is some evidence that John also conducted miracles (Mark 6:14–17).[71]

It cannot be maintained, therefore, that prophecy was defunct in Paul's time. Rather, for Paul and his contemporaries, prophecy in a number of different forms was "in luxuriant bloom," as Adolf von Harnack put it.[72] Further, we have seen that the charismatic prophets sought to be involved in actions of miraculous deliverance, and that seers or prophets among the Essenes and Pharisees predicted the future, for example. Notably, even though the scriptural prophets were no longer with them—though they were expected in the future (e.g., 1 Macc. 4:46; 1QS IX, 9–11)—in their successors such as Jesus ben Ananias, John the Baptist, and Jesus of Nazareth the oracular prophets were also known in Paul's time. Since this particular form of the prophetism, also associated with the miraculous, most directly informed Paul and was important in how he expected his readers to understand his ministry, we need to explore more fully the perceived relationship between scriptural prophecy, prophets, and the miraculous in his world.

3.3 The Classic Prophets and Their Heirs

Our question is, in what ways would Paul's understanding himself as a prophet in the line of the classical tradition have caused him to have particular attitudes in relation to the miraculous? Or, if those receiving his letters considered him a prophet in this tradition, what expectations would they have had of Paul in relation to the miraculous? Although it has been supposed that only Sirach has associated the classic prophets with miracles,[73] a number of sources—the Dead Sea Scrolls, Sirach, Ezekiel the Tragedian, Philo, *Lives of the Prophets*, *Liber antiquitatum biblicarum*, and Josephus—show that, in the time of Paul, the scriptural prophets were understood to be involved in the miraculous, including conducting miracles. So far as the limited information permits, I will treat this material chronologically.

---

70. See esp. John P. Meier, *A Marginal Jew: Rethinking the Historical Jesus*, vol. 2, *Mentor, Message, and Miracles* (ABRL; New York: Doubleday, 1994), part 3.

71. Graham H. Twelftree, "Jesus the Baptist," *JSHJ* 7 (2009): 112–14.

72. Adolf von Harnack, *The Expansion of Christianity in the First Three Centuries*, trans. and ed. James Moffat, 2 vols. (New York: Arno, 1904–5), 1:415.

73. David Satran, *Biblical Prophets in Byzantine Palestine: Reassessing the Lives of the Prophets* (SVTP 11; Leiden: Brill, 1995), 58.

(a) The Dead Sea Scrolls. Judging by the number of copies of prophetic books found or represented among the scrolls, the prophets of old were highly honored at Qumran (e.g., 1QS I, 1–3). Of the 206 biblical manuscripts recovered from Qumran, one-fifth are of the so-called classical prophets, including twenty-one copies of Isaiah, and six each of Jeremiah and Ezekiel.[74] Moreover, as we will see, the importance of prophecy in the Qumran texts is seen in the evidence of prophetization: describing or designating as prophets figures not, or not normally, accorded the status in the traditional literature.[75]

The close relationship that the movement saw between being a classic prophet and a miracle worker is obvious in some of the portraits of the prophets. For example, Moses, who is remembered as involved in the miracles associated with the exodus,[76] is numbered among the prophets,[77] even though the title is not applied directly to him.[78] Elijah, as the forerunner to the Messiah, is assumed to be a prophet. He is also associated with the miraculous in that miracles are expected to accompany his coming (4Q558 1 II, 4–5). In this, the *Messianic Apocalypse* (4Q521), a text we have already noted (§2.5 above), is of particular interest. God's anointed one is said to usher in a period of receiving sight, of being straightened, and of the Lord performing marvelous acts, healing and raising the dead (4Q521 2 II, 1–14). In that the speaker of this composition is the new Elijah,[79] the prophet is associated with the miraculous.

David is nowhere explicitly identified as a prophet in the extant scrolls; in fact, in the line "the Books of the Prophets and David" (4Q397 14–21 10) a distinction may be intended. Yet his portrait includes a direct connection between prophecy and the miraculous. In 11Q5 he is associated with exorcism, being said to compose four "songs for making music over the stricken"[80] (11Q5 XXVII, 9–10). Notably, for us, the text goes on to say, "All these he uttered through [ב] proph-

74. Including manuscripts whose identity is uncertain, the total number could be 213. See James C. VanderKam, *The Dead Sea Scrolls Today* (Grand Rapids: Eerdmans, 2010), 48.

75. See John C. Reeves, "Scriptural Authority in Early Judaism," in *Living Traditions of the Bible: Scripture in Jewish, Christian, and Muslim Practice*, ed. James E. Bowley (St. Louis: Chalice, 1999), 72–74. NT writers also prophetize. Luke, e.g., says David was a prophet (Acts 2:30).

76. E.g., 4Q226 1, 2–4; 4Q365 2 // Exod. 8:13–19; 4Q365 3 // Exod. 9:9–12; 4Q365 4 // Exod. 10:19–20; 4Q377 // Exod. 19:16–19; 20:18–22; 4Q504 1–2 I, 8; 1–2 II, 12.

77. CD-A V, 21; 4Q504 1–2 III, 11–14; 1QS I, 3; 4Q375 I, 1; 4Q397 14–21 10; 4Q398 14–17 I, 2–4. Cf. George J. Brooke, "Parabiblical Prophetic Narratives," in *The Dead Sea Scrolls after Fifty Years: A Comprehensive Assessment*, ed. Peter W. Flint and James C. VanderKam, 2 vols. (Leiden: Brill, 1999), 1:272–75.

78. James E. Bowley, "Prophets and Prophecy at Qumran," in *The Dead Sea Scrolls after Fifty Years: A Comprehensive Assessment*, ed. Peter W. Flint and James C. VanderKam, 2 vols. (Leiden: Brill, 1999), 2:361.

79. Cf. 4Q521 2 III, 2 and Mal. 4:6 (MT 3:24; LXX 3:23).

80. Or הפגועים ("the possessed"). Cf. 1 Sam. 16:14–23; 11Q11 V, 2; *y. Šabb.* 6:8b; *y. 'Erub.* 10:26c; *b. Šebu.* 15b.

ecy [נבואה][81] which was given him from before the Most High."[82] In this, if not the miracle working, at least the texts used for the miraculous are seen to arise "through" or "in" (ב) prophecy, perhaps in a prophetic trance.[83]

Daniel, who is called "the prophet" (הנביא) in *4QFlorilegium* (4Q174 1 II, 3, 24, 5.3), is probably portrayed as a healer or diviner (גזר) in the *Prayer of Nabonidus* (4Q242 1–3 4).[84] Abraham, however, though not called a "prophet," would have been understood as one (cf. Gen. 20:7)[85] and is portrayed as functioning as such in the *Genesis Apocryphon*. As could be expected of a prophet, his dreams are predictive, and he has visions (1Q20 XXI, 8; XXII, 27). That this prophetic figure was thought to be involved in miracles is clear from the story of him healing Pharaoh (1Q20 XX). Moreover, Qumran's contemporary interest in connecting the prophetic figure with miraculous healing is seen in the story not simply repeating the Genesis tradition, but introducing the ideas of the laying on of hands and also making it an exorcism, for an evil spirit is said to be removed from the king.

Clearly, the Qumran library connects the miraculous with being a prophet, both in the great figures of the past and in their involvement in the eschaton. Also, as we have just noted, the figure of Daniel, and the editing of the story of Abraham healing Pharaoh, suggest a contemporary interest in associating prophecy and miracle working. However, most of the references to miracle working (see §2.1 [a] above) are not associated with prophets or prophecy, and not all prophets are regarded as involved in the miraculous. For example, we read nothing of Elisha, Isaiah, Jeremiah, Ezekiel, or the twelve Minor Prophets on this subject.

There may have been, then, some caution in promoting too strong a connection between prophecy and the miraculous. Indeed, there was likely healing activity taking place in the community, including exorcisms by the leaders,[86] and the prophet interpreted Scripture through revelation,[87] and also the Teacher

81. Only here in the Dead Sea Scrolls. Cf. 11Q5 XXVII, 4.

82. 11Q5 XXVII, 11.Cf. 4Q397 14–21 10; 4Q398 14–17 I, 3.

83. Cf. 1 Sam. 10:1–16; 19:20–24; 1 Kings 22:12; Jer. 29:24–28; see Robert R. Wilson, "Prophecy and Ecstasy: A Reexamination," *JBL* 98 (1979): 321–37.

84. Only here in the Qumran literature; but see, e.g., Dan. 2:27; 4:7 (MT 4:4); 5:7, 11. On גזר as "diviner," rather than exorcist, see Brooke, "Prophetic Narratives," 292.

85. See, e.g., Gerhard von Rad, *Genesis: A Commentary*, trans. John H. Marks (London: SCM, 1972), 228–29.

86. Cf. 11Q11; 4Q510; 4Q511; 6Q18; on which, see Graham H. Twelftree, "Jesus the Exorcist and Ancient Magic," in *A Kind of Magic: Understanding Magic in the New Testament and Its Religious Environment*, ed. Michael Labahn and Bert Jan Lietaert Peerbolte (LNTS 306; London: T&T Clark, 2007), 63–64.

87. George J. Brooke, "Prophecy," in *Encyclopedia of the Dead Sea Scrolls*, ed. Lawrence H. Schiffman and James C. VanderKam, 2 vols. (New York: Oxford University Press, 2000), 2:695.

was taken to have divine inspiration and authority,[88] special revelation, unmediated access to the divine, and to be an exegete of the prophetic word.[89] Yet, we have no evidence that the title "prophet" was either claimed by or attributed to the Teacher or any other member of the community.[90]

This caution in not taking up the title "prophet" and its explanation may be reflected in some lines from the *Temple Scroll*. In selecting, as well as editing, the laws of the Torah so that they are spoken directly by God, the redactor of the *Temple Scroll* has provided immediate divine revelation for his own time.[91] In doing so, the redactor has retained the mandate in Deuteronomy 13:1–7 on testing prophets. Of particular interest to us, he maintains the material that says, "If a prophet or a dreamer appears among you and presents you with a sign or a portent, even if the sign or portent comes true, when he says, 'Let us go and worship other gods whom you have not known!' do not listen to the words of that prophet or that dreamer" (11Q19 LIV, 8–11; cf. §2.1 [a] above). Moreover, even though the redactor has omitted everything that he considered repetitious,[92] he goes on to include another mention of false prophecy (11Q19 LXI, 1–5 // Deut. 18:20–22). Further, another text is a list of seven false prophets known from biblical texts (e.g., Balaam) and one, perhaps John, son of Simon (i.e., Hyrcanus I), from recent times (4Q339).[93] This merging of the biblical and the contemporary suggests a more than theoretical interest in the topic.[94] Perhaps, then, although the people of Qumran saw a close relationship between prophets and the miraculous, experience of misleading individuals claiming the relationship had given them cause for caution (cf. 4Q339; 4Q375).[95]

(b) Sirach. What was originally an independent canticle (cf. 11Q5 XXI–XXII), now identified as Sirach 44:1–50:29, in most Greek manuscripts bears the heading "Hymn in Honor of Our Ancestors" (πατερων υμνος). Beginning, "Let us now sing the praises of famous men" (44:1), the early second-century BCE[96]

88. 1QpHab VII, 4–5; 1QS VIII, 12; CD-A VI, 7; VII, 18.

89. Bowley, "Prophets," 371, 373, citing 1QpHab VII, 4–5; 1QHᵃ IV, 26; VI, 25; IX, 21; X, 10–18; XII, 23, 27–28; XV, 26–27; XVI, 16–19; XVII, 32; XX, 12–13; XXIII, 10–14; cf. 1QpHab II, 8–9.

90. Cf., e.g., Jassen, "Prophets," 309n34, and those cited there.

91. Johann Maier, *The Temple Scroll: An Introduction, Translation and Commentary* (JSOT-Sup 34; Sheffield: JSOT Press, 1985), 3.

92. Michael O. Wise, *A Critical Study of the Temple Scroll from Qumran Cave 11* (SAOC 49; Chicago: Oriental Institute of the University of Chicago, 1990), 200.

93. On the restoration of this damaged text, see Michael O. Wise, "False Prophets in Israel: 4Q339," in Michael O. Wise, Martin Abegg Jr., and Edward Cook, *The Dead Sea Scrolls: A New Translation* (San Francisco: HarperSanFrancisco, 1996), 323–25.

94. Bowley, "Prophets," 365, 372.

95. 1Q22; 1Q29; 4Q375; 4Q376 may have been written as guides for testing prophets; see ibid., 373–76.

96. E.g., David S. Williams, "The Date of Ecclesiasticus," *VT* 44 (1994): 563–66.

author (prologue 8) from Jerusalem (50:27) provides a series of short biographies. Sirach's string of vignettes involves Enoch, Noah, Abraham, Isaac, Jacob, Moses, Aaron, Phinehas, Joshua, Caleb, "the judges," Samuel, Nathan, David, Solomon, Elijah, Elisha, Hezekiah, Isaiah, Josiah, Jeremiah, Ezekiel, Job, "the twelve prophets," Zerubbabel, Jeshua, Nehemiah, Enoch (again), Joseph, Shem, Seth, Enosh, Adam, and Simon son of Onias.

Of the thirty individuals mentioned, eight are identified as prophets or as prophesying: Moses (cf. Sir. 46:1),[97] Joshua (46:1), Samuel (46:13, 15, 20), Elijah (48:1), Elisha (48:8),[98] David (48:22), Isaiah (48:20b–25, esp. 48:23), and Jeremiah (49:7).[99] Of these, all but David and Jeremiah are associated with miracles,[100] and the stories of Elijah (48:1–11) and Elisha (48:12–16) are dominated by the miraculous.[101] In turn, Elisha's miracles (48:12) form the heart of his mission to the people of God.[102] In this, Sirach is portraying a strong relationship between prophecy and the miraculous.[103] Moreover, on the one hand, all of the miracles are related in some way to a prophet.[104] On the other hand, of the other great men, Aaron (45:6–22, esp. 45:19), Hezekiah (48:17–22, esp. 48:20–21), and perhaps Enoch (44:16; 49:14) are the only ones said to be involved in or associated with the miraculous, suggesting a strong relationship between prophets and the miraculous.

The kinds of miracles associated with these figures vary. Some of the miracles in Sirach are interruptions in the expected course of nature: hailstones (46:5), thunder (46:17), drought (48:3), and the sun going backward in the sky (48:23). Others are military victories (45:19; 48:20) or healings (48:6, 23) or raising the dead (48:5) or prophesying (48:13–14) or are unspecified (45:19).[105] However, by and large, the miracles do not so much benefit individuals as influence and direct national affairs.[106] The way the miracles are carried out also varies. Aaron does

97. On Moses not being directly named as a prophet, see Burton L. Mack, *Wisdom and Hebrew Epic: Ben Sira's Hymn in Praise of the Fathers* (CSJH; Chicago: University of Chicago Press, 1985), 30–32.

98. On the Greek translator introducing the plural προφήτας, see Patrick W. Skehan and Alexander A. Di Lella, *The Wisdom of Ben Sira: A New Translation with Notes* (AB 39; New York: Doubleday, 1987), 531.

99. Cf. Mack, *Wisdom*, 28.

100. Moses (Sir. 44:23b–45:5, esp. 44:3), Joshua (46:1–8, esp. 46:5), Samuel (46:13–20, esp. 46:17), Hezekiah (48:17–25, esp. 48:23–25) and Isaiah (48:20b–25, esp. 48:20, 22–23).

101. Eric Eve, *The Jewish Context of Jesus' Miracles* (JSNTSup 231; Sheffield: Sheffield Academic Press, 2002), 110. On Sir. 48:12, see 76n109 below.

102. Erkki Koskenniemi, *The Old Testament Miracle-Workers in Early Judaism* (WUNT 2/206; Tübingen: Mohr Siebeck, 2005), 36, 38.

103. Also Eve, *Jewish Context*, 111, 115.

104. Mack, *Wisdom*, 212.

105. Ibid.

106. Koskenniemi, *Miracle-Workers*, 29, 33.

not perform any miracles, the Lord performs them against his enemies (45:19), and God takes up Enoch from the earth.[107] However, Moses (45:3)[108] and Elijah (48:6) are directly responsible for miracles, though Elijah also performs them "by the word of" the Lord (48:3, 5–6), and Joshua (46:5) and Samuel (46:16) call on God. So important is the miraculous in the portrait of Elisha that he is even said to prophesy and perform wonders after his death (48:13–14).

Despite this interest in the miraculous, Sirach has not introduced the theme to any of the portraits of his characters whom he found in his Scriptures. Moreover, in translating the Hebrew into Greek, Jesus ben Sira also shows no particular interest in the miraculous. For example, a special interest in miracles would likely have caused him not to leave out, but rather to maintain, Sirach 48:12cd, at least in a revised form: "He [Elisha] performed twice as many signs [as Elijah], and marvels with every utterance of his mouth."[109] Perhaps for the very reason that Sirach's attention is not on prophets or the miraculous, but more broadly on the values of traditional Jewry, his views are more reliable in conveying what was thought about prophets and the miraculous.

In determining Jesus ben Sira's perspective on prophets and miracles, we have to set aside the idea that the miraculous is used primarily to praise the Creator acting in history and nature,[110] not least because God is only indirectly praised (cf. Sir. 50:22).[111] The miracles that interrupt nature or history come about either by the person calling on God (46:5, 16; 48:20), or the miracle is used to reflect positively on the person (45:3, 19–20; 48:23); and it is the person's relationship with God rather than divine vocation[112] that is applauded. We are obliged, then, to take the first line of the hymn seriously. The writer is seeking not to praise God, at least not directly, but to "sing the praises of famous men" (44:1): prophets, priests, kings, and judges. Notwithstanding, the underlying

107. Sir. 49:14, ἀνελήμφθη (aorist passive, "was taken up"); cf. 44:16, μετετέθη (aorist passive, "was transferred").

108. In the Greek, Moses is said to have "caused signs to cease" (σημεῖα κατέπαυσεν [Sir. 45:3]), perhaps understood to be a reference to Moses asking God to remove the portents of frogs, flies, hail, and locusts (Exod. 8:12, 31; 9:33; 10:19). See John G. Snaith, *Ecclesiasticus, or The Wisdom of Jesus Son of Sirach* (CBC; London: Cambridge University Press, 1974), 221.

109. "G may have omitted 48:12cd . . . because this bicolon seems to make Elisha a greater person that Elijah" (Skehan and Di Lella, *Ben Sira*, 534).

110. The view of, e.g., Teresa R. Brown, "God and Men in Israel's History: God and Idol Worship, in *Praise of the Fathers* (Sir 44–50)," in *Ben Sira's God: Proceedings of the International Ben Sira Conference, Durham, Ushaw College, 2001*, ed. Renate Egger-Wenzel (BZAW 321; Berlin: de Gruyter, 2002), 214.

111. E.g., Thomas R. Lee, *Studies in the Form of Sirach 44–50* (SBLDS 75; Atlanta: Scholars Press, 1986), 242.

112. As supposed by John Barton, *Oracles of God: Perceptions of Ancient Prophecy in Israel after the Exile* (Oxford: Oxford University Press, 2007), 101n12.

purpose of the theme of the miraculous is not the legitimization of the various figures as men of God in general or prophets in particular.[113] Rather, as Jesus ben Sira says at the end of the hymn (50:27–29), and as exemplified in Simon the high priest (50:1–24),[114] he intends the personal piety of the characters in his anthology of biographies to be emulated (50:27–29).[115] In sum: in relation to prophecy and the miraculous, Jesus ben Sira conveys to his readers the idea that prophets and the miraculous are strongly related; that the greatest miracle workers in the scriptural traditions (Moses, Elijah, and Elisha) were prophets; that most of the Scriptural prophets were miracle workers, and that miracle working was the most important activity of these prophets; and that these figures, including their miracle working, were expected to be taken as models for life by his readers.

   (c) *Ezekiel the Tragedian.* The *Exagōgē* (*Exodus*), by Ezekiel the Tragedian, is a drama on the exodus from Egypt. Principally through Eusebius quoting the work from Alexander Polyhistor (c. 105–35 BCE), perhaps one quarter (269 lines) of the text has been preserved.[116] Noting affinities with Daniel and *Jubilees* (both from mid-second century BCE), recent discussions on the dating of this tragic drama have left the matter open.[117] Also, in that we are dealing with a writer who bears a thoroughly Jewish name,[118] who is writing about Jewish history in which he is well versed, who seeks to promote Jewish heroes, and who was known by Clement of Alexandria as a composer of Jewish tragedies (*Strom.* 1.23.155), it is highly likely this Ezekiel was a Jew.[119] We do not know where he was writing, though with the Egyptians as antiheroes, it is not likely to be in Alexandria.[120]

   In Ezekiel retelling the story of the exodus (Exod. 1–15), Moses is involved in the "miraculous" (σημεῖον) or "great portent" (τεράστιον μέγιστον) of the burning bush (Ezek. Trag. 90–91). He has a hand that becomes leprous and is restored, and a rod through which the miraculous occurs (120–132, 225–226);

---

113. Cf. also Mack, *Wisdom*, 22.

114. Cf. Alon Goshen-Gottstein, "Ben Sira's Praise of the Fathers: A Canon-Conscious Reading," in Egger-Wenzel, *Ben Sira's God*, 235–67.

115. E.g., Benjamin G. Wright III, *Praise Israel for Wisdom and Instruction: Essays on Ben Sira and Wisdom, the Letter of Aristeas and the Septuagint* (JSJSup 131; Leiden: Brill, 2008), chap. 8.

116. Bruno Snell and Richard Kannichtemend emend frg. 13, line 9, to give 270 lines (*Tragicorum Graecorum Fragmenta*, 4 vols. [Göttingen: Vandenhoeck & Ruprecht, 1986–71], 1:295n143).

117. Pieter W. van der Horst, "Some Notes on the *Exagoge* of Ezekiel," *Mnemosyne* 37 (1984): 356–57.

118. On the possibility of "Ezekiel" being a pseudonym, see ibid., 355–56.

119. Carl R. Holladay, *Fragments from Hellenistic Jewish Authors*, vol. 2, *Poets: The Epic Poets Theodotus and Philo and Ezekiel the Tragedian* (TTPS 12; Chico, CA: Scholars Press, 1989), 301–4.

120. Ibid., 312–13.

he also takes part in the wonders and portents of the exodus (e.g., 220–241). Yet, the miracles of the hand and the rod are used not to authenticate Moses before his people (as in Exod. 4:1–9),[121] but to convince Pharaoh and to "end the arrogance of this evil people" (Ezek. Trag. 148; cf. 89, 149).

At the same time, though not specifically called one, Moses is described as a prophet. Most notably, he has a vision of a great throne (Ezek. Trag. 67–82). There is considerable speculation as to the significance of this vision for Ezekiel. For example, the astral symbolism could be features of divinity pointing to a cosmic ruler. Or, in portraying Moses having dreams and visions as in Jewish and Greek sources, he may be attempting to portray him as human rather than divine. Or, it could be that Moses is being portrayed as a king, or someone in the tradition of *merkabah* mysticism. However, although it is likely that the vision would have conveyed multiple messages about Moses, portraying him as a prophet was probably one of the most important ones.[122]

In that the vision (Ezek. Trag. 68) or dream (82) is placed at the beginning of Moses' career, and that, without a break, the text goes on to interpret the vision in terms of a call (83–89)—including that he will see "what is, what has been and what shall be" (89)—two of the great prophets of old (Isaiah and Ezekiel) are recalled who received visions of the heavenly throne as part of their calls (Isa. 6:1–13; Ezek. 1:4–28). In concert with this portrayal as a prophet, Moses is also said to hear God's voice (Ezek. Trag. 102–103) and to converse with him (90–130). Also consistent with being represented as a prophet is his being called and sent by God with a message (109) and being told he will be a "leader of people" (καθηγήση βροτῶν, 86).[123]

From this we see a writer of the period portraying a classic prophet hearing God's voice, having visions and dreams, being sent by God with a message, and performing miracles to persuade his audience. Even though we have no direct evidence of whether or not the author thought such individuals could be his contemporaries, Ezekiel is important in establishing that scriptural prophets were thought to have been heavily involved in the miraculous.

(d) Philo. As with each of the bodies of literature we are passing under review, our interest is not in what Philo says either about prophets or prophecy, or about miracles or the miraculous in general. Rather, our interest is in

---

121. Cf. Koskenniemi, *Miracle-Workers*, 68–69.

122. Cf. ibid., 81–86; also Erich S. Gruen, *Heritage and Hellenism: The Reinvention of Jewish Tradition* (HCS 30; Berkeley: University of California Press, 1998), 134.

123. For καθηγέομαι ("lead") in the sense of "explain" or "guide" that could signify a "role as preeminent prophet who provides inspired guidance for the people," see Holladay, *Poets*, 448–49, citing Plato, *Ep.* 312C; Herodotus, *Hist.* 7.183; Xenophon, *Anab.* 7.8.9; Plutarch, *Mor.* 2.120A; Strabo, *Geogr.* 14.5.14; Dionysius of Halicarnassus, *1 Amm.* 5.16.

what he has to say about the relationship between a classic prophet and the miraculous or conducting of miracles. Apart from God, for whom all things are possible (*Abr.* 175), only Moses and, to a lesser extent, Aaron (*Migr.* 85; *Somn.* 2.235) are miracle workers.[124] Like others of his time, Philo calls Moses a prophet.[125] He also calls Moses "the prophet"[126] as well as "the archprophet"[127] and prophet of the highest quality.[128] Philo considers prophecy or "divine utterances" (*Mos.* 2.188) to be communicated either through God himself speaking (with his prophet interpreting, 2.187–188), or through question and answer between the prophet and God (2.192–245), or by the prophet being "inspired and transported out of himself" (2.188).[129] This last category is particularly important to our enquiry for, on the one hand, it is in virtue of this ecstacy that a person "is chiefly and in the strict sense considered a prophet" (2.191). On the other hand, it is in being "taken out of himself by divine possession" that Moses utters "inspired words" (2.250), and "what he prophesied came to pass through divine power" (θείαις δυνάμεσι, 2.253) in the form of a miracle. In one case this is the parting of the Red Sea (2.246–257), in another it was food from heaven (2.258–262), and in two other examples it was food from heaven in relation to the Sabbath (2.263–269). Another example is a story of the earth opening up and swallowing 250 men who had led a sedition, immediately after Moses had been inspired and "transformed into a prophet" (μεταβαλὼν εἰς προφήτην, 2.280) to see and speak of their destruction (2.275–287).

In each of these cases, however, where Moses is being portrayed as a prophet, it is God, not Moses, who performs the miracles (cf. 2.253, cited above).[130] Moses, through inspired speech, only anticipates God's miracles.[131] Moreover, miracles verify God's presence and power—only indirectly do they authenticate Moses as a prophet (e.g., 1.71–84). Insofar as Philo takes the miracles to reflect on Moses, it is his virtue rather than his being a prophet that is considered established (2.284). That Philo is not wishing to establish a necessary link be-

---

124. Eve, *Jewish Context*, 73–74, 84.

125. Philo, *Leg.* 2.1; *Mos.* 2.213; *Contempl.* 64; 87; *Praem.* 1.

126. ὁ προφήτης (Philo, *Fug.* 140). See also *Her.* 4; *Mut.* 11; *Somn.* 2.277; *Mos.* 1.156; 2.229, 250, 257, 275; *Virt.* 51; *Gig.* 49; cf. *QG* 4.245; *QE* 1.11; 2.44.

127. ὁ ἀρχιπροφήτης (Philo, *Mut.* 103; 125; *Somn.* 2.189). Cf. *QG* 4.8 (ὁ ἀρχιπροφήτης καὶ ὁ ἀρχάγγελος, "the chief prophet and the chief messenger"); *QG* 1.86 (ὁ πρωτοπροφήτης, "the primary prophet").

128. Superlative of δόκιμος, "approved, genuine, esteemed" (Philo, *Mos.* 2.187 [cf. 2.234]).

129. ἐπιθειάσαντος καὶ ἐξ αὐτοῦ κατασχεθέντος. Cf. Philo, *Mos.* 2.191: ἐνθουσιώδης, "ecstatic" by reason of divine inspiration or possession. See LSJ 566–67.

130. Eve, *Jewish Context*, 65–66, 73.

131. Cf. Philo, *Mos.* 2.253, 262, 263, 269, 284.

tween being a prophet and conducting miracles is seen in Noah, Isaac, Jacob, and Abraham being accorded the status of true prophets, yet they are not said to perform miracles (*Her.* 260–266). Also, while Philo describes himself as a prophet, and heir of Moses,[132] he gives no hint that he conducted miracles.

Moses, however, is Philo's primary hero, calling him divine, holy (*QE* 2.54), a god-man or man of God (θείου ἀνδρός, *Virt.* 1.177), and portraying him as having an unmediated relationship with God (*Deus.* 109–110) and, as God's friend, sharing his possessions (*Mos.* 1.156; cf. *Somn.* 2.227–228). Thus, if God is a miracle worker, it is not surprising that Philo also gives this role to Moses, his partner, as well as to Aaron, the prophet's brother (e.g., *Det.* 126) and mouthpiece (e.g., *Det.* 39; *Migr.* 76).[133] What emerges from this discussion of prophets in Philo is that although Moses—because of his unique relation with God—is a prophet credited with involvement in miracles that God performs, Philo sees no necessary link between prophecy and miracle working, either in his sacred writings or in his own time.

(e) Lives of the Prophets. Along with all the texts we are examining, the usefulness of this document in helping us understand Paul depends not only on the text associating prophecy and the miraculous, but also in it reflecting his cultural world. *Lives*, which probably was written in Greek,[134] has been variously dated, including to the fourth century of our era, and attributed to Epiphanius, bishop of Salamis (c. 315–403 CE).[135] However, given that the political and cultural situation of *Lives* reflects the Hasmonean and Roman period, and that the description of the prophets is consistent with the period, it is probable that the book had its origins in the first century CE.[136] Given the accurate information conveyed about Palestine, it is likely this book originated there.[137]

132. See Philo, *Migr.* 34–35; *Her.* 264–265; *QG* 3.9; *Spec.* 1.65; 4.49.

133. Cf. Philo, *Leg.* 3.128: Ἀαρὼν—δεύτερος γάρ ἐστι Μωυσῆ ("Aaron—second to Moses").

134. D. R. A. Hare ("The Lives of the Prophets," *OTP* 2:380) notes that there is little evidence of mistranslation, and that there are instances of the text being closer to the Greek than Hebrew versions of the Bible. On *Lives of the Prophets* having a Hebrew original, see Charles C. Torrey, *The Lives of the Prophets: Greek Text and Translation* (SBLMS 1; Philadelphia: Society of Biblical Literature and Exegesis, 1946), 1, 6–7, 16–17.

135. Codex Paris Gk. 1115, or E[1] (copied 1276) and Codex Coisl. 120, or E[2] (tenth century). The case by Satran (*Biblical Prophets*) that *Lives of the Prophets* is essentially a Byzantine document taking up early Jewish traditions has not been well received. See the review by William Horbury, *VT* 46 (1996): 422–23.

136. Marinus de Jonge, *Pseudepigrapha of the Old Testament as Part of Christian Literature: The Case of the Testaments of the Twelve Patriarchs and the Greek Life of Adam and Eve* (SVTP 18; Leiden: Brill, 2003), 44–47.

137. Torrey, *Lives*, 11.

That the biographies forming *Lives* are thoroughly Jewish, short and simple, do not glorify the characters, and that the Christian elements[138] can be easily removed,[139] supports the increasing agreement that *Lives* is Jewish,[140] even though a minority continue to see it as a Christian document.[141] *Lives*, then, is able to help us see how scriptural prophets and the miraculous were related in the time of Paul.

This text associates many of the Old Testament prophets with the miraculous. Codex Marchalianus (referred to as Q),[142] the most important text of what is now known as *Lives of the Prophets*, says that it contains "The names of the prophets, and where they are from, and where they died and how, and where they lived" (superscription).[143] The prophets mentioned are Isaiah, Jeremiah, Ezekiel, Daniel, the twelve Minor Prophets, and seven other biblical prophets: Nathan, Ahijah, Joad, Azariah, Elijah, Elisha, and Zechariah son of Jehoiada.

In some of these biographies the miraculous element is absent. The brief lives of Micah, Amos, Joel, Obadiah, Jonah, Nahum, Joad, and Azariah have no miracle stories associated with them. However, it is said of Hosea, Habakkuk, and Zechariah that each "gave a portent,"[144] and Zephaniah, Haggai, and Malachi prophesy (13:2; 14:1; 16:3). Nathan is hindered by Beliar (17:2) and knows what David has done (17:3). Abijah has a vision (18:3) and foretells aspects of Solomon's life (18:4).

The three writing prophets, along with Daniel, whose stories open *Lives*, are all more obviously involved in the miraculous. Although Isaiah's biography does not include the Old Testament miracle stories associated with him,[145] it remains dominated by the story of him praying for water to drink. Isaiah having prayed, the narrator says, "God worked the sign [σημεῖον] of Siloam for the prophet's sake" (1:2) enabling him and the nation, but not the foreigners, to drink (1:3–7). Another mention of the miraculous, again expected to be by God not the prophet, comes in the climax of the story.

138. Anna Maria Schwemer, *Vitae Prophetarum* (JSHRZ 1/7; Gütersloh: Gütersloher Verlagshaus, 1997), 553.

139. Though to the contrary, see Satran, *Biblical Prophets*, e.g., 75–76.

140. Koskenniemi, *Miracle-Workers*, 160.

141. See the discussion by Koskenniemi (*Miracle-Workers*, 161n9) of particularly Satran, *Biblical Prophets*, and Anna Maria Schwemer, *Studien zu den frühjüdischen Prophetenlegenden Vitae prophetarum* (TSAJ 49; Tübingen: Mohr Siebeck, 1995).

142. For critical texts of Q, see James H. Charlesworth, *The Pseudepigrapha and Modern Research, with a Supplement* (SBLSCSS 7; Chico, CA: Scholars Press, 1981), 175–77.

143. Hare, "Lives," 379.

144. ἔδωκε τέρας (*Liv. Pro.* 5:2; cf. 12:10; 15:1, 4). See Schwemer, *Vitae prophetarum*, 551–53.

145. Isa. 38:1–22 // 2 Kings 10:1–11; Isa. 37:14–37 // 2 Kings 19:14–37.

Isaiah is buried near the pool "so that through his prayers even after his death they might enjoy the benefit of the water" (1:8; cf. Sir. 48:13–14). Jeremiah, whose miraculous activity in the Old Testament is limited to his prophecies, becomes a miracle worker in *Lives*, thereby gaining high esteem (2:2).[146] For example, he is said to have prayed, and asps and crocodiles left the Egyptians (2:3). He is also said to have seized the ark of the law and caused a rock to swallow it and its contents (2:11). Although Ezekiel is not a miracle worker in the Old Testament, in *Lives* he is said to stop a river for the people to cross, but for the enemies to be drowned (3:8–9). Then, "through prayer" he supplied people with fish (3:10), and he stopped the enemies of the people through terrifying prodigies (3:11). He may even be credited with raising the dead.[147] Ezekiel is also credited with visionary powers (3:13), of being transported from the Far East to Jerusalem (3:14), and of causing snakes to devour infants and animals (3:17). Daniel's only specific miracle is, through prayer, to cause Nebuchadnezzar's sentence of suffering (perhaps demonic in origin, 4:6) to be reduced (4:12–13), though it is said that "he wrought many prodigies" (4:17).

Toward the end of *Lives of the Prophets* the biographies of Elijah and Elisha also involve the miraculous. Legendary elements adorn the story of Elijah's birth (21:2–3), and all the biblical miracles associated with him are listed.[148] There are also legendary features associated with the story of Elisha's birth (22:1–3), which is followed by a summary of his biblical miracles.[149] However, since the work of Charles C. Torrey, doubts remain as to whether or not either the material on the miraculous or the entire sections on these two prophets are to be taken as part of the earliest version of the text.[150] Even if we exclude this material from consideration, *Lives* gives ample evidence of associating miracle working with prophets, generally portraying them not as independent miracle workers but as people of God praying to him for miracles. However, this association was not a necessary part of the portrayal of a prophet.

(f) Liber antiquitatum biblicarum (Pseudo-Philo). This text is greatly interested in miracles and the miraculous, but it bears repeating that our interest

---

146. *Liv. Pro.* 2:8 and 9 ("through a savior, a child born of a virgin, in a manger. Wherefore even to this day they revere a virgin giving birth and, placing an infant in a manger, they worship") is a Christian addition. See Torrey, *Lives*, 36; Hare, "Lives," 387 note n.

147. καὶ πολλοῖς ἐκλείπουσι ζωὴν ἐκ θεοῦ παρεκάλεσεν (*Liv. Pro.* 3:10b), which Hare ("Lives," 389) translates as "and for many who were at the point of dying he entreated that life should come from God," may be intended to refer to raising the dead.

148. *Liv. Pro.* 21:4–14; cf. 1 Kings 10:6; 17:1, 6, 8–16, 17–24; 2 Kings 1:1–17; 2:8, 11; 9:3.

149. *Liv. Pro.* 22:4–17; cf. 1 Kings 19:16; 2 Kings 2:13–14, 19–24; 4:1–7, 48–51; 5:1–27; 6:1–23; 13:20–21.

150. Torrey, *Lives*, 8; Koskenniemi, *Miracle-Workers*, 184–86.

here is in how it relates the theme to the classic prophets. Along with his miracles, the story of Moses takes up chapters 9–19, nearly 20 percent of the text. Later in the text Samuel calls Moses "my master Moses" (*dominus meus Moyses*, perhaps אדני משה; *L.A.B.* 57:2).[151] Given that this is spoken by a prophet (57:4), Moses is being cast as the master of prophets.

Even the announcement of his birth associates Moses with miracles. However, God says that it is he who "will perform through him signs and wonders for my people that I have not done for anyone else" (*L.A.B.* 9:7; cf. 9:10). It is also God who sends the plagues (10:1). Then again, at the crossing of the Red Sea, as in Exodus 14:21, although God tells Moses to hold up his rod and strike the sea, using the language of Psalm 106:9, it is God who threatens the sea[152] to effect the miracle to save his people (*L.A.B.* 10:5).[153] In relation to the desert miracles of bread and quail from heaven, which are passed over quickly, Moses is not mentioned (10:7). However, the miracle of the ground swallowing up the rebellious Korah and his people, which is related at some length, is not for the benefit of Moses, but to legitimize the law (16:1–7).[154]

Although Joshua is not designated a prophet, as Elisha succeeds Elijah as prophet, so Joshua takes on the garments of wisdom and knowledge from Moses. Like a prophet,[155] he is changed to become another man (*L.A.B.* 20:2–3; cf. 1 Sam. 10:6). Later, in the song of Deborah, at Joshua's command, the sun and moon stand still to give light to God's children, but darkness to their enemy (*L.A.B.* 32:9–10; cf. Josh. 10:12–15).

Kenaz, a little-known figure in the Old Testament,[156] is credited not only with being a prophet (*L.A.B.* 28:6–9), but also with asking for wonders (27:7). In battle he is clothed with the spirit of power, and the Lord sent angels to aid in the defeat of the Amorites (27:10). The miracle is in the magnitude of the defeat (27:7, 13) and is portrayed as taking place "in the last days" (*in novissimis diebus*, 27:7).

Looking back over the miracles in *Liber antiquitatum biblicarum*, we see an obvious interest in connecting the prophets of old with the miraculous.

151. Howard Jacobson, *A Commentary on Pseudo-Philo's Liber Antiquitatum Biblicarum, with Latin Text and Translation*, 2 vols. (AGJU 31; Leiden: Brill, 1996), 2:1157.

152. *L.A.B.* 10:5: *comminatus est Deus mari et siccatum est mare* ("God rebuked the sea, and the sea was dried up"). Cf. Ps. 106:9: ויגער בים סוף ויחרב ("And he rebuked the Red Sea, and it dried up"). See Richard Bauckham, "The Liber Antiquitatum Biblicarum of Pseudo-Philo and the Gospels as Midrash," in *Studies in Midrash and Historiography*, ed. R. T. France and David Wenham (GP 3; Sheffield: JSOT Press, 1983), 43.

153. Jacobson, *Liber Antiquitatum Biblicarum*, 1:440.

154. Cf. Koskenniemi, *Miracle-Workers*, 198–99.

155. Cf. *L.A.B.* 27:10; 28:6, 10; 62:2; Philo, *Mos.* 2.272.

156. See Gen. 36:11, 15, 42; Josh. 15:17; Judg. 1:13; 3:9, 11; 1 Chron. 1:36, 53; 4:13, 15.

However, the miracles are not healings or events of compassion. Rather, they serve a political (and eschatological) purpose: they are God's method of advancing the political agenda of his people "in the last days." It is this perspective that may explain the little interest in the miracles of the desert when there were no political enemies or issues at stake. In line with this, it is notable that although the miracles take place through and in relation to work of the prophet, it is God who does them, a perspective we will see again when we turn to Paul's testimony.

(g) *Josephus*. Largely reflecting the distribution of miracle stories in Josephus's Scriptures, Eric Eve has noted that most of the miracle stories in Josephus—60 to 70 percent of them in *Antiquities of the Jews*—are associated with great prophetic figures: Moses, Samuel, Elijah, Elisha, and Daniel, with Moses accounting for around 36 to 43 percent.[157] However, Josephus makes it clear that it is God and not Moses who performs the miracles. For example, Moses does not strike the waters of the Nile (Exod. 7:17); it is at God's command that they are turned into blood (*Ant.* 2.294). As the author of miracles, God can use them to save people.[158] Josephus does not show any intention of playing down the supernatural aspects of the stories of the plagues or the water coming from the rock (3.38; cf. Exod. 17:1–7; Num. 20:1–13), though traits of rationalization appear in the story of water at Marah, in that it is the larger part of the water drained off that is drinkable.[159] The revolt led by Korah (Num. 16:1–17:31) is expanded by Josephus to provide a lesson in the political consequences of rebellion (*Ant.* 4.11–66).[160] Moses, however, is not simply a miracle worker, he is also a political leader. Perhaps this explains why Josephus omits miracle stories about Moses from *Against Apion*: his status did not depend on the miracles.[161] Nevertheless, for the Hebrews and Moses' opponents, miracles legitimize Moses, who also is unable to doubt the promises of God because of the miracles (*Ant.* 2.275; cf. 2.280, 286).[162]

Miracles associated with Samuel—an earthquake engulfing the enemy and a storm to deafen and blind them—are also credited to God by Josephus (*Ant.* 6.27). Samuel's foretelling of the safety of Saul's asses (6.53–57) presumably is possible because of prayer (6.49), and learning the location of Saul's hiding place is credited to God (6.65; cf. 6.143–146, 151).

157. Eve, *Jewish Context*, 34–35.
158. Josephus, *Ant.* 2.223: σωζομένους δ' ἐκ παραδόξου.
159. Josephus, *Ant.* 3.7–8; cf. Exod. 15:22–27. See also §2.1 (c) above.
160. Koskenniemi, *Miracle-Workers*, 244.
161. Ibid., 247.
162. See Louis H. Feldman, *Josephus's Interpretation of the Bible* (HCS 27; Berkeley: University of California Press, 1998), 428.

In his portrait of Elijah, Josephus retells all the biblical miracle stories associated with him. In the case of the raising of the widow's son, he says God conducted the miracle and that it legitimized the prophet (*Ant.* 8.327; cf. 9.60). However, Josephus severely abbreviates the story of Elijah's ascension (9.28; cf. 2 Kings 2:1–18), and he does not mention the biblical expectation of his return (cf. Mal. 4:5). As Elijah was identified with the zealous Phinehas,[163] including by the author of *Liber antiquitatum biblicarum*, a contemporary of Josephus (*L.A.B.* 48:1–2),[164] it is likely that Josephus would want to play down this politically sensitive idea that might be interpreted to support revolt against Rome.[165]

In relation to Elisha, Josephus includes stories of the widow in debt (*Ant.* 9.47–50; cf. 2 Kings 4:1–7), the prophet's warning King Joram (*Ant.* 9.51–59; cf. 2 Kings 6:8–23), and Elisha prophesying help for a starving city (*Ant.* 9.61–86; cf. 2 Kings 6:24–7:20). However, despite the eulogy, a great number of biblical stories related to Elisha are missed: the cursed boys (2 Kings 2:23–25), the Shunammite woman (4:8–37), the poisoned food (4:38–41), the miraculous feeding (4:42–44), the healing of Naaman, the punishment of Gehazi (5:1–27), and the floating axe head (6:1–7). Not only may Elisha have been an insignificant figure in the period,[166] it is quite likely that there is a lacuna in Josephus's text involving the material in 2 Kings 4:8–6:8,[167] and not an attempt to tone down the miracles of Elisha.[168]

Though associating himself (Josephus, *J.W.* 3.405, 4.625) and Daniel with "the mantics" (τοὺς μάντεις; *Ant.* 10.195; cf. 10.197) and their technical skill and training,[169] Josephus calls Daniel one of the greatest prophets (10.266–268). He is said to escape from the fiery furnace and the lions' den by divine providence (10.214, 260, 262). Daniel's ability to prophesy and interpret dreams also is credited to God (10.272, 277).

From this brief sketch of what Josephus has to say about the great prophets in relation to miracles, it is obvious that although others conducted miracles,

163. Martin Hengel, *The Zealots: Investigations into the Jewish Freedom Movement in the Period from Herod I until 70 A.D.*, trans. David Smith (Edinburgh: T&T Clark, 1989), 162–68. On the reputed zeal of Phinehas, see 1 Macc. 2:54; 4 Macc. 18:12.

164. See Louis H. Feldman, "Josephus' Portrait of Elijah," *SJOT* 8 (1994): 64.

165. Louis H. Feldman (*Studies in Josephus' Rewritten Bible* [JSJSup 58; Leiden: Brill, 1998], 302–3) notes that Josephus removed reference to Elijah's zealot features. See 1 Kings 18:40; 19:10, 14; Josephus, *Ant.* 8.343, 350, 352; Koskenniemi, *Miracle-Workers*, 270n209.

166. In the NT Elisha is mentioned only in Luke 4:27, he is not mentioned in the Mishnah and rarely in the Tosefta (*t. Yoma* 1:6; *t. Sanh.* 2:9; 14.10; *t. Soṭah* 4:7; 12:5–6).

167. Christopher T. Begg, "Elisha's Great Deeds According to Josephus," *Hen* 18 (1996): 74–75.

168. As supposed by Feldman, *Studies*, 345.

169. Gray, *Prophetic Figures*, 108–9.

and miracles were thought to take place up to the present, they were associated primarily with these prophets of old. We have noted the miracle stories contributing to the political agenda of Josephus, as well as some evidence of rationalization. However, Erkki Koskenniemi is probably right to say that there is "no reason to believe that he consistently tried to remove the miraculous to please his Gentile readers."[170] In any case, Josephus—someone from Paul's time—is shown not only closely associating miracle working with the classical prophets, but also seeing miracles and the miraculous as activities of God and legitimatizing the prophets. Before I draw conclusions from this discussion, a puzzle mentioned earlier in this chapter (§3.1 above) requires attention.

3.4 Paul's Caution

Why did Paul, though so obviously considering himself a prophet, consciously functioning as one, and acknowledging that others would claim the title for themselves (1 Cor. 14:37), not use the title for himself? Both those responsible for the Dead Sea Scrolls and Josephus show a similar reluctance, as well as suggest the most likely explanation for Paul's caution.

As we have noted, despite the high regard for prophets and prophecy, both in the past and in the eschaton, as well as in the present, the title "prophet" (נביא) is not applied to anyone at Qumran. Not even the Teacher of Righteousness is called a prophet (see §3.3 [a] above). However, using prophetic terminology, the authors of the scrolls could describe their enemies as "lying prophets" (נביאי כזב).[171] Yet, they are refuted not by a counterclaim to being (true) prophets, but by setting the false prophets over against the law (1QH^a XII, 10) or God's word (1QH^a XII, 17). In this the authors have taken the polemic from the personal to one where the opponents are seen to be self-proclaimed prophets in conflict with God,[172] a tack that the prophet Micah also took in his polemic against false prophets (Mic. 3:5–8).[173] This is evidence of a mind-set that does not claim the prophet's title because of the claim or activity of others and, hence, the fear of being deemed illegitimate. Further, it could be, as George Brooke has suggested, that the Teacher of Righteousness, fictional or real, particularly in the second or first centuries BCE, had a mediating role in a small but pluralist movement (cf.

---

170. Koskenniemi, *Miracle-Workers*, 278.
171. 1QH^a XII, 16; cf. XII, 5–XIII, 4. See the discussion by Jassen, "Prophets," 311–17.
172. Cf. ibid., 311.
173. Cf. A. S. van der Woude, "Micah in Dispute with the Pseudo-Prophets," *VT* 19 (1969): 244–60; Ralph L. Smith, *Micah-Malachi* (WBC 32; Waco: Word, 1984), 33–34.

4Q171 IV, 23–24).[174] The Teacher was seen as the focal identity of the community rather than as a prophet, a perception that would have placed him too sharply over against the community.[175]

Also, although in *Jewish War* Josephus describes himself as "chosen" (3.354), "sent," a "messenger" (3.400), and, notably, "inspired" (ἔνθους, 3.353) and claimed to be able to predict the future (3.351–354, 399–408), he does not call himself a prophet. Also, Josephus is reserved in the use of the title for others in his period,[176] using it only of some hired stooges whom he parallels with false prophets (6.281–287) and of Cleodemus (*Ant.* 1.240–241),[177] whom he may regard as a successor to those of the Scriptures,[178] for his history is said to be "in conformity with the narrative of . . . Moses" (1.240). Instead, Josephus uses "seer" or "prophet" (μάντις) terminology in relation to himself as well as others.[179] This hesitancy on the part of Josephus to call himself and other contemporaries "prophets" may be an expression of the distinction he sees between the great prophets of Scripture and those of the present (*Ag. Ap.* 1.41), whom, by comparison, he takes to be unworthy of the appellation.[180] Thus, he may be wishing to distance himself from those who claimed to be prophets[181] but were, from his perspective, impostors.[182]

The general perspective we see in the Dead Sea Scrolls and Josephus probably can be taken, *mutatis mutandis*, to apply to Paul. First, while he saw himself and his ministry in the tradition of the classical prophets—claiming revelations, prophesying, and having direct access to God—he would also most probably have been aware of the contemporary abuses by, and suspicion of, self-proclaimed prophets who were often deemed impostors. Paul would also have known that some of the great prophets of the past eschewed the

---

174. George J. Brooke, "Was the Teacher of Righteousness Considered to Be a Prophet?" in *Prophecy after the Prophets? The Contribution of the Dead Sea Scrolls to the Understanding of Biblical and Extra-Biblical Prophecy*, ed. Kristin de Troyer and Armin Lange (CBET 52; Louvain: Peeters; 2009), 96.

175. Ibid., 77–97, esp. 96.

176. Gnuse, *Dreams*, 25.

177. Josephus says he is quoting from Alexander Polyhistor. See David E. Aune, "The Use of ΠΡΟΦΗΤΗΣ in Josephus," *JBL* 101 (1982): 419–21.

178. Ibid., 421.

179. See Josephus, *Ant.* 4.102–130, 157–158; 5.253; 6.327–342; 10.195; *J.W.* 3.405; 4.625; and the discussion by Gray, *Prophetic Figures*, 107–10.

180. So also Gray, *Prophetic Figures*, 109.

181. Marinus de Jonge, "Josephus und die Zukunftserwartungen seines Volkes," in *Josephus-Studien: Untersuchungen zu Josephus, dem antiken Judentum und dem Neuen Testament, Otto Michel zum 70. Geburtstag gewidmet*, ed. Otto Betz, Klaus Haacker, and Martin Hengel (Göttingen: Vandenhoeck & Ruprecht, 1974), 208; Aune, "ΠΡΟΦΗΤΗΣ"; Louis H. Feldman, "Prophets and Prophecy in Josephus," *JTS* 41 (1990): 410; Gnuse, *Dreams*, 25.

182. Josephus, *J.W.* 2.259, 261; 6.285–286; on which, see Gray, *Prophetic Figures*, 136.

title,[183] and that it was the fraudulent in the present who claimed the title, so he probably would have been aware that questions might have been raised about his own specific claims.[184]

Second, analogous to the Teacher of Righteousness, Paul exercised another role that likely would have been compromised if he openly portrayed himself as a prophet. That is, Paul also took on a mediating role among his readers (e.g., 1 Cor. 1:10–4:21), so that readily portraying himself as a prophet may have placed him too much over against his readers to mediate successfully.

Third, Paul's hesitation in taking up the title "prophet" may result from his view that there was a subtle but profound distinction between himself and the prophets of old. For, outside 1 Corinthians 12–14, he uses the term "prophet" for those who wrote Scripture (Rom. 1:2; 3:21; cf. 16:26) or, soberingly, who were killed by their own people![185] Moreover, Paul had come to the conclusion that he was living in a new age (2 Cor. 5:17) to which the scriptural prophets had looked forward.[186] To act as a prophet who, true to type, was involved in the miraculous was one thing, but to claim the title in the present may have given the impression that the old age persisted. Over against this reluctance to take up the title of prophet, Paul eagerly and publicly held onto the title "apostle" (see §5.4 [a] below). As we will see, in doing so, he understood himself to be functioning as a prophet in the scriptural tradition.[187]

3.5 Conclusions: Prophets, Prophecy, and the Miraculous

Since prophecy and prophesying were important aspects of Paul's self-understanding, in this chapter I have been enquiring whether such a role would have involved the miraculous. My investigation regarding how Paul and his readers would have understood the relation between prophets, prophecy, and the miraculous has produced some significant results. First, not only is the view that prophecy was not part of the Judaism of Paul's time to be set aside as unfounded, but we can also see that various forms of prophecy were flourishing in the activities of charismatic (or sign) prophets, seers, and oracular

183. See Amos 7:14; Zech. 13:5; cf. Homer, Od. 1.200–202; Philostratus, Vit. Apoll. 4.44. See Aune, "ΠΡΟΦΗΤΗΣ," 421; Gnuse, Dreams, 25.
184. Cf. Lester L. Grabbe, "Poets, Scribes, or Preachers: The Reality of Prophecy in the Second Temple Period," in Knowing the End from the Beginning: The Prophetic, the Apocalyptic and Their Relationships, ed. Lester L. Grabbe and Robert D. Haak (JSPSup 46; London: T&T Clark, 2003), 203–4.
185. Rom. 11:3; 1 Thess. 2:15. See Ashton, Religion of Paul, 184–85.
186. Sandnes, Paul, 243–44.
187. Cf. Aune, Prophecy, 202–3, 248.

prophets in the tradition of the classical prophets. Since an important part of Paul's self-understanding was that he stood in the tradition of the classical or scriptural prophets, I have sought to see how those who breathed the same cultural air as Paul related these prophets and the miraculous.

Second, we have seen that there was a strong and widespread connection made between the scriptural prophets and the miraculous, for the Dead Sea Scrolls, Sirach, Ezekiel the Tragedian, Philo, *Lives of the Prophets*, *Liber antiquitatum biblicarum*, and Josephus, classic prophets were involved in the miraculous and in conducting miracles. However, scriptural prophecy and miracle working were not taken as synonymous. None of the writers supposed that all scriptural prophets were miracle workers or associated with the miraculous. Even though, for ben Sira, miracle working was the most important activity of a prophet and the greatest miracle workers were prophets, not all prophets were miracle workers. Or, from the perspective of the Dead Sea Scrolls, not only were not all the prophets connected with the miraculous, but most references to miracle working are not linked with prophets or prophecy.

Moreover, even though a relationship between prophecy and the miraculous might be assumed for the past, this connection was not always affirmed for the present. We cannot, then, follow Ludwig Bieler to conclude that the miracle was a *conditio sine qua non* for the sage and prophet.[188] In particular, Philo portrays himself as a prophet and heir of Moses—whom he describes as a miracle worker—yet he does not in any way describe himself as involved in the miraculous. On the other hand, ben Sira not only connected prophecy and the miraculous in history, he also expected the figures of the past whom he applauded to be emulated by his readers. From what was noted earlier in this chapter (§3.2 above), this spectrum of possible relationships between prophecy and the miraculous would also have been familiar to Paul's non-Jewish audience, even though Paul was expecting them to understand him using scriptural categories.

The implication of this for our understanding of Paul and the miraculous is that although Paul lived and moved in a tradition that made firm and frequent connections between being a contemporary prophet and involvement in the miraculous, considering himself a prophet did not determine that he would be involved in performing miracles. Rather, taking up the role of a prophet or

---

188. Ludwig Bieler, ΘΕΙΟΣ ΑΝΗΡ: *Das Bild des "göttlichen Menschen" in Spätantike und Frühchristentum* (Vienna: Höfels, 1935), followed by Ernst Bammel, "John Did No Miracle," in *Miracles: Cambridge Studies in Their Philosophy and History*, ed. C. F. D. Moule (London: Mowbray, 1965), 181; and John Lierman, *The New Testament Moses: Christian Perceptions of Moses and Israel in the Setting of Jewish Religion* (WUNT 2/173; Tübingen: Mohr Siebeck, 2004), 53.

being seen as one only opened up the possibility, albeit a strong one, that Paul would be involved in the miraculous. How Paul using the probably equivalent term "apostle" for himself modifies this conclusion will become clear later (see §5.4 [a] below).

Third, in a number of bodies of literature we have seen that although prophets were associated with the miraculous, appearing to perform miracles, it is made clear that God was responsible for the marvel. Nevertheless, although it was God who was often credited with the miracle, the happening was also sometimes taken to legitimize the prophet. The miracle, though the work of God, could also reflect positively on the prophet.

Therefore, if the miraculous was part of Paul's ministry it is likely to have been seen by him, as well as by his readers, as God at work. Concomitantly, given that involvement in the miraculous was considered to reflect positively on the credibility of the prophet, Paul and his readers would likely, then, take any occurrence of the miraculous associated with his ministry as divine legitimation of it. Whether or not Paul took up the option to be involved in the miraculous beyond prophecy itself we will not discover until we examine his testimony (chap. 7). For the present, however, the task in the next chapter is to test whether or not Paul's missionary activity could be expected to involve the miraculous.

4

Proselytizing, Propaganda, and the Miraculous

The purpose of this chapter is to enquire if being involved in missionary preaching itself would have caused Paul, or those who knew him, to assume an involvement in the miraculous. In looking for connections Paul and his readers may have made between the miraculous and preaching or proselytizing, or having a message, as we noted at the beginning of chapter 2, we have to take into account that Paul was a citizen of a complex world. He traveled, preached, and worked, perhaps as a leather worker,[1] in a Greek world. Yet, he was also nurtured in, and had a message that arose from, the Jewish world; and he moved through the Mediterranean world primarily along the threads and knots of the Jewish Diaspora. Therefore, we need to enquire about the connections, if any, that both Jewish culture and other cultures of Paul's time made between propagandizing and the miraculous. We begin with the Jewish world, and the results are not as positive as one might expect.

4.1 A Jewish Mission?

Arguably, there were a number of factors causing Gentiles to become Jews: Jewish missionaries, Jewish literature, the synagogue and education, attractive

---

1. Luke says Paul was, like Priscilla and Aquila, a tentmaker (Acts 18:3), which Ronald F. Hock (*The Social Context of Paul's Ministry: Tentmaking and Apostleship* [Philadelphia: Fortress, 1980], e.g., 66) has shown to be leather working. Paul says only that he worked with his hands: "we grow weary from the work of our own hands" (κοπιῶμεν ἐργαζόμενοι ταῖς ἰδίαις χερσίν [1 Cor. 4:12]).

worship, good deeds, marriage, adoption, and force.[2] Also, God's direct intervention, in terms of miraculous activity or events, was thought to cause conversions to Judaism in the present,[3] as well as at the end of history.[4] However, our question is this: Were there Jewish missionaries at the time who combined preaching and miracle working so that those who heard Paul could have expected, or would not have been surprised, that he also performed miracles? For most of the twentieth century, the long-standing consensus was that in terms of "activity intended to win converts,"[5] the Judaism of Paul's time was a lively missionary religion.[6] According to George Foot Moore, for example, Judaism was "the first great missionary religion of the Mediterranean world."[7] Also, Joachim Jeremias begins his monograph *Jesus' Promise to the Nations* saying, "At the time of Jesus' appearance an unparalleled period of missionary activity was in progress in Israel."[8] In turn, it has been widely held that the Christian mission in which Paul was involved, to proselytize the Gentiles, was modeled on the Jewish mission to the nations.[9]

There had been some lone and largely unheard voices raising doubts about this view.[10] However, it was not until the last years of the twentieth century that

2. Scot McKnight, *A Light among the Gentiles: Jewish Missionary Activity in the Second Temple Period* (Minneapolis: Fortress, 1991), 50–68.

3. See Philo, *Mos.* 1.147; Josephus, *Ant.* 11.285–286; *J.W.* 2.454.

4. See Jdt. 11:23; 14:6–10; Tob. 13:11; Sir. 36:1–17; *2 Bar.* 54:18; *1 En.* 48:4–5; 50:1–5; 62:9–13; 90:30–33; 91:14; McKnight, *Light*, 50–51.

5. Rainer Riesner, "A Pre-Christian Jewish Mission," in *The Mission of the Early Church to Jews and Gentiles*, ed. Jostein Ådna and Hans Kvalbein (WUNT 127; Tübingen: Mohr Siebeck, 2000), 223.

6. E.g., Karl G. Kuhn, "προσήλυτος," *TDNT* 6:731 and n. 26; and A. Bertholet, W. Bousset, W. G. Braude, J. J. Collins, F. Hahn, D. Georgi, A. von Harnack, J. Jeremias, O. Michel, A. Oepke, K. G. Kuhn and H. Stegmann, J. S. Raisin, J. R. Rosenbloom, H. J. Schoeps, and M. Simon, cited by McKnight, *Light*, 2–3; and S. W. Baron, J. Juster, and Victor A. Tcherikover, cited and followed by Elizabeth Schüssler Fiorenza, "Miracles, Mission, and Apologetics: An Introduction," in *Aspects of Religious Propaganda in Judaism and Early Christianity*, ed. Elizabeth Schüssler Fiorenza (SJCA 2; Notre Dame, IN: University of Notre Dame Press, 1976), 2, 20n3. See also a discussion of the debates by Riesner, "Jewish Mission," 211–20.

7. George Foot Moore, *Judaism in the First Centuries of the Christian Era: The Age of the Tannaim*, 3 vols. (Cambridge, MA: Harvard University Press, 1958), 1:324.

8. Joachim Jeremias, *Jesus' Promise to the Nations*, trans. S. H. Hooke (SBT 24; London: SCM, 1967), 11; cf. 12–19. Cf. Dieter Georgi says that Judaism was "the greatest missionary religion to precede Christianity" ("Forms of Religious Propaganda," in *Jesus in His Time*, ed. Hans Jürgen Schultz, trans. Brian Watchorn [Philadelphia: Fortress, 1971], 126).

9. E.g., Jeremias, *Jesus' Promise*; Dieter Georgi, *The Opponents of Paul in Second Corinthians: A Study of Religious Propaganda in Late Antiquity* (Philadelphia: Fortress, 1986); John P. Dickson, *Mission-Commitment in Ancient Judaism and in the Pauline Communities: The Shape, Extent and Background of Early Christian Mission* (WUNT 2/159; Tübingen: Mohr Siebeck, 2003).

10. E.g., Joseph Dérenbourg, *Essai sur l'histoire et la géographie de la Palestine: D'après les Thalmuds et les autres sources rabbiniques* (1867; repr., Farnborough: Gregg International, 1971),

the tide began to turn against the consensus with a succession of publications. Notably, Scot McKnight argued that "Judaism never developed a clear mission to the Gentiles," concluding that "there is no evidence that could lead to the conclusion that Judaism was a 'missionary religion' in the sense of aggressive attempts to convert Gentiles or in the sense of self-identity."[11] The next year Édouard Will and Claude Orrieux arrived at the same conclusion.[12] In the following year Martin Goodman's investigation of a universal proselytizing mission among the Jews concluded similarly.[13] He went on to say that, "It was only in the third century that we can be certain that some rabbis began assuming the desirability of a mission to proselytize."[14] A review of the evidence supports these conclusions.

(a) Matthew 23:15. One of the centerpieces of evidence—for some, the only convincing evidence[15]—for the case for a pre-Christian Jewish mission to the Gentiles, which Paul may have modeled, has been Matthew 23:15: "Woe to you, scribes and Pharisees, hypocrites! For you cross sea and land to make a single convert [προσήλυτος], and you make [γένηται ποιεῖτε] the new convert twice as much a child of hell as yourselves." Yet, even if this saying can be traced back to Jesus,[16] it is open to question whether or not he had in mind the Pharisees attempting to convert Gentiles.[17] As McKnight, for example, argued, it is plausible that it refers to Pharisees attempting to make proselytes out of God-fearers.[18] Or, as Goodman argued, it could refer to Pharisees' "trying to persuade *other Jews* to follow Pharisaic halakha."[19] Other evidence for a Jewish mission that Paul could have emulated, on closer examination, also proves insecure.

(b) Horace. There is the statement by Horace (65–8 BCE) that is taken as evidence for a Jewish mission to the Gentiles: "We, like the Jews, will

---

227–28; Johannes Munck, *Paul and the Salvation of Mankind*, trans. Frank Clarke (London: SCM, 1959), 266–67; David Rokéah, *Jews, Pagans, and Christians in Conflict* (StPB 33; Jerusalem: Magnes; Leiden: Brill, 1982).

11. McKnight, *Light*, 116–17.

12. Édouard Will and Claude Orrieux, *Prosélytisme juif? Histoire d'une erreur* (Paris: Belles Lettres, 1992).

13. Goodman, *Mission and Conversion: Proselytizing in the Religious History of the Roman Empire* (Oxford: Clarendon, 1994). Cf. Martin Goodman, "Proselytising in Rabbinic Judaism," *JJS* 40 (1989): 175–85; L. J. (Bert Jan) Lietaert Peerbolte, *Paul the Missionary* (CBET 34; Louvain: Peeters, 2003), 19–53.

14. Goodman, *Mission*, 152. Cf. Goodman, "Proselytising."

15. Dérenbourg, *Essai*, 228, discussed by Riesner, "Jewish Mission," 211.

16. So, e.g., McKnight, *Light*, 106–8; Goodman, *Mission*, 69.

17. As interpreted by, e.g., James Carleton Paget, "Jewish Proselytism at the Time of Christian Origins: Chimera or Reality?" *JSNT* 62 (1996): 94–97.

18. McKnight, *Light*, 106–8.

19. Goodman, *Mission*, 70, emphasis original.

compel you to make one of our throng" (*veluti te Iudaei cogemus in hanc concedere turbam*, *Sat.* 1.4.142–43).[20] However, Horace makes no mention of Gentiles being compelled and could have in mind Jews using mass intimidation in lawsuits,[21] for the context of his discussion is politics and personal advantage, not religious propaganda.[22] Thus, Horace is of no help in providing evidence for a Jewish mission to the Gentiles in Paul's time or before.

(c) Synagogues. Open to the Gentiles, synagogues have also been taken as centers for proselytizing and the basis for seeing Judaism as a great missionary religion. Dieter Georgi, for example, attempted to make the case that the synagogues, particularly the worship, was the engine of Jewish missionary endeavor.[23] However, his evidence cannot bear the weight of his assertions.[24] For example, he makes use of Horace, whom we have just seen does not mention the Gentiles. Horace also makes no mention of the synagogue (*Sat.* 1.4.142–43).[25] Otherwise, where the evidence mentions the synagogue, there is nothing about the Gentiles (Philo, *Mos.* 2.909–916; *Hypoth.* 7.13); and where there is mention of the Gentiles, it is not in relation to the synagogue (Philo, *Mos.* 2.17–27). Further, the evidence is equally elusive when trying to show that Jews used the synagogues to educate Gentiles in order to make them proselytes.[26]

(d) Jewish Literature. The argument that Jewish literature written in Greek was used to win the Gentiles[27] need not detain us, for Paul did not use his letters to evangelize. In any case, even though this literature could lead to conversion to Christianity, as the Septuagint did for Tatian (*Oratio Graeco*

20. So, e.g., Menahem Stern, *Greek and Latin Authors on Jews and Judaism*, vol. 1, *From Herodotus to Plutarch* (Jerusalem: Israel Academy of Sciences and Humanities, 1974), §§127, 323; Georgi, *Opponents of Paul*, 97. The passage in Horace has been the subject of considerable attention; see H. Rushton Fairclough, *Horace* (LCL; Cambridge, MA: Harvard University Press; London: Heinemann, 1978), 60–61.

21. Further, and also on Philo, *Mos.* 2.25–44, see Goodman, *Mission*, 74–77.

22. E.g., John Nolland, "Proselytism or Politics in Horace Satires I, 4, 138–143?" *VC* 33 (1979): 353.

23. Georgi, *Opponents of Paul*, 83–90.

24. See Josephus, *J.W.* 7.45; Horace, *Sat.* 1.4.138–43; Juvenal, *Sat.* 14.96–106; Philo, *Mos.* 2.17–25, 26–27, 209–216; *Spec.* 2.62–63; *Hypoth.* 7.13.

25. Juvenal (*Sat.* 14.96–106) also says nothing about the synagogue or the Torah. See McKnight, *Light*, 64–65.

26. See Philo, *Mos.* 2.26–44; Josephus, *J.W.* 2.120; McKnight, *Light*, 66–67.

27. See, e.g., P. Dalbert, *Die Theologie der hellenistisch-jüdischen Missionsliteratur unter Ausschluss von Philo und Josephus* (TF 4; Hamburg-Volsdorf: Herbert Reich, 1954); Fergus Miller, "'God-Fearers' and 'Proselytes,'" in Emil Schürer, *The History of the Jewish People in the Age of Jesus Christ (175 B.C.–A.D. 135)*, trans. T. A. Burkill et al., 3 vols. (Edinburgh: T&T Clark, 1973–86), 3.1:160.

29),[28] long ago, Victor Tcherikover successfully showed that it is more than likely that the literature was addressed to Greek-speaking Jews.[29]

(e) Paul's competitors. Even though we are not finding evidence of a pre-Christian Jewish mission to the Gentiles, there are glimpses in Paul's writings of competitors who could be examples of Jewish missionary activity.[30] First, Paul accepts that his readers may have heard the gospel from one of the Twelve (1 Cor. 15:3–11), suggesting that he assumes other Jewish Christians were missionaries. Paul is also frustrated that the Galatians are being confused by some proclaiming a "different" gospel (Gal. 1:6–9; cf. 2:1–10). However, even though these are Jews (before there was a clear distinction between Jews and Christians) teaching Paul's readers to live like Jews (Ἰουδαΐζειν, "to Judaize," 2:14), they are still Christians. There is no evidence to conclude other than that, as Judaizers, they were most probably galvanized into action by Paul's work and, therefore, taking up a reactionary mission.[31]

Another place in the Pauline corpus where there may be more solid evidence of Jewish missionary activity is in the letter to the Colossians.[32] The author is combating circumcision (2:11–12) and teachings about asceticism, angel worship, festivals, and philosophy, for example (2:8, 16–18, 20), all of which are compatible with what might be propagated by Jewish preachers or missionaries in competition with Paul.[33] However, these missionaries are not trying to win Gentiles to their faith, but are seeking to correct Jews as well as Gentiles who have already joined (cf. 2:16–23) what they consider an aberrant form of Judaism. Given that we have no other evidence for traveling Jewish missionaries, it is most reasonable to assume that these missionaries came from the area that was heavily populated by Jews.[34] It turns out, then, that in

---

28. Cf. Goodman, *Mission*, 80.

29. Victor A. Tcherikover, "Jewish Apologetic Literature Reconsidered," *Eos* 48 (1956): 169–93. For a well-argued minority position, maintaining the importance of literature in winning Gentiles, see Louis H. Feldman, "Jewish Proselytism," in *Eusebius, Christianity, and Judaism*, ed. Harold W. Attridge and Gohei Hata (StPB 42; Leiden: Brill; Detroit: Wayne State University Press, 1992), 381–86.

30. Michael F. Bird, *Crossing over Sea and Land: Jewish Missionary Activity in the Second Temple Period* (Peabody, MA: Hendrickson, 2010), 136.

31. Bird (ibid., 136n8) anticipates this argument against his case, but he does not appear to appreciate the strength of the point that these Jewish missionaries were part of the Jesus movement.

32. Cf. ibid., 140–48. Regardless of whether or not Paul wrote the letter, the evidence is not changed in a way that would have any implications for the present study. On the authorship of Colossians, see §9.1 below.

33. See James D. G. Dunn, "The Colossian Philosophy: A Confident Jewish Apologia," *Bib* 76 (1995): 153–81, esp. those cited in 153n3.

34. See Cicero, *Flac.* 28.68; Josephus, *Ant.* 12.147–153. Cf. Paul R. Trebilco, *Jewish Communities in Asia Minor* (SNTSMS 69; Cambridge: Cambridge University Press, 1991), 8, 13–16;

Colossians we do not have evidence of a pre-Christian Jewish mission to the Gentiles, but further evidence of Jews seeking to correct those who want to belong to their faith.[35]

(f) Paul's pre-Christian Gentile Mission? Before his conversion, Paul himself may have been an example of Jewish missionary activity to the Gentiles. He protests to the Galatians, "Why am I still persecuted if I am still preaching circumcision?" (Gal. 5:11), implying in "still preach" (ἔτι κηρύσσω) that he had once been a Jewish preacher of circumcision.[36] It has been suggested this is evidence Paul had been a missionary to the Gentiles.[37] Without any other evidence that Paul had once been engaged in a mission to the Gentiles,[38] and it being unlikely that he preached circumcision after his conversion (see §6.6 below),[39] it is more likely that Paul is referring to his persecution of the church (1:13–14, 23; Phil. 3:4–6)—that is, his zeal to see "God-fearers" complete their conversion by undergoing circumcision.[40] In short, Paul's testimony is not evidence for the existence of a Jewish mission to Gentiles.

(g) Conclusions. There are other kinds of evidence that, in spite of an interest in the Gentiles who joined their communities,[41] suggest, in Paul's time, the Jews were not actively involved in a mission to the Gentiles. First, we know of no individual Jewish missionary in antiquity other than Paul.[42] Second, Philo and Josephus say nothing about mission to the Gentiles.[43]

What the evidence does show is Jews seeking to win sympathy among the Gentiles. For example, Josephus tells of a Jewish merchant, Ananias, trying to persuade Izates the king of Adiabene and his family to worship God (τὸν θεὸν σέβειν, *Ant.* 20.34). However, Ananias wished no more than to win the king's sympathy, for Josephus says Ananias was opposed to his conversion

Clinton E. Arnold, *The Colossian Syncretism: The Interface between Christianity and Folk Belief at Colossae* (Grand Rapids: Baker Academic, 1996), 196.

35. Contrast Bird, *Sea and Land*, 147–48.

36. E.g., Richard N. Longenecker, *Galatians* (WBC 41; Dallas: Word, 1990), 232–33.

37. E.g., Hans Joachim Schoeps, *Paul: The Theology of the Apostle in Light of the Jewish Religious History*, trans. Harold Knight (London: Lutterworth, 1961), 219; Günther Bornkamm, *Paul*, trans. D. M. G. Stalker (London: Hodder & Stoughton, 1971), 12.

38. Martin Hengel, *The Pre-Christian Paul* (London: SCM, 1991), 58–59.

39. To the contrary, e.g., McKnight, *Light*, 104–5.

40. Ibid.

41. E.g., CD-A IX, 1; XI, 15; XII, 6, 9; XIV, 5–6; XV, 5–6; Josephus, *Ag. Ap.* 2.209–210, 261; *J.W.* 2.560–561; 7.45. See McKnight, *Light*, 38, 41.

42. Ernst Barnikol (*Die vorchristliche und frühchristliche zeit des Paulus: Nach seinen geschichtlichen und geographischen selbstzeugnissen im Galaterbrief* [FEUNTK 1; Kiel: W. G. Mühlau, 1929], 18–20) proposed to read out of Gal. 1:13–16 the idea that Paul had already been a Jewish missionary preacher of circumcision to the Gentiles. Schoeps (*Paul*, 64n2) cautions that although this possibility cannot be excluded, "Unfortunately we know just nothing about it."

43. Goodman, *Mission*, 85–90, esp. 85.

(20.38–41).[44] Therefore, while Jewish theology was inherently universal,[45] and there are some texts that show a theological consciousness of mission,[46] in terms of activity by Jews intended to win converts, although not all are convinced,[47] Rainer Riesner is correct to conclude that the evidence "does not allow us to speak of a pre-Christian Jewish mission."[48]

If the Jewish religion of Paul's day was not a lively missionary religion, if there were no missionaries attempting to persuade the Gentiles to be converted, at least on these grounds, not only was his seeking to convert Gentiles novel,[49] we also cannot expect to find him, or those who knew him, making any assumptions about a relationship between his proselytizing and the miraculous. However, this conclusion may require nuancing in light of what we know of activities in the wider Greek world.

4.2 Greek Peripatetic Philosophers and the Miraculous

Cult centers where, among other things, the voice of the gods and miracles of healing were sought were part of the cultural landscape of the Hellenistic world.[50] Greek history is also well endowed with stories of seers, healers, and miracle workers. For example, Melampus is said to have had mantic skills,[51] Menecates healed epileptics,[52] and Euphemus the Argonaut ran over the sea without getting his feet wet.[53] Also, taking the early philosophers, such as Aristeas (Herodotus, *Hist.* 4.13–15) and Zalmoxis (Plato, *Charm.* 156d–158b),

---

44. See also Josephus, *Ant.* 8.117; *J.W.* 7.45; and the brief discussion by Goodman, *Mission*, 86–87.

45. See Gen. 1:1–2:3; Sir. 18:13; Philo, *Decal.* 41–42, 64–65; Josephus, *Ant.* 2.94, 122, 152; 3.281; *Ag. Ap.* 2.146; McKnight, *Light*, 26.

46. See Wis. 18:4; *2 En.* 33:9; 48:7–8; Philo, *Spec.* 2.162–167; *Somn.* 1.175–178; McKnight, *Light*, 46–47.

47. E.g., David Rokéah, "Ancient Jewish Proselytism in Theory and Practice," *TZ* 52 (1996): 206–24, esp. 223–24.

48. Riesner, "Jewish Mission," 211–50.

49. Paula Fredriksen, "Judaism, the Circumcision of Gentiles, and Apocalyptic Hope: Another Look at Galatians 1 and 2," *JTS* 42 (1991): 532–64.

50. On healing in the sanctuaries, see, e.g., Fritz Graf, "Heilungtum und Ritual: Das Beispiel der griechisch-römischen Asklepieia," in *Le sanctuaire grec: Huit exposés suivis de discussions*, ed. Albert Schachter (EAC 37; Geneva: Fondation Hardt, 1992), 158–203, esp. 186–93.

51. E.g., Homer, *Od.* 11.281–97; 15.222–42.

52. E.g., Plutarch, *Ages.* 21; *Apoph. Iac.* 213A; Athenaeus, *Deipn.* 7.289a–f.

53. E.g., Pindar, *Pyth.* 4.61. Further, see, e.g., the lists in Barry L. Blackburn, "'Miracle Working ΘΕΙΟΙ ΑΝΔΡΕΣ' in Hellenism (and Hellenistic Judaism)," in *The Miracles of Jesus*, ed. David Wenham and Craig Blomberg (GP 6; Sheffield: JSOT Press, 1986), 185–218, esp. 187; Barry L. Blackburn, *Theios Anēr and the Markan Miracle Traditions* (WUNT 2/40; Tübingen: Mohr Siebeck, 1991), 13–96.

as the heirs of the wise seer or shaman, the Greeks had long associated the philosopher and the preternatural.[54]

Our interest, however, is not simply in the miracle workers or even with those who were also philosophers. Rather, our interest is in individuals who combined traveling with miracle working and philosophizing or propaganda. We can expect these individuals as a type, or stories about them, to have caused those who knew Paul to understand him in a particular way, to expect the work of this traveling preacher to be accompanied by the miraculous or miracle working. It is widely agreed that such individuals existed in large numbers.

Dieter Georgi says that, in Paul's time, "not only the cult places, but also the alleys and markets of the ancient cities, as well as the rest areas on the more important long-distance and rural roads, were full of the noise and bustle of the most diverse religious and philosophical recruiters." He also goes on to say that, "Healings and exorcisms were offered as exceptional deals, as well as magic arts, astrological knowledge and practices, oracles, and more."[55] More pointedly in relation to our interests, Elizabeth Schüssler Fiorenza tells us, "In the Greco-Roman world the wandering preachers and missionaries sought to attract the attention of their audience and to demonstrate the exceptional character of their message by miraculous deeds and powerful speech."[56]

However, the evidence we have that can reliably inform us about what would have been known by Paul and his contemporaries concerning those who combined traveling and philosophizing or preaching with the miraculous in some way, suggests we should draw a more restrained and nuanced conclusion. For, as we will see, much of the evidence is indirect. That is, the evidence comes from literature that is either from before or after Paul's time. If these sources are to be useful to us, they must be shown to reflect what Paul and his contemporaries would have known.

(a) Abaris. To begin with, there is the legendary peripatetic figure Abaris, who healed with "charms" (ἐπῳδοί, Plato, Charm. 158b; cf. Herodotus, Hist. 4.36).[57] Given that this shadowy figure does not emerge with any clarity or association with philosophy until the third century of our era (e.g., Iamblichus, Vit. pyth. 20), it is unlikely that stories of him informed Paul or those who knew him.

---

54. See E. R. Dodds, *The Greeks and the Irrational* (Berkeley: University of California Press, 1951), 135–78; F. M. Cornford, *Principium sapientiae: The Origins of Greek Philosophical Thought* (Cambridge: Cambridge University Press, 1952), 65, 88–126.

55. Georgi, *Opponents of Paul*, 152, relying on Arthur Darby Nock, *Conversion: The Old and the New in Religion from Alexander the Great to Augustine of Hippo* (Oxford: Oxford University Press, 1933), 83–91, 101–5. Nock, however, offers scant support for Georgi's statements.

56. Schüssler Fiorenza, "Miracles," 10.

57. See, e.g., Erwin Rohde, *Psyche: The Cult of Souls and the Belief in Immortality among the Greeks*, trans. W. B. Hillis (1925; repr., London: Routledge, 2001), 300–303, esp. 300n108.

(b) Pythagoras. Potentially more important are the traditions about Pythagoras, who lived in sixth-century BCE Croton, an Achaean colony on the "toe" of Italy.[58] Early stories about Pythagoras mention his travel to Egypt (Isocrates, *Bus.* 11.28; cf. Herodotus, *Hist.* 2.81.2) and, perhaps, to other places, including to Croton from the Aegean island Samos, his place of birth.[59] According to Antiphon a century later, he was already teaching while he was still on Samos (Porphyry, *Vit. pyth.* 9). Dicaearchus, a pupil of Aristotle, says Pythagoras was a powerful and captivating speaker.[60] And miracle working was also early associated with him in that his near contemporary Heraclitus saw him as the "chief of charlatans" or liars (κοπίδων ἀρχηγός, frg. 81.4) and also thought him a "fraud" (κακοτεχνία),[61] using a word that brings to mind the wonder worker.[62] In the fourth century BCE Aristotle took this well-traveled philosopher to be involved in the miraculous, saying that he was seen by many people in two different places at the same time, that he had a golden thigh, prophesied, and killed a poisonous snake by biting it.[63] These Pythagorean stories of peripatetic preaching involving the miraculous are also found in the works of Diogenes Laertius, writing in the first half of the third century of our era,[64] and in Porphyry, writing toward the end of that century,[65] and Iamblichus (c. 245–c. 325 CE),[66] writing a little later. This shows that these stories probably remained in circulation through the period in which Paul lived, and they likely formed part of the interpretive grid for those who knew him and his work.

(c) Empedocles. Next to take into account are fragments of the poetry of Empedocles (c. 494–c. 434 BCE).[67] In one fragment, addressing a crowd in his

58. For extant sources for Pythagoras, see Walter Burkert, *Lore and Science in Ancient Pythagoreanism*, trans. Edwin L. Minar Jr. (Cambridge, MA: Harvard University Press, 1972), 109n64.

59. Aristoxenus, frg. 16 // Porphyry, *Vit. pyth.* 9; Herodotus, *Hist.* 4.95; Dicaearchus, frg. 33 // Porphyry, *Vit. pyth.* 18. See the discussion in Burkert, *Lore and Science*, 112n16.

60. Dicaearchus, frg. 33 // Porphyry, *Vit. pyth.* 18. See Geoffrey S. Kirk, J. E. Raven, and M. Schofield, *The Presocratic Philosophers: A Critical History with a Selection of Texts*, 2nd ed. (Cambridge: Cambridge University Press, 1983), 226–27.

61. Heraclitus, frg. 129 // Diogenes Laertius, *Vit.* 8.6.

62. Burkert, *Lore and Science*, 161–62.

63. Aristotle, frg. 191 // Apollonius Paradoxographus, *Hist. mir.* 6; Kirk, Raven, and Schofield, *Presocratic Philosophers*, 228–29 (#274).

64. David T. Runia, "Diogenes Laertius," *New Pauly* 4 (2004): 452.

65. See Michael Chase, "Porphyrius," *New Pauly* 11 (2007): 646–47.

66. Iamblichus, *Vit. pyth.* 28. See Massimo Fusillo and Lucia Galli, "Iamblichus (2)," *New Pauly* 6 (2005): 666.

67. On the fragments, see Brad Inwood, *The Poem of Empedocles: A Text and Translation with Introduction* (Toronto: University of Toronto Press, 2001). On the identity and date of Empedocles, see Aristotle, *Metaph.* A3, 984a11; Diogenes Laertius, *Vit.* 8.51, 58, 74; Simplicius,

home, Acragas in Sicily, Empedocles describes himself as a peripatetic and as
teaching, as well as performing healings. He says: "I go about among you all an
immortal god, mortal no more. . . . Whenever I enter the prosperous townships
with these my followers, men and women both, I am revered; they follow me
in countless numbers, asking where lies the path to gain, some seeking prophecies, while others, for many a day stabbed by grievous pains, beg to hear the
word that heals all manner of illness" (frg. 112).[68] Even if this fragment cannot
be traced back to Empedocles,[69] its awkward fit in Diogenes Laertius, as well
as parts of the fragment being quoted in part elsewhere,[70] suggest that he has
taken it up and is maintaining an established tradition.[71] The miracle working
that Empedocles is said to be associated with is not so much healing *in situ* as
suggesting cures. For, the question "where lies the path to gain" (πρὸς κέδρος
ἀταρπός) is the general question that includes the questioner wanting a remedy
for sickness rather than expecting Empedocles to heal on the spot.[72]

   In another fragment, also found in Diogenes Laertius, Empedocles promises
a follower that he will "learn all the drugs that are a defense to ward off ills
and old age" (frg. 111).[73] On the grounds that Empedocles's work shows an
interest in the human body and its functions,[74] and that later writers see him
as the founder of the Sicilian medical school, it may be reasonable to conclude that he was early thought to have acumen in healing.[75] In the traditions
related to Empedocles, therefore, we probably have an example of the idea of
the combination of itinerant teaching and miracle working stretching back
across and including the time of Paul.

   (d) Plato. A generation after Empedocles, early in the fourth century BCE,
Plato writes of itinerant priests going door-to-door with a message claiming
that they could atone for offenses, and that their initiations were effective
against suffering in the afterlife. As well, with some cynicism, Plato says they
claimed to be able to injure an enemy (*Resp.* 364b–365a) and cure madness

---

In Phys. 25.19; and discussion by, e.g., M. R. Wright, *Empedocles: The Extant Fragments* (New
Haven: Yale University Press, 1981), 3–6.
   68. Diogenes Laertius, *Vit.* 8.54, 61, 66; cf. 8.52; Diodorus Siculus, *Bib. hist.* 13.83.2; Clement,
Strom. 6.30.3. See Wright, *Empedocles*, 134.
   69. For an argument that the fragment is a reliable reflection of Empedocles, see Simon
Trépanier, *Empedocles: An Interpretation* (New York: Routledge, 2004), 48–49.
   70. See above, and also the discussion by Wright, *Empedocles*, 134, 264–67.
   71. Cf. Jørgen Mejer, *Diogenes Laertius and His Hellenistic Background* (HE 40; Wiesbaden:
Steiner, 1978), 2–29.
   72. Wright, *Empedocles*, 266–67.
   73. Diogenes Laertius, *Vit.* 8.59. See Wright, *Empedocles*, 261–63.
   74. E.g., frg. 2 (Sextus Empiricus, *Math.* 7.123); frg. 4 (Sextus Empiricus, *Math.* 7.125).
   75. W. K. C. Guthrie, *A History of Greek Philosophy*, 6 vols. (Cambridge: University Press,
1962–81), 2:132 and n. 3.

(*Phraedr*. 244d–245a).[76] Although Plato does not give the number of these wandering priests who could heal, his point is made on their being well known. In that Plato was widely read in the Hellenistic world,[77] it is probable that his portrait of traveling speakers involved in the miraculous was also well and widely known in Paul's time.

(e) *Cynics*. Sometimes Cynics and Cynicism are taken to be important in helping understand Christian beginnings, including Paul.[78] However, for two centuries before Paul Cynicism had experienced a period of obscurity that continued until its revival after his time, in the last quarter of the first century CE.[79] Nevertheless, in Paul's time the memory of Cynicism probably was available and important in understanding him. For, Diogenes Laertius maintains the tradition that the Cynic Menippus of Gadara, who probably flourished in the first half of the third century BCE,[80] was accomplished in "wonder working" or "quackery" (τερατεία, Diogenes Laertius, *Lives* 6.102).[81] Diogenes Laertius also claims that Menippus had come back from Hades and would return there to report on sins committed (*Lives* 6.102; cf. Lucian, *Men.* 1). Writing a little earlier, Lucian of Samosta[82] says Menippus sought out a wise and skilled Chaldean who, acting much like those described in the magical papyri—invoking spirits, sprinkling blood, and whispering and then shouting, often meaningless multisyllabic words[83]—paves the way for

76. On setting "Orphic" (in the *Republic*) and "Dionysiac" (in the *Phraedrus*) side by side, as also in Strabo, *Geogr.* 10.3.23, see Walter Burkert, "Craft Versus Sect: The Problem of Orphic and Pythagoreans," in *Jewish and Christian Self-Definition*, vol. 3, *Self-Definition in the Graeco-Roman World*, ed. Ben F. Meyer and E. P. Sanders (Philadelphia: Fortress, 1982), 4–5.

77. See, e.g., John Dillon, *The Middle Platonists: 80 B.C. to A.D. 220* (Ithaca, NY: Cornell University Press, 1996).

78. Cf., e.g., F. Gerald Downing, *Jesus and the Threat of Freedom* (London: SCM, 1987); F. Gerald Downing, *Cynics and Christian Origins* (Edinburgh: T&T Clark, 1992); F. Gerald Downing, *Cynics, Paul, and the Pauline Churches: Cynics and Christian Origins II* (London: Routledge, 1998).

79. Donald R. Dudley, *A History of Cynicism: From Diogenes to the Sixth Century A.D.* (1938; repr., Hildesheim: G. Olms, 1967), 117–42.

80. Diogenes Laertius most probably confuses Menedemus with Menippus. See the corresponding description of Menippus by Lucian, *Menippus*, and the *Suda*; see Immanuel Bekker, *Suidae Lexicon* (Berolini: G. Reimeri, 1854), 1078 (φαιός, "dark"), citing Diogenes, *Vit.* 6.102. Cf., e.g., Dudley, *History of Cynicism*, 61; Joel C. Relihan, "Menippus in Antiquity and the Renaissance," in *The Cynics: The Cynic Movement in Antiquity and Its Legacy*, ed. R. Bracht Branham and Marie-Odile Goulet-Cazé (Berkeley: University of California Press, 1996), 275; cf. 279n45.

81. See LSJ, "τερατεία," 1776.

82. Lucian was born between 115 and 125 CE and died between the late 180s and the early 190s. See Heinz-Günther Nesselrath, "Lucianus of Samosata," *New Pauly* 7 (2005): 836–37.

83. See Graham H. Twelftree, "Jesus the Exorcist and Ancient Magic," in *A Kind of Magic: Understanding Magic in the New Testament and Its Religious Environment*, ed. Michael Labahn and Bert Jan Lietaert Peerbolte (LNTS 306; London: T&T Clark, 2007), 63–78.

the return visit to Hades (Lucian, *Men.* 9–10). We cannot be certain how much, if any, of this characterization is to be traced back to Menippus.[84] Notwithstanding, in that both Diogenes Laertius and Lucian are relying on earlier sources and are agreed on his preternatural journey, it is reasonable to assume this is evidence that the memory of peripatetic Cynics was part of Paul's world, and that they were taken to have been involved in at least this kind of miraculous activity. How this memory could have been realized can be seen in Peregrinus.

(f) *Peregrinus.* Lucian of Samosata says that Peregrinus, whose life ended with self-immolation (Lucian, *Peregr.* 35–36) at the 165 CE Olympic games (20), met and joined the Christians in Palestine, soon becoming a leader (11).[85] Peregrinus was clearly a traveler, as his Latin name ("foreigner" or "stranger") implies.[86] However, the involvement of Peregrinus in miracles is mentioned only after he had become a Christian: "It would be nothing unnatural if, among all the dolts that there are, some should be found to assert they were relieved of quartan fevers by him" (28). Nevertheless, Lucian portrays Peregrinus coming to the Christians fully accomplished: "In a trice he made them all look like children; for he was prophet, cult-leader, head of the synagogue, and everything, all by himself" (11). Lucian probably, then, intended his readers to assume that, before becoming a Christian, Peregrinus was already involved in the miraculous as a Cynic, and that the speaking and the miraculous combined to make him attractive.

With so many parallels between Lucian's portrait of Peregrinus and Alexander the false prophet, including their miracle working (Lucian, *Peregr.* 28; *Alex.* 5–6),[87] it is difficult to be sure of any details. Further, we are suspicious of the miraculous in Lucian's portrait of Peregrinus when we take into account what Aulus Gellius says around the same time. In his *Attic Nights* Gellius says Peregrinus was "a man of dignity and fortitude, living in a hut outside the city. And visiting him frequently, I heard him say many things that were in truth helpful and noble" (*Noc. att.* 12.11.1–6). Here there is no hint of the wonders and showy leadership.

84. William D. Desmond (*Cynics* [Berkeley: University of California Press, 2008], 37) is "dubious." Joel C. Relihan (*Ancient Menippean Satire* [Baltimore: Johns Hopkins University Press, 1993], 45 and n. 38) is more confident because of a reference in the *Suda*, "φαιός."

85. See, e.g., C. P. Jones, *Culture and Society in Lucian* (Cambridge, MA: Harvard University Press, 1986), 117–32.

86. E.g., Cicero, *De or.* 1.249; Horace, *Ep.* 1.17.62; Tacitus, *Dial.* 1.7.4.

87. Graham Anderson, *Lucian: Theme and Variation in the Second Sophistic* (MBCBSup 41; Leiden: Brill, 1976), 72–74. On Alexander Abonouteichus, see Louis Robert, *À travers l'Asie Mineure: Poètes et prosateurs, monnaies grecques, voyageurs et géographie* (BEFAR 239; Athens: École française d'Athènes, 1980), 393–421.

Yet, not only could Cynicism and Neo-Pythagoreanism have been fused at the time, but Peregrinus (the Cynic) may also have modeled himself on Pythagoras,[88] whom we have just seen was associated with the miraculous. Moreover, Athenagoras, addressing his *Embassy for the Christians* to Marcus Aurelius in about 177, supports his reputation as a miracle worker. Only a dozen years after the death of Peregrinus, Athenagoras tells of the statue of Peregrinus at Troy giving oracles, and associates it with other statues that healed the sick.[89] In short, it is reasonable to conclude that although we may have little confidence in the details of Lucian's portrait, Peregrinus probably was associated with miracle working. His existence, then, helps contribute to our knowledge of what would have been known, if not in Paul's time about traveling teachers who were involved in the miraculous, at least how the memory of Cynicism could have been realized.

(g) Apollonius of Tyana. From nearer Paul's time, Apollonius, born early in the first century CE at Tyana (around ninety-five miles [153 kilometers] north of Tarsus),[90] is the best known and documented example of an itinerant speaker involved in the miraculous.[91] Much that survives about Apollonius is considered secondary.[92] Nevertheless, the various traditions are agreed that he was a prophet and performed miracles, including exorcisms (Philostratus, *Vit. Apoll.* 4.10; Lactantius, *Epit.* 5.3),[93] though there is nothing to suggest any relationship between the speaking and the miraculous.

Even though it is difficult to establish the authenticity of any one of the stories associated with him, taking into consideration independent traditions, the stories that most likely belong to the historical Apollonius are him knowing (in Ephesus) of the murder of Domitian in Rome (Dio Cassius, *History* 67.18.1; Philostratus, *Vit. Apoll.* 8.26) and, also in Ephesus, of him learning from the twitter of birds that grain had been spilt some distance away (Porphyry, *Abst.* 3.3; Philostratus, *Vit. Apoll.* 4.2–3). There is also some independent agreement that he was thought to provide talismans.[94] That he is independently associated

88. See Hazel H. Hornsby, "The Cynicism of Peregrinus Proteus," in *Die Kyniker in der modernen Forschung: Aufsätze mit Einführung und Bibliographie*, ed. Margarethe Billerbeck (BSP 15; Amsterdam: B. R. Grüner, 1991), 173–76.
89. Athenagoras, *Leg.* 26.3–5; see cf. Hornsby, "Peregrinus Proteus," 167. On the dating of Athenagoras's *Embassy for the Christians*, see Bernard Pouderon, *Supplique au sujet des chrétiens; et, Sur la résurrection des morts* (SC 379; Paris: Cerf, 1992), 23–30.
90. W. W. Ramsay, "Cilicia, Tarsus, and the Great Tarsus Pass," *Geographical Journal* 22 (1903): 357–413, esp. 388.
91. Ewen Bowie, "Apollonius of Tyana: Tradition and Reality," *ANRW* II.16.2 (1978): 1652–99.
92. Ibid.; Maria Dzielska, *Apollonius of Tyana in Legend and History*, trans. Piotr Pienkowski (PRSA 10; Rome: L'Erma di Bretschneider, 1986).
93. Bowie, "Apollonius of Tyana," 1686–87.
94. Ibid., 1686n135.

with mainland Greece, Ephesus, Antioch, Byzantium, Tyana, and, less securely, other places[95] suggests he was known as a philosopher and miracle worker who traveled a great deal in the same regions and period as Paul.

(h) Conclusions. This examination of what was known in the Hellenistic world about traveling teachers who were also thought to be involved in the miraculous has shown that we have no direct evidence from the second century BCE to the second century CE of any such figures. Indirectly, however, we have second-century CE evidence of Apollonius of Tyana, one of Paul's contemporaries, probably combining his peripatetic philosophizing with some miracle working and the miraculous. We cannot conclude that no other such figures existed. However, no evidence has turned up to support the view that, in the time of Paul, the roads were full of the noise of wandering preachers using miracles to attract attention.[96]

Instead, from the second and third centuries CE, when there was a revival of interest in such figures, we have literature—with roots in the sometimes-distant past that probably remained in circulation across the period in which Paul lived—carrying the memory of wandering preachers or philosophers who were thought to be associated with the miraculous. This is probably sufficient to show that, while it could not be said that for Paul to travel about as a preacher he would have been expected to be involved in the miraculous, any miracle working and preaching of his could have been well accommodated and understood as expressions of different aspects of his skill. However, we have found nothing to suggest that the miracles had any particular connection between the message and the miraculous or would have been assumed to prove anything beyond contributing to the reputation of the individual.

4.3 Conclusions

In this chapter I set out to see if Paul's involvement in missionary preaching would have given rise to the expectation that the miraculous would be part of his work. For, the claim is made that Paul and his audience would have been very familiar with traveling preachers who offered healings and exorcisms to gain attention and followers. However, my endeavor to identify connections that Paul and those who knew him would have made between proselytizing and

95. Ibid., 1686–87.
96. See 98nn55–56 above. Cf. Eric Eve, who says, "The evidence for other miracle-working figures in Israel of Jesus' day is quite sparse. Apart from exorcist the only known candidates from contemporary miracle-workers are the charismatic holy men depicted in rabbinic literature and the sign prophets reported by Josephus" (*The Healer from Nazareth: Jesus' Miracles in Historical Context* [London: SPCK, 2009], 12–13).

miracle working that would have required or encouraged Paul to be involved in the miraculous has not been as fruitful as some would have expected.

On the one hand, it is not likely that, as Jews, Paul or his audience would have assumed he would be involved in the miraculous simply on the basis of his being a missionary to the Gentiles. There was no Jewish mission directed to the Gentiles that could have provided a model for their thinking; Paul is the first known Jewish missionary. Nor, on the other hand, were there models in the wider world on which to draw that would have given rise to the expectation that Paul would have been a miracle worker. Despite claims to the contrary that we noted, we also have no direct evidence from Paul's period of any peripatetic teachers in the wider Hellenistic world including the miraculous in their work. Nevertheless, although there may have been no living models for what Paul was doing, there were memories. From what can be gleaned from later sources, it is likely that there were traditions available in Paul's time that carried the memory of earlier associations between proselytizing and the miraculous. Therefore, it is important for the present project to note that Paul's traveling and preaching for converts would not raise expectations of the miraculous. Although any such activity would have been understood in light of the traditions as one of his skills attracting attention, it would not have proved anything in particular. To understand any impulse to be involved in the miraculous, and what that might mean for Paul and his readers, we have to turn elsewhere. And as we turn to consider the impact on Paul of the Christianity that he inherited, it will become obvious that the conclusions to this chapter need to be refined significantly.

5

The Christianity Paul Inherited

Jesus had the reputation of a powerful and prolific miracle worker. Yet, with his earliest known interpreter apparently saying little or nothing about miracles and the miraculous in his own ministry, it is not unreasonable to suppose that Paul had little or no knowledge of Jesus, and certainly not of his miracle working. Paul, then, was not so much an interpreter of Jesus,[1] but an innovator,[2] the second founder of Christianity,[3] developing a Christianity that did not include an interest in the miraculous. Also, it could be, as Albert Schweitzer long ago supposed, that the Christianity Paul inherited had a diminished interest in the miraculous, playing a decisive role in explaining the difference between Paul and Jesus.[4] Or, as James Dunn supposes, the allusiveness in Paul's use of Jesus tradition is because "substantial amounts" were "in the common discourse and worship of the churches" so that Paul rarely needed to cite it.[5] Therefore, in order to see in what ways the Christianity Paul inherited, and the Jesus he knew, could have influenced his views and practice in relation to the miraculous, in this chapter I will do three things.

1. Victor P. Furnish ("The Jesus-Paul Debate: From Baur to Bultmann," in *Paul and Jesus: Collected Essays*, ed. Alexander J. M. Wedderburn [JSNTSup 37; Sheffield: JSOT Press, 1989], 47) cites Gloatz, Wellhausen, Harnack, and Deissmann as holding this view.

2. Furnish (ibid., 47), cites F. W. Nietzsche, who called Paul "crafty," Ray Knight, who said he was "profound," as did F. C. Baur, H. Weinel, and P. Wernle.

3. Cf. William Wrede, *Paul*, trans. Edward Lummis (1908; repr., Eugene, OR: Wipf & Stock, 2001), 197.

4. Albert Schweitzer, *Paul and His Interpreters: A Critical History*, trans. W. Montgomery (London: Black, 1912), 160.

5. James D. G. Dunn, *The Theology of Paul the Apostle* (Grand Rapids: Eerdmans, 1998), 17; cf. 183–89.

First, given that Paul's conversion and call took place somewhere between 30 and 35 CE,[6] and that he was executed in the early 60s CE,[7] I will attempt to describe the place of miracles and the miraculous in Christian traditions in this period. Second, I will marshal evidence, slight though it be, showing that Paul was aware of and influenced by this Christianity. I may not be able to offer a definitive answer on the degree of this influence, but we will be able to see something of the nature and likely extent of this influence. Third, we will see if, and in what ways, the knowledge and relationship Paul supposed that he had concerning Jesus would have influenced the place of the miraculous in his ministry. However, before proceeding to discuss the miraculous in the Christianity Paul inherited, there is a problem to be solved.

5.1 Paul and Early Christianity

Paul appears to make conflicting statements about the origin of his gospel, or his relationship to earlier Christians. In 1 Corinthians 15:3 he sets out what is generally agreed to be a statement he has taken up from earlier Christians: "that Christ died for our sins . . . that he was buried . . . that he was raised . . . and that he appeared . . ." (15:3–5).[8] Yet, in Galatians 1:11–12 Paul is at pains to stress that the gospel he proclaims "is not of human origin" (1:11), that he did not receive it from a human source, nor, he says, was he taught it (1:12; cf. 1:16–17). In this Paul may be expressing his distance from early Christian traditions, making it futile, or at least not very productive, to explore the possibility that he was positively influenced by them.

However, here in Galatians Paul is not defending the origins of the tenets or the verbal content of his message.[9] From his phrase "is not of human origin" (1:11),[10] and what he goes on to say about God being pleased to reveal his Son

6. See the discussion and those cited in Rainer Riesner, *Paul's Early Period: Chronology, Mission Strategy, Theology*, translated by Doug Stott (Grand Rapids: Eerdmans, 1998), §1, §4.2; Rainer Riesner, "Pauline Chronology," in *The Blackwell Companion to Paul*, ed. Stephen Westerholm (Malden, MA; Chichester: Wiley-Blackwell, 2011), 9–29, suggesting 31/32 CE.

7. Udo Schnelle, *Apostle Paul: His Life and Theology*, trans. M. Eugene Boring (Grand Rapids: Baker Academic, 2005), 55–56, 381–86; Robert Jewett, *Dating Paul's Life* (London: SCM, 1979), 102.

8. E.g., see the influential treatment by Oscar Cullmann, "The Tradition," in *The Early Church: Five Essays*, ed. A. J. B. Higgins, trans. A. J. B. Higgins and S. Godman (London: SCM, 1966), 59–75; and more recently, Anders Eriksson, *Traditions as Rhetorical Proof: Pauline Argumentation in 1 Corinthians* (ConBNT 29; Stockholm: Almqvist & Wiksell, 1998), 86–97.

9. As supposed by Dunn, *Theology of Paul*, 177.

10. Paul's phrase οὐκ ἔστιν κατὰ ἄνθρωπον made use of a familiar Greek idiom meaning "human." Otherwise in Paul, see Rom. 3:5; 1 Cor. 9:8; Gal. 3:15. See also BDAG, "ἄνθρωπος," 1(c), and the discussion by James D. G. Dunn, *Galatians* (BNTC; Peabody, MA: Hendrickson, 1993), 52.

to him so that he might proclaim him among the Gentiles (1:13–16), the issue Paul is attempting to establish is not the content of his gospel. Rather, he is concerned to establish that it was his commission that he received from God rather than humans. This is all but confirmed in that, having established that it was God who had set him apart (1:15–16), Paul concludes his case by repeating the earlier point: "I did not immediately consult flesh and blood, nor did I go up to Jerusalem to those who were apostles before me" (1:16–17, my translation).

Also to consider in Paul's understanding of his relationship with earlier Christians is 1 Corinthians 11:23. Paul says, "For I received from [ἀπό] the Lord what I also handed on to you." Initially, it might be concluded that Paul is saying the ensuing information about the Lord's Supper was communicated to him directly from the Lord.[11] Codex Bezae (early fifth century),[12] for example, probably took it this way and clarified the point by replacing Paul's "from" (ἀπό) with "from the side of" (παρά). However, it is generally agreed that Paul is taking for granted that the normal processes of transmission of traditions are involved.[13] Not only is Paul's language—"receive" (παραλαμβάνω) and "hand on" (παραδίδωμι)—characteristic for transmitting human traditions,[14] but his choice of words suggests he is also conveying information that is most probably also known independently of him (cf. Mark 14:22–24).[15] Further, given that something directly "from the Lord" probably would be conveyed in distinctly Pauline language, it is surprising that what Paul says he is handing on carries many distinctly un-Pauline features.[16] Moreover, it is also possible that in the phrase "that also I handed over to you" (ὃ καὶ παρέδωκα ὑμῖν) Paul is implying

11. See, e.g., Otfried Hofius, "The Lord's Supper and the Lord's Supper Tradition: Reflections on 1 Corinthians 11:23b–25," in *One Loaf, One Cup: Ecumenical Studies of 1 Cor 11 and Other Eucharistic Texts; The Cambridge Conference on the Eucharist, August 1988*, ed. Ben F. Meyer (NGS 6; Louvain: Peeters, 1993), 75–115.

12. Bruce M. Metzger and Bart D. Ehrman, *The Text of the New Testament*, 4th ed. (Oxford: Oxford University Press, 2005), 70; cf. 70–74.

13. E.g., Cullmann, "The Tradition," 61.

14. 1 Cor. 11:23; 15:3. Παραλαμβάνειν and παραδιδόναι represent, respectively, the rabbinical technical terms קבל and מסר (cf. *m. 'Abot* 1:1); see Ernst Käsemman, "The Pauline Doctrine of the Lord's Supper," in *Essays on New Testament Themes*, trans. W. J. Montague (SBT 41; London: SCM, 1964), 120. Just as significantly, the terms were also used together in the Hellenistic world for the transmission of traditions (cf. Josephus, *Ant.* 19.31). See Gerhard Delling, "παραλαμβάνω," *TDNT* 4:10–11.

15. On the relationship between the accounts of the Last Supper, see Joachim Jeremias, *The Eucharistic Words of Jesus*, trans. Norman Perrin (London: SCM, 1966), chap. 2.

16. Jeremias (ibid., 101–3) points out a number of un-Pauline features: (1) the phrase ὑπὲρ τῶν ἁμαρτιῶν ἡμῶν ("for our sins"); (2) the phrase "according to scriptures"; (3) the perfect passive ἐγήγερται ("he was raised"); (4) the phrase τῇ ἡμέρᾳ τῇ τρίτῃ ("on the third day") has the number of the day placed after the noun; (5) the third person aorist passive ὤφθη ("he appeared," from ὁράω, "to see"); (6) "the twelve"; and (7) considerable evidence of being a translation of a Semitic original.

that he is handing on the tradition in the way he received it,[17] as he seems to be suggesting in 1 Corinthians 11:2, where he commends his readers for maintaining the traditions "just as" (καθώς) he has handed them on (cf. Phil. 4:9; 1 Thess. 2:13). It is reasonable, then, to suggest that he has received this material on the Lord's Supper from earlier Christians. Indeed, at many places in his letters there appears to be material he has taken up from earlier Christians: Jesus' identity, his last meal, his death for our sin, his burial, resurrection and appearance, and present status and role, as well as the poem on love, the general resurrection, and the cry "Our Lord, come!"[18] In other words, although Paul wishes to claim unquestionably that his call or commission came from God, he readily acknowledges that he has been influenced by and is dependent on traditions from earlier Christians.[19] This point will come into clear view again when we consider Paul saying that he is an imitator of Jesus (see §5.4 [d] below).

From this section on Paul's relationship with early Christianity we are able to see that, while Paul takes his commission for mission to have come from God, not human beings, he still acknowledges he is reliant on traditions that he inherited from earlier followers of Jesus. Perhaps, then, if Albert Schweitzer was correct (see 106n4 above), it is these traditions that account for Paul saying little or nothing about the miraculous. Therefore, we turn to examine the place of the miraculous in early Christian traditions that Paul could have known.

5.2 Miracles and the Miraculous in Early Christianity

In seeking to discover what influence in relation to the miraculous Paul may have received from the first generation of followers of Jesus, our task is to enquire what Christian traditions about miracles and the miraculous are likely to have been circulating before and during the time of Paul's ministry. To answer this question, we are dependent on the Gospel traditions; I will deal first with the Synoptic material and then turn to the Fourth Gospel.

Despite periodic challenges, and not all similarities and differences among the first three Gospels being explained by it, the two-source theory remains the most

17. Hans Conzelmann, *1 Corinthians: A Commentary on the First Epistle to the Corinthians*, trans. James W. Leitch, ed. George W. MacRae (Hermeneia; Philadelphia: Fortress, 1975), 196n30.

18. Rom. 1:3–5; 4:24–25; 8:34; 10:8–9; 1 Cor. 8:6, 11b; 10:16; 11:23–25; 12:3; 13; 15:3–7; 16:22; Gal. 1:4; Phil. 2:6–11; 1 Thess. 4:14; 5:9; cf. Eph. 5:14. To this list can be added the faith, hope, and love triad that appears in 1 Cor. 13:13; 1 Thess. 1:3; 5:8; Rom. 5:1–5; Gal. 5:5–6; Col. 1:4–5; Eph. 4:2–5. Cf. Heb. 6:10–12; 10:22–24; 1 Pet. 1:3–8, 21–22; Barn. 1.4; 11.8; Pol. *Phil.* 3.2–3.

19. Birger Gerhardsson, *Memory and Manuscript: Oral Tradition and Written Transmission in Rabbinic Judaism and Early Christianity; with, Tradition and Transmission in Early Christianity*, trans. Eric J. Sharpe (Grand Rapids: Eerdmans; Livonia, MI: Dove, 1998), 288–323.

widely accepted solution to the Synoptic Problem.[20] That is, Mark and Q are the major sources used by Matthew and Luke. In turn, Mark and Q are generally taken to be independent of each other, with Q being the earlier source, even though, of the two, Mark may contain witness to an earlier tradition. Moreover, it is sometimes supposed, though with less certainty, that Matthew and Luke had access to their own unique sources, designated M and L, respectively.[21]

(a) Pre-Matthean tradition. As they stand, Matthew and Luke are of little use to us, for it is generally agreed they were written in the last quarter of the first century,[22] too late to influence Paul. Matthew's sources also turn out to be of little help to us. Nearly a century ago M, Matthew's special source, was an important component of the solution to the Synoptic Problem,[23] and there remain attempts to see its usefulness.[24] However, since the rise of redaction criticism, much of the material unique to Matthew has been attributed to his creativity.[25] The remaining data, not easily marshaled into a coherent whole, more reasonably reflect a plurality of traditions rather than a single theoretical source.[26]

Of this potentially pre-Matthean material, only Matthew 10:5-6, which presupposes a mission, is of possible interest to us: "Go nowhere among the Gentiles, and enter no town of the Samaritans, but go rather to the lost sheep of the house of Israel." We might have been able to use this as corroborative evidence for an early mission that involved performing miracles (see below). However, although there is distinctive phraseology,[27] the vocabulary and gram-

20. See, e.g., Robert A. Derrenbacker Jr., *Ancient Compositional Practices and the Synoptic Problem* (BETL 186; Louvain: Leuven University Press; Dudley, MA: Peeters, 2005), esp. the conclusions, 257-58. For recent challenges see, e.g., Mark S. Goodacre and Nicholas Perrin, eds., *Questioning Q: A Multidimensional Critique* (Downers Grove, IL: InterVarsity, 2004).

21. Robert H. Stein, *The Synoptic Problem: An Introduction* (Grand Rapids: Baker Academic, 1994).

22. For brief discussions on the dating of Matthew, see, e.g., David C. Sim, *The Gospel of Matthew and Christian Judaism: The History and Social Setting of the Matthean Community* (SNTW; Edinburgh: T&T Clark, 1998), 33-40. For a discussion of the dating of Luke, taking into account that a number of passages almost certainly presuppose the fall of Jerusalem (Luke 13:1-5; 19:41-44; 21:20-24; 23:27-31), see, e.g., Joseph A. Fitzmyer, *The Acts of the Apostles: A New Translation with Introduction and Commentary* (AB 31; New York: Doubleday, 1998), 51-55.

23. See esp. B. H. Streeter, *The Four Gospels* (London: Macmillan, 1924), 223-70.

24. E.g., Stephenson H. Brooks, *Matthew's Community: The Evidence of His Special Sayings Material* (JSNTSup 16; Sheffield: JSOT Press, 1987).

25. E.g., see W. D. Davies and Dale C. Allison, *The Gospel According to Matthew*, 3 vols. (ICC; Edinburgh: T&T Clark, 1988-97), 1:121-24.

26. Brooks (*Matthew's Community*, chap. 7) was able to suggest no less than three distinct traditions reflected in M. Reasonably, Ulrich Luz concludes, "In my opinion it [M] may be filed away" (*Matthew 1-7: A Commentary*, trans. Wilhelm C. Linss [Edinburgh: T&T Clark, 1990], 48).

27. εἰς ὁδὸν ἐθνῶν ("to the way of the Gentiles") is unique in the NT; πόλιν Σαμαριτῶν ("Samaritan town") is only found here; and τὰ πρόβατα τὰ ἀπολωλότα οἴκου Ἰσραήλ ("the lost

mar[28] suggest this saying was created by Matthew.[29] We look in vain, then, for any pre-Matthean material on miracles and the miraculous that would have been part of early Christian traditions that could have influenced Paul.

(b) L material. For the existence of L, Luke's special source, there is somewhat more confidence.[30] In any case, within the Lukan material that is not found in Mark or Q, there are five stories and a saying of interest to us. The saying is Jesus' message to Herod: "Listen, I am casting out demons and performing cures today and tomorrow" (Luke 13:32). Although this may not have been created by Luke, there is little evidence on which to make a decision regarding its earlier history.[31]

One of the miracle stories, that of the large catch of fish (Luke 5:1–11), I will leave until discussing the Fourth Gospel, where, as a post-Easter story, its early history is more easily traced (see §5.2 [e] below). For the other four stories unique to Luke—the raising of the widow's son at Nain (7:11–15),[32] the healing of the crippled woman (13:10–17),[33] the healing of the man with dropsy (14:1–6),[34] and the healing of the ten lepers (17:11–19)[35]—a good case can be made that, although modified by Luke, none of them appears to have been created by him.[36]

Moreover, there are features of these stories that are consistent with an early date: all of the stories presuppose the importance of the Jewish law, and three of the four involve the problem of the violation of the law (Luke 13:10–17;

---

sheep of the house of Israel") is echoed only in Matthew 15:24. See Brooks, *Matthew's Community*, 49, 141nn8–9.

28. See ὁδόν ("way"), ἐθνῶν ("nations"), πόλιν ("town"), πρόβατα ("sheep"), ἀπολωλότα ("lost"); the participle form λέγων to introduce direct speech; the nominative participle πορευόμενοι (Matt. 10:7), which also "strikingly corresponds to πορευθέντες in Matthew's version of the great commission (8:19)" (Robert H. Gundry, *Matthew: A Commentary on His Literary and Theological Art* [Grand Rapids: Eerdmans, 1982], 184).

29. Cf. Gerhard Barth, "Matthew's Understanding of the Law," in *Tradition and Interpretation in Matthew*, by Günther Bornkamm, Gerhard Barth, and Heinz Joachim Held, trans. Percy Scott, 2nd ed. (London: SCM, 1982), 100–101n4; Brooks, *Matthew's Community*, 140n5.

30. E.g., see Kim Paffenroth, *The Story of Jesus According to L* (JSNTSup 147; Sheffield: Sheffield Academic Press, 1997), and the cautious reviews by Robert A. Derrenbacker, *CBQ* 61 (1999): 375–76; Mark S. Goodacre, *JBL* 118 (1999): 363–64; Christopher M. Tuckett, *NovT* 41 (1999): 191–92.

31. Graham H. Twelftree, *Jesus the Miracle Worker: A Historical and Theological Study* (Downers Grove, IL: InterVarsity, 1999), 274.

32. John P. Meier, *A Marginal Jew: Rethinking the Historical Jesus*, vol. 2, *Mentor, Message, and Miracles* (ABRL; New York: Doubleday, 1994), 790–98. Less confident is François Bovon, *Luke 1: A Commentary on the Gospel of Luke 1:1–9:50*, trans. Christine M. Thomas, ed. Helmut Koester (Hermeneia; Minneapolis: Fortress, 2002), 267, 270.

33. Meier, *Mentor, Message, and Miracles*, 684–85.

34. I. Howard Marshall, *The Gospel of Luke: A Commentary on the Greek Text* (NIGTC; Exeter: Paternoster, 1978), 578. Less confident is Meier, *Mentor, Message, and Miracles*, 711; Joseph A. Fitzmyer, *The Gospel of Luke I–IX* (AB 28A; Garden City, NY: Doubleday, 1985), 1038–39.

35. Meier, *Mentor, Message, and Miracles*, 706.

36. Cf. Paffenroth, *Story of Jesus*, 104–11.

14:1–6; 17:11–19). While there is evidence of anti-Torah attitudes among early Christians[37]—perhaps beginning with Jesus[38]—and, on the other hand, of later Gentile Christians adhering to the law, the tendency over time was for the law to be of decreasing importance among Christians.[39] Therefore, on balance, these stories are likely to reflect an earlier time, as seen in Galatians, for example, when the law was more significant for Christians.[40] Thus, even if all these stories could not be traced back to the historical Jesus,[41] they are all early enough to have been part of the Christian traditions in Paul's time.

(c) Pre-Markan material. Moving back through time, next we can consider Mark's Gospel. As it stands, Mark is not of much value in establishing what could have been available to Paul. For, the near consensus is that Mark wrote somewhere in the 60s and 70s CE,[42] with the key issue being whether or not the Gospel—chapter 13 in particular—was written before[43] or after the fall of Jerusalem.[44] Indeed, it has been Paul's influence on Mark's Gospel that has long been discussed.[45]

However, even though Mark probably does not take us back into the period of Paul's ministry, there is considerable material in this Gospel relating to the miraculous that not only most probably pre-dates Mark, but also is to be traced back to the earliest traditions about Jesus. The presuppositions of the stories of the leper cleansed (Mark 1:40–45), the paralytic forgiven and healed (2:1–12),

37. For an argument that Stephen and the Hellenists attacked the cult and the ritual law, even in Jerusalem, see Martin Hengel, *Between Jesus and Paul: Studies in the Earliest History of Christianity*, trans. John Bowden (London: SCM, 1983), 54–58.

38. E. P. Sanders (*Jesus and Judaism* [London: SCM, 1985], 252–55, 267–69) identifies Matt. 8:22 // Luke 9:60 ("Let the dead bury their own dead") as the only instance in which Jesus demanded transgression of the law. However, now see Crispin H. T. Fletcher-Louis, "'Leave the Dead to Bury Their Own Dead:' Q 9.60 and the Redefinition of the People of God," *JSNT* 26 (2003): 39–68. Fletcher-Louis concludes, "There are ways in which Jesus' saying would be heard as typical of one who is zealous for Torah and its correct application to the true Israel" (p. 67).

39. Cf. Martin Hengel, "φάτνη," *TDNT* 9:53, citing Matt. 12:11–12; Luke 14:5.

40. Cf. Paffenroth, *Story of Jesus*, 155–56.

41. For the story of the cleansing of the ten lepers (Luke 17:11–19), it is difficult to establish an early history. See Twelftree, *Miracle Worker*, 274, 312–313. On the three stories of the raising of the widow's son (Luke 7:11–15), of the healing of a crippled woman (Luke 13:10–17), and of the healing of the man with dropsy (Luke 14:1–6) being part of the earliest traditions about Jesus, see Twelftree, *Miracle Worker*, 308, 296–97, 325–26, respectively.

42. See, e.g., M. Eugene Boring, *Mark* (NTL; Louisville: Westminster John Knox, 2006), 14–15.

43. See, e.g., Adela Yarbro Collins, *Mark: A Commentary*, ed. Harold W. Attridge (Hermeneia; Minneapolis: Fortress, 2007), 11–14.

44. See, e.g., Morna D. Hooker, *A Commentary on the Gospel According to St. Mark* (BNTC; London: Black, 1991), 7–8. For earlier dates, see those cited by John S. Kloppenborg, "*Evocatio Deorum* and the Date of Mark," *JBL* 124 (2005): 419–50, esp. 419n1.

45. E.g., Vincent Taylor, *The Gospel According to St. Mark: The Greek Text, with Introduction, Notes and Indexes* (London: Macmillan, 1952), 125–29.

and the withered hand cured (3:1–6) involve internal Jewish issues rather than those of a later Jewish-Gentile dialogue from the time of Paul.[46] The core of the remaining stories can also be shown to be early and part of the reliable traditions about Jesus: an exorcism in the synagogue at Capernaum (1:21–28), Peter's mother-in-law cured (1:29–31), a leper cleansed (1:40–45), a paralytic forgiven and healed (2:1–12), a withered hand cured (3:1–6), a Gerasene exorcism (5:1–20), a woman healed of a hemorrhage and Jairus's daughter raised to life (5:21–43), a Syrophoenician woman's daughter exorcised from a distance (7:24–30), a deaf mute healed (7:31–37), a blind man healed at Bethsaida (8:22–26), the exorcism of the so-called epileptic boy (9:14–29), and sight restored to Bartimaeus (10:45–52).[47]

There is also sayings material attributed to Jesus we can take into account. First, the parable of the strong man (Satan) about exorcism has good claim to being part of the earliest Jesus traditions: "But no one can enter a strong man's house and plunder his property without first tying up the strong man; then indeed the house can be plundered" (Mark 3:27; cf. Matt. 12:29 // Luke 11:21–22).[48] Second, the request for Jesus to provide a sign, which was probably always part of the stories about him,[49] is of interest to us because it was taken to have arisen out of a misunderstanding of the miracles Jesus performed.[50] Further, his refusal to provide some "proof" of his identity through using his powers shows that it would have been known that he did not want to use his powers to draw a following.[51]

To all this it is tempting to add Jesus' mission charge (Mark 6:7–12).[52] It is not that there is considerable debate about the origins of this story that could remove it from our discussion; its historicity seems quite defensible. In Jesus inaugurating the eschatological regathering of the tribes of Israel, there is good reason to think that he would have sent his immediate followers on a similar mission.[53] Rather, the issue for us is that the version we have in

46. Cf. James D. G. Dunn, "Mark 2.1–3.6: A Bridge between Jesus and Paul on the Question of the Law," NTS 30 (1984): 395–415; reprinted with an additional note in James D. G. Dunn, Jesus, Paul and the Law (London: SPCK, 1990), 10–36, esp. 28.

47. Twelftree, Miracle Worker, 328–29.

48. Of the historicity of this saying, see ibid., 269–70, esp. n71.

49. Ibid., 274–75. See also §5.3 (f) below.

50. See Matt. 15:32–16:4; Mark 8:1–12; Luke 11:14–16, 29.

51. E.g., A. E. Harvey, Jesus and the Constraints of History (London: Duckworth, 1982), 111–12. See §5.3 (f) below.

52. The four existing reports probably arose from Mark 6:7–12 (followed by Luke 9:1–6) and Q (Luke 10:1–11), with Matthew 10:1–15 conflating them. See Risto Uro, Sheep among the Wolves: A Study on the Mission Instructions of Q (AASF 47; Helsinki: Suomalainen Tiedeakatemia, 1987), 21–23.

53. See John P. Meier, A Marginal Jew: Rethinking the Historical Jesus, vol. 3, Companions and Competitors (ABRL; New York: Doubleday, 2001), 148–54, 158.

Mark has been so rewritten by him that it is difficult to show that the aspects relating to the miraculous predate him.[54] Nevertheless, I will return to this theme as I discuss Q.

In any case, already we are seeing from pre-Markan material that the Christian traditions likely to have been known by Paul in the period when he joined the followers of Jesus were flush with material about miracles and the miraculous. Furthermore, if we take up the increasingly popular view that Mark was composed not in Rome but in the East[55]—Damascus has even been speculated[56]—the likelihood is increased that this material would have formed part of the fabric of the Christianity to which Paul was introduced.

(d) The Q tradition. Turning to Q, we are on even more secure ground in being able to establish that, from the time he became a follower of Jesus, Paul would have known a Christianity in which miracles and the miraculous were important. To begin with, although the compositional history of Q is likely to have been complex,[57] in its latest edition the future of Jerusalem is hopeful (Luke 13:35b), and there are no signs of the conflict of the 60s. Further, there is probably an awareness of the charismatic prophets and their movements (11:29–30; 17:23–24), beginning in the mid-40s (see §3.2 [a] above). Therefore, a date for its publication as early as the 50s is a reasonable supposition.[58] In any case, the earlier traditions—written or oral or both[59]—taken up in Q help us describe aspects of the Christianity to which Paul would have been introduced.

Even though Q is dominated by sayings material, thaumaturgical themes and traditions are integral and important to it.[60] The level of importance of miracle in Q is seen when we take into account that of only two major narratives in Q, one is a miracle story (the healing of the centurion's servant, Luke

54. The vocabulary and style of Mark 6:7b ("and he gave them authority over the unclean spirits") suggest it is composed by Mark (see Taylor, *St. Mark*, 303) to compliment his version of the call of the Twelve, to which he has most likely added the idea that they had "authority to cast out demons" (Mark 3:15). On it being unlikely that the instruction that the Twelve are to anoint with oil is early, see Boring, *Mark*, 176.

55. Boring, *Mark*, 15–20.

56. Gerd Theissen, *The Gospels in Context: Social and Political History in the Synoptic Tradition*, trans. Linda M. Maloney (Minneapolis: Fortress, 1991), 244–45.

57. Cf. John S. Kloppenborg Verbin, *Excavating Q: The History and Setting of the Sayings Gospel* (Edinburgh: T&T Clark, 2000).

58. Cf. David R. Catchpole, "The Question of Q," *STRev* 36 (1992): 36–37; Dale C. Allison, *The Jesus Tradition in Q* (Harrisburg, PA: Trinity Press International, 1997), 49–54.

59. Ronan Rooney and Douglas E. Oakman, "The Social Origins of Q: Two Theses in a Field of Conflicting Hypotheses," *BTB* 38 (2008): 114–21.

60. Ronald A. Piper, "Jesus and the Conflict of Powers in Q: Two Q Miracle Stories," in *The Sayings Source Q and the Historical Jesus*, ed. A. Lindemann (BETL 158; Louvain: Leuven University Press, 2001), 317–49, esp. 319–21.

7:1–10), the other is the temptation story (4:1–13).[61] Also, the only other very brief narrative is the mention of Jesus "casting out a demon that was mute" (11:14). Both of these miracle narratives probably predate Q.[62]

Following the story of the healing of the centurion's servant there is the answer to John the Baptist's enquiry about the identity of Jesus in which, borrowing messianic hopes expressed in Isaiah, Jesus' ministry is summarized as dominated by miracle working: "the blind receive their sight, the lame walk, the lepers are cleansed, the deaf hear, the dead are raised, the poor have good news brought to them" (Luke 7:22).[63] It is also probable that the history of this statement predates Q.[64]

Then, following the brief report of an exorcism there is considerable material not only defending Jesus' exorcisms, but also establishing their eschatological significance as the arrival of the kingdom of God (Luke 11:15–26, esp. v. 20). Jesus says, "But if in God's Spirit I cast out the demons, then has come upon you the kingdom of God" (my translation; Matt. 12:28 // Luke 11:20; see below).[65] This views the exorcisms of Jesus as the expression of the kingdom of God being brought about by the Spirit. From this material in Q we can see not only that traditions about Jesus and the miraculous would have been circulating among early Christians during Paul's ministry, but also that Jesus' miracles were thought to be empowered by the Spirit and connected with, and understood as, the realization of the end-time salvation.

To this discussion so far there are two further aspects of the Synoptic traditions to be considered as most probably forming part of the early Christianity Paul knew and, therefore, could have informed his views on miracles and the miraculous. First is the story of the disciples being sent on mission before Easter. In the discussion of Mark I noted that even though the details are no longer recoverable from Mark, the historicity of a mission is not difficult to establish (see 113n53 above). Also, even though it is no longer possible to recover the

---

61. Kloppenborg Verbin (*Excavating Q*, 87), suggests that Luke 4:1–13 may be a late addition to Q.

62. On Luke 7:1–10, see Fitzmyer, *Luke I–IX*, 648; Bovon, *Luke 1*, 259. On Luke 11:14, see Meier, *Mentor, Message, and Miracles*, 657, 713–14.

63. Cf. Isa. 26:19; 29:18; 35:5–6; 42:18; 61:1.

64. Meier, *Mentor, Message, and Miracles*, 832–37.

65. Recent discussions generally conclude that Matthew's "Spirit of God," rather than Luke's "finger of God," reflects Q. See the summary discussion by John Nolland, *Luke 9:21–18:34* (WBC 35B; Dallas: Word, 1993), 639. On the historicity of this saying, see James D. G. Dunn, "Matt. 12:28/Luke 11:20—A Word of Jesus?" in *Eschatology and the New Testament: Essays in Honor of George Raymond Beasley-Murray*, ed. W. Hulitt Gloer (Peabody, MA: Hendrickson, 1988), 29–49; to the contrary, see Heikki Räisänen, "Exorcisms and the Kingdom: Is Q 11:20 a Saying of the Historical Jesus?" in *Symbols and Strata: Essays on the Sayings Gospel Q*, ed. Risto Uro (PFES 65; Helsinki: Finnish Exegetical Society; Göttingen: Vandenhoeck & Ruprecht, 1996), 119–42.

charge that Jesus gave to his followers, it is almost certain that all concerned would have assumed they were involved in the same kind of end-time ministry that included performing miracles.[66] However, in the Q saying "cure the sick who are there" (Luke 10:9)[67] we can see the idea that healing was involved in the understanding of the mission of the disciples.[68] Notably, that no attempt has been made to conform this simple charge to perform cures either to the more complex ministry attributed to Jesus (cf. Matt. 10:8) or to the connection elsewhere in Q between exorcism and the kingdom of God (Luke 11:20) suggests its antiquity. It is also notable that in Q the charge to cure the sick and, then, preach is an order of priority likely to have been part of earliest Christianity,[69] for Mark independently also shares this perspective (Mark 6:7). It is highly probable, then, that the Christianity of the time that Paul came to know included the idea that the followers of Jesus had been sent out on a mission to perform healings, as well as announce the kingdom of God. This leads to a second point about the Synoptic traditions.

Not only is the kingdom of God the center of Q's theology,[70] but there are also occurrences of the "kingdom of God" theme in the Gospel traditions that most probably have a history that goes back to the historical Jesus.[71] Notably for us, as in the mission charge (Luke 10:9), the theme was also associated with Jesus' miracles, especially the exorcisms (Matt. 12:28 // Luke 11:20; see 115n65 above). This association was understood not to be one in which the miracles prepared for the coming of the kingdom of God, or were signs or evidence or proof of the coming of God's reign. Instead, the miracles themselves were understood to be the kingdom of God expressed in the lives of those healed.[72]

(e) The Fourth Gospel. Finally, we turn to the Fourth Gospel in search of material on miracles and the miraculous that may have been part of Christian traditions influencing Paul early in his ministry.[73] Whatever their origins, three

66. Graham H. Twelftree, *In the Name of Jesus: Exorcism among Early Christians* (Grand Rapids: Baker Academic, 2007), 49–51.

67. On Luke 10:9 well reflecting Q, see Uro, *Sheep among the Wolves*, 82.

68. John S. Kloppenborg, *The Formation of Q: Trajectories in Ancient Wisdom Collections* (Philadelphia: Fortress, 1987), 192–97, 391–93.

69. On Matthew reordering healing and teaching to give priority to teaching, see Harry T. Fleddermann, *Q: A Reconstruction and Commentary* (BibTS 1; Louvain: Peeters), 413–14.

70. The term βασιλεία ("kingdom" or "reign") occurs in Q at least in Luke 4:5; 6:20; 7:28; 10:9, 11; 11:2, 17, 18, 20; (11:52?); 12:31; 13:18, 20, 28, 29; 16:16 (17:20, 21?).

71. Meier, *Mentor, Message, and Miracles*, chaps. 15–16.

72. See Graham H. Twelftree, "The Miracles of Jesus: Marginal or Mainstream?" *JSHJ* 1 (2003): 118.

73. On the relationship between Paul and Johannine theology, see Pierre Benoit, "Paulinisme et Johannisme," *NTS* 9 (1962–63): 193–207; Frank J. Matera, "Christ in the Theologies of Paul and John: A Study in the Diverse Unity of New Testament Theology," *TS* 67 (2006): 238–40.

miracle stories have to be left aside—Jesus turning water into wine (John 2:1–12), the feeding of a multitude (6:1–15), and Jesus walking on the sea (6:15–21)—for it does not seem possible to trace a sufficiently early history of them.[74]

On the other hand, the story of the healing of the official's son (4:46–54) is quite likely to have been part of Christian traditions from the beginning.[75] Also, although the story of the healing of the paralytic at Bethesda (5:1–18) is found only in the Fourth Gospel, it is likely always to have been part of the earliest traditions about Jesus.[76] Similarly, the story of the man born blind (9:1–7), though attested only here, probably can be included in the Christian traditions that would have been known in Paul's time.[77]

The story of the raising of Lazarus from the dead (11:1–57) presents overwhelming difficulties for twenty-first-century readers. Yet, even though the puzzle remains why the Synoptic tradition does not carry this story,[78] it has aspects that suggest a history going back to the historical Jesus: the naming of the person involved (which is uncommon in the Gospels),[79] topographical details (11:18), the extra suffering caused by the delay in Jesus' response (11:6, 21), Jesus taking part in the mourning and weeping (11:35), and the hesitancy to take away the stone (11:39).[80]

Tracing the story of the large catch of fish, found at the end of the Fourth Gospel (John 21:4–14; cf. Luke 5:1–11), to the very early life of the church depends considerably on the veracity of a resurrection appearance to Peter. Given that, only a generation after Easter, Paul hands on independent information, which he is prepared to have verified (1 Cor. 15:5–7), that Peter had seen the risen Jesus, lends weight to the historical reliability of the core of this story. Moreover, that the appearance of Jesus should be in the context of fishing adds to our confidence in the early history of the story.[81]

(f) Conclusions. To test the view that it was the early Christianity Paul inherited that accounts for the low profile of miracles and the miraculous in his writings, the task in this section has been to set out what Christian traditions concerning miracles and the miraculous are likely to have been circulating

---

74. Twelftree, *Miracle Worker*, 326–28, 318–20, 320–22.

75. Ibid., 296.

76. Raymond E. Brown, *The Gospel According to John: Introduction, Translation, and Notes*, 2 vols. (AB 29, 29A; London: Geoffrey Chapman, 1971), 1:209.

77. C. H. Dodd, *Historical Tradition in the Fourth Gospel* (Cambridge: Cambridge University Press, 1963), 174–80.

78. Twelftree, *Miracle Worker*, 309.

79. Cf. Richard Bauckham, *Jesus and the Eyewitnesses: The Gospels as Eyewitness Testimony* (Grand Rapids: Eerdmans, 2006), 39–91, esp. 84.

80. Twelftree, *Miracle Worker*, 308–10.

81. Ibid., 325.

before and during Paul's ministry. I cannot suppose to have identified the entire range of material likely to have been available to influence Paul. Nevertheless, I have been able to draw attention to sufficient material (particularly miracle stories) to conclude that the theme of miracles and the miraculous was a very significant part of the Christianity to which Paul would have been introduced. Within this material we have seen a number of clear themes dominate: exorcism and healing are recurring topics, and even raising the dead is part of the tradition. In addition to this list, note can be made of the possibility of miracle stories such as the large catch of fish forming part of the tradition.

Notably, the tradition holds both that Jesus took his miracles, particularly his exorcisms, to be the kingdom of God in operation, and that his followers had been involved in a similar ministry. Moreover, as the form critics have taught us, this material would not have been circulating in a vacuum, but would have reflected the practical interests of its communities.[82]

This conclusion can be put another way. Taking as a rough guide the material that I have identified, it would have been difficult for Paul to escape coming in contact with a Christianity shot through with an interest in miracle. Numbers of stories about Jesus being a miracle worker, sayings about this aspect of his ministry, as well as the tradition about Jesus sending out his followers on a mission—duplicating his own—that included performing miracles and proclaiming the kingdom of God, give evidence that early Christianity had a lively and practical interest in the miraculous that was taken to have originated in Jesus and had been carried on by his followers. In short, we cannot follow Harnack and Schweitzer in supposing that the responsibility for the distance between Paul and Jesus in relation to miracles and the miraculous is to be laid at the feet of primitive Christianity. However, we still have to enquire about the actual influence of this Christianity on Paul.

5.3 Paul and the Early Christian Miracle Traditions

Having set out the extent and some of the significance of the early Christian traditions about miracles and the miraculous most likely circulating around the time of Paul's conversion, it is reasonable to assume that this material would have influenced him. Notwithstanding, in this section I will attempt to probe behind the assumption to detect what response, if any, he had to this tradition. We can expect that any response by Paul that I am able to establish will help to interpret him in relation to the miraculous.

82. Christopher Tuckett, *Reading the New Testament: Methods of Interpretation* (London: SPCK, 1987), 95–115.

To begin with, Paul neither makes a reference to, nor even alludes to, any of the miracle stories of Jesus.[83] Nevertheless, the long-standing debate on Paul's use of the Jesus tradition continues, perhaps increases,[84] some arguing for a great deal of contact between Paul and the traditions,[85] others seeing minimal connections.[86] As we will see, a median position probably more accurately reflects the evidence.

Discussions to date have drawn attention to a number of themes and places in Paul's letters that may show not only his knowledge of the Jesus tradition, but also his knowledge of the miracle tradition in particular, and that this influenced his understanding of his ministry. First, however, in the hope of establishing a reasonable base for approaching this data, I begin with the issue of plausibility.

(a) Paul and the miracles of Jesus: Plausibilities. Those such as Johannes Weiss and James Hope Moulton, for example, who sought to establish that Paul knew the historical Jesus[87] have not been considered successful.[88] The matter is different with Paul's knowledge of the immediate followers of Jesus. Not only does Paul know about the Twelve, and Peter and James in particular (1 Cor. 15:5–7), he also claims to have met and had discussions with Peter, James, and John (Gal. 1:18–19; 2:9), and perhaps other leaders in Jerusalem (2:2), including Barnabas, whom he considers an apostle (1 Cor. 9:5–6).[89] Given what we have seen of the place of miracles in the ministry of Jesus and the mission of his followers, it is very plausible that Paul had heard about the miracles of Jesus and his first followers, along with their significance. For,

83. Twelftree, *Name of Jesus*, 60–64.
84. Bruce N. Fisk, "Paul: Life and Letters," in *The Face of New Testament Studies: A Survey of Recent Research*, ed. Scot McKnight and Grant R. Osborne (Grand Rapids: Baker Academic; Leicester: Apollos, 2004), 312–13; Todd D. Still, ed., *Jesus and Paul Reconnected: Fresh Pathways into an Old Debate* (Grand Rapids: Eerdmans, 2007).
85. E.g., Paul W. Barnett, *Paul: Missionary of Jesus* (Grand Rapids: Eerdmans, 2008), 11–22.
86. E.g., Frans Neirynck, "Paul and the Sayings of Jesus," in *L'Apôtre Paul: Personalité, style et conception du ministère* (BETL 73; ed. Albert Vanhoye; Louvain: Peeters, 1986), 265–321.
87. Johannes Weiss, *Paul and Jesus*, trans. H. J. Chaytor (New York: Harper, 1909), 40–50. On the history of the debate on the relationship between Paul and Jesus see, Furnish, "Jesus-Paul Debate."
88. Rudolf Bultmann, "The Significance of the Historical Jesus for the Theology of Paul" (1929), in Rudolf Bultmann, *Faith and Understanding*, ed. Robert W. Funk, trans. Louise Pettibone Smith (Philadelphia: Fortress, 1987), 220–46; Margaret E. Thrall, *A Critical and Exegetical Commentary on the Second Epistle to the Corinthians*, 2 vols. (ICC; London: T&T Clark, 1994–2000), 1:416.
89. Our information about Barnabas is so meager, especially from Paul, that we can only speculate that he was both well connected with Jerusalem (plausible from 1 Cor. 9:5–6) and one through whom Paul learned about Christianity. See Acts 4:36; 9:27; 11:22, cf. 11:30; 12:25; 15:2 (2x), 12, 22, 25; also 1 Cor. 9:6; Gal. 2:1, 9, 13; Martin Hengel and Anna Maria Schwemer, *Paul between Damascus and Antioch: The Unknown Years* (London: SCM, 1997), 205–21.

as C. H. Dodd famously quipped, "At the time he [Paul] stayed with Peter for a fortnight, . . . we may presume they did not spend all the time talking about the weather."[90] While this does not establish that Paul knew the traditions about the miracles of Jesus and his early followers, it does suggest high plausibility for the idea and gives us confidence in pursuing a more detailed examination of the issue.

(b) Paul and Q.[91] If we could be confident Paul knew Q, we could reasonably conclude that he would have been aware of its thaumatological themes. However, some of the Jesus sayings he may have known appear not only in Q but also in pre-Markan tradition, and therefore do not immediately help establish Paul's knowledge of Q.[92] Then, in places where Paul is likely to be echoing material now found only in Q,[93] he could be relying on other unknown sources.[94] We need to be able to show that Paul was aware of Q material in the context of Q.[95] For that, Dale Allison points us to the Q pericope about the killing of the prophets and sages (set out below),[96] a passage long argued to have parallels in Paul (1 Thess. 2:14–16).[97]

---

90. C. H. Dodd, *The Apostolic Preaching and Its Developments*, 3rd ed. (London: Hodder & Stoughton, 1963), 16.

91. For the ongoing discussion of the relationship between Paul and Q, see, e.g., Christopher M. Tuckett, "1 Corinthians and Q," *JBL* 102 (1983): 607–19; Allison, *Jesus Tradition*, 54–60.

92. The saying about judging others or causing them to stumble (Rom. 14:13; 1 Cor. 8:13) may not only be echoed in Q (Luke 17:1–2), but could also be part of the pre-Markan material (Mark 9:42). See Dale C. Allison, "The Pauline Epistles and the Synoptic Gospels: The Pattern of Parallels," *NTS* 28 (1982): 13–15.

93. (1) Cf. Luke 10:7 ("the laborer deserves to be paid") and 1 Cor. 9:14 ("the Lord commanded that those who proclaim the gospel should get their living by the gospel"); on which, see §5.3 (c) below. (2) Cf. Luke 16:18 and 1 Cor. 7:10 (a saying prohibiting divorce). On the difficulty of determining whether Paul knows the Markan version or what is now in the Q tradition, see Tuckett, "1 Corinthians and Q," 613 and n. 32. On what is judged to be the unsuccessful attempt by David L. Balch ("Backgrounds of 1 Cor. VII: Saying of the Lord in Q; Moses as an Ascetic ΘΕΙΟΣ ΑΝΗΡ in II Cor. III," *NTS* 18 [1972]: 351–64) to find a link between Q and ascetic views of marriage in Paul, see Tuckett, "1 Corinthians and Q," 615.

94. Bultmann, "Historical Jesus," 222.

95. Allison, *Jesus Tradition*, 55, 60. To be set aside from consideration is Luke 10:16 ("whoever rejects me rejects the one who sent me"); cf. 1 Thess. 4:8 ("whoever rejects this rejects not human authority but God"). This is not, as David R. Catchpole ("The Mission Charge in Q," *Semeia* 55 [1991]: 166–67) suggests, evidence of Paul's knowledge of a late redaction of Q (see the discussion by Allison, *Jesus Tradition*, 56), for parallels between Luke 10:16 and 10:10 suggest it was part of an early Q version of this story to which 10:12–15 was subsequently added.

96. Luke 11:47–51 // Matt. 23:29–32, 34. See Allison, *Jesus Tradition*, 57–60.

97. Christopher M. Tuckett, "Synoptic Tradition in 1 Thessalonians," in *The Thessalonian Correspondence*, ed. Raymond F. Collins (BETL 87; Louvain: Leuven University Press, 1990), 165n23. For the debate about 1 Thess. 2:15–16 being a later interpolation, see, e.g., Carol J. Schlueter, *Filling Up the Measure: Polemical Hyperbole in 1 Thessalonians 2:14–16* (JSNTSup 98; Sheffield: JSOT Press, 1994), 13–24.

The order of the Q material in this passage is a matter of debate, though, as set out below, Matthew's order is probably to be preferred.[98] Within this material, the place of Matthew 23:32 ("Fill up, then, the measure of your ancestors") is also a problem. Although this statement is sometimes judged to be of Matthew's creation,[99] it probably was part of Q.[100] On the one hand, the vocabulary is not particularly Matthean;[101] on the other hand, the sentiment of the saying—that listeners will finish what their ancestors started—is implicit in Q (Luke 11:49–51). Luke, then, presumably deleted it as he abbreviated the saying about the building of tombs to the prophets (Luke 11:47 // Matt. 23:29–32).[102]

Paul's potential borrowing from Q is more easily considered when we set the texts in parallel:[103]

Luke 11 [47]"Woe to you! For you build the tombs of the prophets, but your forefathers killed them. [48]Thus you witness against yourselves that you are the sons of your forefathers. [Matt. 23 [32]Fill up, then, the measure of your ancestors.] [49]Therefore also Wisdom said, 'I will send them prophets and sages, and some of them they will kill and persecute,' [50]so that a settling of accounts for the blood of all the prophets poured out from the founding of the world may be required of this generation, [51]from the blood of Abel to the blood of Zechariah, murdered between the sacrificial altar and the House. Yes, I tell you, an accounting will be required of this generation! 13[34]"Jerusalem, Jerusalem, who kills the prophets and stones those sent to her!"

1 Thessalonians 2 [14]For you, brothers and sisters, became imitators of the churches of God in Christ Jesus that are in Judea, for you suffered the same things from your own compatriots as they did from the Jews, [15]who killed both the Lord Jesus and the prophets, and drove us out; they displease God and oppose everyone [16]by hindering us from speaking to the Gentiles so that they may be saved. Thus they have constantly been filling up the measure of their sins; but God's wrath has overtaken them at last.

Common to Paul and Q are the Judeans (Paul) or Jerusalem (Q) killing (ἀποκτείνω) and persecuting (διώκω)[104] the prophets (προφῆται) and apostles (ἀπόστολοι, Paul says "us," ἡμᾶς), and the filling up the measure (broken

98. Allison, *Jesus Tradition*, 201–3. On the idea that in Q, Luke 13:34 immediately followed Luke 11:49–51, see ibid.

99. E.g., Tuckett, "Synoptic Tradition," 166.

100. See Davies and Allison, *Matthew*, 3:313; Allison, *Jesus Tradition*, 59; Fleddermann, *Q*, 543.

101. πληρόω ("fulfill"), though characteristic of Matthew (16x; cf. Mark 2x; Luke 9x; John 15x), is rarely used by him other than in relation to the fulfillment of Scripture (see Matt. 3:15; 13:48; 23:32); and μέτρον ("measure") is of no particular interest to him (Matt. 7:2; 23:32).

102. Cf. Allison, *Jesus Tradition*, 58 and n. 265; Davies and Allison, *Matthew*, 3:303–9.

103. The English text of Luke (Q) is taken from James M. Robinson, Paul Hoffmann, and John S. Kloppenborg, eds., *The Critical Edition of Q: Synopsis Including the Gospels of Matthew and Luke, Mark and Thomas with English, German, and French translations of Q and Thomas* (Hermeneia; Minneapolis: Fortress; Louvain: Peeters, 2000), 282–88, 420.

104. Paul (1 Thess. 2:15) has ἐκδιώκω. Notably, A D W Ψ f[13] and the Majority Text also have ἐκδιώκω at Luke 11:49, which, if part of Q, would strengthen the case for Pauline borrowing.

underlining above).[105] Strengthening the ties between these two passages is not only this vocabulary (double underlining above), including "drive out" or "persecute" (ἐκδιώκω), which is a *hapax legomenon* for Paul, and ἀποκτείνω, not his usual word for the death of Jesus.[106] Also, the basic thought, including the harsh view of Israel, and the shared progression of the ideas over a short span of text (esp. italics above) suggest Paul is echoing the Q passage.[107] In Paul the order of ideas is Judea, persecution, filling up, and warning; in Q the order is reversed. It could be that Paul is depending on a third document or tradition for any one of these ideas. However, the echoing of a set of ideas (including its vocabulary), though in reverse order, makes it reasonable to conclude that Paul most likely knew these ideas from Q.[108] In view of the number of links in the chain of this argument—some of them not strong— my conclusion needs to be expressed in terms of "most likely" rather than anything more confident.

Nevertheless, in turn, we have arrived at the point where it may be said that since Paul most likely knows a late redaction of Q, he is most likely to have been aware of its thaumaturgical themes: healing (Luke 7:1–10), including of the blind, lame, skin diseased, deaf, and the raising of the dead (7:22), exorcism (11:14) and its ambiguity (11:15) and it being both an expression of the coming of the kingdom of God and the defeat of Satan (11:17–20), and also that miracles could lead to repentance (10:13).

Importantly, it is not simply that Paul is most likely to have been informed by this piece of literature or oral tradition. As we have already noted, the form critics have taught us that these traditions have been preserved because communities found the material useful and would have expressed the values of these traditions in their views and activities. This means that Paul is most likely to have been familiar not only with these themes from the Q tradition, but also with people for whom the miraculous was an important part of Christianity. This leads to the next point at which we can probably see Paul's knowledge of the miracles and the miraculous in early Christianity.

---

105. Paul (1 Thess. 2:16) has εἰς τὸ ἀναπληρῶσαι αὐτῶν τὰς ἁμαρτίας πάντοτε ("they have constantly been filling up the measure of their sins"). Matt. (Q?) 23:32 has καὶ ὑμεῖς πληρώσατε τὸ μέτρον τῶν πατέρων ὑμῶν ("Fill up, then, the measure of your ancestors").

106. Paul uses ἀποκτείνω four times: Rom. 7:11; 11:3; 2 Cor. 3:6; 1 Thess. 2:15; cf. Eph. 2:16. For the death of Jesus, see ἀποθνήσκω (Rom. 5:6, 8; 6:8, 9, 10 [2x]; 8:34; 14:9, 15; 1 Cor. 8:11; 15:3; 2 Cor. 5:14 [2x], 15; Gal. 2:21; 1 Thess. 4:14; 5:10; cf. Col. 2:20); θάνατος (Rom. 5:10; 6:3, 4, 5, 9; 1 Cor. 11:26; 2 Cor. 1:9; Phil. 2:8 [2x]; 3:10; cf. Col. 1:22; 2 Tim. 1:10).

107. Cf. Karl P. Donfried, "Paul and Judaism: I Thessalonians 2:13–16 as a Test Case," *Int* 38 (1984): 249; Schlueter, *Filling Up the Measure*, 72; to the contrary, Tuckett, "Synoptic Tradition," 165–67.

108. Also Allison, *Jesus Tradition*, 60.

(c) The pre-Easter mission of the followers of Jesus. Broadly, Paul calling
the leaders at Jerusalem "apostles" (1 Cor. 15:7–9), a word given its Christian
content from the Old Testament idea of being sent by God to a particular
people with a special message or task (see §5.4 [a] below), suggests that he
would have understood that those who were followers of Jesus before him had
been charged with a mission. There is more specific support for this suggestion
in other parts of 1 Corinthians.

It is generally accepted that Paul's statement "the Lord commanded that
those who proclaim the gospel should get their living by the gospel" (1 Cor.
9:14), refers to the Synoptic saying now in the missionary discourse: "for the
laborer deserves to be paid" (Luke 10:7a).[109] What is not agreed is whether
Paul knew this saying as part of the Synoptic missionary discourse (10:1–16)[110]
or as part of an unknown collection of sayings, or even as an isolated saying
(cf. 1 Tim. 5:17–18; *Did.* 13:1–2).[111]

In order to show that Paul was aware of the mission discourse, we have to
be able to show that he was aware of the saying in this context. Although the
debate on the issue is complex,[112] a number of points establish the probability
that Paul knew this saying from the mission discourse.

First, we are already predisposed to think that Paul knew the mission discourse, for we have just seen that he most likely knew the Q tradition. Second,
Paul makes a strong association between his discussion about the rewards of a
missionary and the Jesus tradition; he says "the Lord commanded" the wages
(1 Cor. 9:14). Third, although the statement "the laborer deserves to be paid" is
an abstract generalization, it is both integral to Q's mission discourse[113] and is,
for Paul, a statement about missionaries. Fourth, Paul's vocabulary and ideas,[114]
particularly those concerning a missionary having the right to food and drink,
are also to be found in the missionary discourse (Luke 10:7a // 1 Cor. 9:4, 7, 13).
Fifth, there is supporting evidence that Paul knew the mission discourse in his

109. E.g., David R. Catchpole, "The Mission Charge in Q," *Semeia* 55 (1991): 147–74.

110. So, e.g., Biörn Fjärstedt, *Synoptic Tradition in 1 Corinthians: Themes and Clusters
of Theme Words in 1 Corinthians 1–4 and 9* (Uppsala: Teologiska Institutionen, 1974), 67–70;
Dale C. Allison, "The Pauline Epistles and the Synoptic Gospels: The Pattern of Parallels," *NTS*
28 (1982): 1–32; and those cited by Allison, *Jesus Tradition,* 105n7.

111. So, e.g., Christopher M. Tuckett, "Paul and the Synoptic Mission Discourse," *ETL*
60 (1984): 376–81; and the response by Dale C. Allison, "Paul and the Missionary Discourse,"
ETL 61 (1985): 369–75.

112. Tuckett, "Mission Discourse"; Allison, "Missionary Discourse."

113. Note the introductory γάρ ("for") linking Luke 10:7b with the mission theme in 10:7a:
"Remain in the same house." See A. E. Harvey, "'The Workman Is Worthy of His Hire': Fortunes
of a Proverb in the Early Church," *NovT* 24 (1982): 219–21.

114. See the evidence set out by Fjärstedt, *Synoptic Tradition,* 65–77; and the summary
discussion by Allison, "Missionary Discourse," 371–72.

statement, "whoever rejects this rejects not human authority but God" (1 Thess. 4:8). This is a clear echo of "the one who rejects you rejects me, and the one who rejects me rejects the one who sent me" (Luke 10:16), which probably was in Q's mission discourse.[115] In short, it is reasonable to conclude that Paul knew of a pre-Easter mission of the followers of Jesus through the Q tradition.[116] This means that Paul would have understood the Christianity he had inherited involved a mission initiated by Jesus, and that healing—miracle working that was linked with announcing that the kingdom of God had come near—was part of that mission.

(d) Romans 15:18–19: Echoes of the miracle stories of Jesus. The clearest example that Paul most probably echoes knowledge of Jesus performing miracles is Romans 15:18–19: "what Christ has accomplished through me to win obedience from the Gentiles, by word and deed, by the power of signs and wonders, by the power of the Spirit of God."[117] It might be thought that, in using "Christ" instead of "Jesus," Paul is referring only to the present, risen Christ working through him. However, not only was "Christ" no longer simply a title but a personal name for Paul, as well as for the Hellenistic church,[118] he also readily links the name with the earthly existence (Rom. 1:3) and crucifixion of Jesus.[119] Therefore, anticipating my more detailed discussion that concludes Paul is talking about his own involvement in the miraculous (see §7.8 below), it is reasonable to propose that this statement has force only if Paul held the view that Christ conducted miracles.[120]

Moreover, from this statement of Paul in Romans 15:18–19 it is important to note how he refers to the Spirit. He says the Gentiles were won "by word and deed" (15:18). This is followed by a parallel construction:

> in the power [ἐν δυνάμει] of signs and wonders
> in the power [ἐν δυνάμει] of the Spirit [of God][121]

---

115. E.g., Bultmann, *History*, 143; David R. Catchpole, "The Poor on Earth and the Son of Man in Heaven: A Re-appraisal of Matthew 25:31–46," *BJRL* 62 (1979): 357–58.

116. Allison, "Missionary Discourse," 375.

117. What follows is intended as a development of Twelftree, *Name of Jesus*, 61, 65–66. When discussing Paul's testimony in relation to his ministry, I will have cause to return to this passage in §7.8 below.

118. Leonhard Goppelt, *Theology of the New Testament*, trans. John E. Alsup, ed. Jürgen Roloff, 2 vols. (Grand Rapids: Eerdmanns, 1982), 2:67–68.

119. E.g., Rom. 5:3–4; 1 Cor. 15:3; Gal. 2:20; 3:13. Cf. Walter Grundmann, "χρίω, κτλ.," *TDNT* 9:544–45.

120. Cf. David Wenham, *Paul: Follower of Jesus or Founder of Christianity?* (Grand Rapids: Eerdmans, 1995), 351.

121. On the textual support for θεοῦ ("of God"), see NA[27]; Bruce M. Metzger, *A Textual Commentary on the Greek New Testament*, 2nd ed. (Stuttgart: Deutsche Bibelgesellschaft; New York: United Bible Societies, 1994), 473.

The import of this parallel is not so much to establish that Paul's ministry, as a whole, was accomplished in the power of the Holy Spirit.[122] Nor is Paul describing the signs and wonders simply as conducted in the power of the Spirit.[123] For, in the parallel, Paul is expressing (tautologically) the point that the signs and wonders are the same as the power of the Spirit.[124] This is precisely the relationship between miracles and the Spirit we have seen made in the Jesus tradition, now in Q, in relation to Jesus conducting exorcisms (Matt. 12:28 // Luke 11:20): the miracles are the activity or expression of the Spirit. Also, we note in passing that these parallel statements are explaining the origin of both the word and the deed. In this the word and deed are of a piece, not set over against each other, the latter confirming the former.[125] They are both the work of the Spirit.

(e) The kingdom of God. Paul's use of the term "kingdom of God" may be another point at which we are able to detect his response to early Christian miracle traditions.[126] The importance of the kingdom of God to Jesus is generally agreed.[127] However, the term "kingdom of God" does not appear to be of central importance to Paul as it was for Jesus.[128] Therefore, that Paul, one of Jesus' early followers, has so little to say on the subject is one of the factors

122. As suggested by C. E. B. Cranfield, *A Critical and Exegetical Commentary on the Epistle to the Romans*, 2 vols. (ICC; Edinburgh: T&T Clark, 1975, 1979), 2:759n5.

123. E.g., Robert Jewett, *Romans: A Commentary* (Hermeneia; Minneapolis: Fortress, 2007), 911.

124. Cf. Ernst Käsemann: "ἐν δυνάμει πνεύματος sums up an epexegetical genitive, asserting almost tautologically the miraculous power of the exalted Lord" (*Commentary on Romans*, trans. and ed. Geoffrey W. Bromiley [London: SCM, 1980], 394).

125. Contra C. E. B. Cranfield, *Romans: A Shorter Commentary* (Edinburgh: T&T Clark, 1985), 366.

126. See, e.g., Richard Bauckham, "Kingdom and Church According to Jesus and Paul," *HBT* 18 (1996): 1–26; Karl P. Donfried, "The Kingdom of God in Paul," in *The Kingdom of God in 20th-Century Interpretation*, ed. Wendell Willis (Peabody, MA: Hendrickson, 1987), 175–90, republished in *Paul, Thessalonica, and Early Christianity* (Grand Rapids: Eerdmans, 2002), 233–52; Peter Wolff, *Die frühe nachösterliche Verkündigung des Reiches Gottes* (FRLANT 171; Göttingen: Vandenhoeck & Ruprecht, 1999), 9–34.

127. See, e.g., Bruce Chilton, *Pure Kingdom: Jesus' Vision of God* (Grand Rapids: Eerdmans; London: SPCK, 1996), ix; E. P. Sanders, *The Historical Figure of Jesus* (New York: Penguin, 1993), 169–204. Exceptions include Burton L. Mack, *A Myth of Innocence: Mark and Christian Origins* (Philadelphia: Fortress, 1988), 69–74; Marcus J. Borg, *Jesus, a New Vision: Spirit, Culture, and the Life of Discipleship* (San Francisco: HarperOne, 1991), 202–3n20.

128. Cf., e.g., Rudolf Bultmann, *Theology of the New Testament*, 2 vols. (London: SCM, 1952–55), 1:76, 189; Wenham, *Paul*, 71–72. For the "kingdom" of God (or heaven) in the Gospels: Matthew 40x; Mark 14x; Luke 32x; John 5x. Outside the Gospels, "kingdom" (of heaven, God or his son, or "my [Jesus] kingdom") occurs in the NT thus: Acts 8x; Paul 8x (Rom. 14:17; 1 Cor. 4:20; 6:9, 10; 15:24, 50; Gal. 5:21; 1 Thess. 2:12). In the remainder of the NT, see Eph. 5:5; Col. 1:13; 4:11; 2 Thess. 1:5; 2 Tim. 4:1, 18; Heb. 1:8; 12:28; James 2:5; 2 Pet. 1:11; Rev. 1:6, 9; 5:10; 11:15; 12:10.

that appears to put a distance between these two figures[129]—Gerd Lüdemann terms it a "doctrinal dissonance."[130]

For example, in Romans, when Paul is writing the most sustained and reflective statement of his thinking, the notion of the kingdom of God plays no real part, occurring only once (Rom. 14:17). Of course, it could be that, as Rudolf Bultmann suggested, the concept of the "righteousness of God" (δικαιοσύνη θεοῦ) corresponds to the kingdom of God.[131] Further, aspects of Paul's use of this phrase increase his distance from Jesus. For example, in two places Paul defines the kingdom of God antithetically (Rom. 14:17; 1 Cor. 4:20) in a way not seen in the Jesus tradition.[132]

Notwithstanding these differences between Paul and Jesus in the use of the term, Paul mentioning the kingdom of God only eight times[133] probably does not reflect its considerable importance to him and his readers, nor obscure that he associates it with miracle. Introducing the phrase "kingdom of God" with "for" (γάρ) as a way of summarizing his argument of 1 Corinthians 4:1–21 shows that it was a term well understood and shared by Paul and his readers. In 1 Thessalonians Paul's description of his activities in Thessalonica occupies the first part of the body of the letter (2:1–12; cf. 1:2–10, esp. v. 5). At the end of his description of his ministry he says the readers will remember (cf. 2:9) that he pleaded with them to "lead a life worthy of God, who calls you into his own kingdom" (2:12). He makes a similar point in Galatians 5:21: "I am warning you, as I warned you before: those who do such things will not inherit the kingdom of God." Thus, although the term "kingdom" is mentioned only once in each of these recollections of his preaching, the importance of the theme to Paul and his readers is such that he is able to introduce it casually[134] and use it as a catchphrase to help readers recall a significant aspect of his preaching.[135]

129. A well-known statement by Alfred Loisy comes to mind: "Jesus foretold the kingdom, and it was the Church that came" (*The Gospel and the Church*, trans. Christopher Home, 2nd ed. [New York: Scribner, 1912], 166).

130. Gerd Lüdemann, *Paul, the Founder of Christianity* (Amherst, NY: Prometheus, 2002), 194.

131. Bultmann, "Historical Jesus," 232; see also Alexander J. M. Wedderburn, "Paul and Jesus: The Problem of Continuity," in Wedderburn, *Paul and Jesus*, 99–115, esp. 102, 103–13.

132. Günter Haufe, "Reich Gottes bei Paulus und in der Jesustradition," *NTS* 31 (1985): 467–72.

133. Rom. 14:17; 1 Cor. 4:20 (ἡ βασιλεία τοῦ θεοῦ); 1 Cor. 6:9 (θεοῦ βασιλείαν); 6:10 (βασιλείαν θεοῦ); 15:24 (τὴν βασιλείαν τῷ θεῷ); 15:50 (βασιλείαν θεοῦ); Gal. 5:21 (βασιλείαν θεοῦ); 1 Thess. 2:12 (τὴν ἑαυτοῦ βασιλείαν). In the larger Pauline corpus see Eph. 5:5 (τῇ βασιλείᾳ τοῦ Χριστοῦ καὶ θεοῦ); Col. 1:13 (τὴν βασιλείαν τοῦ υἱοῦ τῆς ἀγάπης αὐτοῦ); 4:11 (τὴν βασιλείαν τοῦ θεοῦ); 2 Thess. 1:5 (τῆς βασιλείας τοῦ θεοῦ); 2 Tim. 4:1 (τὴν βασιλείαν αὐτοῦ); 4:18 (τὴν βασιλείαν αὐτοῦ).

134. Cf. James D. G. Dunn, "Paul's Knowledge of the Jesus Tradition: The Evidence of Romans," in *Christus Bezeugen: Festschrift für Wolfgang Trilling zum 65. Geburtstag*, ed. Karl Kertelge, Traugott Holtz, and Claus-Peter März (Leipzig: St. Benno, 1989), 204.

135. Cf. Donfried, "Kingdom of God," 241.

Anticipating my later conclusions that Paul's preaching about the kingdom of God was associated with miracles is probably clearest in 1 Corinthians 4:20: "the kingdom of God is not in talk but in power" or miracles (further see §7.4 below). The same connections are found in 1 Thessalonians, where Paul recalls his message of the gospel coming in words, "in power" (or "miracle"), and "in the Holy Spirit" (1 Thess. 1:5; see §7.1 below), which he goes on to associate with God's kingdom (1 Thess. 2:12). The kingdom of God and the Spirit are also brought together in Romans 14:17: "For the kingdom of God is not food and drink but righteousness and peace and joy in the Holy Spirit."[136] In the traditions about Jesus' ministry we see the same association of ideas: Spirit, miracles, or power[137] and the kingdom of God (Matt. 12:28 // Luke 11:20).[138] Moreover, it is notable that although the kingdom of God can have a future aspect for Paul,[139] in passages where the possible connection to miracles is the closest, the present tense is used,[140] as it is in the Jesus tradition (Matt. 12:28 // Luke 11:20). In light of these associations between the kingdom of God, miracles, power, and the Spirit, in both Paul and the Jesus tradition as well as his knowledge of Q, it is reasonable to suppose that early Christian traditions about the miracles of Jesus have influenced Paul through his inheritance of this matrix of ideas.

(f) "Jews demand signs." In seeking to determine if Paul had been influenced by the miracle traditions associated with Jesus, David Wenham takes into account that in the Synoptic traditions Jesus rejects any demand (from Jews) to perform a sign,[141] and in 1 Corinthians 1:22 Paul says that "Jews demand signs."[142] Two problems present themselves, however, in supposing that this is evidence of Paul knowing about the miracles of Jesus.

---

136. Cf. Jason A. Wermuth, "*The Spirit and Power: Addressing Paul's Vision of the Kingdom of God through a Pneumatological Approach*" (MA thesis, Regent University, 2010).

137. See Mark 6:5 (on which, see C. E. B. Cranfield, *The Gospel According to Saint Mark: An Introduction and Commentary* [CGTC; Cambridge: Cambridge University Press, 1966], 197) and Mark 9:39 (on which, see Graham H. Twelftree, *Jesus the Exorcist: A Contribution to the Study of the Historical Jesus* [WUNT 2/54; Tübingen: Mohr Siebeck; Peabody, MA: Hendrickson, 1993], 40–43).

138. E.g., Dunn, "Paul's Knowledge," 204.

139. 1 Cor. 6:9, 10; 15:24, 50; Gal. 5:21; cf. 2 Thess. 1:5.

140. 1 Cor. 4:20; cf. Rom. 14:17; 1 Cor. 15:24. In 1 Thess. 2:12, where even if the aorist (καλέσαντος, "who called") variant reading is accepted (cf. 1 Thess. 4:7; Gal. 1:6) (see the discussion by Ernest Best, *First and Second Epistles to the Thessalonians* [BNTC; Peabody, MA: Hendrickson; London: Continuum, 1986], 107–8), Paul would still be describing the kingdom of God as present to his readers.

141. See Matt. 12:38–39; 16:1–4; Mark 8:11–13 // Luke 11:16, 29; John 6:30; cf. 2:12–22.

142. Wenham, *Paul*, 353–54, citing Matt. 12:38, 39 // Luke 11:16, 29–32; Matt. 16:1–4 // Mark 8:13.

First, the notion of Jews seeking signs was more widely attested than in the Jesus traditions,[143] therefore Paul need not be dependent on Christian sources for this idea. However, some time ago, James M. Robinson noted that it is rather striking that "signs," "wisdom," and "kerygma" are associated only in two places in early Christianity: 1 Corinthians 1:17–25 and Q (Luke 11:29–32).[144] This not only suggests that Paul knew this particular Q passage but it strengthens my earlier general case that Paul most likely was aware of the Q traditions.

Another problem in supposing that Paul's saying "Jews demand a sign" indicates he knew the miracle tradition of Jesus is that seeking signs was not the same as asking for a miracle. For, in this context, a sign was something God was thought to do for or through a prophet to establish the prophet as authentic and that his words would be fulfilled.[145] For example, for Moses there were a number of signs: the staff, the leprous hand, and the water turning to blood; for Gideon and Elijah it was a fire; and for Isaiah it was the sun moving backward.[146] Closer to Paul's time, Theudas, for example, expected the Jordan to divide (Josephus, *Ant.* 20.97–99), and an Egyptian claimed the walls of Jerusalem would collapse.[147] Nevertheless, since in Q (as in Mark 8:1–12) the Jews' request for a sign arose directly out of Jesus performing a miracle, and Paul was most likely aware of Q, there is at least the possibility that the statement "Jews demand signs" reflects Paul's awareness of the miracle traditions about Jesus.

(g) Faith to remove mountains. Given that Paul is the author of the love lyrics in 1 Corinthians 13,[148] in his saying "if I have all faith, so as to remove mountains" (13:2), he may be alluding to a saying in the Jesus tradition, though there is some debate as to whether it is the version now in Mark 11:23[149] or Q (Luke 17:6)[150] or, more likely, Matthew 17:20.[151] In turn, that Paul understands this saying to be connected to the miracle tradition of Jesus (as it is in Mat-

143. In the canon see, e.g., Exod. 4:1–9; 14:13; Deut. 18:15–22; Judg. 6:17–22; 1 Sam. 10:1–9; 1 Kings 18:30–39; 2 Kings 20:5–11; Isa. 7:10–17, all discussed by Morna D. Hooker, *The Signs of a Prophet: The Prophetic Actions of Jesus* (London: SCM, 1997), 5–6.
144. James M. Robinson, "Kerygma and History in the New Testament," in *The Bible in Modern Scholarship: Papers Read at the 100th Meeting of the Society of Biblical Literature, December 28–30, 1964,* ed. James Philip Hyatt (Nashville: Abingdon, 1965), 129. In the two passages in question the data is as follows: κήρυγμα ("kerygma"): Matt. 12:41 // Luke 11:32; 1 Cor. 1:21; σοφία ("wisdom"): Matt. 12:42 // Luke 11:31; 1 Cor. 1:17, 19, 20, 21 (2x), 22, 24, 30; σημεῖον ("sign"): Matt. 12:38 // Luke 11:16; Matt. 12:39 (3x) // Luke 11:29 (3x), 30; 1 Cor. 1:22.
145. See the discussion by Hooker, *Signs of a Prophet,* 2–4.
146. See Exod. 4:1–9; Judg. 6:17–22; 1 Kings 18:30–39; 2 Kings 20:5–11.
147. Josephus, *Ant.* 20.168–172; *J.W.* 2.261–263; cf. Acts 21:38.
148. See Anthony C. Thiselton, *The First Epistle to the Corinthians: A Commentary on the Greek Text* (NIGTC; Grand Rapids: Eerdmans, 2000), 1027–32 (including bibliography).
149. Allison, *Jesus Tradition,* 54n242.
150. Wenham, *Paul,* 82.
151. Tuckett, "1 Corinthians and Q," 614.

thew and Mark) seems possible in that he has been discussing the miraculous and faith (1 Cor. 12:1–31; cf. 12:9).[152] However, it is just as likely that Paul is using a widely available proverbial saying (e.g., *b. Ber.* 64a; *b. Sanh.* 24a),[153] or a recognizable variation of it, so that we cannot be sure that this is evidence that he had the miracle tradition of Jesus in mind.

(h) The compassion of Jesus and his care of the weak. David Wenham has also suggested that the phrase "the compassion [σπλάγχνον] of Christ Jesus" (Phil. 1:8) may be a hint of Paul's knowledge of the miracles of Jesus.[154] For, in the Gospel miracle traditions Jesus has "compassion"[155] for a leper (Mark 1:41), for crowds,[156] for a demoniac and his family (9:22), for two blind men (Matt. 20:34), and for the widow of Nain (Luke 7:13).

Turning to Paul, we see that he says he and Titus have compassion for the Corinthians, and that he has the same attitude toward the Philippians.[157] Although it is possible that the notion of compassion may be reminiscent of the traditions about compassion motivating the miracles of Jesus, it is more likely Paul has in mind God's redemptive compassion in Jesus, which is seen also in the parables where a slave receives compassion (Matt. 18:27), and the Samaritan (Luke 10:33) and the father of the prodigal exercise compassion (15:20). For, in the period the σπλάγχνον word group could be used for God's mercy,[158] and there is no hint otherwise of the idea of miracle being associated with Paul's use of the word.

Wenham further proposes that in Paul urging his readers to help the "weak" (ἀσθενής; 1 Thess. 5:14), it is possible Paul sees himself continuing Jesus' healing ministry.[159] For, in the Gospels "weak" was used of the physically sick.[160]

---

152. See the extended discussion by Wenham, *Paul*, 81–83.

153. See John Lightfoot, *A Commentary on the New Testament from the Talmud and Hebraica: Matthew—1 Corinthians*, 4 vols. (1859; repr., Grand Rapids: Baker, 1979), 2:282–83. For a not altogether convincing case to the contrary, see Maureen W. Yeung, *Faith in Jesus and Paul: A Comparison with Special Reference to "Faith That Can Remove Mountains" and "Your Faith Has Healed/Saved You"* (WUNT 2/147; Tübingen: Mohr Siebeck, 2002), 23–30, and the review by Timothy Gombis, *JETS* 47 (2004): 536.

154. Wenham, *Paul*, 351.

155. σπλαγχνίζομαι (verb): Matt. 9:36; 14:14; 15:32; 18:27; 20:34; Mark 1:41; 6:34; 8:2; 9:22; Luke 7:13; 10:33; 15:20.

156. Mark 6:34 // Matt. 9:36 // 14:14; Mark 8:2 // Matt. 15:32.

157. σπλάγχνον (noun): 2 Cor. 6:12; 7:15; Phil. 1:8; cf. 2:1; Philem. 7, 12, 20.

158. See Luke 1:78 (σπλάγχνον); Eph. 4:32 (εὔσπλαγχνος, also in the NT in 1 Pet. 3:8). See Markus Bockmuehl, *The Epistle to the Philippians* (BNTC; Peabody, MA: Hendrickson, 1998), 65, citing Luke 1:78; James 5:11 (πολύσπλαγχνος); *T. Zeb.* 8:2; *T. Naph.* 4:5; *T. Levi* 4:4; Pr. Man. 7; *Let. Arist.* 211; *1 Clem.* 29:1.

159. Wenham, *Paul*, 352.

160. See Matt. 25:43, 44; Luke 9:2; 10:9; cf. Acts 4:9; 5:15, 16. In the NT ἀσθενής also occurs in Mark 14:38; Rom. 5:6; 1 Cor. 1:25, 27; 4:10; 8:7, 9, 10; 9:22 (3x); 11:30; 12:22; 2 Cor. 10:10; Gal. 4:9; 1 Thess. 5:14; Heb. 7:18; 1 Pet. 3:7.

However, Paul almost always uses ἀσθενής as a contrast to strength, not health.[161] Only in one place does "weakness" most probably refer to sickness: Paul explains that it is the improper approach to the Lord's Supper that has caused many of the Corinthians to be "weak," ill, and some to have died (1 Cor. 11:30; see §6.3 below). In another place Paul cites his opponents as saying that "his bodily presence is weak" (2 Cor. 10:10), which also could mean that he was sick.[162] However, when Paul urges the Thessalonians to "help the weak," it is in the context of encouraging the care of the idle, the fainthearted, and the weak (1 Thess. 5:14), which is most likely to mean not the sick but those who are spiritually weak. In short, neither Paul's use of "weak" nor his idea of the compassion of Christ is probably helpful in establishing any connection between him and the miracle traditions of Jesus and his first followers. Notwithstanding, in this section we have ample evidence that Paul knew of the motifs of the miraculous, as well as of mission, in the Christian traditions he inherited.

If Paul was introduced to a Christianity that included tradition in which Jesus was firmly and frequently associated with miracle working and the miraculous, we can turn to setting out the relationship that Paul understood he had with Jesus in order to see what implication it is likely to have for his understanding of the miraculous in relation to this ministry.

5.4 Jesus and Paul

In this section we will be able to see that the relationship Paul describes himself having with Jesus makes it highly probable that Paul was involved in the miraculous. In doing so, we keep in mind that, in line with the Christianity Paul inherited, Jesus was already affirmed as the Christ. This is obvious when, for example, he writes to the Corinthians that the tradition he had received from earlier Christians was that *Christ* died and was raised.[163] Yet, he can also say that *Jesus* died and rose again,[164] showing that he could use the names "Jesus" and "Christ" interchangeably, as he does most obviously in the parallel phrases "who raised Jesus . . . who raised Christ" (Rom. 8:11).[165]

---

161. 1 Cor. 1:25, 27; 4:10; 8:7, 9, 10, 22 (3x); 12:22; Gal. 4:9; cf. 2 Cor. 10:10. For his comparable use of the noun ἀσθένεια, see Rom. 6:19; 8:26; 1 Cor. 2:3; 15:43; 2 Cor. 11:30; 12:5, 9 (2x), 10; 13:4; Gal. 4:13.

162. Cf. Gal. 4:13: ἀσθένειαν τῆς σαρκός ("weakness of the flesh"). However, see 2 Cor. 12:1–10, where "weakness" rather than "sickness" is the better translation of the noun ἀσθένεια.

163. 1 Cor. 15:3–4; cf. 1:23; 2:2; 15:12–17, 20; Rom. 6:4, 9; 7:4. See also Eph. 1:20; Col. 3:1.

164. 1 Thess. 4:14; cf. 1:10; Rom. 4:24; 10:9; 2 Cor. 4:14.

165. Rom. 8:11: τοῦ ἐγείραντος τὸν Ἰησοῦν . . . ὁ ἐγείρας Χριστόν. Cf. 1 Cor. 4:15; Gal. 2:16; Phil. 2:5–11; 3:8. Also see Eph. 1:3; 2:13; 2 Thess. 1:12.

The issue here is not so much what Paul knew about Jesus;[166] I have already established that he most probably knew Jesus to have been a miracle worker (see above). Instead, here I expect to be able to show that the way Paul understood his relationship with Jesus—as ambassador, "in" Christ, imitator of Jesus, a prophet, and especially his wish to be seen as an apostle[167]—makes it most probable that Paul would have included the miraculous in his own ministry.

(a) Apostle. Paul's most cherished and closely guarded designation for himself was that of "apostle."[168] He uses it often to introduce himself,[169] especially when asserting his leadership,[170] as he does most notably in the Corinthian correspondence.[171] Later, as its use by Luke and in the literature written by Paul's followers suggests,[172] it was the title by which he was best remembered, and was thought to describe him most accurately.

For our purposes, Paul's use of ἀπόστολος ("apostle") is significant in two ways. First, the word, though not common before being taken up by Christians, had already assumed the connotation of an emissary.[173] For example, in the

166. For a generous list of the information Paul probably had about Jesus, see Barnett, *Paul*, 18–19.

167. On the fluidity and flexibility of Paul's understanding of his multiple identities, see Caroline Johnson Hodge, "Apostle to the Gentiles: Constructions of Paul's Identity," *BibInt* 13 (2005): 270–88.

168. For ἀπόστολος in the Pauline corpus, see Rom. 1:1; 11:13; 16:7; 1 Cor. 1:1; 4:9; 9:1, 2, 5; 12:28, 29; 15:7, 9 (2x); 2 Cor. 1:1; 8:23; 11:5, 13; 12:11, 12; Gal. 1:1, 17, 19; Eph. 1:1; 2:20; 3:5; 4:11; Phil. 2:25; Col. 1:1; 1 Thess. 2:7; 1 Tim. 1:1; 2:7; 2 Tim. 1:1, 11; Titus 1:1. In the rest of the NT see Matt. 10:2; Mark 3:14; 6:30; Luke 6:13; 9:10; 11:49; 17:5; 22:14; 24:10; John 13:16; Acts 1:2, 26; 2:37, 42, 43; 4:33, 35, 36, 37; 5:2, 12, 18, 29, 40; 6:6; 8:1, 14, 18; 9:27; 11:1; 14:4, 14; 15:2, 4, 6, 22, 23; 16:4; Heb. 3:1; 1 Pet. 1:1; 2 Pet. 1:1; 3:2; Jude 1:17; Rev. 2:2; 18:20; 21:14. The importance to Paul of the idea of being an apostle can be further seen in his using this theologically pregnant word, including the verb ἀποστέλλω (1 Cor. 1:17; cf. Rom. 10:15), but nevertheless rich πεμπ ("send") words for his ministry. For Paul's use of πέμπω, see Rom. 8:3; 1 Cor. 4:17; 16:3; 2 Cor. 9:3; Phil. 2:19, 23, 25, 28; 4:16; 1 Thess. 3:2, 5; cf. Eph. 6:22; Col. 4:8; 2 Thess. 2:11; Titus 3:12. Note also προπέμπω in Rom. 15:24; 1 Cor. 16:6, 11; 2 Cor. 1:16; Titus 3:13.

169. Rom. 1:1; 1 Cor. 1:1; 2 Cor. 1:1; Gal. 1:1.

170. See the discussion by Ernest Best, "Paul's Apostolic Authority—?," *JSNT* 27 (1986): 10–12. Best (*Paul and His Converts* [Edinburgh: T&T Clark, 1988], 19–20) does not take 1 Cor. 9:1–2 into account when stating that, in exercising authority among his converts, Paul "never reinforces what he says by claiming to be an apostle."

171. Of Paul's fifteen uses of the term in relation to himself (including Colossians), nine occur in the Corinthian correspondence, in which his leadership is most at stake: Rom. 1:1; 11:13; 1 Cor. 1:1; 4:9; 9:1, 2, 5; 15:9 (2x); 2 Cor. 1:1; 12:12; Gal. 1:1, 17; Col. 1:1; 1 Thess. 2:7. Notably, he does not use the term of himself in his letter to the Philippians, addressed to a church with which he was manifestly pleased (1:3–11) and that supported him (4:10–20).

172. Acts 14:4, 14; Eph. 1:1; 2:20; 3:5; 4:11; 1 Tim. 1:1; 2:7; 2 Tim. 1:1, 11; Titus 1:1.

173. See Karl H. Rengstorf, "ἀπόστολος, κτλ.," *TDNT* 1:407–8, citing, e.g., Dionysius of Halicarnassus, *Ant. rom.* 9.59; Jan-Adolf Bühner, "ἀπόστολος," *EDNT* 1:142–46. This is not to argue that, in Paul's time, there was a legal institution of ambassador. See the discussion by

only appearance of ἀπόστολος in the Septuagint, it translates שָׁלַח (šālaḥ, "to be let go," or "sent off").[174] With an emphasis on the sending in conjunction with the one sent, the prophet Ahijah says, "I am charged with heavy tidings for you."[175] Notably, "apostle" is used here as a technical term for the prophet commissioned by God with a message from him.[176] Also, in the call of Isaiah, which was important to Paul (Isa. 6:8; see §3.1 above), the idea of a prophet being sent (using the verb ἀποστέλλειν) is seen most clearly,[177] and in rabbinic Judaism a little after Paul's time a prophet could be called an envoy or agent.[178]

Further, in his only certain use of the word, Josephus describes a "delegation" (ἀπόστολος) of fifty Jewish ambassadors[179] sent to petition the emperor Augustus to allow their nation to live by their own laws.[180] Here the intimate connection, even identity, between those sending and those sent is apparent. Philo expresses the same close connection between sender and sent in a description of angels and demons as "ambassadors" (πρεσβευταί) moving "backwards and forwards between men and God" (Philo, Gig. 16). He goes on to cite Psalm 78:49 (LXX 77:49), where God sends his wrath "through an apostleship [ἀποστολή] of evil angels."[181] As Karl Rengstorf described this use of "apostle," "The one who is sent is of interest only to the degree that in some measure he embodies in his existence as such the one who sent him."[182]

That Paul understood his use of "apostle" for his ministry to express this dependent and intimate relationship with God in Christ is seen in his use of "to send out" (ἐξαποστέλλειν) for God sending Jesus (Gal. 4:4). That is,

---

Anthony Bash, *Ambassadors for Christ: An Exploration of Ambassadorial Language in the New Testament* (WUNT 2/92; Tübingen: Mohr Siebeck, 1997), esp. 12–13.

174. Rengstorf, "ἀπόστολος, κτλ.," 400. On the debate regarding the role of שליח in the origins of the NT concept of apostle, see Francis H. Agnew, "The Origin of the NT Apostle-Concept: A Review of Research," *JBL* 105 (1986): 75–96.

175. LXX 3 Kgdms. (ET 1 Kings) 14:6 [A]: και εγω ειμι αποστολος προς σε σκληρος.

176. Cf., e.g., LXX Gen. 32:4 (ET 32:3); Num. 20:14; Josh. 7:22; Judg. 6:35; 7:24; 9:31; 2 Chron. 36:15; Mal. 3:1.

177. Cf. LXX Exod. 3:10; Judg. 6:8; Isa. 6:8; Jer. 1:7; Ezek. 2:3; Hag. 1:12; Zech. 2:15 (ET 2:11). Cf. Rom. 11:13; 1 Cor. 9:1.

178. See the discussion by Jan-Adolf Bühner, *Der Gesandte und sein Weg im 4. Evangelium: Die kultur- und religionsgeschichtlichen Grundlagen der johanneischen Sendungschristologie sowie ihre traditionsgeschichtliche Entwicklung* (WUNT 2/2; Tübingen: Mohr Siebeck, 1977), 283–99; Bühner, "ἀπόστολος," 145. Also, in Isa. 18:2 Symmachus (late second to early third century CE) uses ἀπόστολος to translate שָׁלַח (šālaḥ).

179. Josephus, *Ant.* 17.300, using both πρεσβεία ("embassy" [feminine singular]) and πρέσβεις ("ambassadors" [masculine plural]).

180. Josephus's other possible use of ἀπόστολος is in *Ant.* 1.146, where τὸν ἀπόστολον (or τὴν ἀποστολήν) may be read in place of τὸν ἀποδασμόν. See Rengstorf, "ἀπόστολος," 413.

181. Philo, *Gig.* 17, my translation. The LXX has the verb ἐξαποστέλλω ("send out").

182. Rengstorf, "ἀπόστολος," 401.

for Paul, as God has sent his Son, so Christ has sent him. The reverberation through Paul's letters of this mind-set is apparent in the way he describes his "apostolic" ministry as obedience to God's will,[183] as an obligation (1 Cor. 9:16–17), and as slavery to Christ (Rom. 1:1; cf. 2 Cor. 4:5; Titus 1:1) rather than as something of human origin (Gal. 1:10–17; see §5.1 above). Further, being under obligation to God, as a slave to Christ and his emissary, is of a piece with Paul's view that God is present in his ministry (Rom. 15:18; 1 Cor. 15:9–10), working through him (Gal. 2:8), and that the glory of Christ is seen in his ministry (2 Cor. 3:6–8; 4:4–6).[184] It is reasonable to suppose, then, knowing the ministry of Jesus involved miracles, as his apostle, Paul would have expected them in his.

Second, Paul's use of the title "apostle" is significant to us in that he uses it as a way of including himself among the first, or at least first wave of, followers of Jesus and to cause his readers to compare him favorably with Peter, James, and the other early leaders.[185] He says that he has seen the Lord (1 Cor. 9:1), who appeared to him, as he had to all the apostles (15:7–8). He asserts his and Barnabas's right to material support (9:4) and to be accompanied by a believing wife,[186] "as do the other apostles [ἀπόστολοι] and the brothers of the Lord and Cephas" (9:5).[187] Although here "apostles" could refer to the wider group of mission workers,[188] he includes Peter in comparing himself with others. In other words, Paul considered himself neither derivative of nor subordinate to them (esp. Gal. 1:11–17, on which, see §5.1 above), but rather one of the

183. 1 Cor. 1:1; 2 Cor. 1:1; Col. 1:1; cf. Eph. 1:1; 2 Tim 1:1.
184. From the opposite perspective, it could be that Paul sees his ministry conducted before or in "God's presence" (κατέναντι [2 Cor. 2:17; 12:19]). However, on the basis of Paul implying that he is willing to defend himself, even before God, David A. Renwick (*Paul, the Temple, and the Presence of God* [BJS 224; Atlanta: Scholars Press, 1991]) is right to conclude that, "although Paul might well have sensed that God's presence was a reality, and not merely hypothetical, the major thrust of his use of κατέναντι in both cases would not have been to assert that reality, but to defend his integrity" (p. 62). For such a reading of Rom. 4:17, the only other place where Paul uses κατέναντι, see Douglas A. Campbell, "Towards a New, Rhetorically Assisted Reading of Romans 3.27–4.25," in *Rhetorical Criticism and the Bible*, ed. Stanley E. Porter and Dennis L. Stamps (JSNTSup 195; Sheffield: Sheffield Academic Press, 2002), 381–83. See also Murray J. Harris (*The Second Epistle to the Corinthians: A Commentary on the Greek Text* [NIGTC; Grand Rapids: Eerdmans; Milton Keynes: Paternoster, 2005], 255n79), who associates κατέναντι with the omniscience ("in God's sight") rather than his omnipresence ("in the presence of").
185. Best, "Apostolic Authority–?" 7–8.
186. Literally, "sister wife" or "sister as a wife" (ἀδελφὴν γυναῖκα). See Thiselton, *First Epistle to the Corinthians*, 679–80.
187. On the notion that Paul does not see Peter and James as apostles, see Walter Schmithals, *The Office of Apostle in the Early Church*, trans. John E. Steely (Nashville: Abingdon, 1969), 80–81. On the other hand, see Gordon D. Fee, *The First Epistle to the Corinthians* (NICNT; Grand Rapids: Eerdmans, 1987), 403n35.
188. Eduard Lohse, "Ursprung und Prägung des christlichen Apostolates," *TZ* 9 (1953): 267.

group to which Peter, James, and the other first followers of Jesus belonged.[189]
Moreover, from 1 Corinthians 4:21—"let no one boast about human leaders
. . . whether Paul or Apollos or Cephas"—Paul is aware that at least some of
his readers see him in the same league as Peter (Gal. 2:7–9).

In turn, I have already established that Paul knew these apostles or followers
had been commissioned by Jesus to heal, as well as to preach (see §5.2 above).
Therefore, for Paul to call himself an apostle on a level with these—even if
the last or least (1 Cor. 15:8–9)[190]—it would be surprising if he did not also
take his commission to involve healing. Indeed, as we will see when we look
more closely at what Paul appears to say about miracles, it is to his being an
apostle that he links performing signs: "signs of a true apostle" (2 Cor. 12:12;
see §7.7 below). In short, Paul's use of the title "apostle" for himself would
have carried with it the shared assumption with his readers that, like Jesus,
who called him, he also conducted miracles, or they were at least involved in
his ministry. This conclusion is considerably strengthened when we look at
other ways he describes himself in 2 Corinthians.

(b) *Ambassador.* In 2 Corinthians 5:20 Paul describes his ministry: "for
Christ, then, we are ambassadors" (ὑπὲρ Χριστοῦ οὖν πρεσβεύομεν) (my
translation).[191] That Paul means his ministry to be understood as "in place of
Christ,"[192] rather than simply "serving Christ,"[193] is suggested by four factors.[194]
First, as in the saying "a man's agent is like to himself,"[195] an ambassador
was regarded in the same way as the sender.[196] Second, more particularly,

---

189. Richard N. Longenecker, *Galatians* (WBC 41; Dallas: Word, 1990), 34.

190. In Gal. 1:17 he writes of τοὺς πρὸ ἐμοῦ ἀποστόλους ("those apostles before him," my
translation), by which he means at least Peter and James (Gal. 1:18–19). Cf. Rom. 16:7.

191. In Philem. 9 Paul appeals to Philemon as a πρεσβύτης, often translated "old man" (e.g.,
NRSV) (cf. Luke 1:18; Titus 2:2). However, πρεσβύτης is more reasonably rendered "ambassador."
Cf. LXX 2 Chron. 32:31 [B]; 1 Macc. 14:22; 15:17 [ℵ]; 2 Macc. 1:34; see Günther Bornkamm,
"πρέσβυς, κτλ.," *TDNT* 6:683n2. First, at the time, πρεσβύτης was used interchangeably with
πρεσβευτής, the usual word for "ambassador." See the discussion, as well as those cited, by Peter T.
O'Brien, *Colossians, Philemon* (WBC 44; Milton Keynes, UK: Word,1987), 290. Second, Paul is
unlikely to appeal to a man, likely of similar age, on the basis of his age. Third, taking Paul to
be referring to his ambassadorial role makes more sense of the contrast involved in the conjunction νυνὶ δὲ καί ("but now also") between being an ambassador and a prisoner (cf. Eph. 6:20).

192. E.g., Rudolf Bultmann, *The Second Letter to the Corinthians*, trans. Roy A. Harrisville
(Minneapolis: Augsburg, 1985), 163; Thrall, *Second Epistle to the Corinthians*, 1:437.

193. E.g., Jean Héring, *The Second Epistle of Saint Paul to the Corinthians*, trans. A. W.
Heathcote and P. J. Allcock (London: Epworth, 1967), 44.

194. On the complexities and broader implications of Paul using the term "ambassador" of
himself, see the discussion by Bash, *Ambassadors*, esp. 104–16.

195. *b. Ber.* 5:5. See also e.g., Matt. 10:40–43; Mark 9:37; Luke 10:16; John 5:23, 43; 7:18;
Did. 11:4; Philo, *Legat.* 369.

196. See Margaret M. Mitchell, "New Testament Envoys in Their Context of Greco-Roman Diplomatic and Epistolary Conventions: The Example of Timothy and Titus," *JBL* 111 (1992): 645–47.

Paul has just said he is doing what God had done: God, having reconciled Paul to himself through Christ, has given Paul the ministry of reconciliation (2 Cor. 5:18). Third, ambassadors—often introduced as "for" (ὑπέρ) in relation to the authority who had commissioned them—legally represented and acted for the one sending them, in order to bring a message or to negotiate in their stead.[197] Then, fourth, Paul goes on immediately to say that God is making his appeal "through us" (δι᾽ ἡμῶν, 5:20). In other words, at least in his preaching, which is immediately in view here (cf. παρακαλέω, "call" or "invite"), Paul sees himself not simply conveying a message, but speaking in Christ's place.

This same conclusion is to be drawn from Paul's next paragraph. In summarizing the nature of his ministry, Paul appeals (παρακαλέω) to his readers on the basis of working together (συνεργέω).[198] He does not say with whom he is working. In that the working together is the basis of his call to the readers, it is not likely to be them. Nor is there anyone else in view, such as fellow evangelists,[199] with whom readers would think he was working. Since he has just said, using the same word (παρακαλέω), that it is God who is calling his readers through him (2 Cor. 5:20), it is most likely that Paul is representing his ministry of preaching as working together with God (cf. 1 Thess. 3:2).[200]

That Paul sees his ministry involving not only speaking in Christ's stead, but also acting for him, is clear from Romans 15:18. He writes of "what Christ has accomplished through me . . . by word and deed."[201] As with his speaking, it is not simply that Paul has been acting in the service of Christ (cf. Rom. 15:16), but that what Paul has done has been Christ himself actually working through him.[202] Paul expresses the strong sense of Christ carrying out the work in using the compound verb κατεργάζομαι ("achieve, accomplish, bring about").[203] This

197. Bornkamm, "πρέσβυς," 381.
198. 2 Cor. 6:1. Paul uses the noun συνεργός in Rom. 16:3, 9, 21; 1 Cor. 3:9; 2 Cor. 1:24; 8:23; Phil. 2:25; 4:3; 1 Thess. 3:2; Philem. 1, 24; cf. Col. 4:11. Otherwise in the NT this word occurs only in 3 John 8. The verb συνεργέω is used in the NT in Mark 16:20; Rom. 8:28; 1 Cor. 16:16; 2 Cor. 6:1; James 2:22.
199. As supposed by F. F. Bruce, 1 and 2 Corinthians (NCB; London: Oliphants, 1971), 211, citing 1 Cor. 3:9. See also Rom. 16:3, 9, 21; 2 Cor. 8:23; Phil. 2:25; 4:3; Philem. 1, 24; cf. Col. 4:11.
200. E.g., Ralph P. Martin, 2 Corinthians (WBC 40; Waco: Word, 1986), 165; Thrall, Second Epistle to the Corinthians, 1:451n1824. More difficult to interpret is Paul's θεοῦ γάρ ἐσμεν συνεργοί ("for we are God's fellow-workers," my translation) in 1 Cor. 3:9. See Thiselton, First Epistle to the Corinthians, 305–7.
201. Rom. 15:18: ὧν οὐ κατειργάσατο Χριστὸς δι᾽ ἐμοῦ εἰς ὑπακοὴν ἐθνῶν, λόγῳ καὶ ἔργῳ. Further, see §7.8 below.
202. Cranfield, Romans, 2:758.
203. For κατεργάζομαι in the Pauline corpus, common in Romans and 2 Corinthians, see Rom. 1:27; 2:9; 4:15; 5:3; 7:8, 13, 15, 17, 18, 20; 15:18; 1 Cor. 5:3; 2 Cor. 4:17; 5:5; 7:10, 11; 9:11; 12:12; Phil. 2:12; cf. Eph. 6:13. In the remainder of the NT James 1:3; 1 Pet. 4:3.

leads us to note a characteristic Pauline idea that also shows that Paul saw himself as acting in Christ's place.

(c) Identifying with Jesus Christ. The importance to Paul of a series of phrases—"in Christ Jesus," "in the Lord," "in the Lord Jesus," "with Christ," "through Christ," "into Christ," for example, as well as, particularly, "in Christ"—is well known.[204] Sometimes Paul uses the "in Christ" phrase to refer particularly to the saving work of Christ. He says, for example, "God was in Christ reconciling the world" (2 Cor. 5:19), and he writes of "the will of God in Christ for you" (1 Thess. 5:18). A subjective use of the phrases occurs in him saying of believers, "you are in Christ Jesus" (1 Cor. 1:30), or that we have freedom "in Christ" (Gal. 2:4), portraying "the most intimate possible fellowship," as Adolf Deissmann put it.[205]

Of particular interest to us is Paul's use of the "in Christ" phrase to describe his own activity. He says, for example, he has fellow workers "in Christ" (Rom. 16:3); and he says "in Christ" he became father to the Corinthians (1 Cor. 4:15), and that they are his work "in the Lord" (9:1). Especially from this last statement, it is not only that Paul is saying that Christ is expressing himself in him, as Deissmann described it.[206] This would be how Paul describes his work as being "through" (διά) Christ—acting as a conduit between God and his people (e.g., Rom. 15:18; 2 Cor. 5:20).[207] Rather, a point that has important implications for our study: Paul identifies his work with the work of Christ or the Lord. That is, in his ministry Paul considers himself as no less than acting as Christ.[208] What he does, Christ is doing; and what Christ does, he is doing.

Paul also reminds the Corinthians "of my ways in Christ" (τὰς ὁδούς μου τὰς ἐν Χριστῷ, 1 Cor. 4:17). Here "ways" (ὁδοί) refers not simply to his thinking or teaching.[209] "Way" (ὁδός) was a rich word with a breadth of possible meanings, and it was widely used figuratively for a way or manner of life.[210] It

204. The precise phrase "in Christ" (or "in Christ Jesus") is used seventy-three times in the Pauline corpus (Rom. 3:24; 6:11, 23; 8:1, 2, 39; 9:1; 12:5; 15:17; 16:3, 7, 9, 10; 1 Cor. 1:2, 4, 30; 3:1; 4:10, 15, 17; 15:18, 19, 31; 16:24; 2 Cor. 2:17; 3:14; 5:17, 19; 12:2, 19; Gal. 1:22; 2:4, 17; 3:14, 26, 28; Eph. 1:1, 3; 2:6, 7, 10, 13; 3:6, 21; 4:32; Phil. 1:1, 13, 26; 2:1, 5; 3:3, 14; 4:7, 19, 21; Col. 1:2, 4, 28; 1 Thess. 2:14; 4:16; 5:18; 1 Tim. 1:14; 3:13; 2 Tim. 1:1, 9, 13; 2:1, 10; 3:12, 15; Philem. 8, 20, 23), while in the remainder of the NT it appears only in 1 Pet. 3:16; 5:10, 14. For a summary discussion of Paul's language of participation, see Dunn, *Theology of Paul*, 390–412 (including bibliography).

205. Adolf Deissmann, *Paul: A Study in Social and Religious History*, trans. William E. Wilson (1926; repr., New York: Harper, 1957), 140.

206. Ibid., 135, citing 1 Cor. 1:24; 4:4; 2 Cor. 12:9; Phil. 3:10.

207. See Dunn, *Theology of Paul*, 406.

208. See ibid., 398.

209. As supposed by, e.g., Wilhelm Michaelis, "ὁδός, κτλ.," *TDNT* 5:87–88.

210. E.g., Plato, *Resp.* 10.600a; Isocrates, *Demon.* 5.5; Thucydides, *Hist.* 3.64.4; LXX Exod. 18:20; Deut. 5:33; Jer. 4:18; Philo, *Gig.* 64; *Leg.* 3.253; *Mos.* 1.195; Josephus, *J.W.* 5.402; *Ant.*

was the equivalent to "custom"[211]—that is, a moral way of life. It was used in this way by early Christians.[212] Paul, therefore, would probably have in mind his ethical standards, as well as his ideas and teaching.[213] However, since he has been cataloging his sufferings (1 Cor. 4:11–13), it is likely that these also are in mind as part of the model for his readers.[214] Further, however, since he goes straight on to contrast "talk" (λόγος) and "power" (δύναμις), and to define his gospel ("kingdom of God") (4:20; see §5.3 [e] above) as power rather than talk, it is highly likely that to remind his readers of his ways, he had in mind drawing attention to his whole pattern of life and ministry, including the miracles as well as his sufferings.

This identification of Paul's work with that of Christ's is also clear in Paul's statement about the Corinthians: "you are a letter of Christ [ἐπιστολὴ Χριστοῦ], prepared by us" (2 Cor. 3:3). Given that Paul's interest is the existence rather than the contents of the letter,[215] the Corinthians are a letter written by Christ, not about him.[216] Yet, Paul says that the letter was "cared for by us" (διακονηθεῖσα ὑφ' ἡμῶν, 3:3).[217] Bultmann catches the essence of Paul's thinking in saying that, "Paul's work is basically not his own, but that of Christ . . . for which he merely assumes the role of διάκονος" ("servant").[218] Put another way, Paul sees not only his own experience, but also his ministry as the expression and, therefore for his converts, the experience of Jesus at work.

13.290. See F. J. Helfmeyer, "הָלַךְ," TDOT 3:388–403, esp. 391–92; Wilhelm Michaelis, "ὁδός, κτλ.," TDNT 5:48–65.

211. E.g., LXX Exod. 18:20; Jer. 33:13 (ET 26:13); Jastrow, "הֲלָכָה," 353. Also see Boykin Sanders, "Imitating Paul: 1 Cor. 4:16," HTR 74 (1981): 353–63; Willis Peter de Boer, The Imitation of Paul: An Exegetical Study (Kampen: Kok, 1962), 148.

212. See, e.g., Matt. 7:13–14; 22:16; Mark 12:14; Luke 20:21; Acts 13:10; 14:16; Rom. 3:16–17; Heb. 3:10; James 1:7–8; 5:20; 2 Pet. 2:2, 15, 21; Jude 11; Barn. 4:10; 5:4 (2x); 10:10; 11:6 (2x); 12:4; 18:1 (2x); 19:1 (2x), 2; 20:1 (2x); 1 Clem. 16:6; 18:13; 35:5; 53:2; 57:6; 2 Clem. 5:7; Did. 1:1 (2x), 2; 4:14; 5:1; 6:1; Herm. 6:6; 35:2, 3, 4 (2x), 5; 75:1.

213. See, e.g., Fee, First Epistle to the Corinthians, 189 and n. 37; Thiselton, First Epistle to the Corinthians, 374.

214. William D. Spencer, "The Power in Paul's Teaching (1 Cor. 4:9–20)," JETS 32 (1989): 51–61, esp. 59.

215. Victor P. Furnish, II Corinthians: Translated with Introduction, Notes, and Commentary (AB 32A; Garden City, NY: Doubleday, 1984), 182.

216. On the discussion of the genitive Χριστοῦ ("of Christ") being objective (written about Christ) or, more likely, subjective (written by Christ), see Thrall, Second Epistle to the Corinthians, 1:224, and those cited.

217. The word διακονηθεῖσα could be translated "prepared by" (NRSV), "delivered by" (e.g., NEB), "supplied by us" (C. K. Barrett, The Second Epistle to the Corinthians [BNTC; London: Black, 1973], 96, 108), for example. It is unlikely to mean "written" (Harris, Second Epistle to the Corinthians, 263), for Paul goes on to say that the letter has been "written not with ink but with the Spirit of the living God" (2 Cor. 3:3).

218. Bultmann, Second Letter to the Corinthians, 72.

My conclusion is maintained when we take into account those places where Paul talks not of his being in Christ, but of Christ being in him.[219] Most dramatically he says in Galatians 2:20: "and it is no longer I who live, but Christ lives in me" (my translation).[220] Paul has just said that he has been crucified with Christ (2:19). He now explains this not only means death to the Mosaic law (2:19), but also that his "I" has been killed and, as James Dunn puts it, "replaced by a new focus of personality."[221] While Paul understands that there is a certain tension in his existence, in that his life is still lived "in the flesh,"[222] Christ is now the new personal center of his life.[223]

We can also take into account that although Paul uses the phrase "with Christ" (Phil. 1:23; cf. Col. 2:20; 3:3) or "with him"[224] to refer primarily to the future of believers,[225] in Romans 6:8 his present life is seen as "with Christ," in that he says "we have died with Christ."[226] Paul's interest in his present identification with Christ is also seen in his using the present active tense, we "suffer with" (συμπάσχομεν) him (Rom. 8:17). He writes also in the present tense of "being conformed to" (συμμορφιζόμενος) Christ's death (Phil. 3:10). And in Romans 8:29 being "conformed [συμμόρφους] to the image of his Son" is an ongoing experience.[227] The import of this language is that Paul is giving expression to the understanding that his life and activities are a participation in the whole life of Jesus.[228] It is inconceivable, therefore, that Paul would have understood his ministry without including miracles, and that they would not have been a significant aspect of his work.

(d) *Imitator of Jesus.* A number of times Paul specifically urges his readers to imitate him,[229] and there are hints of the idea in other places.[230] In both Paul's

219. See Rom. 8:10; 2 Cor. 13:5; cf. John 17:23; Eph. 3:17; Col. 1:27. Though, at the level of experience it amounts to the same thing, Paul more commonly writes of the Spirit living or acting in a believer, e.g., Rom. 5:5; 8:9, 11, 15–19, 23, 26.
220. Gal. 2:20: ζῶ δὲ οὐκέτι ἐγώ, ζῇ δὲ ἐν Χριστός.
221. Dunn, *Galatians*, 145.
222. Gal. 2:20: ἐν σαρκί; cf. Rom. 8:11; 2 Cor. 4:11.
223. Ulrich Luz, "Paul as Mystic," in *The Holy Spirit and Christian Origins: Essays in Honor of James D. G. Dunn*, ed. Graham N. Stanton, Bruce W. Longenecker, and Stephen C. Barton (Grand Rapids: Eerdmans, 2004), 139.
224. Rom. 8:32; 2 Cor. 13:4; 1 Thess. 4:14; 5:10; cf. Col. 2:13; 3:4. In 2 Cor. 4:14 Paul uses "with Jesus," and 1 Thess. 4:17 "with the Lord."
225. This is also expressed through some of his many σύν- ("with") compound words. See Phil. 3:21 (σύμμορφος, "have the same form"); Rom. 8:17 (συγκληρονόμος, "inherit together"; συνδοξάζω, "glorify with"). On Paul's σύν- ("with") compounds, see Dunn, *Theology of Paul*, 402–4.
226. Cf. Rom. 6:4: συνθάπτω ("bury with").
227. Jewett, *Romans*, 428–29.
228. We need not be diverted by the debate about Paul and mysticism. See, e.g., Luz, "Paul as Mystic," 139.
229. 1 Cor. 4:16; 11:1; Phil. 3:17; 1 Thess. 1:6.
230. Gal. 4:12; Phil. 1:30; 2:18; 3:17; 4:9; cf. Eph. 4:32–5:1; 2 Thess. 3:7, 9. E.g., see Sanders, "Imitating Paul"; Kathy Ehrensperger, *Paul and the Dynamics of Power: Communication and*

Jewish and Hellenistic heritages a pupil not only received instruction but also was expected to imitate and live out the life modeled by the teacher.[231] Not surprisingly, then, Paul offers himself as a model to his readers to guide them in their behavior (Phil. 3:17), including being selfless (1 Cor. 11:1; cf. 4:16), as well as to encourage them in facing suffering (1 Thess. 1:6; 2:14; cf. 2 Thess. 3:7–9). It is not, however, that readers should become his disciples or followers, an idea he abhors (1 Cor. 1:12–13).[232] Rather, as is sometimes quite obvious, the rationale for this call is his imitation of Christ,[233] so that both Paul and his readers are engaged in imitating Christ. In concluding a section in 1 Corinthians on how readers are to behave without offense toward others he says, "Be imitators of me, as I am of Christ" (1 Cor. 11:1). And in 1 Thessalonians 1:6 he says that his readers have become "imitators of us and of the Lord."

Though the idea of imitating God is foreign to the Old Testament, where God is inimitable (cf. Isa. 14:14; 46:5),[234] in the Greco-Roman world of Paul's time the idea of imitating a teacher or ancestor, or even a deity,[235] was well established.[236] A number of times Philo assumes or says that people should imitate God.[237] Philo also explains that imitation involved more than copying a person's words or even character. In noting that Jacob "harkened" (εἰσήκου-σεν)[238] to his parents in going to Mesopotamia, Philo explains that while the "mimic" (or "hearer," ἀκροατής) is determined only by what the person says (*Congr.* 70), an "imitator" (μιμητής) models the whole "life" (βίος)[239] and can resemble a person (cf. *Virt.* 66).

That Paul thought his and his readers' lives, including their behavior, should resemble that of Jesus is the import of Philippians 2:1–18.[240] Although Paul is

---

Interaction in the Early Christ-Movement (LNTS 325; London: T&T Clark, 2007), chap. 8, esp. 151–54.

231. 2 Macc. 9:23; Josephus, *Ant.* 1.68; 8.315; Philo, *Virt.* 66; *Congr.* 70. See Wilhelm Michaelis, "μιμέομαι, κτλ.," *TDNT* 4:659–74.

232. See David M. Stanley, "'Become Imitators of Me': The Pauline Conception of Apostolic Tradition," *Bib* 40 (1959): 859n5.

233. Gordon F. Fee says, "In every case 'imitation' of Paul means 'as I imitate Christ'" (*Paul's Letter to the Philippians* [NICNT; Grand Rapids: Eerdmans, 1995], 364.

234. Nor does Josephus write of imitating God (see *Ant.* 1.19; *Ag. Ap.* 2.191); later, the rabbis talk of imitating God. See Michaelis, "μιμέομαι," 663n7, 666; Gerhard Kittel, "ἀκολουθέω, κτλ.," *TDNT* 1:212, citing, e.g., *b. Soṭah* 14a; *Lev. Rab.* 25 on 19:23; *Mekilta Exod.* 15:2.

235. E.g., Terence, *Eun.* 3.5, cited by Augustine (*Conf.* 1.16) in his development of the notion. See also *Let. Arist.* 188, 210, 280, 281.

236. See Philo, *Virt.* 66; 4 Macc. 9:23; Josephus, *Ant.* 1.68; 8.315; *2 Bar.* 18:2.

237. E.g., Philo, *Decal.* 111, 120; *Leg.* 1.48; *Spec.* 4.73; *Virt.* 168.

238. LXX Gen. 28:7 has ἤκουσεν ("he heard").

239. See the brief discussion by Michaelis, "μιμέομαι," 665–66.

240. The idea that the passage is to be taken as kerygmatic rather than exemplary has been shown to rest on an overly simplistic view of imitation. E.g., Ernst Käsemann, "A Critical Analysis

urging his readers to adopt the "mind-set" (φρονέω, 2:5)[241] he sees in Christ
Jesus, it is an attitude that is to be expressed in behavior (2:7–9); he uses the
words "slave" (δοῦλος) and "obedient" (ὑπήκοος) to describe the expression
of the mind-set of Jesus. Moreover, it is notable for our study that Paul is
not supposing that it is the character of a heavenly Christ figure that is to be
emulated.[242] The emphasis in his description is on "Jesus."[243] If it is not the
name "Jesus" itself that is "the name which is above every name" (2:9)—although that is what a straightforward reading of the text suggests[244]—then
certainly it is Jesus who receives the name "Lord" ("Yahweh"), and Jesus to
whom all are to be subject (2:10–11).[245] In Paul's view, then, it is the human
life of Jesus, not "the pre-existent Christ who is the pattern," as Bultmann
thought,[246] that is to be impressed on the life of his followers.[247] The same
conclusion is reached in taking into account Paul's admonition to "put on"
(ἐνδύω) the Lord Jesus Christ (Rom. 13:14). Apart from one other use by Paul
(Gal. 3:27), the only known previous expression of putting on a person is by
Dionysius of Halacarnassus (c. 60–at least 8/7 BCE), who used it of an actor
assuming the role of another person.[248]

Further, that Paul thought his activities were shaped by the concrete human
career of Jesus, rather than simply by his words or by a vague heavenly Christ
figure, comes into view clearly in 1 Thessalonians. In the opening thanksgiving
he says he is thankful for their "work of faith and labor of love" (1:3). For
Paul, "labor"—probably not to be distinguished from "work"[249]—is often

---

of Philippians 2:5–11," *JTC* 5 (1968): 45–88, and Ralph P. Martin, *Carmen Christi: Philippians ii 5–11 in Recent Interpretation and in the Setting of Early Christian Worship* (Grand Rapids: Eerdmans, 1983), 84–88.

241. For a similar use of φρονέω, see Matt. 16:23; Mark 8:33; Rom. 8:5; 12:3, 16; Phil. 3:19; Col. 3:2.

242. John B. Webster, "The Imitation of Christ," *TynBul* 37 (1986): 110.

243. Jean-François Collange, *The Epistle of Saint Paul to the Philippians*, trans. A. W. Heath-cote (London: Epworth, 1979), 106.

244. C. F. D. Moule, "Further Reflexions on Philippians 2:5–11," in *Apostolic History and the Gospel: Biblical and Historical Essays Presented to F. F. Bruce on His 60th Birthday*, ed. W. Ward Gasque and Ralph P. Martin (Exeter: Paternoster, 1970), 270.

245. Bockmuehl, *Philippians*, 142–44.

246. Bultmann, "Historical Jesus," 239.

247. John Webster comments, "Jesus Christ is not here envisaged simply as a lordly redeemer whose authority is confessed, but as one whose human history is to be impressed on the histories of those who participate in his life" ("Imitation of Christ," 110). However, David Stanley ("'Become Imitators,'" 859–77) notes that the imitation rarely refers to the earthly career of Jesus.

248. Dionysius of Halacarnassus, *Ant. rom.* 11.5.2. See LSJ, "ἐνδύω," 562; cf. Albrecht Oepke, "δύω, κτλ.," *TDNT* 2:319–20.

249. F. F. Bruce, *1 & 2 Thessalonians* (WBC 45; Waco: Word, 1982), 12. Cf. 1 Cor. 15:58, where ἔργον ("work") and κόπος ("labor") are synonymns for ministry or the work of the Lord. See also 1 Cor. 16:10 and Phil. 2:30, where ἔργον refers to ministry or the work of the Lord.

his missionary activity[250] or that of others,[251] which is probably what is meant here.[252] For, he goes on to mention their faith in God becoming known in every place (1:8), despite persecutions (1:6).[253] It is this that he applauds in saying the Thessalonians have become "imitators of us and of the Lord" (1:6). The imitation of the Lord that Paul has in mind, then, is not general behavior but missionary work.[254] And, Paul is saying that what the Thessalonians have been able to imitate from him is something that Paul, in turn, was imitating from Jesus. That is, Paul sees his work as an outworking of the mission of Jesus.[255] Reinforcing this would have been Paul's seeing himself as a prophet in the traditions of the Old Testament: on the model of the scriptural prophets, notably Elijah and Elisha (1 Kings 17–19; 21; 2 Kings 1–2), what the master had done, the follower continued.[256]

Not only does this general perspective of imitating the ministry of Jesus suggest that miracles are probably in mind but Paul describing his own ministry in terms of "in word . . . and in power" (ἐν λόγῳ . . . καὶ ἐν δυνάμει, 1 Thess. 1:5) increases the probability. How probable the miraculous is in mind here as Paul describes his ministry will become clear when we turn more directly to Paul's testimony in relation to the miraculous (see §7.1). For the present, we have been able to see that in Paul describing his life and ministry activity in terms of imitating Jesus, it is most probable that miracles would have been a component of that imitation. However, I must explain a motif in Paul's writing that is in tension with this conclusion before it can be allowed to stand.

250. κόπος (noun): 1 Cor. 3:8; 2 Cor. 6:5; 11:23, 27; 1 Thess. 2:9; 3:5; cf. 2 Thess. 3:8. Also, κοπιάω (verb): 1 Cor. 4:12; 15:10; Gal. 4:11; Phil. 2:16; cf. Col. 1:29; 1 Tim. 4:10.

251. κόπος (noun): 1 Cor. 3:8; 15:58; 2 Cor. 10:15; 1 Thess. 1:3. Also, κοπιάω (verb): Rom. 16:6, 12; 1 Cor. 15:10; 16:16; 1 Thess. 5:12; 1 Tim. 5:17.

252. Stanley, "'Become Imitators,'" 865.

253. Paul uses θλῖψις of his "trouble" related to missionary activity in 2 Cor. 1:8; 4:17; 6:4; 7:4; Phil. 1:17; 4:14; 1 Thess. 3:3, 7. Otherwise, θλῖψις occurs in the NT in Matt. 13:21; 24:9, 21, 29; Mark 4:17; 13:19, 24; John 16:21, 33; Acts 7:10, 11; 11:19; 14:22; 20:23; Rom. 2:9; 5:3; 8:35; 12:12; 1 Cor. 7:28; 2 Cor. 1:4; 2:4; 8:2, 13; Eph. 3:13; Col. 1:24; 1 Thess. 1:6; 2 Thess. 1:4, 6; Heb. 10:33; James 1:27; Rev. 1:9; 2:9, 10, 22; 7:14.

254. Cf. Earl J. Richard, *First and Second Thessalonians* (SP 11; Collegeville, MN: Liturgical Press, 1995), 67.

255. So J. Ross Wagner, "The Heralds of Isaiah and the Mission of Paul: An Investigation of Paul's Use of Isaiah 51–55 in Romans," in *Jesus and the Suffering Servant: Isaiah 53 and Christian Origins*, ed. William H. Bellinger and William R. Farmer (Harrisburg, PA: Trinity Press, 1998), 198.

256. Bert Jan Lietaert Peerbolte, "Paul the Miracle Worker: Development and Background of Pauline Miracle Stories," in *Wonders Never Cease: The Purpose of Narrating Miracle Stories in the New Testament and Its Religious Environment*, ed. Michael Labahn and Bert Jan Lietaert Peerbolte (LNTS 288; London: T&T Clark, 2006), 190.

5.5 Boasting in Weakness

Consistent with a ministry that likely involved the miraculous, we have seen
Paul insist he is an apostle (1 Cor. 9:1–2), for example, and describe himself
in terms of a prophet (cf. Gal. 1:15 and Isa. 49:1). Yet, appearing to fly in
the face of this high view of his calling, and his claimed intimate relationship with divinity that would make miracle working a natural part of his
ministry, we have to take into account Paul's apparent low view of himself.
He says in 2 Corinthians, for example, that he is not competent to claim
anything as coming from himself (3:5), being no more than a mere clay pot
(4:7). Indeed, a well-known thread running through his letters is his self-
abasement and boasting in weakness,[257] which does not appear consistent
with a miracle worker.

Paul's self-effacement can be seen at the level of written expression in taking up the literary plural ("we")[258] when referring to himself in saying, "we
have received grace and apostleship" (Rom. 1:5).[259] At another level, Paul uses
the first-person plural ("we") to identify himself with his readers, not only
to include them in the theological reality he describes,[260] but also in what
C. E. B. Cranfield called "the first person plural of humility."[261] For example,
in talking about life in the Spirit in Romans, Paul says, "*we* are debtors, not
to the flesh" (8:12), "*we* cry, 'Abba! Father!'" (8:15), and "*we* are children of
God" (8:16). Then, readily sinking his individuality in that of the others, Paul
habitually uses "we" to identify himself with his fellow workers (e.g., Phil. 3:3,
17; 1 Thess. 2:16).[262] However, in the first nine chapters of 2 Corinthians the
frequent occurrence of the first-person plural becomes part of Paul's means
of establishing the nature of his ministry over against his opponents.[263]

---

257. See, e.g., Paul's use of ἀσθεν- words: 1 Cor. 2:3; 4:10; 9:22; 2 Cor. 10:10; 11: 29 (2x), 30;
12:5, 9, 10; 13:4, 9; cf. Rom. 5:6; 8:26; 1 Cor. 1:25; Gal. 4:13.

258. See BDF §280; Thrall, *Second Epistle to the Corinthians*, 1:105–7.

259. Also, see Charles E. B. Cranfield, "Changes of Person and Number in Paul's Epistles,"
in *Paul and Paulinism: Essays in Honour of C. K. Barrett*, ed. Morna D. Hooker and Stephen G.
Wilson (London: SPCK, 1982), 286–87, citing Rom. 3:8–9; 1 Cor. 9:11–12; 2 Cor. 1:4–14, 18,
24; 7:5–7; 7:12–8:8; 9:3.

260. E.g., Rom. 8:15; Gal. 4:5; 1 Thess. 1:9–10.

261. Cranfield, "Changes of Person," 284.

262. On Phil. 3:3, see Fee, *Philippians*, 365n14; though see the discussion by Gerald F. Hawthorne, *Philippians* (WBC 43; Waco: Word, 1983), 160–61.

263. 2 Cor. 1:4 (2x), 6 (2x), 8 (2x), 9 (2x), 10, 12, 13, 14, 24 (2x); 2:11, 15, 16, 17 (2x); 3:1
(2x), 4, 5, 12, 18; 4:1 (2x), 2, 5, 7, 11, 13, 16; 5:1 (2x), 2, 3, 4 (2x), 6, 7, 8 (2x), 9, 11 (2x), 12, 13
(2x), 16, 20 (2x), 21; 6:1, 9, 16; 7:1, 2 (3x), 13 (2x), 14; 8:1, 5, 17, 18, 21, 22 (2x); 9:1, 4; cf. 10:1,
3, 10, 11, 12, 13, 14 (2x); 11:4 (2x), 21; 12:1, 12, 18, 19 (2x); 13:4 (2x), 6, 7 (3x), 8, 9 (3x). See
Jeffrey A. Crafton, *The Agency of the Apostle: A Dramatistic Analysis of Paul's Responses to
Conflict in 2 Corinthians* (JSNTSup 51; Sheffield: JSOT Press, 1991), 62–63, 67–68.

Unlike his opponents, Paul does not claim that the legitimacy of his ministry depends on his words and deeds; rather, his ministry is a means for God to be perceived.[264] In order to make it clear that it is God who is manifest in his ministry, Paul uses a number of metaphors of weakness to describe himself and his work. It is in paying close attention to his use of these metaphors that we gain insight into how Paul understands his acknowledged powerless weakness is related to a high sense of calling that could involve miracle working.

First, Paul begins a description of his ministry (2 Cor. 2:14–4:6) by saying that God, in Christ, "always leads us in triumphal procession" (θριαμβεύοντι, 2:14). The verb θριαμβεύειν[265] corresponds to the Latin verb *triumphare* ("celebrate" or "lead in a triumph").[266] Although there are no examples of its metaphorical use in Greek until this point,[267] given the great number of triumphs that took place,[268] and the metaphor being in active use among Latin writers,[269] Paul probably is taking up the image to describe his ministry in terms of being led by a general in a victory parade in Rome. Also, given that when the verb is followed by an accusative (ἡμᾶς, "us"), the image is never used of a person triumphing or celebrating,[270] Paul is likening his ministry to the humiliation and shame involved in a conquered slave being publicly ridiculed before execution.[271] He sees himself, therefore, as a mere trophy, as evidence of the glory of the conquering hero (cf. Livy, *Hist.* 45.39.10).

Second, following the trophy image, Paul immediately says "and through us revealing in every place the fragrance [τὴν ὀσμήν] that comes from knowing him" (2 Cor. 2:14b, my translation). Since Paul is describing God's continuing activity in the coordinated participles, "leading in triumph" (2:14a) and "revealing" (2:14b), he probably means the image of fragrance still to be understood

264. See ibid., 62–63, 67–68.

265. On the much-discussed θριαμβεύειν, which occurs only here and in Col. 2:15 in the NT, see Martin, *2 Corinthians*, 46–47.

266. Peter Marshall, "A Metaphor of Social Shame: ΘΡΙΑΜΒΕΥΕΙΝ in 2 Cor. 2:14," *NovT* 25 (1983): 302–17, esp. 303n6.

267. Rory B. Egan, "Lexical Evidence on Two Pauline Passages," *NovT* 19 (1977): 38n15; Marshall, "Metaphor," 303.

268. Peter Marshall notes, "Approximately 350 triumphs are recorded in their [Greek and Roman] literature and they were most sought after and frequent in the Republican Period" ("Metaphor," 304). Plutarch (*Aem.* 32–34) provides a graphic account of triumph.

269. See Cicero, *Clu.* 5.14; *Att.* 9.16.2; *Mur.* 5.1; *Fam.* 2.12.3; Seneca, *Ben.* 2.11.1.

270. Lamar Williamson, "Led in Triumph: Paul's Use of *thriambeuō*," *Int* 22 (1968): 318–22.

271. Frank J. Matera, *II Corinthians: A Commentary* (NTL; Louisville: Westminster John Knox, 2003), 73. Cf. J. M. Scott, "The Triumph of God in 2 Cor. 2.14: Additional Evidence of Merkabah Mysticism in Paul," *NTS* 42 (1996): 260–81. Scott proposes, "Paul uses the metaphor of a Roman triumphal procession to conjure up an image of the throne-chariot of God" (p. 281). Cf. Ps. 68:18–19; Eph. 4:8.

in light of a Roman triumph.[272] Indeed, along the route of a triumph the air was filled with the odors of incense being burned, of the spices carried from the conquered territories, as well as from the garlands of flowers scattered and perfume being sprinkled along the streets.[273]

The importance of the "fragrance" (ὀσμή) image is not only that it is associated with his death but the close connection of ὀσμή with "aroma" (εὐωδία)[274] enables Paul to develop the idea in saying, "we are the aroma [εὐωδία] of Christ to God" (2 Cor. 2:15a). So closely was εὐωδία associated with the burnt offering sacrifices[275] that Paul's readers would have understood him to say that he is the fragrance of the burnt offering ascending to God. Paul's ministry is the odor of Christ.[276] In both aspects of this image—the odor of the triumph and the aroma of the sacrifices—being associated with his being led to death, and with death itself, he is describing his ministry as doing no more than reflecting the glory of the victor and being evidence of the burnt offering.

Third, toward the end of the description of his ministry (2 Cor. 2:14–4:6) Paul says not only is it God's mercy that has engaged him in his ministry (4:1) but also that "we do not proclaim ourselves, but Jesus Christ as Lord" (4:5, my translation). In his proclamation he describes himself as an "earthen vessel" (ὀστράκινος σκεύεσιν, 4:7); a fragile (cf. LXX Ps. 30:13 [ET 31:12]), cheap, often unattractive, earthenware container (cf. LXX Lev. 11:33). Yet, he says that in this vessel he[277] has "this" (τοῦτον) treasure, most likely the "glory of God in the face of Jesus Christ" (4:7), which he has just mentioned (4:6).[278] The purpose of being such an unattractive, disposable container is "in order that the extraordinary power is from God and not from us" (4:7, my translation).[279] In other words, Paul sees value in his ministry only to the extent that the "glory of God in the face of Jesus" is seen in it.

272. Harris, *Second Epistle to the Corinthians*, 246.

273. Ibid., 245 and n. 32, citing Horace, *Carm.* 4.2.50–51; Suetonius, *Nero* 25.2; Appian, *Punica* 66.

274. Elsewhere in the NT εὐωδία occurs in Eph. 5:10 and Phil. 4:18, each time with ὀσμή. Here in 2 Cor. 2:15 the words are in direct proximity to each other and, to some extent, in parallel.

275. Both words of the nearly technical term for the burnt offering, ὀσμὴ εὐωδίας ("pleasant odor"), had sacrificial connotations: LXX Gen. 8:21; Exod. 29:18; Lev. 1:9, 13, 17; Num. 15:3, 7, 10; cf. Eph. 5:2; Phil. 4:18.

276. Thrall, *Second Epistle to the Corinthians*, 1:200.

277. Paul uses ἔχομεν ("we have"), the first-person plural.

278. On the various possible referents of "this" (τοῦτον [2 Cor. 4:7]), see Harris, *Second Epistle to the Corinthians*, 339 and nn. 4–7.

279. On the translation of ἵνα ἡ ὑπερβολὴ τῆς δυνάμεως ᾖ τοῦ θεοῦ καὶ μὴ ἐξ ἡμῶν without supplying "to show" after ἵνα, see Crafton, *Agency*, 90n2.

Fourth, perhaps still developing the thought of the "we have" (ἔχομεν) at the beginning of the sentence,[280] Paul continues the theme of his human frailty with a series of four antitheses: "afflicted in every way, but not crushed; perplexed, but not driven to despair; persecuted, but not forsaken; struck down, but not destroyed" (2 Cor. 4:8–9).[281] Each contrasting relief of these particular hardships suggests divine deliverance (see 1:8–9; 4:16) and, again, contributes to his conclusion that Jesus, including his death and his life, is visible in Paul's body in ministry (4:10).

Fifth, of the other references Paul makes either to boasting in, or being contentedly aware of, his weakness,[282] the image of the thorn shows clearest how he understood his ministry in relation to Jesus (2 Cor. 12:7–9; further, see §6.2 below). Paul says he appealed to the Lord three times that a thorn in the flesh would leave him. That Paul means he has appealed to (the risen) Jesus is clear from his resultant boast in "the power of Christ" (12:9).[283] However, Paul says the Lord's answer was "My grace is sufficient for you, for power is made perfect in [ἐν] weakness" (12:9). It is not so much that Paul's weaknesses are the means to allow Christ's power to reach its potential. Rather, his resultant ongoing contentment (εὐδοκῶ, present tense) and boasting in his weaknesses ("whenever I am weak, then I am strong," in the present tense, 12:10), and his being happy always (πάντοτε) to carry (περιφέροντες, present tense) the death of Jesus in his body so his life can be visible (4:10–11), suggest that it is in the ongoing presence or sphere of weakness that the power of Jesus is seen for what it is or reaches its fulfillment (τελέω, 12:9). Jeffrey Crafton says it well: "As Paul is consumed, the gospel is propagated . . . as Paul disappears into the task of ministry, the divine activity is allowed to flow freely through him."[284] From the perspective of our interests, what Paul understands is taking place in his (weak) ministry is Jesus' (powerful) ministry; he is a clay pot bringing the power of God.[285]

These images of weakness with which Paul describes himself—a mere trophy, the aroma of a burnt offering, a disposable clay pot, being crushed,

---

280. Barrett, *Second Epistle to the Corinthians*, 138.

281. Cf. 2 Cor. 4:9–13; 6:3–10. Harris (*Second Epistle to the Corinthians*, 247n36) notes 2 Cor. 1:4; 4:7–12, 16; 6:8–10; 7:4, 8; 8:2, 9, 15; 10:3; 12:9–10, 15; 13:4, 8 as examples of the irresistible appeal of such paradoxes to Paul.

282. See, e.g., Rom. 8:26; 1 Cor. 1:18–25; 2:3; 4:10; 9:23; 2 Cor. 10:1, 10; 11:30; 12:5; 13:4; Gal. 4:13.

283. See Harris, *Second Epistle to the Corinthians*, 860; see also §6.2 below in relation to Paul's experience of miracle.

284. Crafton, *Agency*, 70.

285. Cf. Timothy B. Savage, *Power through Weakness: Paul's Understanding of the Christian Ministry in 2 Corinthians* (SNTSMS 86; Cambridge: Cambridge University Press, 1996), 63–64.

for example, and experiencing a thorn—are in apparent stark contrast to the other side of the coin of his self-understanding of being an apostle like Peter, an ambassador of Christ or identifying with him, and functioning as a prophet. However, in attending to Paul's use of these images, we can see that the apparent tension between the weaknesses in which he boasts and the confidence in who he was is resolved in his view that *Jesus and all his power are at work in the sphere of his human weakness*—a perspective on ministry that could readily encompass not only the miraculous but also Paul's involvement in miracle working.

In the resolution of this tension I am able to allow my earlier conclusion to stand, that in seeing his life and work as imitating Jesus, it is most probable that miracles would have been seen as an aspect of that imitation (§5.4 above), not least because he understood he was imitating one in whom the power of God was seen because of his weakness (Phil. 2:1–11). In short, in view of Paul identifying his attitudes and activities with Christ, whom he knew to have been a miracle worker, we have at least circumstantial evidence that it probably would have been incomprehensible to Paul for his ministry not to have involved the miraculous: whatever Paul knew about Jesus he would have expected and wanted to express through his ministry. In other words, the picture of Paul that is emerging from this enquiry into his self-understanding is not of a missionary or someone with a ministry limited to speaking or conveying ideas through the spoken word. Rather, the Paul whom we glimpse through his own eyes understands the gospel to be "word and deed," speech and act, which involved his lifestyle, his suffering, and also, most probably, miracles.

5.6 Conclusions

We have been able to see that the cause of Paul appearing to say little or nothing about the miraculous is not to be found in either a miracle-free Christianity he inherited or in his lack of knowledge of Jesus or perceived relationship to him. Quite to the contrary, we have seen, first, there is ample evidence that the Christian traditions in existence during the period of Paul's ministry were well laden with miracle stories as well as some sayings related to them and the miraculous. Material from the Jesus tradition that found its way into Mark included a number of healing and exorcism stories, as well as the view that exorcism is linked to the defeat of Satan. However, we have also seen in this material related to Jesus that miracles were recognized to be of ambiguous value and could lead to misunderstandings. This point will become important when we turn to Paul's testimony in relation to the miraculous.

Along with two miracle stories, the Christian traditions reflected in Q mentioned healing the blind, the lame, the skin diseased, the deaf, and the raising of the dead. Q also held exorcism to be important, though of ambiguous significance, and that for the Christians it expressed both the demise of Satan and the coming of the kingdom of God. Further, in Q being a follower of Jesus involved conducting a healing and preaching mission initiated by Jesus and, like his ministry, had eschatological significance. Q also carried the idea that the miracles were able to provoke repentance. Early traditions now in the Fourth Gospel also testify to the importance of healing including, perhaps, the raising of the dead in this period. If the story of the large catch of fish existed this early, it provided an example of a "nature" miracle.

From this it is clear that it would have been hard for Paul to avoid forming the view that miracles and the miraculous were an important part of his Christian heritage. Not only did the material give evidence of Jesus performing many miracles, but also that these miracles, especially the exorcisms through the Spirit, were the kingdom of God in operation. Moreover, these traditions carried the view that, at his direction, Jesus' first followers carried out a similar mission. It is in this heritage that we are to see the conception of Paul's understanding of mission, which, as we will see in the next chapter, was given birth in his conversion and call experience.

Second, we have seen not only that Paul acknowledged his dependence on earlier Christian tradition, but also that he had met and had discussions with key followers of Jesus who had become leaders in Jerusalem, making it quite plausible, indeed probable, that he was aware of the miracle traditions in early Christianity. In particular, although only at Romans 15:18–19 does Paul seem to echo the miracles of Jesus, not least because he shows signs that he most likely knew Q and, therefore, those who valued this tradition, I have been able to suggest that Paul inherited from his predecessors the view that being a follower of Jesus involved following a figure who conducted miracles. In turn, Paul most likely alluding to the Q mission charge means that he would have understood that Jesus sent his followers on a mission of healing in relation to proclaiming the coming of the kingdom of God. Taking up the theme of the kingdom of God, which was more important in his preaching than is suggested by the few times the phrase is mentioned, Paul also is seen to take up the view that the activity of the Spirit included the miraculous, associating the ideas of Spirit, kingdom of God, and miracles, as in Jesus' ministry.

Third, it is demonstrable that, while he had no contact with the historical Jesus, Paul had knowledge of traditions about Jesus, including as a miracle worker. He probably had received the view that Jesus, empowered by the Spirit, conducted miracles that expressed the realization of the end-time kingdom of

God, and he expected his followers to emulate this ministry. Further, Paul's relationship to Jesus as apostle, ambassador, and as being "in Christ," for example, as well as seeing himself as an imitator of Jesus, makes it most probable that miracle working was part of his life and ministry—a life and ministry, however, that is no more than a clay pot carrying God's extraordinary power.

Moreover, in the convergence of these three kinds of evidence—that there was a great deal of Christian material on miracles and the miraculous circulating in the middle third of the century, that Paul gives clear evidence of knowing about it, and that he understood himself to be an ambassador for and imitator of a figure (of weakness) who was a miracle worker who sent his followers out on mission—it is hard to conclude other than that he would have understood that he had inherited a Christianity in which miracles and the miraculous in association with being on mission were of critical importance. We have also begun to catch glimpses of Paul promoting this form of Christianity.[286] Whether or not these glimpses turn out to be of a ministry that is on a recognizable trajectory from that seen in the traditions associated with Jesus and the early Christians, or whether Paul's understanding of miracle working and the miraculous was of a different order, requires turning directly to Paul's writings, which we will do in chapters 6 and 7, the next part of this study.

5.7 So Far . . .

In order to read as sensitively as possible what little Paul appears to say about the miraculous, I have set out on three interrelated areas of enquiry: Paul's inheritance in relation to the miraculous; Paul's testimony about the miraculous; and what Paul's early interpreters say about his involvement in the miraculous. So far, in the first of these steps, we have seen that Paul probably inherited a variety of views on the miraculous.

First, continuing to be proud of his Jewish tradition, we can be assured that Paul remained convinced God's power could be apparent in the miraculous, including speaking to people, and in healings or exorcisms, even if he may have had limited involvement in them before becoming part of the Jesus movement. In any case, convinced that the coming of Jesus was part of an eschatological shift, he probably would have been alert to an anticipated increase in miraculous activity.

Second, seeing himself as called and functioning in the tradition of scriptural prophets at least opened up the strong possibility, though not inevitability,

---

286. In this I am able to support Dunn, *Theology of Paul*, 17 (noted in the opening paragraph of this chapter), that this material was in the discourse that Paul shared with his readers.

that Paul and those who knew him would have expected the miraculous to be part of his ministry. It would have been assumed that whatever miraculous phenomena may have been involved was the responsibility of God, not the prophet. This is a point that will turn out to be of central importance in understanding Paul in relation to the miraculous.

Third, we saw neither evidence of Jewish missionaries nor any direct evidence of traveling Hellenistic teachers involved in the miraculous in Paul's time. The "rest areas on the more important long-distance and rural roads" were not, as Dieter Georgi claimed, "full of the noise and bustle of the most diverse religious and philosophical recruiters" offering exceptional deals in the miraculous.[287] However, indirect evidence from the second- and third-century CE revival of interest in such individuals in the Hellenistic world shows that while a traveling preacher such as Paul may not have been expected to be associated with the miraculous, any such activity would have been readily understood as part of his skill set. Viewed through the lens of the combination of speaking and involvement in the miraculous, we found nothing to suggest that miracles would either have been conceptually connected with his teaching or had any particular meaning if Paul was involved in the miraculous, save that it likely enhanced his public appeal.

Fourth, these results stand in stark contrast to the traditions Paul received from earlier followers of Jesus, and on which he acknowledged dependence, which were flush with the miraculous, both in terms of how Jesus was perceived and in the reported activity of his first followers. In light of the variety of Paul's inheritance, for the second area of enquiry we turn to his testimony, first of his experience and then in relation to his ministry.

---

287. Dieter Georgi, *The Opponents of Paul in Second Corinthians: A Study of Religious Propaganda in Late Antiquity* (Philadelphia: Fortress, 1986), 152.

Part 3

PAUL'S TESTIMONY

6

The Experience of Paul

Paul's self-perception as a zealous Jew who received a call from God to proclaim a message about Jesus with eschatological significance has caused me to take into account traditions most likely influencing his views and practice on the miraculous and miracle working. Taking a second step toward understanding Paul and the miraculous, I turn to his letters. In the first of two chapters, examining aspects of Paul's religious experience, I take into account his expected or reported inner feelings or tangible events, experienced corporately or individually, that he assumes were caused by, or were responses to, the divine.[1] However, I am not seeking to explore the whole range of Paul's religious experience,[2] which would include a discussion of, for example, his experience of grace,[3] ecstasy (2 Cor. 5:13),[4] intimacy with God (Rom. 8:15–16;

1. On the problems involved in defining religious experience, see Joachim Wach, "The Nature of Religious Experience," in *The Comparative Study of Religions*, ed. Joseph M. Kitagawa (New York: Columbia University Press, 1958), 27–30. Cf. Mark Batluck, "Religious Experience in New Testament Research," *CurBR* 9 (2010): 339–63.

2. For broader treatments of Paul's religious experience, see, e.g., Albert Schweitzer, *The Mysticism of Paul the Apostle*, trans. William Montgomery (Baltimore: Johns Hopkins University Press, 1998); James D. G. Dunn, *Jesus and the Spirit: A Study of the Religious and Charismatic Experience of Jesus and the First Christians as Reflected in the New Testament* (London: SCM, 1975), 199–258; John Ashton, *The Religion of Paul the Apostle* (New Haven: Yale University Press, 2000); Clint Tibbs, *Religious Experience of the Pneuma: Communication with the Spirit World in 1 Corinthians 12 and 14* (WUNT 230; Tübingen: Mohr Siebeck, 2007), esp. 77–111.

3. E.g., Rom. 5:2; 1 Cor. 15:10; 2 Cor. 12:9; Gal. 2:9.

4. Recently, see Colleen Shantz, *Paul in Ecstasy: The Neurobiology of the Apostle's Life and Thought* (Cambridge: Cambridge University Press, 2009).

cf. Gal. 4:6), and his positive experience resulting from suffering.[5] Instead, I will bring into play Paul's reports of his experience of the miraculous. In doing so, I am asking what impact, if any, the experience of the miraculous is likely to have had on his life, theology, and mission.

We have already seen that, in Paul's time, a miracle was something considered humanly impossible or extraordinary from God that had meaning. Also, I have argued that the scope of Paul's notion of miracle included not only healings and "miracles" (works or expressions of power), but also accomplishing the impossible and experiences associated with revelation (see §1.5 above).

So far as I can tell, Paul gives no reports of his experience of the miraculous in terms of faith to remove mountains or do the ordinarily impossible (1 Cor. 13:2; cf. 12:9). He mentions, for example, his ancestors passing through the sea (10:2; cf. Exod. 14:19–22), their miraculous food and drink,[6] and Abraham in old age and Sarah though barren becoming parents (Rom. 4:19; cf. Gen. 15:5; 18:1–15). But from Paul's letters we know of no such feats of faith related to his own life.[7] Nevertheless, he gives other examples of his experience of the miraculous. Moreover, he gives both positive examples (from his life and others) and what could be called negative examples where a miracle might be expected but does not take place or is not reported. Indeed, in one place he interprets sickness and death in terms of miracle.

Therefore, I will take into account (1) his illness (Gal. 4:13–14); (2) the thorn in his flesh not being taken away (2 Cor. 12:1–10); (3) sickness and death as punishment (1 Cor. 11:30); (4) rescue from his afflictions in Asia (2 Cor. 1:8–11); and (5) the recovery of Epaphroditus (Phil. 2:26–27). Since revelatory experience was of a piece with miracle for Paul (see §1.5 above), I will also take into account what he says of his revelatory experiences. However, from all the possible references Paul makes to his experiences of revelation,[8] I will take into account only those passages where he is clear about both the experience and its implications, that is (6) his conversion and call and (7) his experience of *charismata* (esp. 1 Cor. 14:6, 18; 2 Cor. 13:3).[9] I will argue that

5. Rom. 5:3–5; 8:17; 2 Cor. 1:3–8; 4:10; Phil. 3:10–11; cf. Col. 1:24. Paul's statement "worship [λατρεύοντες] in the Spirit" (Phil. 3:3) is a reference not to his Spirit-empowered liturgical experience, but to his devoted service to God as a whole. See BDAG, "λατρεύω"; Gordon D. Fee, *God's Empowering Presence: The Holy Spirit in the Letters of Paul* (Peabody, MA: Hendrickson, 1994), 751–53.

6. 1 Cor. 10:3–4; cf. Exod. 16:4–30; 17:1–7; Num. 20:2–13.

7. In his Acts narrative Luke has, of course, amply made up for this lack. See chap. 8 below.

8. Notably, Paul's experience of conversion and call (1 Cor. 9:1; 15:8; Gal. 1:13–16; Phil. 3:4–11); visions and revelations (1 Cor. 2:13; 7:40; 2 Cor. 5:13; 12:1–4, 7; Gal. 2:2), and *charismata* (esp. 1 Cor. 14:6, 18; cf. 2 Cor. 13:3).

9. 2 Cor. 3:18—"And all of us [ἡμεῖς δὲ πάντες], with unveiled faces, seeing [κατοπτριζόμενοι] the glory of the Lord as though reflected in a mirror, are being transformed into the same image

Paul's experience of miracle dramatically changed his life, determined his mission, and significantly contributed to and modified his theology.

I enter the arena with those debating the relationship between religious experience and belief formation and modification.[10] On one side are those who hold that religious experiences are not causative factors for beliefs and practices, but only confirmation of already held views.[11] On the other side are those supposing that, while beliefs may inform experience, there are reports of experience that are at odds with, or go beyond, received tradition. Philip Almond, citing Teresa of Avila having to set out criteria to deal with experiences at variance with tradition, concludes that experience "may be decisive in the formulation or revision of doctrinal frameworks, and . . . provide the impetus also for important changes in the societal and cultural framework as a whole."[12]

In relation to Paul, James Dunn has argued strongly for the creative force of Paul's religious experience, calling it "a furnace which melted many concepts in its fires and poured them forth into new moulds."[13] My discussion of Paul's experience of miracle will lend support for this view. Seyoon Kim, however, has argued that it was the Damascus Christophany experience that was theologically creative for Paul, other revelatory experiences being of little significance.[14] However, my discussion of Paul's experience of miracles will show that his life, theology, and mission had a base in religious experience that was broader than his vision of the risen Christ.

6.1 Illness (Galatians 4:13–14)

Paul gives glimpses of his experience of illness, the clearest in Galatians, where he says that "physical infirmity" (ἀσθένειαν τῆς σαρκός) was associated with his

---

from one degree of glory to another; for this comes from the Lord, the Spirit"—is excluded from our discussion. Paul is not, as assumed by some (e.g., Luke Timothy Johnson, *Religious Experience in Earliest Christianity: A Missing Dimension in New Testament Studies* [Minneapolis: Fortress, 1998], 4–8; Ashton, *Religion of Paul*, 135–38), describing any particular visionary experience (or experiences), but the ongoing "seeing" (κατοπτριζόμενοι, present participle) of Jesus by "all" (πάντες) believers. Cf. the discussion by Margaret E. Thrall, *A Critical and Exegetical Commentary on the Second Epistle to the Corinthians*, 2 vols. (ICC; London: T&T Clark, 1994–2000), 1:282–95.

10. Larry W. Hurtado, "Religious Experience and Religious Innovation in the New Testament," *JR* 80 (2000): 183–205.

11. Paul A. Rainbow, "Jewish Monotheism as the Matrix for New Testament Christology: A Review Article," *NovT* 33 (1991): 86–87.

12. Philip C. Almond, *Mystical Experience and Religious Doctrine: An Investigation of the Study of Mysticism in World Religions* (New York: Mouton, 1982), 183; cf. 166–68.

13. Dunn, *Jesus and the Spirit*, 4.

14. On 2 Cor. 12:1–4, e.g., see Seyoon Kim, *The Origin of Paul's Gospel*, 2nd ed. (WUNT 2/4; Tübingen: Mohr Siebeck], 1984), 56, 78–79, 86–87.

announcing the gospel to them (Gal. 4:13–14; cf. 2 Cor. 12:1–10, on which see §6.2 below). In twice specifying that his "weakness" (ἀσθένεια), which might otherwise mean limitation or frailty,[15] was of the "flesh" (σάρξ, Gal. 4:13–14), Paul makes it almost certain that he was suffering from some physical illness.[16]

It is unclear what Paul means by saying it was "through" or "on account of" (διά, with the accusative) his illness that he first preached the gospel to the Galatians (4:13). It could be that Paul went to Galatia to recuperate or that he was delayed there by his sickness.[17] In any case, his sickness was significant enough to have considerable impact on his life.

Attempting to diagnose Paul's illness has given rise to many suggestions: malaria, migraine, epilepsy, chronic brucellosis, hysteria, depression, severe sciatica, rheumatism, poor hearing, leprosy, stammering, and solar retinitis, for example.[18] Two of the most likely suggestions warrant discussion. Paul says the Galatians would have torn out their eyes and given them to him (4:14). It is possible, therefore, that Paul was suffering from some ophthalmic complaint.[19] In support of this diagnosis is the subscription to Galatians, where Paul says he writes using "large letters" (6:11).[20] Alternatively, it could be that Paul, generally working with his hands, found that writing was not easy for him. However, it is more likely that Paul was emphasizing a point.[21] In any case, since eyes were considered the most valuable organ,[22] and gouging out eyes was an act of self-sacrifice (1 Sam. 11:2), notably as a demonstration of friendship (Lucian, Tox. 40–41), it is reasonable to take his reference to the Galatians being prepared to give their eyes as the equivalent to our saying we would give our "right arm" for a friend.[23]

We probably get no further in diagnosing Paul's illness through noting that he says the Galatians did not "spit [him] out" (ἐκπτύω). Some think the Galatians were tempted to see Paul as demonized because of his sickness,[24]

---

15. Cf. 1 Cor. 15:43; 2 Cor. 11:30; 12:5, 9–10.

16. See, e.g., P. H. Menoud, "L'écharde et l'ange satanique (2 Cor. 12,7)," in *Studia Paulina: In honorem Johannis de Zwaan septuagenarii*, by Willem C. van Unnik et al. (Haarlem: De Ervem F. Bohn N.V., 1953), 165; David Alan Black, *Paul, Apostle of Weakness: Asthenia and Its Cognates in the Pauline Literature* (AUS 7/3; New York: Peter Lang, 1984), 67–79.

17. Cf. W. M. Ramsay, *St. Paul the Traveller and the Roman Citizen* (London: Hodder & Stoughton, 1908), 92–97.

18. Audrey Dawson, *Healing, Weakness and Power: Perspectives on Healing in the Writings of Mark, Luke and Paul* (PBM; Milton Keynes: Paternoster, 2008), 193–95.

19. See, e.g., J. B. Lightfoot, *Saint Paul's Epistle to the Galatians* (London: Macmillan, 1881), 333.

20. Noted by Richard N. Longenecker, *Galatians* (WBC 41; Dallas: Word, 1990), 290.

21. See the discussion by C. Keith, "'In My Own Hand': Grapho-Literacy and the Apostle Paul," *Bib* 89 (2008): 39–58.

22. See Deut. 32:10; Ps. 17:8; Zech. 2:8; *Barn.* 19:9; Dawson, *Healing*, 194.

23. Thrall, *Second Epistle to the Corinthians*, 2:814.

24. Heinrich Schlier, "ἐκπτύω," *TDNT* 2:448–49.

perhaps epilepsy,[25] since ejecting saliva was used to ward off evil (Theocritus, *Id.* 6.39). However, spitting was more often used as an expression of contempt,[26] and we have no other hint that Paul connected his health problems with the demonic.[27] In any case, Paul is using "spit out" (ἐκπτύω) as a synonym for "despise" (ἐξουθενέω),[28] and in contrast to the welcome (δέχομαι) he received (4:14). It is more reasonable, therefore, to suppose that Paul is using "spit out" (ἐκπτύω) metaphorically for "despise" (NRSV) or "disdain."

Even though we are unable to diagnose Paul's illness from this passage, we can be certain he suffered physically, and we are able to see its impact on him. Paul does not say that he has prayed for healing, but if this illness is the same as his thorn (see 160n53 below), we can assume he did. Moreover, his experience is that his sickness is not healed. Although he probably expected a miracle, it did not take place.

What is more certain is that Paul's sickness caused him anxiety, in part because of its potential threat to his mission. Perhaps based on previous experience of rejection related to his infirmity, in coming to the Galatians, he expected the possibility of being held in contempt or being despised rather than finding hospitality (4:13–14). The welcome of hospitality was honored in Paul's world, to the point of being sacred.[29] The Greeks took Zeus to be overseeing the practice of hospitality or the kind treatment of travelers and strangers.[30] For the Jews, Abraham provided the example (Gen. 18:1–16),[31] and a guest could be associated with God or his angels.[32] Reflecting Paul's era, Rab Judah said, "Hospitality to wayfarers is greater than welcoming the presence of the Shechinah" (*b. Šabb.* 127a).

For Paul not to be welcomed, therefore, would have been to suffer not only the humiliating denial of an accepted social courtesy, but also the rejection of the God he represented. Further, not only did Jesus (Matt. 8:20 // Luke 9:58)

25. E.g., William Wrede, *Paul*, trans. Edward Lummis (Eugene, OR: Wipf & Stock, 2001), 22–23.

26. BDAG, "ἐκπτύω," 309.

27. On 2 Cor. 12:7 ("a thorn was given me . . . a messenger of Satan"), see §6.2 below.

28. Also *Jos. Asen.* 2:1. 𝔓[46] omits ἐξεπτύσατε, perhaps seeing it as redundant. See Longenecker, *Galatians*, 188, 192.

29. Cf. Walter Grundmann, "δέχομαι, κτλ.," *TDNT* 2:57–58; also Xenophon, *Oec.* 5.8; Homer, *Od.* 19.316–21.

30. Homer, *Od.* 6.207–10; cf. 3.4–485; 13:47–125; Andrew E. Arterbury, *Entertaining Angels: Early Christian Hospitality in Its Mediterranean Setting* (NTM 8; Sheffield: Sheffield Phoenix, 2005), 15–54, esp. 51–54.

31. John Koenig, *New Testament Hospitality: Partnership with Strangers as Promise and Mission* (Philadelphia: Fortress, 1985), 15–16.

32. Gen. 18:1–16; 19:1–23; Judg. 13:16; Josephus, *Ant.* 1.196; Origen, *Hom. Gen.* 4.1; see Arterbury, *Entertaining Angels*, 91.

and his early followers[33] rely on hospitality for the success of their missions, but Paul's whole mission strategy also depended on the hospitality of those he encountered. Not to have been welcomed would have ended Paul's work. The ongoing nature of the illness suggests that Paul lived under the constant threat of rejection and the termination of his mission (cf. 1 Thess. 2:18).

However, in relation to the Galatians, Paul's fears are not realized. Using the adversative ἀλλά ("but"), he contrasts what he feared with what he received. Paul says he experienced a welcome as a messenger of God (4:13–14); he goes on to recall their reception as "their blessing" (ὁ μακαρισμὸς ὑμῶν; 4:15).[34] In this we are probably able to see the relief that Paul experienced.

6.2 A Thorn in the Flesh (2 Corinthians 12:1–10)

From 2 Corinthians 12 we may be able to come to some conclusions about the nature of Paul's illness.[35] Having related his ecstatic experiences of being caught up in the third heaven,[36] Paul says, "To keep me from being too elated, a thorn was given me in the flesh, a messenger of Satan to torment me, to keep me from being too elated" (12:7).

As with Paul's illness (Gal. 4:13–14), there have been numerous suggestions as to the nature of the "thorn" (σκόλοψ).[37] These suggestions have sometimes been grouped in three categories.[38] First, Chrysostom proposed that the thorn

33. Matt. 10:7–8, 10b–13, 40 // Luke 10:5–9, 16; cf. 1 Cor. 9:5.

34. James D. G. Dunn, *Galatians* (BNTC; Peabody, MA: Hendrickson, 1993), 235.

35. See also Graham H. Twelftree, "Healing, Illness," *DPL* 379.

36. See, e.g., John W. Bowker, "Merkabah Visions and the Visions of Paul," *JSS* 16 (1971): 157–73; Helmut Saake, "Paulus als Ekstatiker: Pneumatologische Beobachtungen zu 2 Kor 12:1–10," *NovT* 15 (1973): 153–60; Alan F. Segal, *Paul the Convert: The Apostolate and Apostasy of Saul the Pharisee* (New Haven: Yale University Press, 1990), 34–71; Klaus Berger, *Identity and Experience in the New Testament*, trans. Charles Muenchow (Minneapolis: Fortress, 2003), 108–14; Ashton, *Religion of Paul*, 116–23. Against the generally accepted view that in 2 Cor. 12:1–10 Paul is the person experiencing the "visions and revelations of the Lord" (12:1), Michael D. Goulder ("Visions and Revelations of the Lord [2 Corinthians 12:1–10]," in *Paul and the Corinthians: Studies on a Community in Conflict; Essays in Honour of Margaret Thrall*, ed. Trevor J. Burke and J. Keith Elliott [NovTSup 109; Leiden: Brill, 2003], 303–12) argues that Paul is appealing to "the rapture of a friend" (p. 312).

37. See the discussions, especially by E.-B. Allo, *Saint Paul: Seconde épître aux Corinthiens*, 2nd ed. (Ebib; Paris: Gabalda, 1956), 313–23 (excursus 16, "La maladie de Saint Paul," including bibliography); Thrall, *Second Epistle to the Corinthians*, 2:809–18; and those cited by Reimund Bieringer, Emmanuel Nathan, and Dominika Kurek-Chomycz, *2 Corinthians: A Bibliography* (BTS 5; Leuven: Peeters, 2008), 251–52.

38. See, e.g., Victor P. Furnish, *II Corinthians: Translated with Introduction, Notes, and Commentary* (AB 32A; Garden City, NY: Doubleday, 1984), 548–50; Thrall, *Second Epistle to the Corinthians*, 2:809–18.

was Paul's experience of persecution, including from the Corinthians (*Hom. 2 Cor.* 26.2).[39] This interpretation pays attention to Paul describing the thorn as a "messenger" (ἄγγελος) of Satan,[40] noting that "Satan" means "adversary" (Gk. σατανᾶς; Heb. שָׂטָן). This interpretation also notes that "to torment or batter" (κολαφίζειν)[41] is a personal activity, implying an individual or group. Further, Paul's statement comes in the context of writing about his struggles with opponents (2 Cor. 10–13), and the Septuagint uses the term "thorn" for enemies of the people of God (Num. 33:55; Ezek. 28:24).[42] However, Paul's experience of persecution appears to have been almost constant, so he is unlikely to relate the thorn to one over against other opponents. Also, the thorn is likely to have been given to Paul nearer the time of the ecstatic experiences he describes—he associates the two—before he was confronted by his opponents.[43] Also, Paul is unlikely to represent his opponents in the singular, "thorn" and "angel."[44]

Second, John Calvin is right to suppose that the thorn was not the temptation to lust.[45] Paul does not otherwise give the impression that he struggled with sexual temptation (cf. 1 Cor. 7:7). Also, this interpretation of the flesh—"that part of the soul which has not yet been regenerated"[46]—relies on too narrow a view of "flesh" (σάρξ). Moreover, Paul is not likely to boast about this kind of difficulty.[47] Other psychological conditions suggested—a troubled mind,[48] the failure of the Jewish mission,[49] anger,[50] and Calvin's view that it was temptation in general,[51]

39. More recent advocates are discussed by Thrall, *Second Epistle to the Corinthians*, 2:811–13. A range of views held by the ancient fathers is assembled by Gerald Bray, ed., *1–2 Corinthians* (ACCS 7; Downers Grove, IL: InterVarsity, 1999), 304–8.

40. Cf. 2 Cor. 11:14, where Satan is an "angel of light" (ἄγγελον φωτός).

41. For a summary of interpretations of the use of this word in 2 Cor. 12:7, see BDAG, "κολαφίζω," 555 (2).

42. See also LXX Josh. 23:13; Song 2:2; Ezek. 2:6. Cf. Terence Y. Mullins, "Paul's Thorn in the Flesh," *JBL* 76 (1957): 302–3.

43. Cf. Ralph P. Martin, *2 Corinthians* (WBC 40; Waco: Word, 1986), 415.

44. Cf. Thrall, *Second Epistle to the Corinthians*, 2:812.

45. John Calvin, *Calvin's Commentaries*, vol. 20, *Commentary on the Epistles of Paul the Apostle to the Corinthians* (Grand Rapids: Baker, 1979), 373. Lightfoot (*Galatians*, 188) notes that Martin Luther probably is correct that the Latin (*stimulus carnis*) of σκόλοψ τῇ σαρκί is likely responsible for the prevalence of this interpretation in the Middle Ages, found in Thomas Aquinas, Robert Bellarmine, Cornelius a Lapide, and Guilherme Estius.

46. Calvin, *Paul the Apostle to the Corinthians*, 373–74.

47. Thrall, *Second Epistle to the Corinthians*, 2:817.

48. E.g., Adolf Schlatter, *Paulus, der Bote Jesu: Eine Deutung seiner Briefe an die Korinther*, 4th ed. (Stuttgart: Calwer, 1969), 666–67.

49. Menoud, "L'écharde et l'ange satanique," 163–71.

50. E. Kamlah, "Wie beurteilt Paulus sein Leiden? Ein Beitrag zur Untersuchung seiner Denkstruktur," *ZNW* 54 (1963): 218–19, citing *T. Sim.* 2:7.

51. Calvin, *Paul the Apostle to the Corinthians*, 373.

for example—are to be rejected because Paul's language refers to physical not emotional torment.[52]

Third, since Tertullian (*Pud.* 13.15–16), most interpreters have taken the thorn to be some form of physical illness. In favor of this view is Paul describing the thorn as related "to the flesh" (τῇ σαρκί). Also, in Paul's world, as is most obvious in the Synoptic Gospels, physical illness and Satanic activity were related (e.g., Mark 9:14–29; Luke 10:17–20). Further, other evidence for Paul suffering physical illness, which was an ongoing problem for Paul (see §6.1 above), not only favors the same interpretation here, but also that he is alluding to the same illness.[53] The view of Sir William Ramsay (1851–1939) that Paul had contracted recurrent malaria in Pamphilia has gained considerable acceptance.[54] This diagnosis accounts for the physicality of the thorn, its ongoing battering nature (κολαφίζῃ, present active tense), and it being humiliating and, therefore, probably obvious to an observer, while not impeding his rigorous mission work. In short, Paul is probably saying he suffered from some ongoing, obvious, physical, painful illness.

As we seek to understand Paul's view of the miraculous, there are some further clues in 2 Corinthians 12 about Paul's understanding of his illness. First, he says that it humbled him. That is, not only was it physically painful, but it also had repercussions as to how he viewed himself and, as we will see, his ministry. On the one hand, he was the recipient of revelatory experiences (12:1–7), yet, on the other hand, he faced innumerable difficulties (12:10), in particular an ongoing physical problem that caused him to see himself as weak (12:9). Second, he indirectly attributes the illness to Satan. He does not say that the thorn was from Satan, but that "a thorn was given me . . . a messenger of Satan" (12:7). In the passive, "was given" (ἐδόθη), there is probably a veiled allusion to the illness being given by God.[55] Paul resolves this paradox by saying that the Lord's grace is shown to be sufficient, even in the face of three requests for the thorn's removal.

Praying three times (τρίς) could mean he prayed often and earnestly.[56] However, in that he does not use "frequently" (πολλάκις), and that for Jews and

---

52. C.f. Christian Wolff, *Der zweite Brief des Paulus an die Korinther* (THKNT 8; Berlin: Evangelische Verlagsanstalt, 1989), 246.

53. Cf. Dunn, *Galatians*, 233; Thrall, *Second Epistle to the Corinthians*, 2:814.

54. Ramsay, *St. Paul the Traveller*, 94–97. See the brief discussion by Dawson, *Healing*, 194.

55. Wolff, *Korinther*, 246; Martin, *2 Corinthians*, 416; Thrall, *Second Epistle to the Corinthians*, 2:806 and n. 260; cf. Murray J. Harris, *The Second Epistle to the Corinthians: A Commentary on the Greek Text* (NIGTC; Grand Rapids: Eerdmans; Milton Keynes: Paternoster, 2005), 854.

56. Chrysostom, *Hom. 2 Cor.* 26.3 (on 2 Cor. 12:8); Calvin, *Paul the Apostle to the Corinthians*, 376; C. K. Barrett, *The Second Epistle to the Corinthians* (BNTC; London: Black, 1973), 316.

Greeks the threefold utterances of words or prayers made them definitive and gave them full validity and power,[57] it is best to assume that Paul means he prayed in the most efficacious and earnest way he knew.[58] Also, that Paul uses the aorist tense in saying that he "prayed" or "appealed" (παρεκάλεσα) suggests that he no longer prayed for a miracle.[59]

Especially since the thorn is probably a physical illness, what is particularly interesting for our project is that Paul has prayed unsuccessfully for healing—a miracle had not materialized. Paul's praying shows that, initially, he did not take the sickness to be other than a physical problem to be solved through a miracle.

The way Paul casts the response from the Lord is probably significant. He introduces the Lord's reply to his prayer with "and his answer to me has been" (καὶ ἔιρηκέν μοι, 2 Cor. 12:9). The perfect tense suggests, as James Hope Moulton put it many years ago, that the phrase "sets forth with the utmost possible emphasis the abiding results of the event."[60] That is, in the face of not experiencing a healing miracle, Paul nevertheless still has ringing in his ears[61] the answer to his prayer: "My grace is sufficient for you, for power is made perfect in weakness" (12:9).

There is no disappointment that the hoped-for miracle was not a healing. Rather, Paul is given reason to boast in the ongoing experience of God's powerful presence that becomes apparent in his weakness.[62] It is not surprising then that, as we have just noted, in speaking of the thorn, Paul uses the passive as a probable veiled allusion to the illness being given by God.

Notably, the answer to his prayer transforms a messenger of Satan, if not into a gift from God, into an explanation for other unanswered prayers. Whereas he might once have fought these things in prayer, having seen God's power in his weaknesses in relation to the thorn, he says, "therefore" (διό) he is "content"

---

57. For the Jews, e.g., see LXX Num. 6:24–26; 3 Kgdms. (1 Kings) 17:21. For the Greeks, e.g., see Euripides, *Hipp.* 46. Further, see Hans Windisch, *Der zweite Korintherbrief*, 9th ed. (KEK 6; Göttingen: Vandenhoeck & Ruprecht, 1970), 389–90; Gerhard Delling, "τρεῖς, κτλ.," *TDNT* 8:216–17; Hans Dieter Betz, "Eine Chrustus-Aretalogie bei Paulus (2 Kor. 12, 7–10)," *ZTK* 66 (1969): 292–93.

58. The suggestion by Furnish (*II Corinthians*, 529), that Paul is referring to the Jewish practice of praying three times a day (Ps. 55:16–17; Dan. 6:10, 13; 1QS X, 1–7; 1QHᵃ XII, 3–9), does not capture the urgency conveyed by Paul.

59. On the use of the aorist, see J. W. Voelz, "Present and Aorist Verbal Aspect: A New Proposal," *Neot* 27 (1993): 153–64; K. L. McKay, "Observations on the Epistolary Aorist in 2 Corinthians," *NovT* 37 (1995): 154–58, esp. 155; F. Beetham, "The Aorist Indicative," *GR* 49 (2002): 236.

60. James Hope Moulton, et. al., *A Grammar of New Testament Greek*, 4 vols. (Edinburgh: T&T Clark, 1908–76), 1:137.

61. The phrase is from Martin, *2 Corinthians*, 418.

62. Cf. Gerald G. O'Collins, "Power Made Perfect in Weakness, 2 Cor. 12:9–10," *CBQ* 33 (1971): 537.

(εὐδοκῶ) with, or takes pleasure in,[63] other weaknesses—"insults, hardships, persecutions, and calamities" (2 Cor. 12:10)—in which (through God's grace and power) he is strong (12:10; cf. 11:30).

Not only does Paul take the answer of grace and power to apply to his thorn in the flesh or sickness (ἀσθένεια, singular), but also he immediately applies it more widely to other areas in his life where God's grace and power are evident. In other words, the theme with which he begins (12:5), and to which he returns (12:9b, 10), is boasting in his "weaknesses" (ἀσθενείας), and the thorn scenario is an example not only of his weaknesses, but also of unanswered prayers. If this reading of Paul is correct, he will have had many experiences of unanswered prayers or expected miracles not taking place. This is significant for this project in that it shows that Paul's experience of miracles not taking place significantly modified his understanding both of God and of his own suffering and difficulties. Notwithstanding, Paul reports other aspects of his experience of miracle.

6.3 Miracles of Punishment (1 Corinthians 11:30)

I have argued that for Paul, a miracle was, broadly, a phenomenon brought about by and revealing God (see §1.5 above). He reports such experiences not only in relation to their absence (see above), but also in their positive, though painful, presence. In 1 Corinthians 11, having said that "all who eat and drink [the Lord's Supper] without discerning the body, eat and drink judgment against themselves" (11:29), he says, "For this reason [διὰ τοῦτο] many of you are weak [ἀσθενής] and ill [ἄρρωστος], and some have died [κοιμάω]" (11:30). In that this striking situation is brought about "by [the] Lord" (ὑπὸ [τοῦ] κυρίου, 11:32), he is describing the miraculous.[64] If the notion of miracles by an interfering god is troubling for our enlightened times, even more challenging is what appears to be the idea of miracles of punishment or discipline. Moreover, if this is correct, the chastisement is said to come through taking part in the Lord's Supper, otherwise associated with salvation and healing, not sickness and death.[65]

There is no need here to explore all aspects of this much-discussed passage;[66] I need only to establish that Paul considers he is describing miracles of punish-

---

63. Gottlob Schrenk, "εὐδοκέω," *TDNT* 2:738–43; Harris, *Second Epistle to the Corinthians*, 866.
64. Cf. Gordon D. Fee, *The First Epistle to the Corinthians* (NICNT; Grand Rapids: Eerdmans, 1987), 566. On the state of the text in relation to the article τοῦ, see NA[28], 541.
65. Cf. Dale B. Martin, *The Corinthian Body* (New Haven: Yale University Press, 1995), 190–91.
66. As well as the classic article by C. F. D. Moule, "The Judgment Theme in the Sacraments," in *The Background of the New Testament and Its Eschatology*, ed. W. D. Davies and D. Daube

ment. The significant paranomasia (i.e., using a number of words with the same root, in this case κριν-)[67] makes judgment the obvious and inescapable theme of the passage (11:27–34). The judgment that the Corinthians brought on themselves (11:29) is not simply a natural consequence of their actions, perhaps the result of drunkenness and gluttony (cf. 11:21).[68] Rather, as we have just noted, Paul makes clear that the judgment has been from the Lord (11:32).

In deciding the nature of the judgment Paul has in mind, we probably need to set aside the idea that "weakness," "illness," and "death" are mere metaphors of spiritual ailments.[69] The physicality Paul assumes can be associated with spiritual transactions is already clear in him saying, for example, "You are to hand this man over to Satan for the destruction of the flesh" (5:5).[70] And his vocabulary in the passage in question suggests physical weakness, sickness, and death rather than spiritual ailments.[71]

Admittedly, although "weakness" (ἀσθενής) can mean physical sickness (e.g., Luke 10:9),[72] for Paul, this is not obviously so. Paul uses the word for spiritual (e.g., 1 Cor. 8:7, 9, 10) or general weakness (e.g., 1 Cor. 9:22) or even vulnerability (e.g., 1 Cor. 12:22). However, the few uses of ἄρρωστος in the New Testament always mean "sick" or "ill,"[73] and for Paul, κοιμάω was always a euphemism for physical death and dying.[74] In short, as disturbing as the idea may be, it is not possible to conclude other than that Paul interprets weakness, sickness, and death at Corinth as miracles of judgment.[75]

(Cambridge: Cambridge University Press, 1956), 464–81, see Mark P. Surburg, "Structural and Lexical Features in 1 Corinthians 11:27–32," *ConcJ* 26 (2000): 200–217, and the literature cited.

67. See κρίνω (1 Cor. 11:31, 32); κρίμα (11:29, 34); διακρίνω (11:29, 31); κατακρίνω (11:32).

68. Cf. Anthony C. Thiselton, *The First Epistle to the Corinthians* (NIGTC; Grand Rapids: Eerdmans, 2000), 894.

69. Against the majority view, Sebastian Schneider ("Glaubensmängel in Korinth: Eine neue Deutung der 'Schwachen, Kranken, Schlafenden' in 1 Kor 11,30," *FilNeot* 9 [1996]: 3–19) interprets ἀσθενής ("weakness"), ἄρρωστος ("sick"), and κοιμάω ("sleep") metaphorically.

70. Cf. C. K. Barrett, *The First Epistle to the Corinthians* (BNTC; London: Black, 1971), 275. See also 2 Cor. 12:1–10.

71. Raymond F. Collins (*First Corinthians* [SP 7; Collegeville, MN: Liturgical Press, 1999], 439) reasonably suggests that Paul lists the afflictions in order of increasing intensity.

72. For ἀσθενής in the NT, see Matt. 25:43, 44; 26:41; Mark 14:38; Luke 9:2; 10:9; Acts 4:9; 5:15, 16; Rom. 5:6; 1 Cor. 1:25, 27; 4:10; 8:7, 9, 10; 9:22 (3x); 11:30; 12:22; 2 Cor. 10:10; Gal. 4:9; 1 Thess. 5:14; Heb. 7:18; 1 Pet. 3:7.

73. Matt. 14:14; Mark 6:5, 13; 16:18; 1 Cor. 11:30.

74. See 1 Cor. 7:39; 11:30; 15:6, 18, 20, 51; 1 Thess. 4:13, 14, 15; elsewhere in the NT see Matt. 27:52; John 11:12; Acts 7:60; 13:36; 2 Pet. 3:4. In Matt. 28:13; Luke 22:45; John 11:12; Acts 12:6 κοιμάω is used to indicate for sleeping. See also, e.g., *1 Clem.* 24:3; 26:2; 44:2; *Herm.* 32:1. Cf. BDAG, "κοιμάω," 551.

75. Cf. Richard B. Hays, *First Corinthians* (IBC; Louisville: John Knox, 1997), 201, 205–6. The suggestion by Barrett (*First Epistle to the Corinthians*, 275), that the Corinthians have opened themselves up to the demonic, would relieve God of some of the responsibility of the

6.4 Rescue from Afflictions (2 Corinthians 1:8–11)

In customary fashion, Paul begins Second Corinthians with a salutation (1:1–2) followed by an opening thanksgiving (1:3–7).[76] Uncharacteristically, he focuses on the experience of God's mercies and consolation in his own life rather than in those of his readers. Then, connecting his example with "for" (γάρ), Paul says that in "the affliction [θλῖψις] we experienced in Asia . . . we despaired of life itself" (1:8). It is not immediately obvious what Paul is referring to: Being life-threatening and in the past—he uses the aorist (γενομένης, "happened" or "experienced")[77]—it is unlikely to be mental or spiritual anguish.[78] Also, Paul probably is not referring to his "thorn" (12:7). In contrast to the thorn, the affliction alluded to here was life-threatening and a specific event.[79] Using the word "affliction" (θλῖψις), which is rarely employed in relation to illness,[80] and comparing his suffering to Christ (1:5) also make it unlikely he is referring to sickness.[81] Instead, Paul probably is referring to an experience of extreme or life-threatening persecution, the details of which are unknown to us.[82]

What is of interest to us is that Paul describes this scenario in terms of his concept of miracle, something carried out by God that was extraordinary and had meaning (see §1.5 above). He says he despaired of life; in other words, he did not expect to survive (1:8–9). Also, he says God, who raises the dead, "rescued" (ἐρρύσατο) him[83] from a deadly peril (1:10).[84] By inference, in describing God as one who raises the dead, Paul draws attention to the severity of the life-threatening situation. Also, the use of "rescue" (ἐρρύσατο), which, consistent with the Septuagint, always has God as the author in the New Testament,[85] draws attention to God being responsible for his safety. The meaning Paul gave to this

suffering Paul describes, but there is nothing in the text to support the idea. Nevertheless, cf. 1 Cor. 5:5, where Paul expresses a similar idea.

76. See P. Arzt, "The Epistolary Introductory Thanksgiving in the Papyri and in Paul," *NovT* 36 (1994): 29–46.

77. See McKay, "Epistolary Aorist in 2 Corinthians," 155.

78. Thrall, *Second Epistle to the Corinthians*, 1:115n238.

79. Ibid., 1:116, esp. n248.

80. See BDAG, "θλῖψις," 457; Colin Kruse, *The Second Epistle of Paul to the Corinthians: An Introduction and Commentary* (TNTC; Leicester: Inter-Varsity; Grand Rapids: Eerdmans, 1987), 68.

81. Against Dawson, *Healing*, 197.

82. Cf. Thrall, *Second Epistle to the Corinthians*, 1:117.

83. On Paul's use of the literary plural "us" (ὑμᾶς) see 142n258 above.

84. On the problems of the textual variants θανάτου ("death") and θανάτων ("deaths"), see Thrall, *Second Epistle to the Corinthians*, 1:120–21.

85. Matt. 6:13; 27:43 (cf. Ps. 21:9 [ET 22:8]; Luke 1:74 (cf. Ps. 17:1 [ET 18 superscription]; 3 Macc. 6:10; 2 Kgdms. [ET 2 Sam.] 22:18; Judg. 8:34); Rom. 7:24; 11:26 (cf. Isa. 59:20); 15:31; 2 Cor. 1:10 (cf. Ps. 55:14 [ET 56:13]; Job 5:20); Col. 1:13; 1 Thess. 1:10; 2 Thess. 3:2 (cf. Isa. 25:4); 2 Tim. 3:11 (cf. Ps. 33:20 [ET 34:19]); 4:17–18 (cf. 1 Macc. 2:60); 2 Pet. 2:7, 9.

experience is that God will continue to rescue him (1:11). In other words, Paul has had the experience of a miracle in God rescuing him from mortal danger, giving him confidence in the occurrence of further such miracles.

6.5 The Recovery of Epaphroditus (Philippians 2:25–30)

In order to be cheered by news of the Philippians, Paul says he intends to send Timothy to them (2:19).[86] In the meantime, since Epaphroditus, Paul's co-worker and the one who brought the Philippians' gift to Paul (2:25; 4:18), has been distressed on learning that the Philippians heard he was ill, Paul will send him to the Philippians with the letter in question (cf. 2:29). Epaphroditus has not only been sick (ἀσθενέω, cf. §6.1 above); but he came "near to death" (παραπλήσιον θανάτῳ, 2:27), "having risked his life" (παραβολευσάμενος τῇ ψυχῇ, 2:30).[87] Although the nature of the severe sickness is not specified, Paul says it came in relation to or "through the work of Christ" (διὰ τὸ ἔργον Χριστοῦ, 2:30)—that is, in the present context, the bringing of the Philippians' gift to Paul. The reasonable supposition is that Epaphroditus, becoming ill on the road, took the risk of completing his journey, which nearly killed him (2:30).[88]

To suggest that Paul's anxiety shows that he could not heal Epaphroditus, and therefore healing was not part of the ministry of the church,[89] is an ill-conceived argument.[90] Paul says nothing about his, or anyone else's, involvement

86. The question of the possible composite nature of Philippians need not detain us. See, e.g., Loveday C. A. Alexander, "Hellenistic Letter-Forms and the Structure of Philippians," *JSNT* 37 (1989): 87–101.

87. παραβολευσάμενος (the verb occurs in the NT only in Phil. 2:30) could mean "gambling" with his life; see J. B. Lightfoot, *Saint Paul's Epistle to the Philippians* (London: Macmillan, 1879), 124–25. More likely, in light of the same form of the word, meaning "daring to expose oneself to danger," being found in a second-century CE inscription from Olbia on the Black Sea, it means "risking." See Adolf Deissmann, *Light from the Ancient East: The New Testament Illustrated by Recently Discovered Texts of the Graeco-Roman World*, trans. Lionel R. M. Strachan (London: Hodder & Stoughton, 1910), 84–85; and the discussion by Gerald F. Hawthorne, *Philippians* (WBC 43; Waco: Word, 1983), 118. On the less reliable variant reading παραβουλευσάμενος τῇ ψυχῇ ("having no concern for his life"), see Henk Jan de Jonge, "Eine Konjektur Joseph Scaligers zu Philipper II 30," *NovT* 17 (1975): 297–302.

88. Cf. George B. Caird, *Paul's Letters from Prison: Ephesians, Philippians, Colossians, Philemon* (NClarB; Oxford: Oxford University Press, 1976), 129. The argument by, e.g., R. Alan Culpepper ("Co-Workers in Suffering: Philippians 2:19–30," *RevExp* 77 [1980]: 356), that the sickness was the result of imprisonment with Paul, does not take sufficiently into account the notion of risk and bringing the gift that Paul associates with the sickness.

89. Gary W. Derickson, "The Cessation of Healing Miracles in Paul's Ministry," *BSac* 155 (1998): 309.

90. Without evidence, H. C. G. Moule (*The Epistle to the Philippians* [CGTSC 11; Cambridge: Cambridge University Press, 1897], 53) suggests Paul was unable to heal Epaphroditus.

in the recovery that enabled Epaphroditus to travel again (2:28–29). Rather, he attributes the change directly to God acting mercifully (ἐλεέω, 2:27),[91] therefore seeing the health of Epaphroditus as a miracle (see §1.5 above). Although it probably outruns the evidence to suggest the miracle was due to "gifts of healings" (1 Cor. 12:9, 28, 30),[92] in light of the prayers in the Gospels asking for mercy (or healing, see n. 91 below) it is not unreasonable to assume that prayers for God's mercy in relation to Epaphroditus had been offered.[93]

6.6 Conversion and Call (1 Corinthians 9:1; 15:8; Galatians 1:13–16; Philippians 3:4–11)

We have already seen that Paul's description of his call experience shows he saw himself belonging to the tradition of the scriptural prophets (§3.1). Here, through paying attention to key texts,[94] we will also see that he took it to be a conversion experience.[95] It is not that Paul had his plagued conscience

91. For other NT writers using ἐλεέω ("mercy") to describe God's activity resulting in healing, see Matt. 9:27; 15:22; 17:15; 20:30–31; Mark 5:19; 10:47–48; Luke 16:24; 17:13; 18:38–39.

92. As suggested by Gordon D. Fee, *Paul's Letter to the Philippians* (NICNT; Grand Rapids: Eerdmans, 1995), 279. See the sober comments by Peter T. O'Brien (*The Epistle to the Philippians: A Commentary on the Greek Text* [NIGTC; Grand Rapids: Eerdmans, 1991], 336) about our ignorance of the details.

93. Cf. Jean-François Collange, *The Epistle of Saint Paul to the Philippians*, trans. A. W. Heathcote (London: Epworth, 1979), 121.

94. 1 Cor. 9:1; 15:8; Gal. 1:13–16; Phil. 3:4–11. On the one hand, Jerome Murphy-O'Connor (*Paul: A Critical Life* [Oxford: Oxford University Press, 1996], 70) considers Paul refers to his conversion and call only at 1 Cor. 9:1; 15:8 and Gal. 1:12–16, and J. Christiaan Beker (*Paul the Apostle: The Triumph of God in Life and Thought* [Edinburgh: T&T Clark, 1980], 4) cites 1 Cor. 15:9–10; Gal. 1:15–16; Phil. 3:4–11, and Walter Schmithals (*The Office of Apostle in the Early Church*, trans. John E. Steely [Nashville: Abingdon, 1969], 56) says that "in contrast to the prophets, Paul can relate no experience of his call." On the other hand, Seyoon Kim (*Paul's Gospel*, 3–31) finds reference to Paul's experience at Rom. 10:2–4; 12:3; 15:5; 1 Cor. 1:4; 3:10; 9:16–17; 2 Cor. 3:16; 4:6; 5:16; Gal. 2:9; Eph. 3:1–13; Phil. 3:4–12; Col. 1:23–29, and in the opening statements of Romans, 1–2 Corinthians, Galatians, Ephesians, and Colossians. See also the summary discussion by Ron Elsdon, "Was Paul 'Converted' or 'Called'? Questions of Methodology," *PIBA* 24 (2001): 18–19.

The discussion of the long-standing and complex problem of the place of Rom. 7:7–25 in Paul's autobiography is summarized by Robert Jewett, *Romans: A Commentary* (Hermeneia; Minneapolis: Fortress, 2007), 441–45, affirming the view of Troels Engberg-Pedersen that "Paul is describing an experience of living under the Mosaic Law as seen from the Christ-believing perspective" ("The Reception of Graeco-Roman Culture in the New Testament: The Case of Romans 7.7–25," in *The New Testament as Reception*, ed. Mogens Müller and Henrik Tronier [JSNTSup 230; London: Sheffield Academic Press, 2002], 37).

95. Referring to, e.g., Krister Stendahl, *Paul among Jews and Gentiles* (London: SCM, 1977), 7–23; Hans Dieter Betz, *Galatians: A Commentary on Paul's Letter to the Churches in Galatia* (Hermeneia; Philadelphia: Fortress, 1979), 64; Dieter Georgi, *Theocracy in Paul's Praxis and Theology*, trans. David A. Green (Minneapolis: Fortress, 1991), 19. Jerome Murphy-O'Connor

quieted,[96] or defected from Judaism and changed religions,[97] but as the most life-changing event of his life, the experience gave his Judaism a new center of gravity.[98] In particular, my interest is in establishing that Paul understood his conversion and call not just as an ecstatic experience, but also one that was miraculous—from God and meaningful or revelatory. If, further, we can identify the place that Paul gave to this experience, we will have an indication of the place Paul gave to miracle in his life and theology.

In Philippians Paul alludes to his conversion, describing a complete reorientation or transformation of his life because of knowing Christ (3:4–11),[99] obviously regarding it as life changing.[100] He says that, in light of knowing Christ, "I have suffered the loss of all things, and I regard them as rubbish" (3:8). The clearest account Paul gives of his conversion from Pharisaism "to a particular kind of Gentile community of God-fearers living without the law," as Alan Segal put it,[101] is in Galatians 1:13–16. Paul says, in part: "God, who had set me apart before I was born and called me through his grace, was pleased to reveal his Son to me, so that I might proclaim him among the Gentiles" (1:15–16). Even without the introduction of "God" (1:15),[102] from the echo of Isaiah 49:1,[103] and reference to "his Son" (υἱὸν αὐτοῦ, Gal. 1:16), it is obvious that God is the subject of the parenthetical clause ("he who set me apart . . . and called me through his grace," 1:15). In other words, Paul takes this experience to have been from God.[104] What Paul says that God

---

(*Paul: A Critical Life*, 70n2) says that "some scholars have pedantically denied that Paul was converted."

96. Krister Stendahl, "The Apostle Paul and the Introspective Conscience of the West," *HTR* 55 (1962): 119–215, also in *Paul among the Jews and Gentiles* (London: SCM, 1977), 78–96. Note Krister Stendahl, "Sources and Critiques," in *Paul among Jews and Gentiles*, 129–33, in which his views are summarized in debate with Ernst Käsemann, "Justification and Salvation History in the Epistle to the Romans," in *Perspectives on Paul*, trans. Margaret Kohl (London: SCM, 1971), 60–78.

97. Segal, *Paul the Convert*, e.g., xiii–xiv.

98. Albert Schweitzer, *Paul and His Interpreters: A Critical History*, trans. W. Montgomery (London: Black, 1912), 227. See the brief summary discussion by Larry W. Hurtado, "Convert, Apostate or Apostle to the Nations? The 'Conversion' of Paul in Recent Scholarship," *SR* 22 (1993): 281–83.

99. See Segal, *Paul the Convert*, 22; O'Brien, *Philippians*, 383.

100. E.g., Heikki Räisänen, "Paul's Call Experience and His Later View of the Law," in *Jesus, Paul and Torah: Collected Essays*, trans. David E. Orton (JSNTSup 43; Sheffield: JSOT Press, 1992), 15.

101. Segal, *Paul the Convert*, 117.

102. A number of manuscripts (e.g., ℵ A D) have ὁ θεός (Gal. 1:15).

103. Gal. 1:15: ἐκ κοιλίας μητρός μου καὶ καλέσας ("from my mother's womb and calling"); cf. Isa. 49:1: ἐκ κοιλίας μητρός μου ἐκάλεσεν ("from my mother's womb and called") (my translations). See also LXX Isa. 44:2; 49:5; Ps. 70:6 (ET 71:6).

104. Cf. Stephen J. Chester, *Conversion at Corinth: Perspectives on Conversion in Paul's Theology and the Corinthian Church* (SNTW; London: T&T Clark, 2003), esp. 59–112.

"was pleased" (εὐδόκησεν) to do was reveal his Son to him. Thus, at least in retrospect, years later Paul understood and wanted to convey this experience as both from God and revelatory or meaningful—in other words, miraculous.[105]

Just what revelation was involved in Paul's miraculous experience is not obvious or agreed and the subject of ongoing debate.[106] It is argued that Paul's theology, especially his law-free gospel, was conceived in or immediately after this experience.[107] However, Paul likely made little of this aspect of his gospel, for up until the dispute at Antioch (Gal. 2:11–14), involving a breach with Barnabas (2:13), it is probable that Paul's theology was similar to other Antiochene Christians.[108] Yet, Paul portrays his theology and practice of mission arising, not in relation to being sent out from Antioch (Acts 13:1–3),[109] but in (or very soon after)[110] his conversion experience.[111] Also, if Paul's Gentile mission had not arisen as he portrays it here, but was a more recent interpretation of his experience, he would have given grounds for his opponents to see him as a self-made apostle and to question why he was only now taking this position. Therefore, it is likely that Paul took his law-free gospel straight from the furnace of his conversion experience, even though he continued to shape his message on the anvil of the trials of ministry.[112]

Indeed, the import of his defense of the origin of his gospel (Gal. 1:11–24) is not only that the Son had been revealed to him, but also that he could not have received his gospel from humans, since immediately after his conversion he did not confer with any one (1:16) but began his Gentile mission. In going beyond mention of the revelatory experience to include a discussion of his Gentile mission in his defense shows that he saw it as inseparably related to, and probably having its rise in, the revelatory experience.[113]

105. For a review discussion of the reliability of Paul's account of his conversion, see Matthew W. Mitchell, *Abortion and the Apostolate: A Study in Pauline Conversion, Rhetoric, and Scholarship* (GD 42; Piscataway, NJ: Gorgias, 2009), esp. 56–71.

106. See the discussion by Räisänen, "Paul's Call Experience," esp. 21–25, and Elsdon, "Was Paul 'Converted' or 'Called'?"

107. As supposed by, e.g., Kim, *Paul's Gospel*, 269, and those cited in n. 1.

108. Heikki Räisänen, *Paul and the Law*, 2nd ed. (WUNT 29; Tübingen: Mohr Siebeck, 1987), 253–54; Räisänen, "Paul's Call Experience," 24.

109. As supposed by Nicholas Taylor, *Paul, Antioch and Jerusalem: A Study in Relationships and Authority in Earliest Christianity* (JSNTSup 66; Sheffield: JSOT Press, 1993), 92–93.

110. Even though the reliability of Paul's interpretation of his experience is open to question (see, e.g., the discussion by Mitchell, *Abortion and the Apostolate*, 56–66), Paul sees and wishes to portray a very close connection between his conversion experience and his Gentile mission.

111. Cf., e.g., Martin Hengel and Anna Maria Schwemer, *Paul between Damascus and Antioch: The Unknown Years* (London: SCM, 1997), 47–50, 107–120.

112. Cf. Räisänen, "Paul's Call Experience," esp. 45–47.

113. Cf., e.g., Segal, *Paul the Convert*, 127.

For, in Jewish literature the conversion of the Gentiles was associated with the eschaton.[114] Also, Paul's almost exact quotation from Isaiah's call and sharing ideas in common with Isaiah—God's prenatal knowledge, a call to speak, and a mission to the Gentiles (Isa. 49:1–6)—shows not the unlikely scenario that the contemplation of the call of Isaiah contributed to Paul's missionary convictions, and that he took his experience and understanding of it to have similar life-changing repercussions.[115] This contemplation would have either been fueled by what he already knew or been confirmed by what he came to know about the significant missionary component of the Jesus movement he joined. Further, in Paul's two other clear, though brief, references to his conversion he also relates the revelatory experience to his mission. In one case, his being an apostle is said to be dependent on seeing Jesus (1 Cor. 9:1), and in the other the appearance of Christ is taken to be the grounds for counting himself among the apostles—those sent on mission (15:8). Notably, this understanding of his conversion was available to Luke, who picked it up in each of his stories of Paul's conversion (Acts 9:15; 22:21; 26:17).[116]

What Paul says about his conversion giving rise to his mission is borne out by what he says he did immediately after the experience: "I went away at once into Arabia, and afterwards I returned to Damascus" (Gal. 1:17). In that Paul is describing how he fulfilled the call to "proclaim him among the Gentiles" (1:16), he intends his readers to understand that this is what he was doing in Arabia. He was not merely reflecting and studying, as is sometimes suggested.[117] Also, Paul says of the whole period during which he was in Arabia, Damascus, briefly in Jerusalem, and also in Syria and Cilicia (1:17–21) that in Judea they were "hearing (ἀκούοντες, present active participle) it said, 'The one who formerly was persecuting us is now proclaiming the faith he once tried to destroy'" (1:23). Further, that Paul had incurred the wrath of Aretas IV, the Nabatean (Arabian) king and had to flee from him in Damascus (2 Cor. 11:32; cf. Acts 9:24–25) is strong support for the idea that Paul had been engaged in mission work to the Gentiles immediately after his conversion experience.[118]

---

114. E.g., Ps. 96:3, 10; Isa. 11:10; 40:5; 45:20, 22; 51:4; 60:3; Jer. 3:17; Tob. 13:11; *1 En.* 48:4. See the discussion of the primary data by Joachim Jeremias, *The Eucharistic Words of Jesus* (NTL; London: SCM, 1966), 56–73.

115. Cf. Kim, *Paul's Gospel*, 60.

116. Cf. Gustav Stählin, *Die Apostelgeschichte: Übersetzt und erklärt*, 10th ed. (NTD; Göttingen: Vandenhoeck & Ruprecht, 1962), 310–11.

117. E.g., Taylor, *Paul*, 73.

118. Cf., e.g., F. F. Bruce, *The Epistle of Paul to the Galatians: A Commentary on the Greek Text* (NIGTC; Exeter: Paternoster; Grand Rapids: Eerdmans, 1982), 96.

Paul's reflections on his conversion and call, and his subsequent mission activities among the Gentiles, show not only that he thought he had experienced a miracle but also that it had changed his life (cf. Phil. 3:4–11). Moreover, reminiscent of Isaiah before him, the experience also shaped Paul's theology and practice of mission. Since there is no evidence of a Jewish mission to the Gentiles in the time of Paul (see §4.1 above), the significance of the impact of this miraculous experience on his theology and mission is profound and ought not be lost: the miracle had given rise to an entirely new impulse for Paul's mission practice. In this case, miracle, not practice, was the mother of theology, as well as of practice.

6.7 *Charismata* (1 Corinthians 2:9–13; 14:6, 18; 2 Corinthians 13:3)

In assembling evidence of Paul's experience of miracle, we need to take into account his discussion of *charismata* in 1 Corinthians 12–14. For, Paul describes the gifts in terms of miracle: God activates them (12:4); they are extraordinary in that the class includes, for example, healing (12:9) and working miracles (12:10); and they have meaning in that they manifest the Spirit for the common good (12:7) (see §1.5 above).

However, we have to set aside the view, at least as old as Augustine (354–430),[119] that Paul had experience of all, or even most of,[120] the gifts or expressions of the Spirit he mentions. First, his description of the distribution of the gifts—"to one is given . . . and to another . . . to another . . . to another . . ." (12:8–10)—assumes that people have different gifts. Second, if he considered that he or anyone could lay claim to all the gifts, he would not need to describe the Spirit as allotting gifts "to each one individually just as the Spirit chooses" (12:11). Third, the whole point of his body metaphor is to demonstrate the implication of individuals having gifts that differ from each other (12:12, 14). Fourth, most obviously making the point that no one person has all the gifts, he finishes his discussion of variety in the church by asking if all, for example, work miracles or possess gifts of

---

119. Though Augustine (*Pelag.* 32) objected to the Pelagian view that "every individual has the ability to possess all powers and graces," he proposed that only an apostle, including Paul, possessed all the gifts.

120. As supposed by, e.g., Hermann Gunkel, *The Influence of the Holy Spirit: The Popular View of the Apostolic Age and the Teaching of the Apostle Paul*, trans. Roy A. Harrisville and Philip A. Quanbeck II (Philadelphia: Fortress, 1979), 77; cf. 112; Ashton, *Religion of Paul*, 210; Craig A. Evans, "Paul the Exorcist and Healer," in *Paul and His Theology*, ed. Stanley E. Porter (PSt 3; Leiden: Brill, 2006), 365.

healing (12:30). Beginning each question with μή ("not"), Paul is requiring a negative answer, translated something like, "Not all work miracles, do they?"[121] Paul's point is not that there is a range of gifts, but that no one has all the gifts.[122]

Although his view is that no one person has all the gifts, given that he considers every person has one (12:7) or more (14:1–5) gifts, which did Paul have? It may be significant for the present project that in the section where Paul uses himself as an example (14:6–33) there is no hint that he claimed to work miracles or possess the gift of healing. However, it is more likely he does not mention these gifts because his concern is only with the value of and protocol for the use of tongues, which he discusses in relation to other verbal contributions members bring to meetings.

It could be that in saying, "But now, brothers, if I come to you speaking in tongues, how will I benefit you unless I speak to you in a revelation or knowledge or prophecy or teaching?" (14:6, my translation), Paul is claiming a concrete example of his use of these gifts.[123] However, the sentence is cast hypothetically ("if I come," ἐὰν ἔλθω).[124] Therefore, Paul's statement falls short of unequivocal evidence that he claims to speak revelation, knowledge, prophecy, or teaching. Notwithstanding, there is other evidence he used these and other gifts.

(a) Tongues. Paul must have considered he spoke in tongues a great deal to claim to use the gift more than his readers (14:18; cf. 14:6, 14) for they highly valued the practice (cf. 14:1–33). In saying he spoke in tongues more than his readers, "but" (ἀλλά, a strong adversative) "in the assembly" (ἐν ἐκκλησίᾳ) he would rather speak five words with his mind (14:18–19), implies he is thankful for its personal use (cf. 14:2, 28b).[125] It is not that Paul is proscribing the use of tongues in the assembly (cf. 14:27). Instead, in calling for them to "be silent" (σιγάτω) and to "speak to themselves and to God" (ἑαυτῷ δὲ λαλείτω καὶ τῷ

---

121. Cf. Thiselton, First Epistle to the Corinthians, 1022–23. Though losing Paul's subtlety, the TEV expresses Paul's intent well: "They are not all apostles or prophets or teachers. Not everyone has the power to work miracles or to heal diseases or to speak in strange tongues or to explain what is said" (1 Cor. 12:29–30).

The traditional Pentecostal interpretation that speaking in tongues in private was for everyone, and that Paul's "no" relates only to speaking in tongues in the assembly, is to be dismissed as special pleading. For, as Max Turner (The Holy Spirit and Spiritual Gifts, Then and Now [Carlisle: Paternoster, 1996], 234–35) asks, "Are apostles only apostles in the assembled church, etc. (1 Cor. 12:28a)?"

122. Thiselton, First Epistle to the Corinthians, 1023.

123. Cf., e.g., David E. Aune, Prophecy in Early Christianity and the Ancient Mediterranean World (Grand Rapids: Eerdmans, 1991), 249.

124. Cf. Thiselton, First Epistle to the Corinthians, 1101.

125. Ibid., 1117.

θεῷ) if there is no interpreter available (14:28),[126] Paul means that those who have this gift are to use it in private, at home.[127]

In its private or personal use, Paul says of tongues, which for him included singing (14:14–15),[128] was a means of speaking to God (14:2)[129]—that is, prayer in its broadest sense.[130] He also says tongues "builds up" (οἰκοδομέω) the speaker (14:4). In light of his own positive experience (14:18), and encouraging others to speak in tongues (14:5, 28), Paul is unlikely to mean this pejoratively[131] or with any sarcasm.[132] Rather, he means tongues can edify or build up the individual,[133] as a prophecy (14:3), a hymn, a lesson, a revelation, or an interpreted tongue can edify others in the assembly (14:26).[134] In view of the parallel structure of his statement[135]—"those who prophesy speak to other people for their edification and encouragement and consolation. Those who speak in a tongue edify themselves, but those who prophesy build up the church" (14:3–4, my translation)—Paul probably sees edification as involving encouragement and consolation, for tongues as well as prophecy. Indeed, interpreted for others in the assembly, tongues approximates the function of prophecy (cf. 14:5–6).[136]

In public, Paul's use of translated tongues (spoken or sung, 14:14–15) was for blessing or offering thanksgiving, which edifies others (14:17). Another public use of tongues, which Paul contrasts with prophecy, is that it is a sign to the unbelievers (14:22).[137] We need not be detained by determining the

126. Paul's comment in 1 Cor. 14:2 that the person speaking an uninterpreted tongue is πνεύματι δὲ λαλεῖ μυστήρια ("speaking mysteries in the Spirit") is probably to be understood not as referring to speaking hidden truths (Barrett, *First Epistle to the Corinthians*, 315–16), but rather, since comprehension is the issue for Paul, as "Nobody understands a word he says" (Calvin, *Paul the Apostle to the Corinthians*, 436). See the discussion by Thiselton, *First Epistle to the Corinthians*, 1086.

127. It is generally agreed that by ἑαυτῷ ("to himself" [1 Cor. 14:28]) Paul means the person is to use the gift in private or at home. See Thiselton, *First Epistle to the Corinthians*, 1139–40.

128. 1 Cor. 14:14–15 is not only rhetorical but also autobiographical, see 14:18–19. Cf. ibid., 670, 674.

129. Fee (*God's Empowering Presence*, 218) draws attention to Paul's view of tongues as speaking to God as counter to the contemporary Pentecostal view that tongues is a message from God.

130. Cf., e.g., Dunn, *Jesus and the Spirit*, 245; Fee, *First Epistle to the Corinthians*, 656.

131. Cf. Otto Michel, "οἰκοδομέω," *TDNT* 5:141.

132. John MacArthur, *1 Corinthians* (Chicago: Moody, 1984), 372.

133. So Chrysostom, *Hom. 1 Cor.* 35.1; Fee, *First Epistle to the Corinthians*, 657.

134. Edification is a theme threaded through Paul's discussion of tongues. See 1 Cor. 14:3, 5, 12, 17.

135. Fee, *God's Empowering Presence*, 217–18.

136. Cf., e.g., Turner, *Holy Spirit*, 231.

137. Against Thomas R. Edgar (*Miraculous Gifts: Are They for Today?* [Neptune, NJ: Loizeaux, 1983], chap. 7), who asserts that tongues has one function as a sign that aids in evangelism, see Turner, *Holy Spirit*, 232–34.

precise meaning of tongues as a sign to unbelievers.[138] Paul's general intent is clear: untranslated tongues are unhelpful to unbelievers. By inference (14:24), translated tongues would have the same impact on an unbeliever as prophecy: secrets would be revealed, the person would bow down and worship God, declaring him to be present (14:25).

From this we can see that Paul's experience of the miracle of tongues is part of his experience of prayer, contributing to his edification, encouragement, and consolation. Untranslated in public, tongues is unhelpful; translated tongues functioned as prophecy, also edifying, encouraging, and consoling believers, as well as causing unbelievers to worship God.

(b) Prophecy. We have already seen that although he did not claim the title, Paul saw himself as a prophet and prophesied (§3.2 above). In light of his plea that his readers strive especially for the gift of prophecy, Paul probably would have claimed the *charisma* (14:1, 6 [see above]). Therefore, as with tongues, identifying the contribution of prophecy to Paul's life, theology, and mission, we are probably gaining insight into his understanding of the impact of miracle on him.

Paul's references to prophesying (προφητεύω, "prophesy") are concentrated in 1 Corinthians 14.[139] There he describes the activity: "Let two or three prophets speak, and let the others weigh what is said. If a revelation is made to someone else sitting nearby, let the first person be silent. For you can all prophesy one by one, so that all may learn and all be encouraged" (14:29–31). For Paul, then, prophesying was the spontaneous reception and speaking of a "revelation" (ἀποκάλυψις).[140] The context makes it obvious the revelation is understood to come from God (e.g., 14:25), and Paul refers to the result as prophecy (προφητεία, esp. 14:6, 22).

At least part of Paul's understanding of the function of prophecy can be seen in his description of its outcome: edification, encouragement, and consolation (14:3; cf. 1 Thess. 4:18).[141] The word "edification" (οἰκοδομή), an image familiar from house construction,[142] which Paul used for his ministry (1 Cor. 3:10–15; 2 Cor. 10:8) and for prophecy in particular (1 Cor. 14:3; cf. 1 Thess.

---

138. For various attempts to deduce Paul's particular intent, see the summary discussion by Thiselton, *First Epistle to the Corinthians*, 1123–26.

139. προφητεύω: 1 Cor. 14:1, 3, 4, 5 (2x), 24, 31, 39; cf. 11:4, 5; 13:19; in the remainder of the NT: Matt. 7:22; 11:13; 15:7; 26:68; Mark 7:6; 14:65; Luke 1:67; 22:64; John 11:51; Acts 2:17, 18; 19:6; 21:9; 1 Pet. 1:10; Jude 14; Rev. 10:11; 11:3.

140. For other definitions of prophecy, see, e.g., Aune, *Prophecy*, 247–48; Turner, *Holy Spirit*, 197.

141. Cf. E. Cothenet, "Prophétisme et ministère d'après le Nouveau Testament," *La Maison-Dieu* 107 (1971): 50.

142. E.g., see Epictetus, *Diatr.* 1.28; 2.15; Philo, *Gig.* 30; *Mut.* 211; *Somn.* 2.8.

5:11), carried the idea of strengthening against difficulties.[143] This shows he probably understood prophecy strengthened believers to withstand the disasters and difficulties of life (cf. 1 Thess. 4:13–5:11). "Encouragement" (παράκλησις)[144] and "consolation" (παραμυθία, "close conversation")[145] cannot be sharply distinguished and probably are synonyms,[146] contributing a relational warmth to the edifying function of prophecy. In short, Paul understood prophecy to have a pastoral function, instrumental in caring for and encouraging believers.

Other functions of prophecy for Paul can be seen from examples in his letters. David E. Aune has suggested criteria for identifying fragments of prophetic material in Paul's letters. Given that prophetic material could be recognized if it (1) was attributed to a supernatural being, (2) consisted of predictions or knowledge of the past not ordinarily accessible, and (3) was introduced by formulae otherwise used to introduce prophetical material, there are a number of passages in Paul's letters that can be described as prophetic:[147] Romans 11:25–26; 1 Corinthians 12:3; 14:37–38; 15:51–52; 2 Corinthians 12:9; Galatians 5:21; and 1 Thessalonians 3:4; 4:2–6, 16–17.[148]

The theologically creative function of prophecy is evident for Paul in Romans 11:25b–26a: "I want you to understand this mystery: a hardening has come upon part of Israel, until the full number of the Gentiles has come in. And so all Israel will be saved." Perhaps coming to Paul as he was writing this section,[149] the prophecy both introduces into early Christian literature the only place where the idea of all Israel being saved is found[150] and reverses the order in which Jews expected salvation to take place,[151] here having the Jews follow the Gentiles. The prophecy also contrasts with, and goes beyond, the notion earlier in Paul's argument of a "remnant" (λεῖμμα [Rom. 11:5; cf., e.g., 9:6–29]) or "some" (τινες, 11:17) or a "part" (μέρους, 11:25) to "all" (πᾶς, 11:26) of Israel being saved.[152]

143. Cf. Matt. 7:24–27; 'Abot R. Nat. 24. See Michel, "οἰκοδομέω."

144. Paul uses the verb παρακαλέω ("encourage" [1 Cor. 14:31; 1 Thess. 4:18; cf. 5:11, 14) and the noun παράκλησις ("encouragement" [1 Cor. 14:3]) as the intention and the outcome of prophecy.

145. παραμυθία occurs in the NT only here in 1 Cor. 14:3.

146. Cf. Phil. 2:1; and note the use of the verbs παρακαλέω ("entreat" or "urge") and παραμυθέομαι ("encourage" or "exhort") in 1 Thess. 2:12 as synonyms. See Gustav Stählin, "παραμυθέομαι," TDNT 5:820.

147. Aune, Prophecy, 247–48.

148. Ibid., 261, 441 and n. 47. For other attempts at establishing criteria, see Calvin J. Roetzel, "The Judgment Form in Paul's Letters," JBL 88 (1969): 305–12, and Aune, Prophecy, 261–62.

149. Suggested by Bent Noack, "Current and Backwater in the Epistle to the Romans," ST 19 (1965): 165–66.

150. Aune, Prophecy, 252–53.

151. See, e.g., Mic. 4:2; Zeph. 3:9; Zech. 2:11; 14:16–18; Tob. 13:11; 14:6–7; Pss. Sol. 17:34; Sib. Or. 3:772–75.

152. Cf. Otto Hofius, "'All Israel Will Be Saved': Divine Salvation and Israel's Deliverance in Romans 9–11," PSB supplement 1 (1990): 33–39.

The theological contribution of prophecy is also seen in 1 Thessalonians 4:16–17, where Paul goes beyond the idea of resurrection, which was already the hope and belief of the readers (4:13–14), to set the time of the resurrection before the parousia.[153] In 1 Corinthians 15:51–52 prophecy is used to convey similar ideas,[154] the particular contribution being on the change for the living ("in the twinkling of an eye," 15:52) necessary so they can, with the dead, inherit the kingdom of God (15:50).[155]

The predictive function of prophecy for Paul is seen in relation to persecution (1 Thess. 3:4). In other places it functions variously as parenesis (4:2–6), teaching (1 Cor. 14:37–38;[156] cf. §6.2 above on 2 Cor. 12:9), as warning (Gal. 5:21), as assurance (2 Cor. 12:9), and as a recognition oracle ("Jesus is Lord," 1 Cor. 12:3).[157] Along with tongues, then, prophecy as part of Paul's experience of miracle was profoundly important to Paul.

(c) Teaching. Only here in 1 Corinthians 14:6 does Paul imply he has the gift of teaching.[158] However, it is notable that the list of gifts in Romans 12:6–8, which is a remarkably good fit to Paul's work, includes teaching along with prophecy, ministry, exhortation, giving, leading, and compassion.[159] Further, Paul clearly took teaching to be a gift of considerable importance, claiming to use it everywhere he went (1 Cor. 4:17).[160]

(d) Wisdom. There is no direct evidence that Paul considered himself a bearer of the charisma of wisdom. However, the indirect evidence is particularly strong. Early in 1 Corinthians Paul has been contrasting his proclamation of the wisdom of God—Christ crucified (1:23–24)—with the rhetorical wisdom so highly valued by his readers (1:25; 2:1). As part of his defense he claims to "speak God's wisdom, secret and hidden, which God decreed before the ages for our glory" (2:7; cf. 2:6). Paul goes on to say that this wisdom has been revealed to him by the Spirit (2:10), and that he speaks these things "not taught

---

153. Ernest Best, *The First and Second Epistles to the Thessalonians* (BNTC; Peabody, MA: Hendrickson; London: Continuum, 1986), 180–82.

154. Charles Masson, *Les deux épîtres de Saint Paul aux Thessaloniciens* (CNT 11A; Neuchâtel: Delachaux & Niestlé, 1957), 63.

155. Also, see Helmut Merklein, "Der Theologe als Prophet: Zur Funktion prophetischen Redens im theologischen Diskurs des Paulus," *NTS* 38 (1992): 402–29, esp. 427.

156. On the scope of the subject of Paul's statement in 1 Cor. 14:37–38, see Aune, *Prophecy*, 257–58.

157. Ibid., 257.

158. Collins, *First Corinthians*, 498.

159. Although the 1 Cor. 12:8–10 and 28–29 lists are more likely to reflect the interests of, and Paul's correction of, the Corinthians, Ashton (*Religion of Paul*, 210), on the other hand, supposes that the lists in 1 Cor. 12 would have been seen as reflecting Paul's activities.

160. On Paul's reputation as a teacher and promoter of the activity, see Col. 1:28; 3:16; 1 Tim. 2:7; 2 Tim. 4:11.

by human wisdom but taught by the Spirit" (2:13; cf. 2:10; 2 Cor. 1:12). This description of wisdom is in line with his description of the *charismata*, which he describes as activated by God and as manifestations of the Spirit (1 Cor. 12:6–7).[161] It is highly likely, therefore, that Paul's readers would have seen this gift as what Paul has been describing as the essence of his proclamation. It is not surprising, then, that the first *charisma* in his list is wisdom (12:8–10), not only because of its inherent interest to the Corinthians, but also, arguably, because in a letter that involves Paul defending his notion of wisdom, it would be natural and important for Paul to mention it first.

Against the identification of Paul's message of wisdom with the *charisma* of wisdom it might be supposed that, early in his letter, Paul has been describing a wisdom that could be characterized by considered and controlled articulation, whereas the gift of wisdom is a different and spontaneous gift for the moment. However, even though the *charismata* might be used spontaneously in the moment,[162] a point emphasized by James Dunn, among others,[163] the gifts are not given in the moment but are associated over time with particular individuals (1 Cor. 12:28–30). As Anthony Thiselton put it: the "gifts are *not* given primarily *in* the moment for their use, but *for* such a moment."[164] There is, then, good reason to suppose that Paul understood that he had the gift of wisdom. If this is correct, the very heart of his message—the crucified Christ—was not (only) a repeated tradition but had a miraculous origin, revealed by God through the Spirit's teaching (2:10, 13).

6.8 Conclusions

The significance of the experience of the miraculous for Paul can hardly be overestimated. He claims to have had a range of experiences of the miraculous—extraordinary and meaningful experiences he attributed to God. Of the miracle of healing, Paul had firsthand experience of one of his valued co-workers miraculously recovering (Phil. 2:25–30), perhaps as the result of prayers offered. His own personal experience of a miracle is of God not only

161. Support for this point comes from those who see the content of wisdom being the same for Paul's preaching and for the *charisma*. See, e.g., Archibald Robertson and Alfred Plummer, *A Critical and Exegetical Commentary on the First Epistle of St. Paul to the Corinthians* (ICC; Edinburgh: T&T Clark, 1914), 264–65; E. Earle Ellis, "'Wisdom' and 'Knowledge' in I Corinthians," *TynBul* 25 (1974): 82–98.

162. E.g., Paul uses the singular λόγος, "a word" (of wisdom), usually translated "utterance" (e.g., NRSV).

163. Dunn, *Jesus and the Spirit*, 221; Siegfried S. Schatzmann, *A Pauline Theology of Charismata* (Peabody, MA: Hendrickson, 1987), 35.

164. Thiselton, *First Epistle to the Corinthians*, 942–43, emphasis original.

rescuing him from unspecified life-threatening afflictions in Asia but also of subsequently having confidence that God would continue to provide such miracles (2 Cor. 1:8–11).

In relation to his thorn in his flesh, Paul's experience of the miraculous is of a different order (2 Cor. 12:1–10; Gal. 4:13–14). In view of what he says to the Galatians, his condition probably caused him anxiety, particularly as a potential threat to his mission. And if, as is most probable, the thorn was physical illness, Paul prayed earnestly, and unsuccessfully, for healing. He expected a miracle, but it did not materialize. Nevertheless, the experience of God's grace and power in the face of his ongoing sickness, while not the answer to prayer he anticipated, transformed his attitude toward this and his other weaknesses—for which he had also likely prayed unsuccessfully—from one of attempted escape, even to delight or pleasure. His not experiencing a miracle also considerably changed his view of God as not always answering prayers as anticipated. Yet, his rescue from afflictions gave him the confidence of God repeating the miracle in the future.

I have argued that Paul's concept and experience of miracle extended to include *charismata*, of which we can be confident that Paul claimed for himself tongues, prophecy, teaching, and probably wisdom. Notable for this study, I have found no comment by Paul that suggests he claimed the gifts of healing or exorcism, for example.[165] We need to be careful in drawing conclusions from Paul not appearing to give examples of his experience of "faith"—the ability to accomplish the ordinarily impossible (1 Cor. 12:9; 13:2). But we can at least say that although he saw such faith as important to his ancestors, it probably was not significant to him.

Paul's considerable use of tongues was not only part of his personal experience of prayer, edifying him; but translated tongues in the assembly functioned as prophecy, including causing unbelievers to worship God. From his description of the outcome of prophecy, and from some of the identifiable examples of prophecy, we can judge that Paul saw it as an instrument of pastoral care in his churches. Also, notably, from what appear to be cases of prophecy in his letters, we can conclude that Paul's theology came not only from received Christian and Jewish tradition, or from the contemplation of his Scriptures. Rather, prophecy was also theologically generative, contributing ideas to his theology not otherwise available to him, most obviously: all Israel being saved, after the Gentiles; the resurrection taking place before the parousia;

165. Cf. Stefan Schreiber, *Paulus als Wundertäter: Redaktionsgeschichtliche Untersuchungen zur Apostelgeschichte und den authentischen Paulusbriefen* (BZNW 79; Berlin: de Gruyter, 1996), 268.

the instant change of the living at the parousia; and predicting persecution. Moreover, the fundamental creative function of the miraculous for Paul is seen in his change of life and his mission to the Gentiles originating in, and being inaugurated as the direct and immediate result of, the miraculous, a revelatory experience.[166] The creative function of miracle is also seen in Paul equating his proclamation with wisdom, which he describes as a *charisma*, revealed by God and taught by the Spirit (1 Cor. 2:10, 13).

The contribution of the miraculous to Paul's life, theology, and mission is, to say the least, profound. Paul's religious experience is not simply an inner activity of the mind; it is something he considered to have tangible realization. As important as are Paul's mystical experiences, he was more than a mystic. His description of their impact shows that he did not understand the rise of his theology only in terms of ideas and literary expressions. Nor did he take the foundation of his theology and gospel to be one or more inherited ideas he had remixed to preach and write about. To nuance Christiaan Beker's view: Paul brought into play with his traditions not only his primordial experience of the Christ event, but also the range of his experience of the miraculous.[167] For Paul, miracle was a fundamentally generative factor for his life, theology, and mission.

166. 1 Cor. 9:1; 15:8; Gal. 1:13–16; Phil. 3:4–11.
167. Beker, *Paul*, 15–16.

7

The Ministry of Paul

From Paul's experience of the miraculous I turn to examine those places in his letters where he arguably mentions his involvement in or conducting of miracles.[1] In light of what has been concluded in previous chapters, I come to this exercise with significant presuppositions. First, as a zealous Jew and Pharisee, Paul was at least sensitive to the possibility of miracles taking place; and, attending synagogues, he may have witnessed them. Second, since he considered the eschaton to have been at least partially realized, he would have been expecting an increase in the incidence of the miraculous. Third, since he implied that he saw himself in the line of scriptural prophets, it is also highly likely he expected miracles to be associated with his ministry. Fourth, Paul had inherited a Christian tradition in which miracles were seen as integral both to its origins and in its ongoing mission, making it likely that, seeing himself as part of that tradition, he expected miracles to take place in his own ministry. Moreover, fifth, although he reported the experience of the absence of the miraculous in his life, he also reports its presence, including in his conversion experience and in the lives of other followers of Jesus. We would not be surprised, therefore, to find Paul referring to conducting miracles and seeing them as related in some way to his ministry.

The purpose of this chapter is to examine the statements in Paul's letters that appear to relate to the miraculous and also those that have been the focus

---

1. Cf. Bernd Kollmann, "Paulus als Wundertäter," in *Paulinische Christologie: Exegetische Beiträge; Hans Hübner zum 70. Geburtstag*, ed. Udo Schnelle, Thomas Söding, and Michael Labahn (Göttingen: Vandenhoeck & Ruprecht, 2000), 78.

179

of debate about him performing miracles in relation to his ministry. Against those who suppose that miracle was of little or no importance to Paul, we will see that Paul takes not only miracles but also the miraculous broadly, to be an inherently essential aspect and expression of the coming of the gospel. We will also see that he becomes increasingly clear and forthright about the fact and importance of miracle as he increasingly needs to defend his call. Notwithstanding, it will be important to note precisely what Paul has to say about his involvement in the miraculous and the significance of this aspect of his ministry. Taking the material in chronological order, I will examine 1 Thessalonians 1:5; Galatians 3:1–5; 1 Corinthians 2:1–5; 1 Corinthians 4:19–20; 1 Corinthians 12–14; 2 Corinthians 6:6–7; 2 Corinthians 12:11–12; and Romans 15:18–19.[2] I begin with 1 Thessalonians, Paul's earliest letter and the oldest extant Christian text.[3]

7.1 1 Thessalonians 1:5

In the statement that is of interest to us Paul says, "Our gospel[4] came to you not in word only, but also in power and in the Holy Spirit and with full conviction" (1 Thess. 1:5a, my translation). Though some are uncertain,[5] it is generally agreed that this is not a reference to miracles.[6] However, with a

2. For an earlier and less developed engagement with some of these texts, see Graham H. Twelftree, *In the Name of Jesus: Exorcism among Early Christians* (Grand Rapids: Baker Academic, 2007), chap. 3.

3. On the chronology of Paul's letters, see, e.g., Rainer Riesner, *Paul's Early Period: Chronology, Mission Strategy, Theology*, trans. Doug Stott (Grand Rapids: Eerdmans, 1998, 26). On the generally older and minority view that James is to be dated earlier than Paul's letters, see the summary discussion and tabular representation of twentieth-century views on the dating of James by Peter H. Davids, *The Epistle of James: A Commentary on the Greek Text* (NIGTC; Grand Rapids: Eerdmans; Exeter: Paternoster, 1982), 2–34. For the dating of Jude, sometimes taken to precede Paul, see the brief discussion by Richard J. Bauckham, *Jude, 2 Peter* (WBC 50; Waco: Word, 1983), 13–16.

4. Bruce M. Metzger (*A Textual Commentary on the Greek New Testament*, 2nd ed. [Stuttgart: Deutsche Bibelgesellschaft; New York: United Bible Societies, 1994], 561) notes that, despite a diversity of witnesses, some scribes seem to have been offended by Paul's term τὸ εὐαγγέλιον ἡμῶν ("our gospel").

5. E.g., Pelagius (see Alexander Souter, *Pelagius's Expositions of Thirteen Epistles of St. Paul*, 3 vols. in 1 [TS 9/1–3; Cambridge: Cambridge University Press, 1922], 418); Robert L. Thomas, "1 Thessalonians," in *The Expositor's Bible Commentary*, vol. 11, *Ephesians through Philemon*, ed. Frank E. Gaebelein (Grand Rapids: Zondervan, 1978), 244; I. Howard Marshall, *1 and 2 Thessalonians* (NCBC; Grand Rapids: Eerdmans, 1983), 53–54.

6. See, e.g., E. J. Bicknell, *The First and Second Epistles to the Thessalonians* (WC; London: Methuen, 1932), 6; A. L. Moore, *1 and 2 Thessalonians* (NCB; London: Nelson, 1969), 27; D. E. H. Whiteley, *Thessalonians* (NClarB; Oxford: Oxford University Press, 1969), 36; Ernest Best, *The First and Second Epistles to the Thessalonians* (BNTC; Peabody, MA: Hendrickson;

minority,[7] I will argue that it is more than likely that Paul's description of the coming of the gospel involves a reference to miracles.

Having only recently established the church at Thessalonica (1 Thess. 2:17),[8] perhaps in 49 CE, and then having been prevented in some way by Satan (2:18) from making a return visit,[9] Paul sent Timothy to "strengthen and encourage" (3:2) the Christians in the face of persecution (3:3–5) and, possibly, opponents (2:1–12).[10] At the time of writing, perhaps in 50 or 51 CE,[11] Timothy has just returned with news for Paul, who has been anxious to hear of their "faith and love" (3:6).[12] Receiving good news (3:6–8), Paul writes not to chastise (cf. 3:6–10), but to urge them on (3:12; 4:1, 10).[13] In the face of their difficulties (3:3–5), including internal tensions (5:12–15),[14] Paul does not restore what they lack (as supposed by the NRSV), but urges them on

London, Continuum, 1986), 75; F. F. Bruce, *1 & 2 Thessalonians* (WBC 45; Waco: Word, 1982), 14; Leon Morris, *The First and Second Epistles to the Thessalonians* (NICNT; Grand Rapids: Eerdmans, 1991), 57; Gordon D. Fee, *God's Empowering Presence: The Holy Spirit in the Letters of Paul* (Peabody, MA: Hendrickson, 1994), 43; Stefan Schreiber, *Paulus als Wundertäter: Redaktionsgeschichtliche Untersuchungen zur Apostelgeschichte und den authentischen Paulusbriefen* (BZNW 79; Berlin: de Gruyter, 1996), 266, 274; Günter Haufe, *Der erste Brief des Paulus an die Thessalonicher* (THKNT 12/1; Leipzig: Evangelische Verlagsanstalt, 1999), 26; Victor Paul Furnish, *1 & 2 Thessalonians* (ANTC; Nashville: Abingdon, 2007), 44–45.

7. E.g., Charles H. Giblin, *The Threat of Faith: An Exegetical and Theological Reexamination of 2 Thessalonians 2* (AnBib 31; Rome: Pontifical Biblical Institute, 1967), 45; Charles A. Wanamaker, *The Epistles to the Thessalonians: A Commentary on the Greek Text* (NIGTC; Grand Rapids: Eerdmans; Exeter: Paternoster, 1990), 79; Petrus J. Gräbe, *The Power of God in Paul's Letters* (WUNT 2/123; Tübingen: Mohr Siebeck, 2000), 215–16; Karl P. Donfried, *Paul, Thessalonica, and Early Christianity* (Grand Rapids: Eerdmans, 2002), 91–92; cf. 189, 239–40.

8. See the discussion by Best, *Thessalonians*, 8–11. On πρὸς καιρὸν ὥρας ("a short time") combining πρὸς καιρόν ("a set time" [cf. Luke 8:13; 1 Cor. 7:5]) and πρὸς ὥραν ("briefly" [cf. 2 Cor. 7:8; Gal. 2:5; Philem. 15]), see ibid., 124.

9. Paul does not provide any details. W. M. Ramsay (*St. Paul the Traveller and the Roman Citizen* [London: Hodder & Stoughton, 1908], 230–31) uses Acts 17:1–15 to suggest Paul saw satanic agency in the politarchs' actions.

10. Cf., e.g., Seyoon Kim, "Paul's Entry (εἴσοδος) and the Thessalonians' Faith (1 Thessalonians 1–3)," *NTS* 51 (2005): 519–42. For earlier debates, see Best, *Thessalonians*, 16–22, and more recently, Todd D. Still, *Conflict at Thessalonica: A Pauline Church and Its Neighbours* (JSNTSup 183; Sheffield: Sheffield Academic Press, 1999).

11. E.g., Robert Jewett, *Dating Paul's Life* (London: SCM, 1979), esp. "Graphs of Dates and Time-Spans," following p. 160. For an earlier dating of the ministry (41–44 CE) and, hence, the letter writing, see Karl P. Donfried and I. Howard Marshall, *The Theology of the Shorter Pauline Letters* (NTT; Cambridge: Cambridge University Press, 1993), 9–12.

12. On the possibility that the Thessalonians had also written to Paul, see the discussion by Best, *Thessalonians*, 14.

13. On the integrity of 1 Thessalonians, see Raymond F. Collins, "Apropos the Integrity of 1 Thess," in *Studies on the First Letter to the Thessalonians* (BETL 66; Louvain: Leuven University Press, 1984), 96–135.

14. Cf. Still, *Conflict at Thessalonica*, 275–80.

by "supplying" (καταρτίζω)[15] the instruction that they "need" (ὑστέρημα),[16] for their faith (3:10).

The pleasure with which Paul recalls their reception of the gospel, as well as his delight in Timothy's positive report, is evident in the introductory thanksgiving (1:2–10),[17] in which he mentions the gospel coming to them in "not only words, but also in power and in the Holy Spirit and with full conviction" (1:5). The issue for us is whether or not in this statement Paul is referring to miracles.

It could be that, as at Corinth, Paul's more ecstatic critics had pointed out that he was no pneumatic; he only talked.[18] To this, arguably, Paul's refutation comes in the statement we are examining: "the gospel came to you not in word only, but also in power" (1:5). By this, it is argued, he means not miracles, but the preached word's inherent miraculous power (or God's power) working through the preaching,[19] which brought about joy, faith, and serious discipleship.[20]

There probably were ecstatics among the believers in the church (cf. 1 Thess. 5:19).[21] However, rather than criticize them, in this letter Paul is urging the Thessalonians not to quench or "extinguish" (σβέννυμι) the Spirit, by which he means the *charismata*, including particularly prophecy (cf. 5:20).[22] If Paul was attempting to counter an attack from the pneumatics—that he had not displayed sufficient demonstrations of power—this comment is unlikely to have been understood as such by them or their sympathizers.[23] Rather, if the

15. For καταρτίζω ("complete" or "prepare") in Paul's writings, see Rom. 9:22; 1 Cor. 1:10; 2 Cor. 13:11; Gal. 6:1; 1 Thess. 3:10; otherwise in the NT see Matt. 4:21; 21:16; Mark 1:19; Luke 6:40; Heb. 10:5; 11:3; 13:21; 1 Pet. 5:10. On the range of meanings, see BDAG, "καταρτίζω," 526–27.

16. For ὑστέρημα ("need" or "shortcoming") in Paul's writings, see 1 Cor. 16:17; 2 Cor. 8:14 (2x); 9:12; 11:9; Phil. 2:30; 1 Thess. 3:10; cf. Col. 1:24; otherwise in the NT see Luke 21:4. See BDAG, "ὑστέρημα," 1044.

17. On the structure of 1 Thessalonians, including this now generally agreed compass of the introductory thanksgiving, see the brief discussions by David Luckensmeyer, *The Eschatology of First Thessalonians* (NTOA/SUNT 71; Göttingen: Vandenhoeck & Ruprecht, 2009), 56–60, and those cited. Although the majority view is that the epistle is a unit (e.g., Kieran J. O'Mahony, "The Rhetorical Dispositio of 1 Thessalonians," *PIBA* 25 [2002]: 81–96), a respectable few argue against the unity of the letter (e.g., Walter Schmithals, "The Historical Situation of the Thessalonian Epistles," in *Paul and the Gnostics*, trans. John E. Steely [Nashville: Abingdon, 1972], 123–218).

18. See Schmithals, "Historical Situation," 139–40; Robert Jewett, *The Thessalonian Correspondence: Pauline Rhetoric and Millenarian Piety* (Philadelphia: Fortress, 1986), 102.

19. Moore, *1 and 2 Thessalonians*, 27.

20. E.g., Schmithals, "Historical Situation," 140–41; Whiteley, *Thessalonians*, 36.

21. Willem C. van Unnik, "'Den Geist löschet nich aus' (1 Thessalonicher v. 19)," *NovT* 10 (1968): 255–69.

22. E.g., Whiteley, *Thessalonians*, 84.

23. Best, *Thessalonians*, 20.

pneumatics were a problem to him, as in 2 Corinthians 12:1–13, Paul could be expected to oppose them more directly and in more detail when dealing with other problems (cf. 1 Thess. 4:3–5:11).[24] Even though Paul is probably not, therefore, countering a criticism of failing to provide ecstatic demonstrations of power by affirming the preached word's life-transforming power, it is not immediately clear what Paul means by his assertion that "the gospel came . . . in power and in the Holy Spirit and with full conviction" (1:5).

A number of times Paul uses "Spirit" and "power" together,[25] mostly of the gospel or its coming to people.[26] They appear to be synonyms, as they were for others. Much earlier, in Micah, "power" (כח, δυναστεία) and "Spirit" (רוח, πνεῦμα) are treated as synonyms: "I am filled with power, with the spirit of the Lᴏʀᴅ" (Mic. 3:8; cf. 1 Sam. 11:6).[27] In Paul's time, Luke uses "Spirit" and "power" as synonyms. John the Baptist is expected to have "the spirit and power of Elijah" (Luke 1:17); and an angel says to Mary, "The Holy Spirit will come upon you, and the power of the Most High will overshadow you" (1:35; cf. 4:14; Acts 1:8). In Acts Jesus is said to have been anointed "with the Holy Spirit and with power" (10:38). In the *Thanksgiving Hymns*, from among the Dead Sea Scrolls, the Holy Spirit and power or strength are also closely associated.[28] In short, it is most likely that Paul is using the terms synonymously, so that his phrase "of Spirit and of power" is to be taken as a hendiadys.[29]

The use of "power" (δύναμις) and (Holy) "Spirit" as synonyms and, in turn, these being contrasted with "word alone" suggest Paul is referring not

24. Cf. ibid., 237, against Schmithals, "Historical Situation," 124–26.

25. Rom. 1:4; 15:13, 19; 1 Cor. 2:4; 5:4; Gal. 3:5; 1 Thess. 1:5. See also Eph. 3:16; 2 Tim. 1:7.

26. Rom. 1:4; 15:19; 1 Cor. 2:4; 1 Thess. 1:5. Paul indirectly associates Spirit, power, and his preaching in 2 Cor. 6:47. See Murray J. Harris, *The Second Epistle to the Corinthians: A Commentary on the Greek Text* (NIGTC; Grand Rapids: Eerdmans; Milton Keynes: Paternoster, 2005), 476.

27. Against, e.g., Hans Walter Wolff, *Micah: A Commentary*, trans. Gary Stansell (CC; Minneapolis: Augsburg, 1990), 91–92. Delbert R. Hillers (*Micah: A Commentary on the Book of the Prophet Micah* [Hermeneia; Philadelphia: Fortress, 1984], 45nk), e.g., makes the argument that metrically את רוח יהוה ("the spirit of Yahweh") does not overload and unbalance the verse and therefore need not be a gloss. Even if את רוח יהוה ("the spirit of Yahweh") is a gloss, the text as it stands exhibits the parallel.

28. 1QHᵃ IV, 28–29, 34–38; VII, 25–26; XIII, 38; XV, 9–10. See also 1 Sam. 11:6; Jud. 3:10. Cf. Menahem Mansoor, *The Thanksgiving Hymns* (STDJ 3; Grand Rapids: Eerdmans, 1961), 76–77; Heinz-Wolfgang Kuhn, "Die Bedeutung der Qumrantext für Verständnis der Ersten Thessalonicherbriefes," in *The Madrid Qumran Congress: Proceedings of the International Congress on the Dead Sea Scrolls, Madrid, 18–21 March, 1991*, ed. Julio Trebolle Barrera and Luis Vegas Montaner (STDJ 11; Leiden: Brill; Madrid: Editorial Complutense, 1992), 342–43.

29. Rudolf Bultmann, *Theology of the New Testament*, 2 vols. (London: SCM, 1952–55), 1:156; Michael A. Bullmore, *St. Paul's Theology of Rhetorical Style: An Examination of 1 Corinthians 2.1-5 in Light of First Century Graeco-Roman Rhetorical Culture* (San Francisco: International Scholars Publications, 1995), 213–14.

simply to the divine reality of the gospel,[30] or potency of the word,[31] but to miracles. Doubts about this interpretation arise, however, when we note that it is not the singular, as here, but rather the plural "powers" (δυνάμεις) that generally was used to speak of miracles.[32]

Yet, the singular "power" (δύναμις) could be used not only to denote the cause or source of miracles[33]—in the New Testament this is particularly true in Luke's writings[34]—but also to refer to the miracles themselves.[35] In another place Paul also appears to use the singular with the miraculous in mind. In 1 Corinthians 4:19 he contrasts "talk" (λόγος) and "power" (δύναμις), going on immediately to link power with the kingdom of God. In view of Paul's Christian tradition firmly linking the kingdom of God and miracles (see §5.1 above), we cannot rule out that in using "power" in 1 Thessalonians 1:5, Paul is referring to miracles.

In Paul's statement the expression "in Holy Spirit" (ἐν πνεύματι ἁγίῳ) is anarthrous—it lacks an article. This could mean that Paul was referring not to the Holy Spirit, but to a divine, inspiring spirit.[36] For Luke this can be true.[37] Yet, for Paul, in this phrase perhaps echoing a Semitic idiom (cf. 1Q28b II, 24),[38] it is almost always obvious he is referring to the Holy Spirit,[39] as, therefore,

30. As supposed by James E. Frame, *A Critical and Exegetical Commentary on the Epistles of St. Paul to the Thessalonians* (ICC; New York: Scribner, 1912), 81.

31. So Stefan Schreiber, *Paulus als Wundertäter: Redaktionsgeschichtliche Untersuchungen zur Apostelgeschichte und den authentischen Paulusbriefen* (BZNW 79; Berlin: de Gruyter, 1996), 252–66.

32. For the plural δυνάμεις ("powers") for miracles in the NT, see Matt. 7:22; 11:20, 21, 23; 13:54, 58; 14:2; 24:29; Mark 6:2, 14; Luke 10:13; 19:37; Acts 2:22; 8:13; 19:11; cf. 1 Cor. 12:10, 28, 29; Gal. 3:5; Heb. 2:4. See also, e.g., Justin, *1 Apol.* 26.2; *Dial.* 11.4; 35.8; 115.4; 132.1; Irenaeus, *Epistle to Florinus*, cited by Eusebius, *Hist. eccl.* 5.20.6; Hippolytus, *Haer.* 7.23; Origen, *Cels.* 1.46.

33. See Gerhard Friedrich, "δύναμις," EDNT 1:357–58; BDAG, "δύναμις," esp. (3). Cf. Walter Grundmann, "δύναμαι, κτλ.," TDNT 2:311–12. In Mark 6:14 // Matt. 14:2 the plural, "powers" (δυνάμεις), is used for the source or power for miracles.

34. Luke 5:17; 6:19; 8:46 (// Mark 5:30); Acts 10:38; cf. Acts 2:22; Heb. 1:3.

35. For the singular δύναμις as "miracle" or its cause, see Mark 5:30; 6:5; 9:39; Luke 5:17; 6:19; 8:46; 9:1; Acts 3:12; 4:7; 6:8; 10:38; Rom. 15:19 (see §7.8 below); 1 Cor. 4:20 (see §7.4 below); 2 Thess. 2:9, on which, see Best, *Thessalonians*, 305–6; cf. 1 Cor. 6:4. See Grundmann, "δύναμαι," 302–4, 310–13; Friedrich, "δύναμις," 357–58; BDAG 263.

36. Best, *Thessalonians*, 75, depending on an incomplete reading of James Hope Moulton, et al., *A Grammar of New Testament Greek*, 4 vols. (Edinburgh: T&T Clark, 1908–76), 3:175–76.

37. Moulton, *Grammar*, 3:175–76, citing Luke 1:15, 35, 41, 67; 2:25; 3:16; 4:1; 11:13; Acts 1:2; 4:25; 6:5; 7:55; 8:15, 17, 19; 10:38; 11:24; 19:2.

38. Robert Jewett, *Romans: A Commentary* (Hermeneia; Minneapolis: Fortress, 2007), 558n37.

39. Besides 1 Thess. 1:5, see Rom. 9:1; 14:17; 15:16; 1 Cor. 12:3. Only in 2 Cor. 6:6 is it unclear that Paul is referring to the Holy Spirit. For the anarthrous ἐν πνεύματι ἁγίῳ in the NT, see Matt. 3:11; Mark 1:8; Luke 3:16; John 1:33; Acts 11:16; 1 Pet. 1:12; Jude 1:20.

probably here.[40] In this case, the result of leaving out the article gives Paul three parallel phrases[41] over against (or to balance) the statement "not . . . in word alone, but" (οὐκ . . . ἐν λόγῳ μόνον ἀλλά):

also in power (καὶ ἐν δυνάμει)
also in Holy Spirit (καὶ ἐν πνεύματι ἁγίῳ)
also in much fullness (καὶ ἐν[42] πληροφορίᾳ πολλῇ)

This repetition of nouns with the same preposition (ἐν, "in") could mean that each component was intended to refer to something different.[43] However, the Greek of Paul's time was not constrained by this convention.[44] In any case, if "power" is likely to have brought to mind the source of miracle (if not miracle itself), in association with "Holy Spirit" a reference to the miraculous becomes unavoidable. The third phrase ("also in much fullness") is not in itself obviously a reference to miracles and requires some explanation.

Since Paul uses the verb πληροφορέω to mean "make certain,"[45] and in non-Christian literature πληροφορία (the noun) means "certainty,"[46] it would seem reasonable to assume that the noun also had this meaning for Paul (cf. NRSV).[47] However, the verb's earliest Christian use after the New Testament frequently refers to "fullness."[48] The three other occurrences of the noun in the New Testament other than the one under discussion also mean "fullness" (Col. 2:2; Heb. 6:11; 10:22). In particular, in Colossians 2:2 (at least Pauline, if not by Paul)

40. So also, e.g., Bruce, *1 & 2 Thessalonians*, 14; Earl J. Richard, *First and Second Thessalonians* (SP 11; Collegeville, MN: Liturgical Press, 1995), 48; Donfried, *Paul, Thessalonica*, 79, 85, 152.
41. Cf. Raymond F. Collins, "Recent Scholarship on Paul's First Letter to the Thessalonians," in *Studies on the First Letter to the Thessalonians* (BETL 66; Louvain: Leuven University Press, 1984), 59n305.
42. Though not accepted in NA[25], more recently NA[26], NA[27], and NA[28] conjecture ἐν is, with A C D F G Ψ, e.g., to be read here.
43. George B. Winer, *A Grammar of the Idiom of the New Testament: Prepared as a Solid Basis for the Interpretation of the New Testament* (Andover, MA: Draper; London: Trübner, 1877), 420.
44. A. T. Robertson, *A Grammar of the Greek New Testament* (Nashville: Broadman, 1934), 566, citing, e.g., Acts 26:29; Phil. 1:7, where the ideas are similar; and Matt. 7:16; 1 Cor. 2:5, where the ideas are dissimilar.
45. Rom. 4:21; 14:5; cf. Col. 4:12; 2 Tim. 4:5, 17. See also Luke 1:1 and C. Spicq, "πληροφορέω, πληροφορία" *TLNT* 3:121, citing *1 Clem.* 42:3; Ign. *Magn.* 8:2; *Martyrdom of Pionius* 4.17.
46. E.g., Giessen Papyri 87.25–26; *Rhet. Gr.* VII.108.3; Gerhard Delling, "πληροφορία," *TDNT* 6:310; BDAG, "πληροφορία," 827. The LXX does not use the noun πληροφορία; the verb πληροφορέω is used for מלא ("complete" or "fill") in Eccl. 8:11.
47. The Geneva New Testament (1557), which I earlier favored (see Twelftree, *Name of Jesus*, 70), has "muche certaintie of persuasion."
48. See *1 Clem.* 54:1; Ign. *Magn.* 11:1; Ign. *Phld.* prologue; cf. Ign. *Smyrn.* 1.1.

πληροφορία is a synonym for "riches" (πλοῦτος).[49] Moreover, in the statement under discussion Paul is not describing his attitude of certainty in bringing the gospel (1 Thess. 1:5),[50] as the translations "conviction"[51] or "assurance"[52] suggest. If that was his intention he would have written "in all confidence" (ἐν πάσῃ παρρησίᾳ, cf. Phil. 1:20).[53] Nor is Paul describing the reception of the gospel,[54] that does not come into view until the next verse (1 Thess. 1:6). Rather, in using "it came" (ἐγενήθη)[55] "to you" (εἰς ὑμᾶς) with πληροφορία, he is describing something about the gospel's coming—in particular, the manner of its coming—that is independent of both himself and the Thessalonians. The New Jerusalem Bible captures at least this in the phrase "with great effect."

On these three phrases we can conclude that, with "power" by itself readily implying the miraculous and more so placed in parallel with "Holy Spirit," the third phrase ("in much fullness") should most probably be construed in the same way.[56] "Fullness," then, suggests a richness or breadth of the miracles experienced by the Thessalonians. From what Paul says about the activity of the Spirit in other places, this wider expression of the coming of the gospel in terms of the miraculous would have gone beyond miracles in terms of healings and exorcisms to include, for example, phenomena such as inspired speech, prophecy, words of wisdom, generosity, diligence, joy (cf. Rom. 12:6–8; 1 Thess. 1:6), faith, discernment of spirits, and tongues and interpretation (cf. 1 Cor. 12:8–10).

This understanding of "much fullness" leads me to conclude more generally on Paul's statement not simply that the experience of the coming of the gospel was "that of being addressed by God's Spirit, of being grasped by divine power," as James Dunn put it.[57] Rather, Paul's description of the full or unimpaired com-

49. Cf. Eduard Lohse, *Colossians and Philemon: A Commentary on the Epistles to the Colossians and to Philemon*, trans. William R. Poehlmann and Robert J. Karris, ed. Helmut Koester (Hermeneia; Philadelphia: Fortress, 1971), 81; A. van Roon, *The Authenticity of Ephesians* (NovTSup 39; Leiden: Brill, 1974), 246.

50. William Tyndale (1534) translated it "moche certayntie."

51. E.g., ESV, NAB, NIV, NRSV, RSV; and widely followed by, e.g., Best, *Thessalonians*, 64, 75; Bruce, *1 & 2 Thessalonians*, 10; John R. Levison, *Filled with the Spirit* (Grand Rapids: Eerdmans, 2009), 280.

52. E.g., ASV, KJV, TEV, NASB, NKJV, NLT.

53. Cf. 2 Cor. 3:12; 7:4; Philem. 8; see *TLNT* 3:120.

54. As supposed by Bruce, *1 & 2 Thessalonians*, 14.

55. Ἐγενήθη is third-person, singular, first aorist, passive, deponent, indicative. For discussions of deponent verbs—middle or passive voice with an active meaning—see Moulton, *Grammar*, 1:153; Robertson, *Grammar*, 811–13.

56. Delling, "πληροφορία," 310. Earl Richard (*Thessalonians*, 48) reasonably suggests that "Holy Spirit" and "fullness" stand in apposition to "power," describing two of its aspects.

57. James D. G. Dunn, *Jesus and the Spirit: A Study of the Religious and Charismatic Experience of Jesus and the First Christians as Reflected in the New Testament* (London: SCM, 1975), 226.

ing of the gospel in terms of not only word but also of power (cf. Rom. 1:16),[58] Holy Spirit, and completeness meant that he understood the gospel came not only in his preaching: the gospel came in the words he conveyed to his listeners and also—simultaneously,[59] we probably are to assume—in the miraculous expressions of the Spirit's presence. These went beyond the miracles such as healing and exorcism, for example, to include the breadth and unimpaired entirety of the miraculous as Paul understood it (see §1.5 above). No doubt with his own experience as a measure, he was recalling that the coming of the gospel was no less powerful, confronting, transforming, and complete for the Thessalonians than it had been for him. The same conclusion is reached when we turn to his correspondence with the Galatian Christians.

7.2 Galatians 3:1–5

Paul writes to the Galatians to defend his gospel. He is so concerned about the situation in Galatia that after the salutation (1:1–5) he sets aside the traditional thanksgiving, turning immediately to the defense of his teaching and authority (1:6–2:21). He challenges the Galatians to consider the evidence: "You foolish Galatians! Who has bewitched you? . . . does God supply you with the Spirit and work powers among you by your doing the works of the law, or by your believing what you heard?" (3:1, 5).[60]

In an earlier defense of his mission Paul had confronted Peter at Antioch (Gal. 2:11–14). If Paul had won that battle, he could be expected to mention Peter's support here. But he does not. There was also probably a subsequent breakdown in Paul's relationship with the Jerusalem leaders. He writes about "those who were supposed [δοκούντων][61] to be acknowledged leaders (what

58. Cf. the discussion by Bert Jan Lietaert Peerbolte, "Paul the Miracle Worker: Development and Background of Pauline Miracle Stories," in *Wonders Never Cease: The Purpose of Narrating Miracle Stories in the New Testament and Its Religious Environment*, ed. Michael Labahn and Bert Jan Lietaert Peerbolte (LNTS 288; London: T&T Clark, 2006), 196.

59. Though the French of Lucien Cerfaux (*Le Christ dans la théologie de Saint Paul* [LD 6; Paris: Cerf, 1951], 216), "les phénomènes extraordinaires qui ont accompagné l'entrée du christianisme," does not support the translation "simultaneous" in Lucien Cerfaux, *Christ in the Theology of St. Paul*, trans. Geoffrey Webb and Adrian Walker (New York: Herder & Herder, 1959), 286, it is probably a fair representation of what Paul was conveying.

60. If, with the majority, Acts 15 and Gal. 2 are taken to refer to the same events in Jerusalem, then Galatians is dated in the mid-50s. See Raymond E. Brown, *An Introduction to the New Testament* (ABRL; New York: Doubleday, 1997), 474–77. On the relationship between the events behind Acts 15 and Gal. 2, see, e.g., Matti Myllykoski, "James the Just in History and Tradition: Perspectives of Past and Present Scholarship (Part I)," *CurBR* 5 (2006): 90–97.

61. In itself the intransitive use of δοκέω (for "to count for something" or "to be of repute") suggests no irony (cf. Josephus, *Ant.* 19.307; *J.W.* 4.141, 159; Epictetus, *Ench.* 33.12).

they actually were makes no difference to me; God shows no partiality)—those leaders contributed nothing to me" (2:6).[62] That Paul was not on good terms with the leaders in Jerusalem is suggested by Luke's report of Paul and Barnabas going their separate ways soon after the Jerusalem council (Acts 15:36–41). Barnabas, having a long history with the Jesus movement in Jerusalem, probably remained loyal to the leaders there.[63]

With the Galatian Christians bewitched (Gal. 3:1),[64] perhaps by people from Jerusalem (cf. 1:8–9, 12),[65] the battle for Paul's gospel has shifted to Galatia. In defending himself and his ministry, he first argues that the gospel he has proclaimed to them—"a person is justified not by the works of the law but through faith in Jesus Christ" (2:16)—is not of human origin but was received through a revelation of Jesus Christ (1:11–2:21).[66] In this, Paul incorporates his own life as an embodiment of his gospel of freedom and as a paradigm for the exhortation of his readers (1:13–2:21; cf. 4:12–20).[67] Then, before appealing to Scripture (3:6–29), Paul draws attention to their own experience in relation to the coming of the Spirit (3:1–5).[68]

See Gerhard Kittel, "δοκέω, κτλ.," *TDNT* 2:233. Cf. Frank J. Matera, *Galatians* (SP 9; Collegeville, MN: Liturgical Press, 1992), 75. However, Paul's fourfold repetition of the word (Gal. 2:2, 6, 9; 6:3), probably indicating it is a slogan coined by his opponents, and the disparaging use of δοκέω in Gal. 6:3 contribute to the supposition that Paul's statement is meant with some sarcasm.

62. James D. G. Dunn, *Galatians* (BNTC; Peabody, MA: Hendrickson, 1993), 12. Hans Dieter Betz, (*Galatians: A Commentary on Paul's Letter to the Churches in Galatia* [Hermeneia; Philadelphia: Fortress, 1979], 92), noting the parallel beginnings to Gal. 2:4 and 6, says that "Paul begins this section (2:6–10) with a characterization of the Jerusalem authorities analogous to the characterization of the opponents (2:4). Notably, the characterization is much more objective and also less hostile."

63. Cf. Acts 4:36; 9:27; 11:22, 30; 12:25; 15:2, 12, 22, 25.

64. Paul uses βασκαίνω ("bewitch"), which could describe opponents and their sophistry; see Betz, *Galatians*, 131, citing, e.g., Demosthenes, *Chers.* 19; *Meg.* 19; *Cor.* 108, 132, 139, 189, 242, 252, 307, 317; *Lept.* 24; *Mid.* 209; Philostratus, *Vit. Apoll.* 6:12; Lucian, *Philops.* 35; Philo, *Mos.* 1.4. However, in view of Paul saying that it was "before your eyes" that Jesus was exhibited, it is more likely he has in mind the more common notion of the evil eye or glance that brought harm; see LXX Deut. 28:54, 56; Sir. 14:6, 8; and the material cited by MM, "βασκαίνω," 106, and LSJ, "βασκαίνω," 310.

65. Cf. Gal. 1:7; 3:1; 4:17; 5:7–12; 6:12–13; on which, see Matera, *Galatians*, 7–11.

66. On the superiority of the divine source of knowledge, cf. Plato, *Phaedr.* 244D, cited by Betz, *Galatians*, 62n68.

67. George Lyons, *Pauline Autobiography: Toward a New Understanding* (SBLDS 73; Atlanta: Scholars Press, 1985), esp. 170–76; cf. 164–68; Beverly R. Gaventa, "Galatians 1 and 2: Autobiography as Paradigm," *NovT* 28 (1986): 309–26.

68. Although Gal. 3:6 begins with καθώς ("as" or "just as"), connecting what follows with what precedes (see Sam K. Williams, "Justification and the Spirit in Galatians," *JSNT* 29 [1987]: 92–93), a development of the argument in a change of subject suggests that Paul is beginning a new section.

Characteristic of his approach seen in other letters,[69] and consistent with rhetorical practice in making a case,[70] Paul asks a series of confronting questions. The answers to these questions are self-evident and, in not needing answers, make his case. The initial questions are about the Galatians' experience, which centered around their reception of the Spirit (3:2–3); his use of the aorist indicative tense signals that he has in mind their experience in the past.[71] Notably, Paul takes this "experience" (πάσχω) to have been "so great" (τοσοῦτος, 3:4), not unreasonably characterized as a Galatian Pentecost.

In partly mirroring his first question ("from works of the law . . . ?"),[72] and in using "therefore" (οὖν) to introduce his final question, Paul signals not that he is summarizing their initial experience,[73] but drawing a conclusion from it: "Therefore, does the One who richly supplies to you the Spirit and works powers [δυνάμεις] among you (do so) on the basis of works of the law, or of faith from a hearing?" (Gal. 3:5, my translation).[74] In this question Paul is concluding that if, as must be agreed, God acted among them initially on the basis of faith, then his ongoing action among them will have the same basis.

The present active participles used of God (ὁ, "the One") "richly supplying" (ἐπιχορηγῶν)[75] the Spirit and "working" (ἐνεργῶν) powers among them, without a main verb to restrict the time of the action, implies that what happened in the initial coming of the Spirit was part of an ongoing experience.[76] Although Paul is not specific about their initial experience, he is assuming it is consistent with their continued experience of the Spirit and powers.[77] What is important to us is that it is generally agreed that Paul's description of their

69. See Rom. 3:1–9, 27–31; 4:1, 9–10; 6:1–3, 15–16; 7:1, 7; 8:31–35.

70. Cf. Cicero, *Inv.* 1.31.51; Quintilian, *Inst.* 5.11.3–5, cited by Betz, *Galatians*, 129n19.

71. Cf. J. Louis Martyn, *Galatians* (AB 33A; New York: Doubleday, 1997), 285.

72. Gal. 3:2: ἐξ ἔργων νόμου τὸ πνεῦμα ἐλάβετε ἢ ἐξ ἀκοῆς πίστεως;
Gal. 3:5: τὸ πνεῦμα . . . ἐξ ἔργων νόμου ἢ ἐξ ἀκοῆς πίστεως;
See Betz, *Galatians*, 135; Ronald Y. K. Fung, *The Epistle to the Galatians* (NICNT; Grand Rapids: Eerdmans, 1988), 130.

73. As supposed by Richard N. Longenecker, *Galatians* (WBC 41; Dallas: Word, 1990), 105.

74. Literally, "from hearing faith" (ἐξ ἀκοῆς πίστεως). This probably is a Semitic idiom, "a sort of hearing which issues in belief" (C. F. D. Moule, *An Idiom-Book of New Testament Greek* [Cambridge: Cambridge University Press, 1959], 175).

75. Even the simple χορηγέω carries the notion of abundant supply. See BDAG, "χορηγέω," 1086, citing, e.g., Sir. 1:10, 26; 1 Macc. 14:10; *Let. Arist.* 259; Philo, *Mos.*1.255; Josphus, *Ant.* 7.279; 2 Cor. 9:10; 1 Pet. 4:11. The compound, therefore, formed with ἐπι-, further intensifies χορηγέω (cf. 2 Cor. 9:10; for the noun, ἐπιχορηγία, see Eph. 4:16; Phil. 1:19). See Harris, *Second Epistle to the Corinthians*, 640–41.

76. F. F. Bruce, *The Epistle of Paul to the Galatians: A Commentary on the Greek Text* (NIGTC; Grand Rapids: Eerdmans; Exeter: Paternoster, 1982), 151.

77. The attempt by K. Gatzweiler ("La conception paulinienne du miracle," *EphTheolLou* 37 [1961]: 813–46, esp. 819–21) to draw a distinction between the initial and ongoing miracles is unconvincing.

ongoing experience as "working powers" (ἐνεργῶν δυνάμεις) refers to miracles.[78] For, as we have already noted, the plural δυνάμεις was a well-known term for "miracles" (see 184n32 above).

This means not only that miracles were part of the experience of the Galatians when they received the Spirit—in 3:3 Paul says, "from the beginning" (ἐναρξαμενοι)[79]—but also that miracles remained part of their experience. We are also bound to notice that, with only one article (ὁ, "the One") governing both elements, the supply of the Spirit and the working of powers are, for Paul, if not synonymous, inextricably associated (cf. 1 Cor. 12:10).[80] The implication, then, of Paul asking, "Having begun with the Spirit, are you now continuing [ἐπιτελέω][81] with the flesh?" (Gal. 3:3b) is that if they continue with the flesh, their experience of the miracles (δυνάμεις) will not continue.

Paul says the miraculous powers were at work "in you" (ἐν ὑμῖν). Whether Paul means that the miraculous powers were at work in the Galatians,[82] or that the miracles occurred among them,[83] it amounts to the same thing: the Galatians were performing or experiencing miracles. For, in Paul also saying the Spirit was supplied "to them" (or "for them," ὑμῖν, dative), it is the Galatians, not Paul, who are assumed to perform or "accomplish" (ἐπιτελέω) the miracles, as John Chrysostom put it.[84] Indeed, Paul's argument, which depends

78. See 184n32 above. Many years ago, Kenneth W. Clark ("The Meaning of ἘΝΕΡΓΕΩ and ΚΑΤΑΡΓΕΩ in the New Testament," *JBL* 54 [1935]: 93–101) observed that in every case where ἐνεργέω was used in the NT "the context bears the atmosphere of supernatural forces at work" (p. 95), so that it has the meaning of "to infuse with supernatural spirit" (p. 101). To the contrary, without support, see Hans Dieter Betz, *Der Apostel Paulus und die sokratische Tradition: Eine exegetische Untersuchung zu seiner "Apologie" 2 Korinther 10–13* (BHT 45; Tübingen: Mohr Siebeck, 1972), 71.

79. James D. G. Dunn says, "ἐνάρχομαι cannot refer to anything other than the moment of becoming a Christian" (*Baptism in the Holy Spirit: A Re-examination of the New Testament Teaching on the Gift of the Spirit in Relation to Pentecostalism Today* [London: SCM, 1970], 108). However, David John Lull convincingly argues that "Paul implies that his converts in Galatia received the Spirit ἐξ ἀκοῆς πίστεως"—that is, in relation to his proclamation rather than at their baptism (*The Spirit in Galatia: Paul's Interpretation of Pneuma as Divine Power* [SBLDS 49; Chico, CA: Scholars Press, 1980], 54).

80. Peter Rhea Jones, "Exegesis of Galatians 3 and 4," *RevExp* 69 (1972): 474; Donald Guthrie, *Galatians* (NCBC; Grand Rapids: Eerdmans; London: Marshall, Morgan & Scott, 1973), 94; Longenecker, *Galatians*, 105.

81. See Gerhard Delling, "τέλος, κτλ," *TDNT* 8:61–62.

82. Cf. J. B. Lightfoot, *Saint Paul's Epistle to the Galatians* (London: Macmillan, 1881), 136, citing Matt. 14:2; Mark 6:14; 1 Cor. 12:6, 10, 28, 29.

83. Ernest de Witt Burton, *A Criticial and Exegetical Commentary on the Epistle to the Galatians* (ICC; Edinburgh: T&T Clark, 1921), 152; Theodor Zahn, *Der Brief des Paulus an die Galater*, 3rd ed. (1922; repr., Wuppertal: Brockhaus, 1990), 147; Betz, *Galatians*, 135; Longenecker, *Galatians*, 105.

84. John Chrysostom, *Hom. Gal.* 3.5 (PG vol. 61, p. 650, line 25): καὶ θαύματα ἐπετελέσατε τοσαῦτα ("and accomplish such wonders").

on the Spirit working in the Galatians, would be severely undermined if he was implying that the miracles were restricted to him or his presence.[85] In turn, we may suppose that it was the Galatians, rather than, or as well as, Paul, who were active in the initial miracles.[86] As Anitra Kolenkow put it, in this approach "Paul shows that the full range of powers attributed to Jesus were possibilities for individual members of the church."[87] This point will become more significant when we examine 1 Corinthians 12–14; 2 Corinthians 12:12; and Romans 15:18–19 (see §§7.5, 7, 8 below).

Paul does not specify the kind of miracles involved. Probably not thinking a spell had been put on his readers (Gal. 3:1; see 188n64 above), it is unlikely Paul was thinking primarily of exorcism.[88] Also, even though Paul's later statement about the fruit of the Spirit shows that he sees the Spirit's work as wider than the miraculous (5:22),[89] in the nature of his argument in which he is appealing to the dramatic—note his words "so much" (τοσαῦτα, plural) and "powers" (δυνάμεις)—he probably has in view the whole range of not simply the ecstatic productions of the Spirit[90] or the charismatic gifts,[91] but particularly the more dramatic manifestations of the Spirit.[92]

From these few lines to the Christians in Galatia we learn, first, that Paul gives testimony to a considerable amount of miraculous activity in relation to his ministry (3:4–5). For Paul, God is the author of these miracles. Also, they take place on the basis of the faith of those involved or receiving them (3:5). Further, Paul implies that miracles not only took place as part of the initial coming of the Spirit, but also continue as part of the readers' ongoing experience of the Spirit (3:3). From this it is clear that, for Paul, the experience of miracles is inextricably linked—even synonymous—with the coming and continuing work of the Spirit. Put another way: Paul takes the occurrence of miracles as evidence of God's activity. We can also note a point that will become increasingly important in this discussion: nowhere does Paul lay claim to conducting the miracles himself or suggest that he is directly involved in their performance. Indeed, his argument would lose its force if the miracles depended on him.

85. Cf. Shirley Jackson Case, *The Evolution of Early Christianity* (Chicago: University of Chicago Press, 1914), 149n1; Longenecker, *Galatians*, 105–6.

86. Cf. de Witt Burton, *Galatians*, 152; Schreiber, *Wundertäter*, 269.

87. Anitra Bingham Kolenkow, "Relationships between Miracle and Prophecy in the Greco-Roman World and Early Christianity," *ANRW* II.23.2 (1980): 1503.

88. As supposed by Heinrich Schlier, *Der Brief an die Galater* (KEK 7; Göttingen: Vandenhoeck & Ruprecht, 1971), 126.

89. Cf. de Witt Burton, *Galatians*, 151.

90. As suggested by Walter Schmithals, "The Heretics at Galatia," in *Paul and the Gnostics*, 47.

91. As assumed by Franz Mussner, *Der Galaterbrief* (HTKNT 9; Freiburg: Herder, 1974), 211.

92. Lightfoot, *Galatians*, 136.

7.3 1 Corinthians 2:1–5

In this passage there is a potential reference to the miraculous in Paul saying that his proclamation had come to the Corinthians with "a demonstration of Spirit and of power" (1 Cor. 2:4).[93] Having been refounded in 44 BCE by Julius Caesar,[94] Corinth, by Paul's time, was again true to its ancient reputation as a wealthy city (e.g., Strabo, *Geogr.* 8.6.20–23). With Silvanus and Timothy (2 Cor. 1:19), Paul probably arrived from Athens (Acts 18:1) in this busy center of trade at the crossroads of international communication (Aelius Aristides, *Or.* 46.24), sometime between 50 and 52 CE (Acts 18:1–2, 12).[95]

(a) Paul and the Corinthians. Apart from this passage (1 Cor. 2:1–5), Paul has nothing to say about the beginning of the church at Corinth (cf. Acts 18:1–17). Though, from the names he mentions, we can deduce that both Greeks and Jews joined the Christian community (16:15–18).[96] It is also in this passage that Paul gives the most details of his approach to ministry.[97] From the extensive correspondence between Paul and the Corinthians of up to thirteen, but more likely five, letters from Paul,[98] and from the topics treated, the Corinthians appear enthusiastic and keen to know the implications of their faith.[99] However, perhaps a combination of Paul's imprecision

93. This passage and the early sections of 1 Corinthians have been the focus of considerable scholarly attention. See the literature cited by Timothy H. Lim, "Not in Persuasive Words of Wisdom, But in the Demonstration of the Spirit and Power," *NovT* 29 (1987): 137–38n2; see also Anthony C. Thiselton, *The First Epistle to the Corinthians* (NIGTC; Grand Rapids: Eerdmans, 2000), 206–7; H. H. Drake Williams III, *The Wisdom of the Wise: The Presence and Function of Scripture within 1 Cor. 1:18–3:23* (AGJU 49; Leiden: Brill, 2001).

94. E.g., Diodorus Siculus, *Bib. hist.* 32.27.1; Strabo, *Geogr.* 8.6.23c.

95. See the discussion of the edict of Claudius (Suetonius, *Claud.* 25; Dio Cassius, *Hist.* 60.6.6; Orosius, *Hist.* 7.6.15–16) and the Delphi or Gallio inscription (*SIG* 2.108) by Jerome Murphy-O'Connor, *St. Paul's Corinth: Text and Archaeology*, 3rd ed. (Collegeville, MN: Liturgical Press, 2002), 118–19, 152–55, 161–69, 219–21.

96. Gordon D. Fee, *The First Epistle to the Corinthians* (NICNT; Grand Rapids: Eerdmans, 1987), 831–32.

97. Cf. Rom. 15:18–19; on which, see §7.8 below. See also Duane A. Litfin, *St. Paul's Theology of Proclamation: 1 Corinthians 1–4 and Greco-Roman Rhetoric* (SNTSMS 79; Cambridge: Cambridge University Press, 1994), 204.

98. See the summary discussion by Brown, *New Testament Introduction*, 515, 548–51. On the integrity of 2 Corinthians and the movements of Paul in relation to the Corinthians, see also Margaret E. Thrall, *A Critical and Exegetical Commentary on the Second Epistle to the Corinthians*, 2 vols. (ICC; London: T&T Clark, 1994–2000), 1:1–77, esp. 47–49 ("Survey of Major Critical Theories"); Harris, *Second Epistle to the Corinthians*, 8–51, esp. 42–43, citing those holding this traditional view.

99. In 1 Cor. 7:1 Paul refers to a letter from the Corinthians (cf. 7:25; 8:1; 12:1; 16:1, 12) to which he is responding. See Margaret M. Mitchell, "Concerning περὶ δέ in 1 Corinthians," *NovT* 31 (1989): 229–56, and the brief discussion by Thiselton, *First Epistle to the Corinthians*, 483–94.

in preaching and their genius for misunderstanding him gave rise to his most exasperating church. As Jerome Murphy-O'Connor supposes: "Virtually every statement he made took root in their minds in a slightly distorted form, and from this defective seed flowed bizarre approaches to different aspects of the Christian life."[100]

At least according to Luke, after a considerable time in Corinth, Paul sailed for Ephesus (Acts 18:18–21). Paul says he wrote to the Corinthians (1 Cor. 5:9), a letter now lost. Still in Ephesus (16:8), Paul hears "from Chloe's people" (ὑπὸ τῶν Χλόης, 1:11). In response, and informed by a letter from the Corinthians (7:1) through the hands of Stephanus, Forunatus, and Achaicus (16:17–18), Paul writes what we know as 1 Corinthians.

Paul had heard that, in the time since he had been in the city, perhaps after the arrival of Apollos,[101] his relations with the church had soured. There had been criticisms of him,[102] and opposition to him had arisen among the Corinthians.[103] Early in his letter, therefore, Paul makes a case that the status of the believers at Corinth and his message about the cross being the power of God (1:18) are very different from their present understanding (1:18–31).[104] As part of his case, in the section that requires our attention (2:1–5), Paul recalls for them that, in contrast to the tactics of others,[105] he "decided to know nothing among you except Jesus Christ, and him crucified" (2:2). This is not, as Anthony Thiselton points out, an expression of anti-intellectualism, a lack of imagination, or inflexible communication.[106] Instead, perhaps reflecting on the Greek funeral oration (Plato, *Menex.* 234c–235c),[107] Paul sets aside embellished words to single out the aspect of his message on which his argument depends: the crucifixion and its expression in his ministry characterized by suffering and weakness.[108] And, despite appearing to leave the topic of division

100. Murphy-O'Connor, *Paul: A Critical Life*, 252.
101. Cf. Acts 19:1; 1 Cor. 1:12; 3:3–6, 22.
102. Cf. the implied criticisms in 1 Cor. 1:17; 2:1, 4; 3:2; 4:8.
103. 1 Cor. 1:12; 3:18–23; 4:3, 6, 18–20; 9:3; 10:29–30; 14:37; 15:12.
104. Cf. David A. Ackerman, *Lo, I Tell You a Mystery: Cross, Resurrection, and Paraenesis in the Rhetoric of 1 Corinthians* (Eugene, OR: Pickwick, 2006), e.g., Ackerman argues that the basic cause of the problems at Corinth was a lack of spiritual maturity.
105. C. K. Barrett, *The First Epistle to the Corinthians* (BNTC; London: Black, 1971), 64.
106. Thiselton, *First Epistle to the Corinthians*, 212. Nor is this signaling a change of tactics in light of indifferent success in Athens, a view for which "there is no evidence whatsoever" (Barrett, *First Epistle to the Corinthians*, 63).
107. See the discussion by Kenneth E. Bailey, *Paul through Mediterranean Eyes: Cultural Studies in 1 Corinthians* (Downers Grove, IL: IVP Academic, 2011), 93–101.
108. John H. Schütz, *Paul and the Anatomy of Apostolic Authority* (SNTSMS 26; Cambridge: Cambridge University Press, 1975), 193.

(cf. 1:18–3:2),[109] in line with rhetorical practice,[110] using the phrases "lofty words" or "rhetorical speech" (ὑπεροχὴν λόγου, 2:1),[111] "persuasive words of wisdom" (πειθοῖ[ς][112] σοφίας [λόγοις], 2:4)[113] and "human wisdom" (σοφίᾳ ἀνθρώπων, 2:5), Paul continues to refer covertly both to the self-centered divisive power plays around key figures in Corinth (Paul, Cephas, Apollos)[114] and to his weakness that mirrors Christ's, a theme that will not find its full treatment until later in this correspondence (2 Cor. 12:1–10).

(b) Redefining wisdom and power. Paul's argument against the Corinthians is that the message of the cross destroys all human wisdom (cf. 1 Cor. 1:22–23),[115] for, against expectation, rhetoric skill and wisdom are not to be equated.[116] However, it is not that Paul presents the good news of the cross as an irrefutable message from heaven. Astonishingly, at least for readers in our time, Paul submits the message of the cross to the Corinthians for their empirical assessment based on their experience.[117]

Part of the Corinthians' experience to which he appeals—when he says "consider your own call" (1:26)—is that, contrary to what they would have expected, not many of the "powerful" (δυνατοί) or "noble" (εὐγενεῖς) were called by the message. In line with biblical traditions of power expressed in weakness,[118] this demonstrates that Paul is arguing for both God's rejection of human wisdom and the strength of the message of the cross (1:27–28).[119]

109. Cf. Wilhelm Wuellner, "Greek Rhetoric and Pauline Argumentation," in Early Christian Literature and the Classical Intellectual Tradition: In Honorem Robert M. Grant, ed. William R. Schoedel and Robert L. Wilken (Paris: Beauchesne, 1979), 177–88. V. P. Branick ("Source and Redaction Analysis of 1 Corinthians 1–3," JBL 101 [1982]: 251–69) supposes that 1 Cor. 1:18–3:2 was originally written for a different audience and inserted into this letter.

110. A number of studies of Paul's rhetorical style have been focused on this section of 1 Corinthians. See, e.g., Bullmore, Rhetorical Style, 5–15, and those cited.

111. See Diodorus Siculus, Bib. hist. 34/35.5.5, discussed by Stephen M. Pogoloff, Logos and Sophia: The Rhetorical Situation of 1 Corinthians (SBLDS 134; Atlanta: Scholars Press, 1992), 132.

112. πειθοῖς (adjective). Cf., e.g., Philostratus, Vit. soph. 488, 503, 521, 536, 576, where πείθω (the verb) is used frequently of the persuasive skill of rhetoricians.

113. There is considerable confusion in the text at this point. The most likely reading is: οὐκ ἐν πειθοῖ[ς] σοφίας. See NA[28]; Metzger, Commentary, 481.

114. "Christ" is probably not one of the figures but a rhetorical addition by Paul. Cf. Peter Lampe, "Theological Wisdom and the 'Word about the Cross': The Rhetorical Scheme in 1 Corinthians 1–4," Int 44 (1990): 117–31.

115. See the helpful discussions by Edwin A. Judge, "Paul's Boasting in Relation to Contemporary Professional Practice," ABR 16 (1968): 37–50; Lampe, "Theological Wisdom."

116. Samuel IJsseling, Rhetoric and Philosophy in Conflict: An Historical Survey (The Hague: M. Nijhoff, 1976), 40, followed by Bullmore, Rhetorical Style, 208.

117. Lampe, "Theological Wisdom," 126.

118. See Exod. 4:10; 19:4–6; Deut. 26:5; Isa. 6:5, see the discussion by Graydon F. Snyder, First Corinthians: A Faith Community Commentary (Macon, GA: Mercer University Press, 1992), 32.

119. Lampe, "Theological Wisdom," 126.

Reinforcing his proposition through continuing his appeal to the experience of his readers,[120] Paul goes on to say that his speech and preaching were "not in persuasive words of wisdom but in demonstration of Spirit and of power" (2:4, my translation). To "persuade" (πειθώ) was the purpose of rhetoric.[121] For Paul's readers the "persuasive words of wisdom" would have been the skillful rhetorical arguments used to persuade hearers,[122] for they would have expected power to have been in the spoken word (cf. Quintilian, *Inst.* 2.15.3).[123]

However, in line with his commitment to the principle in his tradition and in his experience (esp. 2 Cor. 12:1–10) that God's power is encountered in weakness, and also over against what his readers are likely to have anticipated (cf. 1 Cor. 1:22), portraying himself as a kind of "anti-rhetor,"[124] Paul is asserting that the proof of his case is to be sought not in the persuasive or wise words he might have used but in the demonstration or proof of Spirit and of power (1 Cor. 2:4). The noun "demonstration" or "proof" (ἀπόδειξις), not otherwise found in the New Testament,[125] was frequently used in rhetoric in relation to demonstrating or proving an argument from agreed premises.[126] Quintilian (born c. 35 CE) explained, "An ἀπόδειξις is a clear proof [*est evidens probatio*] . . . a method of proving what is not certain by means of what is certain" (*Inst.* 5.10.7). Of central import to us is the question: What was the demonstration or proof of Paul's speech and proclamation that he describes as "of Spirit and of power" (πνεύματος καὶ δυνάμεως, 1 Cor. 2:4)?[127]

120. On 1 Cor. 2:1–5 not being a digression, see Lars Hartman, "Some Remarks on 1 Cor. 2:1–5," *SEÅ* 39 (1974): 111. Also, noting the parallels between 1 Cor. 1:17 and 2:4–5, Litfin (*Theology of Proclamation*, 189–90) argues for the inherent unity of Paul's argument across the section.

121. Pogoloff, *Logos and Sophia*, 137.

122. See Pogoloff (*Logos and Sophia*, 137), who also notes the number of linguistic parallels between Aristotle, *An. post.* 1.2.16–25; *Top.* 1.1 (100a.18–100b.23), 1.4 (101b.11–16), 1.8 (103b.1–7), 1.11 (104b.1–3); *Rhet.* 1.1.1–3 (1354a), 1.1.11 (1355a), and Paul in 1 Corinthians (ἀπόδειξις, γνῶσις, ἔνδοξος, λόγος, πειθώ, πίστις, and σοφός), not to suggest that Paul and his readers were involved in philosophical discussions, but that "Aristotle's language and categories were widely influential" (p. 138).

123. See Raymond F. Collins (*First Corinthians* [SP 7; Collegeville, MN: Liturgical Press, 1999], 120), who also mentions Gorgias, Isocrates, and other Sophists.

124. The term is from Hartman, "Remarks on 1 Cor. 2:1–5," e.g., 120.

125. For the cognate verb ἀποδείκνυμι in the NT, see Acts 2:22; 25:7; 1 Cor. 4:9; 2 Thess. 2:4.

126. See, e.g., Aristotle, *Eth. nic.* 1.3; Quintilian, *Inst.* 5.10.7; Diogenes Laertius, *Vit.* 7.45; Plato, *Tim.* 40e; *Phaed.* 77c, and the discussion by Lim, "Not in Persuasive Words," 147.

127. In attempting to determine if the genitives are objective ("spirit and power demonstrate") or subjective ("demonstrates spirit and power"), Moulton says, "It is well to remember that in Greek this question is entirely one of exegesis, not of grammar" (*Grammar*, 1:72). In any case, Paul may not have wished the distinction to be made (notably, Barrett, *First Epistle to the Corinthians*, 65). For, as Thiselton points out, this "interpretation coheres well with Paul's wider theology of the Holy Spirit. The Holy Spirit witnesses to his own presence and activity precisely

(c) Spirit and power? Early church fathers could read Paul's reference to Spirit and power in different ways. In one place Origen (c. 185–c. 254), the first church father known to cite this verse,[128] takes Paul's reference to the Spirit to be prophecies, especially those referring to Christ, and power to be "the prodigious miracles" (*Cels.* 1.2). Further on, however, Origen relates the power to that possessed by successful preachers (6.2; cf. 3.68; 7.60). Similarly, Eusebius (c. 260–c. 340) can imply that Paul is referring to miracles through associating Paul with "the wonder-working power of Christ" (*Hist. eccl.* 3.24.3). But Eusebius can also use Paul's statement to establish that he is following Paul in deprecating "deceitful and sophisticated plausibilities and to use proofs free from ambiguity" (*Praep. ev.* 1.3.5).[129]

Modern commentators are as divided as the early fathers, some not specifying what Paul had in mind by "of Spirit and of power,"[130] others supposing that the miraculous is not in view,[131] or that the phrase "of Spirit and of power" is to be explained by taking "and of power" (καὶ δυνάμεως) as epexegetic, or an additional explanation to Paul's description of the Spirit.[132] Some take Paul to be referring to miracles, alluding to 2 Corinthians 12:12 for support: "The signs of a true apostle were performed among you . . . signs and wonders and mighty works."[133] Indeed, "Spirit" and "power" often are used together in the context of the Spirit being responsible for unusual or miraculous activity.[134] My earlier

---

by witnessing to Christ, to the effectiveness of the gospel, and to other effects which are themselves the work of the trinitarian God" (*First Epistle to the Corinthians*, 222).

128. For a list of citations by Origen, see J. Allenbach, *Biblia patristica: Index des citations et allusions bibliques dans la littérature patristique* (Paris: Centre National de la Recherche Scientifique, 1975), 385; cf. J. Allenbach, *Biblia patristica: Index des citations et allusions bibliques dans la littérature patristique [Vol.] 2 Le troisième siècle (Origène excepté)* (Paris: Centre National de la Recherche Scientifique, 1977).

129. Cf. Cyril of Jerusalem, *Catech.* 13.3; 17.29–32.

130. E.g., James Moffatt says the apostolic gospel was "charged with power divine" (*The First Epistle of Paul to the Corinthians* [MNTC; London: Hodder & Stoughton, 1938], 24).

131. E.g., Fee, *First Epistle to the Corinthians*, 92; Schreiber, *Wundertäter*, 252, 274.

132. As supposed by Ulrich Wilckens, "Zu 1 Kor 2,1–16," in *Theologia Crucis, Signum Crucis: Festschrift für Erich Dinkler zum 70. Geburtstag*, ed. Carl Anderson and Günter Klein (Tübingen: Mohr Siebeck, 1979), 505–6.

133. See, e.g., Wilfred L. Knox, *St. Paul and the Church of the Gentiles* (Cambridge: Cambridge University Press, 1939), 115; Bultmann, *Theology*, 1:161; Ulrich Wilckens, *Weisheit und Torheit: Eine exegetisch-religionsgeschichtliche Untersuchung zu 1. Kor. 1 und 2* (BHT 26; Tübingen: Mohr Siebeck, 1959); Axel von Dobbeler, *Glaube als Teilhabe: Historische und semantische Grundlagen der paulinischen Theologie und Ekklesiologie des Glaubens* (WUNT 2/22; Tübingen: Mohr Siebeck, 1987), 33–38; E. Earle Ellis, *Prophecy and Hermeneutic in Early Christianity* (Grand Rapids: Baker Academic, 1993), 65; Gräbe, *Power of God*, 64. On 2 Cor. 12:12, see §7.7 below.

134. Cf. 1 Sam. 11:6; Luke 1:17, 35; 4:14; Acts 1:8; 10:38; Rom. 1:4; 15:19; 1 Thess. 1:5. This point is strengthened if Paul is intentionally echoing Zech. 4:6. See Williams, *Wisdom*, 133–56.

discussion of "Spirit" and "power" being used together (§7.1 above) at least predisposes us to take this phrase to refer to miracles. However, taking "of Spirit and of power" as a reference to the miraculous faces a number of challenges.

One obstacle to taking the phrase as a reference to miracles could be Paul's earlier negative comment that "Jews demand signs and Greeks desire wisdom" (1 Cor. 1:22).[135] However, on the one hand, from his contrasting use of the phrases "those who are perishing" and "those who are being saved" (1:18), Paul's metanarrative in this paragraph (1:18–25) is neither the mundane nor simply the situation in Corinth, but the cosmological and eschatological (cf. Rom. 1:16, 18; Phil. 1:27).[136] As we have already noted, in an eschatological context, for Jews, a sign was not a miracle, such as a healing or an exorcism, but a cosmological event—the sun going in reverse, or a river parting, for example—that God performed to authenticate his messenger (see §2.5 above).

Nevertheless, on the other hand, in the face of the Jews demanding signs and the Greeks desiring wisdom, Paul offers the single response of Christ crucified (1 Cor. 1:23). This, he says, is not only the wisdom of God, clearly expected to satisfy the Greeks, but also the power of God (1:24), presumably expected to satisfy the Jews. Not surprisingly, Paul goes on most obviously to discuss wisdom (1:18–3:4).[137] However, in twice describing Christ crucified as God's power (1:17, 24),[138] Paul also prepares his readers for taking the discussion of his proclamation in nonlofty words, and his coming with fear and trembling, as well as the demonstration of the Spirit and power, as the proper interpretation of the power of God (2:1–5). That is, Paul claims to answer not only the Greeks' desire for wisdom, but also the Jews' demand for eschatological signs in the proclamation of Christ crucified, which, in turn, is accompanied by a demonstration of Spirit and power.

If this reading of Paul is correct, then a reference to miracles would not, as Gordon Fee supposes, "play directly into the Corinthians' hands, to build up the very issue he is trying to demolish (cf. 2 Cor. 12:1–10)," that "his preaching exhibited 'the weakness of God' that is stronger than human strength (1 Cor. 1:25)."[139] Rather, a reference to miracles would set them in their place as a demonstration of (and by) the power of God over against his poor preaching and personal showing. In any case, we will see from later in this letter that, in his discussions with the Corinthians, Paul has no wish to set aside miracles and the miraculous (1 Cor. 12–14; see §7.5 below). Instead, he takes them to

---

135. See ibid., 154.
136. Cf. Collins, *First Corinthians*, 91–92.
137. Collins, *First Corinthians*, 106.
138. Litfin, *Theology of Proclamation*, 190.
139. Fee, *First Epistle to the Corinthians*, 92.

be one of the experiences of the Spirit's presence, a point that has already emerged in discussing Galatians 3:1–5 (see §7.2 above).

Another supposed obstacle to reading "of Spirit and of power" as a reference to miracles is "power" occurring in the singular (δυνάμεως, "of power," 1 Cor. 2:4).[140] Prima facie, it would be unusual for Paul to use the singular to refer to miracles.[141] However, we have already noted that there are examples in early Christian literature of the singular "power" being used, not only for the source of a miracle (see 184n33 above), but also for a miracle itself (see 184n35 above). Also, as we will see later, in Romans 15:19 Paul uses "power" in referring to miracles in a phrase with "signs and wonders," and also in parallel with "the power of the Spirit" (§7.8 below). To say the least, it would not be out of the question, then, that in the phrase "of Spirit and of power" (in the singular) Paul had miracle in mind.[142]

The question arises then as to why Paul does not say "with a demonstration of the Spirit and powers." He probably did not use this expression in the plural because it would have given rise to a potential contrast, or at least a difference, between the Spirit and the miracles. The singular ("power") maintains the phrase as a hendiadys (cf. §7.1 above on 1 Thess. 1:5). That is, in Paul's phrase, "power," which could refer to miracle, is an expression of Spirit, and "Spirit" is seen in power or the miraculous.

A further potential obstacle to taking "Spirit and power" as a reference to "signs and wonders" is the context of "weakness" in Paul's discussion.[143] However, the context (both of this particular passage and of the Corinthian correspondence generally) is not one of weakness, but of contrasts.[144] In the Corinthian correspondence contrasts or antitheses—explicit and implicit—undergird Paul's writing: contrasts between the world and heaven (e.g., 1 Cor. 15:40–49), between this age and the next (e.g., 1 Cor. 2:6–8; 2 Cor. 4:17–18), and between people and God (e.g., 1 Cor. 2:5; 9:8).[145] In the passage of interest to us there is a contrast, for example, between God and people (2:5), and in "persuasion" (πειθώ) and "demonstration" (ἀπόδειξις) being set over against each other (2:4).[146] Notably, Paul contrasts his not using lofty words with his

140. Reginald St. John Parry, *The First Epistle of Paul the Apostle to the Corinthians*, 2nd ed. (CGTSC; Cambridge: Cambridge University Press, 1926), 50.

141. For the plural δυνάμεις ("powers") as miracles in the NT, see Matt. 7:22; 11:20, 21, 23; 13:54, 58; 14:2; Mark 6:2, 14; Luke 10:13; Acts 8:13; 19:11; 1 Cor. 12:28, 29; Gal. 3:5.

142. For Luke's use of "Spirit" and "power" together as the source of Jesus' miracles, see Acts 10:38.

143. So Fee, *First Epistle to the Corinthians*, 95.

144. Litfin, *Theology of Proclamation*, 174–78.

145. See the list of antitheses in ibid., 174–75.

146. Cf. Hartman, "Remarks on 1 Cor. 2:1–5," 116; Pogoloff, *Logos and Sophia*, 138.

proclamation of Christ crucified (2:1–2), which he has just identified with the power of God (1:23–24, cf. 1:17). Then he contrasts his weakness (1 Cor. 2:3)[147] or poor showing as a person (cf. 2 Cor. 10:10), his fear and trembling (1 Cor. 2:3),[148] and his unpersuasive words (cf. 2 Cor. 11:6) with a demonstration or proof of Spirit and of power (1 Cor. 2:4).

The parallel in this argument between Christ crucified and what is demonstrated suggests that the demonstration was the action of God or Christ (1 Cor. 2:5). This parallel is consistent with other places where Paul mentions his weakness as a contrast to the activity of God.[149] Indeed, even though he may be writing "un chef-d'œuvre rhétorique"[150] in saying that he came proclaiming "the testimony about God"[151] (τὸ μαρτύριον τοῦ θεοῦ, 2:1),[152] Paul would have signaled to readers that his appeal could be to more than words, and that he could have in mind experience beyond the normal human range.

Yet, even if Paul is appealing to more than words, "of Spirit and of power" is not likely to be a reference "to the convicting power of the gospel," as supposed by John Polhill.[153] If that was Paul's intention, he more likely would

147. In view of 2 Cor. 10:10, and perhaps his thorn in the flesh (12:7), his weakness is probably neither deliberate nor feigned. Cf. Snyder, *First Corinthians*, 31.

148. In the NT the phrase φόβος καὶ τρόμος ("fear and trembling"), or some variation of it, is distinctly Paul's. See also 2 Cor. 7:15; Phil. 2:12; cf. Eph. 6:5; also Mark 16:8. For the variety of reasons suggested for Paul's fear and trembling (e.g., failure, nervousness, panic), see David E. Garland, *1 Corinthians* (BECNT; Grand Rapids: Baker Academic, 2003), 85. More likely, although in the present context (in parallel with ἀσθένεια, "weakness") the fear and trembling probably would have been taken to refer primarily to Paul's human frailty, readers familiar with the LXX (Gen. 9:2; Exod. 15:16; Deut. 2:25; 11:25; Jdt. 2:28; 15:2; 1 Macc. 7:18; 4 Macc. 4:10; Ps. 2:11; 54:6 [ET 55:5]; Odes 1:16; Isa. 19:16; 54:14; Dan. 4:19, 37) would also likely have heard in the phrase a reference to Paul coming in awe of his message from God and its demonstration (note 1 Cor. 2:7–13).

149. See Rom. 7:7–25; 8:17–27; 1 Cor. 4:9–13; 2 Cor. 4:7–12; 6:4–10; 11:30; 12:1–10; 13:4; Gal. 4:13–14; Phil. 1:29–30; Col. 1:24–27.

150. Jean-Noël Aletti, "Sagesse et mystère chez Paul: Réflexion sur le rapprochement de deux champs lexicographiques," in *La sagesse biblique de l'Ancien au Nouveau Testament*, ed. Jacques Trublet (LD 160; Paris: Cerf, 1995), 382.

151. The variant reading τοῦ Χριστοῦ ("of Christ"), in place of τοῦ θεοῦ ("of God"), is to be explained as an assimilation to 1 Cor. 2:1. See Fee, *First Epistle to the Corinthians*, 35n2. As in 1 Cor. 1:6, the genitive ("of Christ") is probably to be taken as an objective: "witness about God." See Barrett, *First Epistle to the Corinthians*, 63.

152. I am persuaded by Fee (*First Epistle to the Corinthians*, 88n1) that this reading is to be preferred to τὸ μυστήριον τοῦ θεοῦ ("the mystery of God") on the grounds that it is difficult to imagine a scribe replacing μυστήριον ("mystery") with μαρτύριον ("witness"), though the opposite could be expected, and, following Barrett (*First Epistle to the Corinthians*, 62–63) and Günther Zuntz (*The Text of the Epistles: A Disquisition upon the Corpus Paulinum* [London: Oxford University Press, 1953], 101) the use of μυστήριον in 1 Cor. 2:7 would lose much of its force if Paul had already used it in 2:1.

153. John B. Polhill, "The Wisdom of God and Factionalism: 1 Corinthians 1–4," *RevExp* 80 (1983): 331.

have simply said his speech and proclamation were with Spirit and power. The introduction of the idea of a "demonstration" or "proof" suggests something other than his speech, most likely a visible effect, is involved.[154] Indeed, in 1 Thessalonians 1:5 "word" and "Spirit and power" together were complementary terms describing the presentation of Paul's gospel and also, probably, how he would have come to the Corinthians.[155]

Moreover, Paul does not set up the Corinthians' response or conversion as the demonstration of Spirit and power.[156] Rather, the power of the preaching was demonstrated in Spirit and power, "in order that" (ἵνα, 1 Cor. 2:5) not many wise, powerful, and noble (1:26) Corinthians were able to respond to the call of God in his gospel (2:5). In short, as a demonstration or proof that came with Paul's proclamation, "of Spirit and of power" was neither a power inherent in the message nor any response by the Corinthians; rather, the phrase refers to the miraculous expression of the message of the power of God.

(d) A "theologia gloriae" and a "theologia crucis." Before drawing conclusions on 1 Corinthians 2:1–5, I can note that it contains one of Paul's clearest expressions of how he relates a "theology of glory" (theologia gloriae) and a "theology of the cross" (theologia crucis).[157] In his previous paragraph Paul has said that the Corinthians' call experience illustrates and establishes that, contrary to expectation, God chooses the low and despised so that no one might boast before God (1:26–29), who is the source of their life in Christ Jesus (1:30). Firmly tying this paragraph with the next (using κἀγώ, "and so I," 2:1),[158] Paul shows that this source of life involves another paradox: it is seen in the crucifixion (cf. 1:30 and 2:2). In turn, this paradox is reflected in his own ministry. Paul says he was not using lofty words (about the wisdom, righteousness, sanctification, and redemption of God in Christ Jesus[159] or

154. Cf. Helge Kjaer Nielsen, "Paulus' Verwendung des Begriffes Δύναμις: Eine Replik zur Kreuzestheologie," in Die Paulinische Literatur und Theologie, ed. Sigfred Pedersen (TeolSt 7; Århus: Aros; Göttingen: Vandenhoeck & Ruprecht, 1980), 154.

155. Richard A. Horsley, "Wisdom of Word and Words of Wisdom in Corinth," CBQ 39 (1977): 230–31. Cf. §7.1 above.

156. Argued by, e.g., Fee, First Epistle to the Corinthians, 95.

157. On the pair of contrasting terms, theologia gloriae and theologia crucis, which Luther used in his Heidelberg Disputation (1518), see John G. Strelan, "Theologia Crucis, Theologia Gloriae: A Study in Opposing Theologies," LTJ 23 (1989): 99–113.

158. Fee, First Epistle to the Corinthians, 90 and n. 8.

159. There are no grammatical reasons for this word order. Given that Paul uses this form for his initial mention of Jesus in Romans, 1 Corinthians, 2 Corinthians, and Philemon, and his followers do the same in Ephesians, Colossians, 1 Timothy, and 2 Timothy, it probably was used for emphasizing who Jesus is: the Christ. See C. E. B. Cranfield, A Critical and Exegetical Commentary on the Epistle to the Romans, 2 vols. (ICC; Edinburgh: T&T Clark,

the risen Lord), but proclaiming Jesus crucified (2:1–2). Yet (κἀγώ, 2:3), his message brought in weakness and without plausible words of wisdom was proved by the Spirit and power. In other words, as the power of God in Jesus is seen in the crucifixion of Jesus, so the power of the message of the crucifixion brought without lofty words or wisdom is demonstrated in the Spirit and power. Paradoxically, then, just as the life of God is clear in the crucifixion, so also in the weakness of Paul the Spirit and power of God are seen in the miraculous. At least in this passage the relationship between the message of the cross and the glory of God is encapsulated and said to be experienced in the miraculous associated with a powerless messenger.

(e) Conclusions. From Paul's paragraph contrasting his weakness with the power of God (1 Cor. 2:1–5) we have learned that his phrase "a demonstration of Spirit and of power" (2:4) does not refer to the convicting power of the gospel or to the Corinthians' response to it. The expression is a reference to miracles that accompanied and were the demonstration or proof of his proclamation. By implication, Paul is writing in a social context that assumes miracles legitimate a message, and thus he is able to remind the Corinthians that the coming of the gospel was not in or authenticated by rhetorical skill, but in the Spirit's power materialized in the miraculous. As Hermann Gunkel put it: "The presence and activity of the Spirit in the world are for Paul a divine guarantee of the Christian faith."[160] Thus, on the one hand, the truth of the proclamation of a crucified Messiah by a messenger without rhetorical skill rested on the power of God seen in the miraculous that was associated with Paul's ministry. On the other hand, the Corinthians were not responding to human wisdom or a message only, but to the power of God (2:5). Or, as we have just noted in the way Paul related the cross and the glory of Christ, as the life and power of God are seen in the crucifixion, so through the weakness of Paul's ministry the miraculous power of the Spirit of God is seen. The next place Paul appears to mention the miraculous is at the end of this part of 1 Corinthians.

1975, 1979), 2:836. Concomitantly, William Sanday and Arthur C. Headlam (*A Critical and Exegetical Commentary on the Epistle to the Romans* [ICC; Edinburgh: T&T Clark, 190], 3) noted that earlier texts use "Jesus Christ." Moreover, "Christ Jesus" also carries with it the notion of Jesus as risen Lord. Cf. 1 Cor. 1:1; see Fee, *First Epistle to the Corinthians*, 27n3. The same conclusion is reached when we take into account the number of times "in Christ Jesus," but never "in Jesus Christ," occurs ("in Jesus" is found only in Rev. 1:9). That is, Paul sees the intimate relationship that a follower has with Jesus is with God's risen Anointed One. Also, see Selly Vernon McCasland, "Christ Jesus," *JBL* 65 (1946): 377–83.

160. Hermann Gunkel, *The Influence of the Holy Spirit: The Popular View of the Apostolic Age and the Teaching of the Apostle Paul*, trans. Roy A. Harrisville and Philip A. Quanbeck II (Philadelphia: Fortress, 1979), 81.

7.4 1 Corinthians 4:19–20

In these verses Paul is drawing to a close the first section of his letter (1 Cor. 1:10–4:21) in which he has been addressing the problem of the readers' quarreling over their leaders (1:10–12), perhaps in terms of assessing them as teachers of wisdom (cf. 1:18; 2:1–5).[161] Since, for Paul, the greatest implication of this quarreling is not only the misunderstanding of the gospel, but also of the church and its leadership,[162] as we have just seen, to deal with the problem he sets out the nature of the gospel (1:18–25) and the readers' experience of it (1:26–2:5). He also explains that, for the mature, the gospel is wisdom revealed by the Spirit. However, the gospel is foolishness for the immature, those who are jealous and quarreling over the leadership (2:6–3:4). Finally, after hints along the way (esp. 2:1–5), Paul turns more squarely to confront their divisions that have involved assessing his leadership (3:5–23). In doing so, he sets his ministry over against their error in not seeing him as a servant of Christ (4:1), which has led them to judge him (4:1–13). Paul ends with an assertion of his leadership in terms of being their father (4:14–21), and that, contrary to the expectation of some of them, he intends visiting Corinth soon to "find out not the talk of these arrogant people but their power. For the kingdom of God consists not in talk [λόγος] but in power [δύναμις]" (4:19–20, my translation).[163]

The question for us to answer is whether or not Paul had miracles in mind when he mentions "power" in connection with the kingdom of God (4:20). C. K. Barrett supposes that by "power," Paul refers to "the power of the Holy Spirit (cf. Rom. 14:17), by which God's purpose is put into effect and the future anticipated in the present."[164] But this begs the question as to what effects Paul had in mind. For in contrasting power with talk, Paul probably implies some manifestation.[165]

Giving attention to the immediate context (1 Cor. 4:11–13), as well as the larger background of Paul's letters, William Spencer suggests that in "power"

---

161. On Paul's argument in 1 Cor. 1–4, see Fee, *First Epistle to the Corinthians*, 47–51.

162. As Garland is right to point out, "Fee's reference to the 'ringleader' is overblown, and wrongly assumes some nefarious plot to usurp Paul's authority" (*1 Corinthians*, 148).

163. The second sentence lacks a verb: οὐ γὰρ ἐν λόγῳ ἡ βασιλεία τοῦ θεοῦ ἀλλ' ἐν δυνάμει (literally: "for not in word the kingdom of God but in power"). As in other examples (Matt. 27:25; John 14:11; 21:21; Acts 10:15; 18:6; 19:28, 34; Rom. 4:9; 5:18; 13:7; 1 Cor. 5:12; 2 Cor. 1:18; 8:15; 9:7; 11:6; Gal. 2:9; Phil. 4:5; Rev. 1:4), either εἰμι (the verb "to be") or γίνομαι (to be translated variously as, e.g., "become," "happen," "appear," "be") usually can be supplied. See Robertson, *Grammar*, 1202; cf. Winer, *Grammar*, 586. However, the translation adopted here takes into account that ἐν can mean "amounting to" or "consisting in" (1 Macc. 3:19; Epictetus, *Diatr.* 2.1.4; Mark 4:8, 20; Acts 7:14; Eph. 2:15). See Moulton, *Grammar*, 3:265.

164. Barrett, *First Epistle to the Corinthians*, 118, and those listed by William D. Spencer, "The Power in Paul's Teaching (1 Cor. 4:9–20)," *JETS* 32 (1989): 51n1.

165. Cf. Spencer, "Power," 53, and those cited.

Paul refers to his life of suffering as an imitation of Christ.[166] However, this ignores the earlier connection that Paul made between power and Christ crucified, and that the demonstration of power and Spirit was something from God, to be seen in Paul's particular activity or weakness (see 2:1–5 and §7.3 above).

The way forward in understanding what Paul had in mind using the word "power" is noting that he is using it with "kingdom of God" as part of a definition of the gospel—his message. We have seen that his previous use of the word "power," earlier in this section, was also in a summary definition of his message (1 Cor. 2:1–5). There, "power" was linked with "Spirit" as a synonym. In this summary definition of the gospel, therefore, readers could be expected to read "power" as a shorthand description of what power and Spirit implied in Paul's earlier definition of the gospel.[167] That this was Paul's intention is seen in taking into account that even earlier, in his letter to the Thessalonians, he had associated power and the Holy Spirit in this way (1 Thess. 1:5; see §7.1 above).

Moreover, "power" being used with "kingdom of God" all but assures us not only that he intended his readers to take the notion of Spirit to be involved, but also that the miraculous was implied. As we have seen, the term "kingdom of God" is much less common in Paul than in the Jesus traditions (see 125n128 and 126n133 above). However, as we have also noted, its unannounced and casual introduction—here as a summary of the gospel—is strong support for a case that Paul and his readers shared it as a synonym for the gospel, sometimes regarding its present and sometimes its future expression (see §5.3 [e] above). Here the term has a present reference, as is clear from the kingdom being set over against words or talking. In that Paul does not appear to be offering an exhaustive definition of the kingdom of God, but an aphorism (cf. Rom. 14:17), he is likely drawing attention to an essential feature for the immediate context.[168]

With such a strong relationship in Jesus' ministry between the kingdom of God and miracles—and to a lesser extent Spirit (Matt. 12:28/Luke 11:20)[169]— remembered in a number of early Christian traditions,[170] it would be surprising

166. Ibid., 51–61.
167. E.g., Barrett, *First Epistle to the Corinthians*, 118; John Ruef, *Paul's First Letter to Corinth* (PNTC; London: SCM, 1977), 37.
168. Hans Conzelmann, *1 Corinthians: A Commentary on the First Epistle to the Corinthians*, trans. James W. Leitch, ed. George W. MacRae (Hermeneia; Philadelphia: Fortress, 1975), 93.
169. James D. G. Dunn, "Spirit and Kingdom," *ExpTim* 82 (1970–71): 36–40.
170. See particularly the so-called Beelzebul controversy, which is found in Mark (Mark 3:22–27 // Matt. 9:32–34) and Q (Matt. 12:22–30 // Luke 11:14–23) and reflected in Matthew and Luke. See also Jesus' answer to John the Baptist (Matt. 11:2–6 // Luke 7:18–23) and the

if any early Christian readers did not associate Paul's collocation of kingdom
and power or Spirit with the miraculous (Rom. 14:17). Also, I have already
established that the Christianity Paul inherited included the idea that Jesus
commissioned his followers to perform miracles in association with announcing
the kingdom of God (§5.2 [d] above). Further, we have seen that "power," both
in the plural and sometimes in the singular, was used for miracle (§7.1 above).
Moreover, we have seen that this connection Paul has made between power and
Spirit a little earlier in this letter (1 Cor. 2:4–5) is likely to imply the miraculous
for the readers (§7.3 above). Therefore, it is quite probable that, in saying "the
kingdom of God consists not in talk but in power" (4:20), Paul intended his
readers to see in the word "power" a reference to the miraculous.[171] This has
the support of John Chrysostom (*Hom. 1 Cor.* 14.3) taking "power" to refer
to "signs" (σημηεῖα).

It can reasonably be assumed that included in this inference to the miraculous were miracles, such as healings and exorcisms. However, Paul probably
did not intend to limit the reference to miracles,[172] or he could be expected to
use the phrase "signs and wonders" or even "powers." Therefore, for Paul,
while the kingdom of God could be equated with the power (of God) or the
miraculous, it was more than the miracles.[173] If this reading of Paul is correct,
we catch a glimpse of his understanding of the place and function of miracles
and the miraculous in the gospel. In the last section (§7.3 above) we saw that the
miraculous was the proof or demonstration of the gospel. Here the manifestation of power in the miraculous is the kingdom of God, a view that found its
origin in Jesus' ministry.[174] That is, for Paul, as well as for Jesus before him, in
the miraculous the gospel or the kingdom of God was expressed or realized.

7.5 1 Corinthians 12–14

I have already been able to establish that although Paul does not (and is
unlikely to) claim to be involved in all the *charismata*, he claims to speak in

discussion by Graham H. Twelftree, "The Miracles of Jesus: Marginal or Mainstream?" *JSHJ*
1 (2003): 117–22.

171. Cf. Craig A. Evans, "Paul the Exorcist and Healer," in *Paul and His Theology*, ed.
Stanley E. Porter (PSt 3; Leiden: Brill, 2006), 365.

172. As assumed by, e.g., Gräbe, *Power of God*, 66–70; Thomas R. Schreiner, *Paul, Apostle of
God's Glory in Christ: A Pauline Theology* (Downers Grove, IL: InterVarsity; Leicester: Apollos,
2001), 93; Udo Schnelle, *Apostle Paul: His Life and Theology*, trans. M. Eugene Boring (Grand
Rapids: Baker Academic, 2005), 153.

173. Though not mentioning the miraculous, see the helpful discussion on "power" in 1 Cor.
4:20 by Fee, *First Epistle to the Corinthians*, 192.

174. See Twelftree, "Miracles of Jesus," 114–22.

tongues and, most probably, to prophesy and teach. I also argued that he would have been understood to exercise the gift of wisdom (see §6.7 [c] above). In view of his interest in combating the Corinthians' preoccupation with rhetorical wisdom and his claim to speak God's secret and hidden wisdom (cf. 1 Cor. 2:7), it is not surprising that Paul would lay claim to speaking gifts. However, if my conclusions are correct that the "demonstration of the Spirit and of power" (2:4) carried an implicit reference to the miraculous expression of God's power as the demonstration or proof of Paul's proclamation (see §7.3 [c] above)—carried out in the context of his acknowledged weakness—it is not surprising that he does not lay claim to other *charismata*. My tentative conclusion probably should be, therefore, that Paul was not directly involved in any of these gifts—faith, healing, or miracles, for example.[175] That is, while he claims the miraculous took place in relation to his ministry, it was not through his touch or prayer. As we have already seen from his letter to the Galatians, Paul had democratized the miraculous (see §7.2 above).

7.6 2 Corinthians 6:6–7

To understand what Paul is saying in the two passages that require our attention in 2 Corinthians we do not need to untangle the chronology of Paul's complex relationship with the Corinthian Christians. We also do not need establish the number and extent of letters in this probably composite letter (cf. 192n98 above). Assuming the unity of chapters 1–8,[176] all we need to take into account here is that, having just defended his ministry on the grounds that he is an ambassador of Christ (5:11–21), he now offers a list of hardships and positive characteristics related to his ministry to support his appeal (6:1–13).[177] For, it is obvious that the relationship between the Corinthians and Paul is strained to breaking point (e.g., 6:11–13; 7:2). After his introductory statement ("as servants of God we have commended ourselves in every way," 6:4), it is generally agreed that Paul has four supporting stanzas[178] written in an elevated style.[179] This structuring suggests not so much a previous formulation of this material as Paul's careful composition.[180]

175. See §7.7 (c) below for a development of this idea.
176. Thrall, *Second Epistle to the Corinthians*, 1:48–49, and those listed.
177. Sometimes 2 Cor. 6:4b–10 is inaccurately called a hardship list. See the discussion by Frank J. Matera, *II Corinthians* (NTL; Louisville: Westminster John Knox, 2003), 147.
178. 2 Cor. 6:4b–5, 6–7a, 7b–8a, 8b–10.
179. Ralph P. Martin, *2 Corinthians* (WBC 40; Waco: Word, 1986), 161.
180. Thrall, *Second Epistle to the Corinthians*, 1:454, 457.

Following the first stanza, a list of hardships (6:4b–5), in the second stanza Paul has eight positive aspects of his life or character, which he marshals to commend himself "in every way" (6:4). In effect he says that as a servant of God he has commended himself in every way: "by[181] purity, by knowledge, by patience, by kindness, by Holy Spirit, by sincere love, by true speech, by God's power" (6:6–7a). The issue for us is whether or not "by God's power" (ἐν δυνάμει θεοῦ) Paul means miracles, as some have concluded.[182]

Each one of the last four means through which Paul has commended himself—Holy Spirit, sincere love, true speech, and God's power—is a paired term, the first and last pair being connected with the divine. This pairing suggests that in these four terms Paul had in mind a chiastic or criss-cross relation between them.[183] In turn, this means that "Holy Spirit" and "God's power" are to be read as similar ideas, informing each other. Our confidence in this observation is increased when we take into account that in Romans 15:19 ("by the power of signs and wonders, by the power of the Spirit"), "Spirit" and "power" are almost tautological.[184]

However, some have argued that by "holy spirit" (πνεύματι ἁγίῳ) Paul means (his) "holiness of spirit."[185] For, as C. K. Barrett notes, Paul appears to be listing "a series of [his] human ethical qualities."[186] Yet, others argue Paul has in mind "the Holy Spirit,"[187] for he often uses "holy spirit," without the article, in referring to "the Holy Spirit."[188] Moreover, if he meant that he had a "spirit of holiness," he could be expected to use the term πνεῦμα ἁγιωσύνης (so Rom. 1:4).

181. Paul uses ἐν ("in"), in the dative, the most common preposition in the NT, and variously translated. See BDAG, "ἐν," 326–30.

182. E.g., Rudolf Bultmann, *The Second Letter to the Corinthians*, trans. Roy A. Harrisville (Minneapolis: Augsburg, 1985), 231.

183. Martin, *2 Corinthians*, 162. Though the use of a crosswise interchange of four clauses was ancient and evident in the OT (e.g., Ps. 20:2–5; 51:7), the term "chiasmus" first appears somewhere between the second and fourth centuries CE in Pseudo-Hermogenes, *On Invention* 4.3. See George A. Kennedy, *New Testament Interpretation through Rhetorical Criticism* (Chapel Hill: University of North Carolina Press, 1984), 28. On the dating of Pseudo-Hermogenes, *On Invention*, see Michael Weissenberger, "Hermogenes of Tarsus," *New Pauly* 6 (2005): 235.

184. See §7.8 below. Cf. Ernst Käsemann, *Commentary on Romans*, trans. and ed. Geoffrey W. Bromiley (London: SCM, 1980), 394.

185. E.g., NAB, NRSV; in the JB, "spirit of holiness." Alfred Plummer, *A Critical and Exegetical Commentary on the Second Epistle of St. Paul to the Corinthians* (ICC; Edinburgh: T&T Clark, 1915), 196: "a spirit that is holy"; NAB (2nd ed.): "by a spirit of holiness"; Barrett, *Second Epistle to the Corinthians*, 186–87: "a holy spirit." See the discussion by Harris, *Second Epistle to the Corinthians*, 475.

186. Barrett, *Second Epistle to the Corinthians*, 187.

187. So, e.g., ASV, KJV, ESV, NASB, NASU, NET, NIV, NJB, NKJV, NLT, RSV.

188. See Rom. 5:5; 9:1; 14:17; 15:13, 16; 1 Cor. 6:19; 12:3; 2 Cor. 13:13; 1 Thess. 1:5, 6; 4:8; cf. 2 Tim. 1:14; Titus 3:5.

The resolution of this apparent paradox is in noting two things. First, all the occasions in the New Testament (including in Paul) where the Holy Spirit is described in terms of power, often miraculous power, the definite article is not used.[189] Second, as we have just noted, Paul probably intends this reference to the Holy Spirit to be taken chiastically with "the power of God." In short, both "Holy Spirit" and "God's power"—along with genuine love and truthful speech—refer to the Spirit powerfully at work or expressed in Paul's life and ministry[190] in the face of, and in order to endure, the hardships just mentioned (2 Cor. 6:4b–5; cf. 6:8).[191]

In turn, given that we have already seen the close association between Spirit and power that Paul uses to refer to miracles (see §7.1 above), it is most probable they are also in view here. However, in view of the broad context (Paul's ministry in general) and subtlety of the relationship of Spirit and power, he may have in mind the widest spectrum of the miraculous. In any case, yet again, in view of his using this list to commend himself, Paul is using the miraculous as at least part of what he understands to constitute his ministry.

7.7 2 Corinthians 12:11–12

In countering that he is "not at all inferior to these super-apostles" (2 Cor. 12:11), Paul says that even though he is nothing, "Indeed [μέν],[192] the signs of the apostle were performed among you with utmost patience, signs and wonders and mighty works" (12:12a). This statement, and asking "How have you been worse off than the other churches?" (12:13),[193] suggests Paul is responding

---

189. Matt. 1:18, 20; Luke 1:35; Acts 1:2; Rom. 15:13; 1 Cor. 12:3; 1 Thess. 1:5–6; Heb. 2:4; 2 Pet. 1:21, cited by D. Pitt Francis, "The Holy Spirit: A Statistical Inquiry," *ExpTim* 96 (1985): 136. Francis notes, "In all these cases, the Holy Spirit is clearly 'power' rather than 'person' (in the personified or personalized sense), if we take 'joy in the Holy Spirit' as meaning 'joy' effected in people by the Holy Spirit (1 Thess. 1:6)" (p. 137).

190. Martin, *2 Corinthians*, 177; Matera, *II Corinthians*, 153.

191. John T. Fitzgerald observes, "The reference to the 'power of God' in 6:6 is a conscious cross-reference to the catalogue of 4:7–12" (*Cracks in an Earthen Vessel: An Examination of the Catalogues of Hardships in the Corinthian Correspondence* [SBLDS 99; Atlanta: Scholars Press, 1988], 195).

192. Cf. Jan Lambrecht (*Second Corinthians* [SP 8; Collegeville, MN: Liturgical Press, 1999], who notes that the postpositive μέν, even without the corresponding δέ, "could point to the concessive nature of the sentence, e.g., 'It is true that signs of the apostle were performed among you (but that did not take away my weakness)'" (p. 211). Barrett (*Second Epistle to the Corinthians*, 320) takes the uncorrelated μέν to give the sense "at least." In contrast to classical style, in biblical Greek μέν and δέ are rarely correlated. See Moulton, *Grammar*, 3:331.

193. On this part of Paul's so-called foolish or boastful discourse (*Narrenrede*), a title attributed to Hans Windisch—so Paul W. Barnett, *The Second Epistle to the Corinthians* (NICNT;

to criticisms from the Corinthians.[194] They had failed to see him as a bearer of the Spirit who, through signs and wonders, was able to confirm that Christ spoke through him (13:3).[195] Although the phrases "signs of an apostle" and "signs and wonders" are confined to this passage of the correspondence, suggesting they were introduced to the Corinthians by Paul's opponents,[196] hints of questions of deficiencies in Paul's ministry in relation to the supernatural are found early in his extant letters (e.g., 1 Cor. 1:22),[197] suggesting that the Corinthians had long-standing criticisms that Paul's opponents had sharpened and articulated along the lines expressed in the phrases he is using here.[198]

With this verse (2 Cor. 12:12), there is generally more confidence that Paul is referring to miracles, such as healings and exorcism.[199] Paul is not ceding the advantage to the miracle-working super-apostles.[200] For example, on the basis of this verse, Hans von Campenhausen concluded that performing miracles was

---

Grand Rapids: Eerdmans, 1997), 494n1—see Margaret M. Mitchell, "A Patristic Perspective on Pauline περιαυτολογία," *NTS* 47 (2001): 354–71.

194. Cf., e.g., Dieter Georgi, Erhardt Güttgemanns, Ernst Käsemann, Walter Schmithals, and Ulrich Wilckens, cited by Jacob Jervell, "The Signs of an Apostle: Paul's Miracles," in *The Unknown Paul: Essays on Luke-Acts and Early Christian History* (Minneapolis: Augsburg, 1984), 94 and 172n44. More recently, see Barrett, *Second Epistle to the Corinthians*, 321; Calvin J. Roetzel, "The Language of War (2 Cor. 10:1–6) and the Language of Weakness (2 Cor. 11:21b–13:10)," *BibInt* 17 (2009): 77–99.

195. Wilckens, *Weisheit und Torheit*, 218; Anitra Bingham Kolenkow, "Paul and His Opponents in 2 Cor. 10–13: THEIOI ANDRES and Spiritual Guides," in *Religious Propaganda and Missionary Competition in the New Testament World: Essays Honoring Dieter Georgi*, ed. Lukas Bormann, Kelly Del Tredici, and Angela Standhartinger (NovTSup 74; Leiden: Brill, 1994), 362–64.

196. Ernst Käsemann, "Die Legitimität des Apostels: Eine Untersuchung zu II Korinther 10–13," *ZNW* 41 (1942): 35; Derk William Oostendorp, *Another Jesus: A Gospel of Jewish-Christian Superiority in II Corinthians* (Kampen: Kok, 1967), 15; Bultmann, *Second Letter to the Corinthians*, 231; Thrall, *Second Epistle to the Corinthians*, 2:838; and, with less confidence, Victor P. Furnish, *II Corinthians: Translated with Introduction, Notes, and Commentary* (AB 32A; Garden City, NY: Doubleday, 1984), 555.

197. Cf. Michael D. Goulder, *Paul and the Competing Mission in Corinth* (LPS; Peabody, MA: Hendrickson, 2001), 251–52.

198. On the phrases originating with the Corinthians, see C. K. Barrett, "Paul's Opponents in II Corinthians," *NTS* 17 (1971): 245; Martin, *2 Corinthians*, 435.

199. See, e.g., Hans Windisch, *Der zweite Korintherbrief*, 9th ed. (KEK 6; Göttingen: Vandenhoeck & Ruprecht, 1970), 397; Barrett, *Second Epistle to the Corinthians*, 321; Bultmann, *Second Letter to the Corinthians*, 232; Barnett, *Second Epistle to the Corinthians*, 579–80; Friedrich Avemarie, "Warum treibt Paulus einen Dämon aus, der die Wahrheit sagt? Geschichte und Bedeutung des Exorzismus zu Philippi (Acts 16,16–18)," in *Die Dämonen: Die Dämonologie der israelistisch-jüdischen und frühchristlichen Literatur im Kontext ihrer Umwelt* [= *Demons: The Demonology of Israelite-Jewish and Early Christian Literature in Context of Their Environment*], ed. Armin Lange, Hermann Lichtenberger, and K. F. Diethard Römheld (Tübingen: Mohr Siebeck, 2003), 571; Matera, *II Corinthians*, 289; Harris, *Second Epistle to the Corinthians*, 875.

200. Calvin J. Roetzel, *Paul: The Man and the Myth* (Minneapolis: Fortress, 1999), 164.

a matter of expectation for the apostle.[201] Yet, Walter Schmithals contended that, apart from this formula ("signs and wonders"), which he sees as unclear and modified by Paul, there is no suggestion in his letters that he practiced healing or exorcism. Therefore, according to Schmithals, the possibility must remain open that, in this statement, Paul simply refuses to take the trouble to give specific content to a traditional formula.[202] With a similar result, others take the "signs of an apostle" to be the miracle of the word or proclamation.[203]

In view of this divergence of opinion, again we must seek to establish for ourselves whether or not Paul had miracles in mind when referring to "signs and wonders and mighty works" (2 Cor. 12:12b). If so, due to some aspects of what he says, we can also enquire about his relationship to them.

(a) *"Signs and wonders."* The phrase "signs and wonders," first used in the New Testament here by Paul,[204] is first known in Polybius (c. 200–c. 118 BCE) referring to the superstitious rites of the Romans.[205] Josephus uses the phrase of God warning and directing his people before the war with Rome (*J.W.* 1.28). Josephus has in mind, for example, a star resembling a sword that stood over the city, a comet that continued for a year, a brilliant light shining at night around the altar to make it seem as light as day, a cow giving birth to a lamb, the large and heavy eastern gate of the inner court of the temple opening by itself at night, chariots and armed battalions hurtling through the sky, and a peasant standing in the temple for years incessantly crying out a message of doom (6.288–309). Josephus also uses the phrase "wonders and signs" to describe the activities of impostors at the time deceiving people (*Ant.* 20.168), and probably for this reason he completely avoids using the terms for the exodus events (cf. 2.284; 4.43).[206] Plutarch (before 50–after 120 CE), the philosopher and biographer, uses the words "signs" and "wonders" synonymously (*Mor.* 2.149C; cf. Josephus, *Ant.* 10.28).

201. Hans von Campenhausen, "Der urchristliche Apostelbegriff," *ST* 1 (1948): 111.

202. Walter Schmithals, *The Office of Apostle in the Early Church*, trans. John E. Steely (Nashville: Abingdon, 1969), 37.

203. See the discussion by Jervell, "Signs," 91, 171n37, citing Hans D. Betz, Günther Bornkamm, and Walter Schmithals.

204. For the phrase "signs and wonders" and its variations in the NT, see Matt. 24:24; Mark 13:22; John 4:48; Acts 2:19, 22, 43; 4:30; 5:12; 6:8; 7:36; 14:3; 15:12; Rom. 15:19; 2 Cor. 12:12; 2 Thess. 2:9; Heb. 2:4.

205. E.g., Polybius, *Hist.* 3.112.8; cf. Plutarch, *Alex.* 75.1. Cf. Selly Vernon McCasland, "Signs and Wonders," *JBL* 76 (1957): 149–52; Molly Whittaker, "'Signs and Wonders': The Pagan Background," in *Studia Evangelica V: Papers Presented to the Third International Congress on New Testament Studies Held at Oxford, 1965*, ed. F. L. Cross (TUGAL 103; Berlin: Akademie-Verlag), 155–58; Wolfgang Weiss, *Zeichen und Wunder: Eine Studie zu der Sprachtradition und ihrer Verwendung im Neuen Testament* (WMANT 67; Neukirchen-Vluyn: Neukirchener, 1995).

206. See Karl H. Rengstorf, "σημεῖον, κτλ," *TDNT* 7:224.

Notwithstanding, for Paul and his readers, the phrase "signs and wonders" probably would have been known primarily from the Septuagint,[207] where it was generally used for the miracles associated with Moses leading God's people to freedom.[208] Deuteronomy has the largest number of occurrences of the phrase, all but two of which are in the singular and are related to the miracles of the exodus (LXX Deut. 13:3 [ET 13:2]; 28:46). In Exodus the phrase also occurs a number of times for the plagues and miracles instigated by Moses.[209] Not surprisingly, Philo uses the phrase as a traditional description of the miracles in Egypt[210] and also of portents such as "dreams or oracles" (*Aet.* 2).

(b) Salvific miracles. We can see that the traditional phrase "signs and won-ders" could refer to a wide range of marvels, from the wonders of the exodus to the portents of the Greco-Roman world and also to those associated with opponents. Notably, Paul adds to the phrase the modification "and mighty works" (καὶ δυνάμεσιν, 2 Cor. 12:12). This addition does not, as Rudolf Bult-mann thought, denote the power to do miracles,[211] but most probably it is a deliberate restricting of the meaning of the terms "signs and wonders" to echo the redemptive exodus miracles as described by Deuteronomy (LXX Deut. 9:29; 26:8).[212] This becomes even clearer when we see that Baruch, more obviously using the language and theology of the Deuteronomic tradition,[213] also adds "and in great power" (καὶ ἐν δυνάμει μεγάλη) to the traditional phrase to form the same triad of "signs," "wonders," and "power" (Bar. 2:11)[214] found in Deuteronomy (LXX) for the miracles related to the exodus.[215] Although Paul's phrase "signs and wonders and mighty works" is, therefore, almost certainly a deliberate recalling of the miracles of Moses associated with the exodus, a further factor was most probably determining how the readers would have understood Paul.

207. For the phrase "signs and wonders" and its variations in the LXX, see Exod. 7:3, 9; 11:9, 10; Deut. 4:34; 6:22; 7:19; 11:3; 13:2, 3 (ET 13:1, 2); 26:8; 28:46; 29:2 (ET 29:3); 34:11; Esther 10:3–4; Ps. 77:43 (ET 78:43); 104:27 (ET 105:27); 134:9 (ET 135:9); Wis. 8:8; 10:16; Isa. 8:18; 20:3; Jer. 39:20, 21 (ET 32:20, 21); Bar. 2:11; Dan. 4:2 (Θ), 37, 37a; 6:28 (Θ); cf. 3 Macc. 6:32.

208. LXX Exod. 7:3, 9; 11:9, 10; Deut. 4:34; 6:22; 7:19; 11:3; 26:8; 29:2 (ET 29:3); 34:11; Ps. 77:43 (ET 78:43); 104:27 (ET 105:27); 134:9 (ET 135:9); Wis. 10:16; Isa. 20:3; Jer. 39:20, 21 (ET 32:20, 21); Bar. 2:11; cf. 3 Macc. 6:32.

209. LXX Exod. 7:3, 9; 11:9, 10.

210. Philo, *Mos.* 1.95; *Spec.* 2.218; cf. *Mos.* 1.178.

211. Bultmann, *Second Letter to the Corinthians*, 231.

212. See the discussions by John William Wevers, *Notes on the Greek Text of Deuteronomy* (SBLSCSS 39; Atlanta: Scholars Press, 1995), 405–6, and J. G. McConville, *Deuteronomy* (ApOTC 5; Leicester: Apollos; Downers Grove, IL: InterVarsity, 2002), 112.

213. Cf. Anthony J. Saldarini, "The Book of Baruch: Introduction, Commentary and Reflec-tions," *NIB* 6:955, citing Deut. 6:21–23; Jer. 32:20–21; Dan. 9:15.

214. Noted also by Evans, "Paul the Exorcist," 366.

215. Cf. Dan. 9:15; on which, see André Kabasele Mukenge, *L'unité littéraire du livre de Baruch* (Etudes Bibliques 38; Paris: Gabalda, 1998), 130n54.

There was, at least among some Jews just before Paul's time, the expectation that the signs and wonders of the exodus would be repeated in later times.[216] In particular, early Christians began to use variations of the phrase for the miracles of Jesus. Luke, using a distinctly Christian triadic combination,[217] describes Jesus as "a man attested to you by God with deeds of power, wonders, and signs" (δυνάμεσι καὶ τέρασι καὶ σημείοις, Acts 2:22). The Fourth Gospel, in which "sign" is the usual word for Jesus' miracles,[218] uncharacteristically uses "signs and wonders" (John 4:48) of miracles sought by Jesus' audience, suggesting it was a traditional phrase for Jesus' miracles. However, this single and negative use of the phrase—"Unless you see signs and wonders you will not believe"—suggests that the author has similar sensibilities to Josephus (see §2.1 [c] above) and wishes to distance Jesus' miracles from marvels or portents of others, or from false prophets of the time (cf. Mark 13:22 // Matt. 24:24).[219] The *Epistle of Barnabas* (c. 130 CE) also describes Jesus as teaching Israel, and performing "great wonders and signs" (τηλικαῦτα τέρατα καὶ σημεῖα, *Barn.* 5:8).[220] Further, the phrase "signs and wonders" was also used by some early Christians of miracles attributed to Christians[221] and to Satan (2 Thess. 2:9; *Did.* 16:4).[222] In that Luke's use of the phrase is unevenly distributed across his work, and found mostly in the early chapters of Acts, suggests he is picking up a feature of earlier tradition rather than using terms that he is introducing to his work,[223] and therefore could have been familiar to Paul and his readers.

From this discussion it is hardly to be doubted that, in using the phrase "signs and wonders and mighty works," Paul had miracles in mind, and that his readers would have taken him to mean miracles. However, Paul's modification of the traditional phrase, in order to call to mind the miracles associated with the exodus, both distances the notion of "signs and wonders" from the omens and portents of

216. LXX Esther 10:3–4; Sir. 36:5; Dan. 4:2; 6:28 (Θ); 3 Macc. 6:32.

217. The earliest combined use "signs," "wonders," and "deeds of power" is found in the NT: Acts 2:22; 6:8; Rom. 15:19; 2 Cor. 12:12; 2 Thess. 2:9; Heb. 2:4; see also Bar. 2:11.

218. For σημεῖον ("sign") in the Fourth Gospel, see John 2:11, 18, 23; 3:2; 4:48, 54; 6:2, 14, 26, 30; 7:31; 9:16; 10:41; 11:47; 12:18, 37; 20:30.

219. See the brief discussion in Graham H. Twelftree, *Jesus the Miracle Worker: A Historical and Theological Study* (Downers Grove, IL: InterVarsity, 1999), 227–28.

220. For the dating of the *Epistle of Barnabas*, see the summary discussion by Bart D. Ehrman, ed. and trans., *The Apostolic Fathers*, 2 vols. (LCL; Cambridge, MA: Harvard University Press, 2003), 2:6–7.

221. Acts 2:43; 4:30; 5:12; 6:8; 14:3; 15:12; cf. Heb. 2:4; on which, see §9.5 below.

222. For the dating of the *Didache* at the turn of the first and second centuries CE, see Huub van de Sandt and David Flusser, *The Didache: Its Jewish Sources and Its Place in Early Judaism and Christianity* (CRINT 3/5; Assen: Van Gorcum; Minneapolis: Fortress, 2002), 48, and those cited in n128.

223. Variations of the phrase "signs and wonders" occur in Luke's writing in Acts 2:19, 22, 43; 4:30; 5:12; 6:8; 7:36; 14:3; 15:12.

charlatans of the period and claims salvific significance for the miracles. Moreover, given that Paul and his readers probably shared knowledge of Jesus' miracles being called "signs and wonders," it is equally probable that Paul's readers would also have understood his reference to miracles to include the kinds of activities known to be associated with Jesus—healings and exorcism, for example.

(c) Paul and the miracles. Despite the confidence we can have in this conclusion that Paul is referring to miracles in relation to his ministry, there are aspects to what he writes that probably require an important nuance to how he understood himself in relation to the miracles. To begin with, the claim "Indeed, the signs of the apostle were performed among you" (2 Cor. 12:12a) follows his comment "even though I am nothing" (εἰ καὶ οὐδέν εἰμι, 12:11b).[224] Paul's intention in this self-deprecation depends on the identity of the "super-apostles" with whom he is reluctantly comparing himself.[225] If they are the first apostles (Peter, James, and John),[226] then Paul would mean that he was the least significant of them (cf. 1 Cor. 15:5–9).[227] However, on the one hand, it is unlikely that, despite his altercation with Peter (Gal. 2:11–14, see §7.2 above), he would be so contemptuous of them in the term "super-apostles" (ὑπερλίαν ἀποστόλων, 2 Cor. 11:5; 12:11). On the other hand, it is unlikely he would need to concede that they were more polished orators than he (12:6) if they were Jews from Palestine.[228] More likely, then, the so-called super-apostles are his rival missionaries,[229] for they are portrayed as his direct competitors.[230] And, in that they are Jews (11:22), they probably are Hellenistic Jews, as the Corinthians had accepted them as eloquent speakers (11:6).[231]

224. In regard to whether the phrase εἰ καὶ οὐδέν εἰμι is to be taken as the end of 2 Cor. 12:11 or the beginning of 12:12, Plummer says, "The μέν, and the very awkward asyndeton that would arise if εἰ καί is prefixed to v. 12, are decisive against this arrangement" (*Second Epistle of St. Paul to the Corinthians*, 358).

225. Even if the reference to himself as οὐδέν ("nothing") may reflect the sentiments of his opponents (so R. V. G. Tasker, *The Second Epistle to the Corinthians* [TNTC 8; Grand Rapids: Eerdmans, 1958], 180), the view is in line with Paul's self-assessment. Cf. 1 Cor. 3:7; 15:8–9; 2 Cor. 10:1–2; 12:9–10; see also 1 Cor. 13:2.

226. So John Chrysostom, *Hom. 2 Cor. XXIII* (PG 61.556), and more recently, e.g., John M. Court, "The Controversy with Adversaries of Paul's Apostolate in the Context of His Relations to the Corinthian Congregation (2 Corinthians 12,14–13,13)," in *Verteidigung und Begründung des apostolischen Amtes (2 Kor 10–13): XII Colloquio ecumenico Paolino*, ed. Eduard Lohse (Rome: Abtei St. Paul vor den Mauern, 1992), 96.

227. Cf. the discussion by Thrall, *Second Epistle to the Corinthians*, 2:835–36.

228. Furnish, *II Corinthians*, 505; Thrall, *Second Epistle to the Corinthians*, 2:674.

229. If these missionaries traced their roots back to Jerusalem, where the miraculous probably was important, miracles would be important to them. See Jean Héring, *La seconde épître de saint Paul aux Corinthiens* (CNT 8; Neuchâtel: Delachaux & Niestlé, 1958), 98n1.

230. Thrall, *Second Epistle to the Corinthians*, 2:674.

231. Jerry L. Sumney, *"Servants of Satan," "False Brothers," and Other Opponents of Paul* (JSNTSup 188; Sheffield: Sheffield Academic Press, 1999), 113. On methodological issues involved

Therefore, in saying he is nothing, Paul arguably is to be read in light of the ancient philosophical principle,[232] known in Paul's time, that self-knowledge enables a person to admit nothingness in relation to divine power.[233] Yet, contrary to what is often supposed, Paul does not intend a false modesty and its accompanying irony that would cause his readers to take him to mean the opposite.[234] Rather, most obviously in light of what he has just said about his weakness and God's power (12:9–10), he is saying that although he is (in fact) nothing in relation to the divine power,[235] the signs of an apostle (still) took place (cf. Rom. 15:18–19, on which, see §7.8 below). This leads to another point that helps us understand Paul's relationship to these miracles.

In the verse we are examining Paul says, "Indeed, the signs of the apostle were performed among you" (2 Cor. 12:12a). The aorist "were performed" (κατειργάσθη) points to Paul's initial ministry in Corinth.[236] However, what is notable is that Paul uses the passive "were performed."[237] Especially in light of the criticism of his spiritual weakness that he is countering, we might have expected Paul to say, "Despite being nothing before God, I performed [κατειργασάμην] signs and wonders and mighty works."[238] It could be, therefore, that Paul intends the passive to have theological significance, implying that God performed the miracles.[239] Indeed, saying the signs were performed "with utmost patience" (ἐν πάσῃ ὑπομονῇ, 12:12) would have brought to mind a characteristic of God (Rom. 15:4–5; cf. Col. 1:11) obvious in his weakness (2 Cor. 12:9).[240] For although in the New Testament "patience" is generally attributed to human beings,[241] it was a gift of God, "grounded in the work of

---

in identifying Paul's opponents, see Jerry L. Sumney, "Paul and His Opponents: The Search," in *Paul Unbound: Other Perspectives on the Apostle*, ed. Mark D. Given (Peabody, MA: Hendrickson, 2010), 55–70, and literature cited.

232. See Plato, *Phaedr.* 234E; Epictetus, *Diatr.* 3.9.14; 4.8.25.

233. Betz, *Paulus*, 128–30.

234. See, e.g., Martin, *2 Corinthians*, 427, 433.

235. Cf. Matera, *II Corinthians*, 288.

236. Barnett, *Second Epistle to the Corinthians*, 577, 581.

237. Moulton, *Grammar*, 3:58.

238. Cf. Plummer, *Second Epistle of St. Paul to the Corinthians*, 358.

239. Plummer, *Second Epistle of St. Paul to the Corinthians*, 358; Georg Bertram, "κατεργάζομαι," *TDNT* 3:635; Schreiber, *Wundertäter*, 275; Harris, *Second Epistle to the Corinthians*, 874.

240. Cf. Martin, *2 Corinthians*, 435–36; Sumney, *Opponents of Paul*, 123n263. Paul's use of ὑπομονή ("patience" or "endurance") is unlikely to be a description of the way he performed the miracles (as supposed by Thrall, *Second Epistle to the Corinthians*, 2:839), but of his ministry, or a general characteristic of it (as it is in 2 Cor. 6:4; cf. 1:6). We can note here that this is particularly appropriate in the context of portraying his apostleship as one of strength in weakness (12:5–10). Paul's ministry, including the miraculous, arose not out of triumphalism, but out of weakness and patiently enduring suffering.

241. Luke 8:15; 21:19; Rom. 2:7; 5:3, 4; 8:25; 15:4, 5; 2 Cor. 1:6; 6:4; 12:12; Col. 1:11; 1 Thess. 1:3; 2 Thess. 1:4; 1 Tim. 6:11; 2 Tim. 3:10; Titus 2:2; Heb. 10:36; 12:1; James 1:3,

Christ in bearing reproaches for others," as Robert Jewett puts it,[242] given in the face of difficult circumstances (cf. Rom. 15:4–5; Col. 1:11).[243] Thus, although it is undoubtedly partly the case that in the passive "were performed" Paul has in mind God performing the miracles (cf. §7.8 below on Rom. 15:18–19),[244] this probably is not the entire explanation. For, on the one hand, Paul is quite happy to use active terms in referring to Christ sending him to proclaim the gospel (1 Cor. 1:17), and to write of his eagerness to preach the gospel (Rom. 1:15), and to say that he proclaims it.[245] In fact, only once does Paul use the passive of his preaching the gospel.[246] However, he goes on to say it was he who was proclaiming it (Gal. 1:11).[247] On the other hand, Paul is happy to use the active form "accomplished" or "performed" (κατειργάσατο) when Christ is the subject of the verb (Rom. 15:18, on which, see §7.8 below).[248]

Further, taking into account the miracle working of the super-apostles, against whom he is pitting himself, brings into sharper relief what we should probably conclude from Paul's description of his miracle working in passive terms. For the plain sense of his statement—"I am not at all inferior to these super-apostles. . . . Indeed, the signs of the apostle were performed among you . . ." (2 Cor. 12:11–12)—is that they also performed miracles.[249] This statement also assumes that miracles were generally taken as evidence of apostleship.[250] Also, for Paul's argument to have its impact, he would be assuming the miracles of the super-apostles were similar to the ones he claims. However, the methods of his opponents, likely derived from the earliest followers of Jesus, may have been different from his.

Implying that his opponents had encroached on his God-given responsibilities to the Corinthians (2 Cor. 10:13), which he understood was recognized

---

4; 5:11; 2 Pet. 1:6; Rev. 1:9; 2:2, 3, 19; 3:10; 13:10; 14:12; contrast 2 Thess. 3:5, where Jesus is the subject.

242. Jewett, *Romans*, 882, discussing Rom. 15:4.

243. Cf. W. Radl, "ὑπομονή," *EDNT* 3:405–6.

244. In line with this, Bultmann (*Second Letter to the Corinthians*, 232) suggests that the passive "indicates that Paul is not conscious of himself as θεῖος ἀνήρ."

245. Rom. 10:8; 15:20; 1 Cor. 1:23; 9:16; 15:11; 2 Cor. 2:12; 4:5; 10:16; Gal. 1:8, 16; 2:2; cf. Phil. 1:15–16.

246. Bultmann, therefore, is not correct to suggest that "the passive κατειργάσθη is characteristic" of Paul (*Second Letter to the Corinthians*, 232).

247. Gal. 1:11: τὸ εὐαγγέλιον τὸ εὐαγγελισθὲν ὑπ' ἐμοῦ ("the gospel proclaimed by me").

248. Cf. Fee, *God's Empowering Presence*, 628n469.

249. Dieter Georgi, *The Opponents of Paul in Second Corinthians: A Study of Religious Propaganda in Late Antiquity* (Philadelphia: Fortress, 1986), 278, 289n54. According to Adolf Schlatter (*Die korinthische Theologie* [BFCT 18; Gütersloh: Bertelsmann, 1914], 110–11), the adversaries did not perform signs and wonders because they were false apostles; but this begs the question. See Georgi, *Opponents of Paul*, 294n118. Barnett (*Second Epistle to the Corinthians*, 580) assumes that Paul's opponents did not perform miracles.

250. E.g., Sanday and Headlam, *Romans*, 406.

by the Jerusalem leaders (Gal. 2:8–9; cf. 1:16; Acts 15:1–35), suggests Paul connects his opponents with Jerusalem.[251] From this connection, and perhaps from Peter's visit (1 Cor. 9:5),[252] whose reputation remained important to some (1:12; 3:22),[253] they would likely have been familiar with the importance of miracles to Jesus and his first followers, as well as their methods of miracle working. These methods most often, though not always (see below), centered around the miracle worker using a source of power-authority and being actively involved in directing it to particular supplicants to effect a healing or exorcism.[254]

Keeping in mind his self-deprecation, his not claiming any *charism* related to miracle working (see above), and his passive description of the miracles, could it not be that, in contrast to the active involvement of the super-apostles in their miracle working, Paul was not as directly involved in the miracles as in the proclaiming? That is, while he proclaimed the gospel, he did not also set out to heal and cast out demons like others, including Jesus. Nevertheless, as part of the response to his message, the Holy Spirit was received, and healings and exorcisms, for example, took place spontaneously among the people.

Such passive miracle working is not unknown in early Christian traditions. Notably, as Mark tells the story, initially without Jesus' knowledge and without his active involvement, a woman was healed by touching his clothing (Mark 5:25–34 // Matt. 9:20–22 // Luke 8:43–48). Luke says that people "even carried out the sick into the streets, and laid them on cots and mats, in order that Peter's shadow might fall on some of them as he came by" (Acts 5:15). Although the shadow was seen as an extension of the person,[255] Peter is not portrayed as actively involved in the miracle working. Further on, when describing the coming of the Spirit to the household of Cornelius, Luke says that "while Peter was still speaking, the Holy Spirit fell upon all who heard the word" (10:44). In that Luke does not portray Peter as directly

---

251. Cf. Barrett, *Second Epistle to the Corinthians*, 278.

252. Peter is singled out in 1 Cor. 9:5; on which Barrett comments, "It is hard to see why he should have been singled out for special mention here if he had not himself visited Corinth" (*First Epistle to the Corinthians*, 204).

253. See the discussion by Fee, *First Epistle to the Corinthians*, 404.

254. See the discussion of exorcistic techniques in Twelftree, *Name of Jesus*, 51–52. Though in relation to Luke's portrayal of Paul not acting on his own authority, cf. Lietaert Peerbolte, "Paul the Miracle Worker," 187.

255. See, e.g., Cicero, *Tusc.* 312.26; Virgil, *Ecl.* 10.75–76; Pliny, *Nat.* 17.18; 28.69; Dio Chrysostom, *2 Glor.* 4–5; Aelian, *Nat. an.* 6.14; Philostratus, *Her.* 1.3; Porphyry, *Antr. nymph.* 26; Pseudo-Aristotle, *Mir. ausc.* 145 (157), and the discussion by Pieter W. van der Horst, "Peter's Shadow: the Religio-Historical Background of Acts 5:15," *NTS* 23 (1976–77): 204–12.

involved either through prayer or the laying on of hands, the miracle of the coming and experience of the Spirit takes place apart from, yet associated with, Peter. Paul is also portrayed by Luke as indirectly involved in miracle working. Even though Paul was not present, handkerchiefs and aprons that had touched Paul's skin were said to be effective in healings and exorcisms (19:11–12). I can suggest, therefore, that Paul was not actively involved in healings and exorcism. Rather, as he preached the gospel in Corinth, miracles, including the obvious coming of the Spirit, and healings and exorcisms took place among the people.

(d) The function of miracles. If Paul is reminding the Corinthians that miracles did take place among them in relation to his initial ministry, in order to understand more of Paul's view of miracles, we need to ask what function they had for him. Ralph Martin argued that although Paul does not belittle them, because of the importance of miracle to others,[256] Paul does not put forward signs and wonders as evidence of his apostleship. Rather, for Paul, the primary evidence of his apostleship was his life and the changed lives that resulted from his preaching.[257] To the contrary, however, the natural reading of what Paul is saying is to bring the miracles into full view as central in authenticating his apostolic ministry.[258] Most obviously, the first appearance of "signs" early in the sentence ("the signs of the apostle . . . ," 2 Cor. 12:12) is used in the primary sense of "distinguishing marks."[259] In other words, Paul is saying that "The miracles that took place among you in relation to my ministry were the distinguishing marks of the apostle."

We also note that Paul says the miracles were "the signs" (τὰ . . . σημεῖα) of "the apostle" (τοῦ ἀποστόλου). The articles with "signs" and "apostle" indicate they are generic terms.[260] It is not, then, that Paul claims miracles as the distinguishing mark of his apostleship. Rather, Paul is implying that it was generally known that miracles were the distinguishing signs of all apostles.[261]

256. Martin suggests that "the idea of θεῖοι ἄνδρες, 'divine men,' or something like it, was present at Corinth" (*2 Corinthians*, 434).

257. Cf. Käsemann, "Die Legitimität des Apostels," 62.

258. Thrall, *Second Epistle to the Corinthians*, 2:840.

259. BDAG, "σημεῖον," 920, citing from the NT Matt. 16:3; 24:3, 30; 26:48; Mark 13:4; Luke 2:12, 34; 11:29, 30; 21:7; Rom. 4:11; 1 Cor. 14:22; 2 Cor. 12:12a; 2 Thess. 3:17. On the different uses of σημεῖον in 2 Cor. 12:12, see Plummer, *Second Epistle of St. Paul to the Corinthians*, 359; Lambrecht, *Second Corinthians*, 211–12; Harris, *Second Epistle to the Corinthians*, 873.

260. See Robertson, *Grammar*, 408; cf. 757; Thrall, *Second Epistle to the Corinthians*, 2:837n508.

261. Contrast N. N. Taylor, "Apostolic Identity and the Conflicts in Corinth and Galatia," in *Paul and His Opponents*, ed. Stanley E. Porter (PSt 2; Leiden: Brill, 2005), 105. Taylor suggests it is not clear to what extent the criteria of apostleship were generally current in the early church.

Further, for Paul, apostles are not confined to the Twelve (Rom. 16:7; 1 Cor. 5:9; 15:7); apostles are those to whom the risen Lord (1 Cor. 9:1)[262] gave particular commissions (2 Cor. 10:13–16; cf. 1 Cor. 15:8–9) to found churches (1 Cor. 9:2).[263] Thus, the function of miracles as marking out apostles meant that for Paul, miracles would have been characteristic of his ministry,[264] and that he would have considered them to have been as widespread as the reach of the mission of the apostles.

However, Paul does not portray the performance of miracles as the only or even most important distinguishing feature of the apostle. For Paul, the most important qualifications for claiming to be an apostle are seeing the risen Lord and being called by him,[265] and enduring many hardships (2 Cor. 11:23–27).[266] He also points to converts or churches that result from the work of an apostle[267] and to visions and revelations (12:1)[268] as evidence of apostleship.[269] We have also seen that he appears to acknowledge that his opponents also conducted miracles. Even if essential, miracles are, then, only one of a number of features of his life and ministry that Paul saw as authenticating his ministry. Moreover, from what he says in other places, it is the visionary call experience of the risen Lord that held the key to his and others' apostleship (1 Cor. 15:7–9; Gal. 1:11–17), not the miracles.

Further, in deliberately using the miracles of the exodus as the interpretive grid for the miracles that took place during his ministry, Paul is claiming that they had, in themselves, a salvific function.[270] That is, as the miracles of Moses were the means of salvation for those involved, and also the miracles of Jesus were the realization of salvation for the supplicant, so Paul saw the apostolic

262. Fee, *First Epistle to the Corinthians*, 394–95.

263. James D. G. Dunn, *The Theology of Paul the Apostle* (Grand Rapids: Eerdmans, 1998), 540–41.

264. See Georgi, *Opponents of Paul*, 281.

265. 1 Cor. 9:1; 2 Cor. 10:13–16; cf. 1 Cor. 15:8–9.

266. "Miracles were one part of the badge of the apostle; endurance was the other" (Barnett, *Second Epistle to the Corinthians*, 580) captures only a part of Paul's perspective.

267. 1 Cor. 9:2; 2 Cor. 3:2; cf. 1 Cor. 4:15; 1 Thess. 2:19–20.

268. See the discussion by Thrall, *Second Epistle to the Corinthians*, 2:774–75.

269. Paul does not accept the Corinthians' view that a person being financially supported by the church was a sign of an apostle (cf. 2 Cor. 11:7–11; 12:13–21). See Sumney, *Opponents of Paul*, 118–20. Paul's emphatic αὐτὸς ἐγώ ("I myself") in 2 Cor. 12:13 may be intended as a contrast to false apostles (see Martin, *2 Corinthians*, 439).

270. In view of Luke using the same triadic description of the work of Jesus (Acts 2:22), it may be possible to suggest that Paul was also echoing the salvific work of Jesus. However, Barnett goes beyond any evidence that we have to suggest, "The effect of giving this triad [signs, wonders, and mighty works] as 'the signs of the apostle' is to tie the apostle to God's great redemptive event under the new covenant, focussed on Christ's death and resurrection" (*Second Epistle to the Corinthians*, 581).

miracles, including of his ministry, having the same function: miracles were realized soteriology.

(e) Conclusion. The basis of a criticism from the Corinthians appears to be that in light of the super-apostles' ministry involving the active performance of signs of their apostleship, they did not see Paul doing the same thing. They concluded Paul was neither spiritual nor an apostle through whom Christ spoke. In offering proof that Christ was speaking through him (2 Cor. 13:3), and that he was not inferior to the super-apostles, Paul has argued on two fronts. On the one hand, he has just argued that his weakness enabled the power of God to be seen in his life (12:9–10). On the other hand, I have suggested that Paul, admitting he is weak and nothing (12:11), challenges the Corinthians to recall that though he may not have been actively involved in them, salvific authenticating miracles—most probably not unlike those known in the Jesus tradition—characteristically did take place among them in association with his ministry (12:12).

Elsewhere Paul stakes the authenticity of his apostolic ministry on his call and vision of Jesus[271] and the conversion of his hearers (see 217n267 above). The present context, in which he is answering criticism of his supernatural abilities, demands that he bring the miracles into play as authenticating marks characteristic of his ministry.[272] In doing so we can also see that he took the miracles to be salvific, or realized soteriology. In terms of performing miracles, the essential difference between Paul as a miracle worker and his charismatic opponents (and some other Christians) is that he took the costly personal risk of not claiming to perform them or that they were his, even though they took place in relation to his ministry. There remains one more place in Paul's correspondence where he appears to mention the miraculous.

7.8 Romans 15:18–19

In the letter to the Romans we have Paul's most mature writing, his last extant letter, probably drafted in late 57 or early 58 CE[273] when he was in Corinth.[274] Whatever Paul's reasons for writing—preparation for a western mission, support for the collection for Jerusalem (Rom. 15:14–33), or an exercise in diplomacy to bring about unity (10:14–21; 11:13–36), for example[275]—they

271. 1 Cor. 1:1; 9:1; 2 Cor. 1:1; cf. Gal. 1:1; see also Col. 1:1.
272. Cf. Thrall, *Second Epistle to the Corinthians*, 2:840–41.
273. See, e.g., the brief discussion by Jewett, *Romans*, 18–23, esp. 18, and those cited in n. 87.
274. See esp. Rom. 16:23; cf. Acts 18:7; 1 Cor. 1:14, and the discussion in ibid., 21–22.
275. For a brief though thorough summary of the debate concerning Paul's purpose for writing Romans, see ibid., 80–91.

included a desire to set out a most sustained and reflective defense of his gospel (1:16–17).[276]

Near the end of letter, coming to the paragraph of interest to us (15:14–33), Paul's theological discourse is complete. Paul returns in a recapitulation to reinforce themes he set out in his introduction:[277] his ministry to the Gentiles (1:13; cf. 15:15–21), the frequent hindrances to his visit to Rome (1:13; cf. 15:22)—which he hopes will be mutually beneficial (1:11–12; cf. 15:23–24, 28–29)—and his prayer for them (1:9–10), as well as his request for prayer from them (15:30–32).[278] In the first section of this paragraph (15:14–16) Paul is "undisguisedly wooing the reader," as Ernst Käsemann put it.[279] In the second section (15:17–21) Paul gives a succinct description of his ministry strategy that includes the statement that is of particular importance to us. In what Robert Jewett calls an "involuted sentence,"[280] with a double negative, Paul awkwardly expresses his self-consciousness in speaking about his ministry:[281] "For I will not presume to speak about anything that Christ has not accomplished through me, to win obedience from the Gentiles, word and deed, in the power of signs and wonders, in the power of the Spirit of God" (15:18–19a, my translation).[282]

In the last section we saw that, in defending his apostleship before the Corinthians, Paul was "content with weakness . . . for the sake of Christ" (2 Cor. 12:10; see §7.7 above). Here the same self-effacing approach to ministry, which directs attention to the work of Christ, remains an important interpretive frame for him (Rom. 15:18–19). Paul encapsulates the winning of the "obedience" (ὑπακοή, cf. 1:5) of the Gentiles as the "accomplishment" (κατεργάζομαι) of Christ "through me" (δι᾽ ἐμοῦ) as "word and deed" (λόγῳ καὶ ἔργῳ).[283] Contrary to English translations, Paul does not say that what Christ accomplished was "through" word and deed (e.g., NRSV), which has the effect of distancing the word and deed from Christ. Rather, Paul says "Christ accomplished through me . . . word and deed" (15:18b), keeping

276. See Dunn, *Theology of Paul*, 25.

277. Jewett, *Romans*, 902.

278. James D. G. Dunn (*Romans 9–16* [WBC 38B; Dallas: Word, 1988], 857) presses the material in finding further parallels.

279. Käsemann, *Romans*, 391.

280. Jewett, *Romans*, 909.

281. Cranfield, *Romans*, 2.758; N. T. Wright, "The Letter to the Romans," *NIB* 10:754.

282. On this convoluted sentence, see C. K. Barrett, *The Epistle to the Romans*, 2nd ed. (BNTC; London: Black, 1991), 253; and the discussion by Goulder, *Competing Mission*, 252–53.

283. Without justification, Joseph Fitzmyer translates λόγῳ καὶ ἔργῳ as "either in word or in deed" (*Romans: A New Translation with Introduction and Commentary* [AB 33; New York: Doubleday, 1993], 713).

Christ firmly connected to the word and deed as "the hidden author," as Franz Leenhardt put it.[284]

From the wider use of the two words in association with each other, "word and deed" is shown to be a common Greek phrase encompassing a person's entire activity,[285] so that Paul is describing the entirety of what Christ has accomplished (through him). At this point readers might assume Paul had in mind not only the spoken word, but also his traveling, his sufferings, his letter writing, and his care of them that constituted the accomplishments of Christ.[286] Even if this were at least part of what Paul intended to convey, he immediately goes on to give a more precise description of Christ's accomplishments and to explain their means: "in the power of signs and wonders" (15:19).[287] Although some commentators, particularly those in an earlier generation, pass over this statement making little or no comment,[288] in light of my discussions so far we would be hard pressed to avoid seeing in this unmodified phrase a deliberate reference to miracles (see §7.7 above).[289] What these miracles are we do not know, though from what we have seen so far we can reasonably assume that Paul considered them salvific or redemptive[290] and similar to those conducted by Jesus (cf. §5.4 above).[291] In any case, the precise nature of the miracles is not important in what Paul is saying. For, having explained that Christ's accomplishments were "in the power of signs and wonders," he continues with a parallel phrase: "in the power of the Spirit [of God]."[292]

284. Franz J. Leenhardt, *The Epistle to the Romans: A Commentary*, trans. Harold Knight (London: Lutterworth, 1961), 369. The christocentric nature of the entire paragraph is noted by Fee, *God's Empowering Presence*, 628, citing Rom. 15:14, 16, 17, 18, 19, 21, 29, 30.

285. See BDAG, "ἔργον," 390, citing, e.g., Cebes, *Tab.* 2.2; Lucian, *Tox.* 35; Sir. 3:8; 16:12; 4 Macc. 5:38; *T. Ab.* 9:4; Josephus, *Ant.* 17.220; *Ag. Ap.* 2.12; *2 Clem.* 17:7. See also, e.g., Homer, *Od.* 2.273; Josephus, *Ant.* 17.47; *J.W.* 7.343; *Ag. Ap.* 2.1; Philo, *Leg.* 3.44; *Post.* 87, 181; *Plant.* 156; *Somn.* 1.182; 2.302; *Mos.* 1.151; *Prob.* 74; *Praem.* 119; *Virt.* 56; *QE* 2.16; cf. *1 Clem.* 30:3; *2 Clem.* 13:3. In the NT see Luke 24:19; Acts 7:22; Rom. 15:18; Col. 3:17; 2 Thess. 2:17; 1 John 3:18.

286. Cf. Cranfield, *Romans*, 2:759; Jewett, *Romans*, 910.

287. Cf. Fitzmyer, *Romans*, 713; Fee, *God's Empowering Presence*, 629.

288. E.g., C. H. Dodd, *The Epistle of Paul to the Romans* (MNTC; London: Hodder & Stoughton, 1932), 227; Karl Barth, *The Epistle to the Romans*, trans. Edwyn C. Hoskins (London: Oxford University Press, 1933), 532–33.

289. See Origen, *Comm. Rom.* 10.12; Sanday and Headlam, *Romans*, 406; Barrett, *Second Epistle to the Corinthians*, 321; Cranfield, *Romans*, 2:759; Fee, *God's Empowering Presence*, 630; Schreiber, *Wundertäter*, 269.

290. Cf. Dunn, *Romans 9–16*, 868; Schreiber, *Wundertäter*, 202.

291. So also Colin G. Kruse, *New Testament Foundations for Ministry* (London: Marshall, Morgan & Scott, 1983), 128; Eduard Lohse, *Der Brief an die Römer* (KEK 4; Göttingen: Vandenhoeck & Ruprecht, 2003), 395.

292. Rom. 15:19a: ἐν δυνάμει σημείων καὶ τεράτων ἐν δυνάμει πνεύματος [θεοῦ]. On the status of θεοῦ in the text, see Metzger, *Commentary*, 473.

Though a chiasmus is not perfectly formed, Paul may have intended his ideas to be read chiastically:

A what Christ has accomplished through me
  B to win obedience from the Gentiles
    C word and deed[293]
  B′ in the power of signs and wonders
A′ in the power of the Spirit of God[294]

A number of points on Paul's understanding of the miraculous emerge, reinforced by the rough chiasmus. First, linking Christ's accomplishments with the power of the Spirit enables Paul to describe his ministry—winning the obedience of the Gentiles through signs and wonders—while keeping before the readers his concern to attribute that ministry to Christ. The miracles are not his doing, but are of Christ or the Spirit.[295] In this point, along with our noting that in Galatians 3:5 Paul attributes the miracles to God (see §7.2 above), there is support for my suggestion in the last section that the miracles of Paul were not performed directly by him, but took place spontaneously as he preached (see §7.7 above).

Second, Paul says that his ministry is "in the power" (ἐν δυνάμει) of signs and wonders, and the Spirit. Keeping in mind that the two phrases using ἐν δυνάμει form a hendiadys—"signs and wonders" and "the Spirit" each nuancing the meaning of the other—and the wider use of "in the power" in his letters,[296] where it is used either in relation to miracles (Rom. 15:19; 1 Cor. 2:5) or the resurrection (1 Cor. 15:43) or in contrast to speech (1 Cor. 4:20), we can suppose that Paul probably is not saying that his ministry was attested by signs and wonders.[297] Instead, he probably is saying that his ministry was based on or conducted on the basis of, or strength of, the miracles (or Spirit). It is, therefore, not so much that the miracles proved his ministry of words,

293. In view of "word" and "deed" forming a recognizable phrase for Paul's readers, it is probably unwise to follow Rengstorf ("σημεῖον," 259) in dissolving the phrase so that "word" refers to the Spirit and "deed" to the signs and wonders. Cf. Leenhardt (*Romans*, 369n§) offers a similar suggestion. Moreover, this approach to the chiasm is undermined by Cranfield (*Romans*, 2:758–59), noting that nowhere else in the Pauline corpus is ἔργον used of miraculous work.

294. On Paul intending a chiasm here, see the various suggestions by, e.g., Leenhardt, *Romans*, 369; Dunn, *Romans 9–16*, 857. Cf. Cranfield, *Romans*, 2:758–59.

295. In proposing that the signs are the "work" of the apostles and the "word" is inspired by the Spirit, Matthew Black (*Romans* [NCB; London: Oliphants, 1973], 175) misses Paul's point of attributing all his ministry to Christ (or the Spirit).

296. Ἐν δυνάμει occurs in Paul's letters in Rom. 1:4; 15:13, 19 (2x); 1 Cor. 2:5; 4:20; 15:43; 2 Cor. 6:7; 1 Thess. 1:5; cf. Col. 1:29; 2 Thess. 1:11.

297. Cranfield, *Romans*, 2:759.

but that his ministry arose out of the miraculous or the power of the Spirit. The significance of this point is not only that it establishes the fundamental centrality of the miracles in the ministry of Paul—the miracles as much as the speaking was the ministry—but also that just as Jesus saw his ministry as miracle based,[298] so also did Paul.

Third, despite the paucity of references to miracles in his letters, in this paragraph Paul makes clear that he saw the miracles not only as the basis of his work but also as central to, and profoundly important in, the routine of his ministry.[299] The theme "signs and wonders" finding a place in a recapitulation and summary statement that restates motifs from his introduction, as well as echoing ideas from his Corinthian correspondence,[300] shows that Paul is drawing on the core matrix of his values and concerns when he mentions miracles. Also, given that Paul is attempting, at least in part, to convey his understanding of the gospel to readers who are likely to have limited knowledge of him (Rom. 16:3–13),[301] and that he provides so little information to them, is the strongest evidence not only that miracles are a high-profile, integral, and regular part of his thinking and ministry strategy,[302] but also that he presumes he shares this understanding with his readers.[303]

Fourth, it is to be noted that Paul does not see his ministry of proclaiming the gospel (as he sometimes calls it) as confined to, or understood only in terms of, his words or the verbal message he preaches. Indeed, in the final

298. See Twelftree, "Miracles of Jesus," 104–24.

299. See also Fee, *God's Empowering Presence*, 632; Jewett, *Romans*, 911.

300. Note γνῶσις ("knowledge") in Rom. 15:14; e.g., 1 Cor. 1:5; 8:1, 7, 10, 11; 12:8; 13:2, 8; 14:6; 2 Cor. 2:14; 4:6; 6:6; 8:7; 10:5; 11:6; τολμᾶν ("to presume") in Rom. 15:18; e.g., 2 Cor. 10:2, 12; 11:21; ὑπακοή ("obedience") in Rom. 1:5; 15:18; e.g., 2 Cor. 7:15; Paul's authority in Rom. 15:18–19; e.g., 1 Cor. 9:1–2; 15:9; 2 Cor. 12:12; 13:3; cf. Gal. 1:1, 11–16; the character and scope of his mission including the Gentiles in Rom. 15:16, 18, 19, 20, 21, 24, 26, 27; e.g., 1:5, 13; 1 Cor. 1:23; 3:10; 2 Cor. 10:15–16; προπέμπειν ("to send on one's way") in Rom. 15:24; e.g., 1 Cor. 16:6; 2 Cor. 1:16; and the collection for Jerusalem in Rom. 15:25–29; 1 Cor. 16:1–4; 2 Cor. 8–9; cf. Gal. 2:10. See also, Fee, *Presence*, 629; Dunn, *Romans 9–16*, 857.

301. Peter Lampe, *From Paul to Valentinus: Christians at Rome in the First Two Centuries*, trans. Michael Steinhauser, ed. Marshall D. Johnson (Minneapolis: Fortress, 2003), 167–68. Although in the nineteenth century there was considerable support for regarding Rom. 16 as a separate letter, it is now generally viewed as an original part of Paul's letter to the Romans. For a brief history, as well as summary of the recent debate on the relationship of the various parts of the final chapter (Rom. 16:1–27) to the remainder of the letter, see Harry Y. Gamble Jr., *The Textual History of the Letter to the Romans: A Study in Textual and Literary Criticism* (Grand Rapids: Eerdmans, 1977), and Peter Lampe, "Zur Textgeschichte des Römerbriefes," *NovT* 27 (1985): 273–77.

302. Cf. Fee, *God's Empowering Presence*, 630; N. T. Wright, "The Letter to the Romans," *NIB* 10: 754.

303. Also, see Jewett, *Romans*, 911.

clause where he describes the result of his ministry—"so that [ὥστε][304] from Jerusalem and as far around as Illyricum[305] I have fulfilled [πεπληρωκέναι] the gospel of Christ" (Rom. 15:19b)—he allows word and deed, signs and wonders, to stand for his entire ministry. For Paul, therefore, (fulfilling or proclaiming) the gospel involves not only words or propositions, but also actions or deeds empowered by the Spirit,[306] in particular miracles. Moreover, in this statement Paul makes clear to his readers in Rome that the miraculous involved in the coming of the gospel was not an occasional aspect of his work but characterized his ministry "from Jerusalem and as far around as Illyricum" (15:19b), in other words, wherever he preached. Although he sees Paul conducting the miracles himself, Jacob Jervell is surely right to see in this survey of his work that Paul is saying miraculous activity was everywhere and regularly part of his ministry.[307]

7.9 Conclusions

In this chapter I have examined Paul's statements that have been part of the scholarly discussion regarding his involvement in, and understanding of, the miraculous. I came to this exercise with significant and arguably credible presuppositions. Notably, Paul's Jewish heritage, his eschatological perspective, the information he had received from earlier followers of Jesus, and his own experience of the miraculous made it highly likely that the miraculous would have played a significant role in his ministry. However, the broad view of Paul's occasional correspondence—the wide-angled view of Paul's ministry taken from the vantage point of the twenty-first century—does not allow the casual viewer to see the place of the miraculous in Paul's life and ministry. A more finely focused telephoto lens, nevertheless, picks up not only the details of the miraculous, but also how the miracles function in the whole view of Paul's ministry.

With varying degrees of clarity, the passages that I examined brought into focus the importance and function of the miraculous in Paul's ministry. In the earliest letter we have from Paul he describes the coming of the gospel to his readers in terms not only of word but also of power, Holy Spirit, and

304. Although it is uncertain how far back ὥστε ("so that") reaches in Rom. 15:19b (15:15 or 15:18), it will encompass his description of his ministry in 15:18–19a. Cf. Cranfield, *Romans*, 2:760.

305. On the debate about the sweep of Paul's grandiose claims see Dunn, *Romans 9–16*, 863–64.

306. Cf. Fee, *God's Empowering Presence*, 629.

307. Jervell, "Signs," 91–92.

completeness, or lacking nothing (1 Thess. 1:5). This was, we saw, not only more than a description "of being grasped by divine power," as Dunn described it;[308] it was also more than a limited reference to miracles such as healings or exorcisms. I argued that since the gospel was, for Paul, an unhindered realization or expression of the Spirit, its coming would have been thought to involve the full panoply of what he understood as the work of the Spirit, which included the inherently miraculous *charismata*, as well as the so-called fruit of the Spirit.

From the letter to the Galatians, it appears that Paul so linked the experience of the miraculous with the coming of the gospel that it could be seen as coincidental with the coming and work of the Spirit and, therefore, as evidence of God's activity (3:1–5). Concomitantly, in 1 Corinthians Paul reminds his readers that the gospel was put before them not in the garb of rhetorical skill but in the authenticating power of the Spirit (1 Cor. 2:1–5). Therefore, in defending himself against those who were looking for a miracle-working rhetorician, Paul points out that as the power of God is seen in the crucifixion, so through his (Paul's) weakness the power of the Spirit of God is materialized in the miraculous. As a result, the Corinthians were able to respond to and depend not on human wisdom, but on the power of God (cf. 2 Cor. 6:6–7).

We probably see something of Paul's view concerning the function of the miraculous in his equating the kingdom of God with power (1 Cor. 4:19–20). As with Jesus before him, Paul understood the miracles to express or realize God's powerful presence. The kingdom of God was not attended by miracles, but it was the expression of power in the miraculous. Similarly, in using the exodus to interpret the miracles associated with his ministry, Paul claims for them a salvific function. As the miracles of Moses and Jesus were the realization of salvation for those involved, Paul saw the miracles of his ministry as realized soteriology. It is not surprising, then, that he firmly links the miraculous with the authenticity and function of his apostleship. This link between miracles and his apostleship shows how fundamentally important the miracles were for his ministry and his self-understanding. The link also explains why the miracles come into clear focus only occasionally and when his apostleship and credentials are under question or, as in Romans, when he wants to establish his credentials.[309]

---

308. Dunn, *Jesus and the Spirit*, 226. See also Kendell H. Easley, "The Pauline Usage of *Pneumati* as a Reference to the Spirit of God," *JETS* 27 (1984): 304.

309. In Paul's three earliest letters (1 Thessalonians, Philippians, Philemon) there is neither clear reference to miracle (cf. 1 Thess. 1:5) nor does he introduce himself as an apostle or seek to defend his apostleship. However, in the four later letters, when his credentials are either in question (1 Cor. 9:1; 2 Cor. 12:11) or needing to be established (Rom. 1:1–6; Gal. 1:11–24),

From the last reference we have of Paul's concerning the miraculous (Rom. 15:18–19) it becomes clear that, despite the few references through his writings, Paul saw the miraculous as an integral and profoundly important aspect of his day-to-day ministry, wherever he went.[310] We cannot avoid concluding that Paul did not consider his gospel to be merely preaching. Nor were the miracles secondary to the preaching.[311] Instead, the gospel was always word and deed: a message of salvation realized in and (therefore) authenticated by the Spirit's manifestation or materialization in the miraculous.

Yet, we still have to explain why Paul does not mention performing miracles. At least we can say that in failing to qualify what mention he does make of the miraculous, it cannot be that he is trying to minimize the importance of this aspect of his ministry.[312] Also, in light of the claimed importance of the miraculous (before and outside the Corinthian correspondence), we have to explain why his critics, as well as the Corinthians, did not see Paul as a miracle worker. Indeed, at least superficially, the picture that emerges from Paul's letters is of a preacher, who is probably physically poor, not using the best rhetorical skills. It is also very clear that he is careful never to lay claim to conducting miracles or to suggest that he was directly involved in their performance. At least in writing to the Galatians, his argument would have been undercut had he suggested the miracles were restricted to him or his presence. Moreover, in one of the clearest descriptions of the miracles taking place in relation to his ministry there is his puzzling use of the passive "were performed" (2 Cor. 12:12).

I have suggested that the resolution of this puzzle—the scenario that brings the pieces together—is that although miracles took place in association with his ministry, Paul neither set out to perform them nor orchestrated those that took place. Rather, as he preached, the Spirit's powerful presence was spontaneously manifested in the miraculous. This was God's doing, not Paul's. In the simplest terms, if pressed, Paul might say that the gospel was proclaimed when he did the preaching and Christ, through the Spirit, performed the miracles. In the next part of this study we turn to early interpreters of the apostle to see how they help us understand the historical Paul.

Paul begins by asserting his apostleship (Rom. 1:1; 1 Cor. 1:1; 2 Cor. 1:1; Gal. 1:1). Schreiber (*Wundertäter*, 271) is not quite correct in saying that Paul mentioned his miracles always in connection with his appearance as an apostle.

310. Cf. L. J. (Bert Jan) Lietaert Peerbolte, *Paul the Missionary* (CBET 34; Louvain: Peeters, 2003), 250.

311. As supposed by Käsemann, "Die Legitimität des Apostels," 33–71; Schreiber, *Wundertäter*, 274, 278.

312. Roetzel, *Paul*, 164.

Part 4

PAUL'S INTERPRETERS

8

Luke: Paul's Earliest Interpreter

R elative to the paucity of literature preserved from antiquity, there is a wealth of extant material offering interpretations of Paul: pseudepigraphal and epistolic texts, narratives about Paul, writings representing anti-Paulinism, and Paul as an object of interpretation.[1] And there has developed nothing short of an industry considering the history of the reception or influence (*Wirkungsgeschichte*) of Paul:[2] his life, his theology, and the texts that bear his name or seek to interpret him.[3]

We turn to Paul's early interpreters because from them we anticipate help in recovering the historical Paul in relation to the miraculous. However, among

---

1. The recent full discussion by Richard I. Pervo, *The Making of Paul: Constructions of the Apostle in Early Christianity* (Minneapolis: Fortress, 2010), takes into account the pseudepigraphal material (Colossians, Ephesians, 2 Thessalonians, 1 Timothy, 2 Timothy, Titus, *3 Corinthians*, *Laodiceans*, *Alexandrians*, the correspondence between Paul and Seneca); the epistolic tradition in early Christianity (Hebrews, James, 1 Peter, *1 Clement*, Ignatius of Antioch, Polycarp of Smyrna, 2 Peter, Dionysius of Corinth); the narratives about Paul (canonical Acts, the *Acts of Paul*, the *Epistula Apostolorum*, the *Acts of Peter*, the *Acts of Barnabas*, the *Acts of Titus*, the *Acts of Xanthippe*, Apocalypses, the *Pseudo-Clementines*); writings representing anti-Paulinism (Matthew and Hegesippus); and Paul as an object of interpretation (Marcion of Sinope, Paul among the "gnostics," and Irenaeus of Lyon).

2. Cf. Christopher Rowland, "Wirkungsgeschichte: Central or Peripheral to Biblical Exegesis?" *ScrB* 36 (2006): 1–11; Mark Knight, "*Wirkungsgeschichte*, Reception History, Reception Theory," *JSNT* 33 (2010): 137–46. Among recent discussions of the early reception of Paul, see William S. Babcock, ed., *Paul and the Legacies of Paul* (Dallas: Southern Methodist University Press, 1990); Andrew Gregory and Christopher Tuckett, eds., *The Reception of the New Testament in the Apostolic Fathers* (NTAF 1; Oxford: Oxford University Press, 2005); Andrew Gregory and Christopher Tuckett, eds., *Trajectories through the New Testament and the Apostolic Fathers* (NTAF 2; Oxford: Oxford University Press, 2005); Pervo, *Making of Paul*; Michael F. Bird and Joseph R. Dodson, eds., *Paul and the Second Century* (LNTS 412; London: T&T Clark, 2011). See also the discussion of recent research by Jens Schröter, "Actaforschung seit 1982. IV, Israel, die Juden und das Alte Testament: Paulusrezeption," *TRu* 73 (2008): 27–59.

3. For the three-part typology (letters, life, and theology) of reception, see Daniel Marguerat, "Paul après Paul: Une histoire de réception," *NTS* 54 (2008): 321–23.

themselves and in relation to Paul they offer conflicting reports and interpretations about his involvement in the miraculous. My task, then, is to examine and evaluate these varying interpretations to see what light they might shed on the historical Paul's relation to the miraculous.

While recognizing that earlier material is not free from dogmatic concerns, and not denying that later material can contain historically reliable material,[4] given the decay and tricks of human memory, as well as the introduction and change of ideas that take place during the transmission of traditions, we can expect the material in the canon—the earliest that we have about Paul—to be generally the most reliable in recovering the historical Paul. The next chapter will include a look into the second century for data that can help us understand the historical Paul in relation to the miraculous (see §9.7 below).

Included among the canonical interpreters of Paul is the Acts of the Apostles, which engages Paul in narrative form.[5] In this chapter we begin with Acts, not only because it is probably the earliest extant interpretation of Paul, but also because the text has been fundamentally important in the history of the interpretation of Paul and unavoidably brings to the fore a very apparent discrepancy between interpreters of Paul and what Paul himself has to say about the miraculous and his involvement in it.[6]

8.1 Luke and the Historical Paul

It is obvious from the amount of attention given to him, and the overall narrative thrust of Acts, that Luke was a great admirer of Paul and his abilities as a miracle worker.[7] However, our interest is not how Luke understands Paul

---

4. In relation to Jesus, see the criticism of Heinrich J. Holtzmann, notably his *Die synoptischen Evangelien: Ihr Ursprung und geschichtlicher Charakter* (Leipzig: Engelmann, 1863), by Ben F. Meyer, who says that Holtzmann and his generation "remained mesmerized by a siren song: the lure of early sources, the critical importance of reducing to a minimum the time-lag between event and account. . . . The earlier one went back, the better things got" (*The Aims of Jesus* [London: SCM, 1979], 37–38).

5. Cf. Daniel Marguerat, ed., *Reception of Paulinism in Acts* [= *Réception du Paulinisme dans les Actes des Apôtres*] (BETL 229; Leuven: Peeters, 2009); Thomas E. Phillips, *Paul, His Letters, and Acts* (LPS; Peabody, MA: Hendrickson, 2009).

6. Differences between the Paul of Acts and of the letters have long been recognized. Note the recent detailed and balanced treatment by Phillips, *Paul.*

7. For literature on the miraculous and the Acts of the Apostles, see that cited by Augustin George, "Le miracle dans l'oeuvre de Luc," in *Les miracles de Jésus selon le Nouveau Testament*, ed. Xavier Léon-Dufour (Paris: Seuil, 1977), 249–68, republished as "Le Miracle," in *Études sur l'oeuvre de Luc* (SB; Paris: Gabalda, 1978), 133–48 (133n1); Gerhard Schneider, *Die Apostelgeschichte*, 2 vols. (HTKNT 5; Freiburg: Herder, 1980–82), 1:304–10; Todd Penner, "Madness in the Method? The Acts of the Apostles in Current Study," *CurBR* 2 (2004): 262–63.

in relation to the miraculous,[8] but how far, if at all, his description is critically credible and reliable and can contribute to a reconstruction of the historical Paul in relation to the miraculous.[9]

In 1845 Ferdinand Christian Baur concluded not only that a comparison of Paul's letters and Luke's Acts "leads to the conclusion that . . . historical truth can only belong to one of them,"[10] but also that Acts is the one that gives a false picture of the apostle.[11] Contrary to Baur, in 1909, Adolf von Harnack concluded not only that as a whole Acts was genuinely historical work, "but even in the majority of its details it is trustworthy." He went on to say, "Except for a few panegyric aberrations in the direction of the Primitive Community, it follows no bias that distorts its representation of the actual course of events, and its author had sufficient knowledge to justify him in coming forward as an historian."[12]

In the ensuing century the historical accuracy of Luke's narrative has continued to be the focus of discussion,[13] with opinions varying greatly. On the one hand, in the tradition of Baur, Dennis MacDonald, for example, argues that Luke had access to traditions and sources, though they were not determinative for him, and that he "composed many of his narratives without traditions to inform him."[14] Also, Gerd Lüdemann, though concluding that "Acts remains an important source for the history of early Christianity alongside the letters of Paul,"[15] credits Luke with constantly twisting real history to theological ends.[16]

8. This is the concern of Stefan Schreiber, *Paulus als Wundertäter: Redaktionsgeschichtliche Untersuchungen zur Apostelgeschichte und den authentischen Paulusbriefen* (BZNW 79; Berlin: de Gruyter, 1996), 13–158.

9. That students of Acts have not shown much interest in the historical Paul behind the text of Acts, see Penner, "Madness," 246.

10. Ferdinand Christian Baur, *Paul the Apostle of Jesus Christ: His Life and Works, His Epistles and Teachings*, 2 vols. in 1 (1845; repr., Peabody, MA: Hendrickson, 2003), 1:5.

11. Ibid., 1:255. For a recent summary of the apparent discrepancies between Acts and Paul, see Marguerat, "Paul après Paul," 318–20.

12. Adolf von Harnack, *The Acts of the Apostles*, trans. J. R. Wilkinson (New York: Putnam, 1909), 298–99. See the brief discussion of Harnack by Jacob Jervell, "The Signs of an Apostle: Paul's Miracles," in *The Unknown Paul: Essays on Luke-Acts and Early Christian History* (Minneapolis: Augsburg, 1984), 78–79.

13. See, e.g., those surveyed by Giuseppe Betori, "La storiografia degli Atti: La ricerca nel nostro secolo: rassegna e valutazioni," *RivB* 33 (1985): 107–23; Joel B. Green and Michael C. McKeever, *Luke-Acts and New Testament Historiography* (IBRBib; Grand Rapids: Baker Academic, 1994), 102–9; also C. K. Barrett, "The Historicity of Acts," *JTS* 50 (1999): 515–34.

14. Dennis R. MacDonald, *Does the New Testament Imitate Homer? Four Cases from the Acts of the Apostles* (New Haven: Yale University Press, 2003), 151.

15. Gerd Lüdemann, *The Acts of the Apostles: What Really Happened in the Earliest Days of the Church* (Amherst, NY: Prometheus, 2005), 397.

16. Ibid., 253. For others who are more skeptical of the historical accuracy, see the discussion by Penner, "Madness," 226–33.

On the other hand, in the tradition of Harnack, in answer to his own question "The Acts of the Apostles: Historical Record or Theological Reconstruction?" F. F. Bruce says that Luke "did not allow his theology to distort his history."[17] Similarly, Colin Hemer concludes in support of "the general reliability of the narrative" of Acts.[18]

In turn, opinion of Luke's portrait of Paul is equally varied.[19] Perhaps, however, most would follow in some way Philipp Vielhauer's general view that there is a material distance between Paul and Acts, if not following his view that Luke "presents no specifically Pauline idea."[20] Others, while recognizing differences between the Paul of Paul and the Paul of Acts, see Luke as complementing or completing what is lacking in the letters. Jacob Jervell, for example, argues that "The Lukan Paul, the picture of Paul in Acts, is a completion, a filling up of the Pauline one, so that in order to get at the historical Paul, we cannot do without Acts and Luke."[21]

Making our way through this minefield—using Acts as a source to help reconstruct the historical Paul in relation to the miraculous—four important points are to be taken into account. First, there are some general historiographical matters. The assumption that I will share with others is that Luke, like all those (ancient or modern) supposing to write about the past, has finite resources. Also, along with his intentions to convey historical information, he has ideological agendas[22] and methodological perspectives (cf. Luke 1:1–4)[23] that have created and maintain an unavoidable distance and dissonance between story and supposed

---

17. F. F. Bruce, "The Acts of the Apostles: Historical Record or Theological Reconstruction?" *ANRW* II.25.3 (1985): 2600.

18. Hemer, *Acts*, 412. On the miracle stories in particular, see, e.g., Jervell, "Signs," 82.

19. The discussion of Luke's portrait of Paul has been extensive and continues. See, e.g., Paul-Gerhard Müller, "Der 'Paulinismus' in der Apostelgeschichte: Ein forschungsgeschichtlicher Überblick," in *Paulus in den neutestamentlichen Spätschriften: Zur Paulus Rezeption im Neuen Testament*, ed. Karl Kertelge (QD 89; Freiburg: Herder, 1981), 157–201; Eckhard Plümacher, "Acta-Forschung 1974–1982 (Fortsetzung und Schluss)," *TRu* 49 (1984): 153–58; Green and McKeever, *Luke-Acts*, 131–40; Barrett, "Historicity of Acts," esp. 532; François Bovon, *Luke the Theologian: Fifty-five Years of Research*, 2nd ed. (Waco: Baylor University Press, 2006), 396–406; Schröter, "Actaforschung," 27–59.

20. Philipp Vielhauer, "On the Paulinism of Acts," in *Studies in Luke-Acts*, ed. Leander E. Keck and J. L. Martyn (London: SPCK, 1968), 48.

21. Jacob Jervell, "Paul in the Acts of the Apostles: Tradition, History, Theology," in *The Unknown Paul: Essays on Luke-Acts and Early Christian History* (1979; repr. Minneapolis: Augsburg, 1984), 70. See also the discussion by Daniel R. Schwartz, "The End of the Line: Paul in the Canonical Book of Acts," in Babcock, *Paul*, 3–24.

22. E.g., that Luke has a "highly charged and theologically sophisticated political" agenda is argued by C. Kavin Rowe, *World Upside Down: Reading Acts in the Graeco-Roman Age* (New York: Oxford University Press, 2009), 4; see also 162–76.

23. Notable on Luke's agenda is Daniel Marguerat, *The First Christian Historian: Writing the "Acts of the Apostles,"* trans. Ken McKinney, Gregory J. Laughery, and Richard Bauckham

event.[24] We cannot, therefore, equate what we read in Acts with "what actually happened."[25] Indeed, in recent decades it has become clear to historiographers that the line between what happened and what was perceived to have happened is not easily drawn.[26] Further, even if the broad outline of Luke's history,[27] or particular details of his narrative,[28] can be shown to be reliable, it remains the obligation of the historian to investigate and test the historicity of any story that is asked to carry some historical burden. Put another way: even if Luke's work as a whole, or one of his stories in particular, can be deemed historical (having a conceptually credible correspondence with his world)—has the "feel" of a real event[29]—the historicity (the reliable reporting of actual events) of the whole or its parts still has to be established at each point.[30]

Second, if we were certain of the date at which Acts was written, we could assess with more confidence its usefulness as a source for reconstructing the historical Paul.[31] But certainty eludes us. Notwithstanding, on the one hand, it is unlikely that Acts can be dated as early as the 60s,[32] at least because in

(SNTSMS 121; Cambridge: Cambridge University Press, 2002), 1–25. Recent discussions of the purpose of Acts are brought together by Penner, "Madness," 258–60.

24. See the discussion, and those cited, by Penner, "Madness," e.g., 253–54. More recently, on Luke among ancient historians, see, e.g., Darryl W. Palmer, "Acts and the Ancient Historical Monograph," in *The Book of Acts in Its Ancient Literary Setting*, ed. Bruce W. Winter and Andrew D. Clarke (BAFCS 1; Grand Rapids: Eerdmans; Carlisle: Paternoster, 1993), 1–29; Marguerat, *Christian Historian*; Ben Witherington III, ed., *History, Literature, and Society in the Book of Acts* (Cambridge: Cambridge University Press, 1996).

25. The infamous phrase "wie es eigentlich gewesen," attributed to Leopold von Ranke (1795–1886), one of the founding fathers of modern history, is to be traced to Thucydides, *Hist.* 2.48.3. See Konrad Repgen, "Über Rankes Diktum von 1824: 'Bloss sagen, wie es eigentlich gewesen,'" *HJ* 102 (1982): 445–49.

26. Generally, see, e.g., Richard J. Evans, *In Defence of History* (London: Granta, 1997), esp. chap. 8, "Objectivity and Its Limits." In particular, see Joel B. Green, "Internal Repetition in Luke-Acts: Contemporary Narratology and Lucan Historiography," in Witherington, *History, Literature, and Society*, 298.

27. Bruce, "Acts," 2576.

28. See ibid., 2569–603; Bruce M. Metzger, "Ancient Astrological Geography and Acts 2:9–11," in *Apostolic History and the Gospel: Biblical and Historical Essays Presented to F. F. Bruce on His 60th Birthday*, ed. W. Ward Gasque and Ralph P. Martin (Exeter: Paternoster, 1970), 123–33; Hemer, *Acts*, esp. chap. 5.

29. See Robert J. Miller, "When Is It Futile to Argue about the Historical Jesus? A Response to Bock, Keener, and Webb," *JSHJ* 9 (2011): 89.

30. See the succinct discussion by Penner, "Madness," 252–55.

31. Cf. Joseph B. Tyson, "Why Dates Matter: The Case of the Acts of the Apostles," *Fourth R* 18, no. 2 (2005): 8–11, 14, 17–18.

32. Joseph A. Fitzmyer (*The Gospel of Luke I–IX* [AB 28A; Garden City, NY: Doubleday, 1985], 54) cites Jerome, M. Albertz, F. Blass, J. Cambier, L. Cerfaux, E. E. Ellis, N. Geldenhuys, G. Godet, B. Gut, A. von Harnack, M. Meinertz, W. Michaelis, B. Reicke, H. Sahlin, J. A. T. Robinson—to which could be added Hemer, *Acts*, 414; and Eckhard J. Schnabel, *Early Christian Mission*, 2 vols. (Downers Grove, IL: InterVarsity, 2004), 1:30–32

writing his first volume Luke is using Mark, who was writing probably around 70 CE.[33] Also, in his Gospel Luke most likely reflects knowledge of the fall of Jerusalem in 70 CE (cf. Luke 19:41–44; 21:20–24).[34] However, confidence in C. K. Barrett's point that the church of Acts has yet to experience the persecutions at the end of the first century[35] diminishes in noting that recent studies find no solid evidence for a persecution of Christians under Domitian.[36] On the other hand, arguments that attempt to date Acts to the first third or more of the second century[37] do not sufficiently take into account that "heresy (probably gnosticism) is little more than a cloud on the horizon (cf. Acts 20:21–31)," as Barrett put it.[38]

Therefore, although I increasingly find the arguments for later dating persuasive,[39] what little evidence we have suggests Luke was writing sometime in the 70s, or even up to the 90s CE, that is, between one and two decades after the death of Paul. This puts the author of Acts at least within reach of living memory of the historical Paul and increases the possibility that he has obtained and maintained historically reliable data about him.

(cf. 31n86)—as concluding that Acts was written before the death of Paul, which Robert Jewett (*Dating Paul's Life* [London: SCM, 1979], 102) puts at March 62 CE, and Jerome Murphy-O'Connor (*Paul: A Critical Life* [Oxford: Oxford University Press, 1996], 368–71) at 67–68 CE.

33. Relatively early dates for the publication of Mark have long been proposed; see those cited by John S. Kloppenborg, "*Evocatio Deorum* and the Date of Mark," *JBL* 124 (2005): 419–50, esp. 419n1. See the brief and balanced discussion of the dating of Mark by Morna D. Hooker, *A Commentary on the Gospel According to St. Mark* (BNTC; London: Black, 1991), 7–8.

34. The classic statement of the case that Luke is dependent not on knowledge of the fall of Jerusalem but the language of the OT is C. H. Dodd, "The Fall of Jerusalem and the 'Abomination of Desolation,'" *JRS* 37 (1947): 47–54; reprinted in his *More New Testament Studies* (Manchester: Manchester University Press, 1968), 69–83.

35. C. K. Barrett, *The Acts of the Apostles: A Shorter Commentary* (London: T&T Clark, 2002), xxv.

36. Cf. Paul Keresztes, "The Jews, the Christians, and the Emperor Domitian," *VC* 27 (1973): 1–28; Leonard L. Thompson, *The Book of Revelation: Apocalypse and Empire* (New York: Oxford University Press, 1990), 96–109; Brian W. Jones, *The Emperor Domitian* (London: Routledge, 1993), 114–17.

37. Joseph A. Fitzmyer (*The Acts of the Apostles: A New Translation with Introduction and Commentary* [AB 31; New York: Doubleday, 1998], 53) lists F. C. Burkitt, G. Klien, H. Koester, J. Knox, J. C. O'Neill, F. Overbeck, P. W. Schmiedel, and J. T. Townsend. More recently, see Richard I. Pervo, *Dating Acts: Between the Evangelists and the Apologists* (Santa Rosa, CA: Polbridge, 2006); Richard I. Pervo, "Acts in the Suburbs of the Apologists," in *Contemporary Studies in Acts*, ed. Thomas E. Phillips (Macon, GA: Mercer University Press, 2009), 29–46; Tyson, "Why Dates Matter"; Joseph B. Tyson, *Marcion and Luke-Acts: A Defining Struggle* (Columbia: University of South Carolina Press, 2006).

38. Barrett, *Acts of the Apostles*, xxv.

39. Nicely summarized by Mikeal C. Parsons, *Acts* (PCNT; Grand Rapids: Baker Academic, 2008), 16–17.

Further, third, if we could be certain that Luke knew Paul or had traveled with him, we would have firsthand knowledge of the apostle. Here the controversial so-called "we-passages" come into view, those apparently firsthand accounts proposing to have been written by the author of Acts.[40] Besides the traditional view,[41] which defends Luke as the author,[42] it is supposed either that Luke has taken up a first-person narrative by someone else, or that the "we-passages" are, if not fictitious,[43] a narrative construct.[44]

While the "we-passages" could point to an eyewitness,[45] if these passages are from an eyewitness, they have been thoroughly reworked by the author of Luke-Acts,[46] who likely did not know Paul. Notably, for example, in Luke's narrative, in Paul's speech at the Areopagus in Athens, the ignorance of the Gentiles is understandable and excusable (Acts 17:22–31), but in Romans Paul says the Gentiles are without excuse (Rom. 1:18–2:16).[47] We can be confident,

40. Acts 16:10–17; 20:5–21:18; 27:1–28:16. For the possibility that the first-person plural is used in Acts 11:28 (in the Western Text, D p w mae); 13:2 and 16:8 (Ir^{lat}), see C. K. Barrett, *A Critical and Exegetical Commentary on the Acts of the Apostles*, 2 vols. (ICC; Edinburgh: T&T Clark, 1994–2002), 1:564, 604; 2:771.

41. That the author of Acts was an eyewitness to events described goes back to the Muratorian Canon: "Luke . . . includes events because they were done in his own presence" (lines 35–37). The date of the Canon Muratori, argued to be either a second-century Roman or, more likely, a fourth-century Eastern document, is a matter of dispute. See Geoffrey M. Hahneman, *The Muratorian Fragment and the Development of the Canon* (OTM; Oxford: Clarendon; New York: Oxford University Press, 1992), esp. 215–18; Geoffrey M. Hahneman, "The Muratorian Fragment and the Origins of the New Testament Canon," in *The Canon Debate*, ed. Lee Martin McDonald and James A. Sanders (Peabody, MA: Hendrickson, 2002), 405–15.

42. E.g., see, John C. Hawkins, *Horae synopticae: Contributions to the Study of the Synoptic Problem*, 2nd ed. (ALBO 2/5; Oxford: Oxford University Press, 1909), 182–89; Colin Hemer, "First Person Narrative in Acts 27–28," *TynBul* 36 (1985): 100; Hemer, *Acts*, chap. 8.

43. See the discussions by Henry J. Cadbury, "'We' and 'I' Passages in Luke-Acts," *NTS* 3 (1957): 128–32; Susan Marie Praeder, "The Problem of First Person Narration in Acts," *NovT* 29 (1987): 193–218; Claus-Jürgen Thornton, *Der Zeuge Des Zeugen: Lukas als Historiker der Paulusreisen* (WUNT 56; Tübingen: Mohr Siebeck, 1991); Alexander J. M. Wedderburn, "The 'We'-Passages in Acts: On the Horns of a Dilemma," *ZNW* 93 (2002): 78–98.

44. William S. Campbell, *The 'We' Passages in the Acts of the Apostles: The Narrator as Narrative Character* (SBL 14; Atlanta: Society of Biblical Literature, 2007), cf. 87–91.

45. Bruce D. Chilton (*Rabbi Paul: An Intellectual Biography* [New York: Doubleday, 2004], 149) suggests that Timothy is a leading candidate for the authorship of the "we-passages." However, the first-person plural could also be a sign of late composition, cf. John 21:24; 2 Pet. 1:16–19. See the discussion by Richard I. Pervo, *Acts: A Commentary*, ed. Harold W. Attridge (Hermeneia; Minneapolis: Fortress, 2009), 394, citing Arthur Darby Nock: "I know only one possible parallel for the emphatic use of a questionable 'we' in consecutive narrative outside literature which is palpably fictional" (*Essays on Religion and the Ancient World*, ed. Zeph Steward, 2 vols. [Cambridge, MA: Harvard University Press, 1972], 2:827–28 [see esp. 828n34]).

46. Hemer (*Acts*, 321) cites Conzelmann, Lindemann, and Lüdemann.

47. Cf. Vielhauer, "Paulinism," 34–37. See also Martin Dibelius, "The Speeches in Acts and Ancient Historiography" (1949), in *Studies in the Acts of the Apostles*, ed. Heinrich Greeven,

then, in saying no more than that Luke idolized Paul, and that he may have some eyewitness accounts of his ministry that he has thoroughly reworked as he integrated them into his narrative. Also, it could be that Luke, though he knew Paul, like others who knew him, misunderstood him (e.g., Rom. 3:8; 1 Cor. 5:9–13).[48] Or, like other witnesses of events, perhaps at times Luke presented accounts at variance to his experience.[49]

In using Acts as a source for reconstructing the historical Paul we also have to take into account, fourth, that on the Greco-Roman cultural map much of Luke's narrative traverses fictional territory:[50] it begins in the "exotic" area of Palestine, draws on the writings of an exotic people, and has characters from a barbarian race and stories from a distant past, for example.[51] At least for educated readers of Acts, to follow Loveday Alexander, "much of the narrative content of Acts would place it in the danger-area of fiction—though with a disturbing undercurrent which suggests it might after all be fact."[52] That is, on the one hand, Acts involves non-Greek traditions, private beliefs, and supernatural events. However, on the other hand, there is a realism to the setting, a lack of a happy ending, and a sober tone to the preface.[53]

To conclude: Even if we were able to establish that Acts was written early by a companion of Paul, and that he had used sources that could be traced to Paul,[54] we would not have established the historical veracity of Luke's writings.[55] To discover Luke's contribution to the historical Paul in relation to the miraculous, we cannot escape the obligation to subject Luke's narrative to careful scrutiny to determine how far his representation of Paul in relation to the miraculous is historically credible and reliable.[56] Moreover, for our historical enquiry to be credible, it is not that we have to approach Acts

---

trans. Mary Ling (London: SCM, 1956), 138–85. Also, though from 1 Cor. 8:1–13 it is clear that Paul is able to adopt different attitudes toward the eating of meat offered to idols, it is hard to believe that a companion of Paul's would think that he consented to a decree that those in his churches "abstain from what has been sacrificed to idols and from blood from what is strangled" (Acts 15:29).

48. Cf. Lüdemann, Acts, 388.

49. Martin Dibelius, "The Acts of the Apostles as an Historical Source" (1947), in Dibelius, Studies, 104.

50. See Richard I. Pervo, Profit with Delight: The Literary Genre of the Acts of the Apostles (Philadelphia: Fortress, 1987).

51. Loveday C. A. Alexander, "Fact, Fiction and the Genre of Acts," in Acts in Its Ancient Literary Context: A Classicist Looks at the Acts of the Apostles (LNTS 298; London: T&T Clark, 2005), 157.

52. Ibid., 161–62.

53. Ibid., 162.

54. Fitzmyer, Acts, 80–88.

55. Cf. Praeder, "First Person Narration," 217.

56. Cf. Baur, Paul, 1:13–14; Barrett, "Historicity of Acts," 525, 534.

skeptically, but critically, and not only be open to positive conclusions, but also vulnerable to negative results.[57] We begin with some points regarding perspective and approach.

8.2 Paul and the Miraculous in Acts

Luke's portrait of Paul's involvement in the miraculous consists of a considerable number of elements, each which I will examine: three conversion or call narratives that together include a visionary experience, a heavenly voice, blindness, and then a healing (Acts 9:1–19a; 22:6–16; 26:9–18); three further call-related stories (13:1–3; 16:6–11; 22:17–21); two stories in which Paul is the subject of a miracle—deliverance from prison (16:25–34) and surviving a viper's bite (28:3–6); a brief story of "extraordinary miracles" (19:11) caused through neckcloths or belts that had touched Paul's skin (19:11–12); a punitive miracle story in which Paul blinds Elymas (13:9–11); three healing stories—the lame man at Lystra (14:8–10), the raising of Eutychus (20:7–12), and the healing of Publius's father of dysentery (28:7–8); an exorcism story (16:16–18); and two summary statements, one about the Lord granting signs and wonders as a testimony to Paul and Barnabas speaking boldly (14:3), and another about the sick on Malta coming to Paul to be healed (28:9).

To begin with, any initial confidence we may have in the historicity of this material is called into question by two factors. One is the long and often-noted apparent stark contrast between Luke's portrait of Paul as a miracle worker and what Paul says of himself.[58] Even though, as personal testimony, we will prefer the witness of Paul himself over against Luke, we have to take into account both that Paul writes with bias and a selective memory, and that Luke may have preserved historically reliable material. In short, in seeking to recover the historical Paul in relation to the miraculous, the perspectives of both Paul and Luke have to be taken into account.

Another factor that raises questions about the historical value of Luke are the parallels, even similarities, that exist between Luke's stories of Paul and

57. Cf. Mark Allan Powell, "Evangelical Christians and Historical-Jesus Studies: Final Reflections," *JSHJ* 9 (2011): 124–36. On the important principle that "the question one puts to evidence should not be biased towards an answer already in mind," see Geoffrey R. Elton, *Return to Essentials: Some Reflections on the Present State of Historical Study* (Cambridge: Cambridge University Press, 1991), 66–67.

58. Frans Neirynck, "The Miracle Stories in the Acts of the Apostles: An Introduction," in *Les Actes des Apôtres: Traditions, rédaction, théologie*, ed. Jacob Kremer (BETL 48; Gembloux: Duculot; Louvain: Leuven University Press, 1979), 173n10, and recently, Pervo, *Making of Paul*, 150.

Luke's stories in which Jesus,[59] and also particularly Peter,[60] are the principal subjects. Even though there is no consensus on which stories relating to Paul are paralleled in Luke's Gospel and elsewhere in Acts,[61] the most inclusive approach in relation to the miraculous gives rise to the following results:

Jesus	Peter	Paul
Baptismal vision (Luke 3:21–22)	Call vision (Acts 10:9–16)	Call vision (Acts 9:1–19; 22:6–11; 26:12–18)
	Call vision (10:9–16)	Holy Spirit's call to mission (13:1–3)
	Condemnation and death of Ananias and Sapphira (5:1–11)	
	Condemnation of Simon the magician (8:18–24)	The blinding of Elymas the magician (13:4–12)
	Summary statement of signs and wonders (2:43; 5:12)	Summary statement of signs and wonders (14:3)
Healing of the lame man (5:17–26)	Healing of the lame man at the temple (3:1–10)	Healing of a lame man at Lystra (14:8–10)
	Wonders and signs by the apostles (2:43)	Signs and wonders through Paul and Barnabas (15:12)
	A trance in Jerusalem (10:9–16; 11:5–10)	Vision-call to Europe (16:6–11)
Recognized by a demoniac (4:34)		Recognized by a demoniac (16:17; note 19:19)
Exorcisms (4:33–37, 41; 8:26–39; 11:20; cf. Acts 10:38)	Apostles cure those tormented by unclean spirits (5:16)	Exorcism of a slave girl (16:16–18)
	Deliverance from prison (12:3–17; cf. 5:17–21)	Deliverance from prison (16:25–34)

59. See Charles H. Talbert, *Literary Patterns, Theological Themes, and the Genre of Luke-Acts* (SBLMS 20; Missoula, MT: Society of Biblical Literature and Scholars Press, 1974), 35–65; Andrew J. Mattill, "Jesus-Paul Parallels and the Purpose of Luke-Acts: H. H. Evans Reconsidered," *NovT* 17 (1975): 15–46; Schneider, *Die Apostelgeschichte*, 1:304–10; Susan Marie Praeder, "Miracle Worker and Missionary: Paul in the Acts of the Apostles," *SBLSP* (1983): 114–20; and the summary and nuanced discussion by Pervo, *Acts*, 9–12.

60. On the long-noted parallel portraits of Paul and Peter by Luke, see the discussion by Floyd V. Filson, "The Journey Motif in Luke-Acts," in Gasque and Martin, *Apostolic History*, 75–76; see also Andrew C. Clark, *Parallel Lives: The Relation of Paul to the Apostles in the Lucan Perspective* (PBM; Bletchley; Waynesboro, GA: Paternoster, 2001).

61. See Neirynck, "Miracle Stories," 170–71; Andrew J. Mattill, "The Purpose of Acts: Schneckenburger Reconsidered," in Gasque and Martin, *Apostolic History*, 108–22.

Jesus	Peter	Paul
	Laying on hands and the coming of the Spirit (8:17)	Laying on hands and the coming of the Spirit (19:6)
Touching Jesus' clothing heals (8:43–48; 6:19)	Peter's shadow falls upon the sick (5:15)	Miracles through hand-kerchiefs and aprons that touched Paul's skin (19:11–12)
An unknown exorcist invokes Jesus' name (9:49–50)		Sons of Sceva associate Paul with exorcism (19:13)
Jairus's daughter raised from the dead (8:40–42, 49–56; cf. 7:11–17)	Tabitha raised from the dead (9:36–42)	Eutychus raised as from the dead (20:7–12)
	A trance in Jerusalem (10:9–16; 11:5–10)	A trance in the temple (22:17–21)
Takes command to save companions in a storm (8:22–25), followed by a successful exorcism		Takes command to save companions in a storm (27:9–44), followed by successful confrontation with evil
		Unharmed by a viper bite (28:3–6)
Simon's mother-in-law healed of high fever (4:38–40)	Aeneas healed of paralysis (9:32–35)	Publius's father healed of fever and dysentery (28:7–8)
Summary statement of healings (4:40; cf. 6:17–19)	Apostles cure the sick (5:16)	Summary statement of the sick on Malta healed (28:9)
The healed provide for the needs of Jesus and his followers (8:2–3)*		The healed provide for the needs of Paul and his companions (28:10)

* The reading αὐτῷ ("his" needs) in, e.g., ℵ A L X, is probably the result of a christologically motivated harmonization with Matt. 27:55 or Mark 15:41. Bruce M. Metzger, *A Textual Commentary* (New York: American Bible Society, 1994), 120–21.

From this chart, at least the rough parallels between these stories relating to Jesus, Peter, and Paul are clear.[62] The parallels between Peter and Paul are particularly obvious, but so also are the differences in the way Paul is portrayed in relation to the earlier characters in the Acts narrative. To a large degree, Peter's portrait is embedded within and arises out of the story of the early apostles.[63]

62. See the brief and nuanced discussion by Pervo, *Acts*, 676.
63. Acts 2:43; 3:1–10; 5:12–16, 17–21. However, Luke also shapes his portrait of Peter so Paul can more easily be seen as his successor. See William O. Walker, "Acts and the Pauline Corpus Reconsidered," *JSNT* 24 (1985): 12, 15, 16–17.

On the other hand, though accompanied by Barnabas (Acts 14:1–3), who is also sometimes in the background (13:7, 13; 14:8–18), and Silas (16:25, 29), as well as others,[64] Paul is the identifiable focus of attention in the narratives. Luke also has more miracle stories attributed to Paul than to Peter or any other figure in Acts.[65] In the chart above, some of the stories of Paul[66] do not have parallels in those attributed to Peter, and the condemnation of Simon (8:18–24), though carrying a theme similar to Paul's blinding Elymas (13:9–12), involves no miracle. However, viewed as a punishment miracle, the blinding of Elymas is paralleled in Peter's condemnation and the deaths of Ananias and Sapphira (5:1–11). Thus, while every miracle of Peter is paralleled in the depiction of Paul,[67] Paul has more miraculous feats attached to him. The impression that Luke leaves on the readers is not of portraits of two similar apostles,[68] but of the marked superiority of Paul as a miracle worker over his predecessors. Indeed, as the dominant character in Acts,[69] Paul embodies Luke's statement "A disciple is not above the teacher, but everyone who is fully qualified will be like the teacher" (Luke 6:40).[70]

Of course, given the inexact parallels, it is possible the parallelism is not an artifice of Luke's[71] but "arises out of the facts," as Richard B. Rackham supposed,[72] or at least through Luke selecting traditional material.[73] Taking into account the biases and interests of both Paul and Luke, my task, therefore, is to examine the stories and references related to Paul and the miraculous to see what can probably be traced back to the initial reports that arose from Paul's ministry.[74] I will take them in the order of Luke's narrative.

64. Acts 16:16; 20:7, 13; 28:1, 11.
65. Also, see Jervell, "Signs," 77–95.
66. Acts 16:17; 19:19; 28:3–6, 10.
67. Cf. Mattill, "Purpose of Acts," 110–11.
68. So ibid., 111.
69. John J. Clabeaux notes, "Paul is the chief character in 60 percent of the content of Acts (seventeen chapters out of twenty-eight)" ("The Story of the Maltese Viper and Luke's Apology for Paul," *CBQ* 67 [2005]: 605).
70. Mattill, "Jesus-Paul Parallels," 41–46; Glenn R. Jacobson, "Paul in Luke-Acts: The Savior Who Is Present," *SBLSP* (1983): 131–46, esp. 145. For a caution against the zeal to overplay the parallels between Paul and Jesus, especially for considering Paul's shipwreck a parallel to the passion of Jesus, see Matthew L. Skinner, *Locating Paul: Places of Custody as Narrative Settings in Acts 21–28* (SBLAB 13; Atlanta: Society of Biblical Literature, 2003), 157–60.
71. As proposed by Baur, *Paul*, e.g., 1:6, 165, 174, 191–92, 202–3, 227.
72. Richard B. Rackham, *The Acts of the Apostles: An Exposition* (WC; London: Methuen, 1951), xlix.
73. Matthias Schneckenburger, reported by R. Rüetschi, "Beiträge zur Erklärung und Kritik der Apostelgeschichte aus dem Nachlasse von D. M. Schneckenburger," *TSK* 28 (1855): 550–51, and cited by Neirynck, "Miracle Stories," 174n13.
74. For a detailed discussion of Luke's intentions in his parallel lives, see Clark, *Parallel Lives*.

8.3 Call, Vision, and Healing (Acts 9:1–19a; 22:6–16; 26:12–18)

Having briefly introduced Paul (as Saul) approving the killing of Stephen and ravaging the church (8:1–9:3), and after the narrative of Philip's ministry (8:1b–40), Luke has the first of three stories of Paul's conversion (9:1–19a).[75] These stories have been subject to considerable discussion.[76] Our interest, however, is limited to what these stories can tell us about the historical Paul and the miraculous.

What can be taken as the miraculous aspects of the first story, told in the third-person singular, are the light from heaven accompanied by a voice of the Lord or Jesus, and Paul's subsequent healing from temporary blindness.[77] Luke's second and third stories, told in the first-person singular, also mention the light and commissioning voice, but his third story does not mention the healing.

From what we have seen of Paul's perspective on his conversion experience (see §6.6 above), Luke agrees that it involved a vision of Jesus and, in some way, a call to a Gentile mission.[78] Yet, Luke nowhere says that Paul saw Jesus, only that Paul heard his voice (9:4–7; 22:7–10; 26:13–18). However, in the first story, through saying that Paul's companions "saw no one" (μηδένα δὲ θεωροῦντες, 9:7), Luke implies that Paul saw a person; and in the third story Luke has Jesus say, "I have appeared to you" (26:16), also implying that Luke understood the vision to involve seeing a person. In this, Luke mirrors Paul's view: "Have I not seen Jesus our Lord?" (οὐχὶ Ἰησοῦν τὸν κύριον ἡμῶν ἑόρακα, 1 Cor. 9:1; cf. 15:8).

The relationship between Paul's visionary experience of Jesus and his call to a Gentile mission is variously portrayed by Luke in Acts. In the first conversion

---

75. See the synopsis of the three stories by Barrett, *Commentary on the Acts*, 1:439–40. On the issues involved in Luke's triple narrative, see, e.g., Ernst Haenchen, *The Acts of the Apostles: A Commentary*, trans. Bernard Noble et al. (Oxford: Blackwell, 1971), 325–29; Charles W. Hedrick, "Paul's Conversion/Call: A Comparative Analysis of the Three Reports in Acts," *JBL* 100 (1981): 415–32; Beverly Roberts Gaventa, *From Darkness to Light: Aspects of Conversion in the New Testament* (OBT 20; Philadelphia: Fortress, 1986), 52–95; Marguerat, *Christian Historian*, 179–204.

76. See the literature listed by Barrett, *Commentary on the Acts*, 1:438–39; 2:1030–31, 1143–44; Fitzmyer, *Acts*, 430–32, 709, 762, and also, e.g., Benjamin Ndiaye, "La conversion de Paul," *Spiritus* 147 (1997): 115–25; Harm W. Hollander, "De bekering van Paulus," *NedTT* 56 (2002): 27–38; P. H. Kern, "Paul's Conversion and Luke's Portrayal of Character in Acts 8–10," *TynBul* 54 (2003): 63–80.

77. On the idea that the healing echoes Tob. 11:10–13, see Hans Conzelmann, *Acts of the Apostles: A Commentary on the Acts of the Apostles*, trans. James Limburg, A. Thomas Kraabel, and Donald H. Juel, ed. Eldon Jay Epp with Christopher R. Matthews (Hermeneia; Philadelphia: Fortress, 1987), 72; James D. G. Dunn, *The Acts of the Apostles* (EC; Peterborough: Epworth, 1996), 124.

78. Cf. Gerd Lüdemann, *Early Christianity According to the Traditions in Acts: A Commentary*, trans. John Bowden (London: SCM, 1989), 115.

story the commission comes later through Ananias (9:15–16). In the second story the vision involves a hint of the mission ("you will be told everything that has been assigned to you to do," 22:10). In the third narrative of Paul's conversion the voice of Jesus says, "I have appeared to you for this purpose, to appoint you to serve and testify to . . . the Gentiles—to whom I am sending you" (26:16–17).[79] In contrast to Acts, Paul's account is simply that God "revealed his son in me, so that [ἵνα] I might proclaim him among the Gentiles" (Gal. 1:16, my translation).[80] Although the implication of the vision and logic of the Gentile mission may have been, for Paul, inherent in the experience,[81] we must resist reading Paul's narrative in light of Acts by putting words into the mouth of the Jesus of his experience.[82] For, on the one hand, given Paul's eagerness to attribute his call to Jesus (cf. 1 Cor. 9:1), if there was an audible call in relation to the vision, we would expect Paul to have reported it.[83] On the other hand, given the Old Testament parallels to vision dialogues,[84] and the common elements with the roughly contemporary Hellenistic-Jewish work *Joseph and Aseneth*[85]—a supernatural light, prostration, a double vocative address, a question ("Who are you?"), the answer ("I am . . ."), the command to get up, the promise of future direction, and the subject standing[86]—the words of Jesus in each of the narratives of Paul's vision are to be attributed to Luke or his tradition, not to Paul.[87]

Paul also tells us nothing about being blind as a result of this experience, nor, therefore, of a healing from blindness. With Paul's keenness to promote his religious experience—what is done to him, though not done by him (see

79. Cf. Stephen G. Wilson, *The Gentiles and the Gentile Mission in Luke-Acts* (SNTSMS 23; Cambridge: Cambridge University Press, 1973), 162.

80. For a discussion of the differences between Acts 9:1–29 and Gal. 1:11–20, see John T. Townsend, "Acts 9:1–29 and Early Church Tradition," in *Literary Studies in Luke-Acts: Essays in Honor of Joseph B. Tyson*, ed. Richard P. Thompson and Thomas E. Phillips (Macon, GA: Mercer University Press, 1998), 87–98.

81. So F. F. Bruce, *Galatians: A Commentary on the Greek Text* (NIGTC; Exeter: Paternoster; Grand Rapids: Eerdmans, 1982), 93.

82. Cf. Hans Dieter Betz, *Galatians: A Commentary on Paul's Letter to the Churches in Galatia* (Hermeneia; Philadelphia: Fortress, 1979), 71–72.

83. On the need for Paul's account to be basically plausible, see Townsend, "Acts 9:1–29," 90; on Paul's purpose being more than conveying autobiographical information, see Jack T. Sanders, "Paul's Autobiographical Statements in Galatians 1–2," *JBL* 85 (1966): 335–43.

84. See Gen. 31:11–13; 46:2–3; Exod. 3:2–10, and the discussion by Gerhard Lohfink, *The Conversion of St. Paul: Narrative and History in Acts*, trans. and ed. Bruce J. Malina (Chicago: Franciscan Herald Press, 1976), 61–65.

85. It is generally agreed that *Joseph and Aseneth* is a Hellenistic-Jewish work. See John J. Collins, "*Joseph and Aseneth:* Jewish or Christian?" *JSP* 14 (2005): 97–112. For the near consensus of the date from between 100 BCE and 100 CE, see Edith M. Humphrey, *Joseph and Aseneth* (GAP; Sheffield: Sheffield Academic Press, 2000), 28–38.

86. Pervo, *Acts*, 235.

87. So also, e.g., Lohfink, *Conversion of St. Paul*, 61–73; John T. Townsend, "Acts 9:1–29," 96.

§7.8 above on Rom. 15:18–19)—if he had been healed of blindness, we could expect it to be mentioned when boasting either of his hardships and rescues (2 Cor. 11:16–33) or his visionary experiences (12:1–7a). On the other hand, Luke would have been aware that bright lights were expected as part of heavenly appearances.[88] And we have just noted the element of a "great and unutterable light" (*Jos. Asen.* 14:3) in a contemporary story with a remarkable resemblance to that of Luke. It is highly likely, therefore, that while we have support for the view that Paul's conversion involved a vision of Jesus, which he took to be a call to a Gentile mission,[89] we have to set aside the ideas that Paul saw a great light, heard a voice, or that he was healed of temporary blindness.[90]

8.4 Call to Mission (Acts 13:1–3)

The beginning of Acts 13 marks a major turn in Luke's narrative. Up to this point Peter, based in Jerusalem, has been the focus of the story; from this point until the end of Acts, Paul and his wider ministry take center stage. In doing so, and to reestablish the view that the mission of the church is empowered and directed by the Spirit, Luke has an episode at Syrian Antioch in which the missionaries are set apart and sent out by the Spirit (13:1–3). The miraculous element in the story is the prophets and teachers, including Paul or Saul, hearing the Holy Spirit speak to them (13:2).[91] Perhaps the Spirit's direction is supposed to have come through a prophecy,[92] voiced by one of those present.[93] Paul's involvement in this is not specified other than that, as a result, he and Barnabas were appointed to go on mission.

Not surprisingly, Luke has left his mark on this story, particularly in the expression "the Holy Spirit said"[94] and in the idea of laying on of hands.[95]

88. See Townsend, "Acts 9:1–29," 96, citing Num. 9:15–16; 2 Kings 2:11–12; 6:17; Ezek. 1:4–28; Luke 2:9; Acts 7:55; Rev. 1:16; 21:23; 22:5.

89. If Luke obtained this information from his Pauline source (so, e.g., Fitzmyer, *Acts*, 420), it was not from the letters of Paul, since there is little echo in Luke's vocabulary of what Paul says about his conversion.

90. See Emmanuel Hirsch, "Die drei Berichte der Apostelgeschichte über die Bekehrung des Paulus," *ZNW* 28 (1929): 311–12; Townsend, "Acts 9:1–29," 95.

91. See the discussion by David E. Aune, *Prophecy in Early Christianity and the Ancient Mediterranean World* (Grand Rapids: Eerdmans, 1991), 265–66.

92. Cf. Dunn, *Acts*, 173.

93. In that those involved are said to be prophets, it is not necessary to take up the suggestion by Pervo (*Acts*, 322) that the oracle came through the mouth of one of those not named.

94. Acts 8:29; 10:19; 11:12; 13:2; cf. Luke 12:12; Acts 4:25; 21:11; 28:25. In the remainder of the NT see John 14:26; Heb. 10:15–17; Rev. 22:17.

95. See Acts 6:6; 8:17–19; 9:12, 17; 19:6; 28:8. The genitive absolute in Acts 13:2 is also probably the work of Luke. See Lüdemann, *Early Christianity*, 146–47.

Luke's interest in fasting also finds expression here,[96] but his preference for associating meals with Christian gatherings[97] suggests that this first mention of fasting (13:2) is probably not of his creation. The second mention of fasting, since it is related to the subsequent commissioning, which involves the laying on of hands (cf. 14:23) and an echo of the Septuagint,[98] is more likely to be of Luke's making.[99]

However, in that apart from Barnabas and Paul, the other names are not essential to the story,[100] the list of the prophets and teachers is likely to be part of Luke's tradition,[101] and in that Antioch was important to Paul (Gal. 2:11), Luke probably is relying on a tradition that involved Paul. Also, in that we know from Paul of his involvement in prophecy (see §3.1 above), at least Luke's story is credible. Moreover, the notion of being set apart, not otherwise used by Luke in the context of a call to mission, is how Paul twice describes himself (Rom. 1:1; Gal. 1:15), suggesting the tradition may have originated with Paul. In short, then, it is likely that Luke has provided a reliable piece of tradition about Paul experiencing prophecy as a means of directing his work.

8.5 The Blinding of Elymas the Magician (Acts 13:4–12)

Having been commissioned, Barnabas and Paul are said to go down the sixteen miles (twenty-six kilometers) to Seleucia, where they could get a boat to Cyprus (13:4), a natural mission destination from Antioch, and for Barnabas, a Cypriot (4:36). At Salamis, on the east coast of Cyprus, "they proclaimed the word of God in the synagogues of the Jews" (13:5). Having made their way to Paphos, on the southwest coast, "they met a certain magician, a Jewish false prophet, named Bar-Jesus" (13:6), who "was with the proconsul, Sergius Paulus" (13:7). However, upon opposing the missionaries speaking to the proconsul, the magician is condemned by Paul and loses his sight for a while (13:9–11). When the proconsul saw this he "believed" (13:12). Our task is to ascertain which if any elements of this story can reasonably be associated with the historical Paul.

96. In the NT the noun νηστεία ("fast") occurs in Luke 2:37; Acts 14:23; 27:9; and in 2 Cor. 6:5; 11:27, and the verb νηστεύω ("fast") in Luke 5:33, 34, 35; 18:12; Acts 13:2, 3; and in Matt. 4:2; 6:16 (2x), 17, 18; 9:14 (2x), 15; Mark 2:18 (3x), 19 (2x), 20.

97. See, e.g., Halvor Moxnes, "Meals and the New Community in Luke," SEÅ 51–52 (1986): 158–67; Graham H. Twelftree, People of the Spirit: Exploring Luke's View of the Church (London: SPCK; Grand Rapids: Baker Academic, 2009), 115–16.

98. Cf. Ernest Best, "Acts XIII. 1–3," JTS 11 (1960): 347.

99. Against Lüdemann, Early Christianity, 147.

100. Barrett, Commentary on the Acts, 1:599.

101. See, e.g., Martin Dibelius, "Style Criticism of the Book of Acts" (1923), in Dibelius, Studies, 11n20; Barrett, Commentary on the Acts, 1:600, 602.

To begin with, there is the broad problem of establishing the historicity of the tour (Acts 13–14). That Paul and Barnabas, driven out of Pisidian Antioch, Iconium, and Lystra, make a return journey to them (14:21–22) without any hint of earlier difficulties suggests Luke may be responsible for constructing this tour and the return journey.[102] However, the towns are listed independently of Luke in the same order in 2 Timothy 3:11, suggesting there was at least a tradition that Paul visited these towns. Paul not mentioning this tour in his report of the early days after his conversion (Gal. 1:13–21) may be because he did not wish to antagonize leaders at Jerusalem by emphasizing his work based out of Antioch.[103] Or, it could be that this tour took place after the Jerusalem settlement (2:1–10).[104] In any case, the details in Luke's narrative are scant, and he describes an unusual choice of taking the difficult southern approach to Derbe[105] rather than the more natural, eastern one,[106] keeping alive doubts about how much reliable tradition was available to him.

In the paired stories of Paul blinding Elymas the magician and the conversion of the proconsul, it is the story of Elymas that is of particular interest to us. The parallels between this story and that of Simon Magus (Acts 8:9–24) are striking. Both stories involve magicians[107] and competition between magic and the mission on the church.[108] In both cases the antagonist attempts to subvert the mission of the apostles: Simon threatens the view that the gift of the Spirit is free (8:20), and Elymas threatens the conversion of the first Gentile (13:8). Both stories stand at the head of a mission: the Simon Magus story stands at the head of Peter's mission outside Jerusalem, to the Samaritans (8:14), and the Elymas story is the first in Paul's encounter with the Gentiles (13:1–4). In turn, being at the head of ministries and involving a battle with Satan[109] over

102. Pervo, *Acts*, 320–21.

103. Ibid., 310.

104. See the discussion by Haenchen, *Acts*, 400–401, 438–39.

105. E.g., F. J. Foakes-Jackson, *The Acts of the Apostles* (MNTC; London: Hodder & Stoughton, 1931), 114.

106. Cf. Pervo, *Acts*, 320.

107. The verb μαγεύω ("to practice magic") is used in Acts 8:9, and the noun μαγεία ("magic") appears in Acts 8:11, their only appearance in the NT. The noun "magician" (μάγος) is found in the NT in Acts 13:6, 8; Matt. 2:1, 7, 16.

108. Graham H. Twelftree, "Jesus and Magic in Luke-Acts," in *Jesus and Paul: Global Perspectives in Honor of James D. G. Dunn for His 70th Birthday*, ed. by B. J. Oropeza, C. K. Robertson, and Douglas C. Mohrmann (LNTS 414; London: T&T Clark, 2009), 46–58.

109. Acts 13:10 explicitly mentions the devil; in the Acts 8:9–24 story Peter describes Simon as in "the chains of wickedness" (σύνδεσμον ἀδικίας, 8:23), a phrase found in LXX Isa. 58:6, another part of which Luke has used to describe Jesus' ministry of exorcism and healing (Luke 4:18; cf. Acts 10:38: καταδυναστευομένους).

future ministry, both stories echo Jesus' initial battle in the temptation story (Luke 4:1–13).[110] In themselves, these parallels do not assign the stories to the category of fiction, for Luke could have selected, placed, and reworked them to suit his purposes. However, along with strong echoes in Luke's story of oracles in Jeremiah 5 and 6,[111] such orchestration heightens already emerging questions about the historicity of the stories.

Elymas is introduced as the false prophet "Bar-Jesus" (Βαριησοῦς, Acts 13:6). Since this means "son of Jesus" in Aramaic, it is highly unlikely that Luke would have created this name for an antagonist in his narrative,[112] for Luke is not given to such irony. Indeed, that Luke does not translate the name (cf. 4:36) suggests it was part of his tradition, the meaning of which he does not want to discuss.[113] That the magician has two names with which Luke struggles is further evidence that they probably were part of his tradition. Despite Luke saying that "Elymas" (Ἐλύμας) was the meaning of his name (13:8), it is neither a Greek word[114] nor a Greek translation of the Semitic "Bar-Jesus." Luke is unlikely to have created such complexity. Theories abound attempting to solve the conundrum.[115] The simplest and most convincing explanation is that Bar-Jesus was known in Jewish circles, significant on Cyprus,[116] by the Aramaic ḥālōma (חלמא), a person supernaturally inspired who could interpret dreams and deliver divine messages revealed in trances.[117] "Elymas" was, then, the Greek vocalization of what was taken to be his sobriquet. That Elymas was "with" (σύν) or in the court of the proconsul is credible, for such court figures were common.[118] However, at-

---

110. Bernard P. Robinson, "Paul and Barnabas in Cyprus," *ScrB* 26 (1996): 70.

111. See Acts 13:6 // Jer. 5:1; Acts 13:7–8 // Jer. 6:17–18; Acts 13:8 // Jer. 5:1, 3, 25; Acts 13:10 // Jer. 5:5, 27; 6:6, 16; Acts 13:11 // Jer. 6:12; see also the discussion by Josep Rius-Camps and Jenny Read-Heimerdinger, *The Message of Acts in Codex Bezae: A Comparison with the Alexandrian Tradition*, vol. 3, *Acts 13.1–18:23: The Ends of the Earth; First and Second Phases of the Mission to the Gentiles* (LNTS 365; London: T&T Clark, 2007), 59.

112. Cf. Haenchen, *Acts*, 402.

113. It is reasonably suggested that, in common with the practice of prophets to identify themselves as the "son of" (e.g., 1 Kings 15:33; 19:19; 2 Kings 19:2; Ezra 6:14), "Bar-Jesus" was the self-designation of this person who considered himself a disciple of Jesus. See, e.g., Rick Strelan, "Who Was Bar Jesus?" *Bib* 84 (2004): 74–75.

114. Ἐλύμας is not cited in LSJ, and the *Thesaurus linguae graecae* cites no occurrence earlier than Acts 13:8.

115. See the reviews by L. Yaure, "Elymas-Nehelamite-Pethor," *JBL* 79 (1960): 297–314, and Metzger, *Commentary*, 355–56.

116. 1 Macc. 15:23; Philo, *Legat.* 282; Josephus, *Ant.* 13.284; cf. Acts 4:36; 11:19–20; 13:4–6; 15:39.

117. Yaure, "Elymas-Nehelamite-Pethor," esp. 304–5.

118. See, e.g., Suetonius, *Tib.* 14.4; *Nero* 36.1; *Otho* 4.1; 6.1; *Vesp.* 25; *Dom.* 15.3; Dio Cassius, *Hist.* 71.8.4.

tempts to verify Sergius Paulus as the proconsul of Cyprus at the time have not been successful.[119]

Despite the likelihood that Luke had at his disposal a story of Paul and Barnabas going on mission to Cyprus and meeting a magician, the core of the story in Acts, a punishment miracle, is of less certain value for it is heavily marked by Luke's hand. The description of Elymas seeking to "mislead" or "pervert" (διαστρέφω, Acts 13:8, 10)[120] both the proconsul and the "straight" (εὐθύς, 13:10) way of the Lord is not only from Luke's hand but, echoing the prophecy of John the Baptist (Luke 3:4), justifies Elymas's title as a "false prophet."[121] The note that Saul was "also known as Paul" (Acts 13:9) is also to be attributed to Luke rather than his tradition in light of the consistency with which the name "Saul" has been used to this point and Paul is now used in the narrative.[122] Also, it is Luke, rather than his tradition, who is responsible for describing Paul as full of the Spirit (13:9),[123] and for saying that he "looked intently" (ἀτενίζω)[124] at Elymas. Paul's address or curse to Elymas also contains clear signals of Luke's composition. He describes Elymas as "full" (πλήρης) of all deceit and "wickedness" (ῥαδιουργία, only here in the New Testament), and as a son of the "devil" (διάβολος), a word that Paul does not use in his letters.[125] Further, we have just noted that the expression "the way of the Lord" (13:10) probably is Luke's doing. Moreover, the phrases "and now behold" (καὶ νῦν ἰδού, 13:11; 20:22, 25), the "hand of the Lord" (χεὶρ κυρίου, Luke 1:66; Acts 11:21; 13:11), and "for a while" (ἄχρι καιροῦ, Luke 4:13; Acts 13:11) are only used by Luke, and "immediately" (παραχρῆμα, Acts 13:11) is decidedly Lukan.[126] Although blindness is a common result of being cursed (see Apuleius, *Metam.* 8.25), in this story it forms part of a frame to Paul's entire ministry of bringing light to "our people and the Gentiles" (Acts 26:23). In this way, the first

119. See the discussions by F. F. Bruce, *The Acts of the Apostles: The Greek Text with Introduction and Commentary*, 3rd ed. (Grand Rapids: Eerdmans; Leicester: Apollos, 1990), 279, and Barrett, *Commentary on the Acts*, 1:613–14.

120. In the NT διαστρέφω occurs in Matt. 17:17; Luke 9:41; 23:2; Acts 13:8, 10; 20:30; Phil. 2:15.

121. Cf. Pervo, *Acts*, 327.

122. Lüdemann, *Early Christianity*, 149.

123. The phrase, "filled with the Spirit," and variations of it, are unique to Luke 1:15, 41, 67; Acts 2:4 (2x); 4:8, 31; 9:17; 13:9.

124. In the NT ἀτενίζω occurs in Luke 4:20; 22:56; Acts 1:10; 3:4, 12; 6:15; 7:55; 10:4; 11:6; 13:9; 14:9; 23:1; 2 Cor. 3:7, 13.

125. For διάβολος in the NT, see Matt. 4:1, 5, 8, 11; 13:39; 25:41; Luke 4:2, 3, 6, 13; 8:12; John 6:70; 8:44; 13:2; Acts 10:38; 13:10; Eph. 4:27; 6:11; 1 Tim. 3:6, 7, 11; 2 Tim. 2:26; 3:3; Titus 2:3; Heb. 2:14; James 4:7; 1 Pet. 5:8; 1 John 3:8, 10; Jude 9; Rev. 2:10; 12:9, 12; 20:2, 10.

126. In the NT παραχρῆμα occurs in Matt. 21:19, 20; Luke 1:64; 4:39; 5:25; 8:44, 47, 55; 13:13; 18:43; 19:11; 22:60; Acts 3:7; 5:10; 12:23; 13:11; 16:26, 33.

miracle story associated with him, Paul is contending with the blind Gentiles as he will be with the blind Jews in the closing lines of this book (28:27).[127]

The result of my investigation of the story of the blinding of Elymas is that although Luke probably has some traditions before him of Paul and Barnabas on a mission trip to Cyprus, where there was a confrontation with a magician Bar-Jesus or Elymas, what Luke has given his readers is a redactional construction[128] in which we can no longer trace the contours of a recognizable story that can be associated with the historical Paul.

8.6 Summary Statement of Signs and Wonders (Acts 14:3)

Having said that in Iconium "unbelieving Jews stirred up the Gentiles and poisoned their minds against the brothers" (14:2), Luke then says: "So they remained for a long time, speaking boldly for the Lord, who testified to the word of his grace by granting signs and wonders to be done through them" (14:3). This disjunction between the trouble in the city (14:2) and Paul and Barnabas nevertheless deciding to stay on (14:3)—which the Western Text attempted to smooth out[129]—has often been noted[130] and need not point to Lukan redaction. It could be that Paul and Barnabas are said to stay because they were needed.[131] However, the entire summary appears to be a creation by Luke: much of the vocabulary[132] and the phrases "a long . . . time"[133] and "to the word of his grace"[134] are strong indicators of Luke's creativity. The phrase "through the hands" (διὰ τῶν χειρῶν), though Semitic,[135] may also be

127. Cf. Pervo, *Acts*, 327.

128. So also Lüdemann, *Early Christianity*, 151.

129. E.g., at the end of Acts 14:2 D gig p w sy^hmg add ὁ δὲ κύριος ἔδωκεν ταχὺ εἰρήνην ("But the Lord quickly gave peace"). See the details in Barrett, *Commentary on the Acts*, 1:669; Rius-Camps and Read-Heimerdinger, *Ends of the Earth*, 136–37.

130. E.g., F. J. Foakes-Jackson and Kirsopp Lake, *The Beginnings of Christianity, Part I: The Acts of the Apostles*, vol. 4, *English Translation and Commentary*, by Kirsopp Lake and Henry J. Cadbury (Grand Rapids: Baker, 1965), 161–62; Dunn, *Acts*, 188; and Barrett, *Commentary on the Acts*, 1:669; Fitzmyer, *Acts*, 525–26; Barrett, *Acts of the Apostles*, 211–13.

131. Barrett, *Commentary on the Acts*, 1:669.

132. In the NT twenty-seven of the thirty-nine occurrences of μὲν οὖν ("so then") are in Acts. Of the thirty-nine occurrences of ἱκανός ("long" or "sufficient"), twenty-seven are in Luke-Acts. Διατρίβω ("stay") is used in the NT once in John and eight times in Acts. In the NT παρρησιάζομαι ("speak freely") is found nine times, seven of them in Acts.

133. The phrase ἱκανὸν . . . χρόνον (in various forms) is used in the NT only by Luke: Luke 8:27; 20:9; 23:8; Acts 8:11; 14:3; 27:9.

134. In the NT the phrase τῷ λόγῳ τῆς χάριτος αὐτοῦ occurs only here in Acts 14:3 and 20:32. On the status of ἐπί, unusually preceding this phrase, perhaps due to Semitic influence (עַל), see Metzger, *Commentary*, 371–72.

135. See Barrett, *Commentary on the Acts*, 1:670.

of Luke's making here.[136] Also, the phrase "signs and wonders" (σημεῖα καὶ τέρατα), though traditional, is one Luke favors.[137] Moreover, it appears that Luke is deliberately echoing his description of the apostles early in his narrative (5:12)[138] in order to extend the apostolate to include Paul and Barnabas. This is confirmed in the next verse when Paul and Barnabas are first called "apostles" (14:4) as they are one other time in Acts, in the same story (14:14).[139] It is hard, then, to avoid the conclusion that this summary statement of miracles is entirely of Luke's creation.[140]

Nevertheless, even though Luke is entirely responsible for this summary, it contains an echo of the approach to the miraculous that we have seen in Paul. Luke describes Paul and Barnabas as speaking openly or boldly. The miracles of Paul and Barnabas are said to be from the Lord—that is, God[141]—testifying or giving his support to them[142] through signs and wonders (14:3). Although this is probably Luke's general assumption (also specified in 19:11), he is perhaps, inadvertently, corroborating the view of the miraculous we have seen that is important to Paul: he does the speaking, and God does the miracles.

8.7 Healing of a Lame Man at Lystra (Acts 14:8–10)

This story is set in the same missionary journey (Acts 13:4–14:28) as the Elymas story.[143] Again, the most significant and long-noted aspect of the story that impinges on questions of historicity is its parallels with the story of Peter healing the lame man at the Beautiful Gate (3:1–10).[144] Not only is there a great deal

136. In the NT the phrase is found in Mark 6:2; Acts 14:3 and 19:11. Cf. 258n212 below.

137. Acts 2:19, 22, 43; 4:30; 5:12; 6:8; 7:36; 14:3; 15:12; cf. 209n204 above. On Luke's use of the phrase "signs and wonders," see, e.g., Karl H. Rengstorf, "σημεῖον, κτλ.," *TDNT* 7:239–43, and §7.7 (a) above.

138. Cf. Acts 5:12: διὰ δὲ τῶν χειρῶν ["through the hands"] . . . ἐγίνετο σημεῖα καὶ τέρατα ["signs and wonders were done"]; and 14:3: σημεῖα καὶ τέρατα γίνεσθαι διὰ τῶν χειρῶν ("signs and wonders to be done through the hands").

139. Cf. Conzelmann, *Acts*, 108; Twelftree, *People of the Spirit*, 25–26.

140. Cf. Haenchen, *Acts*, 422; Lüdemann, *Early Christianity*, 159; Barrett, *Commentary on the Acts*, 1:670; Schreiber, *Wundertäter*, 46–49.

141. Jacob Jervell, *Die Apostelgeschichte*, 17th ed. (KEK 3; Göttingen: Vandenhoeck & Ruprecht, 1998), 370.

142. Cf. Barrett, *Commentary on the Acts*, 1:670.

143. On some of the historical critical problems in Luke's narrative, see S. Dockx, "The First Missionary Voyage of Paul: Historical Reality or Literary Creation of Luke," in *Chronos, Kairos, Christos: Nativity and Chronological Studies Presented to Jack Finegan*, ed. Jerry Vardaman and Edwin M. Yamauchi (Winona Lake, IN: Eisenbrauns, 1989), 209–21.

144. See, e.g., Baur, *Paul*, 1:98–99; Henry J. Cadbury, *The Making of Luke-Acts*, 2nd ed. (London: SPCK, 1961), 231–32; Michael D. Goulder, *Type and History in Acts* (London: SPCK,

of vocabulary common to both stories,[145] but all the elements of the story set in Lystra are also found in the longer story of Peter and John at the temple: a man lame from birth (3:2; 14:8), placed (3:2) or sitting (14:8) in a public place; the man's interest in the miracle worker (3:3; 14:9); the miracle worker looking intently at the man (3:4; 14:9); the direction to stand up (3:6; 14:10);[146] the man jumping (3:8) or springing up (14:10) and beginning to walk (3:8; 14:10).[147] Moreover, these elements are found in the same order in both stories. Further, the elements involve such detail and similarity that, apart from the response of the crowd (3:10; 14:11), they are not to be explained simply as typical of such stories.[148] The exception to this parallel pattern is the mention of faith in the story associated with Paul (14:9), which does not appear in the longer story related to Peter until the very end (3:16). However, with Luke using the Lystra story to draw attention to the stature of Paul (14:11; cf. 14:4), rather than faith in the name of Jesus (3:16; cf. 3:6), it is readily explicable that Luke should use the theme early in the story about Paul.[149]

Although the similarities between these stories and the Gospel story of Jesus healing a lame man (Luke 5:17–26)[150] are not sufficient to conclude with any confidence that the Gospel account is the source for these stories,[151] there are sufficient similarities between all of them to conclude that Luke has crafted the stories so Peter and Paul appear to be modeling Jesus.[152] However, given the shared vocabulary and the parallel order of the elements or ideas in the two Acts stories, we cannot resort to the assumption that Luke has simply selected similar stories from a larger pool available to him.[153] Rather, it is hard to avoid the conclusion that the shorter one related to Paul, occurring later in the narrative, is a redactional construction based on the earlier story

---

1964), 74, 85, 106–7; Charles H. Talbert, *Reading Acts: A Literary and Theological Commentary on the Acts of the Apostles* (New York: Crossroad, 1997), 133; Pervo, *Acts*, 351.

145. "And there was a man" (καί τις ἀνήρ, 3:2; 14:8); "lame from his mother's womb" (χωλὸς ἐκ κοιλίας μητρὸς αὐτοῦ, 3:2; 14:8); "sit" (κάθημαι, 3:10; 14:8); "looked intently" (ἀτενίσας) "at him" (εἰς αὐτόν, 3:4; αὐτῷ, 14:9); "sprang up" (ἐξάλλομαι, 3:8; ἄλλομαι, 3:8; 14:10); "and walk about" (καί περιεπάτει, 3:8; 14:10); the people "seeing" (εἶδον, 3:9; 14:11).

146. Although the formula "in the name of Jesus Christ of Nazareth" (Acts 3:6) is missing from 14:10, the commands "stand up and walk" (ἔγειρε καὶ περιπάτει [3:6]) and "stand up straight on your feet" (ἀνάστηθι ἐπὶ τοὺς πόδας σου ὀρθός [14:10]) are in essence the same. Barrett, *Commentary on the Acts*, 1:675. On the textual status of ἔγειρε καί, see Metzger, *Commentary*, 267.

147. Cf. Lüdemann, *Early Christianity*, 159; Lüdemann, *Acts*, 178–79.

148. As supposed by Haenchen, *Acts*, 430.

149. For this story being used to "reinforce Luke's own claim that Paul is a chosen vessel of God," see Rick Strelan, "Recognizing the Gods (Acts 14:8–10)," *NTS* 46 (2000): 503.

150. See Schneider, *Die Apostelgeschichte*, 1:307–8.

151. See the discussions by Filson, "Journey Motif," 75–76; Neirynck, "Miracle Stories," 182.

152. Cf. Goulder, *Type and History*, 61–62.

153. See the discussion by Neirynck, "Miracle Stories," 172–82; Filson, "Journey Motif," 75.

associated with Peter.[154] As a result, no secure connection can be established between this healing story and the historical Paul.[155]

8.8 Signs and Wonders through Paul and Barnabas (Acts 15:12)

During the so-called Jerusalem council (Acts 15:1–35), called to discuss whether or not Gentile believers were to be circumcised and required to keep the law (15:1, 5), Paul and Barnabas are said to keep the whole assembly in silence listening to them tell "of all the signs and wonders that God had done through them among the Gentiles" (15:12). Luke gives no details, and as his well-used phrase "signs and wonders" (σημεῖα καὶ τέρατα)[156] dominates the summary (including vocabulary he particularly favors),[157] the statement probably is to be attributed to him.[158] This gives us no access, therefore, to any historically reliable material that can be related to the historical Paul and the miraculous.

8.9 The Vision-Call to Europe (Acts 16:6–11)

Luke says that in Troas, during the so-called second missionary journey (Acts 15:40–18:22), Paul had a vision at night in which a man pleaded, "Come over to Macedonia and help us" (16:9).[159] On the one hand, in Philippians Paul refers to the beginning of his mission in Europe (4:15),[160] but he makes no mention of a vision or, what is probably intended to be, a dream.[161] On the other hand, Luke is particularly fond of relating visions.[162] Also, the story—part of the

154. So also Martin Sorof, A. Hilgenfeld, Carl Clemen, Johannes Jüngst, and Alfred F. Loisy, cited by Haenchen, *Acts*, 429. More recently, see Lüdemann, *Early Christianity*, 160; Lüdemann, *Acts*, 179.

155. Also emphasizing Luke's creativity in this pericope is Dean P. Béchard, "Paul among the Rustics: The Lystran Episode (Acts 14:8–20) and Lucan Apologetic," *CBQ* 63 (2001): 84–101. Schreiber (*Wundertäter*, 143 [cf. 67–74]) is more confident in the historicity of this story.

156. Acts 2:19, 22, 43; 4:30; 5:12; 6:8; 7:36; 14:3; 15:12. Cf. 249n137 above.

157. In the NT σιγάω ("be silent") is used six times by Luke and four times by Paul; πλῆθος ("multitude") is used twenty-four times by Luke and seven times in the remainder of the NT; and of the six occurrences of ἐξηγέομαι ("explain") in the NT, all but one are in Luke's corpus.

158. See Rudolf Bultmann, "Zur Frage nach den Quellen der Apostelgeschichte," in *New Testament Essays: Studies in Memory of Thomas Walton Manson*, ed. A. J. B. Higgins (Manchester: Manchester University Press, 1959), 72–73n6; Lüdemann, *Acts*, 188–89.

159. Dunn keeps alive the "pleasing speculation (with a long pedigree) that Luke himself was 'the man from Macedonia'" (*Acts*, 218).

160. Barrett warns that it is "mistaken . . . to make much of a move from Asia into Europe; Paul and his colleagues remained within the one Greco-Roman world" (*Commentary on the Acts*, 2:766).

161. Cf. Dunn, *Acts*, 218.

162. In the NT ὅραμα ("vision") occurs in Matt. 17:9; Acts 7:31; 9:10, 12; 10:3, 17, 19; 11:5; 12:9; 16:9, 10; 18:9; and ἔκστασις ("ecstacy") occurs in Mark 5:42; 16:8; Luke 5:26; Acts 3:10;

"we-passages," which I am taking as likely from someone who did not know Paul (see §8.1 above)—is laden with Lukan language[163] and ideas particularly important to him.[164] It seems reasonable to conclude that we find nothing in this story that we could confidently contribute to the historical Paul in relation to the miraculous.[165]

8.10 Exorcism of a Slave Girl (Acts 16:16–18)

Set in Philippi, during Paul's so-called second missionary journey (Acts 15:36–18:22), Luke has a story of the exorcism of a slave girl.[166] For Luke, the story shows that, as for Jesus (Luke 4:34, 41; 8:28), Paul's identity and message is acknowledged by the supernatural world (Acts 16:17).[167] We will see, though, that this knowledge is flawed. Luke also uses the story to distinguish Paul and the gospel from "soothsaying" or "fortune-telling" (μαντεύομαι, 16:16), a word used long and widely for pagan divination and prophetic activity,[168] and in the Septuagint in relation to false prophets.[169] Further, for Luke, the story shows, again like Jesus (Luke 4:35, 41; 8:29–37), that Paul is superior to these forces (Acts 16:18).[170]

As well suited as the story is to Luke's purposes, there is considerable evidence that it was not only part of his tradition but also that it can credibly be associated with the historical Paul. First, the initial element of the story,

---

10:10; 11:5; 22:17, though in Mark 5:42; 16:8; Luke 5:26; Acts 3:10 it is to be translated "amazement." See also Acts 18:9; 23:11; 27:23.

163. Lüdemann (*Early Christianity*, 177) points to λαλῆσαι τὸν λόγον ("speak the word," 16:6), πορευθῆναι ("to proceed," 16:7), and the accumulation of participles: κωλυθέντες ("preventing," 16:6); ἐλθόντες ("coming," 16:7); παρελθόντες ("passing," 16:8); παρακαλῶν ("calling," 16:9); διαβάς ("going through," 16:9); συμβιβάζοντες ("concluding," 16:10).

164. Lüdemann (ibid.) mentions the Holy Spirit (Acts 16:6) and the Spirit of Jesus (Acts 16:7) demonstrating that salvation history is guided by the Spirit.

165. Cf. Lüdemann, *Acts*, 210–11; Pervo, *Acts*, 391. For a rather cynical review and critique of those who have easily found historically credible material in this story of the call-vision in Macedonia, see Haenchen, *Acts*, 489–91.

166. See also Graham H. Twelftree, *In the Name of Jesus: Exorcism among Early Christians* (Grand Rapids: Baker Academic, 2007), 145–48; Twelftree, "Jesus and Magic," 51–52.

167. Cf. Haenchen, *Acts*, 502.

168. E.g., Aeschylus, *Eum.* 715–16; Pindar, *Ol.* 7.31; Herodotus, *Hist.* 1.46; 4.67, 172; 5.114; Euripides, *Ion* 346, 373, 431; Aristophanes, *Av.* 593; *Vesp.* 159; Plato, *Apol.* 21a; *Phileb.* 64a; Plutarch, *Alex.* 75.1; Arrian, *Anab.* 8.11.1–8; Lucian, *Alex.* 19; *Dial. mort.* 10.1; 23.1; *PGM* 5.50; 7.545–50.

169. In the Septuagint, see μαντεῖον ("oracle"): Num. 22:7; Prov. 16:10; Ezek. 21:27 (ET 21:22); μαντεύομαι ("divinize"): Deut. 18:10; 1 Sam. 28:8; 2 Kings 17:17; Jer. 34:9 (ET 27:9); Ezek. 12:24; 13:6, 23; 21:26, 28, 34 (ET 21:21, 23, 29); 22:28; Mic. 3:11; μάντις ("diviner" or "seer" or "prophet"): Josh. 13:22; 1 Sam. 6:2; Jer. 36:8 (ET 29:8); Mic. 3:7; Zech. 10:2.

170. Cf. Haenchen, *Acts*, 502.

a confrontation, in which the girl is described as "following around"[171] and crying out to Paul and those with him, is part of an exorcism story[172] yet sufficiently unique to suggest that it may have been part of an original report.[173]

Second, the girl describes Paul and the others as "slaves" (δοῦλοι, Acts 16:17) of God, a self-designation taken up by Paul for himself (Rom. 1:1; Gal. 1:10; Phil. 1:1) and other followers of Jesus.[174] Luke shows no particular interest in this description of his characters, using it only one other time in Acts of the followers of Jesus (4:29; cf. 2:18).

Third to consider in relation to the historicity of the story is the description of God as "the Most High God" (τοῦ θεοῦ τοῦ ὑψίστου, Acts 16:17).[175] This title was of little interest to early Christians, being on the margins of their traditions,[176] suggesting that they would have had little cause to introduce it into this story. Yet, on the one hand, it appears to be a title for God that Luke favored.[177] On the other hand, however, in a place where we have access to his source, we can see that Luke has simply taken up the title (Mark 5:7 // Luke 8:28), which he could have done in this Acts story. Moreover, Luke's use of the term shows a sensitivity to its varied use. That is,

171. In the NT κατακολουθέω occurs only in Luke 23:55 and here in Acts 16:17.

172. See Graham H. Twelftree, *Jesus the Exorcist: A Contribution to the Study of the Historical Jesus* (WUNT 2/54; Tübingen: Mohr Siebeck; Peabody, MA: Hendrickson, 1993), 146–48.

173. The suggestion by Friedrich Avemarie ("Warum treibt Paulus einen Dämon aus, der die Wahrheit sagt? Geschichte und Bedeutung des Exorzismus zu Philippi [Acts 16,16–18]," in *Die Dämonen: Die Dämonologie der israelistich-jüdischen und frühchristlichen Literatur im Kontext ihrer Umwelt* [= *Demons: The Demonology of Israelite-Jewish and Early Christian Literature in Context of Their Environment*], ed. Armin Lange, Hermann Lichtenberger, and K. F. Diethard Römheld [Tübingen: Mohr Siebeck, 2003], 552) that, on the basis that all NT references to slave masters are in the singular, here the plural οἱ κύριοι ("the lords," i.e., owners) is an indication of the historical veracity of this story is not convincing. Not only did owners share slaves (see Cicero, *Pro Roscio comoedo*; also Hans-Josef Klauck, *Magic and Paganism in Early Christianity: The World of the Acts of the Apostles*, trans. Brian McNeil [Edinburgh: T&T Clark, 2000], 65), it could be that in light of Luke 16:13 ("no slave can serve two masters") Luke uses the plural to add to the negative portrait of the girl's situation.

174. Rom. 6:16, 17, 20; cf. 1 Cor. 7:23.

175. Note the insightful discussion by Paul R. Trebilco, "Paul and Silas—'Servants of the Most High God' (Acts 16:16–18)," *JSNT* 36 (1989): 51–73.

176. Georg Bertram, "ὕψιστος," *TDNT* 8:620; Ferdinand C. Hahn, *The Titles of Jesus in Christology: Their History in Early Christianity*, trans. Harold Knight and George Ogg (London: Lutterworth, 1969), 291–92; Barrett, *Commentary on the Acts*, 2:786. Jewish Christians later found the term useful, as in, e.g., *Testaments of the Twelve Patriarchs* (see *T. Sim.* 2:5; 6:7; *T. Levi* 3:10; 4:1, 2; 5:1, 7; 8:15 (?); 16:3; 18:7; *T. Jud.* 24:4; *T. Iss.* 2:5; *T. Naph.* 2:3; *T. Gad* 3:1; 5:4; *T. Ash.* 2:6; 5:4; 7:2; *T. Jos.* 1:4, 6; 3:10; 9:3; 10:3; *T. Benj.* 4:5; 9:2.

177. As a title for God, Luke uses the term at Luke 1:32, 35, 76; 2:14; 6:35; 8:28; 19:38; Acts 7:48; 16:17; and in the remainder of the NT the term appears at Mark 5:7; Heb. 7:1; cf. Mark 11:10; Matt. 21:9.

in a Jewish context the title was the simple "Most High" (ὕψιστος) or "the Most High" (ὁ ὕψιστος),[178] but in a Gentile context, as in this Acts story, it was "the God Most High" (τοῦ θεοῦ τοῦ ὑψίστου).[179] This use of the term reflects an awareness that for non-Jews—though used widely, and often of Zeus[180]—the term could also refer to a local deity.[181] At times, therefore, it is not clear which god is in mind.[182] Not surprisingly, then, Josephus only uses the term once (*Ant.* 16.163), and Philo, when not quoting or referring to the Septuagint,[183] used it with careful qualification (*Leg.* 3.82)[184] or when addressing non-Jews.[185] In short, this term for God was quite likely part of Luke's tradition.

Fourth, the girl describing Paul's message as "a way" (ὁδός, Acts 16:17)[186] rather than "the way" (ἡ ὁδός)[187]—implying their proclamation is one among many possibilities for salvation—may also point to the historical veracity of the story. For, consistent with demonic confessions found in his Gospel (Luke 4:34, 41; 8:28), we would expect Luke to provide the more theologically ac-curate statement if it was of his creation. Further, then, given that Luke does not seem to have created the girl's statement, it probably is significant that she says Paul and Barnabas "proclaim" (καταγγέλλω), rather than "preach" (εὐαγγελίζω), which might have been expected.[188]

Fifth, there is an authentic ring to the description of Paul "annoyed" (δι-απονέομαι, Acts 16:18) at being followed for many days by a girl crying after him.[189] On the one hand, the girl was publicizing their mission, but, on the other hand, she also was using an imprecise and misleading description of God along with a deficient grasp of Paul's message. Yet, Paul probably could

178. Reflected in Luke 1:32, 35, 76; 2:14; 6:35; 8:28; 19:38; Acts 7:48; 16:17.

179. Rarely in pagan inscriptions does the term ὕψιστος ("Most High") appear without specification such as θεός ("God") or Ζεύς ("Zeus"). See Trebilco, "Paul and Silas," 59.

180. See Arthur B. Cook, *Zeus: A Study in Ancient Religion*, 2 vols. in 3 (1914–40; repr., New York: Biblo and Tannen, 1964–65), 2:876–90; and a tabular summary by Arthur Darby Nock, Colin Roberts, and T. C. Skeat, "The Guild of Zeus Hypsistos," *HTR* 29 (1936): 56–59.

181. See Franz Cumont, *Hypsistos* (Brussels: Polleunis & Ceuterik, 1897), 1n2 and 3n1; Cook, *Zeus*, 2.2:889; Carsten Colpe, "Hypsistos," in *Der Kleine Pauly: Lexikon der Antike*, vol. 2, *Dicta Catonis bis Juno* (Stuttgart: Druckenmüller, 1967), cols. 1291–92.

182. L. Robert, "Reliefs votifs et cultes d'Anatolie," *Anatolia* 3 (1958): 112–19.

183. Philo, *Leg.* 3.24; *Post.* 89; *Plant.* 59; *Ebr.* 105; *Congr.* 58; *Mut.* 202.

184. See Trebilco, "Paul and Silas," 62, and Klauck, *Magic and Paganism*, 68.

185. Philo, *Legat.* 157, 278, 317; *Flacc.* 46. See Trebilco, "Paul and Silas," 53–54.

186. Also, in Acts 2:28 the article is absent in a citation of LXX Ps. 15:11 (ET 16:11).

187. Acts 9:2; 18:25, 26; 19:9, 23; 22:4; 24:14, 22.

188. However, καταγγέλλω is still a word that Luke prefers. In the NT καταγγέλλω occurs eleven times in Acts and seven times in the Pauline corpus. In the NT εὐαγγελίζω occurs twenty-five times in Luke's writings and twenty-nine times in the remainder of the NT.

189. Cf. Dunn, *Acts*, 220–21.

foresee the response by the owners to an exorcism that would deprive them of their income.[190] Hence, Paul's response to the girl is delayed, reinforced perhaps by ignoring a nameless slave.[191] In any case, Paul's delay leads to the next point.

Sixth, in favor of seeing Luke's story as reflecting an event in the life of the historical Paul is the hesitancy or reluctance with which Paul undertook to perform the miracle. That is, we have seen that Paul does not appear to have sought or taken the initiative to perform miracles. On the principle that this story coheres with what we already know about Paul, it can be taken to reflect the view of the historical Paul.[192]

Finally, at least the core of Paul's command to the spirit in Acts may be authentic.[193] However, its introductory term, "I order" (παραγγέλλω), a favorite of Luke's,[194] is most probably from his hand, as are the use of the name of "Christ" (Χριστός, Acts 16:18)[195] and the description of the spirit coming out "that very hour" (αὐτῇ τῇ ὥρᾳ).[196] Paul, then, may have said something like, "In the name of Jesus, come out!"

Although Luke probably included this story here so that, just as Jesus' public ministry began with preaching (Luke 4:20–30) followed by an exorcism story (4:31–37), so Paul's ministry in Europe could begin with an exorcism signaling the coming of God's rule in the new theater,[197] this is not an argument in itself for Luke or an earlier Christian's creation of the story. Rather, aside from some minor evidence of Luke's hand we have noted, this small story probably can be taken as an authentic contribution to the historical Paul.[198]

190. Cf. Trebilco, "Paul and Silas," 64.

191. Cf. John Byron, "Paul and the Python Girl (Acts 16:16–19)," *ATJ* 41 (2009): 7–9.

192. On the criterion of coherence or consistency, important particularly to students of the historical Jesus, see the discussion by John P. Meier, *A Marginal Jew: Rethinking the Historical Jesus*, vol. 1, *The Roots of the Problem and the Person* (ABRL; New York: Doubleday, 1991), 176–77; Stanley E. Porter, *The Criteria for Authenticity in Historical-Jesus Research* (JSNTSup 191; Sheffield: Sheffield Academic Press, 2000), 79–82.

193. On the brevity of the exorcism incantations among the early Christians, see Twelftree, *Name of Jesus*, e.g., 127–28, 241.

194. In the NT παραγγέλλω ("I order") occurs in Matt. 10:5; 15:35; Mark 6:8; 8:6; Luke 5:14; 8:29, 56; 9:21; Acts 1:4; 4:18; 5:28, 40; 10:42; 15:5; 16:18, 23; 17:30; 23:22, 30; 1 Cor. 7:10; 11:17; 1 Thess. 4:11; 2 Thess. 3:4, 6, 10, 12; 1 Tim. 1:3; 4:11; 5:7; 6:13, 17.

195. It is likely that the earliest Christian exorcisms were carried out only in the name of Jesus. See Twelftree, *Name of Jesus*, e.g., 125–27. In the NT the command ἐν τῷ ὀνόματι Ἰησοῦ Χριστοῦ ("in the name of Jesus Christ") is found only in Acts 3:6; 4:10; 10:48; cf. 16:18 (ἐν ὀνόματι Ἰησοῦ Χριστοῦ).

196. In the NT only Luke uses the phrase αὐτῇ τῇ ὥρᾳ ("that very hour"): Luke 2:38; 10:21; 12:12; 13:31; 20:19; 24:33; Acts 16:18; 22:13; cf. Matt. 8:13; 26:55; Mark 13:32; 14:35; Luke 10:21; John 13:1.

197. Cf. Pervo, *Acts*, 406.

198. Cf. Lüdemann, *Early Christianity*, 182; Schreiber, *Wundertäter*, 88–94, 143.

8.11 Deliverance from Prison (Acts 16:25–34)

This is the third prison escape story in Acts. Early in his narrative Luke says that "during the night an angel of the Lord opened the prison doors" and brought out the apostles, presumably all twelve of them (see Acts 5:19; cf. 5:12). Then, Peter having been arrested and imprisoned by Herod Agrippa I, an angel of the Lord appeared, and a light shone in the apostle's cell. "He tapped Peter on the side and woke him, saying, 'Get up quickly.' And the chains fell off his wrists" (12:7). The angel then led Peter out past the first and second guards, and through the prison door, which opened for them (12:8–10). Then, in the story of interest to us, Paul and Silas, while praying and singing hymns, are released from prison as the result of an earthquake (16:25–26).

The escape stories in Acts have been the subject of considerable attention.[199] For, in Luke's world the motif of a self-opening door was common[200] and used in narratives to promote the legitimacy of minority groups.[201] In his turn, Luke uses his three stories as devices to communicate the legitimacy of the Jesus movement.[202] Our interest, however, is in how far the story of Paul's escape from prison might reflect an event in his life. Although some are happy to accept the historicity of this escape story,[203] two factors weigh heavily against seeing this narrative (as well as the other two stories) as historically credible. First, as Joachim Jeremias pointed out, Luke's picking up many parallels with the stories of his time—"liberation by night, the role of the guards, the falling off of chains, the bursting open of the doors, the shining of bright light, earthquake"—suggests that he is following at least an established topos.[204] Second, if Paul was involved in such an event—humiliating incarceration and eventual escape—it is incredible that he does not mention it along with his escape from Damascus (2 Cor. 11:30–33), which is the climactic example of suffering and humiliation.[205]

---

199. See John B. Weaver, *Plots of Epiphany: Prison-Escape in Acts of the Apostles* (BZNW 131; Berlin: de Gruyter, 2004), 11–22.

200. See, e.g., Euripides, *Bacch.* 433–50, 615–40; Ovid, *Metam.* 691–700; Apollodorus, *Bib.* 3.5.1; and Artapanus, *On the Jews*, frg. 3 (Eusebius, *Praep. ev.* 9.27.23–24). See the discussion by Otto Weinreich, "Gebet und Wunder," in *Religionsgeschichtliche Studien* (Darmstadt: Wissenschaftliche Buchgesellschaft, 1968), 1–298; also the summaries by Joachim Jeremias, "θύρα," *TDNT* 3:175–76; and Weaver, *Plots of Epiphany*, 12–15.

201. Weaver, *Plots of Epiphany*, 90.

202. Acts 5:20–21, 26; 12:11; 16:35–40. Ibid., 144–45, 232, 278.

203. E.g., William Neil, *The Acts of the Apostles* (NCB; London: Oliphants, 1973), 184; I. Howard Marshall, *The Acts of the Apostles: An Introduction and Commentary* (TNTC; Leicester: Inter-Varsity, 1980), 265.

204. Jeremias, "θύρα," 175–76.

205. On the humiliation implied in going down, rather than up, a wall in the face of an enemy, see Edwin A. Judge, "The Conflict of Educational Aims in New Testament Thought," *JCE* 9 (1966): 44–45; and the discussion by Stephen H. Travis, "Paul's Boasting in 2 Corinthians 10–12," in *Studia*

Moreover, there is no hint in the story that the earthquake had any impact on the magistrates or the city,[206] or even the jailer, who is said only to notice the open doors (Acts 16:27);[207] and no mention is made of Timothy, who, along with Silas (15:40), is introduced as a traveling companion of Paul's (16:1).[208] In short, it is not possible for us to connect Luke's story of the miraculous escape with the historical Paul.[209]

8.12 Laying on of Hands and the Coming of the Spirit (Acts 19:6)

Subsequent to about a dozen Ephesian followers of John the Baptist being baptized "in the name of the Lord Jesus" (Acts 19:5), Luke says, "When Paul had laid his hands on them, the Holy Spirit came upon them, and they spoke in tongues and prophesied" (19:6). The general historical credibility of the story as a whole probably is not to be doubted; in the Fourth Gospel followers of the Baptist also transfer their allegiance to Jesus (John 1:35; cf. 3:26; Acts 18:25). Further, Luke's abstract of John's activity and preaching—"John baptized with the baptism of repentance, telling the people to believe in the one who was to come after him, that is, in Jesus" (19:4)—is also consistent with what is otherwise known about him and his message.[210]

However, that followers of John received the Spirit, accompanied by ecstatic speech, when Paul laid his hands on the Ephesians is probably of Luke's making. To begin with, as Luke Timothy Johnson has pointed out, Luke does not seem to have much historical information on hand: the number of disciples of John is a convenient symbolic twelve, they lack names and origin, and play no future role in the story.[211] Then, the notion of laying on of hands is particularly

---

Evangelica VI: Papers Presented to the Fourth International Congress on New Testament Studies Held at Oxford, 1969, ed. Elizabeth A. Livingstone (TUGAL 112; Berlin: Akademie-Verlag, 1973), 527–32.

206. Haenchen, *Acts,* 497; Marshall, *Acts,* 265; Barrett, *Commentary on the Acts,* 2:776. Pervo notes that "Codex Bezae already attempted to set Acts right by having the officials respond to the numinous" (*Profit with Delight,* 147n28).

207. Cf. Pervo, *Acts,* 411.

208. Paul W. Walaskay, *Acts* (WestBC; Louisville: Westminster John Knox, 1998), 159.

209. E.g., Pervo, *Profit with Delight,* 23; Lüdemann, *Early Christianity,* 184; Lüdemann, *Acts,* 217; Pervo, *Acts,* 415. Weaver suggests the escape stories are "mythistory . . . historical narrative configured by traditional stories of collective significance" (*Plots of Epiphany,* 160).

210. Cf. Mark 1:2–8; Matt. 3:1–12 // Luke 3:1–18 (Q); John 1:29–34. See Paul W. Hollenbach, "Social Aspects of John the Baptizer's Preaching Mission in the Context of Palestinian Judaism," *ANRW* II.19.1 (1979): 256–75; W. Barnes Tatum, *John the Baptist and Jesus: A Report of the Jesus Seminar* (Sonoma, CA: Polebridge, 1991), 115–44; John P. Meier, *A Marginal Jew: Rethinking the Historical Jesus,* vol. 2, *Mentor, Message, and Miracles* (ABRL; New York: Doubleday, 1994), 109–10.

211. Luke Timothy Johnson, *The Acts of the Apostles* (SP 5; Collegeville, MN: Liturgical Press, 1992), 342.

Lukan,[212] and only he, and probably the author of 2 Timothy, of the New Testament writers use it in relation to the coming of the Spirit.[213] Further, this scenario concerning the Ephesians probably is part of his agenda to maintain the Pentecost narrative as the model for the reception of the Spirit,[214] for the phrase that he uses here (19:6)[215] he also used a little earlier where he is making the point that it was the same experience as at Pentecost (11:15).[216] Also, the association of the coming of the Spirit with tongues and prophecy fits Luke's paradigm set up in the Pentecost narrative (cf. 10:47; 11:15).[217] On the other hand, we know nothing from Paul of him using the laying on of hands as part of initiation or the coming to faith of his readers. Once again, then, even though Luke probably is working with reliable traditions about some followers of John joining the Jesus movement,[218] we do not have sufficient confidence in the historical veracity of the miraculous elements of Luke's story to attribute the miracle of the coming of the Spirit and ecstatic speech to the activity of the historical Paul.

8.13 Miracles through Neckcloths or Belts (Acts 19:11–12)

In Acts 19, following the conversion of the followers of John, and during Paul's stay in Ephesus, Luke says, "And God did extraordinary powers through the hands of Paul, so that when neckcloths or belts[219] that had touched his skin were brought to the sick, their diseases left them, and the evil spirits came out of them" (19:11–12, my translation). Again, our interest is not in what Luke makes of this story, but in how far it reflects an incident in the life of the historical Paul.

212. A phrase involving the placing or laying (ἐπιτίθημι) of hands (χεῖρες) is used by Luke at Luke 4:40; 13:13; Acts 6:6; 8:17, 19; 9:12, 17; 13:3; 19:6; 28:8. It is also found in Matt. 19:13, 15; Mark 5:23; 6:5; 8:23, 25; 16:18; 1 Tim. 5:22. Cf. 249n136 above.

213. Acts 8:17, 19; 9:12 [cf. 9:17]; 19:6. Cf. 2 Tim. 1:6: "rekindle the gift of God that is within you through the laying on of my hands." See §9.4 below, and the discussion by Raymond F. Collins, *I & II Timothy and Titus* (NTL; Louisville: Westminster John Knox, 2002), 195; I. Howard Marshall with Philip H. Towner, *A Critical and Exegetical Commentary on the Pastoral Epistles* (ICC; London: T&T Clark, 2004), 696–98.

214. See, e.g., Earl J. Richard, "Pentecost as a Recurrent Theme in Luke-Acts," in *New Views on Luke and Acts*, ed. Earl J. Richard (Collegeville, MN: Liturgical Press, 1990), 133–49.

215. Acts 19:6: "the Holy Spirit came upon them" (ἦλθε τὸ πνεῦμα τὸ ἅγιον ἐπ᾽ αὐτούς).

216. Acts 11:15: "the Holy Spirit fell upon them [ἐπέπεσεν τὸ πνεῦμα τὸ ἅγιον ἐπ᾽ αὐτοὺς] as it had upon us at the beginning."

217. Twelftree, *People of the Spirit*, 85–87.

218. Cf. Lüdemann, *Acts*, 252.

219. On the translations of σουδάριον ("neckcloth") and σιμικίνθιον ("belt"), see T. J. Leary, "The 'Aprons' of St. Paul—Acts 19:12," *JTS* 41 (1990): 527–29; and Rick Strelan, "Acts 19:12: Paul's 'Aprons' Again," *JTS* 54 (2003): 154–57.

Since the story involves supposed crude superstition,[220] it has been tempting for modern readers to distance Paul from it by noting that he is portrayed as playing no role in the use of the clothing for healing,[221] or, as F. F. Bruce exonerated the method, "The healing virtue resided not in those pieces of cloth but in the faith of those who used them."[222] However, our disapproval of a practice,[223] or an unwillingness on our part to acknowledge the reality of what could be called the enchanted world of others,[224] might justly be perceived as a form of intellectual colonialism.[225]

Another approach distancing Paul from this story is to call into question its historicity. Hans Conzelmann, for example, sets the story aside as containing no concrete material, but providing a picture of Paul as a miracle worker from a later time.[226] However, Luke and Paul's readers would have been familiar with the idea that objects were thought to take up and transmit spiritual power.[227] Notably, for example, writing at a similar time, Josephus[228] gives evidence of sharing this view when he says that upon receiving Elijah's mantle, "Elisha immediately began to prophesy" (*Ant.* 8.354; cf. 1 Kings 19:19).

In favor of Luke's scenario reflecting an event in the life of the historical Paul, consistent with what we have seen in Paul's letters, the healings take place without his direct involvement (see §7.9 above). For, since the healings take place through the pieces of clothing, Luke's phrase that miracles took place "through the hands of Paul" (διὰ τῶν χειρῶν Παύλου) is not a description of the method of healing but an expression of agency.[229]

Notwithstanding, there are significant problems with associating this narrative with Paul. As is widely agreed, this is a parallel story to one about

220. See, e.g., Haenchen, *Acts*, 562–63.

221. See the discussion by Scott Shauf, *Theology as History, History as Theology: Paul in Ephesus in Acts 19* (BZNW 133; Berlin: de Gruyter, 2005), 110–13.

222. Bruce, *Acts of the Apostles*, 410.

223. Pervo (*Acts*, 475) rightly points out that disapproval is not a valid ground for discrediting the historicity of a story.

224. See the discussion by Charles Taylor, *A Secular Age* (Harvard, MA: Belknap, 2008), 29–30; cf. the review of Taylor by Martin Jay, "Faith-Based History," *HistT* 48 (2009): 76–84.

225. See the discussion by Graham H. Twelftree, "Miracle in an Age of Diversity," in *The Cambridge Companion to Miracles*, ed. Graham H. Twelftree (Cambridge: Cambridge University Press, 2011), 12.

226. Conzelmann, *Acts*, 163.

227. Twelftree, *Name of Jesus*, 148–49.

228. For a discussion of the dates of Josephus, see §2.1 (c) above, and on the dating of the works of Josephus, see Steve Mason, *Josephus and the New Testament*, 2nd ed. (Peabody, MA: Hendrickson, 2003), chap. 3.

229. Against Bruce (*Acts of the Apostles*, 410), who, without evidence, says, "the active use of his hands is implied." See Twelftree, *Name of Jesus*, 148.

the apostles and Peter (Acts 5:12–16).[230] Both stories are introduced with a statement about many (5:12) or extraordinary (19:11) miracles taking place. Both the ensuing stories are summaries rather than specific healings, and both use an extension of the person—the shadow of Peter[231] and the clothing of Paul—as part of the healing method. On closer examination, this pointer to Lukan activity is confirmed, at least in the story of interest to us. That is, the introduction to the story about Paul—"And God did extraordinary powers through the hands of Paul" (19:11)—is probably entirely of Luke's making. The phrase "not the ordinary" (οὐ τὰς τυχούσας)[232] is found nowhere else in the New Testament, but both the litotes (ironically affirming something through a negative),[233] and the word "ordinary" or "happen" (τυγχάνω),[234] and the phrase "through the hands"[235] are all distinctly Lukan, as is the enclitic particle "and" (τέ) in the postpositive position at the beginning of the sentence.[236]

Therefore, whatever we were to make of the historicity of the story of healing at a distance through the use of clothing, with Luke creating the introduction in which Paul is named as the subject, we have no way of being

230. See, e.g., Neirynck, "Miracle Stories," esp. 172–74; Susan Marie Praeder, "Jesus-Paul, Peter-Paul, and Jesus-Peter Parallelisms in Luke-Acts: A History of Reader Response," *SBLSP* 23 (1984): 35–36; Pervo, *Acts*, 472.

231. On the ancient view that the shadow was regarded as a person's "soul, soul-substance, spiritual essence, spiritual double or whatever other term one may use to designate the vital power or life force," see Pieter W. van der Horst, "Peter's Shadow: The Religio-Historical Background of Acts 5:15," *NTS* 23 (1976–77): 207.

232. In view of the ensuing story of the seven sons of Sceva, what was extraordinary for Luke was not the kind of healings or Paul's lack of interest in money, but Paul's effortless success with numerous miracles. Note the plurals: δυνάμεις ("powers"); τὰς τυχούσας ("extraordinary things"); τοὺς ἀσθενοῦντας ("the sick ones"); σουδάρια ("neckcloths"); σιμικίνθια ("belts"); αὐτῶν τὰς νόσους ("their sicknesses"); τά τε πνεύματα τὰ πονηρά ("the evil spirits"). See Twelftree, *Name of Jesus*, 150.

233. A. T. Robertson notes that "Litotes is common enough" (*A Grammar of the Greek Testament* [Nashville: Broadman, 1934], 1205), citing only Acts 1:5; 14:28; 15:2; 19:11, 23, 24; 21:39; 27:14, 20; 28:2. See also Acts 20:12. Cf., e.g., Bruce, *Acts of the Apostles*, 410; Pervo, *Acts*, 472n94.

234. In the NT τυγχάνω ("happen") occurs twelve times, half of them in Luke-Acts: Luke 20:35; Acts 19:11; 24:2; 26:22; 27:3; 28:2. See also the others are in 1 Cor. 14:10; 15:37; 16:6; 2 Tim. 2:10; Heb. 8:6; 11:35.

235. In the NT see Mark 6:2; 14:58; Acts 2:23; 5:12; 7:25; 11:30; 14:3; 15:23; 19:11, 26; Heb. 9:11.

236. The enclitic particle τέ occurs 215 times in the NT: Matthew (3x), Luke (9x), John (3x), Acts (151x), the Pauline corpus (25x), Hebrews (20x), James (2x), Jude (1x), and Revelation (1x). See the discussions by James Hope Moulton, *A Grammar of New Testament Greek* (4 vols.; Edinburgh: T&T Clark, 1908–76), 3:338–39; and K.-H. Pridik, "τέ," *EDNT* 3:339–40. On enclitics and their accents, see D. A. Carson, *Greek Accents: A Student's Manual* (Grand Rapids: Baker Academic, 1985), 47–52.

confident the story can be associated with the historical Paul. Indeed, we have to take into account Ernst Haenchen's point, supported by my discussion in the last chapter, that such healings contradict what we know of the picture Paul's opponents had of him as failing to have miraculous powers.[237] Once again, we are obliged to leave this story aside in our reconstruction of the historical Paul.

8.14 Sons of Sceva Associate Paul with Exorcism (Acts 19:13)

After the story of neckcloths or belts healing the sick and driving out evil spirits, which I have just discussed, Luke says that "some itinerant Jewish exorcists tried to use the name of the Lord Jesus over those who had evil spirits, saying, 'I adjure you by the Jesus whom Paul proclaims'" (19:13). Once again this story cannot be set aside simply because it does not meet with our approval.[238] To the contrary, on the one hand, the incantation in this story fits a type used in the period in which the exorcist recited the history of the invoked power-authority.[239] On the other hand, the incantation in Acts does not easily fit the type in that it does not contain a history but identifies Jesus as he was then known,[240] suggesting that it was not created to fit a type. Also, the slight dissonance between the description of the incantation (using "the name of the Lord Jesus") and the incantation itself ("the Jesus") has not been resolved, suggesting that the less theologically developed one ("the Jesus") is traditional. Moreover, the description of Jesus—"whom Paul proclaims"— does not fit Luke's immediate context, in which Paul is being portrayed as a miracle worker rather than a preacher (19:11–12). Therefore, it is reasonable to conclude that in this incantation Luke is using traditional material. That we can take the next step and suggest it is historically reliable material is probably justified when we note this is a rather indirect association of Paul with the miraculous, a point that we found in Paul's letters. In short, Luke probably has preserved historically reliable material in which Paul is at least associated with exorcism.[241]

237. Haenchen, *Acts*, 563; and the discussion in §7.7 above.
238. So Lüdemann, *Acts*, 255. The historicity of the story is also doubted by, e.g., Conzelmann, *Acts*, 164; Johnson, *Acts*, 340.
239. See, e.g., *PGM* 4.3019–20; 5.99–106; Origen, *Cels.* 1.6; and W. L. Knox, "Jewish Liturgical Exorcisms," *HTR* 31 (1938): 195.
240. Twelftree, *Name of Jesus*, 33–35.
241. Cf. Todd E. Klutz, "Naked and Wounded: Foregrounding, Relevance and Situation in Acts 19:13–20," in *Discourse Analysis and the New Testament: Approaches and Results*, ed. Stanley E. Porter and Jeffrey T. Reed (JSNTSup 170; Sheffield: Sheffield Academic Press, 1999), 278–79.

8.15 Eutychus Raised from the Dead (Acts 20:7–12)

In Acts 20 Luke says that, after the uproar had ceased in Ephesus and Paul had encouraged the disciples there, on the way to Syria he spent time in Macedonia and Greece before returning to Troas (20:1–7), the setting of this story. Although earlier critics took this story of Eutychus to be historically reliable,[242] at least two problems confront the reader in attempting to assign it to the historical Paul. One problem is the absence of reference to "we" in the story (20:9–12),[243] leading to the reasonable conclusion that it is a later, perhaps, secular story inserted into the "we-passage" (20:5–21:18).[244] Indeed, without the Eutychus story, the geographical narrative (20:1–16) is not interrupted (cf. 20:7 and 13). However, on the other hand, the story fits seamlessly into the narrative; and in other parts of the "we-narrative" the first-person plural drops out and returns (see 27:1–28:16; cf. 27:21–26). The other impediments to judging the story useful in contributing to the historical Paul are the parallels between it and other stories. First, the story of Peter raising Tabitha (9:36–42) is said to be parallel to this one about Paul.[245] Indeed, in that both stories have a leading follower of Jesus as the main character, a second main character who is dead (Tabitha and Eutychus),[246] and there is a positive response to both revivals (9:42; 20:12), the stories can be taken as parallel to each other. However, it is highly unlikely that either story was written by Luke, or anyone in his tradition, in order to create a parallel. For, between the two stories verbal parallels[247] are minimal,[248] with some words used quite differently,[249] and the idea of death is expressed differently in each story.[250]

242. Haenchen (*Acts*, 586) cites Zeller, Renan, Wellhausen, and Preuschen.

243. On the puzzling beginning and ends of the "we-passages," see Henry J. Cadbury, "'We' and 'I' Passages in Luke-Acts," *NTS* 3 (1957): 128–32.

244. See the discussions in Lüdemann, *Acts*, 267–68; and Lüdemann, *Early Christianity*, 221–22.

245. See the discussion of earlier works by Neirynck, "Miracle Stories," 174; Praeder, "Jesus-Paul," 25–26.

246. Given that Luke has said Eutychus was taken up dead (Acts 20:9), and that he is relating a miracle story (20:12), the phrase "for his life is in him" (ἡ γὰρ ψυχὴ αὐτοῦ ἐν αὐτῷ ἐστιν [20:10]) refers not to an apparent death (see Dibelius, "Style Criticism," 18; Bruce, *Acts of the Apostles*, 426) but foreshadows the miracle (cf. Luke 8:52). See Conzelmann, *Acts*, 169; Fitzmyer, *Acts*, 669; Barrett, *Commentary on the Acts*, 2:955; and the extended discussion by Andrew Arterbury, "The Downfall of Eutychus," in Phillips, *Contemporary Studies*, 201–21, followed by Parsons, *Acts*, 287–88.

247. Goulder proposes that one of the safeguards against the abuse of the typological method is "the need for the coincidence of actual Greek words between type and antitype, and the rarer the better" (*Type and History*, 10).

248. ὄνομα ("name" [Acts 9:36; 20:9]); ὑπερῷον ("upper room" [9:37, 39; 20:8]); μή ("not" [9:38; 20:10]); ζάω ("live" [9:41; 20:12]).

249. παρακαλέω: "request" (Acts 9:38) and "comfort" (20:12); ἱκανός: "some time" (9:43) and "continue" (20:11).

250. ἀποθνήσκω ("die" [Acts 9:37]); νεκρός ("dead" [20:9]).

Second, the allusions to the Elijah and Elisha stories in the Septuagint[251] are a greater barrier to supposing this story helps us understand Paul. As in Luke's story of Eutychus, there is an "upper room" (ὑπερῷον) in the story of Elijah and the Shunammite woman's son (1 Kings [3 Kgdms.] 17:19; Acts 20:8).[252] Also, in both stories, unusually, "life" (ψυχή) is used in relation to the resuscitations (1 Kings [3 Kgdms.] 17:21; Acts 20:10).[253] Then, in the story of Elisha the boy is first said to sleep and then die (2 Kings [4 Kgdms.] 4:20), as Luke says of Eutychus (Acts 20:9). In both stories the healer's method involves laying on the dead child (2 Kings [4 Kgdms.] 4:34; Acts 20:10).[254]

Yet, these echoes probably were not contrived by Luke. Although, as could be expected, Luke's hand is evident in the beginning (20:7–8)[255] and also at the end (20:12)[256]—pointing readers back to the resurrection of Jesus and his presence[257]—in the body of the story we find few distinctively Lukan features.[258] Also, given that Luke's story has echoes of those of Elijah and Elisha, it is not inherently secular.[259] Further, given that Paul saw himself as a prophet (see §3.1 above), it is not unreasonable to suppose that on being confronted by a situation familiar from the literature of the prophets, Paul used them as a model for his behavior.[260] In short, it is possible that this story of the revival of Eutychus puts us in touch with the historical Paul in relation to the miraculous.

8.16 A Trance in the Temple (Acts 22:17–21)

As part of Paul's self-defense, spoken from the steps of the temple, Luke includes a second narrative of Paul's conversion (22:6–16), which Paul follows by saying,

251. See, e.g., Rackham, *Acts*, 380; G. W. H. Lampe, "Miracles in the Acts of the Apostles," in *Miracles: Cambridge Studies in Their Philosophy and History*, ed. C. F. D. Moule (London: Mowbray, 1965), 163–78; Goulder, *Type and History*, 50; Dunn, *Acts*, 268; Barrett, *Commentary on the Acts*, 2:954–55; Pervo, *Acts*, 512–13.

252. Also, κάθημαι ("sit") is used of Eutychus sitting in the window (Acts 20:9) and of Elijah residing (1 Kings [LXX 3 Kgdms.] 17:19).

253. Pervo, *Acts*, 512.

254. Further, see Barrett, *Commentary on the Acts*, 2:954–55.

255. Note σάββατον, the genitive absolute (Acts 20:7), the upper room (20:8). Cf. Lüdemann, *Early Christianity*, 221; Fitzmyer, *Acts*, 115.

256. Note the litotes, παρεκλήθησαν οὐ μετρίως ("not a little comforted") and παρακαλέω itself (Matt. 9x; Mark 9x; Luke 7x; Acts 22x).

257. So Johnson, *Acts*, 358.

258. See ὀνόματι ("by name") and τίς ("a certain") with a noun (Acts 20:9); on which, see Hawkins, *Horae synopticae*, 44, 47, 177. The reference to Paul returning upstairs after the healing in order to break bread (Acts 20:11) may also be from Luke's hand. See, e.g., Haenchen, *Acts*, 586; Lüdemann, *Acts*, 269.

259. So Pervo, *Acts*, 513, against Lüdemann, *Early Christianity*, 223; and Lüdemann, *Acts*, 267–69.

260. See Dunn, *Acts*, 268.

"After I had returned to Jerusalem and while I was praying in the temple, I fell into a trance and saw Jesus saying to me, 'Hurry and get out of Jerusalem quickly'" (22:17–18a). The most obvious strike against the historical value of this episode is that Paul nowhere relates the motivation of his Gentile mission to the unwillingness of the Jews.[261] Moreover, when discussing Paul's call to Europe (§8.9 above), I noted that Luke has a penchant for relating visions and trances (see 251–52n162 above). To this can be added the point that there is significant Lukan language in this paragraph,[262] leading me to conclude that we are unlikely to find historically reliable material for the reconstruction of Paul in relation to the miraculous.[263]

8.17 Miracles on Malta (Acts 27:39–28:11)

In this section of a "we-passage" (Acts 27:1–28:16) there are four references to Paul and the miraculous: Paul safe in a storm (27:39–28:1), Paul unharmed by a viper's bite (28:3–6), Publius's father healed of fever and dysentery (28:7–8), and a summary of healings on the island (28:9). Given the possibility of miracles, prima facie there is nothing intrinsically improbable about any of these stories.

Paul's statement that he was shipwrecked three times (2 Cor. 11:25) and considerable documentary evidence attesting to details of such a sea voyage suggest this story could reflect an actual journey.[264] For example, an Alexandrian wheat cargo ship (Acts 27:5–7, 38; 28:11) typically headed north for the Lycian ports of Patara or Myra before taking the western journey.[265] Sailing with the currents, but against the prevailing northwesterly winds, under the shelter of the coast of Asia Minor, the Crete to Malta leg was, as in Luke's story, the most hazardous.[266] Also, Luke's narrative carries a number of inconsequential details, such as the wintering of the ship at the island, the figurehead on the ship, and the time spent in Syracuse (28:11–12),[267] that lend credibility to the narrative. Further, the appearance of a snake from firewood is not out of the question. F. F. Bruce quotes T. E. Lawrence saying that, "When the fire

261. See Lüdemann, *Early Christianity*, 239.
262. E.g., ὑποστρέφω ("return"), 35x in the NT, all but three by Luke; ἔκστασις ("trance"), 7x in the NT, five of them by Luke (although translated also as "amazement"); σπεύδω ("hurry"), 6x in the NT, all but one by Luke; ἐν τάχει ("in haste"), 8x in the NT, four of them by Luke; ἐπίσταμαι ("understand") 14x in the NT, nine of them by Luke.
263. Cf. Barrett, *Commentary on the Acts*, 2:1033.
264. F. F. Bruce, *The Book of Acts* (NICNT; Grand Rapids: Eerdmans, 1954), 514–16.
265. Lionel Casson (*Ships and Seamanship in the Ancient World* [Baltimore: Johns Hopkins University Press, 1995], 297; cf. 298n6) says that ships on the Alexandria to Rome route in this period delivered 150,000 tons of wheat annually to the capital.
266. See ibid., 279–99; and the discussion by Hemer, "First Person Narrative," 90–91, 94.
267. See the details discussed by Hemer, "First Person Narrative," 94–102.

grew hot a long black snake wound slowly out into our group; we must have gathered it, torpid, with the twigs."[268] Nor is the allocation of heroic status to Paul by the Maltese unlikely.[269]

In the third story the description of Publius as "the leading man" (τῷ πρώτῳ) of Malta is a title attested epigraphically.[270] Also, the description of the sickness including "fevers" (πυρετοῖς), meaning intermittent attacks,[271] is consistent with malarial and Mediterranean "sand-fly" fever. Along with the mention of "dysentery," Kirsopp Lake and Henry Cadbury commented that "the phenomena which they describe are well known throughout the Mediterranean, and Malta has always a peculiarly unpleasant fever of its own."[272]

However, there are aspects and anomalies to these stories that call into question how far they reflect reports reliably associated with the historical Paul.[273] First, in relation to the story of the sea rescue and the story of the viper's bite, from the Middle Kingdom of Egypt (2055–1650 BCE) there is the tale of a shipwrecked sailor who, on coming ashore on an island, meets a large snake that prophecies his rescue.[274] More notably, Statilus Flaccus, who lived at the beginning of the first century CE,[275] has an epigram attributed to him: "The shipwrecked mariner had escaped the whirlwind and fury of the deadly sea, and as he was lying on the Libyan sand not far from the beach, deep in his last sleep, naked and exhausted by the unhappy wreck, a baneful viper slew him" (*Anth. pal.* 7.290; cf. 9.269).[276]

Similar motifs and the shared basic plot in these narratives suggest they reflect a long-standing and widely held myth. In turn, the epigram, in particular, is so similar in plot and setting to Luke's narrative[277] that it strongly

268. Bruce, *Book of Acts*, 531.

269. See Lily Ross Taylor, *The Divinity of the Roman Emperor* (1931; repr., Chico, CA: Scholars Press, 1981), 35–57; and the discussion by Edwin A. Judge, *The Social Pattern of the Christian Groups in the First Century: Some Prolegomena to the Study of New Testament Ideas of Social Obligation* (TPM; London: Tyndale, 1960), 24–25. Contrast the skepticism of Lüdemann, *Early Christianity*, 262.

270. See *IGRR* 1.512 = *IG* 14.601 (14–37 CE); *CIL* 10.7495.1; Hemer, "First Person Narrative," 100; Hemer, *Acts*, 153n152.

271. Cf. Bruce, *Book of Acts*, 533.

272. Lake and Cadbury, *English Translation and Commentary*, 343.

273. See the brief discussion by Johnson, *Acts*, 456–59.

274. See Miriam Lichtheim, *Ancient Egyptian Literature: A Book of Readings*, vol. 1, *The Old and Middle Kingdoms* (Berkeley: University of California Press, 1975), 211–15, and literature cited. I owe this reference to James McHugh.

275. Maria G. Albiani, "Flaccus: Statilius," *New Pauly* 5 (2004): 448.

276. See Conzelmann, *Acts*, 223; Klauck, *Magic and Paganism*, 114–15. Cf. Lynn Allan Kauppi (*Foreign but Familiar Gods: Greco-Romans Read Religion in Acts* [LNTS 277; London: T&T Clark, 2006], 107–12) on the widespread view that the serpent was an instrument of divine justice; and also L. H. Silberman, "Paul's Viper: Acts 28:3–6," *Forum* (1992): 247–53.

277. Noted since J. J. Wettstein; see Pervo, *Acts*, 674.

suggests his story is modeled on it, or at least on a shared tradition, in order to illustrate that, with God's protection, nothing hinders Paul from reaching Rome.[278] Indeed, the theme of harmful animals would have been familiar to readers and probably is to be taken as traditional rather than a reflection of historical veracity.[279]

Second, there is no evidence whatsoever that there are or ever have been snake species on the Maltese isles that can, or could, inflict a life-threatening bite.[280] Third, although we have seen hints of it (see §8.2 above), here at the climax of his two-volume narrative Luke's intention is obviously to portray Paul as superior to his apostolic predecessors—even drawing parallels with the death of Jesus[281]—to the point of being acclaimed as a god, rather than to offer a dispassionate reporting of stories about Paul. At the conclusion of the episode of the viper bite Luke says that the skeptical crowd "changed their minds and began to say that he was a god" (Acts 28:6). Although readers have already seen this claim countered (14:11–18) and so will read it with caution, Luke not correcting the adulation has the effect of giving his tacit approval to it and, in turn, of enhancing the portrait of Paul.

Moreover, fourth, although readers have been told Paul is a prisoner (Acts 27:42–43), there is no hint of this in these stories.[282] Instead, in line with Luke's portrayal of him in contact with significant people,[283] Paul seems more like the captain of the ship, who, with his companions, is portrayed as an honored guest of the leading figure of the island (28:7).[284] Although it is not out of the question for a large cargo ship to carry 276 crew and passengers (27:37),[285]

278. Cf. Jervell, *Die Apostelgeschichte*, 617.

279. See Plutarch, *Cleom.* 39; Lucian, *Philops.* 11, cited by Conzelmann, *Acts*, 223.

280. Personal communication from Patrick Schembri, department of biology, University of Malta, and Jeroen Speybroeck (http://www.hylawerkgroep.be/jeroen/). See also Thomas A. B. Spratt, *Travels and Researches in Crete*, 2 vols. (London: John van Voorst, 1865), 2:6–7; William M. Ramsay, *Luke the Physician, and Other Studies in the History of Religion* (1908; repr., Grand Rapids: Baker, 1956), 64; Colin J. Hemer, "Euraquilo and Melita," *JTS* 26 (1975): 109–10; Conzelmann, *Acts*, 223; Hemer, *Acts*, 153; Bruce, *Book of Acts*, 531. Over against Angus Acworth, "Where Was St. Paul Shipwrecked? A Re-examination of the Evidence," *JTS* 24 (1973): 190–93, Hemer ("Euraquilo and Melita") convincingly argues for the traditional identification of Malta as the place of the shipwreck.

281. See Clabeaux, "Maltese Viper."

282. Haenchen, *Acts*, 709, 716.

283. Lüdemann, *Acts*, 340.

284. Cf. Matthew L. Skinner, "Unchained Ministry: Paul's Roman Custody (Acts 21–28) and the Sociopolitical Outlook of the Book of Acts," in *Acts and Ethics*, ed. Thomas E. Phillips (NTM 9; Sheffield: Sheffield Phoenix, 2005), 90–93.

285. Josephus (*Life* 15) says that there were six hundred on the ship that took him to Rome. On the size of ancient ships, see Casson, *Ships and Seamanship*, 171–72nn25–26, 183–200. On the textual difficulties associated with Luke's number, 276, see Haenchen, *Acts*, 707n4; Barrett, *Commentary on the Acts*. 2:1210–11; Metzger, *Commentary*, 442; Pervo, *Acts*, 665.

narrative imagination is stretched in portraying them "all" (πάντας) gathered around a fire (28:2) and given hospitality for three days by Publius (28:7). Indeed, the concentration of references to "all" (27:33–37) suggests Luke is serving his interest in universal salvation.[286] And the use of a triangular number, 276 (the sum of the digits from 1 to 23), would have encouraged readers to explore symbolic possibilities of the story.[287] Then, though a prisoner, after three months[288] Paul and his companions leave having received many honors and all the provisions they needed (28:10). Thus, although Luke's story of the voyage and shipwreck is credible, and Paul mentions being shipwrecked three times (2 Cor. 11:25), we are unable to associate the story and the snake bite with the historical Paul. In short, although Paul says he was shipwrecked three times, Luke's story probably does not relate to any of them.

Also, looking more closely at the two stories of Paul involving healing— Publius's father healed of fever and dysentery, and a summary of healings on the island (Acts 28:7–9)—raises questions about their value in contributing to a reconstruction of the historical Paul in relation to the miraculous. To begin with, these two stories—more accurately, a story followed by a summary of healings—are remarkably similar to the Gospel story of the healing of Simon's mother-in-law, which is followed by a summary of healings by Jesus.[289]

Both pairs of stories follow a battle with evil by the main character leading to the adulation of each. In Luke's Gospel, Jesus casts out a demon (4:31–37), which does "no one harm" (μηδὲν βλάψαν, 4:35), leading to adulation (4:36– 37). In Acts, Paul is unharmed (οὐδὲν κακόν, "no evil," 28:5) after shaking off a viper, a terrifying figure, sometimes represented as evil,[290] which also leads to adulation by the crowd of "natives" (βάρβαροι) (28:4, 6).[291]

Further, setting these healing stories in parallel—along with Mark, Luke's source—not only highlights the similarities between the stories but also enables

286. Cf. Susan Marie Praeder, "Acts 27:1–28:16: Sea Voyages in Ancient Literature and the Theology of Luke-Acts," *CBQ* 46 (1984): 698 and n. 42, citing Acts 2:1, 4, 5, 7, (12), 14, 17, 21, 32, (36), 39; 10:2, (2), (8), 12, 33, (33), 35, 36, 38, (39), (41), (43), 43, 44; 17:(22), 24, 25, 26, 30 (2x), 31.

287. Pervo, *Acts*, 665.

288. On the difficulty of this time frame, see ibid., 676.

289. Lake and Cadbury, *English Translation and Commentary*, 343; Mattill, "Jesus-Paul Parallels," 28; Lüdemann, *Early Christianity*, 261–62; Pervo, *Acts*, 675.

290. See, e.g., Theognis, *Elegiac Poems* 595–602; *PGM* 4.2785–90. See Walter Burkert, *Greek Religion*, trans. John Raffan (Cambridge, MA: Harvard University Press, 1985), e.g., 30, 64, 195, 206; James A. Kelhoffer, *Miracle and Mission: The Authentication of Missionaries and Their Message in the Longer Ending of Mark* (WUNT 2/112; Tübingen: Mohr Siebeck, 2000), 340–417; Christian Hünemörder, "Snake," *New Pauly* 13 (2002): 554–55; Jan Bremmer, "Snake: II Myth and Religion," *New Pauly* 13 (2002): 556–58.

291. Although Luke draws the strongest links to his Gospel in these parallels, they by no means exhaust the connections he makes with the Jesus narrative. See Clabeaux, "Maltese Viper."

us to identify more easily Luke's redaction of the Gospel material and, in turn, how he is likely to have contributed to this particular Acts narrative.

Mark 1:29–34a	Luke 4:38–40	Acts 28:8–9
[29]As soon as they left the synagogue, they entered the house of Simon and Andrew, with James and John. [30]Now Simon's mother-in-law was in bed with a <u>fever</u>, and they told him about her at once. [31]He came and took her by the hand and lifted her up. Then the fever left her, and she began to serve them. [32]That evening, at sundown, they brought to him all who were sick or possessed with demons. [33]And the whole city was gathered around the door. [34]And he cured many who were sick with various diseases, and cast out many demons; and he would not permit the demons to speak, because they knew him.	[38]After leaving the synagogue he <u>visited</u> Simon's house. Now Simon's mother-in-law was suffering from a high <u>fever</u>, and they asked him about her. [39]Then he stood over her and rebuked the fever, and it left her. Immediately she got up and began to serve them. [40]As the sun was setting, all those who had any who were <u>sick</u> with various kinds of diseases brought them to him; and he <u>laid his hands</u> on each of them and cured them.	[8]It so happened that the father of Publius lay sick in bed with <u>fever</u> and dysentery. Paul <u>visited</u> him and cured him by praying and <u>putting his hands</u> on him. [9]After this happened, the rest of the people on the island who had <u>sicknesses</u> also came and were cured.

From this synopsis we can see that in both Luke and Acts the lead character visits or enters a home[292] and heals a parental figure of a significant character (Simon and Publius) in the story. In the Gospel story Luke writes the disciples out of the narrative so that Jesus alone is the focus of attention (Luke 4:38; cf. Mark 1:29); and in the Acts story those accompanying Paul, while involved immediately before and after the story (Acts 28:1, 10), are not mentioned so that he alone goes to perform the healing.

Following the individual healings in both Luke and Acts there is a summary of multiple healings (Luke 4:38; Acts 28:9).[293] In each narrative the reader is led to conclude that the crowds came for healing as a result of the success of the healing of the significant individual; in the narrative sequence this is implied in Luke 4:39–40, and in Acts it is made clear that the crowd came "after this happened" (τούτου δὲ γενομένου, Acts 28:9). Then, in the Gospel summary

292. Luke has changed Mark's ἦλθον εἰς ("they came into" [Mark 1:29]) to εἰσῆλθεν εἰς ("he entered into" [Luke 4:38]) and used the same compound word, εἰσελθών ("he going into"), in Acts 28:8.

293. Despite the reference to ἡμᾶς ("us" Acts 28:10) receiving honors following the summary of healings, it is clear from the start of this little narrative (τούτου δὲ γενομένου, "after this happened") that this summary of miracles is intended to relate to Paul, rather than Luke the physician, even with miraculous gifts, as supposed by Harnack, *Acts*, 119.

story Luke omits mention of the demonized in his source (Luke 4:40; cf. Mark 1:34b), and in Acts he mentions only healings, not exorcisms (Acts 28:9).[294]

Further, some of the vocabulary Luke used in reworking Mark he has also used in the Acts summary:[295] "entered into,"[296] "placing his hands," and "sickness"[297] (Acts 28:8). Luke has also increased the severity of the fever to a high fever (Luke 4:38; cf. Mark 1:30), and in Acts the fever is severe in being accompanied by dysentery (Acts 28:8). There are other expressions that are also probably indicative of Luke's creativity in the Acts stories, including the uniquely Lukan initial phrase "it so happened."[298] Also, the infinitive for an activity, here "to lie down" (κατακεῖσθαι) sick,[299] and a considerable amount of the vocabulary are typically Lukan (Acts 28:8–9).[300]

Prayer, which Luke has as part of Paul's healing technique (28:8), is of particular importance to Luke,[301] especially as part of his portrait of key characters,[302] including Paul.[303] Moreover, there are a number of words that, while used too infrequently in the New Testament to judge how important they are to Luke, may be indicative of Luke's hand.[304]

294. It is to be noted that, in contrast to the summary in Luke 4:40, where he uses the active, "he [Jesus] healed" (ἐθεράπευεν), here Luke uses the passive "were cured" (ἐθεραπεύοντο, Acts 28:9). Although this might be taken as an echo of Paul's description of the miraculous using the passive, in the immediate context (Acts 28:8) Luke has established that Paul is active in the healing process.

295. That the parallels are not closer may be, as François Bovon (*Luke 1: A Commentary on the Gospel of Luke 1:1–9:50*, trans. Christine M. Thomas, ed. Helmut Koester [Hermeneia; Minneapolis: Fortress, 2002], 299n2), suggests, because, as a good writer, Luke avoids verbatim repetitions.

296. Of the twenty occurrences of the nominative aorist active participle εἰσελθών ("he entering into") in the NT, ten come from Luke's hand.

297. See n. 300 below.

298. In the NT the phrase ἐγένετο δέ is used thirty-seven times, only by Luke.

299. See Acts 4:5; 9:3, 32, 37, 43; 11:26; 14:1; 16:16; 19:1; 21:1, 5; 22:6, 17; 27:44; 28:8, 17.

300. In the NT: of 12 occurrences of συνέχω ("hold fast"), 9 are by Luke; of 26 occurrences of ἰάομαι ("cure"), 11 are in Luke's Gospel, 4 are in Acts; of 12 occurrences of τυγχάνω ("extraordinary"), 6 are in Luke's writings; of 12 occurrences of προσλαμβάνω ("welcome"), 5 are in Acts; of 21 occurrences of ἐφίστημι ("be present"), 18 are in Luke's writings; of 39 occurrences of ἐπιτίθημι ("put [or lay] upon"), 19 are in Luke's writings; of 8 occurrences of διασώζω ("rescue"), all but 2 are by Luke; of 11 occurrences of ἐάω ("permit"), all but 2 are by Luke; of 16 occurrences of προσδοκάω ("wait"), 11 are by Luke; of 10 occurrences of χωρίον ("place"), 7 are by Luke; of 231 occurrences of ὄνομα ("name"), 94 are in Luke's writings; of 60 occurrences of ὑπάρχω ("exist"), 40 are by Luke; of 10 occurrences of ξενίζω ("receive a guest"), 7 are by Luke; of 43 occurrences of θεραπεύω ("heal"), 19 are by Luke; of 23 occurrences of ἀνάγω ("lead" or "set sail"), all but 3 are by Luke.

301. Cf. Twelftree, *People of the Spirit*, 106n18.

302. Of Jesus praying, see Luke 3:21; 5:16; 6:12; 9:18, 28, 29; 11:1; 22:41, 44; for the apostles praying, see Acts 1:12–14, 15–26; 2:42–47; 3:1; 4:23–31; 6:4, 6; 7:59–60 (Stephen); 8:15; 9:40; 10:9; 11:5; 12:12.

303. For Luke's portrait of Paul praying, sometimes with others, see Acts 9:11; 13:3; 14:23; 16:16, 25; 20:36; 21:5; 22:17; 26:29; 28:8.

304. In the NT ἀποτινάσσω is used in Luke 9:5; Acts 28:5; καταπίπτω is used in Luke 8:6; Acts 26:14; 28:6; ἄφνω is used in Acts 2:2; 16:26; 28:6; ἄτοπος is used in Luke 23:41; Acts 25:5; 28:6;

The result of my examination of the final series of stories in Acts relating to Paul's involvement with the miraculous is that although on a first reading there is nothing inherently improbable about Luke's story of Paul's sea voyage and shipwreck on Malta, on closer examination the story slips through our fingers and cannot, with any confidence, be associated with the historical Paul.[305] Also, in attempting to depict Paul as a worthy successor to the apostles, and particularly Jesus, Luke probably has used the story of Simon's mother-in-law and the ensuing summary of healings as the raw material to create a catena of stories about Paul.

8.18 The Historical Paul?

It bears repeating that my interest in the Acts narrative has been neither Luke's overall portrait of Paul nor even his interpretation of Paul in relation to the miraculous. Rather, my enquiry has been guided by an attempt to recover from Luke's work historically reliable data that can contribute to the reconstruction of the historical Paul in relation to the miraculous.

Despite the assumption or confidence of many, it has become clear that a number of Luke's stories and references to the miraculous in Acts have to be set aside in assembling material that can contribute to a reconstruction of the historical Paul: Paul being healed of blindness (9:18; 22:13), the lame man at Lystra (14:8–10), the report of signs and wonders (15:12), the call to Europe (16:6–11), the escape from prison (16:25–34), the Ephesians receiving the Spirit when Paul laid his hands on them (19:6), the miracles through neckcloths or belts (19:11–12), a trance in the temple (22:17–21), and the miracles on Malta (27:39–28:11). It is to be stressed that I have not been able to conclude that this material is without historical value.[306] Rather, when applying the often blunt tools of historical-critical analysis to the miraculous elements associated with Paul, I was unable to establish them as probably originating in, or being faithful to, firsthand reports of his life. Nevertheless, my investigations have secured a number of arguably reliable pieces of evidence:

- Paul had a visionary experience in or near Damascus that involved seeing and hearing the Lord or Jesus identify himself (9:1–19a; 22:6–16; 26:12–18).
- Paul was involved in prophecy as a means of directing his work (13:1–3).

---

2 Thess. 3:2; χωρίον is used in Matt. 26:36; Mark 14:32; John 4:5; Acts 1:18, 19 (2x); 4:34; 5:3, 8; 28:7.

305. Lüdemann, *Acts*, 340–42; Lüdemann, *Early Christianity*, 261–62.

306. See Schreiber, *Wundertäter*, 143.

- Though we cannot point to the source of his knowledge, Luke corroborates what we see in Paul's epistles: Paul was a preacher, and it was God who was credited with the miracles (14:3).
- The story of the exorcism of a slave girl (16:16–18) probably can be attributed to sources that originated in Paul's ministry, as can Paul's association with exorcism in the story of the sons of Sceva attempting to use his name in an incantation (19:13).
- The story of the revival of Eutychus (20:7–12) is a possible link with the historical Paul, suggesting that he was involved in bringing to life a dead person.

It is particularly obvious that these results are both meager yet highly significant for the present project. On the one hand, I cannot avoid the conclusion that I have been unable to retrieve very much from Luke, Paul's earliest extant interpreter. On the other hand, my conclusion is corroborating what I have already found in the letters of Paul. We turn now to the pseudepigraphical interpretations of the apostle.

9

The Remembered Paul

I n the search for reliable information to help reconstruct the historical Paul
in relation to the miraculous we turn from Acts to other early literature in
which Paul is remembered, primarily the pseudepigraphal Paul. While some
students of the New Testament have concluded that pseudonymity is not to
be found in the New Testament,[1] the vast majority considers there are letters
in the canon carrying Paul's name that were not written by him.[2]

My purpose in considering the Pauline pseudepigrapha is to identify what,
if anything, these writers have to say about Paul and the miraculous as they
recall and use his memory as a vehicle for their message, either to interpret
or reinterpret Paul for their audiences.[3] Of course, letters cannot be read as
biographies or historical narratives. Therefore, while texts not mentioning
the miraculous may raise questions about the importance of the miraculous
for Paul, they cannot be used to establish that the miraculous was not part
of the memory of Paul. The interests of the texts may not have included any

1. E.g., D. A. Carson and Douglas J. Moo, *An Introduction to the New Testament*, 2nd
ed. (Grand Rapids: Zondervan, 2005), 331–50.
2. See the discussions by Terry L. Wilder, *Pseudonymity, the New Testament, and Deception: An Inquiry into Intention and Reception* (Lanham, MD: University Press of America, 2004);
Jörg Frey et al., *Pseudepigraphie und Verfasserfiktion in frühchristlichen Briefen* [= *Pseudepigraphy and Author Fiction in Early Christian Letters*] (WUNT 246; Tübingen: Mohr Siebeck, 2009).
3. Annette Merz, "The Fictitious Self-Exposition of Paul: How Might Intertextual Theory
Suggest a Reformulation of the Hermeneutics of Pseudepigraphy?" in *The Intertextuality of the
Epistles: Explorations of Theory and Practice*, ed. Thomas L. Brodie, Dennis R. MacDonald,
and Stanley E. Porter (NTM 16; Sheffield: Sheffield Phoenix, 2006), 113–32.

topic related to the miraculous. However, if a writer takes up the theme of miraculous, we could expect that if a memory of Paul in relation to the miraculous was available, it would be exploited in some way. If, then, the memory of Paul does not involve him in the miraculous, we will have important data for a reconstruction of the historical Paul.

Taking them in the order in which they may have been written, I will give attention to Colossians, Ephesians, 2 Thessalonians, and the Pastoral Epistles (1 and 2 Timothy and Titus). Besides the Pauline pseudepigrapha, Hebrews also will be considered for, as others have argued, it is written in the tradition of Paul. Also, a brief account needs to be taken of the letter of James, in which Paul is critically engaged. Second Peter is to be included in our discussion, for Paul's letters are possibly alluded to a number of times. Over against some,[4] I will not take 1 Peter into account. For, as John H. Elliott has shown, "the literary composition, historical situation, theological perspective and socioreligious strategy of 1 Peter place it within a broad stream rather than an exclusive Pauline current of early Christian tradition."[5] Similarly, though it is sometimes said to be indebted to Paul for terminology and ideas, Jude will not be taken into account here, for as Richard Bauckham put it, this view "depends on the too ready assumption that ideas and terminology which Paul uses are distinctively Pauline, so that other writers who use them must be dependent on Paul or 'Paulinism.'" Bauckham concludes: "No alleged case of 'Paulinism' in Jude can really be substantiated."[6] The author of 2 Peter knew a number of Paul's letters, considering them to be "scripture" (γραφή) (2 Pet. 3:15–16). However, despite sharing vocabulary and topics with Paul's letters,[7] 2 Peter contains only three, far from certain, allusions to Paul's writings.[8] With the author of 2 Peter speaking positively of Paul ("our beloved brother," 3:15) and his work, but making no use of it, I will also leave this letter out of consideration. Beyond the canon, in the second century, there is material that engages Paul and requires attention in the last major section of this chapter. Acknowledging that dating is far from an exact science, I begin with the earliest pseudepigraphal text in which Paul is remembered.

4. E.g., Helmut Koester, *Introduction to the New Testament*, 2nd ed., 2 vols. (Berlin: de Gruyter, 2000), 2:295–300.

5. John H. Elliott, *A Home for the Homeless: A Social-scientific Criticism of 1 Peter, Its Situation and Strategy*, 2nd ed. (Minneapolis: Fortress, 1990), 271.

6. Richard J. Bauckham, *Jude, 2 Peter* (WBC 50; Waco: Word, 1983), 8.

7. See the list of themes and vocabulary assembled by Jerome H. Neyrey, *2 Peter, Jude: A New Translation with Introduction and Commentary* (AB 37C; New York: Doubleday, 1993), 133–34. See also Albert E. Barnett, *Paul Becomes a Literary Influence* (Chicago: University of Chicago Press, 1941), 222–28.

8. Cf. 2 Pet. 2:19 and Rom. 8:21; 2 Pet. 3:15 and Rom. 12:3; 15:15; 2 Pet. 3:10 and 1 Thess. 5:2.

9.1 Colossians

Of all the letters generally taken to be pseudepigraphal, Colossians is most often argued to have been written by Paul.[9] Raymond E. Brown, however, suggests that about 60 percent of critical scholarship considers that Paul did not write this letter;[10] and this figure probably is growing.[11] Not surprisingly, therefore, of all the Pauline pseudepigraphal material, this is the most like the Paul of the genuine letters. Given the dependence of Ephesians on Colossians,[12] and Ignatius (writing early in the second century)[13] knowing Ephesians,[14] Colossians was written no later than the 80s.[15] Also, the dependence of Colossians on Philemon,[16] which probably was written in Ephesus, makes it most likely both letters originated there.[17]

Even if in matters of style and theology the author was thoroughly acquainted with Paul's principal themes,[18] perhaps as a disciple of Paul,[19] there is little in the letter suggesting Paul was remembered in relation to the miraculous. Notably, the gospel is characterized as "the word,"[20] not as "word and deed,"[21] a phrase Colossians uses to describe behavior (3:17) rather than

9. So, e.g., Werner G. Kümmel, *Introduction to the New Testament*, trans. Howard Clark Kee (London: SCM, 1975), 340–46; For a brief response to those (e.g., Charles Masson, *L'épître de Saint Paul aux Colossiens* [CNT; Paris: Delachaux & Niestlé, 1950]) who attribute elements of the letter to Paul, see F. F. Bruce, *The Epistles to the Colossians, to Philemon, and to the Ephesians* (NICNT; Grand Rapids: Eerdmans, 1984), 28–30.

10. Raymond E. Brown, *An Introduction to the New Testament* (ABRL; New York: Doubleday, 1997), 600.

11. Luke Timothy Johnson, *The Writings of the New Testament: An Interpretation* (Minneapolis: Fortress, 2010), 347.

12. See below, as well as the discussions by C. Leslie Mitton, *The Epistle to the Ephesians: Its Authorship, Origin and Purpose* (Oxford: Clarendon, 1951), 55–74, 279–315; Rudolf Schnackenburg, *Ephesians* (Edinburgh: T&T Clark, 1991), 30–33.

13. Eusebius (*Hist. eccl.* 3.21–22) dates the martyrdom of Ignatius to 107 CE, during the days of the emperor Trajan (98–117 CE). See William R. Schoedel, "Polycarp of Smyrna and Ignatius of Antioch," *ANRW* II.27.1 (1993): 347–58.

14. See Ign. *Pol.* 1:2 // Eph. 4:2; Ign. *Pol.* 5:1 // Eph. 5:25, 29; Ign. *Pol.* 6:2 // Eph. 6:11–17; and the discussion by Ernest Best, *A Critical and Exegetical Commentary on Ephesians* (ICC; Edinburgh: T&T Clark, 2004), 15–16.

15. Brown, *New Testament*, 616.

16. See, e.g., Eduard Lohse, *Colossians and Philemon: A Commentary on the Epistles to the Colossians and to Philemon*, trans. William L. Poehlmann and Robert J. Karris, ed. Helmut Koester (Hermeneia; Philadelphia: Fortress, 1971), 175–77.

17. See Brown, *New Testament*, 616.

18. Though arguing for Pauline authorship, cf. Lohse, *Colossians and Philemon*, 177–83, esp. 182.

19. Brown, *New Testament*, 600.

20. See Col. 1:5 ("word of truth"); 1:25 ("word of God"); 3:16 ("word of Christ"); 4:3 ("the word").

21. Cf. Rom. 15:18; 1 Cor. 2:4; Gal. 3:4–5; 1 Thess. 1:5.

the two aspects of the gospel. Moreover, the coming of the gospel is said to be "heard" (ἀκούω, 1:6, 23) and "learned" (μανθάνω, 1:7),[22] with no suggestion of an accompanying miraculous dimension, as in Galatia, for example, where it was said to be experienced (πάσχω, Gal. 3:4). Also, the defeat of the "principalities and powers" or "rulers and authorities" (τὰς ἀρχὰς καὶ τὰς ἐξουσίας) has already taken place (Col. 2:15; cf. Eph. 1:20–21). Their defeat in the lives of the believers is not through present activity, such as exorcism, but in decisions related to behavior (Col. 2:16–23).[23]

However, there is a hint of the miraculous in the life of the Colossian believers in the writer encouraging readers to "sing spiritual psalms, hymns, and songs to God" (Col. 3:16).[24] The adjective, "spiritual" or "spirit caused" (πνευματικός)[25] in the final position in the (Greek) phrase probably refers not only to "songs,"[26] but to all three words[27] (as just translated), which represent the full range of singing[28] and call to mind the corporate spontaneous worship that Paul describes,[29] with its miraculous features of prophecy, tongues, and revelations (1 Cor. 14:23–33).[30] Therefore, although this letter gives no suggestion either that Paul's gospel came accompanied by the miraculous or that he was remembered as a miracle worker, the reference to Spirit-caused worship singing hints of an ongoing interest at least in this dimension of the miraculous in a church committed to the memory of Paul.

22. See Karl H. Rengstorf, "μανθάνω, κτλ.," *TDNT* 4:406–12; BDAG, "μανθάνω," 615.

23. Perhaps, as Stephen H. Travis suggested to me, the coming of the gospel is not associated with the miraculous because it was Epaphras who founded the church (Col. 1:7). Yet, the point remains that the Pauline tradition carries no memory of the coming of the gospel involving the miraculous, even by a person said to be a fellow servant of Paul (Col. 1:7). On the historicity of Epaphras, see Jerry L. Sumney, *Colossians: A Commentary* (NTL; Louisville: Westminster John Knox, 2008), 39.

24. The psalms, hymns, and songs probably are not to be distinguished from each other. See Lohse, *Colossians and Philemon*, 151, esp. n148.

25. BDAG, "πνευματικός," 837.

26. So Gordon D. Fee, *God's Empowering Presence: The Holy Spirit in the Letters of Paul* (Peabody, MA: Hendrickson, 1994), 653–54, on the grounds that psalms and hymns would naturally be taken to be related to worship, whereas "songs" required the adjective because it was least likely to be associated with worship. However, as Sumney (*Colossians*, 225) points out, the context of the whole statement is worship.

27. Cf. Ralph P. Martin, *Colossians and Philemon* (NCB; Grand Rapids: Eerdmans, 1973), 115–16; Sumney, *Colossians*, 225.

28. Lohse, *Colossians and Philemon*, 151.

29. See the summary discussion of the adjective πνευματικαῖς by Murray J. Harris, *Colossians & Philemon* (EGGNT; Grand Rapids: Eerdmans, 1991), 169.

30. Lohse (*Colossians and Philemon*, 151), who points out that "in your hearts" (Col. 3:16) does not privatize the worship, but, as a Semitic expression, is to be taken as a contrast to worshiping with the lips, a point clarified by the variant singular reading τη καρδια (D² 𝔐 I Clement of Alexandria, *Paed.* 2.4.43).

9.2 Ephesians

A sizable majority of critical scholarship takes Ephesians to be pseude-pigraphical,[31] written around 90 CE[32] for Christians in Asia Minor.[33] Yet, as C. H. Dodd said long ago of the author, "He is at once a powerful and original thinker, and one who has entered into the very heart of Paul's own thought in such a way as to bring the whole course of his theological de-velopment to its predestined climax. For whether the Epistle is by Paul or not, certainly *its thought is the crown of Paulinism*."[34] We might, therefore, expect Ephesians to put the reader in touch with the memory of the historical Paul.[35]

However, in this very Pauline letter, at three points where we may have expected it, there is no hint of interest in the miraculous. First, the work of the Spirit in the coming of salvation is not related to "power" (δύναμις)[36] or to signs of an apostle (cf. 2 Cor. 12:12). Rather, on the one hand, the coming of salvation involves marking the believer "with the seal of the promised Holy Spirit" (Eph. 1:13). "Seal" (σφραγίζω, cf. 4:30) probably does not refer to baptism,[37] but rather the seal of ownership by the Spirit itself.[38] What is notable is that this work of the Spirit is mentioned not because of its present value but because of its value in relation to the future "day of redemption" (4:30).[39] On the other hand, the notion of "power," which

31. Brown (*New Testament*, 621) says the figure is about 80 percent. According to the chart listing those for, against, and uncertain about Pauline authorship by W. Hall Harris (*The Descent of Christ: Ephesians 4:7–11 and Traditional Hebrew Imagery* [AGJU 32; Leiden: Brill, 1996], 198–204), the figure is about 70 percent before 1950 and about 60 percent in the follow-ing forty years.

32. Cf., e.g., Andrew T. Lincoln, *Ephesians* (WBC 42; Dallas: Word, 1990), lxxii–lxxiii; Schnackenburg, *Ephesians*, 33; Brown, *New Testament*, 621.

33. See Ign. *Pol.* 5:1 // Eph. 5:25, 29; Ign. *Eph.* prescript // Eph. 1:3–5; Ign. *Eph.* 9:1 // Eph. 2:20–22; see also the cautious discussion by Schnackenburg, *Ephesians*, 33n38.

34. C. H. Dodd, "Ephesians," in *The Abingdon Bible Commentary*, ed. Frederick C. Eiselen, Edwin Lewis, and David G. Downey (London: Epworth, 1929), 1224–25, emphasis original.

35. Cf. Best, *Ephesians*, 40–44.

36. δύναμις: Eph. 1:19, 21; 3:7, 16, 20 (2x).

37. On the seal as baptism, see, e.g., P. W. Evans, "Sealing as a Term for Baptism," *Baptism Quarterly* 16 (1955): 171–75 (concluding it is not); and D. Mollatt, "Symbolismes baptismaux chez saint Paul," *LumVie* 26 (1956): 205–28 (suggesting it is related to baptism).

38. See, e.g., Geoffrey W. H. Lampe, *The Seal of the Spirit: A Study in the Doctrine of Baptism and Confirmation in the New Testament and the Fathers*, 2nd ed. (London: SPCK, 1967), 3–18, 64–94; Best, *Ephesians*, 150–51; Fee, *God's Empowering Presence*, 670n38; James D. G. Dunn, *Baptism in the Holy Spirit: A Re-examination of the New Testament Teaching on the Gift of the Spirit in Relation to Pentecostalism Today* (London: SCM, 1970), 160; Clinton E. Arnold, *Ephesians* (ZECNT 10; Grand Rapids: Zondervan, 2010), 92–93.

39. On the probable future reference, see Best, *Ephesians*, 458–60.

Paul can relate to salvation (e.g., Rom. 1:16)[40] and its coming in association with the miraculous (e.g., Rom. 15:18–19), is related to God raising Christ from the dead and seating him at his right hand (Eph. 1:19, 21). Indeed, in Ephesians "power" from the Spirit is expected to strengthen the readers' inner being (3:16, 20), having nothing to do with the overtly miraculous. Further, although the phrase "working of power" (ἐνέργειαν τῆς δυνάμεως, 3:7) echoes one of the *charismata* mentioned in the Corinthian correspondence (ἐνεργήματα δυνάμεων, 1 Cor. 12:10), for the author of Ephesians the phrase refers not to miracles but to the mediation of God's grace for ministry.[41]

Second, the list of apostles, prophets, evangelists, pastors, and teachers in Ephesians 4:11 (cf. 2:20; 3:5) resembles Paul's enumerated list headed by apostles, prophets, teachers, deeds of power, and healing in 1 Corinthians 12:28. The similarity between the lists—both beginning with apostles and prophets and then including teachers—suggests Ephesians is dependent on the memory of Paul's thinking.[42] However, not only are the prophets, evangelists, pastors, and teachers of Ephesians not called *charismata* (χαρίσματα)—solidified grace-expressions of the Spirit[43]—but they are roles or people given to the church (Eph. 4:11).[44] Notably, the list does not include those working deeds of power or healing (cf. 1 Cor. 12:28), but instead focuses on speaking and leading.[45]

Moreover, third, in Ephesians 6:12 it would not have been out of place for exorcism to be mentioned in relation to the battle "against the rulers [τὰς ἀρχάς], against the authorities [τὰς ἐξουσίας], against the cosmic powers [τοὺς κοσμοκράτορας] of this present darkness, against the spiritual forces of evil [τὰ πνευματικὰ τῆς πονηρίας] in the heavenly places." These are supranatural powers—equivalent to confronting the devil (6:11)—not civic authorities, even if their influence was thought to have a political dimension.[46] However, the writer expects neither exorcism nor apotropaic means to control these

40. On Paul echoing the miraculous in early Christian tradition, see the discussion by C. K. Barrett, "I Am Not Ashamed of the Gospel," in *On Paul: Aspects of His Life, Work, and Influence in the Early Church* (London: T&T Clark, 2003), 133–34 (this essay was originally published in *Foi et Salut selon S. Paul [Épître aux Romains 1,16]: Colloque œcuménique à l'Abbaye de S. Paul hors les Murs, 16–21 avril 1968* [AnBib 42; Rome: Pontifical Biblical Institute, 1970], 19–41).

41. See the discussion by Lincoln, *Ephesians*, 182.

42. Cf. the discussion by Schnackenburg, *Ephesians*, 182.

43. See Rom. 12:6; 1 Cor. 12:4, 28, 30–31. Cf. 25n125 above.

44. Cf. Schnackenburg, *Ephesians*, 180.

45. Further on the distinction between the Pauline *charismata* and the Ephesian list, see ibid., 180–81.

46. On the extensive literature on principalities and powers, see, e.g., Clinton E. Arnold, *Powers of Darkness: Principalities and Powers in Paul's Letters* (Downers Grove, IL: InterVarsity,

entities. Rather, the decisive victory over them has already been won by God in Christ (1:20–21; cf. Col. 2:15). Apart from being sealed by the ownership of the Spirit (Eph. 1:13),[47] the believers are required only to "withstand" (ἀνθίστημι, 6:13) or "stand" (ἵστημι, 6:11, 13, 14)—that is, preserve or maintain what has been won[48] through using the protective armor of truth, righteousness, proclaiming the gospel, faith, salvation, and the word of God (6:14–17).

Notwithstanding, in the letter's creative dependence on the Pauline corpus,[49] the author of Ephesians has taken up the exhortation from Colossians: "sing spiritual psalms and hymns and songs among yourselves" (Eph. 5:19; cf. Col. 3:16). As in Colossians, the author is referring to Spirit-inspired, probably spontaneous, worship (see §9.1 above). As Rudolf Schnackenburg put it: "The Spirit with his power should take hold of the 'inner person' (cf. 3:16–17) and the outward song should be produced by the inner dynamic."[50] This is all but assured in that the Spirit-inspired worship is compared negatively with drunkenness. Both are states in which the person is under an exterior influence resulting in similar responses, as Philo expresses in saying: "When grace fills the soul, that soul thereby rejoices and smiles and dances, for it is possessed and inspired, so that to many of the unenlightened it may seem to be drunken, crazy and beside itself" (Ebr. 146).[51] Also, as is often pointed out, the present imperatives in the directions in Ephesians 5:18, "do not get drunk" (μὴ μεθύσκεσθε) and "be filled with Spirit" (πληροῦσθε ἐν πνεύματι), suggest this Spirit-inspired worship is not confined to an initial experience, but is an ongoing part of the lives of the readers.[52]

As in Colossians, we look in vain, then, for any help from Ephesians for suggesting that Paul was remembered as involved in the miraculous, either in the coming of the gospel or in the ongoing life of the body of believers. However, as also in Colossians, the miraculous appears evident in the ongoing life of the church in the spontaneous Spirit-inspired worship singing.

1992); Peter T. O'Brien, "Principalities and Powers: Opponents of the Church," *ERT* 16 (1992): 353–84.

47. Cf. Rodney Thomas, "The Seal of the Spirit and the Religious Climate of Ephesus," *ResQ* 43 (2001): 155–66.

48. Lincoln, *Ephesians*, 442–43.

49. See the discussion by Lincoln, *Ephesians*, xlvii–lviii; though see the cautionary article by Ernest Best, "Who Used Whom? The Relationship of Ephesians and Colossians," *NTS* 43 (1997): 72–96.

50. Schnackenburg, *Ephesians*, 238.

51. Cf. 1 Sam. 10:5, 10–12; Acts 2:13–15; 1 Cor. 14:23. See also, Lincoln, *Ephesians*, 344–45; Fee, *God's Empowering Presence*, 720–21.

52. E.g., Markus Barth, *Ephesians: Translation and Commentary on Chapters 4–6* (AB 34A; Garden City, NY: Doubleday, 1974), 582; Lincoln, *Ephesians*, 344–45.

9.3 2 Thessalonians

Relying once more on Raymond Brown, "Scholars are almost evenly divided on whether Paul wrote it, although the view that he did not seems to be gaining ground even among moderates."[53] The majority of those who see 2 Thessalonians as pseudonymous take it to have been written late in the first century, for the Thessalonians were facing severe trials (1:4, 6, 9).[54]

In line with what we have so far seen of the pseudepigraphal Pauline material, there is nothing in 2 Thessalonians that suggests Paul was remembered as a miracle worker or was involved in the miraculous. Indeed, the only mention of the miraculous is placed over against the gospel. The author says that "the lawless one" (2:3, 8),[55] according to the working of Satan, will be apparent "in all false power and signs and wonders" (2:9, my translation).[56] The writer goes on to equate the miraculous with—he says "and in" (καὶ ἐν)—"every kind of wicked deception" and associate them with those who "refused to love the truth and so be saved" (2:10). Associating the miraculous with false Christianities is by no means unique in the New Testament;[57] what is unique is that, in contrast to Paul, the miraculous is seen as an expression not of the Spirit, but of Satan's deception (2:9, 13).[58] Whereas for Paul miracles were part of the coming of the gospel (see chap. 8 above), for the writer of this letter, false miracles will mark the coming of the lawless one (2:9). In line with this, it is not surprising, then, that, if 2 Thessalonians is dependent on 1 Thessalonians,[59] the author has not

53. Brown, *New Testament*, 591; cf. 596.

54. See, e.g., Karl P. Donfried, "The Cults of Thessalonica and the Thessalonian Correspondence," *NTS* 31 (1985): 336–56.

55. In 2 Thess. 2:3 it is generally agreed that ἀνομίας ("of lawlessness," e.g., ℵ B) rather than ἀμαρτίας ("of sin," e.g., A D F G) is the preferred reading. See Bruce M. Metzger, *A Textual Commentary on the Greek New Testament*, 2nd ed. (Stuttgart: Deutsche Bibelgesellschaft; New York: United Bible Societies, 1994), 567.

56. 2 Thess. 2:9: ἐν πάσῃ δυνάμει καὶ σημείοις καὶ τέρασιν ψεύδους. Since the three terms "power(s)," "signs," and "wonders" can be used in a single description (cf. Acts 2:22; 6:8; Rom. 15:19; 2 Cor. 12:12; Heb. 2:4), and since ψεύδους ("false") stands at the end of the phrase in the genitive—for the phrase as a Hebrew genitive see Bruce K. Waltke, *An Introduction to Biblical Hebrew Syntax* (Winona Lake, IN: Eisenbrauns, 1990), §12—it probably qualifies not just "wonders" but all three terms. On the nature of deception, see Alfred Plummer (*A Commentary on St. Paul's Second Epistle to the Thessalonians* [London: Robert Scott, 1918]) who says, "All three are 'lying,' not in the sense that they are shams, but that they are wrought to induce people to believe what is false. . . . Consummate deceit, making evil look like good, is of the very nature of the devil" (67).

57. Matt. 24:24 // Mark 13:22; cf. Rev. 13:13–14; 16:14; 19:20. See Morna D. Hooker, "Trial and Tribulation in Mark 13," *BJRL* 65 (1982): 91.

58. However, in 2 Cor. 11:13–15 Paul associates Satan with false apostles and deceitful workers, whom he probably understood claimed to conduct signs and wonders. See §7.7 above.

59. See the brief discussion by Karl P. Donfried, "2 Thessalonians and the Church of Thessalonica," in Donfried, *Paul, Thessalonica*, 51–52 (this essay was originally published in *Origins*

taken up mention of the message of the gospel coming not only in word but also in power and in the Holy Spirit as evidence of being chosen by God (1 Thess. 1:4–5; cf. 2 Thess. 1:3–4). Instead, in 2 Thessalonians God's choosing, though involving the Spirit, is related to sanctification and belief in the truth (2:13). It is also notable that, in contrast to Paul's use of the term "kingdom of God" for a present reality that involves "the Holy Spirit" (Rom. 14:17) and "power" (1 Cor. 4:20)—terms we have seen him associate with the miraculous (see §§5.3 [e]; 7.4 above)—here "kingdom of God" is associated not with the miraculous but with "suffering" (2 Thess. 1:5). In short, for the writer of 2 Thessalonians, the miraculous is associated with false Christianity and the satanic. It is not surprising, then, that Paul is not associated in any way with the miraculous.

9.4 The Pastoral Epistles

In the face of "a small but stubborn minority," as Luke Timothy Johnson puts it,[60] the vast majority of students of 1 and 2 Timothy and Titus take them to be pseudonymous.[61] In the next generation this minority may well increase,[62] but for this project, it is assumed we have in front of us the work of his disciple or disciples rather than of Paul himself.[63] Even if the Pastorals contain fragments of authentic Pauline material,[64] as they stand, the epistles are to be taken as the remembered Paul rather than the historical Paul.

Each of the three letters is written to a different though broadly similar situation.[65] However, in light of the common outlook of the three letters, and in their appearing not to have circulated as three separate letters,[66] it can also be assumed

and Method: Towards a New Understanding of Judaism and Christianity; Essays in Honour of John C. Hurd, ed. Bradley H. McLean [JSNTSup 86; Sheffield: JSOT Press, 1993], 128–44).

60. Luke Timothy Johnson, The First and Second Letters to Timothy: A New Translation with Introduction and Commentary (AB 35A; New York: Doubleday, 2001), 14. Johnson is to be counted in that minority (see 98–99).

61. About 80 to 90 percent of critical scholarship agrees that Paul did not write the Pastoral Epistles, according to Brown (New Testament, 639).

62. Over half a century ago the same (unfulfilled!) optimism was expressed by E. Earle Ellis, Paul and His Recent Interpreters (Grand Rapids: Eerdmans, 1961), 57.

63. For a recent case for the Pauline authorship of the Pastoral Epistles, see Ben Witherington III, Letters and Homilies for Hellenized Christians: A Socio-Rhetorical Commentary on Titus, 1–2 Timothy, and 1–3 John (Downers Grove, IL: IVP Academic, 2006), 49–75.

64. See, e.g., James D. Miller, The Pastoral Letters as Composite Documents (SNTSMS 93; Cambridge: Cambridge University Press, 1997); I. Howard Marshall with Philip H. Towner, A Critical and Exegetical Commentary on the Pastoral Epistles (ICC; London: T&T Clark, 2004), 92.

65. See Michael Prior, Paul the Letter-Writer and the Second Letter to Timothy (JSNTSup 23; Sheffield: JSOT Press, 1989), 61–67.

66. Richard I. Pervo, The Making of Paul: Constructions of the Apostle in Early Christianity (Minneapolis: Fortress, 2010), 83. The suggestion by William A. Richards (Difference and Distance

that the same author or group of authors is responsible for their composition.[67] Despite the canonical order (governed by the length of each letter),[68] considering its less-developed view of church order (cf. 1 Tim. 3:1–13 and Titus 1:5–16), Titus may have been written before 1 Timothy (as listed in the Muratorian Canon, line 60). The reflective aspect of 2 Timothy (e.g., 4:6–8) could place it last of the three letters.[69] If, as seems probable, Ignatius, writing early in the second century (see 274n13 above), was aware of 2 Timothy,[70] then the Pastorals probably were written toward the end of the first century.[71] Recognizing we can do little more than guess, there is considerable agreement that the writing of the letters is to be associated with Ephesus (1 Tim. 1:3; 2 Tim. 1:18; cf. 4:12)[72] to deal with heresy and opposition to the Pauline gospel there and in Crete (Titus 1:5).[73]

As with the other texts discussed in this chapter, our interest in the Pastorals is in what they can contribute to our knowledge of the historical Paul in relation to the miraculous. Notably for our project, Lloyd Pietersen has proposed that the opponents depicted by the author are not only enthusiasts, of a "holy roller" type of spirituality,[74] but also view Paul as primarily a thau-

---

in Post-Pauline Christianity: An Epistolary Analysis of the Pastorals [SBL 44; New York: Peter Lang, 2002]) that the three epistles were written by three different authors, span as much as six decades, and need to be treated separately, has not been well received. See the reviews by, e.g., Dean P. Béchard, *CBQ* 65 (2003): 651–52; I. Howard Marshall, *Evangel* 21 (2003): 94–95; Perry L. Stepp, *RBL* 5 (2003): 488–91.

67. See the brief discussion by Marshall and Towner, *Pastoral Epistles*, 1. It is sometimes argued that 2 Timothy was written by a different author from the other two Pastoral Epistles. See, e.g., Jerome Murphy-O'Connor ("2 Timothy Contrasted with 1 Timothy and Titus," *RB* 98 [1991]: 403–18), who concludes that "it does not seem possible that 2 Tim. should have been composed by the author of 1 Tim. and Titus" (p. 418).

68. See Robert Morgenthaler, *Statistik des neutestamentlichen Wortschatzes* (Zürich: Gotthelf-Verlag, 1958), 164.

69. See the discussion by Marshall and Towner, *Pastoral Epistles*, 1–2.

70. Ign. *Pol.* 6:2. On the attestation of the Pastoral Epistles in the Apostolic Fathers, see Marshall and Towner, *Pastoral Epistles*, 2–6. For example, it is possible that Titus and 1 Timothy were known to Clement of Rome (see Titus 3:1 // *1 Clem.* 2:7; 1 Tim. 1:17 // *1 Clem.* 61:2; 1 Tim. 2:7 // *1 Clem.* 60:4), who was writing in the mid-90s. See Bart D. Ehrman, ed. and trans., *The Apostolic Fathers*, 2 vols. (LCL; Cambridge, MA: Harvard University Press, 2003), 1:23–25.

71. For discussion of the dating of the Pastoral Epistles, see, e.g., Benjamin Fiore, *The Pastoral Epistles* (SP 12; Collegeville, MN: Liturgical Press, 2007), 19–20.

72. See, e.g., Arland J. Hultgren, *1–2 Timothy, Titus* (ACNT; Minneapolis: Augsburg, 1984), 21–29.

73. Against Marshall and Towner (*Pastoral Epistles*, 41), who take the generally accepted approach that the writer is confronting one broad problem, Jens Herzer ("Juden—Christen—Gnostiker: Zur Gegnerproblematik der Pastoralbriefe," *BTZ* 25 [2008]: 143–68) argues that identifiably different opponents are faced in each letter.

74. So J. Massingberd Ford, "A Note on Proto-Montanism in the Pastoral Epistles," *NTS* 17 (1971): 338–46 (esp. 342). Ford proposes that "the Pastorals may present us with the first attempt to quell Proto-Montanism" (p. 345).

maturge, and that the Pastorals counter with a portrait of Paul as primarily a teacher.[75] This is a potentially important proposal in that the Pastorals are seen to be involved in "a battle for the memory of Paul between those who regarded Paul as primarily a teacher and those who viewed him as primarily a thaumaturge."[76] However, we will see that the Paul of the Pastorals, though not a miracle worker, is also an enthusiast, involved in the miraculous.

There are a number of points at which the opponents, probably Jewish Christians,[77] can be seen as enthusiasts or interested in the miraculous. For example, they may have valued visions. For the threefold denial of the ability to see God (1 Tim. 6:16) suggests the opponents were claiming precisely that.[78] Indeed, the writer says some "pay attention to misleading spirits" (προσέχοντες πνεύμασιν πλάνοις, 4:1), as Paul might have said of those at Corinth involved in misguided ecstasy (1 Cor. 12:1–3).[79] Also, the terms describing meaningless talk[80] may point to ecstatic experiences among the opponents.[81] Further, the comparison of the opponents with Jannes and Jambres, opponents of Moses (2 Tim. 3:8), and the implication that there are "impostors" or "sorcerers" (γόητες, 3:13) among the readers, may point in the same direction. For the names "Jannes" and "Jambres" were associated with working magic before the king of Egypt.[82] Since context determines the meaning of γόης,[83] which for the Pastorals is both the opponents' being likened to magicians (3:8) and a concern for teaching and conduct (3:10–17), including being led astray from it (3:13), the opponents probably are being characterized as sorcerers. The

---

75. Lloyd K. Pietersen, "Despicable Deviants: Labelling Theory and the Polemic of the Pastorals," *SocRel* 58 (1997): 343–52; Lloyd K. Pietersen, *The Polemic of the Pastorals: A Sociological Examination of the Development of Pauline Christianity* (JSNTSup 264; London: T&T Clark, 2004).

76. Pietersen, "Deviants," 343.

77. 1 Tim. 1:4, 7; Titus 1:10, 14. On the history of the debate about the opponents in the Pastoral Epistles, see Pietersen, *Polemic*, 3–26.

78. Michael D. Goulder, "The Pastor's Wolves: Jewish Christian Visionaries behind the Pastoral Epistles," *NovT* 38 (1996): 246; Pietersen, *Polemic*, 119.

79. Cf. Goulder, "Pastor's Wolves," 244.

80. 1 Tim. 1:6 (ματαιολογία, "empty talk"); 1 Tim. 6:20; 2 Tim. 2:16 (κενοφωνία, "empty chatter"); Titus 1:10 (ματαιολόγοι, "idle talkers").

81. Cf. Eusebius, *Hist. eccl.* 5.16.7–8; Epiphanius, *Pan.* 48.3.11; Origen, *Cels.* 7.9; and also the discussion by Pietersen, *Polemic*, 120, 128–31.

82. Though not mentioned in Exod. 7:8–13, Jannes and Jambres first appear in CD-A V, 17–19. See also Pliny the Elder, *Nat.* 30.2.11; Eusebius, *Praep. ev.* 9.8; Tanhuma on Exodus 32.1; *Acts Pil.* 5:1; *Acts Pet. Paul* 34; and the discussions by Kaufmann Kohler, "Jannes and Jambres," *JE* 7:71; Martin Dibelius, *James: A Commentary on the Epistle of James*, rev. Heinrich Greeven, trans. Michael A. Williams, ed. Helmut Koester (Hermeneia; Philadelphia: Fortress, 1976), 116–17; Marshall and Towner, *Pastoral Epistles*, 778–79; and Menahem Stern, "Jannes and Jambres," *EncJud*² 11:78.

83. As noted by Pietersen, *Polemic*, 132, 134; cf. 144–58 (appendix 1).

accumulative impression is, then, that the opponents value the miraculous, broadly defined (see §1.5 above).

However, on two counts it is difficult to follow Lloyd Pietersen—whose main evidence is the Paul of Acts 19–20—and say that the opponents in the Pastorals, viewing the apostle as a wonder worker, also valued wonder working.[84] To begin with, although Ephesus is the likely arena for the debate in these letters (see above), and there are considerable connections between Acts and the Pastorals,[85] the portrait of the opponents does not resonate with the Paul of Acts in Ephesus (19:1–41; cf. 20:17–38). In the Pastorals the miraculous, not miracle working, characterizes the opponents (visions, ecstatic speech, and sorcery [see above]). In Acts, although Paul is involved in the miraculous (19:6), he is primarily a miracle worker, that is, a healer and, by implication (19:13), an exorcist.

Also, the Paul of the Pastorals is not only portrayed as a teacher (1 Tim. 2:7; 2 Tim. 1:11) who values sound teaching or doctrine,[86] supposedly over against the Paul of the opponents. He is also portrayed, not as a miracle worker, but as an enthusiast or charismatic, involved in the miraculous. Three pieces of evidence can be set out.

First, the mention of "prophecies made earlier" about Timothy (1 Tim. 1:18) establishes that prophecy is important to the Paul of the Pastorals, and that prophecy is practiced in the community to which he belongs. Probably in line with this, having mentioned "the mystery of our religion" (3:16), the author begins an oracle by saying, "but the Spirit expressly says" (τὸ δὲ πνεῦμα ῥητῶς λέγει)[87] some will renounce the faith (4:1).[88] In view of the use of the present tense (λέγει, "says"), and the activity of prophets among the readers (1:18; 4:14),[89] as well as Jesus' teaching otherwise being attributed to the Lord (6:3), this probably is not a reference to the Old Testament,[90] or to the words of Jesus,[91] but to Christian prophecy in the community or through the writer.[92]

---

84. Ibid., 139.

85. Ibid.

86. 1 Tim. 1:10; 4:6, 13, 16; 5:17; 6:1, 3; 2 Tim. 3:10, 16; 4:3; Titus 1:9; 2:1, 7, 10; contrast 1 Tim. 4:1.

87. Cf. Acts 21:11; 1 Cor. 12:3; Heb. 3:7; Rev. 2:7, 11, 17; 2:29; 3:6, 13, 22; 14:13; 22:17.

88. David E. Aune, *Prophecy in Early Christianity and the Ancient Mediterranean World* (Grand Rapids: Eerdmans, 1991), 289–90.

89. Fee, *God's Empowering Presence*, 770. Prophecy is not, therefore, only a phenomenon of the past, as supposed by Jürgen Roloff, *Der Erste Brief an Timotheus* (EKKNT 15; Zürich: Benziger; Neukirchen-Vluyn: Neukirchener Verlag, 1988), 220.

90. See the discussion by Fee, *God's Empowering Presence*, 769 and n. 62.

91. So George W. Knight, *The Pastoral Epistles: A Commentary on the Greek Text* (NIGTC; Grand Rapids: Eerdmans; Carlisle: Paternoster, 1992), 188, citing the numerous occurrences of τὸ πνεῦμα λέγει in Revelation (2:7, 11, 17, 25; 3:6, 13, 22) referring to Jesus Christ.

92. Cf. C. K. Barrett, *The Pastoral Epistles* (NClarB; Oxford: Clarendon, 1963), 66–67.

Second, the writer assuming the mantle of Paul also instructs Timothy, "Do not neglect the gift [χάρισμα] in you, which was given to you through prophecy" (1 Tim. 4:14). This statement has been the subject of considerable discussion.[93] What is of interest to us is not only that prophecy is involved but also the nature of the "gift" that was given in the prophecy. It is not uncommon for the gift to be understood as an office or official function.[94] However, Gordon Fee convincingly argues that the writer has in mind not an office but the dynamic character of a *charisma*:[95] the reader is called on to "fan into flame" the gift (2 Tim. 1:6), an unlikely direction in relation to an office;[96] and an office may be external to the person, but here the gift is emphatically "in you" (ἐν σοί).[97] If, as is probable, the gift involves not simply the Spirit, but what has just been listed—the public reading of Scripture, exhorting and teaching (1 Tim. 4:13; cf. 4:16)—they are very similar in kind to those listed by Paul in Romans 12:6–8.[98] In short, we have here an understanding of the gifts as miraculous in a way that is consistent with what we have seen in the historical Paul. However, the notion that the laying on of hands was involved (1 Tim. 4:14; 2 Tim. 1:6), an institutionalization of the charismatic, is something we do not find in Paul.

Third, the statement by the writer taking the role of Paul, that "the Lord rescued me from all" (ἐκ πάντων) of the persecutions he endured (2 Tim. 3:11), reflects a triumphalism—an unqualified positive perspective on the miraculous—beyond even the perspective of Acts, rather than the Paul of the authentic letters (cf. 2 Cor. 1:8–10; 11:23–28). The Paul of the Pastorals is certainly more than a teacher; he is involved in the miraculous.

The contest in the Pastorals, then, is probably not over whether Paul or the Christianity that best reflects his legacy is to be seen in terms of primarily the miraculous (the opponents) or primarily teaching (the Paul of the Pastorals).

93. See those cited by Marshall and Towner, *Pastoral Epistles*, 557, 564–69.

94. See, e.g., E. F. Scott, *The Pastoral Epistles* (MNTC; London: Hodder & Stoughton, 1936), 52–53; Rudolf Bultmann, *Theology of the New Testament*, 2 vols. (London: SCM, 1952–55), 2:108; Hans Conzelmann, "χάρισμα," *TDNT* 9:406; J. N. D. Kelly, *The Pastoral Epistles* (BNTC; London: Black, 1963), 106; James D. G. Dunn, *Jesus and the Spirit: A Study of the Religious and Charismatic Experience of Jesus and the First Christians as Reflected in the New Testament* (London: SCM, 1975), 348–49; Thomas C. Oden, *First and Second Timothy and Titus* (IBC; Louisville: John Knox, 1989), 125; Lorenz Oberlinner, *Die Pastoralbriefe*, vol. 1, *Kommentar zum Ersten Timotheusbrief* (HTKNT 11/2; Freiburg: Herder, 1994), 208, 211.

95. Fee, *God's Empowering Presence*, 772–73.

96. That in 2 Tim. 1:6 τὸ χάρισμα τοῦ θεοῦ ("the gift of God") refers more directly to the Holy Spirit rather than simply the gift of ministry, see ibid., 787.

97. Ibid., 772n79. "The 'enclosed' word order τοῦ ἐν σοὶ χαρίσματος ('the in you gift'), which occurs often in the Pastoral Epistles (e.g., 1 Tim. 3:16; 2 Tim. 2:14; cf. 1 Cor. 6:19 . . .), must be understood as emphatic."

98. So Marshall and Towner, *Pastoral Espistles*, 564. On the relationship between the gift and the Spirit, see Fee, *God's Empowering Presence*, 773.

The Pastorals are not understood simply by supposing, as does James Dunn, that they are "the first example of that progressive institutionalizing which seem to afflict so many movements of spiritual renew . . . when the flexibility of fresh religious experience begins to harden into set forms."[99] For, both sides of the debate in the Pastorals are portrayed as sharing a deep interest in the miraculous. Rather, it is particular teaching or tenets that are to be safeguarded by the reader or readers.

As we seek to identify the notion of the miraculous embedded in the Pastorals, it is to be noted that in these letters "power" (δύναμις) is not related to the miraculous, as we have seen in Paul (chap. 7 above). Instead, "power" is associated with the control of character or lifestyle (2 Tim. 1:7, 8; 3:5). Further, in none of these letters is there any hint that the preaching of the gospel might be associated or accompanied with the coming of the Spirit in a way that could be seen or heard (cf. 1 Tim. 3:16; 2 Tim. 4:1–6; Titus 2:11). Instead, the metaphor of "washing" (λουτρόν, Titus 3:5) is used of the Spirit's coming (3:4–8). That is, the letters could be said to show an interest in the miraculous, but not in miracle working.

What is of particular interest to us is that in these three letters using the memory of Paul to exhort the reader "to guard what was entrusted to you" (1 Tim. 6:20; 2 Tim. 1:14), we have confirmed some aspects of Paul and the miraculous already established. We have seen that not only teaching (2 Tim. 1:11) but also prophecy were taken to be part of his ministry and his churches, and that the gifts of the Spirit, especially relating to teaching, were remembered as associated with Paul. If the opponents reflected in this correspondence are enthusiasts or are involved in the miraculous (broadly conceived), so also is Paul. However, although the miraculous is part of the Pauline tradition of these letters, as Jacob Jervell noted,[100] Paul is not remembered as a miracle worker.

9.5 Hebrews

The time and place reflected in Hebrews cannot be determined with precision or confidence. The upper limit of the time of writing is the mid-90s, when Clement of Rome shows dependence on Hebrews.[101] Noting that Hebrews

---

99. Dunn, *Jesus and the Spirit*, 349.

100. Jacob Jervell, "The Signs of an Apostle: Paul's Miracles," in *The Unknown Paul: Essays on Luke-Acts and Early Christian History* (Minneapolis: Augsburg, 1984), 78.

101. For strong support of this date, see David G. Horrell, *The Social Ethos of the Corinthian Correspondence: Interests and Ideology from 1 Corinthians to 1 Clement* (SNTW; Edinburgh: T&T Clark, 1996), 239–41, including 239n7.

refers to cultic activity in the present tense[102] does not place the writing of
the book before the destruction of the temple. For, the cultic interest of Hebrews is focused on the Old Testament, not on the contemporary temple cult
(e.g., 9:1–10). In any case, cultic activity was not confined to the Jerusalem
temple but is widely attested, even in homes;[103] and other Christians writing
after 70 CE speak of cultic activity in the present tense (*1 Clem.* 40; *Diogn.*
3).[104] More helpful in dating Hebrews is the author saying that he was writing
during the second generation of Christians (Heb. 2:3), suggesting that it was
written somewhere between the late 60s and mid-90s.

From ancient times Palestine was considered the destination of the book.[105]
However, although many alternatives have been suggested,[106] at least on the
evidence of Hebrews 13:24 ("Those from Italy send you greetings") and the
book being first used in Rome (*1 Clem.* 36:1–6),[107] Rome is likely the location
of the readers.[108]

As early as Clement of Rome, Paul was taken to be the author of Hebrews.
Without distinction Clement uses Hebrews, Paul's letter to the Romans, and
his Corinthian correspondence alongside each other.[109] In the second century

102. E.g., Heb. 7:27–28; 8:3–5; 9:7–8, 25; 10:1–3, 8; 13:10–11. See the discussions by Har-
old W. Attridge, *The Epistle to the Hebrews: A Commentary on the Epistle to the Hebrews*
(Hermeneia; Philadelphia: Fortress, 1989), 8; and William L. Lane, *Hebrews 1–8* (WBC 47A;
Dallas: Word, 1991), lxiii.

103. There were Jewish temples in Hellenistic times at Elephantine (*TADAE* A4.7), Leon-
topolis (Josephus, *Ant.* 13.62–73), Shechem, Syrian Antioch (Josephus, *J.W.* 7.43–45), among
"other places" (Josephus, *Ant.* 13.66), which would have been the focus of cultic activity.
Also, sacrifices probably were offered in or near some synagogues (Josephus, *Ant.* 16.164,
168; *J.W.* 7.45; cf. *Ant.* 14.260–261; *CPJ* 467), as well as in homes (Philo, *Spec.* 2.145–149;
QE 1.10).

104. Attridge, *Hebrews*, 8.

105. E.g., Chrysostom, *Hom. Heb.* 1 (PG 63.11); Jerome, *Vir. ill. 5* (PL 23.617); Theodoret,
Interpretatio Epistolæ ad Hebræos (PG 82.675–76); Ceslas Spicq, *L'Épître aux Hébreux*, 2 vols.
(EB; Paris: Gabala, 1952), 1:220–25.

106. Attridge (*Hebrews*, 10) lists Samaria, Antioch, Corinth, Cyprus, Ephesus, Bithynia
and Pontus, and Colossae.

107. For a brief discussion of this and other evidence, see Lane, *Hebrews 1–8*, lviii–lx.

108. E.g., see Alan C. Mitchell, *Hebrews* (SP 13; Collegeville, MN: Liturgical Press, 2007),
6–7. However, see the brief cautionary discussion by James W. Thompson, *Hebrews* (PCNT;
Grand Rapids: Baker Academic, 2008), 6–7.

109. See particularly *1 Clem.* 5:5–6 // 2 Cor. 11:23–25; *1 Clem.* 13:1 // 1 Cor. 1:31; *1 Clem.*
17:1 // Heb. 11:37; *1 Clem.* 24:5 // 1 Cor. 15:36–37; *1 Clem.* 32:2 // Rom. 9:4–5; *1 Clem.* 33:1 //
Rom. 6:1; *1 Clem.* 34:8 // 1 Cor. 2:9; *1 Clem.* 35:5–6 // Rom. 1:29–32; Heb. 1:13; *1 Clem.* 36:1 //
Heb. 3:1; 2:18; *1 Clem.* 36:2–6 // Heb. 1:3, 4, 5, 7, 13; 3:1; 2:18; *1 Clem.* 36:2 // 2 Cor. 3:18; Heb.
1:3–4; *1 Clem.* 37:3 // 1 Cor. 12:29–30; 15:23; *1 Clem.* 37:5; 38:1 // 1 Cor. 12:20–21, 22, 24–25,
28; *1 Clem.* 41:1 // 1 Cor. 15:23; *1 Clem.* 47:1 // 1 Cor. 1:10–12; *1 Clem.* 48:5 // 1 Cor. 12:8–10;
1 Clem. 49:5 // 1 Cor. 13:4–10. See Donald A. Hagner, *The Use of the Old and New Testaments
in Clement of Rome* (NovTSup 34; Leiden: Brill, 1973), 178–220.

Clement of Alexandria (c. 150–c. 215)[110] assigns Hebrews to Paul using the distinctly Pauline title "To the Hebrews" (πρὸς Ἑβραίους),[111] which he said Luke translated from the Hebrew tongue (Eusebius, *Hist. eccl.* 6.14.2–4). In the Chester Beatty papyrus ($\mathfrak{P}^{46}$) from Alexandria, perhaps from as early as 200 CE,[112] Hebrews is placed after Romans in the Pauline corpus.[113]

There are still occasional calls for Paul to be credited with the authorship of Hebrews,[114] sometimes with Luke as a possible amanuensis.[115] However, over against Paul's claim to a direct revelation from Jesus Christ (Gal. 1:1, 12), the author of Hebrews received the gospel secondhand (Heb. 2:3). Also, over against Paul's deep interest in the Gentiles (e.g., Rom. 1:5, 13; 15:16; Gal. 1:16), Hebrews never mentions them.[116] Further, as Ceslas Spicq concluded after his careful analysis of the style and vocabulary, "It is impossible from the linguistic point of view to attribute to Paul the direct paternity of Hebrews."[117] Paul's authorship has, then, been almost universally abandoned.[118]

Yet, in Hebrews there is a convergence of ideas with Pauline traditions.[119] For example: only Hebrews and Paul use "just" (ἔνδικος, Rom. 3:8; Heb. 2:2); Paul's statement that "the last enemy to be destroyed is death" (1 Cor. 15:26) appears to be echoed in Hebrews 2:14: "through death he might destroy the one who has the power of death, that is, the devil"; only Hebrews and Paul use "effective" (ἐνεργής, 1 Cor. 16:9; Philem. 6; Heb. 4:12); only Hebrews and Paul use "permit" (ἐπιτρέπω) of God allowing an activity (1 Cor. 16:7; Heb. 6:3); and only Hebrews and Paul use "fleshly" (σαρκίνης, Rom. 7:14; 1 Cor. 3:1; 2 Cor. 3:3; Heb. 7:16).

110. We know very little about Clement's life, which probably began in Athens about 150 CE (cf. Clement, *Strom.* 1.1.11). See Henny Fiskå Hägg, *Clement of Alexandria and the Beginnings of Christian Apophaticism* (OECS; Oxford: Oxford University Press, 2006), 51–70.

111. Cf. Clare K. Rothschild, *Hebrews as Pseudepigraphon: The History and Significance of the Pauline Attribution of Hebrews* (WUNT 235; Tübingen: Mohr Siebeck, 2009), 5n14.

112. On the dating of $\mathfrak{P}^{46}$, see, e.g., Bruce M. Metzger and Bart D. Ehrman, *The Text of the New Testament*, 4th ed. (Oxford: Oxford University Press, 2005), 54–55.

113. In some other later manuscripts and versions Hebrews is found in varying places in the Pauline corpus. See William H. P. Hatch, "The Position of Hebrews in the Canon of the New Testament," *HTR* 29 (1936): 133–51.

114. Christos S. Voulgaris, "Hebrews: Paul's Fifth Epistle from Prison," *GOTR* 44 (1999): 199–206.

115. David A. Black, "On the Pauline Authorship of Hebrews (Part 1): Overlooked Affinities between Hebrews and Paul," *FM* 16 (1999): 48; David A. Black, "On the Pauline Authorship of Hebrews (Part 2): The External Evidence Reconsidered," *FM* 16 (1999): 84.

116. Lincoln D. Hurst, *The Epistle to the Hebrews: Its Background of Thought* (SNTSMS 65; Cambridge: Cambridge University Press, 1990), 107.

117. Spicq, *Hébreux*, 1:154. For a succinct and detailed comparison of the style and vocabulary of Hebrews and Paul, see also Paul Ellingworth, *The Epistle to the Hebrews: A Commentary on the Greek Text* (NIGTC; Grand Rapids: Eerdmans; Carlisle: Paternoster, 1993), 9–13.

118. Ellingworth, *Hebrews*, 3.

119. Further, see Hurst, *Hebrews*, 108–9.

Even though it is difficult to determine its precise relationship with the Pauline traditions—literary dependence or by a Pauline disciple, for example[120]—the author of Hebrews probably intended his work to be read in the Pauline tradition. The clearest evidence is in the final chapter, for it shares a number of phrases and ideas with Paul.[121] Also, the form of the final pericope—benediction (Heb. 13:20–21a), doxology (13:21b), comments on the body of the text (13:22), personal and travel news (13:23), greetings (13:24), and farewell (13:25)[122]—and its content (including the mention of Timothy, 13:23) further establish the author's intention to be read within the Pauline traditions.[123]

However, various relationships have been suggested between the final chapter and the body of Hebrews—an authentic or pseudephigraphal Pauline piece or pieces added by a different author, for example.[124] Nevertheless, the strong ties between the central section of the chapter (13:7–19) and the body of Hebrews, and the continuity of the final benediction and greeting (13:20–25) with the final chapter and the body of the book,[125] suggest that it was always part of the text. Notwithstanding, whatever the relationship between this chapter and the body of the book, as it stands Hebrews is not pseudepigraphal, for there is neither a Pauline salutation nor the use of his name. Rather, Hebrews is to be taken as written in, and in light of close contact with, the Pauline tradition, reflecting and reinterpreting Paul for a later time.[126]

As a deliberate attempt to write in and for the Pauline tradition, Hebrews provides strong evidence, especially in relation to the coming of salvation, that the miraculous was seen as part of those traditions, and probably contemporary experience as well. Echoing the Pauline interest in tradition being handed on from the Lord to the present (cf. 1 Cor. 11:23; 15:3), Hebrews has the lines: "It [salvation] was declared at first through the Lord, and it was attested to us by those who heard him, God adding his testimony [συνεπιμαρτυρέω] by signs and wonders and various miracles and by apportionments of the Holy Spirit according to his will" (2:3–4, my translation). The author is clearly describing

120. See the discussion by Hurst, *Hebrews*, esp. 109, 124.
121. See Heb. 13:4 // 1 Cor. 5:13; Heb. 13:10 // 1 Cor. 9:4; 11:10; Heb. 13:16 // Phil. 4:18; Heb. 13:20 // 1 Cor. 5:5; Heb. 13:20 // Rom. 10:7. See the discussion by Rothschild, *Hebrews*, 82–89, esp. 82–83.
122. Attridge (*Hebrews*, 405) provides a chart identifying parallels between Heb. 13:20–25 and NT letters, particularly the Pauline corpus.
123. See ibid.
124. A. J. M. Wedderburn, "The 'Letter' to the Hebrews and Its Thirteenth Chapter," *NTS* 50 (2004): 390–405, esp. 390–93.
125. Robert Jewett, "Form and Function of the Homiletic Benediction," *AThR* 51 (1969): 27–30.
126. In that the author of Hebrews does not use or write in the name of Paul, it is incorrect to call the text a "pseudepigraphon," as does, e.g., Rothschild, *Hebrews*.

the origin and nature of the salvation that has come to the readers, which he says involved declaration, and signs and wonders and various powers, as well as "apportionments of the Holy Spirit" (2:4).

From what we have already seen of the composite term "signs and wonders" (σημεῖα καὶ τέρατα, see §7.8 above), as well as in the additional use of "powers" (δυνάμεις, see 25n126 above), Hebrews leaves no doubt that miracles are in mind.[127] Notably, the miracles are portrayed not as the message itself—in the sense that the message was miraculous—but as distinct from the declaration of salvation. Nevertheless, the miracles are an integral part of the coming of salvation.

Positioned at the beginning of the sentence, and being complex and rare, the word συνεπιμαρτυρέω ("testify strongly at the same time") and its different elements probably are significant for the writer.[128] That is, miracles accompany (συν-, "with") and add to (ἐπι-, "upon") the declaration.[129] The tense of this verb (present participle) suggests that God's endorsement through the miracles was taking place at the same time as the declaration. The use of the well-known phrase "signs and wonders" for marvels from God (see §7.7 [a] above), as well as the use of the related "confirm" (ἐπιμαρτυρέω) in the Septuagint for the work of God,[130] probably would have drawn the readers' attention to God, not the human messengers, being the subject of the testimony of miracles. What is accompanied and added through the miracles is God's affirmation of the declaration of salvation. Since the time of the testifying by God is determined by the time of the attesting by "us"—the coming of salvation[131]—the writer is describing the miraculous in relation to the coming of salvation.

This view is seen again in the text when the miraculous reappears. In one of the warnings the writer of Hebrews says, "It is impossible to restore again to repentance those who have once been enlightened, and have tasted the heavenly

---

127. Stefan Schreiber, *Paulus als Wundertäter: Redaktionsgeschichtliche Untersuchungen zur Apostelgeschichte und den authentischen Paulusbriefen* (BZNW 79; Berlin: de Gruyter, 1996), 171, 267; Mitchell, *Hebrews*, 58–59.

128. In the period, the verb is known only in Philo, *Mos.* 2.123; Plutarch, *De laude* 539D.10; Galen, *In Hippocratis de victu acutorum commentaria iv* (Kuhn) 15.583; Athenaeus, *Deipn.* 13.595.e; Clement of Alexandria, *Frag.* 9.15.

129. Ellingworth, *Hebrews*, 141.

130. In the LXX see, e.g., Neh. 9:29, 30; Jer. 39:25 (ET 32:25); Amos 3:13 (through the prophet); Sir. 46:19 (through Samuel).

131. On the interpretation of present participle (συνεπιμαρτυροῦντος, "testify strongly at the same time") being determined by the main verb (ἐβεβαιώθη, "confirmed," aorist indicative) or context, see C. F. D. Moule, *An Idiom-Book of New Testament Greek* (Cambridge: Cambridge University Press, 1959), 99. To the contrary, Lane takes the present participle to imply that "the corroborative evidence was not confined to the initial act of preaching, but continued to be displayed within the life of the community" (*Hebrews 1–8*, 39).

gift, and have shared in the Holy Spirit, and have tasted the goodness of the word of God and the powers of the age to come" (6:4–5). In that the writer is using four aorist participles—"having once been enlightened, and have tasted . . . have shared . . . and have tasted"—the experience described is to be taken as the readers' enlightenment or coming to faith. The experience involves the Holy Spirit, the word of God, and the powers of the age to come. That the "powers" (δυνάμεις, plural) or miracles are "of the age to come" is consistent with the widespread Christian belief that the miracles, first of Jesus, were the present experience of the future (cf. Matt. 12:28 // Luke 11:20). The word of God being paired with miracles is also consistent with what we have seen of Paul's view that the gospel came in word and deed or miracles (Rom. 15:18).

The relationship between the miracles and the other aspects of the coming of salvation at first may appear to be one of subordinating the miracles to the declaration.[132] For we have seen the writer of Hebrews say God added his testimony to the declaration of salvation (2:4). However, it is to be noted that the prefix "with" (συν-) of "testify strongly at the same time" (συνεπιμαρτυρέω) means the declaration and testimony are thought to be taking place at the same time. Further, there is no subordination in the later description of being enlightened (6:4–6); the aspects of the goodness that is tasted—the word of God "and" (τέ) the powers or miracles—are listed almost as one in using the enclitic τέ (6:5), which denotes a closer relationship than "and" (καί).[133]

From this discussion it is clear that, for Hebrews, the coming of salvation involves the human declaration of salvation in association with God's confirmation in the miraculous. That this experience of miracle was thought to go beyond the initial experience of salvation is suggested in the third element in the description of the coming of salvation that I discussed earlier. Along with the declaration and the miraculous, the author says there were "apportionments of the Holy Spirit according to his will" (2:4).[134] The apportionments are said to be "according to his will" (κατὰ τὴν αὐτοῦ θέλησιν)—that is, God's

132. Cf. Ben Witherington III, *Letters and Homilies for Jewish Christians: A Socio-Rhetorical Commentary on Hebrews, James, and Jude* (Downers Grove, IL: IVP Academic, 2007), 137.

133. A. T. Robertson, *A Grammar of the Greek Testament* (Nashville: Broadman, 1934), 1178; BDF §443, τέ (1).

134. On πνεύματος ἁγίου ("of Holy Spirit") being used without the article (also in Heb. 6:4), see Barnabas Lindars, *The Theology of the Letter to the Hebrews* (NTT; Cambridge: Cambridge University Press, 1991), 56. Lindars argues that the absence of the article appears in relation to the readers' participation in Holy Spirit. Whether the phrase πνεύματος ἁγίου ("of Holy Spirit") is taken as an objective genitive ("by Holy Spirit"), as preferred by Ellingworth (*Hebrews*, 142), or a subjective genitive, suggesting the Holy Spirit is distributed (cf. Gal. 3:5), as preferred by F. F. Bruce (*Hebrews*, 2nd ed. [NICNT; Grand Rapids: Eerdmans, 1990], 69n7), the context ("his will") implies the activity of the Spirit is being distributed among believers.

will.[135] Grammatically, the apportionments or "distributions" (μερισμοί) of the Spirit by God are tied to the description of the coming of salvation. However, in using the word μερισμοί, which was used at the time in association with διαιρέω,[136] Paul's word for the distribution of the gifts of the Spirit (1 Cor. 12:11; cf. 12:6), Hebrews is reflecting Paul's description of the distribution of the gifts of the Spirit in the ongoing life of the church.[137] That is, Hebrews probably also has in mind the ongoing presence of the miraculous among the readers.[138] That the author offers no more than these hints of the ongoing place of the miraculous in the life of the believers is probably because his concern is with the beginnings or foundations of the experience of the readers (6:1–2).

From what we have seen, the natural reading of Hebrews is that God's testimony by miracles and the apportionments of the Holy Spirit applies to the horizons both of the Lord and of the author and his readers. The miraculous by God, not the human messengers, accompanies or (perhaps more accurately) is seen as part of the coming of salvation. Notably, there are strong hints that the miraculous was a part not only of the proclamation of the gospel, but also of the ongoing life of the church. It is also notable that, in writing in the tradition of Paul, what is missing from Hebrews is any suggestion that the writer (as Paul) was directly involved in miracle working. This reflects what we have seen of Paul's own testimony of the place of miracle in his experience, thinking, and ministry: though he was not directly involved in or responsible for them, the miraculous was part of the coming of the gospel and the ongoing life of the body of Christ.

9.6 James

As Leonhard Goppelt reminded us, "Hardly any other document of the New Testament is more difficult to classify historically and theologically than the

135. Ellingworth comments, "Aὐτοῦ is best understood as = τοῦ θεοῦ (D*), not as = τοῦ πνεύματος. The unusual order τὴν αὐτοῦ θέλησιν may be intended to carry the reader beyond πνεύματος to θεοῦ as the true antecedent. The order is possibly (though not necessarily . . .) emphatic, as in classical Greek" (*Hebrews*, 142).

136. On the interchangeability of, e.g., the nouns μερισμός and διαίρεσις, see, e.g., LXX Ezra 6:18; Heron, *Def.* 136.49.10–11; Herodian, *Fig.* 94.22.

137. See, e.g., Hans Windisch, *Der Hebräerbrief* (HNT 4/3; Tübingen: Mohr Siebeck, 1913), 116; James Moffatt, *A Critical and Exegetical Commentary on the Epistle to the Hebrews* (ICC; Edinburgh: T&T Clark, 1924), 20; J. H. Davies, *A Letter to the Hebrews* (CBC; Cambridge: Cambridge University Press, 1967), 26; Bruce, *Hebrews*, 69n7; Ellingworth, *Hebrews*, 15; Witherington, *Hebrews, James, and Jude*, 137. To the contrary, Karl H. Rengstorf says "the author has no religious relation to miracles as such" ("σημεῖον, κτλ.," *TDNT* 7:260).

138. Lane, *Hebrews 1–8*, 40.

Epistle of James."[139] Not surprisingly, then, little is agreed about this letter.[140] For example, some accept the simple ascription, "James, a servant of God and of the Lord Jesus Christ" (James 1:1), as well as the Jewish atmosphere of the letter, as pointing to authorship by James of Jerusalem, the Lord's brother (Gal. 1:18–19), who died in 62 CE (Josephus, *Ant*. 20.9; Eusebius, *Hist. eccl*. 2.23).[141] Others note, however, that James of Jerusalem, or James the Just (Eusebius, *Hist. eccl*. 2.23.4) was concerned about the ritual law (Gal. 2:12; Eusebius, *Hist. eccl*. 2.23.4–7), whereas the author of this letter, focusing on the moral aspect of the law, makes no reference to the ritual law (James 1:27; 2:10; cf. Acts 15:13–21). In turn, they conclude that the letter of James is pseudonymous[142] and from late in the first century[143] or even from the middle of the second century.[144]

Concomitantly, the relationship between James and the Pauline corpus is also far from agreed.[145] It is urged by some that James be read on its own terms.[146] Indeed, Richard Bauckham has attempted to show that "James wrote without any reference to the Pauline discussions of faith and works."[147] However, James most probably breathes the same air or literary culture as Paul.[148] There is the shared question-and-answer writing style,[149] and there is the "combination of argument and exhortation composed by means of a fresh combination of appeals to scripture (LXX), experience and common sense," as Margaret Mitchell put it.[150] There is also the infamous Jacobean passage on faith and deeds (James 2:14–26), comprehensible only in light of Paul in general,[151] and

---

139. Leonhard Goppelt, *Theology of the New Testament*, 2 vols. (Grand Rapids: Eerdmans, 1982), 2:199.

140. See the discussion by Peter H. Davids, "The Epistle of James in Modern Discussion," *ANRW* II.25.5 (1988): 3621–45.

141. Richard Bauckham, *James: Wisdom of James, Disciple of Jesus the Sage* (NTR; London: Routledge, 1999), 11–25.

142. See the thorough discussion by Luke Timothy Johnson, *The Letter of James: A New Translation with Introduction and Commentary* (AB 37A; New York: Doubleday, 1995), 89–123.

143. Cf. Brown, *New Testament*, 742.

144. See David R. Nienhuis, *Not by Paul Alone: The Formation of the Catholic Epistle Collection and the Christian Canon* (Waco: Baylor University Press, 2007), 237–38. Note the critical review by Joel Marcus, *CBQ* 70 (2008): 384–85.

145. See the list of options for literary-historical relationships between James and Paul in Margaret M. Mitchell, "The Letter of James as a Document of Paulinism?" in *Reading James with New Eyes: Methodological Reassessments of the Letter of James*, ed. Robert L. Webb and John S. Kloppenborg (LNTS 342; London: T&T Clark, 2007), 77–78.

146. E.g., Mitchell, "Letter of James," 75n1.

147. Bauckham, *James*, 129. See the critical review by James Carleton Paget, *JTS* 53 (2002): 266–72, esp. 271–72.

148. Mitchell, "Letter of James," 83.

149. Ibid., 85, esp. n35.

150. Ibid., 85.

151. Goppelt, *Theology*, 2:200.

of Galatians in particular; and there is probable knowledge of 1 Corinthians,[152] as well as vocabulary shared with Paul,[153] which favor reading James as broadly Pauline rather than as anti-Pauline.[154] In turn, the memory of Paul reflected in James is perhaps of "a flagging Christianity," as Goppelt put it, for which Paul's slogan "faith alone" had become a "quietistic pillow."[155] Into this situation James sought to bring the readers back to their roots.

In relation to our interests in recovering all we can about the historical Paul and the miraculous, James offers us some, even if not strong, evidence. On the one hand, there is some potentially negative evidence. It is notable that for James, the kingdom of God is a future hope (James 2:5),[156] as sometimes in Paul (1 Cor. 6:9–10; 15:24, 50; Gal. 5:21). But, in contrast to Paul (Rom. 14:17; 1 Cor. 4:20; 1 Thess. 2:12), in James there is no hint of a present dimension to the kingdom to which the miraculous might have been associated (see chap. 7 above). Instead, the kingdom is mentioned in terms of God choosing the poor to be heirs of the future kingdom (James 2:5).

On the other hand, there is some more positive evidence that the miraculous was part of the experience of the readers of James. In the section in which James is discussing the nature and scope of faith (2:14–26) he says, "You believe that God is one; you do well. Even the demons believe—and shudder" (2:19). In light of at least two factors—the general interest in evil or the demonic (1:13–14; 3:15; 4:7), which was consistent with exorcistic practice, and the notion of demons shuddering, which is well documented in apotropaic or exorcistic texts (*PGM* 4.3014–19; cf. 12.239–40)[157]—this statement probably reflects exorcistic experience among the readers.[158]

Then, more directly, James says, "Are any among you sick [ἀσθενεῖ]?[159] They should call for the elders of the church and have them pray over them, anointing them with oil in the name of the Lord. The prayer of faith will save [or "heal,"

152. E.g., cf. James 1:16 with 1 Cor. 6:9; 15:33 (cf. Gal. 6:6). Cf. James 1:26 with 1 Cor. 3:18; 11:16; 14:37. Cf. James 2:7 with 1 Cor. 6:11. Cf. James 2:14, 16 with 1 Cor. 15:32. Cf. James 5:7 with 1 Cor. 5:23. Further, see Mitchell, "Letter of James," 89–91.

153. See the discussion by ibid., 85–87.

154. See ibid., 75–98, and those cited at 81–82n27.

155. Goppelt, *Theology*, 2:200.

156. The future is indicated by ἐπηγγείλατο ("he has promised," aorist middle indicative; also in James 1:12). James H. Ropes, *A Critical and Exegetical Commentary on the Epistle of St. James* (ICC; Edinburgh: T&T Clark, 1916), 194.

157. Samson Eitrem, *Papyri Osloenses*, fasc. 1, *Magical Papyri* (Oslo: Norske Videnskaps-Akademi i Oslo, 1925), 98.

158. Graham H. Twelftree, *In the Name of Jesus: Exorcism among Early Christians* (Grand Rapids: Baker Academic, 2007), 179–80.

159. In that the person is assumed unable to go to the elders, the translation "sick" (ἀσθενεῖ) is to be preferred over "weak." Cf. BDAG, "ἀσθένεια," 142.

σῴζω] the sick" (5:14).[160] A few lines later James says, "Pray for one another, so that you may be healed [ἰάομαι]" (5:16). In view of these admonitions, healing may not have been as extensive as the author of James expected, but at least it was understood to be part of Christian experience.

Therefore, although the kingdom of God was conceived as future and not available as a concept to be associated with the practice of miracle working, the hints of exorcism and the encouragement to practice healing are sufficient evidence to suggest that the readers of James, for whom the memory of Paul most probably was important, saw to some extent and understood to a greater extent that the miraculous—healing and exorcism in particular—was part of Christianity.

9.7 Beyond the Canon

The literature, theology, and person of Paul remained of interest beyond the canon. For example, even though he is explicitly mentioned only eight times in the Apostolic Fathers,[161] no other early Christian is referred to as often as Paul.[162] (Peter, the only other apostle named in the Apostolic Fathers, is mentioned three times.)[163] However, our interest is not in the sometimes competing interpretations of Paul, but in what reliable data writers may provide to help us understand the historical Paul in relation to the miraculous. This data— potentially from the Apostolic Fathers, early patristic writers, apocryphal literature, New Testament manuscript introductions, canon lists, and the Mani biography[164]—may be in two forms. We could expect this literature to provide direct references to Paul in relation to the miraculous not found in the New Testament. We could also anticipate that in the later reception of the Pauline literature—by those still living in sociocultural worlds similar to Paul's—the provision of insights into Pauline texts that we might miss.

Not only to keep the amount of material to be examined within manageable limits but also to take into account literature that arose in the same

160. Twelftree, *Name of Jesus*, 180–82.
161. *1 Clem.* 5:5; 47:1; Ign. *Eph.* 12:2; Ign. *Rom.* 4:3; Pol. *Phil.* 3:2; 9:1, 2, 3.
162. Andreas Lindemann, "Paul in the Writings of the Apostolic Fathers," in *Paul and the Legacies of Paul*, ed. William S. Babcock (Dallas: Southern Methodist University Press, 1990), 28.
163. *1 Clem.* 5:4; Ign. *Rom.* 4:3; Ign. *Smyrn.* 3:2. See Paul Hartog, *Polycarp and the New Testament: The Occasion, Rhetoric, Theme, and Unity of the Epistle to the Philippians and Its Allusions to New Testament Literature* (WUNT 2/134; Tübingen: Mohr Siebeck, 2002), 219.
164. On the Mani biography, see Ron Cameron and Arthur J. Dewey, *The Cologne Mani Codex (P. Colon. inv. nr. 4780): Concerning the Origin of His Body* (TTECLS 15/3; Missoula, MT: Scholars Press, 1979), 47–49; Hans Dieter Betz, "Paul in the Mani Biography (Codex Manichaicus Coloniensis)," in *Paulinische Studien: Gesammelte Aufsätze 3* (Tübingen: Mohr Siebeck, 1994), 163–83.

general Greek milieu as Paul, I will take into account literature up to the time of Tertullian (c. 160–c. 225),[165] who began to publish in 196 or 197 CE.[166] Tertullian, the first Christian theologian to write in Latin, is credited with taking Christian thought beyond its Greek roots.[167] In turn, within this period up to the end of the second century, we can expect useful results if we take into account two kinds of material: I will note references to the person or biography of Paul, and I will give attention to the way canonical Pauline passages that, arguably, relate to the miraculous have been treated in relation to the miraculous by these writers.[168] I will leave aside all other citations and echoes of the Pauline writings. Again, so far as our limited resources allow the establishment of dates, I will take the texts in chronological order: *1 Clement*, Ignatius of Antioch, Polycarp, the *Acts of Paul*, the *Epistle of the Apostles*, and Clement of Alexandria.

(a) 1 Clement, written in the mid-90s[169] from Rome to the Corinthians (*1 Clem.*, preface), mentions Paul twice by name, first as an example of endurance (5:5), and then as writing to the Corinthians (47:1). If Clement knew of a tradition of Paul as a miracle worker, he could be expected to have mentioned it in the general description of Paul. However, Clement describes Paul only as a teacher of righteousness (5:6–7), showing no knowledge or interest in him in relation to the miraculous.[170]

(b) Ignatius of Antioch, bishop of Antioch (Ign. *Rom.* 2:2; cf. Eusebius, *Hist. eccl.* 3.22), wrote letters to six churches and one to Polycarp as he was accompanied by ten soldiers on his way to Rome and martyrdom (Ign. *Rom.* 5:1)[171]

---

165. See Timothy D. Barnes, *Tertullian: A Historical and Literary Study* (Oxford: Clarendon, 1985), chap. 5 ("Chronology").

166. See Tertullian, *Or.* 1.17.4; *Apol.* 35.9, 11; 37.4; on which, see ibid., 33–34.

167. Cf. Eric F. Osborn, *Tertullian: First Theologian of the West* (Cambridge: Cambridge University Press, 1997), xiii.

168. The passages of potential value are those discussed above in chap. 6 (1 Cor. 9:1; 11:30; 14:6, 18; 15:8; 2 Cor. 1:8–11; 12:1–10; 13:3; Gal. 1:13–16; 4:13–14; Phil. 2:25–30; 3:4–11), chap. 7 (Rom. 15:18–19; 1 Cor. 2:3–4; 4:19–20; 12:4–11; 2 Cor. 6:6–7; 12:12; Gal. 3:1–5; 1 Thess. 1:5), chap. 8 (Acts 9:1–19a; 13:1–3, 4–12; 14:3, 8–10; 15:12; 16:6–11, 16–18, 25–34; 19:6, 11–12, 13; 20:7–12; 22:6–16, 17–21; 26:12–18; 27:39–28:11), and chap. 9 (Col. 3:16; Eph. 5:19; 2 Thess. 2:9–10; 1 Tim. 1:18; 4:14; 2 Tim. 3:11; Heb. 2:3–4; 6:4–5).

169. See Horrell, *Social Ethos*, 239–41; Ehrman, *Apostolic Fathers*, 1:23–25.

170. Cf. Twelftree, *Name of Jesus*, 210–12.

171. On the three traditional listed recensions of the letters, see William R. Schoedel, *Ignatius of Antioch: A Commentary on the Letters of Ignatius of Antioch*, ed. Helmut Koester (Hermeneia; Philadelphia: Fortress, 1985), 3–4. On the authenticity of the letters, see William R. Schoedel, "Are the Letters of Ignatius of Antioch Authentic?" *RelSRev* 6 (1980): 196–201 (a review article); Caroline P. Hamond Bammel, "Ignatian Problems," *JTS* 33 (1982): 62–97; Mark J. Edwards, "Ignatius and the Second Century: An Answer to R. Hübner," *ZAC* 2 (1998): 214–26. On the identity of the author of *1 Clement*, see Ehrman, *Apostolic Fathers*, 1:21–23.

early in the second century.[172] Ignatius twice mentions Paul.[173] In his letter *To the Ephesians* he says his readers "are fellow initiates with Paul, the holy one who received a testimony and proved worth of all fortune." Ignatius immediately goes on, "When I attain to God, may I be found in his footsteps, this one who mentions you in every epistle in Christ Jesus" (Ign. *Eph.* 12:2).[174] With his attention on his own impending martyrdom (e.g., Ign. *Rom.* 1–2; 8), it is not surprising that, apart from Paul being a letter writer, Paul's death dominates the brief descriptions of the apostle by Ignatius (Ign. *Eph.* 12:2).

In his letter *To the Romans* Ignatius says, "I do not, as Peter and Paul, issue commandments unto you. They were apostles" (Ign. *Rom.* 4:3). Again, there is no mention of the miraculous, nor could it be expected in light of the subject matter of asking his readers not to hinder his martyrdom. In other places Pauline theology probably is influencing Ignatius.[175] However, at no point is he relying on anything related to the miraculous in Paul. Also, there is no evidence that he has other information about the apostle.[176] Notably, he most probably has no knowledge of the book of Acts.[177] In any case, even if he had relevant traditions, with his interests in martyrdom, false teachers (e.g., Ign. *Eph.* 6:2; Ign. *Trall.* 6:1)[178] and the unity of the church (Ign. *Magn.*

172. Eusebius (*Hist. eccl.* 3.21–22) dates the letters in the time of Trajan (98–117 CE), and in his *Chronicon* more specifically to the tenth year of Trajan (107–108 CE). For example, see Timothy D. Barnes, "The Date of Ignatius," *ExpTim* 120 (2008): 126–27.

173. On Paul and Ignatius, see, e.g., Carl B. Smith, "Ministry, Martyrdom, and Other Mysteries: Pauline Influence on Ignatius of Antioch," in *Paul and the Second Century*, ed. Michael F. Bird and Joseph R. Dodson (LNTS 412; London: T&T Clark, 2011), 37–57.

174. If Ignatius knew only 1 Corinthians, Ephesians, and 1 and 2 Timothy, his statement that the Ephesians are mentioned "in every epistle" is reasonable. See Paul Foster, "The Epistles of Ignatius of Antioch and the Writings That Later Formed the New Testament," in *The Reception of the New Testament in the Apostolic Fathers*, ed. Andrew Gregory and Christopher Tuckett (NTAF 1; Oxford: Oxford University Press, 2005), 172. However, Polycarp says "he exulted in you among all his churches" (Pol. *Phil.* 11:3), suggesting hyperbole.

175. Foster, "Epistles of Ignatius," 164–72; Andreas Lindemann, "Paul's Influence on 'Clement' and Ignatius," in *Trajectories through the New Testament and the Apostolic Fathers*, ed. Andrew Gregory and Christopher Tuckett (NTAF 2; Oxford: Oxford University Press, 2005), 18–23.

176. Lindemann, "Paul's Influence," 18.

177. There is only one possible echo of Luke's second volume. Acts 10:41: ὅιτινες συνεφάγομεν καὶ συνεπίομεν αὐτῷ μετὰ τὸ ἀναστῆναι αὐτὸν ἐκ νεκρῶν ("who ate and drank with him after he rose from the dead"), in Ign. *Smyrn.* 3:3: μετὰ δὲ τὴν ἀνάστασιν συνέφαγεν αὐτοῖς καὶ συνέπιεν ("after his resurrection he ate and drank with them").

However, Ignatius is discussing docetic views. Cf. Michael D. Goulder, "Ignatius' 'Docetics,'" VC 53 (1999): 16–30. It is likely, therefore, he is using a phrase common in debates with docetics. See Edouard Massaux, *The Influence of the Gospel of Saint Matthew on Christian Literature before Saint Irenaeus*, vol. 1, *The First Ecclesiastical Writers*, trans. Norman J. Belval and Suzanne Hecht, ed. Arthur J. Bellinzoni (NGS 5; Louvain: Peeters; Macon, GA: Mercer University Press, 1990), 99.

178. See, e.g., Goulder, "Ignatius' 'Docetics.'"

1:2; Ign. *Phld.* 5:2; 8:1),[179] he has no reason to mention Paul in relation to the miraculous.

(c) *Polycarp* (c. 69–c. 155 CE),[180] bishop of Smyrna (Ign. *Magn.* 15), is credited with conversing "with John and with others who had seen the Lord" (Eusebius, *Hist. eccl.* 5.20.6, citing Irenaeus). While this is rather romantic, as Richard Pervo notes,[181] Polycarp makes no mention of it. Rather, Paul is his preferred hero[182] and the only apostle Polycarp names—perhaps not surprising in that he is addressing a church where Paul, the founder, was held in high regard (Phil. 1:7; 4:15–16). Writing early in the second century, at a time when Paul's legacy was a matter of debate,[183] Polycarp is potentially important in recovering historically reliable data from what was known about Paul at the time.

Polycarp's only surviving text,[184] sometimes argued to be the amalgamation of two letters (cf. Pol. *Phil.* 9:1; 13:2),[185] is directed to the Philippians. Michael Holmes, for example, proposes that the author almost certainly uses 1 Corinthians and Ephesians, and that it is highly probable he uses 1 and 2 Timothy and probably knows Romans, Galatians, and Philippians. It is less certain that he knew 2 Corinthians, 2 Thessalonians, and Colossians.[186] The portrait of Paul by Polycarp is of a wise, accurate, and reliable teacher (cf. Pol. *Phil.* 11:2

179. Schoedel, *Ignatius*, 21–22. According to Christine Trevett ("Prophecy and Anti-Episcopal Activity: A Third Error Combatted by Ignatius?" *JEH* 34 [1983]: 1–18; and idem, "Apocalypse, Ignatius, Montanism: Seeking the Seeds," *VC* 43 [1989]: 313–38), Ignatius was combating a third error, prophetic activity that was the seed of Montanism has been discussed and criticized by Schoedel, "Polycarp," 342.

180. See *Mart. Pol.* 9:3 ("For eighty-six years have I been his servant"); and the discussion by Timothy D. Barnes, "A Note on Polycarp," *JTS* 18 (1967): 433–37.

181. Pervo, *Making of Paul*, 139.

182. Cf. D. Richard Stuckwisch, "Saint Polycarp of Smyrna: Johannine or Pauline Figure?" *CTQ* 61 (1997): 125.

183. Hartog, *Polycarp*, 169n118; Michael W. Holmes, "Paul and Polycarp," in Bird and Dodson, *Paul*, 57.

184. The anonymous *Life of Polycarp*, not earlier than the third century, and of doubtful historical value, credits Polycarp with "many treatises and sermons and letters" (*Vit. Poly.* 12). See, e.g., Hartog, *Polycarp*, 32–34. The view of Hans von Campenhausen ("Polykarp von Smyrna und die Pastoralbrief" [1951], in *Aus der Frühzeit des Christentums: Studien zur Kirchengeschichte des ersten und zweiten Jahrhunderts* [Tübingen: Mohr Siebeck, 1963], 197–252), that Polycarp wrote the Pastoral Epistles, has not been accepted. See Holmes, "Paul and Polycarp," 57.

185. In support of P. N. Harrison (*Polycarp's Two Epistles to the Philippians* [Cambridge: Cambridge University Press, 1936]), that chap. 13, and probably chap. 14, formed a cover letter (115 CE) to the Letters of Ignatius, and chaps. 1–12 were written two decades later, after the death of Ignatius, see, e.g., Kenneth Berding, *Polycarp and Paul: An Analysis of Their Literary and Theological Relationship in Light of Polycarp's Use of Biblical and Extra-Biblical Literature* (VCSup 62; Leiden: Brill, 2002), 15–17. Hartog (*Polycarp*, 148–69) and Michael W. Holmes ("Polycarp of Smyrna, Letter to the Philippians," *ExpTim* 118 [2006]: 60–62), e.g., argue for the unity of Polycarp's letter.

186. See Holmes, "Paul and Polycarp," 59.

[Latin MS])[187] of the word of truth, a laborer among the Philippians (11:3, Latin MS), and a letter writer (3:2). The apostles, including Paul, are also to be followed as examples of patience in suffering (8:2–9:1).[188] Paul is, then, a pastor-teacher and an example of patient endurance; there is no hint of the miraculous in connection with Paul.[189]

(d) *The Acts of Paul* perhaps was compiled in Asia Minor (Tertullian, *Bapt.* 17.5),[190] in the last quarter of the second century,[191] from older parts, including "from the oral taletelling of women."[192] The text of *Acts of Paul* is now known only through the extant parts—*The Acts of Paul and Thecla* and *Martyrdom of Paul*, as well as the Heidelberg Coptic Papyrus, the John Rylands Library Coptic fragment, and the Genf Coptic Papyrus[193]—that make up perhaps two-thirds of the original work.[194] From the same time a letter to Paul and his reply, now known as *3 Corinthians*, probably had an independent existence before being incorporated into *Acts of Paul*.[195]

This narrative is of considerable potential interest to us for it contains a number of miracle stories associated with Paul. A man being healed of dropsy dies

---

187. On textual issues relating to Polycarp, *To the Philippians*, see Hartog, *Polycarp*, 67–69.

188. Cf. Berding, *Polycarp and Paul*, e.g., 140.

189. The description of Paul's ministry in *Vit. Poly.* 2 makes no mention of the miraculous. See the brief treatment of Polycarp's reception of Paul by Pervo, *Making of Paul*, 139–43.

190. Hans-Josef Klauck, *The Apocryphal Acts of the Apostles: An Introduction*, trans. Brian McNeil (Waco: Baylor University Press, 2008), 50. On the attestation of *Acts of Paul*, see Tertullian, *Bapt.* 17.5 (c. 200 CE); Hippolytus, *Comm. Dan.* 3.29 (c. 204 CE); and the discussion by A. Hilhorst, "Tertullian on the Acts of Paul," in *The Apocryphal Acts of Paul and Thecla*, ed. Jan N. Bremmer (SAAA 2; Kampen: Kok Pharos, 1996), 150–63. Stevan L. Davies ("Women, Tertullian and the Acts of Paul," *Semeia* 38 [1986]: 139–44) argues that Tertullian more likely refers to a lost pseudepigraphical Pauline letter.

191. Andrew Gregory, "The *Acts of Paul* and the Legacy of Paul," in Bird and Dodson, *Paul*, 169–72.

192. Dennis R. MacDonald, "The Role of Women in the Production of the Apocryphal Acts of Apostles," *Iliff Review* 40 (1984): 21 (cf. 26–35). For a discussion of *Acts of Paul* originating among a community of women, see also Peter W. Dunn, "Women's Liberation, the *Acts of Paul*, and Other Apocryphal Acts of the Apostles: A Review of Some Recent Interpretations," *Apocrypha* 4 (1993): 245–61, along with a response by Shelly Matthews, "Thinking of Thecla: Issues in Feminist Historiography," *JFSR* 17 (2001): 39–55.

193. On the use of these texts in the reconstruction of *Acts of Paul*, see Wilhelm Schneemelcher, "Acts of Paul," in *New Testament Apocrypha*, ed. Wilhelm Schneemelcher, rev. Edgar Hennecke, trans. R. McL. Wilson, 2 vols. (Cambridge: James Clarke; Louisville: Westminster John Knox, 1992), 2:213–70, esp. 216–18; J. Keith Elliott, *The Apocryphal New Testament: A Collection of Apocryphal Christian Literature in an English Translation* (Oxford: Clarendon, 2005), 353–57.

194. In the catalogue in the Codex Claromontanus *Acts of Paul* is said to be 3,560 lines (the Acts of the Apostles is listed as 2,600 lines), and in the Stichometry of Nicephorus *Acts of Paul* (i.e., *The Circuit of Paul*) is 3,600 lines. See Wilhelm Schneemelcher, "General Introduction," in Schneemelcher, *New Testament Apocrypha*, 1:37.

195. See Pervo, *Making of Paul*, 99–102.

and is raised to life, another appears to be raised, Hermippus receives his sight, and perhaps at Paul's prayer half the temple of Apollo at Sindon collapses.[196] The state of the text does not allow for certainty, but in Tyre Paul appears to cause demons to flee and may have healed a man born mute.[197] In Ephesus Paul has a vision and baptizes a lion that subsequently converses with him; a hailstorm does not touch Paul or the lion, but drives off a crowd and kills other animals. Paul also heals a discharging ear.[198] In Philippi Paul raises a girl to life.[199] On the way by boat from Corinth to Italy Paul sees Jesus walk on the water,[200] and in Rome Paul raises to life a youth who had fallen from a window while listening to him teaching.[201] True to his assertion before Caesar, Paul rises from the dead after he is beheaded.[202] The result is, as Richard Pervo said, "a super apostle whose status often approaches, even rivals, that of Christ, working miracles and preaching powerful sermons."[203] Not inappropriately, echoing Martin Kähler's description of the Gospels,[204] Dennis MacDonald calls Acts of Paul "a Pauline passion narrative with a long introduction."[205] However, we are unable to rely on any of this material to contribute to our understanding of the historical Paul.[206] In depending on the Acts of the Apostles or, more likely, traditions or fragments from it,[207] on words and phrases also found in the canonical Gospels and Pauline letters,[208] and on oral traditions shared with the Pastoral Epistles,[209]

196. Acts Paul 4, pp. 28–29, 31, 33; 5, p. 38. Numbers used to refer to the text follow Willy Rordorf, "Actes de Paul," in Écrits apocryphes chrétiens I, ed. François Bovon, Pierre Geoltrain, and Sever J. Voicu (Bibliothèque de la Pléiade 442; Paris: Gallimard, 1997), 1117–77.

197. Acts Paul 6, p. 40.

198. Acts Paul 7, pp. 3, 5.

199. Acts Paul 8, pp. 41–42.

200. Acts Paul 10, p. 7.

201. Acts Paul 11:1–2, pp. 105–10.

202. Acts Paul 11:3–7, pp. 113–17.

203. Pervo, Making of Paul, 101.

204. Martin Kähler wrote, "One could call the Gospels passion narratives with extended introductions" (The So-Called Historical Jesus and the Historic Biblical Christ, trans. and ed. Carl E. Braaten [Philadelphia: Fortress, 1964], 80n11).

205. Dennis R. MacDonald, "Apocryphal and Canonical Narratives about Paul," in Babcock, Paul, 55–70.

206. Also, E. Margaret Howe ("Interpretations of Paul in The Acts of Paul and Thecla," in Pauline Studies: Essays Presented to Professor F. F. Bruce on His 70th Birthday, ed. Donald A. Hagner and Murray J. Harris [Grand Rapids: Eerdmans; Exeter: Paternoster, 1980], 33–49, esp. 46) concludes that Acts of Paul is out of harmony with the historical Paul's attitudes and teaching.

207. Cf. Julian V. Hills, "The Acts of the Apostles in the Acts of Paul," SBLSP 33 (1994): 24–54; Julian V. Hills, "The Acts of Paul and the Legacy of the Lukan Acts," Semeia 80 (1997): 145–58.

208. See, e.g., the discussion by Pál Herczeg, "New Testament Parallels to the Apocryphal Acta Pauli Documents," in Bremmer, Apocryphal Acts, 142–49.

209. Over against older views that saw the author of Acts of Paul depending on the Pastoral Epistles or on written sources behind them, see, e.g., Jeremy W. Barrier, The Acts of Paul and

as well as popular folktales,[210] the author of *Acts of Paul* has engaged in creative storytelling to produce the miracle stories in his narrative.[211] In this the
author probably was not seeking to provide a sequel to the canonical Acts,[212] or
a revision[213] or a rereading of it.[214] Rather, the result, by general consensus at
present, is that the author succeeded in producing a novelistic story or work of
historical fiction, with the canonical Gospels as a significant model,[215] in order
to encourage readers in knowing that God delivers his followers.[216] In this, the
author has maintained a tradition that Paul was a miracle worker.

(e) *The Epistle of the Apostles (Epistula Apostolorum)* was written probably
toward the end of the second century,[217] perhaps in Asia Minor[218] or, considering its free handling of biblical texts, more likely Egypt.[219] In that only the
Acts of the Apostles[220] and Paul's letters[221] appear to be used to tell the story
of Paul's conversion and call to the Gentiles (*Ep. Apost.* 31), the text offers
no independent traditions about Paul and the miraculous.

(f) *Clement of Alexandria* (c. 150–c. 215), theologian and head of the
catechetical school in Alexandria,[222] quotes Paul's statement "The kingdom
of God is not in word but in power" (1 Cor. 4:20). Clement does not, however, associate this with the miraculous but interprets power as truth: "For,"
he says, "the truth alone is powerful" (Clement, *Strom.* 1.54.3; cf. 7.105.2).
Yet, in another place Clement lists the manifestations of the Spirit (*Strom.*
4.21.132; cf. 1 Cor. 12:7–11). He includes "healing" (ἴαμα) and "the working

---

Thecla: A Critical Introdcution and Commentary (WUNT 2/270; Tübingen: Mohr Siebeck,
2009), 33–45.
    210. Ibid., 7–10.
    211. See the discussion by Richard J. Bauckham, "The Acts of Paul as a Sequel to Acts," in
The Book of Acts in Its First Century Setting, vol. 1, *The Book of Acts in Its Ancient Literary
Setting*, ed. Bruce W. Winter and Andrew D. Clarke (Grand Rapids: Eerdmans, 1993), 131–39.
    212. As supposed by Bauckham, "Acts of Paul."
    213. As supposed by Richard I. Pervo, "A Hard Act to Follow: *The Acts of Paul* and the
Canonical Acts," *JHC* 2, no. 2 (1995): 3–32.
    214. As supposed by Daniel Marguerat, "The Acts of Paul and The Canonical Acts: A
Phenomenon of Rereading," *Semeia* 80 (1997): 169–83.
    215. See, e.g., Gregory, "*Acts of Paul*," 189.
    216. Barrier, *Paul and Thecla*, 10–11, 45.
    217. Scholarly consensus assigns the work to the third quarter of the second century. See
Elliott, *Apocryphal New Testament*, 556. More credibly, on the basis of knowledge of early
Christian literature, Pervo (*Making of Paul*, 164) argues for the last quarter of the century.
    218. Charles E. Hill, "The Epistula Apostolorum: An Asian Tract from the Time of Polycarp,"
JECS 7 (1999): 1–53.
    219. C. Detlef G. Müller, "Epistula Apostolorum," in Schneemelcher, *New Testament Apoc-
rypha*, 1:251.
    220. Cf. Acts 9:4–9, 15, 18; 22:7–8, 11; 26:14–15; 13:9; 21:39; 22:3; 26:17.
    221. 1 Cor. 15:9; Gal. 1:13, 16; 2:8–9; Phil. 3:5.
    222. Cf. Clement, *Strom.* 1.1.11; Eusebius, *Hist. eccl.* 5.10.1–4.

of miracles" (ἐνεργήματα δυνάμεων), saying that each manifestation perfects the one receiving it, and that the apostles, including Paul (*Strom.* 4.21.134), are perfected in all manifestations. That is, Clement considers that Paul received all the manifestations. In this conclusion, based on theological speculation, Clement goes beyond what I have been able to establish from Paul's testimony; he did not claim to have the gift of miracles or healing. Nevertheless, though he shows no interest in the Acts stories of Paul, Clement maintains the tradition that Paul had the *charisma* of healing and working miracles.[223] Toward the end of his *Stromata* Clement is also probably assuming Paul was involved in the miraculous in citing Paul, turning a question into a statement: "I shall profit you nothing unless I speak to you, either by revelation, or by knowledge, or by prophecy, or by doctrine" (7.10.59; cf. 1 Cor. 14:6). The same point is made in quoting Paul saying he was rescued by God from deadly peril (Clement, *Strom.* 1.11.50; cf. 2 Cor. 1:10).

(g) *Conclusions.* In this section we have seen that, through citing Paul's involvement in the miraculous,[224] as well as through some theological specula-tion (Clement, *Strom.* 4.21.132, 134), Clement of Alexandria associates Paul with the miraculous. However, in none of this does Clement provide us with data independent of the canon. *Epistle of the Apostles*, also dependent on the canon, tells the story of Paul's conversion. Otherwise, it is only in *Acts of Paul* that Paul is clearly remembered as a miracle worker. However, we have seen that this text is not to be relied upon for historically reliable data in its portrait of Paul as a miracle worker. In short, therefore, we have found no reliable data beyond the canon in the second century to help understand the historical Paul in relation to the miraculous.

With second-century Christian writers maintaining so little in relation to Paul and the miraculous, it is tempting to conclude that the miraculous is, therefore, unlikely to have been significant for the historical Paul. However, it has to be kept in mind that while there is good evidence that the historical Jesus had a well-established reputation as a miracle worker,[225] this is rarely mentioned by the Apostolic Fathers.[226] Rather, we are forced to rely on the letters of Paul and, to a limited extent, the canonical Acts of the Apostles for reliable data on Paul and the miraculous.

---

223. In contrast to this interest in the miraculous in relation to Paul, Clement (*Exc.* 23.3), perhaps writing early in the third century (see John Ferguson, *Clement of Alexandria* [New York: Twayne, 1974], 17), describes the followers of Valentinus as seeing Paul's ministry in terms of preaching.

224. Clement, *Strom.* 1.11.50; 1.54.3; 7.10.59.

225. Cf. Graham H. Twelftree, "The Miracles of Jesus: Marginal or Mainstream?" *JSHJ* 1 (2003): 104–24.

226. Cf. *1 Clem.* 59:4; *Diogn.* 9:6; *Barn.* 5:8.

9.8 Conclusions

From the literature of a later generation seeking to perpetuate the memory of Paul, albeit for purposes of their own, I have garnered some fragments of information that make an important contribution to our knowledge of him and the miraculous. From Colossians, the pseudepigraphon most accurately reflecting the historical Paul, I found nothing that suggested Paul was remembered, perhaps in the late 80s, in bringing a gospel accompanied by the miraculous. However, the letter maintains the memory of Paul's description of worship that involved miraculous features. The letter to the Ephesians, from a few years later, also gives no hint of a memory of Paul in relation to the miraculous other than the ongoing value of Spirit-inspired singing as worship. However, at points where it could be expected, neither letter suggests the miraculous was important in the memory of Paul and his gospel in the Christianity of Asia Minor toward the end of the century. Notwithstanding, at least in the form of Spirit-inspired worship, the miraculous remained important in these Pauline churches.

Then, on the one hand, in 2 Thessalonians the miraculous in a Pauline church is associated with false Christianity and the satanic. On the other hand, the Pastoral Epistles, perhaps written for the Ephesian and Cretan churches toward the end of the first century, show no hint of Paul performing miracles or of the miraculous being associated with the Spirit's coming or him bringing the gospel. However, the author of the Pastorals provides evidence of understanding the "gifts," especially in relation to teaching, reminiscent of the historical Paul. The letters also indicate that prophecy was part of the Pauline tradition reflected in these letters.

With Hebrews and James, the memory of Paul most nearly approximates what we have seen from the letters concerning Paul and the miraculous. Hebrews, written in the Pauline tradition, portrays miracles as accompanying the proclamation of the gospel and, in the form of *charismata*, continuing in the ongoing life of the church. The letter of James, interacting with Pauline Christianity, suggests that the miraculous (in particular, healing and exorcism) was part of the mental furniture and experience of the readers living in the legacy of Paul.

Looking beyond the canon—at least as far as the end of the second century—in the hope of finding reliable data to contribute to our understanding of the historical Paul in relation to the miraculous has proved unfruitful. In view of at least early second-century Christian literature carrying almost no traditions about Jesus as a prolific and powerful miracle worker, I resisted drawing the conclusion that the miraculous would, therefore, have been unimportant to the historical Paul.

Nevertheless, from the fragmentary and not always consistent data of the remembered Paul, it is probably reasonable to conclude that although the miraculous may have been part of the coming of the gospel—apart from the canonically dependent *Acts of Paul*—the miraculous was not sufficiently strongly associated with the memory of Paul himself for him to be accredited with miracle working or for the miraculous to be everywhere recalled as an essential part of his ministry.[227] Indeed, though some Pauline churches maintained a Christianity that included an interest in the miraculous, some did not, and others associated it with false Christianity and the satanic. The important result of this examination of the remembered Paul is that, over against the portrait of Paul by Luke, but consistent with his own letters, I have found no reliable trace of him being remembered as a miracle worker. We are now in a position to draw conclusions to this study.

227. Cf. James A. Kelhoffer, "The Rhetoric of Miracle Discourse in the Writings of Paul," *SBLSP* (2002): 2.

Part 5

PAUL AND THE MIRACULOUS

10

The Paul of History
and the Apostle of Faith

If long-term and widespread influence is a measure, Paul is one of a handful
of the most significant figures in human history. He stands alongside Moses,
Gautama Buddha, Confucius, Jesus, and Muhammad in terms of the number of
people over many centuries who have found, and continue to find, his teaching
important. He is also no less significant in terms of fundamentally shaping a
major religion. If Paul cannot be credited with founding Christianity, it was he
who so interpreted the traditions of the early Jesus movement that it was able
to transcend cultural boundaries to become the largest international religion,
accessible to any who wished to join. Further, Paul's influence on early Christian writings is such that reading the New Testament in chronological order
is, as Raymond Collins put it, "a journey from Paul to Paul." For, the earliest
recorded word in the New Testament is Paul's name (1 Thess. 1:1), and perhaps the last letter written, 2 Peter, refers to him (2 Pet. 3:15–18).[1] Moreover,
in that his surviving writings are now in the Christian New Testament, his
letters have been translated into around 1,185 languages,[2] making him, along

1. Raymond F. Collins, "Paul as Seen through His Own Eyes: A Reflection on the First
Letter to the Thessalonians," in *Studies on the First Letter to the Thessalonians* (BETL 66;
Louvain: Leuven University Press, 1984), 175. Cf. Richard I. Pervo, who notes that of the NT
writings, "Only Mark and John stand quite outside of the Pauline orbit—and a case for indirect
influence upon Mark can be advanced" (*The Making of Paul: Constructions of the Apostle in
Early Christianity* [Minneapolis: Fortress, 2010], xi).
2. See the United Bible Societies' statistics at http://www.ubs-translations.org/about_us/#c165.

with the other New Testament writers, among the most widely known and read figures in any language from any period.

Paul's literary heritage is concerned primarily with ideas he valued and considered under threat, telling us little about his life and not as much as we may wish about his approach to ministry. To date, therefore, Paul has been understood and valued primarily in terms of his intellectual achievement. Along with his traveling, and occasional work to support himself, other aspects of his work are seen as incidental to the fundamental core of his work, his theological enterprise and the preached message, which are taken to be broadly reflected or at least relatively easily accessible in his letters.

This approach to Paul, and the resultant picture of him as theologian and preacher, raise fundamental questions. The most pressing one is how we are to describe his relationship to Jesus. Paul claimed to be an ambassador or an apostle, and an imitator of Jesus, yet, over against Jesus, for whom the performing of miracles was of central importance, Paul has little or no interest in miracles. At least this is how he is almost universally described in the scholarly literature. A complicating factor is introduced by Luke's portrait of Paul. Quite different from the view we get of Paul in his letters, in his second volume, Luke paints the apostle to the Gentiles as a great miracle worker. In turn, this raises questions about the nature of early Christianity. Did it continue as a religion in which the miraculous was thought important, as it appears to have been for Jesus and the movement that immediately followed him, or, as witnessed by Paul's letters, did the miraculous cease to be significant for Christianity?

The vast majority of contemporary and earlier critical studies of Paul depict him almost exclusively in terms of a thinker and theologian, or occasionally also as a missionary. The miraculous has been removed or ignored, or only lip service has been paid to the importance of this element in the reconstruction of the historical Paul. The broad proposal of this study is that the historical Paul is only adequately reconstructed if the miraculous is seen as important and integral to his life, his theological enterprise, and his work as a missionary and pastor. I have arrived at this conclusion guided by a number of specific questions.

Since we have seen that it is credibly argued that experience contributes to ideas and behavior, including for Paul, one of my foundational questions has been (1) What was Paul's experience of and involvement in the miraculous? To answer this question, and throughout this study, the "miraculous" has been used as an all-inclusive term. For the miraculous, as Paul appears to understand it, goes beyond so-called miracles to include a range of experiences extending from those associated with revelation to the ability to accomplish the impossible.[3] Then, supposing that the evidence suggested Paul understood himself to be involved in the miraculous, including being a miracle worker, I sought to discover (2) How important did Paul consider this aspect of his ministry? In turn, I asked, (3) What meaning or significance did Paul give to the miraculous? Further, I enquired, (4) How did Paul relate his theology of weakness, suffering, and the cross to a power-based ministry that involved the miraculous? and (5) How did Paul relate the miraculous to other aspects of his theology and ministry? As part of this endeavor, (6) I set out to see if we could recover what kinds of miracles Paul performed.

I have made no secret of the difficulties besetting a project seeking to answer these questions. Therefore, in order to read Paul with as much sensitivity as possible, my answers have been sought through a three-step approach corresponding to the three central parts of this book: Paul's inheritance, Paul's testimony, and Paul's early interpreters. In this final chapter I will gather together my answers to these questions, though setting them out in an order that focuses on Paul's perspective.

I will begin (§10.1) by setting out what the various aspects of Paul's inheritance are likely to have meant for his views on the miraculous. Then, the results of my examination of Paul's early interpreters (§10.2) and his own testimony will be used in an attempt to give a broad-brushstroke sketch of the historical Paul in relation to the miraculous, taking into account his life, thought, and ministry. This is to be taken as the heart or centerpiece of my conclusion (§10.3). Paul's more recent interpreters will then be engaged in order to argue that the miraculous is critical in a contemporary understanding of Paul's perspective on his life and work (§10.4). Finally, I will offer a solution to the problem of the tension between the various portraits of Paul available to us. In doing so, I will briefly suggest both how Paul and the miraculous is to be understood in relation to Jesus and the miraculous, and what this study can contribute to our knowledge of the nature of the Jesus movement in the time of Paul (§10.5).

10.1 Paul's Inheritance

I undertook an examination of Paul's inheritance in order to see what presuppositions and experiences a well-educated and zealous Jew such as Paul would have brought with him upon becoming part of the Jesus movement. We saw that he could have held a number of views in relation to the miraculous. Having been a Pharisee, he would have viewed God as intervening in life,

---

3. See §1.5 above and §10.2 [a] below.

bringing changes to the natural world, speaking to people, and enabling them to depict the future. Resurrection, angels, and spirits would have been part of his mental furniture; and he may have had some, even if limited, experience of healings and exorcisms, perhaps in the synagogues. Most notably, Paul would have inherited the view that so-called signs and wonders were an expectation of the eschatological age. Since, therefore, he had become convinced that the coming of Jesus was related to an eschatological shift, he would have been expecting an increase in the miraculous.

Given that an important aspect of Paul's self-understanding was seeing himself called and working in the tradition of the scriptural prophets, I set out to discover what he or those who witnessed his ministry would have expected of him in relation to the miraculous. Despite the views of a sizable group of scholars, it was easily shown that in Paul's time the activities of charismatic (or sign) prophets, seers, and oracular prophets not unlike the scriptural prophets are evidence that prophecy in various forms flourished in the Jewish world of Paul's time. However, even though a strong connection was seen between scriptural prophets and the miraculous and performing miracles, seeing himself in this tradition would not have determined that he take up the miraculous in his work, for the connection was not always affirmed. Seeing himself as a prophet would have done no more than open up the possibility, though a strong one, that Paul would understand the miraculous to be part of his ministry. Notwithstanding, a point that we will see in this chapter as fundamentally important to understanding Paul is that in some of the literature we examined where prophecy and the miraculous were brought together, it is God, not the prophet, who was credited with the miracle, even though the miraculous could reflect positively on the prophet. The puzzle that Paul, so obviously seeing himself as a prophet, did not call himself one is easily solved in light of his probably knowing that the classical prophets avoided the title, that it was false prophets who claimed the title, and that taking up the title may have compromised his mediating role with his readers. Moreover, convinced that he was living in the new age, the eschatological age, to call himself a "prophet" may have given the impression he thought the old age remained.

Given, also, that Paul took up the role of a missionary preacher, I asked what obligations such a function would have placed on him in relation to the miraculous. In that Paul is the first known Jewish missionary to the Gentiles, he and his audience would have had no models from the Jewish world to inform and shape their expectations. However, we have seen that probably there were Greco-Roman traditions alive in Paul's time that carried the memory of an earlier period when proselytizing and miracle working were taken together, so that any miraculous elements of Paul's ministry could have been understood as an aspect of his skills, though not proving anything about him or his work. Of course, what he inherited from earlier followers of Jesus would have caused a different conclusion to be drawn.

When we turned to examine what Paul is likely to have inherited from the Jesus movement we saw that there is more than enough evidence to show that if Paul was not involved in the miraculous, it was not because the Christianity he inherited had turned its back on an interest in the miraculous it had inherited from Jesus. To the contrary, the Christianity to which Paul was introduced was replete with stories of and an interest in the miraculous, both as part of its history as well as its ongoing ministry. In other words, as I have already said, it would have been hard for Paul to avoid concluding that the miraculous was taken as a central and essential aspect of the missionary movement he joined. Part of what Paul would have learned from these traditions and from the first wave of followers of Jesus, or had reinforced in his experience, was that the miraculous—especially the work of the Spirit in exorcisms—was the eschatological kingdom of God in operation. Further, picking up the theme of the kingdom of God as a significant part of his ministry supports the reasonableness of concluding that Paul would most probably have taken up the miraculous as part of his ministry. For, the kingdom of God was firmly connected with the miraculous in what Paul would have learned from the Christian traditions. Moreover, since Paul knew some of those called to follow Jesus saw themselves emulating the ministry of Jesus in going on a mission that included performing miracles, it could be expected that Paul would see his call from the risen Jesus also to involve the miraculous.

10.2 Paul's Early Interpreters

One of the issues to be faced in recovering the historical Paul in relation to the miraculous is how to interpret Luke's portrait of him. The image of the apostle of faith set out by Luke is of a powerful and prolific miracle worker, so unlike that of Paul's letters. On close historical investigation, however, we have seen that many of the stories associated with Paul in Acts turn out not to reflect the historical Paul. In his reshaping material so that Paul is consistent with earliest Christian traditions, and able to be viewed as a worthy successor to the first apostles, as well as to Jesus, Luke has made Paul into a miracle worker not unlike Jesus. In this Luke proves to be an unreliable witness in seeking the historical Paul's involvement in the miraculous. Therefore, the difficulty in finding links between the portraits of Paul in Acts and in Paul's letters is not only, as Jacob Jervell supposes, because we are working with an imperfect portrait of the apostle from his letters.[4] Rather, the major responsibility for the dislocation between the Paul of Luke and the Paul of the letters is Luke's attempt to redraw the apostle as a second, miracle-working Jesus.

Nevertheless, I was able to express sufficient confidence in at least the core of a number of the stories in Acts to conclude that Luke conveys some reliable traditions: that Paul had a visionary experience of Jesus identifying himself (9:1–19a; 22:6–16; 26:12–18); that prophecy was a means by which Paul found direction in his work (13:1–3); that Paul was a preacher who credited God with the miracles (14:3); that Paul was associated with the miraculous (19:13), though a reluctant miracle worker (16:16–18); and that he may also have been involved in the revival of a dead person (20:7–12).

Turning from Paul's earliest interpreter to the way he was remembered in the pseudepigraphal literature associated with him, we saw that Colossians (probably the most generally reliable pseudepigraphal reflection of Paul) as well as Ephesians offer no suggestion that Paul was a miracle worker. However, in perpetuating the memory of Paul, these early pseudepigrapha include the importance of worship that involved Spirit-inspired singing that is probably reminiscent of Paul's view (1 Cor. 14:26). The Pastoral Epistles carry no memory of Paul as a miracle worker. Nevertheless, in maintaining his memory, the miraculous remains important in the ongoing use of prophecy, a gift understood in a way suggestive of the historical Paul. In these Pauline pseudepigrapha we have the memory of Paul's interest in the miraculous, but not in him as a miracle worker. We noted that in 2 Thessalonians the miraculous was associated with that which was false (2 Thess. 2:9).

At least in relation to the miraculous, Hebrews and James are the interpreters of Paul most nearly reflecting what we find in the authentic Pauline letters. For Hebrews, written in the Pauline tradition, and reasonably reflecting Paul's views, miracles accompany the proclamation of the gospel and remain part of the life of the church in the *charismata*. In James, a letter from the same literary culture as Paul's and only comprehensible in light of Paul, there are hints of the practice of exorcism and encouragement in healing.

From the early interpreters the conclusion I drew at the end of chapter 9 stands: the miraculous was not sufficiently associated with Paul himself for it to be remembered as part of his portrait in the churches that sought to remain in the Pauline tradition. Those who valued the heritage of Paul interpreted the traditions about him differently. Luke, wishing to establish firm lines of continuity between Jesus and the apostle, has profoundly reshaped the miraculous in

4. Jacob Jervell, "The Signs of an Apostle: Paul's Miracles," in *The Unknown Paul: Essays on Luke-Acts and Early Christian History* (Minneapolis: Augsburg, 1984), 78.

his second volume so that the life of the apostle of faith parallels that of Jesus the Savior. For others who stood in the shadow of Paul, with new concerns, the miraculous was less important, some at best confining it to prophecy, or even associating it with the satanic. Others more nearly reflect Paul's view that the gospel came in word and deed—in speech and in the miraculous. In light of what we have learned from these early interpreters, as well as taking into account his heritage and from weighing his testimony, I can attempt a sketch of the historical Paul in relation to the miraculous.

10.3 Paul and the Miraculous

It bears emphasizing that my sketch of the historical Paul is not an attempt to provide an outline of the life of Paul or even a theological or intellectual biography of him. Rather, using the evidence I have gleaned, my sketch of Paul in very broad brushstrokes will be drawn with an eye only on how the miraculous is to be related to key aspects of his life, his gospel, his approach to miracle working, his theology, and his ecclesiology. I begin with his understanding of the miraculous.

(a) *Miracles and the miraculous.* As we noted early in this study, for biblical writers a miracle was something humanly impossible, striking or surprising, brought about by and giving evidence of the presence of a god (see §1.5 above). Given what Paul experienced and understood took place as a result of the Spirit's presence, he extends this definition.

Even though I have been using the terms interchangeably, the broader term "miraculous" rather than the narrower "miracle" turns out to describe best his understanding of this phenomena. For Paul, the miraculous included not just healings and exorcisms, but also, for example, extraordinary faith, the accomplishment of the impossible, God's provision and protection, and the experience and assessment of revelation that came through prophecy, wisdom, knowledge, and tongues (1 Cor. 12:8–10). Moreover, Paul extends the miraculous to include things such as helps, administration, and tongues (12:28), not, I suppose, because they were thought humanly impossible, but because he considered they had their origin and impact in the Spirit. This shows that, for Paul, the miraculous is identified primarily not by the activity or phenomena but by its source and result, the gracious work of the Spirit of God.[5] Hence comes his use of the term *charismata*

---

5. Cf. Karl Barth writes, "In the Bible a miracle is not some event that is hard to conceive, nor yet one that is simply inconceivable, but one that is highly conceivable, but conceivable only as the exponent of the special new direct act of God in time and history" (*Church Dogmatics,*

(χαρίσματα)[6]—solidified expressions of grace—in relation to the miraculous (see §1.5 above). This also shows that although the existence of the miraculous authenticates the ministry of Paul, the miraculous is valued not because it contributes to the stature of Paul but because it is the means for God's grace to bring health to the body of Christ. In Paul, the miraculous was democratized. Ernst Käsemann has been shown as correct: Paul's notion of miracle, as seen in the *charismata*, undermines the autonomy and self-importance of the miracle worker by directing attention to God's grace and the body of Christ. Further, Käsemann has rightly drawn attention to the miraculous as a point in Paul's thinking and ministry practice, where his experience, theology, soteriology, ecclesiology, and eschatology are brought into direct and productive relationship with each other.[7]

(b) *Miracle and the biography of Paul.* In light of his broad view of the miraculous, it is obvious that Paul would have said the miraculous was central and profoundly important in his life, theology, and work. Moreover, both from what he says and from what can reasonably be implied from his background, one of the surprising results of this study is the clear evidence that the experience of miracle is significant in the life of Paul. Growing up in a Jewish home (Phil. 3:5) and listening to Scriptures read in synagogue, Paul would have heard stories of the miraculous from the Torah and in the work of the prophets that included the miraculous. As a place of meeting, prayer, and community care, the synagogue may also have been a place where he saw healings and the troubles of demoniacs solved. Also, the expectation fueled by Scriptures that the coming of the kingdom of God would involve the miraculous was a living hope in Paul's time, having found its way into literature and undoubtedly into conversations. Further, in the charismatic or sign prophets, and in literature of the time, prophecy associated with the miraculous was a lively part of Paul's cultural landscape.

Even before becoming a Pharisee, Paul shared with his compatriots the view not only that God worked miracles in their history but that God also remained able to effect change in people and creation. In becoming a Pharisee, Paul joined a sect that believed that God spoke to and through individuals and gave foresight and prophecy. As a Pharisee Paul was also among those

---

vol. 1, *The Doctrine of the Word of God*, part 2, ed. G. W. Bromiley and T. F. Torrance [Edinburgh: T&T Clark, 1956], 63).

6. Paul appears to be the first to use the term χαρίσματα (cf. *Thesaurus linguae graecae*), and in the NT it appears only in his letters: Rom. 11:29; 12:6; 1 Cor. 12:4, 9, 28, 30, 31. Cf. Hans Conzelmann, "χάρισμα," *TDNT* 9:402–3; Klaus Berger, "χάρισμα," *EDNT* 3:460.

7. Ernst Käsemann, "Ministry and Community in the New Testament," in *Essays on New Testament Themes*, trans. W. J. Montague (SBT 41; London: SCM, 1964), 66–68.

who practiced exorcism, and for whom belief in the resurrection, angels, and spirits was part of their thought world.

In his zeal for his Jewish traditions, expressed in the persecution of the followers of Jesus (Phil. 3:6), Paul would have come across information about Jesus and the miracle stories associated with him. We have already noted that he would also have become familiar with the Christian mission propagating the view that the kingdom of God had arrived and was thought to be expressed in part in healings and exorcisms.

If Paul had not already experienced the miraculous, he did so in a conversion experience, which, judging from his reports and reflections on it, he took to be miraculous. In turn, Paul's conviction that he was an apostle of Christ was not impressed on him by earlier followers of Jesus nor deduced from his reading of historical texts. Instead, he considered his apostleship arose out of the miraculous (1 Cor. 9:1; Gal. 1:15–16), an experience that would be confirmed in the miraculous phenomena associated with his ministry (2 Cor. 12:12).

Paul's description of his conversion experience echoes prophetic calls in Scripture. He took the call to be from God, revealing Jesus to him (Gal. 1:15–16). The miraculous was, then, not only part of his experience and the basis of his identity, but also the foundation of his work. For, Paul understood his encounter with the Lord to be the rationale not only for claiming to be his apostle, but also the grounds for his mission to the Gentiles (1:16). Seeing himself called in the tradition of the scriptural prophets also opened up to him the option of involvement in the miraculous in his ministry. Indeed, convinced that in the coming of Jesus the kingdom of God had come (e.g., Rom. 14:17; 1 Cor. 4:20), or that there had been an eschatological shift (2 Cor. 5:17), Paul probably would have become sensitive to the increased occurrence of the miraculous. Not surprisingly, then, Paul mentions a coworker miraculously recovering (Phil. 2:25–30); he testifies to God rescuing him from life-threatening afflictions (2 Cor. 1:8–11); and he testifies to prayer answered, even if not in a way he expected (12:8–9), a point that I will explore further in a moment. And from what can be gleaned from his testimony in relation to the *charismata*, tongues, prophecy, and probably wisdom were expressed at least regularly in his own life. Certainly, from my chronological study of his writings, the miraculous appears important throughout Paul's life (1 Thess. 1:5; Rom. 15:19), though as his apostleship comes under attack, attention is drawn to the miraculous (1 Cor. 9:1; 2 Cor. 12:11–12; Gal. 3:1–5).

(c) Paul's gospel. Paul's missionary message can be summarized thus: in Jesus, God sent his Son, who was killed on a cross for the sake of others; but he was raised to life, exalted to heaven, and is expected to return soon. It was

important, therefore, to live ethically sound lives in anticipation of living with Jesus forever.[8] However, *Paul's message was not his gospel.*

The words Paul used to convey this information were not the good news he was bearing, even though words are used to describe and, in part, defend it. He was not attempting to relate an idea or describe the good news or to depict God. In the tradition of the prophets, he considered he was involved in presenting the power of God (cf. Rom. 1:16; Gal. 3:1–5).[9] In defining the gospel in terms of "power of God" (δύναμις γὰρ θεοῦ, Rom. 1:16), Paul directly and closely associates the gospel with the miraculous.

From his letter to the Thessalonians it is clear Paul saw the gospel as an unhindered realization of the Spirit (1 Thess. 1:5; cf. Rom. 15:18–19), which for him, I argued, would have involved the whole range of the miraculous: not only miracles, but also *charismata* (e.g., 1 Cor. 12:4–11) and perhaps the so-called fruit of the Spirit (Gal. 5:22–23). From Galatians we see that the coming of the Spirit and the miraculous could be viewed as one and the same thing (3:1–5). From Romans we also see that Paul understood his gospel as (always) both word and deed, or salvation heard and experienced in proclamation and signs and wonders (Rom. 15:18–19). Or, as he put it in the earliest letter we have, his gospel was word and power in the Spirit (1 Thess. 1:5).

This study has shown that the long-standing and widely held view, attributed in modern times to Bruno Bauer, that Paul thought he was waging war with the word alone[10] is patently false. Paul reminds the Thessalonians that his gospel "did not come to you in word alone" (1 Thess. 1:5). Writing to the Corinthians, he said his preaching, which he admitted was rhetorically unskilled, came in tandem with, or was demonstrated in, "the Spirit and of power" (1 Cor. 2:4). In this, Gordon Fee is shown to be correct in supposing that Paul never would have imagined that the miraculous would not be part of the gospel, or that the gospel could come in either word or deed.[11] Yet, W. D. Davies and Bernd Kollmann are to be deemed incorrect in supposing that,

8. See Rom. 3:23–25; 1 Cor. 2:2; 2 Cor. 5:14; Gal. 3:1; Phil. 3:10–11, 19; 1 Thess. 1:9–10; 4:14–18; 5:23. Cf. E. P. Sanders, *Paul* (Oxford: Oxford University Press, 1991), 21–24, esp. 22.

9. In relation to the scriptural prophets, see Abraham J. Heschel (*The Prophets*, 2 vols. [New York: Harper & Row, 1962], 2.55): "To the prophets, God was not a Being of Whose existence they were convinced in the way in which a person is convinced of the truth of an idea. He was a Being Who is supremely real and staggeringly present. They could not use the language of *essence*; they had to use the language of *presence*. They did not try to depict Him; they tried to present Him, to make Him present"(emphasis original).

10. Bruno Bauer, *Die Apostelgeschichte: Eine Ausgleichung des Paulinismus und des Juden-thums innerhalb der christlichen Kirche* (Berlin: Hempel, 1850), 7–25. See 13n65 above.

11. Gordon D. Fee, *God's Empowering Presence: The Holy Spirit in the Letters of Paul* (Peabody, MA: Hendrickson, 1994), 849–50.

for Paul, the miraculous was subordinate to, or side effects of, the message.[12] Rather, for Paul, miracles, the realization of the presence of the Spirit, were an integral part of, as well as a demonstration of the origin and validity of, the message. The gospel was a composite expression of the audible and the tangible powerful presence of God. *For Paul, no more could the gospel be proclaimed without words than it could come or be experienced without miracles. Without the miraculous, Paul may have had a message, but he would not have had a gospel. Without the miraculous, there was no gospel, only preaching.*[13]

(d) The gospel received. As Paul's gospel was more than his words, so response to it was more than listening. No more could Paul's gospel be propagated by words alone than it could be received as mere words. As both human words and divine activity, not only was the gospel heard and received by believing but it was also received in the miraculous (Gal. 3:2–5). Not only the ears, but the whole— inner and outer—human being was expected to respond to the gospel. (Though beyond the bounds of this study, for Paul, an important aspect of the gospel, and response to it, was behavior.[14] This is captured famously in his "Therefore . . ." [οὖν . . .][15] of Romans 12:1, followed by the ethical implications of the gospel.[16])

(e) Paul the miracle worker? In contrast to Luke's portrait, but more consistent with the Pauline pseudepigrapha, Paul never claimed to perform miracles.[17]

12. W. D. Davies, *Paul and Rabbinic Judaism: Some Rabbinic Elements in Pauline Theology,* 4th ed. (Philadelphia: Fortress, 1980), 213; Bernd Kollmann, "Paulus als Wundertäter," in *Paulinische Christologie: Exegetische Beiträge; Hans Hübner zum 70. Geburtstag,* ed. Udo Schnelle, Thomas Söding, and Michael Labahn (Göttingen: Vandenhoeck & Ruprecht, 2000), 82–83. So also, e.g., Victor P. Furnish, *II Corinthians: Translated with Introduction, Notes, and Commentary* (AB 32A; Garden City, NY: Doubleday, 1984), 556; Calvin J. Roetzel, *Paul: The Man and the Myth* (Minneapolis: Fortress, 1999), 62.

13. Cf. John Ashton, *The Religion of Paul the Apostle* (New Haven: Yale University Press, 2000), 165. The notion that the Christian faith is primarily not a matter of words or ideas to be believed, but something to be and experience, is explored in a masterly book by Andrew Louth, *Discerning the Mystery: An Essay on the Nature of Theology* (Oxford: Clarendon, 1983), see, e.g., p. 74.

14. That Paul's exhortations cannot be regarded as "ethics" distinct from the gospel, see Ernst Käsemann, *Commentary on Romans,* trans. and ed. Geoffrey W. Bromiley (London: SCM, 1980), 171, 323.

15. Cf. Rom. 5:1. See also Rom. 6:1, 12, 15; 14:8, 12, 13, 16, 19; 15:17; 1 Cor. 4:16; 6:15; 1 Cor. 14:23, 26; 2 Cor. 3:12; 2 Cor. 5:6, 10, 20; 7:1; 12:9; Gal. 5:1; 6:10; Phil. 2:1; 1 Thess. 4:1; 5:6. See also Paul's use of ὥστε ("therefore," "so that," or "for this reason") in Phil. 2:12; cf. Rom. 7:4, 6; 13:2; 1 Cor. 5:8; 11:27, 33; 14:39; 15:58; 2 Cor. 2:7; Phil. 4:1; 1 Thess. 1:7; 4:18. See Gerald F. Hawthorne, *Philippians* (WBC 43; Waco: Word, 1983), 97–98; Robert Jewett, *Romans: A Commentary* (Hermeneia; Minneapolis: Fortress, 2007), 727n24.

16. E.g., C. H. Dodd, *The Epistle of Paul to the Romans* (MNTC; London: Hodder & Stoughton, 1932), 190; James D. G. Dunn, *Romans 9–16* (WBC 38B; Dallas: Word, 1988), 705–6, 708.

17. As Jerome Murphy-O'Connor (*Paul: His Story* [Oxford: Oxford University Press, 2005], 238) said in relation to Paul's possible response to *Acts of Paul,* it is not unreasonable to suggest that Paul would have repudiated Luke's portrait of him as a miracle-working apostle.

In line with this, I noted in the conclusion to chapter 6 that Paul did not claim the gifts of healing or exorcism, for example. Even when he could have won an argument by it, Paul did not assert that he had performed miracles (2 Cor. 12:11–13). In this his critics were right: Paul was not a miracle worker, let alone a great miracle worker.[18] Indeed, at least when writing to the Galatians, his argument that the Spirit had been at work in their lives would have been significantly undermined if he was known to hold the view that the miraculous was dependent on him or his presence. Paul clearly did not see himself as a miracle worker; even though he saw himself as an ambassador and imitator of Christ, he did not, as David Aune supposed, present himself as a miracle worker "in continuity with the image of Jesus and the early Christian leaders depicted in Acts."[19]

Yet, Paul was quick to point out that the miraculous was experienced when he was involved in the coming of the gospel. In defending himself against the criticism of those who were looking for a rhetorician with the skills of a miracle worker, he forcefully reminds his readers that even if he was not rhetorically skilled, the gospel came in the authenticating power of the Spirit (1 Cor. 2:4). Contrary to criticisms leveled at Paul, the miracles did take place. However, thoroughly consistent with the views of others of his time, it was God who brought the miracles as the expression of his presence.[20] Notwithstanding, Paul claimed (1 Cor. 2:1–5; 2 Cor. 12:11–13) these works of God reflected positively on him and his ministry. In this Paul shared the view of Jesus and his early followers: the miraculous was both an expression of the kingdom of God and proof of its reality and the credibility of the messenger (Matt. 12:22–32 // Luke 11:14–23; Mark 3:23–27). Just as God's power is seen in the weakness of the crucifixion, so though he is weak, Paul understood the power of God was seen in the miraculous associated with, and authenticating, his ministry.

As I argued, it is Paul's use of the passive and in never laying claim to performing miracles that we see his view: in the event of—or coincidental with—proclaiming the gospel the Spirit comes, obvious in the miracles that God performs. Paul understood that he preached or proclaimed the gospel that was realized by the presence of the Spirit through signs and wonders or the miraculous (Rom. 15:18–19; 1 Cor. 2:4; 1 Thess. 1:5). In the coming of the gospel

18. Cf. Ernst Käsemann, "Die Legitimität des Apostels: Eine Untersuchung zu II Korinther 10–13," *ZNW* 41 (1942): 35.

19. David E. Aune, *Prophecy in Early Christianity and the Ancient Mediterranean World* (Grand Rapids: Eerdmans, 1991), 194; cf. Hans Windisch, who viewed Paul as "a Jesus *redidivus*, a vicar of Christ on earth" ("Paulus und Jesus," *TSK* 196 [1934–35]: 465).

20. See the discussions above of *Liber antiquitatum biblicarum* (§3.3 [f]) and Josephus (§3.3 [g]) respectively.

Paul saw himself doing the speaking and God performing the miracles—though, even his words could be seen as the accomplishments of Christ (Rom. 15:18).

Paul gives us no detailed account of this dramatic coming of the gospel that involved his preaching; he did not need to, his readers had vivid memories of the coming of the gospel in word and deed (Gal. 3:3–5; cf. Rom. 15:18). Though neither from Paul's hand nor about him, Luke's narrative of the Holy Spirit falling while Peter was speaking (Acts 10:44–48) probably well encapsulates the approach that seems to have been taken by Paul: as he spoke, the gospel was also realized in the miraculous through the work of the Spirit.

We do not know, we can only speculate, how Paul came to his view that the miraculous was the responsibility of God, though we have seen that it was a view shared by others at the time (e.g., 4Q521). Perhaps, also, Paul's negative experience of the miraculous restrained him from claiming to be a miracle worker. For, far from being a triumphalist, and even though he tells of his co-worker Epaphroditus miraculously recovering (Phil. 2:25–30) and of God rescuing him from life-threatening afflictions (2 Cor. 1:8–11), Paul experienced physical sickness (Gal. 4:13) and acknowledged that his thorn, or probably illness, was not healed as he had prayed (2 Cor. 12:7–10). In a moment we will see some of the important theological implications Paul drew from this experience.

Notwithstanding, although direct involvement in miracle working was not what characterized Paul's approach to or involvement in the miraculous, the evidence suggests that, perhaps reluctantly, from time to time, he was more directly involved in a healing or exorcism, acting as a miracle worker (cf. Acts 16:16–18; §8.10 above). Yet, from the fragmentary evidence we have that could be reliable (Acts 16:16–18), when Paul chose or thought himself obliged to perform a miracle it was not in a manner consistent with the method of Jesus. For, although on being pressed, Jesus said he used the Spirit of God to perform at least exorcisms (Matt. 12:28 // Luke 11:20),[21] in practice Jesus appeared to operate out of his own resources. His method is clearest in the report of an exorcism in which he says (using the emphatic "I"): "I command you . . ." (Mark 9:25).[22] Paul, however, consistent with miracle workers who

21. On the generally agreed historical reliability of this saying, e.g., see John P. Meier, *A Marginal Jew: Rethinking the Historical Jesus*, vol. 2, *Mentor, Message, and Miracles* (New York: Doubleday, 1994), 413–17.

22. Graham H. Twelftree, "Jesus the Exorcist and Ancient Magic," in *A Kind of Magic: Understanding Magic in the New Testament and Its Religious Environment*, ed. Michael Labahn and Bert Jan Lietaert Peerbolte (LNTS 306; London: T&T Clark, 2007), 57–86, esp. 83; and Graham H. Twelftree, *Jesus the Miracle Worker: A Historical and Theological Study* (Downers Grove, IL: InterVarsity, 1999), 269. See also the discussion by James D. G. Dunn, *Jesus Remembered* (Grand Rapids: Eerdmans, 2003), 695n384.

saw their success dependent on the power-authority they called up rather than their own resources, used the name of Jesus (Acts 16:18). Not surprisingly, then, even though he identified himself with Christ (see §5.4 [c] above), when Paul comes closest to suggesting he performed miracles, he credits his work to Christ: "what Christ has accomplished through me . . . by word and deed, by the power of signs and wonders." He reinforces this point by immediately continuing, "by the power of the Spirit of God" (Rom. 15:18–19). For, as John Chrysostom noted, "See how forcefully everything is shown to be of God, not of himself" (*Hom. Rom.* 29).

The question, therefore, of what kinds of miracles Paul performed is both easily answered and misguided. It is easily answered in that Paul would have taken the whole range of the miraculous to be involved in the coming of the gospel, for the evidence suggests the range or kinds of signs and wonders was wide (1 Thess. 1:5). The question is misguided, however, because it assumes that the miraculous in Paul's ministry is understood in terms of the miracles he performed, for we have seen that the miracles were not from his hand or due to his orchestration. Over against the later interpretation by Luke, who set out to draw parallel portraits of the Savior and the apostle, Paul was not a great miracle worker like Jesus, but he considered the miraculous a great part of his ministry.

(f) The miraculous and the church. The very writing of letters showed that Paul considered his involvement in the ongoing life of the church was important. He sought to encourage, chastise, and correct his readers, as well as to remind them of the traditions they had inherited and what he had taught them.

However, Paul understood that not only the origins of the body of believers (Gal. 3:1–5), but also the ongoing life of the community, was not dependent on or maintained only on the basis of their inherited traditions or his teaching, or through their remembering it, or on the basis of his encouragement, or even by the mutual care of the members. Paul also expected the miraculous to continue among believers as a natural part of their lives—without his presence (Gal. 3:5)—in order to ensure the ongoing health and growth of individuals and the community of believers as a whole. That is, Paul considered that just as the miraculous was part of the coming of the gospel, so too the miraculous remained an experience of the Spirit in a community of believers (1 Cor. 12:7–10; Gal. 3:1–5): the work of the Spirit in bringing salvation and maintaining the life of Christ in the community of believers was equally dependent on the gracious work of the Spirit in terms of the miraculous. For Paul, the edified community of believers, as well as its beginning, was marked by the miraculous. The miraculous was not for the glorification of the individual; the miraculous was only of value insofar as it brought health to the community (1 Cor. 12:7).[23]

The ongoing role and importance of the miraculous in the community is illustrated by the word *charismata* itself, with its root χάρις ("grace"). Paul shows that he sees the miraculous—God's activity among the believers—as an expression of God's grace in an individual for the benefit of the body or community of believers (1 Cor. 12:7). As we have already noted: in Paul the miraculous had been democratized. On the one hand, without the miraculous in the form of *charismata*, the ongoing life of the community would be deprived of wisdom, knowledge, faith, healing, miracles, prophecy, discernment of spirits, tongues, and the interpretation of tongues, for example (cf. 1 Cor. 12:8–10). On the other hand, without their ongoing involvement in the miraculous, believers would have no role or functioning place in the life of the community.[24]

(g) *Paul's theology and the miraculous.* Through this study we have seen that, in various forms, the miraculous was an element in Paul's national history, in his sectarian allegiance as a Pharisee, in his probable experience in the synagogue, in traditions he inherited from followers of Jesus, in his experience of conversion, in his subsequent negative and positive experiences in answer to prayer, and in relation to his experience of missionary preaching. However, it can also be seen that the miraculous formed an essential part of the raw material for his theological speculation.

At the broadest and foundational level, we can see from his letters that Paul chose to see the miraculous as an expression of God's involvement in human life, an expression of God's presence through his Spirit manifest in a wide range of phenomena. Being a Pharisee and with what he probably knew from the Jesus tradition, this could be expected. Seeing the miraculous as God's work and responsibility is consistent with him never claiming to perform a miracle, though he was probably sometimes reported as acting as a miracle worker. It is not unreasonable to conclude that *the most dominant feature of Paul's theology of the miraculous is that he considered these phenomena to be brought about not by himself, but by, and to be the responsibility of, God, who was revealing himself.*

Perhaps one of the surprises of this study is that, negatively, the miraculous can be seen as theologically generative for Paul. As his proof that members of the Corinthian church have been abusing the Lord's Supper, Paul calls up

---

23. Cf. Käsemann, "Ministry and Community," 66.

24. James D. G. Dunn, *Jesus and the Spirit: A Study of the Religious and Charismatic Experience of Jesus and the First Christians as Reflected in the New Testament* (London: SCM, 1975), 260–65.

as evidence the idea that some of the members of the believers are sick or have died. I argued Paul saw these as miracles of punishment (1 Cor. 11:30). The generative function of the negative experience of the miraculous is also expressed in Paul's account of his thorn in the flesh. He says that he prayed three times or earnestly, probably for a healing of his body. However, his prayer was not answered, at least not in the way he expected. Instead of a healing he experienced God's grace and power in the face of continuing illness. It was this unanticipated answer to prayer for a miracle that not only gave him confidence in God answering prayer but also was transformative for Paul: his attitude toward suffering and weakness was transformed from one of wishing to escape from it to delight and pleasure in weakness because in it the power of Christ became evident in him (2 Cor. 12:7–10; cf. Gal. 4:13).

What is notable in Paul not experiencing a miracle in answer to his prayer (2 Cor. 12:7–8) is that we see how Paul, writing as a man of weakness, with a message shot through with the motif of weakness, suffering, and death in relation to Jesus, is to be credited with apparently contradictory works of power. It is not, as E. P. Sanders supposed, that "when pressed for signs of his apostolic authority Paul appealed more to 'weakness' than to miracles."[25] Rather, it is that while acknowledging his weakness, he also points to the miraculous. But he is pointing not to mighty works he has performed but to the miraculous that took place through his weakness and in relation to his apostleship. In other words, *Paul is involved in the miraculous not because he is a man of power but as a man of weakness through whom the power of God works.*

One of the positive functions of the miraculous in generating aspects of Paul's theology can be deduced from his using the term "the kingdom of God"—which he received from the Jesus tradition—as coincidental with power (1 Cor. 4:20). In this term Paul shows that he adopted the view not that the miraculous attended the proclamation of the gospel, but that the miracles were the expression of the kingdom or power of God in those experiencing salvation. That is, the miracles were part of the eschatological shift that had taken place in Jesus; the miracles were not isolated expressions of God's activity as for the scriptural prophets, in whose line Paul saw himself. Rather, in themselves, the miracles were the expression of God's eschatological presence. It is no wonder, then, that he saw his gospel not as a message but as word (preaching) and deed (the miraculous). The message of salvation was both realized or materialized and authenticated in the miraculous.

The theologically generative power of the miraculous is seen also in the role he gives to prophecy. It was prophecy ("the word of the Lord," 1 Thess.

25. Sanders, *Paul*, 25.

4:15) that provided Paul with a timetable and explanation that enabled him to set out how he thought both the dead and the living could be involved in the eschaton. Therefore, alongside his inherited traditions from his Scriptures, his Jewish background, and the followers of Jesus before him, Paul understood prophecy to make unique contributions to theology, in that it revealed God and was a means of the Spirit bringing teaching.

Thus, from Paul's perspective, his theological speculation was not dependent only on intellectual activity (exegesis or hermeneutics, for example) but also included and relied on the miraculous—the activity of God tangibly realized in his experience and that of his readers. Moreover, without the traditions, experiences, and speculations in relation to the miraculous, Paul would not have become a follower of Jesus or considered he had a gospel or a mission or a means to maintain the ongoing life in Christ of his readers.

10.4 Paul's Recent Interpreters

The results of this study show that even though the bandwidth of intellectual receptivity of twenty-first century readers does not detect this motif as often as it should, the miraculous was considered by Paul to be of profound and central importance in terms of its influences on him, his personal experience, and as an aspect of his theology and work. Far from Paul's minimizing the miraculous, as has been suggested,[26] seen from the perspective of his broad understanding of the term, the "miraculous," even when not seen on the surface of the text, is often a subtext of his letters. Thus, over against F. C. Baur, William Wrede, and later Rudolf Bultmann (see §1.2 above), the evidence that I have adduced compels me to assert that the miraculous is central to any credible reconstruction of the historical Paul. Over against J. B. Lightfoot, I must assert that Paul did not consider the miraculous to be a "very poor and mean gift in comparison with the high spiritual powers with which he was endowed."[27] We have seen that, for Paul, the miraculous was as significant as the preaching and cannot, as Albert Schweitzer would suppose, be put in the shadow of "the rational manifestations of the spiritual."[28] Despite the temptation to respond to the reign of rationalism by distancing the motif of the miraculous from Christianity, the evidence does

---

26. So Audrey Dawson, *Healing, Weakness and Power: Perspectives on Healing in the Writings of Mark, Luke and Paul* (PBM; Milton Keynes: Paternoster, 2008), e.g., 243.

27. J. B. Lightfoot, *Notes on Epistles of St. Paul from Unpublished Commentaries* (London: Macmillan, 1895), 13.

28. Albert Schweitzer, *The Mysticism of Paul the Apostle*, trans. William Montgomery (Baltimore: Johns Hopkins University Press, 1998), 171.

not allow the historian to sweep this dimension of Paul's perception of his life and ministry under the carpet of cultural and theological respectability. What Adolf Schlatter said of the early Jesus traditions—that it was not possible to find a miracle-free gospel[29]—applies equally to the early traditions about Paul.

Nevertheless, even those, such as Adolf Schlatter, Martin Dibelius, Werner G. Kümmel, Ernst Käsemann, and, more recently, James D. G. Dunn, N. T. Wright, and Stefan Schreiber, who recognize, at least to some degree, the significance of the miraculous in understanding the historical Paul do not see the miraculous as sufficiently important to find a meaningful place in the biography and theology of Paul. The results of this project provide evidence to make a strong case for proposing that any historical reconstruction of Paul—his experience, his theology, and his ministry—is not credible without giving a high profile to the miraculous. We cannot even take up the view that the miracles are secondary or a subordinate side effect to Paul's ministry.[30] Instead, even though they did not explore the implications, I found the hints of the importance of the miraculous for Paul, identified by Ernst Käsemann, Hans Joachim Schoeps, E. P. Sanders, and especially Gordon Fee and John Ashton, to be important pointers to a historically critical reconstruction of Paul in relation to the miraculous.

Notwithstanding, what at first appears to be a particularly promising conclusion by Jacob Jervell, that "miracles assume a quite central role in Paul's preaching, almost to greater degree than in Acts,"[31] has to be nuanced significantly. For, in depending on the phrase "signs of an apostle" (2 Cor. 12:12) and equating them with the miracle stories of Acts, Jervell has provided a portrait not of the historical Paul but of the miracle worker of Luke's apostle of faith. Craig Evans has also depended heavily on Luke, as has Bert Jan Lietaert Peerbolte, in producing a miracle worker more like that of Jesus than of the historical Paul.[32] Similarly, in an earlier time, through assigning almost all the

29. Adolf Schlatter, *The History of the Christ: The Foundation for New Testament Theology*, trans. Andreas J. Köstenberger (1921; Grand Rapids: Baker Academic, 1997), 174.

30. W. D. Davies, *Paul and Rabbinic Judaism: Some Rabbinic Elements in Pauline Theology*, 4th ed. (Philadelphia: Fortress, 1980), 213; Bernd Kollmann, "Paulus als Wundertäter," in *Paulinische Christologie: Exegetische Beiträge; Hans Hübner zum 70. Geburtstag*, ed. Udo Schnelle, Thomas Söding, and Michael Labahn (Göttingen: Vandenhoeck & Ruprecht, 2000), 82–83.

31. Jervell, "Signs," 91.

32. Craig A. Evans, "Paul the Exorcist and Healer," in *Paul and His Theology*, ed. Stanley E. Porter (PSt 3; Leiden: Brill, 2006), 363–79; Bert Jan Lietaert Peerbolte, "Paul the Miracle Worker: Development and Background of Pauline Miracle Stories," in *Wonders Never Cease: The Purpose of Narrating Miracle Stories in the New Testament and Its Religious Environment*, ed. Michael Labahn and Bert Jan Lietaert Peerbolte (LNTS 288; London: T&T Clark, 2006), 180–99.

gifts of the Spirit to Paul, Hermann Gunkel has aggregated the miraculous too broadly and closely to him.[33]

Rather, my examination of Luke's portrait of Paul the miracle worker vindicates Baur's negative assessment of Acts (see §1.2 [a] above). Luke's portrait of Paul cannot be brought into alignment with Paul's testimony. Paul did not see himself as a miracle worker, let alone a great one, even though from time to time he is likely to have conducted a miracle. Indeed, other than Luke, not one of the writers whom I surveyed remembered Paul as a miracle worker.

In this study I have been able to establish the perceived profound importance of the miraculous to Paul and the Christianity he represented, not through showing that miracle-working stories in Acts accurately portray Paul's ministry, or through being able to show that he exercised all the gifts of the Spirit, but through showing that, without his direct orchestration as a miracle worker, the miraculous in its various expressions was profoundly important to Paul: it was integral to the gospel, its coming and ongoing expression in the life of the community of believers, as well as in his own experience.

10.5 A Resolution

We have before us, then, four conflicting portraits of Paul and the miraculous: (1) Paul's testimony in his letters; (2) Luke's apostle of faith; (3) the Paul remembered in the pseudepigrapha; and (4) a historically reconstructed Paul. Further tension appears in these portraits when they are placed alongside that of Jesus, whom Paul claimed to imitate and work for as an apostle. For, it is not the historical Paul or the Paul of his testimony who most resembles Jesus, but Luke's apostle of faith.

The portrait of the remembered Paul in the Pauline pseudepigrapha is a collection of fragmentary images. Although Colossians, said to be the most generally reliable post-Pauline reflection of him, carries no memory of him as a miracle worker or having a gospel of more than words, it echoes a practice of worship reminiscent of Paul's that also involved the miraculous. Aside from this Spirit-inspired spontaneous worship, Ephesians also gives no hint of the importance of the miraculous to Paul, either in his bringing the gospel or in the ongoing life of the community. However, this could be because these fragments of Paulinism available to us are too small. Only Hebrews carries

---

33. Hermann Gunkel, *The Influence of the Holy Spirit: The Popular View of the Apostolic Age and the Teaching of the Apostle Paul*, trans. Roy A. Harrisville and Philip A. Quanbeck II (Philadelphia: Fortress, 1979), 77; cf. 112.

the memory of what we see in the historical Paul of miracles accompanying the proclamation of the gospel. However, consistent with Paul's testimony, God, not a miracle worker, is responsible for the miraculous. The memory of Paul in relation to the miraculous is similar in the Pastoral Epistles: no memory of him as a miracle worker or bringing a gospel that included the miraculous, but a continued interest in the miraculous in the ongoing value placed on prophecy. James also suggests the miraculous was of ongoing importance to a church living in the shadow of Paul. Only in 2 Thessalonians is the miraculous entirely set aside and associated with false Christianity and the satanic.

Although the pseudepigraphal image of Paul is only fragmentary, we can discern a remarkable consistency with what we learn from Paul himself. The pseudepigrapha agree in carrying no memory of him as a miracle worker, while (at least in the majority of these letters) valuing the miraculous in some, though varying, forms in the ongoing life of the community.

From the evidence I have examined, it turns out that the portrait of the apostle of faith in Acts is a distortion of Paul in relation to the miraculous. On the one hand, depicting Paul's involvement in the miraculous primarily as a miracle worker misrepresents how he understood himself. Though Paul was involved in the miraculous to varying degrees, it was God whom he considered responsible for or who conducted the miracles. He was adamant that (God's) power was realized in (his) weakness (2 Cor. 12:9). In this, the words of Georges Bernanos's country priest are echoed: "Oh, miracle, thus to be able to give what we ourselves do not possess, sweet miracle of our empty hands."[34] On the other hand, the miraculous was more pervasive in Paul's life, theology, and ministry than Luke's portrait suggests. The miraculous was more than a few visions, healings, exorcisms, or escapes from danger, of which Paul was the focus, and which can be set aside without impairing the portrait of the historical Paul. The miraculous was a theme or dimension that pervaded all aspects of what we know of the historical Paul, who believed that, along with the proclamation, it was itself the gospel, and also an integral ongoing expression of the Spirit in the individual believer for the corporate good.

The conflict between the portraits of the historical Paul and the Paul of his letters is resolved in two ways. First, Paul is to be read and interpreted with sensitivity to a first-century reading. Despite more recent readings, the miraculous should more frequently be seen as either the backdrop or the

---

34. Georges Bernanos, *The Diary of a Country Priest*, trans. Pamela Morris (repr., Cambridge, MA: Da Capo Press, 2002), 180.

subject of Paul's attention. Second, we have to take into account that Paul was writing occasional letters,[35] the by-product of his work as an evangelist.[36] While the miraculous was very much a part of Paul's bringing the gospel and an ongoing part of the life of his churches, in that he was addressing issues and values for which he was contending, the miraculous comes to the fore only when connected with those topics, notably when defending his apostleship.

Resolving the tension between the portraits of Jesus and Paul is more complex. What explains the differences between the portraits of Paul and Jesus is not that we have a more rounded picture of Jesus, but from Paul's occasional letters we have only an imperfect view of his dealing predominantly with the ideas and values he considered under threat or in need of particular attention. Though that is part of the answer. If I have correctly interpreted the historical Paul's understanding of his role in relation to the miraculous—involved, yet acknowledging it as God's work and responsibility—we have seen that while Jesus functioned as a powerful and prolific miracle worker in his own right who in his preaching explained the implied good news of the miracles, Paul, in recognizing his dependence on the power of God, proclaimed the good news of Jesus' coming, and God—by his Spirit—realized and affirmed that good news in the experience of the miraculous among the audience.

The tension between the portraits of Jesus and Paul in relation to the miraculous is further resolved when we see each in light of his eschatological perspective. Each shared the religion that was convinced God had recently acted decisively in bringing in his kingdom or powerful presence that involved the miraculous. However, Paul and Jesus saw themselves at different points on the eschatological timetable, and as having different roles in its realization. Initially, Jesus looked expectantly forward to, and was then fundamental to and part of, the coming of the kingdom; Paul looked back to its arrival and initial focus in Jesus, and now lived in its powerful presence—"in a world that was charged with the presence and reality of God," to use the words of Thomas Merton.[37] In turn, in his ministry Paul saw himself imitating the historical Jesus not in inaugurating the new age, but in announcing and experiencing the good news. That he considered his experience of the coming of the gospel and the ongoing life of the church to include the full range of the miraculous, in which he claimed to be involved, is clear from Paul's

35. Cf. Jervell, "Signs," 78, 94.

36. Albert E. Barnett, *Paul Becomes a Literary Influence* (Chicago: University of Chicago Press, 1941), ix.

37. Thomas Merton, *The Seven Storey Mountain* (1948; repr., San Diego: Harcourt Brace, 1999), 208.

letters. Far from being able to conclude that Paul sanitized Christianity of the embarrassing miraculous elements through exchanging a religion of miracles for a religion of ideas and words, the Jesus movement, in his hands, remained a religion of miracle. Moreover, through Paul's democratizing the miraculous, the Jesus movement for which he was responsible exchanged a miracle worker for the miraculous.

Select Bibliography

Achtemeier, Paul J. "The Lukan Perspective on the Miracles of Jesus: A Preliminary Sketch." *JBL* 94 (1975): 547–62.

Ackerman, David A. *Lo, I Tell You a Mystery: Cross, Resurrection, and Paraenesis in the Rhetoric of 1 Corinthians.* Eugene, OR: Pickwick, 2006.

Agnew, Francis H. "The Origin of the NT Apostle-Concept: A Review of Research." *JBL* 105 (1986): 75–96.

Alexander, Loveday C. A. "Fact, Fiction and the Genre of Acts." In *Acts in Its Ancient Literary Context: A Classicist Looks at the Acts of the Apostles,* 133–63. LNTS 298. London: T&T Clark, 2005.

Alkier, Stefan. *Wunder und Wirklichkeit in den Briefen des Apostels Paulus: Ein Beitrag zu einem Wunderverständnis jenseits von Entmythologisierung und Rehistorisierung.* WUNT 134. Tübingen: Mohr Siebeck, 2001.

Allison, Dale C. "Paul and the Missionary Discourse." *ETL* 61 (1985): 369–75.

———. "The Pauline Epistles and the Synoptic Gospels: The Pattern of Parallels." *NTS* 28 (1982): 1–32.

Ashton, John. *The Religion of Paul the Apostle.* New Haven: Yale University Press, 2000.

Aune, David E. *Prophecy in Early Christianity and the Ancient Mediterranean World.* Grand Rapids: Eerdmans, 1991.

Babcock, William S., ed. *Paul and the Legacies of Paul.* Dallas: Southern Methodist University Press, 1990.

Barnett, Albert E. *Paul Becomes a Literary Influence.* Chicago: University of Chicago Press, 1941.

Barnett, Paul W. "The Jewish Sign Prophets—A.D. 40–70: Their Intentions and Origin." *NTS* 27 (1981): 679–97.

Barrett, C. K. "The Acts—of Paul." In *New Testament Essays,* 86–100. London: SPCK, 1972.

———. "The Historicity of Acts." *JTS* 50 (1999): 515–34.

———. "Paul's Opponents in II Corinthians." *NTS* 17 (1971): 233–54.

———. "*Shalia* and Apostle." In *Donum Gentilicium: New Testament Studies in Honour of David Daube*, edited by Ernst Bammel, C. K. Barrett, and W. D. Davies, 88–102. Oxford: Clarendon, 1978.

———. *The Signs of an Apostle: The Cato Lecture, 1969.* London: Epworth, 1972.

Bash, Anthony. *Ambassadors for Christ: An Exploration of Ambassadorial Language in the New Testament.* WUNT 2/92; Tübingen: Mohr Siebeck, 1997.

Baur, Ferdinand Christian. *Paul the Apostle of Jesus Christ: His Life and Works, His Epistles and Teachings.* 2 vols. in 1. Peabody, MA: Hendrickson, 2003.

Beare, F. W. "Jesus and Paul." *CJT* 5 (1959): 79–86.

Becker, Jürgen. *Paul: Apostle to the Gentiles.* Translated by O. C. Dean Jr. Louisville: Westminster, 1993.

Becker, Michael. "Miracle Traditions in Early Rabbinic Literature: Some Questions on Their Pragmatics." In *Wonders Never Cease: The Purpose of Narrating Miracle Stories in the New Testament and Its Religious Environment*, edited by Michael Labahn and Bert Jan Lietaert Peerbolte, 48–69. LNTS 288. London: T&T Clark, 2006.

Beker, J. Christiaan. *Paul the Apostle: The Triumph of God in Life and Thought.* Edinburgh: T&T Clark, 1980.

Berger, Klaus. *Identity and Experience in the New Testament.* Translated by Charles Muenchow. Minneapolis: Fortress, 2003.

Best, Ernest. "Paul's Apostolic Authority—?" *JSNT* 27 (1986): 3–25.

——— "The Power and the Wisdom of God, 1 Cor. 1:18–2:5." In *Paolo a una chiesa divisa (1 Co. 1–4)*, edited by Lorenzo de Lorenzi, 9–41. Rome: Abbazia di S. Paolo, 1980).

Betz, Otto. "Miracles in the Writings of Flavius Josephus." In *Josephus, Judaism, and Christianity*, edited by Louis H. Feldman and Gohei Hata, 212–35. Detroit: Wayne State University Press, 1987.

Bird, Michael F. "The Case of the Proselytizing Pharisees?—Matthew 23.15." *JSHJ* 2 (2004): 117–37.

———. *Crossing over Sea and Land: Jewish Missionary Activity in the Second Temple Period.* Peabody, MA: Hendrickson, 2010.

Bird, Michael F., and Joseph R. Dodson, eds. *Paul and the Second Century.* LNTS 412. London: T&T Clark, 2011.

Borgen, Peder. "Miracles of Healing in the New Testament: Some Observations." *ST* 35 (1981): 91–106.

———. "Openly Portrayed as Crucified: Some Observations on Gal. 3:1–14." In *Christology, Controversy, and Community: New Testament Essays in Honour of David R. Catchpole*, edited by David G. Horrell and Christopher M. Tuckett, 345–53. NovTSup 99. Leiden: Brill, 2000.

Boring, M. Eugene. "What Are We Looking For? Toward a Definition of the Term 'Christian Prophet.'" *SBLSP* (1973): 142–54.

Bornkamm, Günther. *Paul.* Translated by D. M. G. Stalker. London: Hodder & Stoughton, 1971.

Bowers, Paul. "Church and Mission in Paul." *JSNT* 44 (1991): 89–111.

———. "Paul and Religious Propaganda in the First Century." *NovT* 22 (1980): 316–23.

Bowker, John W. "'Merkabah' Visions and the Visions of Paul." *JSS* 16 (1971): 157–73.

Bowley, James E. "Prophets and Prophecy at Qumran." in *The Dead Sea Scrolls after Fifty Years: A Comprehensive Assessment*, edited by Peter W. Flint and James C. VanderKam, 2:354–78. 2 vols. Leiden: Brill, 1999.

Boyarin, Daniel. *A Radical Jew: Paul and the Politics of Identity*. Berkeley: University of California Press, 1994.

Boyce, James L. "Graceful Imitation: Imitators of Us and the Lord (1 Thessalonians 1:6)." *WW* Supplement Series 1 (1992): 139–46.

Brady, Dean. "Paul and Religious Experience." In *The Changing Face of Judaism, Christianity, and Other Greco-Roman Religions in Antiquity*, edited by Ian H. Henderson, Gerbern S. Oegma, and Sara Parks Ricker, 471–90. SJSHRZ 2. Gütersloh: Gütersloher Verlagshaus, 2006.

Brant, Jo-ann. "The Place of Mimesis in Paul's Thought." *SR* 22 (1993): 285–300.

Brawley, Robert L. "Paul in Acts: Aspects of Structure and Characterization." *SBLSP* (1988): 90–105.

Brenk, F. E. "The Exorcism at Philippi in Acts 16.11–40: Divine Possession or Diabolic Inspiration?" *FilNeot* 13 (2000): 3–21.

Bruce, F. F. "Is the Paul of Acts the Real Paul?" *BJRL* 58 (1976): 282–305.

———. *Paul and Jesus*. London: SPCK, 1974.

Bultmann, Rudolf. "The Significance of the Historical Jesus for the Theology of Paul." In *Faith and Understanding*, edited by Robert W. Funk, translated by Louise Pettibone Smith, 220–46. FTMT. Philadelphia: Fortress, 1987.

Burke, Trevor J. "The Holy Spirit as the Controlling Dynamic in Paul's Role as Missionary to the Thessalonians." In *Paul as Missionary: Identity, Activity, Theology, and Practice*, edited by Trevor J. Burke and Brian S. Rosner, 142–57. LNTS 420. London: T&T Clark, 2011.

Byrskog, Samuel. "History or Story in Acts—A Middle Way? The 'We' Passages, Historical Intertexture, and Oral History." In *Contextualizing Acts: Lukan Narrative and Greco-Roman Discourse*, edited by Todd C. Penner and Caroline Vander Stichele, 257–83. SBLSymS 20. Atlanta: Society of Biblical Literature, 2003.

Callan, Terrance. "Prophecy and Ecstasy in Greco-Roman Religion and in 1 Corinthians." *NovT* 27 (1985): 125–40.

Campbell, William S. *The "We" Passages in the Acts of the Apostles: The Narrator as Narrative Character*. SBL 14. Atlanta: Society of Biblical Literature, 2007.

Castelli, Elizabeth A. *Imitating Paul: A Discourse of Power*. Louisville: Westminster John Knox, 1991.

Catchpole, David R. "The Mission Charge in Q." *Semeia* 55 (1991): 147–74.

Cavadini, John C., ed. *Miracles in Jewish and Christian Antiquity: Imagining Truth*. NDST 3. Notre Dame, IN: University of Notre Dame Press, 1999.

Chilton, Bruce D. *Rabbi Paul: An Intellectual Biography*. New York: Doubleday, 2004.

———. "The Kingdom of God in Recent Discussions." In *Studying the Historical Jesus: Evaluations of the State of Current Research*, edited by Bruce D. Chilton and Craig A. Evans, 255–80. NTTS 19. Leiden: Brill, 1998.

Christophersen, Alf, et al., eds. *Paul, Luke and the Graeco-Roman World: Essays in Honour of Alexander J. M. Wedderburn.* JSNTSup 217. London: Sheffield Academic Press, 2003.

Clabeaux, John. "The Story of the Maltese Viper and Luke's Apology for Paul?" *CBQ* 67 (2005): 604–10.

Clark, Andrew C. *Parallel Lives: The Relation of Paul to the Apostles in the Lucan Perspective.* PBM. Bletchley; Waynesboro, GA: Paternoster, 2001.

Cohen, Shaye J. D. "Was Judaism in Antiquity a Missionary Religion?" In *Jewish Assimilation, Acculturation, and Accommodation: Past Traditions, Current Issues, and Future Prospects,* edited by Menachem Mor, 14–23. SJCiv 2. Lanham, MD: University Press of America, 1992.

Cook, L. Stephen. *On the Question of the "Cessation of Prophecy" in Ancient Judaism.* TSAJ 145. Tübingen: Mohr Siebeck, 2011.

Court, John M. "The Controversy with Adversaries of Paul's Apostolate in the Context of His Relations to the Corinthian Congregation (2 Corinthians 12,14–13,13)." In *Verteidigung und Begründung des apostolischen Amtes (2 Kor 10–13): XII Colloquio ecumenico Paolino,* edited by Eduard Lohse, 87–106. Rome: Abtei St. Paul vor den Maurern, 1992.

Crafton, Jeffrey A. *The Agency of the Apostle: A Dramatistic Analysis of Paul's Responses to Conflict in 2 Corinthians.* JSNTSup 51. Sheffield: JSOT Press, 1991.

Cranfield, Charles E. B. "Changes of Person and Number in Paul's Epistles." In *Paul and Paulinism: Essays in Honour of C. K. Barrett,* edited by Morna D. Hooker and Stephen G. Wilson, 280–89. London: SPCK, 1982.

Culpepper, R. Alan. "Co-Workers in Suffering: Philippians 2:19–30." *RevExp* 77 (1980): 349–58.

Davies, W. D. *Paul and Rabbinic Judaism: Some Rabbinic Elements in Pauline Theology.* 4th ed. Philadelphia: Fortress, 1980.

Dawson, Audrey. *Healing, Weakness and Power: Perspectives on Healing in the Writings of Mark, Luke and Paul.* PBM. Milton Keynes: Paternoster, 2008.

Deissmann, Adolf. *Paul: A Study in Social and Religious History.* Translated by William E. Wilson. 1926. Reprint, New York: Harper, 1957.

Dibelius, Martin. *The Book of Acts: Form, Style, and Theology.* Edited by K. C. Hanson. FCBS. Minneapolis: Fortress, 2004.

———. *Paul.* Edited by Werner Georg Kümmel. Translated by Frank Clarke. London: Longmans, 1953.

———. *Studies in the Acts of the Apostles.* Edited by Heinrich Greeven. Translated by Mary Ling. London: SCM, 1956.

Dickson, John P. *Mission-Commitment in Ancient Judaism and in the Pauline Communities: The Shape, Extent and Background of Early Christian Mission.* WUNT 2/159. Tübingen: Mohr Siebeck, 2003.

Dockx, S. "The First Missionary Voyage of Paul: Historical Reality or Literary Creation of Luke." In *Chronos, Kairos, Christos: Nativity and Chronological Studies Presented to Jack Finegan,* edited by Jerry Vardaman and Edwin M. Yamauchi, 209–21. Winona Lake, IN: Eisenbrauns, 1989.

Dominy, Bert. "Paul and Spiritual Gifts: Reflections on 1 Corinthians 12–14." *SwJT* 26 (1983): 49–68.

Donaldson, Terence L. *Paul and the Gentiles: Remapping the Apostle's Convictional World.* Minneapolis: Fortress, 1997.

Donfried, Karl P. *Paul, Thessalonica, and Early Christianity.* Grand Rapids: Eerdmans, 2002.

Dunn, James D. G. *Jesus and the Spirit: A Study of the Religious and Charismatic Experience of Jesus and the First Christians as Reflected in the New Testament.* London: SCM, 1975.

———. "Jesus Tradition in Paul." In *Studying the Historical Jesus: Evaluations of the State of Current Research,* edited by Bruce D. Chilton and Craig A. Evans, 155–78. NTTS 19. Leiden: Brill, 1998.

———. "'A Light to the Gentiles': The Significance of the Damascus Road Christophany for Paul." In *The Glory of Christ in the New Testament: Studies in Christology in Memory of George Bradford Caird,* edited by L. D. Hurst and N. T. Wright, 251–66. Oxford: Clarendon, 1987.

———. "Paul's Knowledge of the Jesus Tradition: The Evidence of Romans." In *Christus Bezeugen: Festschrift für Wolfgang Trilling zum 65. Geburtstag,* edited by Karl Kertelge, Traugott Holtz, and Claus-Peter März, 193–207. Leipzig: St. Benno, 1989.

———. *The Theology of Paul the Apostle.* Grand Rapids: Eerdmans, 1998.

———. "4QMMT and Galatians." *NTS* 43 (1997): 147–53.

Dupont, Jacques. "The Conversion of Paul, and Its Influence on His Understanding of Salvation by Faith." In *Apostolic History and the Gospel: Biblical and Historical Essays Presented to F. F. Bruce on His 60th Birthday,* edited by W. Ward Gasque and Ralph P. Martin, 176–94. Exeter: Paternoster, 1970.

Eckert, Jorst. "Zeichen und Wunder in der Sicht des Paulus und der Apostelgeschichte." *TTS* 88 (1979): 19–33.

Ehrensperger, Kathy. *Paul and the Dynamics of Power: Communication and Interaction in the Early Christ-Movement.* LNTS 325. London: T&T Clark, 2007.

Ellis, E. Earle. *Prophecy and Hermeneutic in Early Christianity.* Grand Rapids: Baker Academic, 1993.

———. "The Role of the Christian Prophet in Acts." In *Apostolic History and the Gospel: Biblical and Historical Essays Presented to F. F. Bruce on His 60th Birthday,* edited by W. Ward Gasque and Ralph P. Martin, 55–67. Exeter: Paternoster, 1970.

———. "Spiritual Gifts in the Pauline Community." *NTS* 20 (1974): 128–44.

Elsdon, Ron. "Was Paul 'Converted' or 'Called'? Questions of Methodology." *PIBA* 24 (2001): 17–47.

Engberg-Pedersen, Troels. *Cosmology and Self in the Apostle Paul: The Material Spirit.* Oxford: Oxford University Press, 2010.

———, ed. *Paul in His Hellenistic Context.* Minneapolis: Fortress, 1995.

Evans, Craig A. "Paul and the Prophets." In *Romans and the People of God: Essays in Honor of Gordon D. Fee on the Occasion of His 65th Birthday,* edited by Sven K. Soderlund and N. T. Wright, 115–28. Grand Rapids: Eerdmans, 1999.

———. "Paul the Exorcist and Healer." In *Paul and His Theology,* edited by Stanley E. Porter, 363–79. PSt 3. Leiden: Brill, 2006.

Eve, Eric. *The Jewish Context of Jesus' Miracles.* JSNTSup 231. Sheffield: Sheffield Academic Press, 2002.

Fee, Gordon D. *God's Empowering Presence: The Holy Spirit in the Letters of Paul.* Peabody, MA: Hendrickson, 1994.

Feldman, Louis H. "Jewish Proselytism." In *Eusebius, Christianity, and Judaism,* edited by Harold W. Attridge and Gohei Hata, 372–408. StPB 42. Leiden: Brill; Detroit: Wayne State University Press, 1992.

Fenton, John C. "Order of the Miracles Performed by Peter and Paul in Acts." *ExpTim* 77 (1966): 381–83.

Francis, D. Pitt. "The Holy Spirit: A Statistical Inquiry." *ExpTim* 96 (1985): 136–37.

Fraser, John W. *Jesus and Paul: Paul as Interpreter of Jesus from Harnack to Kümmel.* Abingdon: Marcham, 1974.

———. "Paul's Knowledge of Jesus: II Corinthians V.16 Once More." *NTS* 17 (1971): 293–313.

Frizzell, Lawrence E. "Paul the Pharisee." In *Jewish-Christian Encounters over the Centuries: Symbiosis, Prejudice, Holocaust, Dialogue,* edited by Marvin Perry and Frederick M. Schweitzer, 45–60. AUS 9/36. New York: Peter Lang, 1994.

Furnish, Victor P. "The Jesus-Paul Debate: From Baur to Bultmann." In *Paul and Jesus: Collected Essays,* edited by A. J. M. Wedderburn, 17–50. JSNTSup 37. Sheffield: JSOT Press, 1989.

———. "On Putting Paul in His Place." *JBL* 113 (1994): 3–17.

Gardner, Percy D. *The Religious Experience of Saint Paul.* London: Williams & Norgate, 1911.

Gatzweiler, Karl. "La conception paulinienne du miracle." *ETL* 37 (1961): 813–46.

Gaventa, Beverly Roberts. *From Darkness to Light: Aspects of Conversion in the New Testament.* OBT 20. Philadelphia: Fortress, 1986.

———. "Galatians 1 and 2: Autobiography as Paradigm." *NovT* 28 (1986): 309–26.

Gempf, Conrad H. "Mission and Misunderstanding: Paul and Barnabas in Lystra (Acts 14:8–20)." In *Mission and Meaning: Essays Presented to Peter Cotterell,* edited by Antony Billington, Tony Lane, and Max Turner, 56–69. Carlisle: Paternoster, 1995.

George, Augustin. "Le miracle dans l'oeuvre de Luc." In *Les miracles de Jésus selon le Nouveau Testament,* edited by Xavier Léon-Dufour, 249–68. Paris: Seuil, 1977. Republished as "Le Miracle." In *Études sur l'oeuvre de Luc,* 133–48. SB. Paris: Gabalda, 1978.

———. "Les récits de miracles. Caractéristiques lucaniennes." In *Études sur l'oeuvre de Luc,* 67–84. SB. Paris: Gabalda, 1978.

Georgi, Dieter. "Forms of Religious Propaganda." In *Jesus in His Time,* edited by Hans Jürgen Schultz, translated by Brian Watchorn, 124–31. Philadelphia: Fortress, 1971.

———. *The Opponents of Paul in Second Corinthians: A Study of Religious Propaganda in Late Antiquity.* Philadelphia: Fortress, 1986.

Getty, Mary Ann. "The Imitation of Paul in the Letters to the Thessalonians." In *The Thessalonian Correspondence,* edited by Raymond F. Collins, 277–83. BETL 87. Louvain: Leuven University Press, 1990.

Gilchrist, J. M. "The Historicity of Paul's Shipwreck." *JSNT* 61 (1996): 29–51.

Gill, D. W. J. "Paul's Travels through Cyprus (Acts 13:4–12)." *TynBul* 46 (1995): 219–28.

Given, Mark D., ed. *Paul Unbound: Other Perspectives on the Apostle*. Peabody, MA: Hendrickson, 2010.

Goodman, Martin. "Jewish Proselytizing in the First Century." In *The Jews among Pagans and Christians in the Roman Empire*, edited by Judith Lieu, John North, and Tessa Rajak, 53–78. London: Routledge, 1992.

———. *Mission and Conversion: Proselytizing in the Religious History of the Roman Empire*. Oxford: Clarendon, 1994.Goulder, Michael D. *Paul and the Competing Mission in Corinth*. LPS. Peabody, MA: Hendrickson, 2001.

———. *St. Paul versus St. Peter: A Tale of Two Missions*. Louisville: Westminster John Knox, 1995.

———. *Type and History in Acts*. London: SPCK, 1964.

———. "Visions and Revelations of the Lord (2 Corinthians 12:1–10)." In *Paul and the Corinthians: Studies on a Community in Conflict; Essays in Honour of Margaret Thrall*, edited by Trevor J. Burke and J. Keith Elliott, 303–12. NovTSup 109. Leiden: Brill, 2003.

Gray, Rebecca. *Prophetic Figures in Late Second Temple Jewish Palestine: The Evidence from Josephus*. Oxford: Oxford University Press, 1993.

Green, William S. "Palestinian Holy Men: Charismatic Leadership and Rabbinic Tradition." *ANRW* II.19.2 (1979): 619–47.

Gruenwald, Ithamar. *Apocalyptic and Merkavah Mysticism*. AGJU 14; Leiden: Brill, 1980.

Gunkel, Hermann. *The Influence of the Holy Spirit: The Popular View of the Apostolic Age and the Teaching of the Apostle Paul*. Translated by Roy A. Harrisville and Philip A. Quanbeck II. Philadelphia: Fortress, 1979.

Gunther, John J. *St. Paul's Opponents and Their Background: A Study of Apocalyptic and Jewish Sectarian Teachings*. NovTSup 35. Leiden: Brill, 1973.

Hahn, Ferdinand C. *Mission in the New Testament*. Translated by Frank Clarke. London: SCM, 1965.

Hamm, D. "Acts 3:12–26: Peter's Speech and the Healing of the Man Born Lame." *PRSt* 11 (1984): 199–217.

Hanson, J. S. "Dreams and Visions in the Graeco-Roman World and Early Christianity." *ANRW* II.23.2 (1980): 1395–427.

Hardon, John A. "Miracle Narratives in the Acts of the Apostles." *CBQ* 16 (1954): 303–18.

Hartman, Lars. "Some Remarks on 1 Cor. 1:1–5." *SEÅ* 39 (1974): 109–20.

Hedrick, Charles W. "Paul's Conversion/Call: A Comparative Analysis of the Three Reports in Acts." *JBL* 100 (1981): 415–32.

Hemer, Colin. *The Book of Acts in the Setting of Hellenistic History*. WUNT 49. Tübingen: Mohr Siebeck, 1989.

———. "First Person Narrative in Acts 27–28." *TynBul* 36 (1985): 79–109.

Hengel, Martin. *Acts and the History of Early Christianity*. Translated by John Bowden. London: SCM, 1979.

———. *The Pre-Christian Paul*. London: SCM, 1991.

Hofius, Otfried. "The Lord's Supper and the Lord's Supper Tradition: Reflections on 1 Corinthians 11:23b–25." In *One Loaf, One Cup: Ecumenical Studies of 1 Cor 11 and*

Other Eucharistic Texts; The Cambridge Conference on the Eucharist, August 1988, edited by Ben F. Meyer, 75–115. NGS 6. Louvain: Peeters, 1993.

Hogan, Larry P. *Healing in the Second Temple Period.* NTOA 21. Freiburg: Universitätsverlag; Göttingen: Vandenhoeck & Ruprecht, 1992.

Holmberg, Bengt. *Paul and Power: The Structure of Authority in the Primitive Church as Reflected in the Pauline Epistles.* Philadelphia: Fortress, 1980.

Holtz, T. "Paul and the Oral Gospel Tradition." In *Jesus and the Oral Gospel Tradition,* edited by Henry Wansbrough, 380–93. JSNTSup 64. Sheffield: Sheffield Academic Press, 1991.

Hooker, Morna D. "A Partner in the Gospel: Paul's Understanding of Ministry." *EpRev* 25 (1998): 70–78.

————. *The Signs of a Prophet: The Prophetic Actions of Jesus.* London: SCM, 1997.

Horsley, Richard A. "'Like One of the Prophets of Old': Two Types of Popular Prophets at the Time of Jesus." *CBQ* 47 (1985): 435–63.

————. "Popular Messianic Movements around the Time of Jesus." *CBQ* 46 (1984): 471–95.

————. "Popular Prophetic Movements at the Time of Jesus: Their Principal Features and Social Origins." *JSNT* 26 (1986): 3–27.

Hughes, Frank Witt. *Early Christian Rhetoric and 2 Thessalonians.* JSNTSup 30. Sheffield: JSOT Press, 1989.

Hurd, John C. "'The Jesus Whom Paul Preaches' (Acts 19:13)." In *From Jesus to Paul: Studies in Honour of Francis Wright Beare,* edited by Peter Richardson and John C. Hurd, 73–89. Waterloo, ON: Wilfrid Laurier University Press, 1984.

Hurtado, Larry W. "Religious Experience and Religious Innovation in the New Testament." *JR* 80 (2000): 183–205.

Jervell, Jacob. "Der schwache Charismatiker." In *Rechtfertigung: Festschrift für Ernst Käsemann zum 70. Geburtstag,* edited by Johannes Friedrich, Wolfgang Pöhlmann, and Peter Stuhlmacher, 185–98. Tübingen: Mohr Siebeck, 1976.

————. "Die Zeichen des Apostels: Die Wunder beim lukanischen und paulinischen Paulus." *SNTSU* 4 (1979): 54–75.

————. "Paul in the Acts of the Apostles: Tradition, History, Theology." In *The Unknown Paul: Essays on Luke-Acts and Early Christian History,* 68–76. Minneapolis: Augsburg, 1984.

————. "The Signs of an Apostle: Paul's Miracles." In *The Unknown Paul: Essays on Luke-Acts and Early Christian History,* 77–95. Minneapolis: Augsburg, 1984.

Johnson, J. F. "Paul's Argument from Experience: A Closer Look at Galatians 3:1–5." *ConcJ* 19 (1993): 234–37.

Johnson, Luke Timothy. *Religious Experience in Earliest Christianity: A Missing Dimension in New Testament Studies.* Minneapolis: Fortress, 1998.

Johnston, G. "'Kingdom of God' Sayings in Paul's Epistles." In *From Jesus to Paul: Studies in Honour of Francis Wright Beare,* edited by Peter Richardson and John C. Hurd, 143–56. Waterloo, ON: Wilfrid Laurier University Press, 1984.

Käsemann, Ernst. "Die Legitimität des Apostels: Eine Untersuchung zu II Korinther 10–13." *ZNW* 41 (1942): 33–71.

————. *Essays on New Testament Themes*. Translated by W. J. Montague. SBT 41. London: SCM, 1964.

Keathley, Naymond H., ed. *With Steadfast Purpose: Essays on Acts in Honor of Henry Jackson Flanders, Jr.* Waco: Baylor University Press, 1990.

Kee, Howard Clark. *Medicine, Miracle, and Magic in New Testament Times*. SNTSMS 55. Cambridge: Cambridge University Press, 1986.

————. *Miracle in the Early Christian World: A Study in Sociohistorical Method*. New Haven: Yale University Press, 1983.

Kelhoffer, James A. "The Apostle Paul and Justin Martyr on the Miraculous: A Comparison of Appeals to Authority." *GRBS* 42 (2001): 163–84.

————. *Miracle and Mission: The Authentication of Missionaries and Their Message in the Longer Ending of Mark*. WUNT 2/112. Tübingen: Mohr Siebeck, 2000.

————. "Ordinary Christians as Miracle Workers in the New Testament and the Second and Third Century Christian Apologists." *JCSBR* 4 (1999): 23–34.

————. "The Rhetoric of Miracle Discourse in the Writings of Paul." *SBLSP* (2002): 1–20.

Kelly, Geoffrey B. "'He Appeared to Me.'" In *Critical History and Biblical Faith: New Testament Perspectives*, edited by Thomas J. Ryan, 108–35. Villanova, PA: College Theology Society, 1979.

Kennedy, Harry A. A. *St. Paul and the Mystery Religions*. London: Hodder & Stoughton, 1913.

Kilgallen, John J. "Reflections on Charisma(ta) in the New Testament." *StM* 41 (1992): 289–323.

Kim, Seyoon. "The Jesus Tradition in 1 Thess. 4.13–5.11." *NTS* 48 (2002): 225–42.

————. *Paul and the New Perspective: Second Thoughts on the Origin of Paul's Gospel*. Grand Rapids: Eerdmans, 2002.

Kirk, John Andrew. "Apostleship Since Rengstorf: Towards a Synthesis." *NTS* 21 (1975): 249–64.

Klauck, Hans-Josef. "With Paul in Paphos and Lystra: Magic and Paganism in the Acts of the Apostles." *Neot* 28 (1994): 93–108.

Kloppenborg, John S. "The Formation of Q and Antique Instructional Genres." *JBL* 105 (1986): 443–62.

Klutz, Todd E. "Naked and Wounded: Foregrounding, Relevance and Situation in Acts 19:13–20." In *Discourse Analysis and the New Testament: Approaches and Results*, edited by Stanley E. Porter and Jeffrey T. Reed, 258–79. JSNTSup 170. Sheffield: Sheffield Academic Press, 1999.

Knox, John. "Rom 15:14–33 and Paul's Conception of His Apostolic Mission." *JBL* 83 (1964): 1–11.

Kolenkow, Anitra Bingham. "Paul and His Opponents in 2 Cor. 10–13: THEIOI ANDRES and Spiritual Guides." In *Religious Propaganda and Missionary Competition in the New Testament World: Essays Honoring Dieter Georgi*, edited by Lukas Bormann, Kelly Del Tredici, and Angela Standhartinger, 351–74. NovTSup 74. Leiden: Brill, 1994.

————. "Relationships between Miracle and Prophecy in the Greco-Roman World and Early Christianity." *ANRW* II.23.2 (1980): 1470–1506.

Kollmann, Bernd. *Jesus und die Christen als Wundertäter: Studien zur Magie, Medizin und Schamanismus in Antike und Christentum.* FRLANT 170. Gottingen: Vandenhoeck & Ruprecht, 1996.

———. "Paulus als Wundertäter." In *Paulinische Christologie: Exegetische Beiträge; Hans Hübner zum 70. Geburtstag,* edited by Udo Schnelle, Thomas Söding, and Michael Labahn, 76–96. Göttingen: Vandenhoeck & Ruprecht, 2000.

Koskenniemi, Erkki. *The Old Testament Miracle-Workers in Early Judaism.* WUNT 2/206. Tübingen: Mohr Siebeck, 2005.

Kourie, Celia. "Christ-Mysticism in Paul." *The Way* Supplement 102 (2001): 71–80.

Kvalbein, Hans. "The Wonders of the End-Time: Metaphoric Language in 4Q521 and the Interpretation of Matthew 11.5 Par." *JSP* 18 (1998): 87–110.

Lampe, G. W. H. "Miracles in the Acts of the Apostles." In *Miracles: Cambridge Studies in Their Philosophy and History,* edited by C. F. D. Moule, 163–78. London: Mowbray, 1965.

Lentz, John Clayton, Jr. *Luke's Portrait of Paul.* SNTSMS 77. Cambridge: Cambridge University Press, 1993.

Liefeld, Walter L. "The Wandering Preacher as a Social Figure in the Roman Empire." PhD diss., Columbia University, 1967.

Lietaert Peerbolte, Bert Jan. "Romans 15:14–29 and Paul's Missionary Agenda." In *Persuasion and Dissuasion in Early Christianity, Ancient Judaism, and Hellenism,* edited by Pieter W. van der Horst et al., 143–59. CBET 33. Louvain: Peeters, 2003.

———. "Paul the Miracle Worker: Development and Background of Pauline Miracle Stories." In *Wonders Never Cease: The Purpose of Narrating Miracle Stories in the New Testament and Its Religious Environment,* edited by Michael Labahn and Bert Jan Lietaert Peerbolte, 180–99. LNTS 288. London: T&T Clark, 2006.

———. *Paul the Missionary.* CBET 34. Louvain: Peeters, 2003.

Liljeström, Kenneth, ed. *The Early Reception of Paul.* Publications of the Finnish Exegetical Society 66. Helkinki: Finnish Exegetical Society, 2011.

Lim, Timothy H. "Not in Persuasive Words of Wisdom, But in the Demonstration of the Spirit and Power." *NovT* 29 (1987): 137–49.

Litfin, Duane A. *St. Paul's Theology of Proclamation: 1 Corinthians 1–4 and Greco-Roman Rhetoric.* SNTSMS 79. Cambridge: Cambridge University Press, 1994.

Longenecker, Richard N., ed. *The Road from Damascus: The Impact of Paul's Conversion on His Life, Thought, and Ministry.* Grand Rapids: Eerdmans, 1997.

Lüdemann, Gerd. *The Acts of the Apostles: What Really Happened in the Earliest Days of the Church.* Amherst, NY: Prometheus, 2005.

———. *Early Christianity According to the Traditions in Acts: A Commentary.* Translated by John Bowden. London: SCM, 1989.

———. *Paul, the Founder of Christianity.* Amherst, NY: Prometheus, 2002.

Lull, David John. *The Spirit in Galatia: Paul's Interpretation of Pneuma as Divine Power.* SBLDS 49. Chico, CA: Scholars Press, 1980.

Luz, Ulrich. "Paul as Mystic." in *The Holy Spirit and Christian Origins: Essays in Honor of James D. G. Dunn,* edited by Graham N. Stanton, Bruce W. Longenecker, and Stephen C. Barton, 131–43. Grand Rapids: Eerdmans, 2004.

Malherbe, Abraham J. *Paul and the Popular Philosophers*. Minneapolis: Fortress, 1989.

Marguerat, Daniel. *The First Christian Historian: Writings of the "Acts of the Apostles."* Translated by Ken McKinney, Gregory J. Laughery, and Richard Bauckham. SNTSMS 121. Cambridge: Cambridge University Press, 2002.

———. "Paul après Paul: Une histoire de reception." *NTS* 54 (2008): 317–37.

———, ed. *Reception of Paulinism in Acts* [= *Réception du Paulinisme dans les Actes des Apôtres*]. BETL 229. Louvain: Peeters, 2009.

Marshall, I. Howard. "The Hope of a New Age: The Kingdom of God in the New Testament." In *Jesus the Saviour: Studies in New Testament Theology*, 213–38. Downers Grove, IL: InterVarsity, 1990.

———. "Luke's View of Paul." *SwJT* 33 (1990): 41–51.

Martin, Ralph P. "The Opponents of Paul in 2 Corinthians: An Old Issue Revisited." In *Tradition and Interpretation in the New Testament: Essays in Honor of E. Earle Ellis for His 60th Birthday*, edited by Gerald F. Hawthorne and Otto Betz, 279–89. Grand Rapids: Eerdmans, 1987.

———. *The Spirit and the Congregation: Studies in 1 Corinthians 12–15*. Grand Rapids: Eerdmans, 1984.

Martyn, J. Louis. "A Gentile Mission That Replaced an Earlier Jewish Mission." In *Exploring the Gospel of John: In Honor of D. Moody Smith*, edited by R. Alan Culpepper and C. Clifton Black, 124–44. Louisville: Westminster John Knox, 1989.

Mattill, Andrew J. "Jesus-Paul Parallels and the Purpose of Luke-Acts: H. H. Evans Reconsidered." *NovT* 17 (1975): 15–46.

———. "The Value of Acts as a Source for the Study of Paul." In *Perspectives on Luke-Acts*, edited by Charles H. Talbert, 76–98. Danville, VA: Association of Baptist Professors of Religion; Edinburgh: T&T Clark, 1978.

McCant, J. W. "Paul's Thorn of Rejected Apostleship." *NTS* 34 (1988): 550–72.

McCasland, Selly Vernon. "Religious Healing in First-Century Palestine." In *Environmental Factors in Christian History*, edited by John Thomas McNeil, Matthew Spinka, and Harold R. Willoughby, 18–34. Port Washington, NY: Kennikat, 1939.

———. "Signs and Wonders." *JBL* 76 (1957): 149–52.

McDermott, John M. "Jesus and the Kingdom of God in the Synoptics, Paul, and John." *EgT* 19 (1988): 69–91.

McKnight, Scot. *A Light among the Gentiles: Jewish Missionary Activity in the Second Temple Period*. Minneapolis: Fortress, 1991.

Metzger, Bruce M. "Considerations of Methodology in the Study of the Mystery Religions and Early Christianity." *HTR* 48 (1955): 1–20.

Miller, Marvin H. "The Character of Miracles in Luke-Acts." ThD diss., Graduate Theological Union, 1971.

Moessner, David P. "Paul and the Pattern of the Prophet like Moses in Acts." *SBLSP* 22 (1983): 203–12.

Moule, C. F. D., ed. *Miracles: Cambridge Studies in Their Philosophy and History*. London: Mowbray, 1965.

Mount, Christopher. *Pauline Christianity: Luke-Acts and the Legacy of Paul*. NovTSup 104. Leiden: Brill, 2002.

Müller, Paul-Gerhard. "Der Paulinismus in der Apostelgeschichte: Ein forschungsgeschichtlicher Überblick." In *Paulus in den neutestamentlichen Spätschriften: Zur Paulus Rezeption
im Neuen Testament*, edited by Karl Kertelge, 157–201. QD 89. Freiburg: Herder, 1981.

Munck, Johannes. *Paul and the Salvation of Mankind.* Translated by Frank Clarke. London: SCM, 1959.

———. "Paul, the Apostles, and the Twelve." *ST* 3 (1949): 96–110.

———. "1 Thess. i.9–10 and the Missionary Preaching of Paul: Textual Exegesis and
Hermeneutic Reflexions." *NTS* 9 (1962): 95–110.

Murphy-O'Connor, Jerome. *Paul: A Critical Life.* Oxford: Oxford University Press, 1996.

Neirynck, Frans. "The Miracle Stories in the Acts of the Apostles: An Introduction." In *Les
Actes des Apôtres: Traditions, rédaction, théologie*, edited by Jacob Kremer, 169–213.
BETL 48. Gembloux: Duculot; Louvain: Leuven University Press, 1979.

———. "Paul and the Sayings of Jesus." In *L'Apôtre Paul: Personalité, style et conception
du ministère*, edited by Albert Vanhoye, 265–321. BETL 73. Louvain: Peeters, 1986.

O'Collins, Gerald G. "Power Made Perfect in Weakness, 2 Cor. 12:9–10." *CBQ* 33 (1971):
528–37.

Oke, C. C. "Paul's Method Not a Demonstration but an Exhibition of the Spirit." *ExpTim*
67 (1955): 85–86.

O'Neill, John C. "The Kingdom of God." *NovT* 35 (1993): 130–41.

O'Toole, R. F. "Parallels between Jesus and His Disciples in Luke-Acts: A Further Study."
BZ 2 (1983): 195–212.

Paget, James Carleton. "Jewish Proselytism at the Time of Christian Origins: Chimera or
Reality?" *JSNT* 62 (1996): 65–103.

Patterson, Stephen J. "Paul and the Jesus Tradition: It Is Time for Another Look." *HTR*
84 (1991): 23–41.

Penner, Todd. "Madness in the Method? The Acts of the Apostles in Current Study."
CurBR 2 (2004): 223–93.

Pervo, Richard I. *The Making of Paul: Constructions of the Apostle in Early Christianity.*
Minneapolis: Fortress, 2010.

———. *Profit with Delight: The Literary Genre of the Acts of the Apostles.* Philadelphia:
Fortress, 1987.

Phillips, Thomas E. *Paul, His Letters, and Acts.* LPS. Peabody, MA: Hendrickson, 2009.

Pilch, John J. *Flights of the Soul: Visions, Heavenly Journeys, and Peak Experiences in the
Biblical World.* Grand Rapids: Eerdmans, 2011.

Porter, Stanley E., ed. *Paul and His Opponents.* PSt 2. Leiden: Brill, 2005.

———. *Paul in Acts.* Peabody, MA: Hendrickson, 2001.

———. *The Paul of Acts: Essays in Literary Criticism, Rhetoric, and Theology.* WUNT
115. Tübingen: Mohr Siebeck, 1999.

Praeder, Susan Marie. "Jesus-Paul, Peter-Paul, and Jesus-Peter Parallelisms in Luke–Acts:
A History of Reader Response." *SBLSP* (1984): 23–39.

———. "Miracle Worker and Missionary: Paul in the Acts of the Apostles." *SBLSP* (1983):
107–29.

Räisänen, Heikki. "Paul's Call Experience and His Later View of the Law." In *Jesus, Paul and Torah: Collected Essays*, translated by David E. Orton, 15–47. JSNTSup 43. Sheffield: JSOT Press, 1992.

———. "Paul's Conversion and the Development of His View on the Law." *NTS* 33 (1987): 404–19.

Reese, J. M. "Paul Proclaims the Wisdom of the Cross: Scandal and Foolishness." *BTB* 9 (1979): 147–53.

Reitzenstein, Richard. "Paul as a Pneumatic." In *Hellenistic Mystery-Religions: Their Basic Ideas and Significance*, translated by John E. Steely, 426–500. Pittsburgh: Pickwick, 1978.

Riesner, Rainer. *Paul's Early Period: Chronology, Mission Strategy, Theology*. Translated by Doug Stott. Grand Rapids: Eerdmans, 1998.

———. "A Pre-Christian Jewish Mission." In *The Mission of the Early Church to Jews and Gentiles*, edited by Jostein Ådna and Hans Kvalbein, 211–50. WUNT 127. Tübingen: Mohr Siebeck, 2000.

Roetzel, Calvin J. *The Letters of Paul: Conversations in Context*. Louisville: Westminster John Knox, 2009.

———. *Paul: A Jew on the Margins*. Louisville: Westminster John Knox, 2003.

———. *Paul: The Man and the Myth*. Minneapolis: Fortress, 1999.

Rokéah, David. "Ancient Jewish Proselytism in Theory and Practice." *TZ* 52 (1996): 206–24.

———. *Jews, Pagans, and Christians in Conflict*. StPB 33. Jerusalem: Magnes; Leiden, Brill, 1982.

Rothschild, Clare K. *Hebrews as Pseudepigraphon: The History and Significance of the Pauline Attribution of Hebrews*. WUNT 235. Tübingen: Mohr Siebeck, 2009.

———. *Luke-Acts and the Rhetoric of History: An Investigation of Early Christian Historiography*. WUNT 2/175. Tübingen: Mohr Siebeck, 2004.

Saake, Helmut. "Paulus als Ekstatiker: Pneumatologische Beobachtungen zu 2 Kor 12:1–10." *NovT* 15 (1973): 153–60.

Sampley, J. Paul, and Peter Lampe, eds. *Paul and Rhetoric*. New York: T&T Clark, 2010.

Sanders, Jack T. *Charisma, Converts, Competitors: Societal and Sociological Factors in the Success of Early Christianity*. London: SCM, 2000.

Sandnes, Karl Olav. *Paul, One of the Prophets? A Contribution to the Apostle's Self-Understanding*. WUNT 2/43. Tübingen: Mohr Siebeck, 1991.

———. "Prophecy—A Sign for Believers (1 Cor. 14:20–25)." *Bib* 77 (1996): 1–15.

Savage, Timothy B. *Power through Weakness: Paul's Understanding of the Christian Ministry in 2 Corinthians*. SNTSMS 86. Cambridge: Cambridge University Press, 1996.

Schäfer, Peter. *The Origins of Jewish Mysticism*. Tübingen: Mohr Siebeck, 2009.

Schatzmann, Siegfried S. *A Pauline Theology of Charismata*. Peabody, MA: Hendrickson, 1987.

Schnabel, Eckhard J. *Early Christian Mission*. 2 vols. Downers Grove, IL: InterVarsity; Leicester: Apollos, 2004.

———. *Paul the Missionary: Realities, Strategies and Methods*. Downers Grove, IL: IVP Academic; Nottingham: Apollos, 2008.

Schnelle, Udo. *Apostle Paul: His Life and Theology.* Translated by M. Eugene Boring. Grand Rapids: Baker Academic, 2005.

Schoeps, Hans Joachim. *Paul: The Theology of the Apostle in Light of the Jewish Religious History.* Translated by Harold Knight. London: Lutterworth, 1961.

Schreiber, Stefan. "Die theologische Signifikanz der Pauluswunder in der Apostelgeschichte." *SNTSU* 24 (1999): 119–34.

———. *Paulus als Wundertäter: Redaktionsgeschichtliche Untersuchungen zur Apostelgeschichte und den authentischen Paulusbriefen.* BZNW 79. Berlin: de Gruyter, 1996.

Schüssler Fiorenza, Elizabeth. "Miracles, Mission, and Apologetics: An Introduction." In *Aspects of Religious Propaganda in Judaism and Early Christianity,* edited by Elizabeth Schüssler Fiorenza, 1–25. SJCA 2. Notre Dame, IN; University of Notre Dame Press, 1976.

Schweitzer, Albert. *The Mysticism of Paul the Apostle.* Translated by William Montgomery. Baltimore: Johns Hopkins University Press, 1998.

———. *Paul and His Interpreters: A Critical History.* Translated by W. Montgomery. London: Black, 1912.

Segal, Alan F. "The Cost of Proselytism and Conversion." *SBLSP* (1988): 336–69.

———. "Paul and Ecstasy." *SBLSP* 25 (1986): 555–80.

———. *Paul the Convert: The Apostolate and Apostasy of Saul the Pharisee.* New Haven: Yale University Press, 1990.

Shantz, Colleen. *Paul in Ecstasy: The Neurobiology of the Apostle's Life and Thought.* Cambridge: Cambridge University Press, 2009.

Sheeley, Steven M. "Getting into the Act(s): Narrative Presence in the 'We' Sections." *PRSt* 26 (1999): 203–20.

Shogren, Gary S. "Is the Kingdom of God about Eating and Drinking or Isn't It?" *NovT* 42 (2000): 238–56.

Spencer, William D. "The Power in Paul's Teaching (1 Cor. 4:9–20)." *JETS* 32 (1989): 51–61.

Stanley, David M. "'Become Imitators of Me': The Pauline Conception of Apostolic Tradition." *Bib* 40 (1959): 857–77.

———. "Pauline Allusions to the Sayings of Jesus." *CBQ* 23 (1961): 26–39.

Stendahl, Krister. "The Apostle Paul and the Introspective Conscience of the West." *HTR* 55 (1962): 119–215.

Sterling, Gregory E. "From Apostle to the Gentiles to Apostle of the Church: Images of Paul at the End of the First Century." *ZNW* 99 (2008): 74–98.

Still, Todd D., ed. *Jesus and Paul Reconnected: Fresh Pathways into an Old Debate.* Grand Rapids: Eerdmans, 2007.

Stolz, Fritz. "Zeichen und Wunder: Die prophetische Legitimation und ihre Geschichte." *ZTK* 69 (1972): 125–44.

Strelan, Rick. "Acts 19:12: Paul's 'Aprons' Again." *JTS* 54 (2003): 154–57.

———. "Recognizing the Gods (Acts 14:8–10)." *NTS* 46 (2000): 488–503.

Sumney, Jerry L. *Identifying Paul's Opponents: The Question of Method in 2 Corinthians.* JSNTSup 40. Sheffield: JSOT Press, 1990.

————. "Paul and His Opponents: The Search." In *Paul Unbound: Other Perspectives on the Apostle*, edited by Mark D. Given, 55–70. Peabody, MA: Hendrickson, 2010.

————. "The Role of Historical Reconstructions of Early Christianity in Identifying Paul's Opponents." *PRSt* 16 (1989): 45–53.

————. *"Servants of Satan," "False Brothers," and Other Opponents of Paul*. JSNTSup 188. Sheffield: Sheffield Academic Press, 1999.

————. "Studying Paul's Opponents: Advances and Challenges." In *Paul and His Opponents*, edited by Stanley E. Porter, 7–58. PSt 2. Leiden: Brill, 2005.

Sweet, John P. M. "A Sign for Unbelievers: Paul's Attitude to Glossolalia." *NTS* 13 (1967): 240–57.

Talbert, Charles H. *Literary Patterns, Theological Themes, and the Genre of Luke-Acts*. SBLMS 20. Missoula, MT: Society of Bibilical Literature and Scholars Press, 1974.

————. "Paul's Understanding of the Holy Spirit: The Evidence of 1 Corinthians 12–14." In *Perspectives on the New Testament*, edited by Charles H. Talbert, 95–108. Macon, GA: Mercer University Press, 1985.

————. *Reading Corinthians: A Literary and Theological Commentary on 1 and 2 Corinthians*. New York: Crossroad, 1987.

————. "What Is Meant by the Historicity of Acts?" In *Reading Luke-Acts in Its Mediterranean Milieu*, 197–217. NovTSup 107. Leiden; Boston: Brill, 2003.

Talbert, Charles H., and John H. Hayes. "A Theology of Sea Storms in Luke-Acts." In *Jesus and the Heritage of Israel: Luke's Narrative Claim upon Israel's Legacy*, edited by David P. Moessner, 267–83. Harrisburg, PA: Trinity Press International, 1999.

Taylor, N. N. "Apostolic Identity and the Conflicts in Corinth and Galatia." In *Paul and His Opponents*, edited by Stanley E. Porter, 99–123. PSt 2. Leiden: Brill, 2005.

Theissen, Gerd. *Miracle Stories of the Early Christian Tradition*. Translated by Francis McDonagh. Edited by John Riches. SNTW. Edinburgh: T&T Clark, 1983.

Thompson, Michael B. "Paul in the Book of Acts: Differences and Distance." *ExpTim* 122 (2011): 425–36.

Thornton, Claus-Jürgen. *Der Zeuge Des Zeugen: Lukas als Historiker der Paulusreisen*. WUNT 56. Tübingen: Mohr Siebeck, 1991.

Thrall, Margaret E. "The Problem of II Cor. vi.14–vii.1 in Some Recent Discussion." *NTS* 24 (1977–78): 132–48.

————. "Super-Apostles, Servants of Christ, and Servants of Satan." *JSNT* 6 (1980): 42–57.

Tibbs, Clint. *Religious Experience of the Pneuma: Communication with the Spirit World in 1 Corinthians 12 and 14*. WUNT 230. Tübingen: Mohr Siebeck, 2007.

Trebilco, Paul R. "Paul and Silas—'Servants of the Most High God' (Acts 16:16–18)." *JSNT* 36 (1989): 51–73.

Tuckett, Christopher M. "1 Corinthians and Q." *JBL* 102 (1983): 607–19.

————. "Paul and the Synoptic Mission Discourse." *ETL* 60 (1984): 376–81.

————. "Synoptic Tradition in 1 Thessalonians." In *The Thessalonian Correspondence*, edited by Raymond F. Collins, 160–82. BETL 87. Louvain: Leuven University Press, 1990.

Turner, Max. *The Holy Spirit and Spiritual Gifts: In the New Testament Church and Today*. Peabody, MA: Hendrickson, 2005.

———. *The Holy Spirit and Spiritual Gifts, Then and Now*. Carlisle: Paternoster, 1996.

Twelftree, Graham H. "Jesus and Magic in Luke-Acts." In *Jesus and Paul: Global Perspectives in Honor of James D. G. Dunn for His 70th Birthday*, edited by B. J. Oropeza, C. K. Robertson, and Douglas C. Mohrmann, 46–58. LNTS 414. London: T&T Clark, 2009.

Tyson, Joseph B. "Why Dates Matter: The Case of the Acts of the Apostles." *Fourth R* 18, no. 2 (2005): 8–11, 14, 17–18.

Verheyden, J., G. Van Belle, and J. G. Van der Watt, eds. *Miracles and Imagery in Luke and John: Festschrift Ulrich Busse*. BETL 218. Louvain: Peeters, 2008.

Vielhauer, Philipp. "On the 'Paulinism' of Acts." *Studies in Luke-Acts*, edited by Leander E. Keck and J. Louis Martyn, 33–50. London: SPCK, 1976.

Vos, Craig S., de. "Finding a Charge That Fits: The Accusation against Paul and Silas at Philippi (Acts 16.19–21)." *JSNT* 74 (1999): 51–63.

Wach, Joachim. "The Nature of Religious Experience." In *The Comparative Study of Religions*, edited by Joseph M. Kitagawa, 27–58. New York: Columbia University Press, 1958.

Walker, William O. "Acts and the Pauline Corpus Reconsidered." *JSNT* 24 (1985): 3–23.

———. "Acts and the Pauline Letters: A Select Bibliography with Introduction." *Forum* 5 (2002): 105–15.

Walter, Niklaus. "Paul and the Early Christian Jesus-Tradition." In *Paul and Jesus: Collected Essays*, edited by Alexander J. M. Wedderburn, 51–80. JSNTSup 37. Sheffield: JSOT Press, 1989.

Weaver, John B. *Plots of Epiphany: Prison-Escape in Acts of the Apostles*. BZNW 131. Berlin: de Gruyter, 2004.

Webster, John B. "The Imitation of Christ." *TynBul* 37 (1986): 95–120.

Wedderburn, Alexander J. M. "Paul and Jesus: The Problem of Continuity." In *Paul and Jesus: Collected Essays*, edited by A. J. M. Wedderburn, 99–115. JSNTSup 37. Sheffield: JSOT Press, 1989.

———. "The 'We'-Passages in Acts: On the Horns of a Dilemma." *ZNW* 93 (2002): 78–98.

Wenham, David. *Paul: Follower of Jesus or Founder of Christianity?* Grand Rapids: Eerdmans, 1995.

———. "The Story of Jesus Known to Paul." In *Jesus of Nazareth, Lord and Christ: Essays on the Historical Jesus and New Testament Christology*, edited by Joel B. Green and Max Turner, 297–311. Grand Rapids: Eerdmans; Carlisle: Paternoster, 1994.

Whitaker, Molly. "Signs and Wonders: The Pagan Background." In *Studia Evangelica V: Papers Presented to the Third International Congress on New Testament Studies Held at Oxford, 1965*, edited by F. L. Cross, 155–58. TUGAL 103. Berlin: Akademie-Verlag, 1968.

Whiteley, D. E. H. *The Theology of St. Paul*. 2nd ed. Oxford: Blackwell, 1974.

Wiles, Maurice F. *The Divine Apostle: The Interpretation of St. Paul's Epistles in the Early Church*. Cambridge: Cambridge University Press, 1967.

Williams, Benjamin E. *Miracle Stories in the Biblical Book Acts of the Apostles*. Lewiston, NY: Edwin Mellen, 2001.

Wilson, Stephen G. "From Jesus to Paul: The Contours and Consequences of a Debate." In *From Jesus to Paul: Studies in Honour of Francis Wright Beare*, edited by Peter Richardson and John C. Hurd, 1–21. Waterloo, ON: Wilfrid Laurier University Press, 1984.

Witherington, Ben, III, ed. *History, Literature, and Society in the Book of Acts*. Cambridge: Cambridge University Press, 2007.

Wrede, William. *Paul*. Translated by Edward Lummis. 1908. Reprint, Eugene, OR: Wipf & Stock, 2001.

Wright, N. T. *Paul: In Fresh Perspective*. Minneapolis: Fortress, 2005.

Young, Brad H. *Paul, the Jewish Theologian: A Pharisee among Christians, Jews, and Gentiles*. Peabody, MA: Hendrickson, 1997.

Ancient Writings Index

Romans

Modern Author Index

Subject Index

Aaron, 38, 75, 79, 80
Abaris, 98
Abraham, 37, 73, 75, 80, 154, 157
Acts of Barnabas, 229n1
Acts of Paul, 15, 16, 229n1, 295, 298–300, 301, 303, 317n17
date, 298
Acts of Peter, 229n1
Acts of the Apostles, 229–71
apostles, 249, 260, 269n302, 270
authority, 19n93
authorship, 19n93, 235–36
date, 233–34
as fiction, 236, 246
historical veracity, 230–37, 261
parallel stories, 237–40, 245–46, 249–50, 256, 259–60, 262–63, 266, 267, 269n295, 312–13, 320
Paul, 3, 7, 8, 11, 13, 326, 232n19
Call or conversion, 241–44, 263–64
Damascus experience, 270
healed, 237, 241–43, 270
healer, 14, 16, 237–40, 249–51, 252–55, 258–61, 262–63, 267–71, 283

historical Paul, 13, 19, 230–37, 270–71
miracle worker, 216, 237, 308, 311, 318n17, 325
and the miraculous, 237–40
prophet, 65, 243–44, 263, 270
snake (viper) bite, 237, 239, 264–67
Adam, 75
administration, gift of, 22
Alexander Abonouteichus, 102
Alexander Polyhistor, 77
ambassador, 131–32, 146
Paul, 134–36, 148, 205, 308, 318
Ananias and Sapphira, 238, 240
anointing, with oil, 114n54, 293
aorist tense, 161n59
Apollonius of Tyana, 103–4
Apollos, 134, 193, 194
"apostle" (ἀπόστολος), 88, 121, 123, 277, 308, 315
false, 214n249, 217n269, 279n58
Jerusalem (the Twelve), 134, 146, 212, 217, 239
Paul, 62, 88, 90, 131–34, 142, 146, 148, 168, 169, 170n20, 214n240, 216, 218, 219, 224, 225n309, 308, 315

Apostolic Fathers, 281n70, 294, 301
apotropaic texts, 37, 277, 293
Aristeas, 97
"aroma" (εὐωδία), of Christ, 144

Barnabas, 119, 133, 168, 188, 237, 238, 239, 243, 244, 245, 247, 248, 249, 251, 254
Barnabas, Epistle, 211
Beelzebul, 50, 203n170
blindness, 36, 57, 84, 113, 115, 117, 122, 129, 147, 237–38, 240–43, 244–45, 247–48, 270

Caleb, 75
charisma (χάρισμα), *charismata* (χαρίσματα), 12, 13, 22, 24, 25n132, 154, 170–78, 182, 204–5, 224, 277, 284, 302, 312, 313–14, 315, 316, 321
defined, 12–13, 25, 277
chiasmus, 206n183, 221
clairvoyance, 10
Clement of Alexandria, 275n30, 295, 300–301
date, 287
Clement of Rome, 57, 229, 281n70, 285, 286, 295
date, 295

384